MW01286291

'In light of numerous excellent recently published commentaries on Proverbs, a question immediately comes to mind: Is there need for another? This work by John Kitchen demands an unqualified Yes. It is committed to the full integrity and authority of the Bible as the written Word of God, to careful exegesis of the text, and to practical application of the truths of biblical wisdom to everyday life.'

EUGENE H. MERRILL,
Old Testament Scholar-in-Residence,
Crisswell College, Dallas, Texas

'Up to now my best helps on Proverbs have been Bridges, Alden and Ross. Now I must add John Kitchen's choice and compendious study in the Mentor Commentary Series. He is clear and probing on the text and always practical. His Appendix on wisdom vs folly is powerful and his Thematic Index of Proverbs opens up the only real preaching possibility for expositors beyond chapter nine of the book. Strings of pearls cannot be taught or preached verse by verse. This is a solid and substantial piece of work, which will deservedly take its place as one of the finest contemporary treatments available.'

DAVID L. LARSEN (1931–2021),
Professor Emeritus of Preaching,
Trinity Evangelical Divinity School, Deerfield, Illinois

'In this commentary on Proverbs, John Kitchen combines careful attention to the text with a warm pastoral concern for his readers. He is familiar with the scholarly discussions on the book, but he avoids technical jargon as he interprets Proverbs for the life setting of the twenty-first century. His lucid exposition expertly focuses on two questions that are too often neglected: How does the message of Proverbs connect with other biblical passages? And, how does this ancient book speak in specific terms to life today? This book will prove helpful for laypeople, students, and scholars alike.'

DANIEL J. ESTES,
Distinguished Professor of Old Testament,
Cedarville University, Cedarville, Ohio

'Dr. John Kitchen's commentary represents a good combination of scholarly research and practical godly admonition. It provides both the experienced biblical scholar and the beginning Bible student a very helpful resource for the study of Proverbs.'

GENNADY PSHENICHNY,
Lecturer in the Old Testament, Former President, Kuban Evangelical Christian
University, Krasnodar, Russia

'In his Mentor series commentary on Proverbs, author John Kitchen readably reflects the fruits of his precise and insightful teacher's mind and his down-to-earth and caring pastor's heart. As I moved through this very thorough treatment of Proverbs, I was consistently challenged to think deeply about the many scholarly issues related to this amazing biblical library of wisdom. But, more than once, I was brought to tears as I was challenged to survey my own life and admit how timely and piercing the practical wisdom of Proverbs remains every day. Kitchen's volume is that rare and beautiful combination: in equal – and very generous – portions, an intellectual feast for the curious mind and a spiritual feast for the needy soul!'

A. BOYD LUTER,
Director of Biblical and Theological Studies, The King's University, Texas

Proverbs

A Mentor Commentary

John A. Kitchen

ⅢENTOR

Copyright © John A. Kitchen 2006

10 9 8 7 6 5

ISBN 978-1-84550-059-7

Published in 2006
Reprinted 2012, 2019, 2021 and 2024
in the
Mentor Imprint
by
Christian Focus Publications Ltd,
Geanies House, Fearn, Ross-shire,
IV20 1TW, Scotland, Great Britain
www.christianfocus.com

Cover design by Moose77.com

Printed and bound by
Bell & Bain, Glasgow

Contents

Abbreviations

Old Testament

Gen.	Genesis	Eccles.	Ecclesiastes
Exod.	Exodus	Song of Sol.	Song of Solomon
Lev.	Leviticus	Isa.	Isaiah
Num.	Numbers	Jer.	Jeremiah
Deut.	Deuteronomy	Lam.	Lamentations
Josh.	Joshua	Ezek.	Ezekiel
Judg.	Judges	Dan.	Daniel
Ruth	Ruth	Hosea	Hosea
1 Sam.	1 Samuel	Joel	Joel
2 Sam.	2 Samuel	Amos	Amos
1 Kings	1 Kings	Obad.	Obadiah
2 Kings	2 Kings	Jonah	Jonah
1 Chron.	1 Chronicles	Mic.	Micah
2 Chron.	2 Chronicles	Nahum	Nahum
Ezra	Ezra	Hab.	Habakkuk
Neh.	Nehemiah	Zeph.	Zephaniah
Esther	Esther	Hag.	Haggai
Job	Job	Zech.	Zechariah
Ps.	Psalm(s)	Mal.	Malachi
Prov.	Proverbs		

New Testament

Matt.	Matthew	1 Tim.	1 Timothy
Mark	Mark	2 Tim.	2 Timothy
Luke	Luke	Titus	Titus
John	John	Philem.	Philemon
Acts	Acts	Heb.	Hebrews
Rom.	Romans	James	James
1 Cor.	1 Corinthians	1 Pet.	1 Peter
2 Cor.	2 Corinthians	2 Pet.	2 Peter
Gal.	Galatians	1 John	1 John
Eph.	Ephesians	2 John	2 John
Phil.	Philippians	3 John	3 John
Col.	Colossians	Jude	Jude
1 Thess.	1 Thessalonians	Rev.	Revelation
2 Thess.	2 Thessalonians		

Bible Translations

ASV	American Standard Version	NIV	New International Version
JB	Jerusalem Bible	NKJV	New King James Version
KJV	King James Version	NLT	New Living Translation
NASB	New American Standard Bible	NRSV	New Revised Standard Version
NEB	New English Bible	RSV	Revised Standard Version

Miscellaneous

c.	*circa*, about	ibid.	*ibidem*, in the same place
cf.	*confer*, compare	i.e.	*id est*, that is
e.g.	*exempli gratia*, for example	LXX	Septuagint
etc.	*et cetera*, and the like	n.d.	no date
ff	following (verses, pages, etc.)	rpt.	reprint

to

Melody, Joe and Clint

May you walk in the fear of the Lord

May you delight in the knowledge of God

Preface

It might be legitimate to question whether anyone ever fully arrives at wisdom in this life. As we live in this world, wisdom is not so much a destination as a journey. If, even for a moment, we think we have arrived at wisdom, we prove we have abandoned the journey. 'Cease listening, my son, to discipline, And you will stray from the words of knowledge' (Prov. 19:27).

This commentary does not represent an arrival at a final destination, other than the publication of a book about what I have learned to this point in my ongoing journey. However, because what I have learned has made a profound impact on my life, these pages do reflect a very significant step along my journey.

Neither does anyone come to wisdom in a vacuum. Certainly, the commentary you now hold in your hands did not arise without the influence of many significant people and works. Naming all of them would be impossible. I do, however, want to express my deepest appreciation for the many people who have invested themselves in my life.

I am grateful for the congregations of the Plymouth Alliance Church and the Stow Alliance Fellowship. Their patience with me as their pastor has made ministry a blessing. They have helped me pursue wisdom, not just in the study, but in the body of Christ, in hands-on, tangible, real-world ways.

My dear wife, Julie, has exhibited patience beyond compare, first in simply sharing life with me and, second, through enduring the many hours, over many years, that have gone into the preparation of this commentary. My dear, you are priceless (Prov. 31:10). I rise up and call you blessed! 'There are many virtuous and capable women in the world, but you surpass them all!' (Prov. 31:29, NLT).

A word about how to best use this commentary is in order. Much of the material in Proverbs receives emphasis through repetition. The many cross-references contained in the commentary alert the reader to rich veins of gold that run throughout Proverbs (and, in many cases, other Biblical books). The investment in tracing out these connections will reward the seeker greatly. The method of repetition is not a sign of scattered and careless work by later editors (Prov. 25:1), but a Divinely inspired pedagogical tool to reinforce that which is most urgent and necessary. Realizing that, rather than reading a commentary from cover to cover, it will be often used in a move-around-all-over-the-place fashion when studying a specific passage, I have attempted at each point in the commentary to provide enough information to link you to other immediately relevant places in Proverbs – and in the commentary – to help you catch these connections and repetitions. From my observation and experience (key aspects of wisdom in Proverbs), this 'pedagogically intentional' repetition only enhances the reader's opportunity to mine out the fuller riches of the wisdom set forth in this priceless, and timeless, book.

Now, may we each set our hearts on a pilgrimage — walking in the fear of the Lord and letting our hearts be satisfied with nothing less than the knowledge of God Himself (Prov. 9:10).

Soli Deo gloria.

Introduction

Few pursuits of the human heart predate our search for wisdom. The tempter was confident that, even in a perfect world, his seductions would find an ear once the woman saw 'that the tree was desirable to make one wise' (Gen. 3:6). The record of our rebel race since that time reveals discoveries of knowledge and technology that are nothing short of breathtaking. Yet, T. S. Eliot still rightly asks: 'Where is the wisdom we have lost in knowledge? Where is the knowledge we have lost in information?'

At the dawn of the nuclear age, General Omar Bradley rightly observed, 'Ours is a world of nuclear giants and ethical infants. If we continue to develop our technology without wisdom or prudence, our servant may prove to be our executioner.' The exponential growth of technological knowledge since that day has rendered us neither wiser nor godlier. We have, however, lost something priceless, something that no amount of mere information can regain for us.

Now, more than ever, we must know wisdom and no better starting point for doing so can be found than the Book of Proverbs. From its pages, God promises to set us on 'The path of life' (Prov. 15:24) and to rescue us from 'the way of death' (14:12; 16:25). In our eagerness to embark on our journey, however, it is prudent to survey the lay of the land we will be traversing.

The Context of Proverbs

Proverbs within the context of the ancient world
The Book of Proverbs was not birthed in a vacuum. Israel's neighbors also sought wisdom and wrote prolifically of their quest. Solomon's wisdom surpassed that of all other nations (1 Kings 4:30), but it did not entirely eclipse it.[1] Scripture acknowledges the aggressive pursuit of wisdom by both Egypt (Gen. 41:8; Exod. 7:11; 1 Kings 4:30; Isa. 19:11, 12) and Babylon (1 Kings 4:30; Jer. 50:35; Dan. 1:4, 17, 20; 2:2-11). Edom likewise had its wise men (Jer. 49:7; Obad. 8). Solomon was pursued by these foreign seekers of wisdom, because his reputation had spread far and wide (1 Kings 4:34; 10:1-13, 24; 2 Chron. 9:23).

It was once widely held that Proverbs must have originated at a late date due to its literary forms. Evidence has since revealed that the literary forms employed by Proverbs are to be found in the wisdom writings of Israel's neighbors and from the time before Solomon.

That Solomon knew of, and appreciated, such writings appears quite likely (1 Kings 4:29-31). Israel's physical location placed her at the crossroads of trade routes between Mesopotamia and Egypt, a fact that heightens the likelihood of not only shared commerce, but intellectual and cultural pursuits as well. Solomon stabilized the nation and ushered in an era of peace, during which such intellectual pursuits flourished (1 Kings 4:33).

Solomon's court had an international flair to it. He showed interest in international trade, including obtaining precious metals, animals, and horticultural items (1 Kings 10:11, 12, 22, 28; 2 Chron. 8:18–9:22). Solomon was not slow to incorporate the best of the skill and technology of neighboring nations (1 Kings 5:6, 7; 7:13ff; 9:26-28). Therefore, given Solomon's appetite for wisdom and the comparisons which exalt him above neighboring wise men (1 Kings 4:30), it seems certain that he knew of, studied, and was influenced by these foreign wisdom writings.

In particular, the Sumerians and Babylonians wrote much concerning their pursuit of wisdom, though neither could match the prolific output of Egypt's wise men. The discoveries of Sumeria likely date from the third millennium BC and those from Babylon from the second millennium BC.[2] The Wisdom of Amenemope is the Egyptian work most commonly compared to Proverbs. It may date from as early as 1300–1200 BC. That it is of such antiquity is apparently confirmed by an extract of its text discovered on an ancient ostracon.[3] It is possible that Solomon's marriage to Pharaoh's daughter may have made for a ready conduit for the delivery of such writings and their culture to Solomon's court (1 Kings 3:1; 7:8; 9:24; 2 Chron. 8:11).

Critical scholars have asserted that features like the extended discourses of Proverbs 1–9 and the personification of wisdom require a late date. Such discourses, they believe, developed out of the shorter sentence sayings characterized in Proverbs 10ff. Yet, the repeated address 'my son' (e.g. Prov. 1:8, 10, 15; 2:1; 3:1, 11, 21) and similar extended discourses are found in other wisdom writings which predate Proverbs by as much as a millennium.[4] Accordingly, Kidner concludes that

> ... it has now been shown beyond reasonable doubt that the literary prototype of such teachings as Proverbs 1–9, and the 'words of the wise' and of King Lemuel's mother (22:17–24:34, and 31:1-9), was not the spoken proverb but the written Instruction, of which many examples survive especially from Egypt.... Here was a long-standing and international form of teaching which, like these sections of Proverbs, addressed the reader as 'my son', setting him a high ethical and professional standard, expounded in straight discourse rather than disconnected aphorisms, and with exhortations rather than bare statements.[5]

Great debate has swirled around the similarities between Proverbs 22:17–24:22 and the Egyptian work The Wisdom of Amenemope. This ancient work was comprised of thirty chapters. Some, who accept an emended Hebrew text, demand that the Biblical text purports to divide the text into thirty sayings (cf. 'Have I not written thirty sayings for you,' NIV, 22:20). The required emendation, however, is not accepted by many.[6] Nor is there universal agreement about how the thirty sayings should be identified. The NIV has arranged its text to represent how it believes these thirty sayings fall out. The supposed parallelisms between the two writings follow no particular order and appear to be selected at random. Neither is there any agreement as to whether the Hebrews borrowed from the Egyptians, the Egyptians from the Hebrews, or both from some other more ancient source(s). What does appear undeniable is that there are some remarkable, though not exact, parallels between this section of Proverbs and The Wisdom of Amenemope. (See the commentary for further details.) However, the exact relationship between Proverbs 22:17–24:22 and The Wisdom of Amenemope remains a mystery and a matter over which commentators can only speculate.

All of this, however, does raise other questions. Should we be alarmed by Scripture's apparent failure to condemn and denounce the wisdom of other nations? Consider its more ruthless countenance toward pagan prophets and priests (e.g. 1 Kings 18; 2 Kings 10:19; 23:5, 17). Should Solomon's apparent affinity toward non-Israelite wisdom concern us? Does the discovery of such writings help legitimize belief in an early date for Proverbs only to then endanger the uniqueness of Scripture?

The answer on all these accounts is negative. Several lines of reasoning steady us here. First, familiarity with, and similarity to, ancient pagan wisdom forms do not imply acceptance of their teachings. Even where the similarities are remarkably close, they prove no more than that Solomon spoke in the midst of a popular cultural milieu which included a trans-national interest in wisdom.

In doing so, did Solomon condescend to unworthy forms and ideas in writing his wisdom? Or is it possible that God stirred an interest in wisdom among the nations in order to provide a platform for His wise man par excellence, guiding him to write and speak in forms that would broaden the appeal, and hasten the spread, of His message? The God behind the Book of Proverbs is One who is sovereign over the nations (e.g. Prov. 21:1). We are, in fact, led to expect just such prudent action from Him.

Secondly, while the words of Proverbs may, at times, sound very much like those of other ancient wisdom writings, the underlying essence of them is fundamentally different. The 'fear of the Lord' is the beginning – and first principle – of all wisdom (Prov. 1:7; 9:10). The writings of the nations establish no such moral, spiritual, and ethical foundation to their wisdom. Indeed, Buzzell writes, 'Wisdom in Proverbs includes practical sagacity, mental acumen, and functional skill, but it also includes moral, upright living which stems from a right relationship to the Lord. The statement "The fear of the Lord is the beginning of wisdom" (9:10) makes the Hebrew concept of wisdom unique.'[7]

Proverbs within the context of the Hebrew world

While the search for wisdom transcended national borders, the Hebrew interest in wisdom was unique. The richness of the Hebrew wisdom culture requires that any interpretation of Proverbs must arise from an understanding of that culture.

From the earliest moments of its history, Israel appreciated her need for wisdom. In Egypt, Joseph was revered among their wise men (Gen. 41:8, 39). Centuries later, God, through Moses, confounded the wise men of Egypt (Exod. 7:10-12). As the nation sat poised to enter the promised land, Moses reminded them, 'See, I have taught you statutes and judgments just as the Lord my God commanded me, that you should do thus in the land where you are entering to possess it. So keep and do them, for that is your wisdom and your understanding in the sight of the peoples who will hear all these statutes and say, "Surely this great nation is a wise and understanding people"' (Deut. 4:5-6).

David was recognized for his wisdom (1 Sam. 18:30), wrote of its value (Ps. 19:7), and retained counselors of wisdom in his administration (1 Chron. 27:32, 33). A wise woman from Tekoa (2 Sam. 14), and another from Abel (2 Sam. 20:16ff), appear without fanfare.

Proverbs fall from the lips of Jotham (Judg. 9:8ff), Samson (Judg. 14:14), David (1 Sam. 24:13), Nathan (2 Sam. 12:1ff), and the common people in Israel (1 Sam. 10:12; 24:19). Wisdom sayings find their way into every stratum of Hebrew Scripture (Num. 21:27-30; Ps. 44:14; 69:11; 1 Kings 9:7; Ezek. 12:22, 23; 16:44; 18:2).

Yet, it was through Solomon that God advanced wisdom in Israel beyond any previous level. Like his father (Ps. 19:7-9), Solomon saw the Law of God as the foundation for a life of wisdom (Prov. 28:4, 7, 9; 29:18). As Moses set life and death before the people (cf. Deut. 30:19, 20; 32:46, 47), so Solomon called upon his readers to choose life and avoid death (e.g. Prov. 12:28; 13:14; 14:27).

But, Solomon did more than stand on past foundations. He launched wisdom to an entirely new level of prominence and influence in Israelite life. Little wonder that some 250 years later, during a period of revival, Hezekiah commissioned his servants to collect and edit the sayings of Solomon (Prov. 25:1). Indeed, Solomon prepared the way for wise men like Daniel to shine when exiled to a foreign land and surrounded by pagan wisdom (Dan. 1:4, 17, 20; 5:7-12).

Proverbs within the context of the Biblical canon
Proverbs is not an isolated text, but one among the sixty-five other books of canonical Scripture. It must be read and interpreted within that larger Biblical context if it is to be rightly understood. Consider the place of Proverbs within the telescoping revelation of God given in His written word.

Proverbs within the context of the Hebrew canon
God through Solomon so elevated the position of the sage that, by the time of Jeremiah, it was recognized within Israelite society as one of three primary sources of divine revelation, standing alongside the priest and the prophet: 'Surely the law is not going to be lost to the priest, nor counsel to the sage, nor the divine word to the prophet!' (Jer. 18:18; cf. Ezek. 7:26).

What, then, was the interplay and relationship between prophet, priest, and sage? It might be said that, while the priest interpreted the Law, quoting and referencing every statement, the prophet fired off lightning bolts, proclaiming thunderously 'Thus saith the Lord!' The sage, on the other hand, made observations, noted repetitions, and pointed out the rhythms of life. The priest's authority was found in God's Law in his hand, the prophet's from a direct revelation from heaven. The sage, however, when asked about his authority might have said, 'Just look around you. Watch. Listen. Observe. See if you don't discover that I'm right.'

Waltke captures the contrasts well, 'Unlike Moses, God did not speak to the sages face to face, and, unlike the prophets, he did not give them visions and auditions. Rather, he spoke to them principally through their observations of the creation and human behavior and their godly reflections, informed by faith, on what they saw.'[8]

We would be remiss, however, in picturing these three at odds with one another. The prophet affirmed everything Moses taught and the righteous priest affirmed what a true prophet declared. Likewise, Solomon rested upon God's Law and understood the essential nature of revelation from God (Prov. 29:18). The true prophet, priest, or sage saw himself not in competition against another, but as engaged in a complementary ministry. The unique contribution of the sage is captured well by Kidner: 'There are details of character small enough to escape the mesh of the law and the broadsides of the prophets, and yet decisive in personal dealings.'[9]

Proverbs fills the need for knowledge of how God's Word looks and acts in the seemingly mundane elements of life. The Law teaches where life comes from and to whom it answers. The prophet set forth what life means and how we may be transgressing its Author. The sage, however, deals in how life is to be lived in the push and shove of daily existence. All three were 'written for our instruction, that through perseverance and the encouragement of the Scriptures we might have hope' (Rom. 15:4). It is in this Hebrew world where every word of God applies to every detail of life that Proverbs stands as the quintessential exhibit of wisdom.

Not surprisingly, the Book of Proverbs is found in every Jewish list of canonical books.[10] It is located in the section called 'the Writings,' though its position within that section varies from list to list.

Proverbs within the context of Hebrew poetic literature

The books of Job, Psalms, Proverbs, Ecclesiastes, and Song of Solomon are generally designated as the Hebrew poetic books. Proverbs makes a unique contribution to this collection. That contribution is best seen in the word 'proverb,' which translates the Hebrew word *m~sh~l*. Some want to trace it to a root word meaning 'to rule' (pointing to a word spoke by a king), but it more likely derives from the root mšl meaning 'to be like.'[11] The proverb makes its point by holding things next to one another and observing likenesses, differences, or other comparisons.

This strategy is easily observed in the sentence literature of Proverbs 10ff. However, the word *m~sh~l* describes more than simply the classic two line proverb. Beyond the borders of the Book of Proverbs the word can describe a popular saying of the common folk (1 Sam. 10:12; 24:13), a byword (Deut. 28:37; 1 Kings 9:7; 2 Chron. 7:20; Ps. 69:11; Jer. 24:9; Ezek. 14:8), a prophet's oracle (Num. 23:7, 18; 24:3, 15, 20-21, 23), a more lengthy taunt (Isa. 14:4ff), an extended discourse (Job 29-31), a parable (Ezek. 20:49), an allegory (Ezek. 17:2), a lament (Mic. 2:4), and is a close cousin to the riddle (Ps. 49:4; Prov. 1:6).

Within Proverbs, we find not only the simple two line proverb (Prov. 10:1–22:16), but also extended instructions (Prov. 1–9; 22:17–24:23; 31:1-9), personification (1:20-33; 8; 9:1-6), numerical sayings (e.g. 30:15-31), and an acrostic poem (31:10-31). It is clear that m~sh~l is a flexible word.

Yet, in its most common sense, it describes the pithy sentence packed with thought-provoking punch. A proverb is compressed truth. Or, to use different imagery, it is a statement of truth stripped to the bare essentials. All qualifications, balancing statements, and explanations are cast aside in order to set a specific truth as starkly and memorably as possible before our minds.

The proverb takes seriously the observation of Ecclesiastes 6:11: 'The more the words, the less the meaning, and how does that profit anyone?' (NIV). In this sense, it accords perfectly with our English word 'proverb.' It represents a saying which opts for the power of brevity over the clarity of verbosity (pro = for; verba = words). The proverb is used in the place of many words which could have spoken more precisely, but perhaps less powerfully, of the same truth.

It has been said that, where Psalms focuses on man in relationship to God, Proverbs shows us man in relationship to man.[12] Perhaps better stated, Proverbs shows us man in relationship with man before and on behalf of God, for in this book God is never far away and wisdom and righteousness are seen as two sides of the same coin. Charles Bridges put it well: 'If the Psalms bring the glow upon the heart, the Proverbs "make the face to shine,"'[13] for here we find the fear of the Lord expressed in the mundane details of life. Indeed, Proverbs aims to make us 'wise because pious, and pious because wise.'[14]

Proverbs within the context of Hebrew wisdom literature
The wisdom literature of the Old Testament is included within the larger designation of poetic literature. The wisdom literature is made up of Job, Proverbs, and Ecclesiastes. These three books share wisdom as a common theme, but they wrestle with it in fundamentally different ways. Where Proverbs uses periods, Job

and Ecclesiastes employ question marks.[15] Proverbs tends to see life as calculable, predictable, almost mathematical, while Job sees it as undecipherable and Ecclesiastes as pointless. Proverbs declares that righteous, wise living will be rewarded in this life. In Job, such talk is found in the mouths of his 'friends,' and seems to miss the point. In Ecclesiastes, Solomon has received many such earthly rewards and finds them empty. Where Proverbs states, Job and Ecclesiastes speculate. Everything appears clear in Proverbs, dark in Job, and pointless in Ecclesiastes.

These are, of course, generalizations. Proverbs is capable of recognizing and wrestling with the inscrutable (e.g. Prov. 13:23; 30:18-20). Likewise, it understands that a life which pursues riches and pleasure for their own sake is empty (e.g. Prov. 10:2; 11:4). And all three books find their common ground in 'the fear of the Lord' (e.g. Job 1:1; 28:28; Prov. 1:7; 9:10; 31:30; Eccles. 3:14; 12:13).

Thus, Proverbs, Job, and Ecclesiastes should not be seen as separate and competing works, but as complementary. They are as three parts of one extended sentence, which, when read alone, are helpful, but are not completely intelligible until the whole has been heard.

A number of Psalms are often recognized as also representative of the wisdom tradition in Israel. Though the number varies from scholar to scholar, at least Psalms 19, 104, and 147 are often recognized as those bearing the characteristics of wisdom writings.

The wisdom tradition continued with strength during Israel's post-Solomonic history. The apocryphal books of Ecclesiasticus (Ben Sirach, c. 180 BC) and the Wisdom of Solomon (c. 1st century BC) have been recognized as later examples of a continuing quest for wisdom among the people of Israel, though they are clearly outside the canon of Scripture.

Proverbs within the total Biblical canon

Proverbs is, of course, not simply one more example of wisdom literature among many others. Nor is it merely a Hebrew book of wisdom. Proverbs is also the Christian book of wisdom, finding its highest demonstration and expression in the Person of Jesus Christ, who is wisdom itself (Matt. 12:42; 1 Cor. 1:24, 30; Col. 2:3).

Jesus often alluded to Proverbs in His teaching. Proverbs 25:6-7 can be heard in His warning about seeking the best seat at a banquet (Mark 14:7-11). Should Proverbs 12:7 or 14:11 be seen standing behind Jesus' parable of the wise and foolish men and their homes (Matt. 7:24-27)? Does Proverbs 27:1 inform the story of the fool who tore down his barn to build bigger ones (Luke 12:19, 20)? Was Jesus thinking of Proverbs 30:4 when He told Nicodemus that only the Son of Man had ascended to heaven?[16] Luke's (2:52) summary of Jesus' childhood years seems to echo Proverbs 3:4.

Jesus' parabolic teaching also reveals His embrace of Proverbs. The Hebrew m~sh~l is translated perhaps most effectively in Greek by parabole, or parable.[17] The root idea ('to be like') in m~sh~l is at the heart of Jesus' parables, which He routinely began by saying one thing 'may be compared to' another (Matt. 13:24; 18:23; 25:1) or that something 'is like' something else (Matt. 13:31, 33, 44, 45, 47, 52).

Paul quoted Proverbs in his writings (Prov. 3:7a = Rom. 12:16; Prov. 25:21, 22 = Rom. 12:20), as did Peter (Prov. 3:34 = 1 Pet. 5:5b; Prov. 10:12 = 1 Pet. 4:8; Prov. 26:11 = 2 Pet. 2:22), James (Prov. 3:34 = James 4:6), and the writer to the Hebrews (Prov. 3:11, 12 = Heb. 12:5, 6). When James quotes Proverbs 3:34 (James 4:6) he presents it as Scripture. New Testament writers quote from the section of the Old Testament called 'the Writings' (in which Proverbs is found) and declare it Scripture.[18]

Jeremiah set forward the priest, the prophet, and the sage as God's vehicles for authoritative revelation (Jer. 18:18). Jesus came declaring Himself the fulfillment of all the Law and Prophets (Matt. 5:17). Similarly, He asserted that, in Himself, 'something greater than Solomon' has come (Matt. 12:42; Luke 11:31). Indeed, Christ is 'the wisdom of God' (1 Cor. 1:24) and 'became to us wisdom from God' (1 Cor. 1:30). Christ is He 'in whom are hidden all the treasures of wisdom and knowledge' (Col. 2:3).

Truly, in Christ, we have embodied all that Proverbs sets forth as wisdom. While the personification of wisdom in Proverbs should not be read as a description of the Second Person of the Trinity per se (see commentary on chapter 8), from the vantage point of the New Testament's progressive revelation we find such wisdom fulfilled perfectly in our Savior.

The Authorship and Date of Proverbs

The authorship and compilation of Proverbs

In modern Hebrew Bibles, Proverbs bears the title *mišlê*, or 'proverbs of.' This is an abbreviation of the fuller and more ancient title *mišlê šᵉlômôh*, 'the proverbs of Solomon,' which is lifted from the opening line of the book (Prov. 1:1). The English name is taken from the Vulgate's Libre Proverbiorum.[19]

The title, however, does not describe all that comes into play when defining the book's authorship. Solomon is designated as the author of large sections of the book (Prov. 1:1; 10:1; 25:1). Just how far these designations are supposed to reach is a matter of some debate. Others clearly are attributed with authorship of portions of the book, such as 'the wise' (Prov. 22:17; 24:23), Agur (30:1), and Lemuel (31:1, 4). One section attributed to Solomon is said to have been compiled during Hezekiah's reign and likely at his command (Prov. 25:1).

It is helpful to move section by section through the whole book and examine the evidence regarding their authorship. Clearly, Proverbs 1–9 constitutes a distinct section of the book. Does, however, Proverbs 1:1-7 serve as an introduction to the entire book or to only the first section? If it was composed to stand over the entire book, it may function not as a signal of authorship (for clearly not all of the book was written by Solomon, cf. 22:17; 24:23; 30:1; 31:1), but as a way of describing its primary author and legitimizing the whole of the work under his name. In that case, the authorship of Proverbs 1–9 would be considered uncertain.

Some champion this position by noting the marked difference in style between the discourses of the first nine chapters and the aphorisms of chapter 10ff. Scholars of the critical tradition have posited that the longer and more complex instructions must, of necessity, have evolved over time from the shorter, more simplistic aphorisms.

Following such logic, they then assert that Proverbs 1–9 could not have been written by Solomon, but must, of necessity, have been composed at a much later date. They usually ascribe the final product to a time following the Babylonian Exile. They hold that the title in Proverbs 1:1 was affixed far after Solomon's day and served not to point to authorship as much as to legitimize the whole of the work under the famous monarch's name.

However, K. A. Kitchen, in his research into the ancient wisdom literature of Israel's neighbors, discovered that they had been using the longer discourse form of instruction alongside the briefer aphorisms for at least a thousand years before Solomon came on the scene.[20] What is more, Kitchen found that such ancient wisdom writings often employed a form which matched that found in Proverbs 1:1–22:16. These writings, like Solomon, employed a preamble (Prov. 1:1-7), a prologue (1:8–9:18), a subtitle (10:1), and, then, the main text (10:2–22:16).[21] It would appear that the weight of evidence points to Solomon employing a common cultural form in authoring the main portion of the Book of Proverbs. Only a pre-judged critical bias sees any need for an author other than Solomon for 1:1–22:16.

Another line of evidence for Solomonic authorship of Proverbs 1–9 is advanced by Andrew E. Steinmann. Through detailed study of the vocabulary, thought, and modes of expression of the author of Proverbs 1–9 and Solomon in 10:1–22:16 and 25:1–29:27, Steinmann found the two sections to be so similar that 'The probabilities of 1–9 coming from someone other than Solomon ... are extremely low.'[22]

The other section ascribed to Solomon is Proverbs 25:1–29:27. It is headed by the statement: 'These also are proverbs of Solomon which the men of Hezekiah, king of Judah, transcribed' (Prov. 25:1). Hezekiah led a revival movement in his day (2 Kings 18–20; 2 Chron. 29–32; cf. Isa. 36–39), showing great interest in restoring Davidic worship forms to the nation (2 Chron. 29:25-30).

Similarly, we learn here that Hezekiah longed also for the wisdom that had guided Solomon. He commissioned his scribes to gather and compile a collection of Solomon's proverbs from the larger body of his literary works. Solomon is credited with writing 3,000 such proverbs (1 Kings 4:32). There appears to be no legitimate reason to doubt the Solomonic authorship of these proverbs, though they were compiled and then added to Solomon's existing work (Prov. 1:1–22:16) at around 700 BC, about 250 years after the time of Solomon. All of these things considered, Waltke puts the overall matter of authorship bluntly: 'Denial of Solomonic authorship is based on academic skepticism inherited from the historical criticism of the last century, not on any scientific data.'[23]

What, then, of the section which separates these works of Solomon (Prov. 22:17–24:34)? This section is clearly marked out by two headings: 'Incline your ear and hear the words of the wise, And apply your mind to my knowledge' (Prov. 22:17) and 'These also are sayings of the wise' (24:23a).

Who were these wise men and how did their work become a part of the canon of Scripture? We have already demonstrated that the ancient Near East abounded with men of wisdom (see above in 'Proverbs within the context of the ancient world') and that many such works predated Solomon's day by a millennium or more.

The exact identity of 'the wise' is impossible to know from our vantage point. There appears, however, no legitimate reason to doubt that Solomon was the collector of these sayings and the one who compiled them into their present form.

This cannot be proven, of course, but the facts that are available to us suggest no better scenario for their existence. Israel had other sages from whom these sayings could have been collected (see above in 'Proverbs within the context of the Hebrew world'). Additionally,

Solomon was clearly a dealer in international wisdom, for 'Solomon's wisdom surpassed the wisdom of all the sons of the east and all the wisdom of Egypt' (1 Kings 4:30; 2 Chron. 9:22, 23).

Just how could it be known that his wisdom 'surpassed' that of other nations if those men or their writings were not consulted? Indeed, we are told that Solomon 'was wiser than all men' and then the text proceeds in naming several of them: 'Ethan the Ezrahite, Heman, Calcol and Darda, the sons of Mahol' (1 Kings 4:31).

The same context tells us of Solomon's far flung international trade networks (1 Kings 10:14, 15; 2 Chron. 9:21). He was sought out by the wise of other nations (1 Kings 10:1–13; 2 Chron. 9:1-12). He clearly had both motive and means for collecting and studying the wisdom writings of other nations. It is natural to assume he might have selected what he considered the best of these writings and edited them into an addendum to his own work. And, does not the text at Proverbs 22:17 suggest as much? 'Pay attention and listen to the sayings of the wise; apply your heart to what *I* teach' (emphasis added). Waltke astutely observes that, if Proverbs 22:17 was written 'by someone other than Solomon, then the "I" who speaks in its prologue (22:17-21) has no antecedent.'[24]

Though the exact identity of these 'wise men' is beyond our scope of knowledge, the evidence we do possess points to none other than Solomon as the most likely compiler and editor of these sayings. This would make it not only reasonable, but probable, that Solomon authored Proverbs 1:1–22:16 and 25:1–29:27, and that he also compiled Proverbs 22:17–24:34 and then affixed it to the main body of his work (1:1–22:16), to which Hezekiah's men then attached Proverbs 25:1–29:27.

This leaves us with the three appendices of the book (Prov. 30:1–31:31). Proverbs 30 claims to be 'The words of Agur the son of Jakeh' (v. 1). Older Jewish commentators routinely understood 'Agur' as a veiled reference to Solomon. But, there appears to be little evidence in favor of this view.

What would be gained by such a cryptic allusion to the one who has been so obviously set forth as the author of the earlier parts of the book? The name 'Agur' appears to be non-Hebrew, and is probably of non-Israelite origin.[25] The name is not otherwise known to us. The only textual help we have in identifying 'Agur' is in the designation 'the son of Jakeh.' But, this is also of little help, for it too seems to be a non-Hebrew name not otherwise found in the Scriptures.

What follows are called 'The words ... the oracle.' The Hebrew word for 'oracle' normally describes a prophetic message given by

God and poured through a messenger (prophet) who personally feels the weight of this message (e.g. Zech. 9:1; Mal. 1:1). It may be translated 'burden' because of its weighty subject matter and import. This would seem to add great gravity to the words that follow in the rest of the chapter. However, because the term is normally reserved for prophetic utterances and not wisdom literature, some (cf. rsv and the niv margin) have seen in it a reference to a personal name (Massa, a son of Ishmael and his clan, Gen. 25:14-16; 1 Chron. 1:30) or a place-name (Massa, the region in northern Arabia where he lived).[26] The same word occurs in Proverbs 31:1, and, if a reference to a place, then Lemuel would have been Agur's ruler.[27]

The second appendix begins with 'The words of King Lemuel, the oracle which his mother taught him' (Prov. 31:1). This 'King Lemuel' is otherwise unknown to us and appears to be, like Agur, of non-Hebrew origin. The words 'the oracle' face the same challenges of interpretation and translation as they do in Proverbs 30:1. Do they refer to a prophetic oracle (e.g. Zech. 9:1) or to a region in northern Arabia? Only here does Proverbs so directly address a king, but such addresses were not uncommon in Egyptian and Mesopotamian literature.[28]

We should take note that this teaching comes from Lemuel's mother, with Lemuel only serving as the reporter. That this comes from 'his mother' is unusual. While Proverbs 1:8 and 6:20 speak of a mother's instruction and while the influence of a king's mother was sometimes substantial (1 Kings 1:11-13; 15:13), this is the only example of a royal oracle coming from the queen mother rather than the king's father.

Many are quick to note that the style of Proverbs 31:10-31 is so distinctive (an acrostic poem) that it likely should not be seen as a part of Lemuel's oracle (vv. 1-9). But, is not the theme of vv. 10-31 consistent with the instruction of Lemuel's mother in vv. 1-9 (cf. especially v. 3)? Both sections share key themes as well ('open your mouth,' vv. 8, 9, 26), and both show concern for the poor (vv. 9, 20).[29] Thus, it seems best to read chapter 31 as a work with two divisions, coming from the same author.

We know nothing else about either Agur or Lemuel. We have no evidence concerning the time of their existence or the means through which their influence came to Israel. No evidence exists to suggest we should view them any differently than the 'wise men' whom we have met in Proverbs 22:17 and 24:23.

That Solomon could have known of and collected these writings as well seems to be a fair conclusion. It seems at least plausible that

Hezekiah's men, as they compiled writings from the larger corpus of Solomon's own work (Prov. 25:1), also came across the works of Agur and Lemuel and thus brought the Book of Proverbs into the basic form in which we enjoy it. If this is so, it would make Solomon the author of the great bulk of the book (Prov. 1:1–22:16 and 25:1–29:27) and the compiler (22:17–24:34) and possible conduit of the rest (30:1–31:1).

The date of Proverbs

Proverbs, in its final form, cannot predate the time of Hezekiah (Prov. 25:1). It is possible that final editing was at an even later date than the work of his men, though there is no way of knowing. As the preceding deductions (see 'The authorship and compilation of Proverbs') reveal, we are not able to identify an exact date for the final editing of the Book of Proverbs into its present form. However, given the available evidence, there appears no good reason that essentially the book's final form could not have been the product of Hezekiah's scribes. This posits a possible date for compilation of c. 700 BC, with the bulk of the book having been written in the time of Solomon (c. 950 BC).

The Audience and Purpose of Proverbs

The audience of Proverbs

Before we can rightly interpret any portion of Scripture, we must discern the audience to whom it was written and to what purpose it was composed. To whom, then, was Proverbs written?

The best starting point for an answer is found in the oft-repeated phrase 'my son.' The phrase is found fifteen times in Proverbs 1–9 (occurring also in the plural four more times as a formal address without the first person singular suffix, cf. Prov. 4:1; 5:7; 7:24; 8:32). The same theme continues throughout the rest of the book, as the phrase is found eight more times. These latter references are found in Solomon's first collection of aphorisms (Prov. 19:27), the first collection of sayings from 'the wise' (23:15, 19, 26; 24:13, 21), Solomon's second collection by Hezekiah's men (27:11), and the instruction of Lemuel's mother (31:2).

It seems unlikely that a singular phrase so widely distributed throughout the book's various sections was merely the work of later editors attempting to give the appearance of literary unity. Rather, it bodes well for the organic unity of the book collected around this intended audience.

Who exactly is intended by 'my son?' Many have suggested that this designation is used metaphorically of the relationship between a teacher and pupil. There is some evidence in other ancient Near Eastern wisdom writings that such formal educational relationships could be designated in this way.

Here, however, the natural, familial relationship of father and son appears to be in view. In favor of this understanding is the fact that the mother stands alongside the father in providing instruction (Prov. 1:8; 6:20). The example of a mother's instruction in Lemuel's account speaks powerfully of a family setting (Prov. 31:1; cf. v. 26).

Further, upon closer examination, the Egyptian examples often cited as designating the relationship between a teacher/sage with a pupil/disciple break down. It may be true that, in many cases, they referred to training in matters of official court business to be inherited from one's father, but they were usually addressed from a specific father and addressed to his son by name.

This also appears to be the case in ancient Akkadian and Assyrian writings when they use the expression 'my son.'[30] Throughout the Old Testament, the father is charged with the responsibility of training the children (e.g. Deut. 6:6, 7; 11:19). There seems, therefore, no compelling reason to restrict the phrase 'my son' to that of a formal educational relationship between sage and disciple. Rather, it should be understood in its most natural sense: as a reference to the relationship of a son to his father.[31]

This having been said, the use of Proverbs among the nation of Israel likely developed over time to include the relationship between teacher/sage and his pupil/disciple. Similarly today, the application of Proverbs appropriately widens and many other relationships are implicated by the book's teaching.

The purpose of Proverbs

At face value, the Book of Proverbs appears to have been written and edited to serve a father in training his son and sending him into the world as a mature, wise follower of the Lord, ready to serve His purposes and advance His kingdom. Waltke sharpens the focus and heightens the drama: 'The "son," probably about twenty years of age, stands on the threshold of full adulthood. The time is at hand when the line must be crossed to move into maturity. Two conflicting worldviews make their appeal: "of Wisdom/Folly, Good/Pseudo-Good, Life/Death," and one must choose between them.'[32] This reveals a sense of urgency about the message of Proverbs. Waltke goes on to say: 'At this juncture when a decision must be made, the young man is most vulnerable to easy sex and easy money, for his sexual passions are at their strongest, and this tendency to be wise in his own eyes has not yet been tempered by reality.'[33]

In this light, should we, therefore, read the opening line ('Solomon the *son* of David,' emphasis added) as more than mere biographical detail? Solomon seems to view his work as the transmission of instruction across three generational lines, from David to Solomon (cf. Prov. 4:3ff) and, then, on to Solomon's sons. Ultimately, this is about the transmission of wisdom from our heavenly Father to those of us who are His sons (Prov. 3:12).

Reading the book from this perspective, it then unfolds and introduces us to the 'foolish son' (Prov. 10:1; 17:25; 19:13), the 'wise son' (13:1; 15:20; 23:24), the 'disgraceful son' (19:26), the 'discerning son' (28:7), and the 'son of my vows' (31:2). Thus, the 'son' we meet has the potential to act wisely, foolishly, or shamefully (Prov. 10:5; 17:2). Which will it be? Proverbs leaves us watching eagerly, praying that the way of wisdom and life will be chosen.

It is no accident that Proverbs closes by setting before us a tantalizing prophetic tidbit suggesting there is a greater Son yet to come, One who will embody the fulness of all the wisdom set forth in these pages (Prov. 30:4). Surely sonship means more than what we observe in our merely human relationships. When the Bible calls God our Father does it intend to measure from man upward to God (using the language of anthropomorphism, lowering and comparing God to a human relationship in order to help us understand Him; cf. Ps. 50:21) or from God to man (assuming an existing divine relationship within the Trinity, in order to raise our expectations about the potential of our human relationships as fathers and sons)?

The Interpretation of Proverbs

Hebrew parallelism in Proverbs
Understanding Proverbs requires appreciating the nature of Hebrew parallelism and the purposes for which it is employed. Though some proverbs have three lines (e.g. Prov. 1:27; 6:13; 19:7; 27:10; 30:20), a few have four (e.g. 30:14, 15, 17, 19), and one has six (30:4), the standard form of the Hebrew proverb is two lines.[34] These two lines are designed to stand in some kind of parallel relationship with one another, in order to achieve a desired affect.

Several kinds of poetic parallelism are employed in Proverbs. Antithetical parallelism sets the two lines in contrast to one another.

The contrast is intended to make a point by moving the reader to reflect on the differences. Proverbs 10:7 is an example: 'The memory of the righteous is blessed, But the name of the wicked will rot.' Consider also Proverbs 12:27: 'A slothful man does not roast his prey, But the precious possession of a man is diligence.' This is the most common type of parallelism in Proverbs and it dominates the scene in Proverbs 10–15.

Synonymous parallelism takes the lesson of the first line and restates it in only slightly different words in the second. The restatement aims at impressing the observation more powerfully upon the mind of the reader. An example is Proverbs 18:7: 'A fool's mouth is his ruin, And his lips are the snare of his soul.' Another is Proverbs 17:4: 'An evildoer listens to wicked lips, A liar pays attention to a destructive tongue.'

Synthetic parallelism uses the second line to amplify or expand upon the lesson of the first: 'The heart of the wise teaches his mouth, And adds persuasiveness to his lips' (Prov. 16:23). Also: 'A man lacking in sense pledges, And becomes surety in the presence of his neighbor' (Prov. 17:18). In addition, the 'how much more' proverbs fit here (Prov. 11:31; 15:11; 19:7; 21:27). This form of parallelism is most common in Proverbs 16:1–22:16.

Emblematic parallelism employs a simile or metaphor in one line to cast light upon the other: 'Like vinegar to the teeth and smoke to the eyes, So is the lazy one to those who send him' (Prov. 10:26). Or: 'Like the cold of snow in the time of harvest Is a faithful messenger to those who send him, For he refreshes the soul of his masters' (Prov. 25:13). Such proverbs bring us nearest to the root meaning of the word ('to be like'; see in 'Proverbs within the context of Hebrew poetic literature'). The goal is to move the reader to meditate on the similarities of the two subjects.

Formal parallelism generally appears to be a full sentence merely expressed in two lines. The 'better than' proverbs fit this description, such as 'Better is a little with righteousness Than great income with injustice' (Prov. 16:8; cf. 12:9; 15:16, 17; 16:16, 19, 32; 17:1; 19:1; 21:9, 19; 25:7, 24; 27:5; 28:6).

Interpreting Proverbs
Proverbs is both like and unlike the other parts of the Bible. It shares with other Scriptures the same inspiration, authority, and divine Author (2 Tim. 3:16). Yet, in its forms and style it is unique from any other portion of God's Word. We must, therefore, take great care in our interpretations and applications of its words.

The text of Proverbs

The Hebrew text of Proverbs, while not without some challenges, is in relatively good condition.[35] The LXX has added approximately 130 additional lines of text, while omitting a few of the lines in the Masoretic Text.[36] Generally, the LXX appears to be a loose translation, tending toward a paraphrase of the Hebrew text.[37] Where emendations have been proposed to resolve challenges in the text, they tend to be speculative in nature.[38] In such places, the Hebrew text is usually 'far more satisfying.'[39] Throughout the commentary, we have endeavored to wrestle with the Hebrew text for understanding rather than being quick to emend it, in order to conform it to the LXX, choosing the latter only when it appears truly necessary.

It should also be noted that in places the LXX also radically rearranges the order of the text. For example, Proverbs 30:1-14 comes immediately after 24:22. Additionally, Proverbs 30:15-33 and 31:1-9 are placed between 24:34 and 25:1.[40]

Principles for Interpreting Proverbs

Proverbs can appear overly mechanical in its description of the universe, God's sovereignty over it, and His dealings with man in it. Its observations are often stated in absolute terms, apparently leaving little room for variance.

For example, consider the sequence in Proverbs 3, which demands that if one fears the Lord he will experience great health (v. 8), material prosperity (v. 10), peaceful sleep (v. 24), and protection from calamity (v. 26). How should we view such sweeping statements? Are these guarantees? Is any lesser experience a sign of moral and spiritual failure?

To arrive at God's intention, several observations should be kept in mind as one interprets and applies Proverbs. First, the proverbs are consistent observations, not categorical absolutes. The proverbs are not always intended as promises, but only as observations of repeated phenomena.

Take Proverbs 22:6: 'Train up a child in the way he should go, Even when he is old he will not depart from it.' Many a parent has been told that, in this verse, God guarantees their wayward child will return to the fold. But, like so many other proverbs, its author is making an observation of consistent behavior and outcomes (i.e. normally children raised in godly homes end up walking with God themselves), not issuing an inviolable law.

It will take discernment to carefully draw the line between divine guarantee and divinely inspired observation.

A helpful path to such wisdom is the balancing of individual proverbs with the fuller witness of Scripture. This leads to a second principle of interpretation: The proverbs must be read in context. Many view the aphorisms as individual nuggets of gold scattered randomly along the path of wisdom. There is, they assert, little help to be found in the context.

However, each proverbial saying does reside within the whole of Proverbs and its teaching. They must be read against the balancing treatment of wisdom in Job and Ecclesiastes, as well as the fuller span of the poetic books. Then, too, the inspired Scriptural circle must be drawn to include the whole of the Old Testament and, ultimately, the entire Bible.

Third, we must understand that, by their very nature, the proverbs are truth stripped to the essentials. They are seldom qualified, balanced by surrounding statements, or extensively defined. They are stripped down, stated, and left to stand – all with the goal of arresting our attention and engaging our minds.

A proverb is truth in its most concentrated form, and thus expects us to add Spirit-illuminated reflection to come to full understanding. A proverb is designed to be 'unpacked' through much meditation, comparison with life, and with other Scriptures. Murphy well says: 'The proverb's declaratory nature catches our attention, but it also conceals, for it achieves only a slice of reality.... The truth of a saying – call it a partial truth – usually needs another saying to counterbalance it.'[41]

Fourth, though Proverbs can appear simplistic to the uninformed reader, we must realize that Proverbs does not intend to present life as void of ambiguities. Consider the juxtaposition of the seemingly contradictory words of Proverbs 26:4-5: 'Do not answer a fool according to his folly, Lest you also be like him. Answer a fool as his folly deserves, Lest he be wise in his own eyes.' The one who comes to Proverbs for simple answers requiring little thought will leave disappointed. We want to know, 'Which is it!? Do I answer him? Or do I not?' Proverbs was written not merely to tell us what to do, but also to make us think. Pure pragmatists may find themselves frustrated, if unwilling to pursue reflective, Spirit-guided meditation.

Fifth, we do well to unearth the assumptions inherent to a proverb. Because a proverb is truth stripped to its irreducible minimum, all helpful qualifying and clarifying statements are implicit rather than explicit. Bullock helpfully observes: 'The first hermeneutical principle is that the theological assumptions of the book are often more important than the textual context.'[42]

For example, until we have carefully absorbed the instructions of Proverbs 1–9, we are not well positioned to rightly interpret the aphorisms of Proverbs 10ff. The theology of Proverbs 1–9 sets the stage for understanding the wisdom of the later sentence literature. We must ask ourselves not only what is stated, but what is assumed about God, His relationship to, and role in, the world around us, and His purposes.

Sixth, while Proverbs is not highly prophetic in nature (though see Prov. 30:4 and the commentary there), it ultimately finds its fulfillment in Jesus Christ, who is the wisdom of God (Isa. 11:2; 1 Cor. 1:24, 30). 'Lady wisdom' in Proverbs 8 is probably best understood as a personification of a divine attribute for didactic purposes, rather than a reference to the second Person of the Trinity specifically (see the commentary at 8:1, 22). Yet, it is only as we embrace Christ through faith that we are then able to enter into the wisdom that His Spirit sets forth here. When Christ becomes our very life (Col. 3:4), we find Him to be the One 'in whom are hidden all the treasures of wisdom and knowledge' (Col. 2:3). We should, therefore, look to the New Testament not only for clarification and balance, but for fulfillment of the wisdom so gloriously set forth in Proverbs.

The Theology of Proverbs

What would I know if all I possessed was the Book of Proverbs? What would I know about God – about His creation, purposes, and ways? Stated negatively, what would remain a mystery and undisclosed to me if all I possessed of God's revelation was this book? What part of reality would I be oblivious to? These questions propel us forward in discerning just what contribution Proverbs makes to the whole of a Biblical theology.

Because of its highly practical nature, some have designated Proverbs as a 'secular' book.[43] While not detracting from its practical nature, it must be said that this could hardly miss the point of the book more badly. Proverbs is highly theological. As A. W. Tozer wisely observed: 'What comes in to our minds when we think about God is the most important thing about us.'[44] This is where we must begin: What came into Solomon's mind when he thought of God? And, what should come into our minds when we read Proverbs?

The God we meet in Proverbs created all things (Prov. 3:19, 20; 14:31; 17:5; 20:12; 22:2), designed a purpose all aspects of His creation were to serve (16:4; 19:21), and actively governs them all

(21:1). Indeed, God established a moral order to His creation and judges (Prov. 10:27, 29; 12:2) and rewards (11:4; 12:11; 14:23; 22:4) according to that order.

But, God does not simply set a moral order in place and step back, but is active in the creation He has made (Prov. 3:9, 10). God avenges wrong (Prov. 25:21, 22) and rewards righteousness (21:21; 22:4). He hears and answers prayer (Prov. 15:8, 29), and receives or rejects worship (15:8; 21:3, 27). God is sovereign over His creation (Prov. 16:4, 9; 19:21). He is sovereign over each individual's life and circumstances (Prov. 3:9, 10), including their health (20:12) and social station (22:2; 29:13, 25). He is sovereign over matters as divergent as a king's decisions (Prov. 21:1) and the roll of dice (16:33). God is sovereign over death and the grave (Prov. 15:11).

God is omniscient (Prov. 5:21; 15:3, 11; 21:2), assaying the heart of every person (15:11; 16:2; 17:3; 20:27). He is holy (Prov. 3:7, 32, 33; 6:16; 8:13; 9:10) and deserving of top honor in all matters (3:9). He is merciful (Prov. 28:13), wise (3:19; 8:22), just (11:1; 16:11), and truthful (12:22). He is both transcendently separate from His creation (Prov. 3:19, 20; 15:29), yet immanently active within it (19:17; 20:27; 22:23). He is inscrutable (Prov. 25:2), and yet knowable, entering into personal relationship with the one who rightly fears Him (2:5; 9:10).

Indeed, God reveals Himself as our Father. As such, He disciplines His sons out of love (Prov. 3:11, 12) and protects His own (3:26; 10:29; 18:10). He provides for their needs (Prov. 10:3), blesses them (10:22), sustains their lives daily (10:27), guides them (16:9), and is the giver of a godly spouse (19:14). God is unchangeably consistent and worthy of trust (Prov. 3:5; 16:3, 20; 22:19; 28:25). He reveals Himself to His creation through His word (Prov. 29:18; 30:5).

God is capable of pleasure (Prov. 16:7) and delight (3:12; 11:1, 20; 12:22; 15:8).

He blesses (Prov. 3:33; 10:22; 16:20) and curses (3:33; 22:14), even cutting short the life of the wicked (10:27; 22:23) and prolonging the lives of the righteous (8:35; 10:27; 14:27; 19:23; 22:4).

In short, in Proverbs, we find God to be the same God presented to us throughout the rest of the Old Testament. In this regard, there is no great divide between the wisdom literature and the Law and Prophets.

Solomon had a particular affinity for Deuteronomy.[45] The wisdom of Proverbs is founded upon the Law (Prov. 28:4; 29:18) and, indeed, its instruction is called torah (1:8; 3:1; 13:14). The close affinity between Proverbs and Deuteronomy finds a plausible explanation in the Law's injunction that the king "write for himself on a scroll a copy of this law" (Deut. 17:18).'[46] The personification of wisdom 'is the closest thing wisdom has to the prophetic formula "Thus says the Lord."'[47]

Israel is never mentioned by name after Proverbs 1:1. Additionally, some bemoan the scarce coverage the covenant gets. However, though it is true that the covenant is not paraded, neither is it avoided. We meet the covenant name of God (i.e. Yahweh) over eighty times in the book. All the rich covenant truths elsewhere communicated in the covenant name are intended here as well.

Further, we are told to follow Moses' instruction by bringing the firstfruits offering to the Lord (Prov. 3:9; cf. Deut. 26:2). The sacrificial system is assumed, even if challenged (Prov. 15:8; 21:3, 27). The differences in emphases may be accounted for by the fact that the sage simply assumed the complementary ministry of the prophets and priests (Jer. 18:18).

Just like the individual aphorism, so the whole of Proverbs does not provide itself with many qualifying, clarifying, and balancing statements. It is content to state the truth in arresting fashion, allowing searching minds to wrestle with it for discernment, insight, and balanced interpretation and application.

Some want to make Proverbs seem exclusively human because of its emphasis on observation and insight. It is true that Proverbs arises from insightful observation of, and reflection on, the created order (Prov. 6:6; 24:30-34; 25:2; 30:18, 19). But, its teaching is founded upon revelation from God (2:6; 8:1ff; 30:5, 6). It is this very revelation that keeps our speculations in check (Prov. 29:18).

While Proverbs shares some forms of expression and literary style with other ancient Near Eastern wisdom writings, it is set apart from and above those of Egypt, Babylon and the like by the recurring theme of 'the fear of the Lord.' They have no corresponding equivalent to this foundational element of Proverbs. Employing the literary technique of inclusio, the book opens (Prov. 1:7) and closes on this theme (31:30). As the opening discourses on wisdom draw to a close it is sounded again (Prov. 9:10). Like a vein of gold the fear of the Lord runs throughout the rest of Proverbs, being found in every stratum of the book.

The fear of the Lord stands in contrast with the fear of man (Prov. 29:25). This holy fear is set forth as a pathway full of countless benefits for its traveler. It is not only the beginning of knowledge (Prov. 1:7, 29; 2:5) and wisdom (9:10; 15:33), but it instills confidence (14:26) and makes rich (22:4). The fear of the Lord prolongs life (Prov. 10:27), is a fountain of life (14:27), leads to life (19:23), and is rewarded with life (22:4). The fear of the Lord purifies, for it is to hate the evil God Himself hates (Prov. 8:13; 16:6; 23:17). The fear of the Lord is a healing balm, for to fear the Lord is to be delivered from other fears (Prov. 19:23). Though you may lose all else, you must gain the fear of the Lord (Prov. 15:16).

To the unredeemed this 'fear' is the terror of having fallen into the hands of the living God (Heb. 10:31). To the child of God this 'fear' is not terror, but a reverential awe that holds his heavenly Father in highest honor. It issues in a heart of submissive worship.

Ed Welch helpfully suggests that the fear of the Lord is a continuum we advance along when we begin to accurately perceive God and the world He has made. He represents it as movement along the following progression of attitudes:

Terror » dread » trembling » astonishment » awe » reverence » devotion » trust » worship.[48]

The fear of the Lord begins as we become aware of the holy justice of God. As we grow in the fear of the Lord, we ever increasingly become aware of the holy love of God, without graduating from the justice of God.[49] Terror is, at one level, appropriate if God is indeed who the Scriptures reveal Him to be, but it is not the ultimate goal of God's self-revelation. His aim is to draw us near in the intimacy of relationship, for the fear of the Lord and the knowledge of God are indivisibly linked (Prov. 2:5; 9:10).

One will never know God without first fearing Him. No one will fear Him without knowing something of Him. To know God is to fear Him. To rightly fear God is to grow in knowledge of Him. Indeed, the fear of the Lord and the knowledge of God are often found as the twin towers of true religion (Isa. 11:2; 58:2), describing 'the poles of awe and intimacy' which God desires.[50]

To possess 'the fear of the Lord' is to embrace reality. It signals the adoption of a Biblical worldview. It defines the perspective of the person who has come to see that 'The earth is the Lord's, and all it contains, The world, and those who dwell in it' (Ps. 24:1). It describes an informed and accurate perspective of who God is and who I am before Him.

In such a world, it is not difficult to understand Proverbs' consistent pairing of wisdom with righteousness (e.g. Prov. 1:3; 9:9; 10:31; 23:24) and folly with sin (e.g. Prov. 10:23; 24:9). To live wisely in the world is to live in harmony with the God who created, sustains, and governs it. The ultimate folly is the attempt to live in God's world without God. Wisdom in Proverbs, therefore, is not cast as a speculative venture, but as a conformity of one's will to a transcendent, unchanging moral order governed by a personal God. Wisdom for this reason is set forth in Proverbs in all or nothing, black or white categories.

How, we may ask, does such a message sound to the ears of our postmodern society? As Van Leeuwen notes, in Proverbs 'Wise folk know the way things "ought to be," and they have a sense of right and wrong.'[51] Such dogmatism is unwelcome in the climate of relativism created by postmodern thinking. Ought-talk finds no welcome among children of the age. Pragmatism ('it works for me') and privatization ('my truth') are twin virtues of postmodern thinking.

Proverbs also values pragmatism, but only in the sense that the God who created and sovereignly governs this world has established a fixed and transcendent moral order which must be understood, appreciated, and conformed to if success in His world is to be enjoyed. Though the pragmatism of postmodern thought and that of Proverbs are vastly different, an appeal to a pragmatic impulse may provide the best common ground between the present cultural climate and the authoritative message of Proverbs. This common longing may provide a good starting point for communicating the message of Proverbs to the people of this age. A successful life is desired by all. The inevitable logical breakdown of postmodern thought can be explored and exposed and then a dialogue begun regarding Proverbs' worldview and prescriptions.

In brief, the purpose of Proverbs is to impart wisdom. Proverbs was written that we might achieve skill in living in God's world (Prov. 1:2-6). The first principle of such wisdom is found in 'the fear of the Lord' (Prov. 1:7) and moves ever increasingly into 'the knowledge of God' (9:10). The great promise held before us is life – both now (Prov. 3:2, 16) and forever (Prov. 12:28; 14:32; 23:17-18). The path we must walk to find it is that of wisdom/ righteousness, while avoiding the way of folly/sin.

The Structure of Proverbs

Understanding the structure of Proverbs is key to rightly interpreting its contents. The argument which informs the following outline is found above (see 'The Authorship and Compilation of Proverbs') and in the commentary at each relevant point.

I. Introduction (1:1-7)
    A. Title (1:1)
    B. Purpose (1:2-6)

End Notes

1. Kidner, Derek, *The Wisdom of Proverbs, Job and Ecclesiastes* (Downers Grove, Illinois: InterVarsity Press, 1985), 15.

2. Bullock, C. Hassell, *An Introduction to the Old Testament Poetic Books: Revised and Expanded* (Chicago: Moody Press, 1979, 1988), 39.

3. Helmbold, A. K., 'Proverbs, Book of,' in *The Zondervan Pictorial Encyclopedia of the Bible* (Grand Rapids, Michigan: Zondervan Publishing House, 1975, 1976), 4:918.

4. Ibid., 4:915.

5. Kidner, 39-40.

6. Whybray, R. N., *Proverbs* (Grand Rapids, Michigan: William B. Eerdmans Publishing Company, 1994), 324, 327-328.

7. Buzzell, Sid S., 'Proverbs' in *The Bible Knowledge Commentary: Old Testament* (Wheaton: Victor Books, 1988), 902.

8. Waltke, Bruce K., 'Proverbs, Theology of,' *New International Dictionary of Old Testament Theology and Exegesis* (Grand Rapids, Michigan: Zondervan Publishing House, 1997), 4:1079.

9. Kidner, Derek, *Proverbs* (Downers Grove, Illinois: InterVarsity Press, 1964), 13.

10. Ross, Allen P, 'Proverbs' in *The Expositor's Bible Commentary* (Grand Rapids, Michigan: Zondervan Publishing House, 1991), 5:890.

11. Brown, Francis, S. R. Driver, Charles A. Briggs, *A Hebrew and English Lexicon of the Old Testament* (Oxford: Clarendon Press, n.d.), 605.

12. Adams, Jay E., *Proverbs* (Woodruff, South Carolina: Timeless Texts, 1997), 2.

13. Bridges, Charles, *A Commentary on Proverbs* (Edinburgh: The Banner of Truth Trust, 1846, reprint 1998), xiii.

14. Whybray, 17.

15. Kidner, *Proverbs*, 14.

16. Ruffle, J., 'Proverbs' in *The New Bible Commentary: Revised* (Grand Rapids, Michigan: William B. Eerdmans Publishing Company, 1970), 550.

17. Ibid.

18. Helmbold, 4:917.

19. Hubbard, D. A., 'Proverbs, Book of,' in *New Bible Dictionary*, 2nd edition (Wheaton, Illinois: Tyndale House Publishers, 1962), 988.

20. Cited in Waltke, 'Proverbs: Theology of,' 4:1081.

21. Ibid.

22. Steinmann, Andrew E., 'Proverbs 1–9 As A Solomonic Composition,' *Journal of the Evangelical Theological Society* 43.4 (2000), 674.

23. Waltke, 'Proverbs: Theology of,' 4:1082.

24. Ibid., 4:1081.

25. Whybray, 407.

26. Kidner, *Proverbs,* 178.

27. Lane, Eric, *Proverbs* (Inverness, Scotland: Christian Focus Publications, 2000), 323.

28. Bullock, 176.

29. Waltke, 'Proverbs: Theology of,' 4:1084.

30. Waltke, Bruce K., 'The Book of Proverbs and Ancient Wisdom Literature,' *Bibliotheca Sacra* 136 (1979), 231.

31. Fox, Michael V., *Proverbs 1–9* (New York: Doubleday, 2000), 9; Kidner, *The Wisdom of Proverbs, Job and Ecclesiastes,* 20; Murphy, Roland E., *Proverbs* (Nashville: Thomas Nelson Publishers, Inc., 1998), xxi; Waltke, Bruce K., 'The Book of Proverbs and Ancient Wisdom Literature,' 8 ; Whybray, 8.

32. Waltke, 'Proverbs, Theology of,' 4:1085.

33. Ibid.

34. Buzzell, 1:903.

35. Ross, 5:890.

36. Whybray, 19.

37. Helmbold, 4:917.

38. Ibid.

39. Ross, 5:890.

40. Murphy, xxvi.

41. Ibid.

42. Bullock, 162.

43. Aitken, Kenneth T., *Proverbs* (Philadelphia: The Westminster Press, 1986), 4.; Fox, 7.

44. Tozer, A. W., *The Knowledge of the Holy* (San Francisco: Harper and Row Publishers, 1961), 1.

45. Waltke, Bruce K., 'The Book of Proverbs and Old Testament Theology,' *Bibliotheca Sacra* 136 (1979): 302-318.

46. Ibid., 318.

47. Bullock, 148.

48. Welch, Edward T., *When People are Big and God is Small* (Phillipsburg, New Jersey: Presbyterian and Reformed Publishing Company, 1997), 96-97.

49. Ibid.

50. Kidner, *Proverbs,* 61.

51. Van Leeuwen, Raymond C., 'The Book of Proverbs' in *The New Interpreter's Bible* (Nashville: Abingdon Press, 1997), 5:24-25.

Proverbs 1

1:1. The proverbs of Solomon the son of David, king of Israel:
The book of wisdom begins by identifying its primary author
– Solomon, son of David, third king of the nation of Israel. With
the hindsight provided by history, we stand amazed that a man like
Solomon would write a book of Wisdom Literature. So many issues
would seem to mitigate against his authoring a book on wisdom.
Exhibit A: his 700 wives and 300 concubines (1 Kings 11:3). One
justly wonders where the wisdom is in that! Yet, later iniquity does
not cancel out previous insight.

A closer examination reveals the source of Solomon's wisdom.
After his father David died, God personally invited Solomon, 'Ask
what you wish me to give you' (1 Kings 3:5b). Solomon's response
was gratefulness for God's faithfulness to his father (v. 6) and
humility (vv. 7-8). Then, the new king made his request, 'So give
Thy servant an understanding heart to judge Thy people to discern
between good and evil' (v. 9). God was pleased (v. 10) and promised
'I have done according to your words. Behold, I have given you a
wise and discerning heart, so that there has been no one like you
before you, nor shall one like you arise after you' (v. 12).

The writer of 1 Kings went on to list Solomon's great achievements
(4:20-34), saying 'Now God gave Solomon wisdom and very great
discernment and breadth of mind, like the sand that is on the
seashore. Solomon's wisdom surpassed the wisdom of all the sons
of the east and all the wisdom of Egypt. For he was wiser than all
men ...' (vv. 29-31a). Among his many remarkable achievements was
the writing of 3,000 proverbs (v. 32). Exactly how these proverbs
were numbered is not stated, though they likely were compiled
into volumes of some kind for preservation. Nor is it stated how the
proverbs mentioned in 1 Kings 4:32 relate to what we find here in
the book of Proverbs, though, undoubtedly, many of those spoken
of in 1 Kings would be included here. We should not, however,
conclude that all of the proverbs of this book are from the pen of
Solomon. Agur (Prov. 30:1-33) and Lemuel (31:1-31) both add theirs
as well (cf. also the comments on Prov. 22:17). Presumably, all of
this took place before Solomon turned his heart away from the Lord
(1 Kings 11:1-11).

What Solomon is said to have given to us are 'proverbs.' A proverb is a compactly constructed sentence packed with practical insight. It is a stubby sentence pregnant with meaning. It is college in a cup. It is wisdom that you can carry with you as you walk through life.

A proverb is a sentence constructed in parallel. See the introduction for how these parallelisms present themselves and what they mean. Proverbs presents us with divinely given nuggets of gold that will make rich the one who prizes them enough to understand and apply them at all cost.

1:2. To show wisdom and instruction, To discern the sayings of understanding,

This begins a series of statements (running through verse 6) that delineate the purpose of this collection of proverbs. Verses 2-6 present ten words that summarize what Proverbs gives the person who heeds its instruction: 'wisdom,' 'instruction,' 'understanding' (v. 2), 'instruction' (v. 3), 'prudence,' 'knowledge,' and 'discretion' (v. 4), 'learning,' 'wise counsel' (v. 5), and 'understand' (v. 6). We will now consider each of these words individually and see what these proverbs are designed to yield in the life of the one who puts them into practice.

'Wisdom' is the first promised result. The basic meaning of the word is 'skill' in living. This skill brings its possessor into success.[1] The Messiah, according to promise, possessed this wisdom (Jer. 23:5), as may the one who possesses 'the mind of Christ' (1 Cor. 2:16). The skill referred to may be in craftsmanship with the hands (Exod. 31:6), in organization (1 Kings 3:28), and in counseling others (2 Sam. 20:22).[2] The root of this term is found forty-two times in the book of Proverbs.

'Instruction' is also guaranteed. An alternative translation is 'discipline.' This discipline is education through correction.[3] Proverbs will step on your toes, but, in doing so, will discipline you and keep your feet in the right path when you walk in their light.[4] Reading this book is profitable, but not comfortable.

'Understanding' refers to the knowledge of something and to the faculty that enables you to come to that knowledge.[5] Proverbs can teach you things you will learn nowhere else. Additionally, 'understanding' may refer to the very object of knowledge.[6] Job asked where the place of understanding is (Job 28:12, 20). Truth is not relative – there is right and wrong, truth and error, understanding and stupidity – and it may be discovered in these proverbs.

'Discernment' is the path to this understanding. Discernment is the ability to look at two things and see what God sees. These proverbs cut through the fog of human reasoning and throw the spotlight of God upon a given situation, revealing God's verdict.[7]

1:3. To receive instruction in wise behavior, Righteousness, justice and equity;
This verse provides the fourth of seven benefits delivered to the door of those who heed the proverbs of this book: 'instruction in wise behavior.' 'Instruction' is the same word as in verse 2. The Hebrew term behind 'wise behavior' is roughly synonymous with the word translated 'discernment' in verse 2. However, there is a distinction to be made. 'Discernment' means to distinguish between two things. 'Wise behavior' refers to an understanding of the reason for the distinction that is made. A good alternative translation may be 'insight.'[8] Feeding on the proverbs not only helps you distinguish God's choice in any situation, but why it is His choice.

This insight is seen as it is actively revealed in 'righteousness, justice and equity.' See Proverbs 2:9 for another use of this trio of moral qualities. '... [W]hatever is true, whatever is honorable, whatever is right, whatever is pure, whatever is lovely, whatever is of good repute, if there is any excellence and if anything worthy of praise, let your mind dwell on these things' (Phil. 4:8). The wisest course of action in any circumstance is bringing your life into conformity with the character and actions of God. Insight is not given for the stuffy halls of academia, but for the trenches of daily life.

1:4. To give prudence to the naïve, To the youth knowledge and discretion,
The fifth item is 'prudence,' a Hebrew word which may be used negatively ('craftily,' Exod. 21:14) or positively as here.[9] The proverbs will make the gullible shrewd and able to avoid the pitfalls of life. The 'naïve' person is one who is open and vulnerable to any influence that the winds may blow upon him. The 'naïve' lack judgment. The proverbs will make them able to see these influences for what they are and to circumvent the disaster they would bring.

The sixth benefit is seen in the 'knowledge' derived from the Proverbs. This is offered to the immature 'youth,' just as 'prudence' is to the gullible. This 'knowledge' is something gained through the senses.[10] The proverbs heighten every part of a person to the truth of God. The immature is given, through the proverbs, what normally only years of experience might grant to the aged.

'Discretion' is the seventh item listed as a benefit to the student of Proverbs. This term is used in the proverbs to describe wisdom's ability to protect its possessor from the harm brought on by foolishly proceeding with an ill-advised plan (cf. Prov. 2:11; 3:21).[11] Positively, 'discretion' is the ability to form a practical plan of action and work it to its end.[12] The proverbs instill common sense.

1:5. A wise man will hear and increase in learning, And a man of understanding will acquire wise counsel,
Not only do the impressionable and immature (v. 4) benefit from the proverbs, but also the one already possessing a degree of wisdom. We are never fully wise.

Two more benefits will come to the one who seeks and keeps on seeking wisdom from God. The eighth is that they will gain additional 'learning.' The root of the word means to 'take' or to 'seize.' The mature person of wisdom gains an ever increasing ability to grasp with their mind the wisdom of God as it relates to their particular circumstances. They will receive 'perception' into the affairs of life.[13]

Also, they will lay hold of 'wise counsel,' the ninth benefit listed. The one who gets this is 'a man of understanding,' the participle of the word translated 'discern' in verse 2. The Hebrew behind 'wise counsel' is related to the word for rope or cord. A metaphor for what is intended comes from the world of sea navigation. Ropes were used to steer a ship, thus the sailor pulled on the ropes to steer a true course. The one who rightly discerns the things of God will, by continuing to study these proverbs, be able to steer a safe and true course through life.[14]

1:6. To understand a proverb and a figure, The words of the wise and their riddles.
This verse ends the litany of benefits that come to the person who absorbs the content of this book (vv. 2-6). The tenth benefit of studying Proverbs is to 'understand.' This is the same word as translated 'discern' in verse 2. Four expressions are then used to describe what we find in this book. A 'proverb' is the term that heads the book (Prov. 1:1). A 'figure' refers to a saying that speaks indirectly to an issue. To the discerning of heart a 'figure' has a sense other than the obvious one.[15] 'The words of the wise' means that the discerning does not give heed to everyone, but only to those who have acquired God's wisdom. The 'riddles' may refer to what is obscure or indirect in its statements, much like the riddles of Samson (Judg. 14:13-14) or the queen of Sheba (1 Kings 10:1).[16]

Instead of describing four different kinds of sayings, it seems rather that the writer is setting up a contrast of two kinds of sayings. The path of wisdom leads not only to understanding plain statements of truth ('proverbs' and 'the words of the wise'), but also more enigmatic, indirect statements that carry a stream of wisdom that lies beneath the surface of the obvious ('a figure' and 'riddles') and is only tapped by the one who meditates upon them.

Let us, then, review what the opening purpose statement of the book reveals. If one considers the verbs of verses 2-6 we discover (1) that studying the proverbs enables one to 'know' certain things, v. 2, (2) to 'discern' God's path, v. 2, (3) to 'receive' the knowledge of God's ways, v. 3; (4) that they 'give' what the naïve and immature need, v. 4; (5) that they 'increase' what the wise have, v. 5; and (6) that they enable their reader to 'understand' God's mind, v. 6.

If one considers the nouns, proverbs grants (1) 'wisdom,' v. 2; (2) 'instruction,' v. 2; (3) 'understanding,' v. 2; (4) 'instruction,' v. 3; (5) 'prudence,' v. 4; (6) 'knowledge,' v. 4; (7) 'discretion,' v. 4; (8) 'learning,' v. 5; (9) 'wise counsel,' v. 5; and (10) understanding,' v. 6.

1:7. The fear of the Lord is the beginning of knowledge; Fools despise wisdom and instruction.
This verse expresses the substance of the entire book of Proverbs: 'The fear of the Lord is the beginning of knowledge.' The fear of the Lord is a repeated theme being found fourteen times throughout the book. The fear of the Lord is an inclusion wrapping itself around the first nine chapters (Prov. 1:7; 9:10), as well as the entire collection (Prov. 1:7; 31:30).

Being contrasted with the fear of man (Prov. 29:25), the fear of the Lord renders countless benefits for its possessor. It is not only the beginning of knowledge (Prov. 1:7, 29; 2:5) and wisdom (9:10; 15:33), but it instills confidence (14:26) and makes rich (22:4). The fear of the Lord prolongs life (Prov. 10:27), is a fountain of life (14:27), leads to life (19:23), and is rewarded with life (22:4). The fear of the Lord is to hate the evil God hates (Prov. 8:13; 16:6, 23:17). Though you may lose all else, gain the fear of the Lord (Prov. 15:16)!

Isaiah echoes these remarkable promises: 'He will be the sure foundation for your times, a rich store of salvation and wisdom and knowledge; *The fear of the Lord is the key to this treasure*' (33:6, niv, italics mine). Oswald Chambers was correct: 'The remarkable thing about fearing God is that when you fear God, you fear nothing else, whereas if you do not fear God, you fear everything else.'[17]

This reverent awe is the 'beginning' of knowledge and wisdom in that it is the 'first and controlling principle, rather than a stage which one leaves behind.'[18] The wise never graduate from the school of instruction and wisdom.

While the fear of the Lord is 'the key to this treasure,' the path of the fool is to 'despise wisdom and instruction.' For the first time, we are introduced to 'the fool,' a personage that will be mentioned repeatedly throughout the book. 'Wisdom' we have already met in verse 1 (and vv. 5, 6, 'the wise'). 'Instruction' has been introduced in verses 2, 3. 'Despise' means to treat with contempt.

1:8. Hear, my son, your father's instruction, And do not forsake your mother's teaching;

This begins the first major section of the book (Prov. 1:8–9:18). While most of the proverbs in the book are short, pithy statements of truth, this section is comprised of more extended discourses, each of which carries a protracted theme. These discourses prepare the reader to receive the proverbs that follow in Proverbs 10:1ff.

The exhortation 'Hear, my son' echoes an oft-repeated call in Proverbs. The word 'son' is used sixty times in the book, and the phrase 'my son' is used twenty-three times. This sense of filial exhortation permeates the entire book. It may apply not only to biological family lines, but also to the relationship of a wisdom teacher and his pupil. Here, however, the addition of 'mother' makes the biological family the primary reference. The home is the primary place for moral instruction. The weight of responsibility for moral instruction of children in wisdom falls upon the father throughout the Book of Proverbs, but here, as in Proverbs 6:20, the mother is also involved and must be respected by the children. See also Proverbs 31:1 for Lemuel's praise of his mother's instruction. With fifteen of the twenty-three occurrences of 'my son' appearing in chapters 1–9, perhaps this section originally served as a text for a father's moral instruction of his son.

The father instills 'instruction,' a word we have already met several times (vv. 2, 3, 7). The primary sense of the word is instruction through correction. Additionally the 'teaching' of the mother is to be heeded. 'Teaching' is the Hebrew word torah and may be cognate to a verb meaning 'to point or direct.'[19] Torah is also the Hebrew word used to refer to God's law. It is possible that the verse means that mothers primarily point out the path of righteousness, but fathers are the primary disciplinarians. It seems more likely, however, that it means that both parents are God's agents on earth to point their children in the right direction and to train them through correction to stay in that path.

Wisdom embraces both tables of God's law and ties them together. To truly fear the Lord (v. 7; cf. the first four commandments) one must rightly relate to others (vv. 8ff; cf. the last six commandments). Likewise, to rightly relate to others one must first rightly relate to God.

1:9. Indeed, they are a graceful wreath to your head, And ornaments about your neck.
To keep the fifth commandment is not only wise, but it adds honor, attractiveness, grace, and esteem to the life of the son or daughter who does so. God makes the honor of father and mother an honor to the child as they pass through life. The two-fold description is first stated as 'a graceful wreath to your head' (cf. Prov. 4:9). The picture is of a crown or wreath placed on the head by those who esteem this person's life. Likewise such a life is adorned as 'ornaments about your neck' might be (cf. Prov. 3:3, 22; 6:21).

Submitting early to the refining process of instruction and discipline of parents removes many of the personal habits and qualities that could spoil relationships later in life. To heed the discipline of father and the instruction of mother yields a happy life full of fruitful and friendly relationships. People will be drawn to you and desire your company.

1:10. My son, if sinners entice you, Do not consent.
Having stated the benefits of heeding the counsel of parents (and perhaps of a wisdom teacher, cf. v. 8), now the instruction grows more specific. Verses 10-14 warn of the attraction of the sinner's ways, but verses 15-19 describe the destruction walking with them brings.

The people bent on leading you astray are called 'sinners,' a word that describes those who make sin their habit.[20] Their alluring call is described by the word 'entice.' The Hebrew verb means to 'be open, spacious, wide.' The resulting description is of one who is open to all kinds of allurements because of their immaturity.[21] The intensive active form, piel, is used, rendering a meaning 'when those seasoned in sin use every trick of their trade to pull you into their path ....'

The prohibition is 'Do not consent.' The Hebrew describes 'the willingness (inclination) to do something under obligation or request.'[22] Do not yield your will to anyone except God! When they do their best to seduce and lead you astray, keep your will bent away from their path.

1:11. If they say, 'Come with us, Let us lie in wait for blood, Let us ambush the innocent without cause;'
Verses 11-14 comprise the verbal enticement of the wicked that was warned of in verses 10. The young often grow weary of being in the place of learning. It is attractive to hear someone call you to take control of your circumstances and become a person to contend with.

The action called for is vicious, the verb 'to lie in wait' is used elsewhere of murder (Deut. 19:11), kidnapping (Judg. 21:20), or seduction (Prov. 23:28).[23] This heinous action is exacted upon 'the innocent' (NIV, 'harmless soul'), showing that it is unprovoked and without cause. By and by, there will be a promise of material gain by these actions (vv. 13-14), but here it is done 'without cause.' The motivation is violence for violence's sake, with the financial benefits of secondary concern. There is illicit pleasure in dominating and intimidating the innocent.[24] How descriptive of the spirit of the age in which we live! We do well to remember it was violence that evoked God's destruction in the days of Noah (Gen. 6:11).

How appropriate verses 8-19 are in the day when gangs seem to have taken over the youth culture of entire cities and, now, even of smaller communities. The call to take control of your life, to become a part of an extended family, to stop being used is an attractive one. How desperately our young people need to hear this wisdom.

Verse 18 contains the answer to this enticement – 'They lie in wait for their own blood; They ambush their own lives.' The treacherous and violent will taste of their own actions. 'He has dug a pit and hollowed it out, And has fallen into the hole which he made. His mischief will return upon his own head, And his violence will descend upon his own pate' (Ps. 7:15-16).

1:12. Let us swallow them alive like Sheol, Even whole, as those who go down to the pit;
The taunting invitation to violence continues. Murder is the plot. 'Sheol' is here not a reference to the afterlife, but to the grave; 'the pit' is a synonym of 'Sheol' found often in Scripture. The two lines are parallel, with the second underscoring the point made by the first. The strategy is an overwhelming show of power and force incapacitating the victim before he can reasonably react to the attack. Confused and engulfed by an attack he did not expect and cannot control, the victim yields up what the attacker wants.

The invitation of the sinner is to lash out at anyone and everyone who comes in your path, then cover all evidence of the wrong.

Beware of the one who promises 'no one need ever know!' You may attempt to bury the evidence, but remember: 'There is no creature hidden from His sight, but all things are open and laid bare to the eyes of Him with whom we have to do' (Heb. 4:13).

1:13. We shall find all kinds of precious wealth, We shall fill our houses with spoil;

The illicit wooing continues. The promise is now that of material wealth untold. The lie is that, if we apply our God-given energies to ill-gotten gain rather than honorable labor, we will come out ahead. This is not the call of a renegade band, but of those who have settled lives in the community and possess their own 'houses.' The plot is to plunder their neighbors, to use them to make their lives plush. That the desired wealth is called 'precious' ('precious, rare, splendid')[25] underscores that they see no earthly way of acquiring it apart from taking matters into their own hands. When God's wisdom is shunned, ever-advancing selfishness is the only path left open to us.

1:14. Throw in your lot with us, We shall all have one purse,

Those whose actions are selfish at their core now promise that such selfishness will not rule among those who cast their lot with them. That is a silly promise, since sin is never so easily compartmentalized. 'Come, let's take advantage of others to our good fortune, but rest assured we will never do you wrong' – This is the final call of the gang. The promise is of common commitment to one another; the reality is never so noble.

1:15. My son, do not walk in the way with them. Keep your feet from their path,

Paternal wisdom now speaks to the ears in which still ring the tempting invitation of sinners. 'My son' echoes the call that began this section in verse 10. Its inclusion adds a tone of pleading seriousness, implying that to go the way of the sinner is to turn your back on family. 'Do not walk in the way' is the opposite of the invitation to 'Come with us' (v. 11). The youth is brought to a critical divide. He must choose between truth and error, light and darkness, righteousness and sin. To go one way is to reject its opposite. To delay decision is to decide. Blessed is the young person whose ears ring with his parents' pleadings when temptation assaults. May the voice of wisdom never be drowned out!

'Keep your feet from their path' answers the first line by simple parallelism. The path of sin rarely looks dangerous at the outset, but it is exceedingly difficult to leave once the journey has begun. Walk a few steps in the path of sin and your life's direction may be settled.

1:16. For their feet run to evil, And they hasten to shed blood.

The father now gives his son a rationale for his counsel. Two components stand out in this verse: their rush and the result. The result they desire is 'to shed blood,' which was their own clearly stated intention (v. 11). This is, as noted earlier, also the end they themselves will face (v. 18). The rationale, then, for avoiding their ways is that they are self-destructive. The very thing they seek to do to others happens to them. The end they design for others becomes their own. The consequences of sin often have a biting irony to them.

The second component of the rationale for not running with these sinners is the urgency they feel to finish their course of evil. Their feet 'run' to evil and they 'hasten' to shed blood. The latter term is in the intensive active form of the verb, adding an even greater sense of urgency and haste to it. While the wicked rush to sin, God is equally speedy when it comes time for judgment (Mal. 3:5). When urgently pressed with temptation, wisdom always asks: 'What's the rush? What will a moment or day of reflection reveal that they don't want me to see?'

This verse is identical to the first two lines of Isaiah 59:7 and is partially quoted in Romans 3:15. The latter utilizes it in its litany of Old Testament quotations to prove the utter lostness of all men apart from Christ. As unwise as their course is, we all run it with them apart from Christ's intervention.

1:17. Indeed, it is useless to spread the net In the eyes of any bird;

An illustration is now employed to make the point, the picture being given here and the point in the following verse. Birds, as well as animals, were caught by use of netting. But, a trap, by necessity, uses the element of surprise, for not even a dumb animal will knowingly place itself in harm's way. This wisdom is not embraced by those provoked onward by their greed (vv. 13-14). 'Those who want to get rich fall into ... a snare' (1 Tim. 6:9). The sad irony is that the snare is of their own making. The one who rushes headlong in greed proves he is less than a bird-brain (Prov. 7:22-23)!

1:18. But they lie in wait for their own blood; They ambush their own lives.

What verse 17 sets forth in picture form is now stated plainly. All of verses 8-17 have been anticipating this. The ultimate reason not to fall in with the sinful and violent is that, what they plot for others (v. 11), becomes their own undoing (v. 18). Note, again, 'lie in wait' and 'ambush' in both verses 11 and 18. The very trap they set for others they spring on themselves.

Sin has a harsh irony to it. 'He who pursues evil will bring about his own death' (Prov. 11:19b). 'In the work of his own hands the wicked is snared' (Ps. 9:16b). 'His own iniquities will capture the wicked, And he will be held with the cords of his sin' (Prov. 5:22). 'Those who sow trouble harvest it' (Job 4:8b). 'They dug a pit before me; They themselves have fallen into the midst of it' (Ps. 57:6b).

1:19. So are the ways of everyone who gains by violence; It takes away the life of its possessors.
The one who cuts off a life in order to gain (the root meaning of 'gains by violence'[26]) discovers that he is cutting his own throat. The very thing you can't live without is the thing you can't live with. Yet how different for the wise: 'He who hates unjust gain will prolong his days' (Prov. 28:16b).

Lest we excuse ourselves because we have never killed another to take their things, we should note that 'ways' refers not simply to action, but also to the thoughts that lead to action. Also 'possessors' refers not simply to possessing unjust gain, but also to being possessed by thoughts of covetousness.[27] Few may carry their thoughts to the extreme of acting them out, but many have secretly nurtured a covetous heart. 'For what is a man profited if he gains the whole world, and loses or forfeits himself?' (Luke 9:25).

1:20. Wisdom shouts in the street, She lifts her voice in the square;
Sin has had its say (vv. 8-19), now wisdom is allowed to raise her voice. Verses 20-33 find wisdom personified as a woman who invites all to listen to and heed her call to life. Wisdom is similarly personified in Proverbs 3:15-18; 8:1-36; 9:1-12.

The word for 'wisdom' is in the plural '... to signify the intensity and comprehensiveness of it all – the "all embracing, eloquent, veracious, and elevated wisdom" ...'[28] Note where she makes her appeal: 'in the street' and 'in the square.' These were public places where the ordinariness of life found its daily expression. 'The square' was the open space inside a city's gates where people gathered to conduct their public business. It was a safe place to seal contracts and close deals because witnesses were readily available. Women did not play a prominent role in public life and for one to raise her voice in a public cry was highly unusual. She must have something urgently important to say! Wisdom is not merely for the haughty halls of academia, but is for life in the streets. Wisdom works in the everyday world of home, work, play, and the struggles of life. Her call is universal; all may come and embrace her.

1:21. At the head of the noisy streets she cries out; At the entrance of the gates in the city, she utters her sayings:
This verse, coupled with the previous one, speaks of the Woman Wisdom in the third person and form the introduction to her extended invitation. Wisdom makes her appeal in 'the noisy streets.' These streets are full of commotion, noise, confusion, and unrest with people shouting and hollering, as they go about transacting their daily business.[29] This is the place that Lady Wisdom speaks her invitation to us. We must tune our ears to hear her voice above the cacophony of life's voices and noises. We must discern the call of wisdom from among a myriad of invitations. What wisdom offers is not for the ivory tower, but literally for the push and shove of life.

The city gate was the place where business was transacted, city affairs were conducted, and people made social interaction. It was the strategic center of the city and its life.[30] Whatever people needed to do in public life, it could be, and probably would be, done at the city gates. The popular attempt by some to shut out the voice of 'religion' from the public arena is wrong and will ultimately prove vain. They might silence individuals, but wisdom will continue to lift her voice in the most public of places.

1:22. 'How long, O naïve ones, will you love simplicity? And scoffers delight themselves in scoffing, And fools hate knowledge?'
Now, after two verses of preparation, at last we hear the appeal of wisdom. She addresses three different groups. 'Naïve ones,' or the 'simple' (*petî*) are those who are gullible, silly and naïve (Prov. 14:15; 22:3). They love to exercise their willfulness and act irresponsibly (Prov. 1:32). They tend to be thoughtless toward others (Prov. 19:25). Indeed, their folly is a source of pleasure to them (Prov. 15:21). They waste their lives chasing after what does not matter (Prov. 15:21). We all begin in the naïveté of the simple. Left undirected and unrestrained, the power of the vortex begins the downward tug of rebellion that will destroy our lives (Prov. 22:3). At this stage the simple are still reachable and able to be rescued from the current of their foolishness (Prov. 19:25).[31] The second group wisdom addresses are the 'scoffers.' The scoffer despises being amended in his actions

or thinking (Prov. 9:7, 8; 13:1; 15:12). His independence makes
movement toward wisdom impossible (Prov. 14:6). The scoffer is no
longer a simpleton who curiously investigates folly here and there,
but is one who has become confirmed in his reviling of all authority
(Prov. 21:24; 22:10; 29:8). The sad verdict awaiting the scoffer is that
the God whom he has scoffed will, in the end, return the favor back
upon his head (Prov. 3:34).[32] The third group is the 'fools.' This is the
most common term referring to the fool in Proverbs. It indicates one
who is thick-headed and stubborn. It is not that the fool is stupid,
but rather that he has, by his refusal to listen to the wisdom of his
parents, chosen a resolutely self-destructive outlook on life. The
source of his problem is a spiritual, not a mental, deficiency. He has
no place for truth in his life and no time for the fear of the Lord
(Prov. 14:8; 1:29). The $k^e s\hat{\imath}l$ brings agony, bitterness and catastrophe
to his parents (Prov. 10:1; 17:21; 17:25; 19:13). Not only does he bring
his parents ruin, he despises them (Prov. 15:20).[33]

The problem lies in our affections. We 'love' what ought to frighten
us, we 'delight' in what should repulse us, and we 'hate' what should
be most cherished. Wisdom rightly queries: 'How long?'

**1:23. 'Turn to my reproof, Behold, I will pour out my spirit on you;
I will make my words known to you.'**
The first verb is not an imperative (as per the NASB), but an imperfect.
It is used conditionally: 'If only you would respond to my reproof'
(NEB). The response to reproof is to 'turn' or perhaps better 'turn
back.' This is the Hebrew word for repentance. 'For better than any
other verb it combines in itself the two requisites of repentance: to
turn from evil and to turn to the good.'[34]

While reproof is distasteful, it can be liberating if embraced. What
we turn from is surpassed by what we receive as we turn to God.
Here God's Spirit and word are promised to those humble enough
to turn toward wisdom. The NASB does not see this as a reference to
God the Spirit, but compare this with Isaiah 11:2: 'The Spirit of the
Lord shall rest upon Him, The Spirit of wisdom and understanding,
The Spirit of counsel and might, The Spirit of the knowledge and
fear of the Lord' (NKJV). God promises to 'pour out' His Spirit when
we turn to Him. The picture is of the 'uncontrollable or uncontrolled
gushing forth'[35] of a spring (cf. Prov. 18:4). 'He who believes in Me,
as the Scripture said, "From his innermost being shall flow rivers of
living water." But this He spoke of the Spirit ...' (John 7:38-39a).

Wisdom also promises 'I will make known my words to you.'
The Spirit and the word always together and always in harmony!

'It is the Spirit who gives life ... the words that I have spoken to you are spirit and are life' (John 6:63). Never object that you can't change – of course you can't! But, once your will is turned toward God, He will enable you by His Spirit and His word to walk in the liberty of His wisdom.

1:24. 'Because I called, and you refused; I stretched out my hand, and no one paid attention;'

This begins a series of four lines describing the rejection of wisdom. Apparently the offer of wisdom has been extended for some time, and rejected all along the way (cf. 'How long?,' v. 22). A final offer has been made (v. 23). Time has been given, but the stubborn refusal to heed wisdom's voice has set in (vv. 24-25), and thus the doom of walking in foolishness appears inevitable (vv. 26-33).

Sometimes the refusal is conscious and calculated: 'I called, and you refused.' Other times it is indifferent and inattentive: 'I stretched out my hand, and no one paid attention.' Whether through conscious rejection or distracted indifference, the rejection of wisdom is costly. The voice of God is heard but not heeded and the providential actions of God are not noticed. Cf. Isaiah 65:1-2.

1:25. 'And you neglected all my counsel, And did not want my reproof;'

The rejection of wisdom begun in verse 24 is matched by two more lines here. The action of wisdom is described as 'counsel' and 'reproof.' It is one thing to spurn the temporal counsel of man, but 'the counsel of the Lord stands forever' (Ps. 33:11a). This counsel is given us in the word of God (Ps. 119:24), and the purposes of God found there will never fail to be accomplished (Isa. 46:10). 'Reproof' describes the correction, rebuke or chastisement God gives to one whose steps lead them from these safe paths of God and into danger.

How foolish, then, when wisdom is 'neglected.' The Hebrew word originally meant to loosen, to release, or to set free.[36] Here it refers to willfully ignoring instructions that are offered and thus coming into the negative consequences of not following them (cf. Prov. 13:18; 15:32).[37] What may appear as 'neglect' of wisdom is in fact simply that we 'did not want' it, i.e. we willfully rebel against it (Deut. 1:26). The picture is of one blindly marching toward a precipice, yet resolutely refusing all offers to help him turn back from his impending doom.

1:26. 'I will even laugh at your calamity; I will mock when your dread comes,'

At first appearing heartless, this verse rather describes the retributive justice of a God who Himself has been mocked by sinners and fools. God laughs at the calamity of the wicked (Ps. 2:4; 37:13; 59:8), but only because they have first laughed at His wisdom (Prov. 29:9). The laughter should not be interpreted as calloused indifference, but as the tragic laughter of the One amazed by such foolish choices. Similarly, those who mock God and His ways (Prov. 14:9; 17:5; 19:28; 30:17) in the end will be mocked by Him.

This verse and the next introduce four words describing the judgment that falls upon those who spurn God's wisdom. 'Calamity' describes the culmination of accumulated judgment as it breaks upon the head of the rebellious (Prov. 6:15; 24:16, 22; 28:14). 'Dread' is the realization of your worst nightmare. It refers both to the overwhelming terror that paralyzes and the person or thing that incites the panic.[38] Such is the lot of those who spurn wisdom, but those who embrace her live securely (v. 33; 3:24, 25).

1:27. 'When your dread comes like a storm, And your calamity comes on like a whirlwind, When distress and anguish come on you.'

The list of words describing the judgment that befalls those who spurn wisdom continues from the previous verse. 'Dread' and 'calamity' are repeated from verse 26. 'Distress' and 'anguish' are new terms. 'Anguish' carries the idea of overwhelming external pressure that hems in and crushes. 'Distress' describes the anguish that comes from being so crushed.[39] This (the combination of the four) 'comes on' the fool. Two of the terms have similes attached to heighten the effect, both giving the same effect but through different pictures. The overwhelming pressure of 'dread' comes upon the fool 'like a storm.' The land of Israel was familiar with the sudden thunderstorm that sent a downpour of rain, overwhelming the dry ground and turning dry river beds into swelling torrents. Suddenly without expectation a wall of water could be upon you. Similarly 'calamity' comes on 'like a whirlwind.' We might call it a tornado. With sudden, unannounced fury, winds of unmanageable speed and power whisk away what was considered secure.

The fool snubs wisdom to his own destruction. The Bible assures that we will reap what we sow (Gal. 6:7) and that we will reap more than we sow: 'They sow the wind, And they reap the whirlwind' (Hosea 8:7).

1:28. 'Then they will call on me, but I will not answer; They will seek me diligently, but they shall not find me,'
Calamity makes one wish for the security of wisdom, but the time for seeking her is then past. Wisdom implored them to come, but they had refused (v. 24). Now it is 'they' (all three times in the emphatic form) who beg for wisdom's help, but she turns a deaf ear to them in their distress. Both 'wisdom' (Prov. 8:1, 4; 9:3) and folly (9:15) call out to us. Likewise, both 'wisdom' (Prov. 8:1-3) and folly (7:15) earnestly seek us. In their own good time, the foolish will reciprocate wisdom's invitation and search. Indeed, we are to 'call' on God for wisdom (Prov. 2:3; 1 Kings 3:9; James 1:5) and we are to 'seek ... diligently' for wisdom (Prov. 2:1-5; 8:17). However, it is their timing that is the problem. They wanted to go their own way and God has granted them their wish. The life and blessing that wisdom bestows on those who have honored her (Prov. 1:33; 3:13; 8:17, 35) must appear a mocking thing (v. 26) to those who have waited too long to embrace her and are suffering the consequences.

1:29. 'Because they hated knowledge, And did not choose the fear of the LORD.'
This judgment of silence (v. 28) may appear severe. Here, however, the truth of its cause comes out. They 'hated' knowledge (Prov. 1:22; 5:12; 8:36; 12:1; 15:10). Hate is '... an emotional attitude toward persons and things which are opposed, detested, despised and with which one wishes to have no contact or relationship. It is therefore the opposite of love. Whereas love draws and unites, hate separates and keeps distant. The hated and hating persons are considered foes or enemies and are considered odious, utterly unappealing.'[40] Some things should be hated; indeed, even God hates some things (Prov. 6:16; 8:13)! We ought to hate as He hates. The fool, however, has embraced what should have been shunned and shunned what should have been embraced.

Likewise they did not 'choose' the fear of the Lord. '... the word is used to express that choosing which has ultimate and eternal significance.'[41] How powerful simple choices can be! How sad, considering the wealth to be had in the fear of the Lord (cf. v. 7). They brought this judgment upon themselves. They exercised their God-given volition to reject God's wisdom. It is not God who is to blame, but themselves.

1:30. 'They would not accept my counsel, They spurned all my reproof.'
Like verse 29, this verse presents two reasons for the non-response of wisdom (v. 28) when called upon. The fool did not 'accept'

counsel and he 'spurned' reproof. This failure to 'accept' refers to an unwillingness to bend the will to an obligation or request.[42] The fool declares, 'No one is going to tell me what to do!' 'Spurned' (Ps. 10:13; 107:11; Prov. 5:12; 15:5; Isa. 5:24) describes the action of one who '... not only "deprecates God's power and ability to carry out his threats," but his contemptuous view of God leads him to prefer sin to God and to express this contempt in conscious contempt of God ...'[43] The scoffer disparages not only God's commands, but God Himself.

1:31. 'So they shall eat of the fruit of their own way, And be satiated with their own devices.'
'Fruit' is a metaphorical reference to the consequences of one's choices (Prov. 8:19; 11:30; 12:14; 13:2; 18:20, 21; 27:18). Experiencing the negative ramifications of one's actions is often referred to as eating the fruit of one's actions (Prov. 4:17; 18:21; 31:27). 'Satiated' represents a word normally reserved for describing the healthy and pleasurable satisfaction of food or the blessings of God (Prov. 3:10; 12:14; 13:25; 19:23; 20:13). However, it also is used negatively, almost satirically, as a reference to being stuffed on the repercussions of sin (Prov. 14:14; 18:20). Temptation creates an appetite for sin that seemingly cannot be satisfied (Prov. 27:20; 30:15, 16), but when the backlash of its ways catch up with us we despise the very thing we once craved (25:16; 27:7).

The worst judgment God may ever pronounce this side of eternity is to allow us to have the full impact of the ways we choose (Rom. 1:24-28). The guarantee of God is that we will reap what we sow (Gal. 6:7).

Note what caused this: 'their own way' and 'their own devices.' 'Devices' refers to counsel, advice, plans and input. The fool does not receive the counsel of others, and especially of God. Rather he blindly assumes the correctness of his ways and plunges headlong into ruin.

1:32. 'For the waywardness of the naïve shall kill them, And the complacency of fools shall destroy them.'
This verse and the next summarize and bring to a close the entire treatise on wisdom (vv. 20ff). This verse sums up the end of the fool and the next the security of the one who embraces wisdom. 'Waywardness' and 'complacency' are the choices that condemn the fool. The first is used elsewhere always of apostasy from Yahweh. Here the fool turns his back on wisdom and walks away, not realizing his defection leads to death. 'Complacency' describes an

attitude of carelessness and false security.[44] The fool assumes his security right up to the moment judgment breaks upon his head. Such was the attitude of Sodom right up to the day God obliterated them (Ezek. 16:49).

The character of those leading themselves to judgment is seen in the names given to them: 'naïve' (cf. v. 4) and 'fools' (cf. v. 22). Their ways 'kill' and 'destroy' them. One's attitude toward God and His wisdom is not a simple matter of preference, but an eternal matter of life and death. To spurn wisdom is spiritual suicide.

1:33. 'But he who listens to me shall live securely, And shall be at ease from the dread of evil.'
How different is the outcome of the one who embraces wisdom! In contrast to the self-destruction of the foolish (v. 32), here we meet the security of the one who heeds wisdom's call. The difference is that the discerning one 'listens' to wisdom. To listen to wisdom was the opening call of the book (v. 8) and is her sustained cry throughout not only this first chapter, but the entire book (e.g. Prov. 4:10; 8:34; 23:19). Contrast the way the fool responded to the invitation to wisdom (vv. 29-30).

The reward is to 'live securely,' a phrase describing '... that sense of well-being and security which results from having something or someone in whom to place confidence.'[45] The wise man has not trusted in self and has found the peace of mind that comes from resting his lot with God. Likewise the prudent live 'at ease from the dread of evil.' 'Evil' here is not used in an ethical sense, but refers to misfortune or harm.[46] 'Ease' translates a word that can mean everything from arrogance to complacency to peaceful ease. Here the idea is clearly positive and it is a peaceful freedom from worry that is intended (Isa. 32:18, 33:20; Jer. 30:10, 46:27).[47] 'And the peace of God ... shall guard your hearts and your minds in Christ Jesus' (Phil. 4:7).

Wisdom's opening invitation has been issued. The contrasting ways and outcomes of wisdom and folly have been established. The remainder of the book of Proverbs will further develop what has been so powerfully introduced to us in this opening chapter. May we now take wisdom's hand and learn from her!

End Notes

1. Louis Goldberg, '*ḥākam*,' *Theological Wordbook of the Old Testament* (Chicago: Moody Press, 1980), 1:282.

2. Ross, Allen P., 'Proverbs,' *The Expositor's Bible Commentary* (Grand Rapids: Michigan: Zondervan Publishing House, 1991), 5:904-905.

PROVERBS 1   55

3. Gilchrist, Paul R., 'yāsar,' *Theological Wordbook of the Old Testament* (Chicago: Moody Press, 1980), 1:386.

4. Ibid., 5:905.

5. Brown, Francis, S. R. Driver, Charles A. Briggs, *A Hebrew and English Lexicon of the Old Testament* (Oxford: Clarendon Press, n.d.), 108.

6. Goldberg, Louis, 'bîn,' *Theological Wordbook of the Old Testament* (Chicago: Moody Press, 1980), 1:103-4.

7. Ibid.

8. Goldberg, Louis, 'śākal,' *Theological Wordbook of the Old Testament* (Chicago: Moody Press, 1980), 2:877.

9. Ross, 5:907.

10. Ibid.

11. Wolf, Herbert, 'zāmam,' *Theological Wordbook of the Old Testament* (Chicago: Moody Press, 1980), 1:244.

12. Whybray, R. N., *Proverbs* (Grand Rapids, Michigan: William B. Eerdmans Publishing Company, 1994), 33.

13. Kaiser, Walter C., 'lāqah,' *Theological Wordbook of the Old Testament* (Chicago: Moody Press, 1980), 1:482.

14. Ross, 5:906.

15. Ibid.

16. Ibid.

17. Draper, Edythe, *Draper's Book of Quotations for the Christian World* (Wheaton, Illinois: Tyndale House Publishers, Inc., 1992), 216.

18. Kidner, Derek, *Proverbs* (Downers Grove, Illinois: InterVarsity Press, 1964), 59.

19. Brown, Driver and Briggs, 434-435, quoted in Ross, 5:907.

20. Livingston, G. Herbert, 'hāta',' *Theological Wordbook of the Old Testament* (Chicago: Moody Press, 1980), 1:277-279.

21. Livingston, G. Herbert, 'pātâ,' *Theological Wordbook of the Old Testament* (Chicago: Moody Press, 1980), 2:742-743.

22. Coppes, Leonard J., ''ābâ,' *Theological Wordbook of the Old Testament* (Chicago: Moody Press, 1980), 1:4.

23. Ross, 5:908.

24. Whybray, 39.

25. Hartley, John E., 'yāqar,' *Theological Wordbook of the Old Testament* (Chicago: Moody Press, 1980), 1:398-399.

26. Whybray, 42.

27. Delitzsch, F., *Proverbs, Ecclesiastes, Song of Solomon* (three volumes in one) in C. F. Keil and F. Delitzsch, vol. 6, *Commentary on the Old Testament* (in ten volumes), (1872; rpt. Grand Rapids, Michigan: William B. Eerdmans Publishing Company, 1980), 1:66-67.

28. Ross, 5:910.

29. Weber, Carl Philip, 'hāmâ,' *Theological Wordbook of the Old Testament* (Chicago: Moody Press, 1980), 1:219-220.

30. Hess, Richard S., 'צָרַ,' *New International Dictionary of Old Testament Theology & Exegesis* (Grand Rapids, Michigan: Zondervan Publishing House, 1997), 4:209.

31. Kidner, 39.

32. Ibid., 41-42.

33. Ibid., 40-41.

34. Hamilton, Victor P., 'shûb,' *Theological Wordbook of the Old Testament* (Chicago: Moody Press, 1980), 2:909.

35. Coppes, Leonard J., 'nāba',' *Theological Wordbook of the Old Testament* (Chicago: Moody Press, 1980), 2:548.

36. Delitzsch, 1:72.

37. Taylor, Richard A., 'פרץ,' *New International Dictionary of Old Testament Theology and Exegesis* (Grand Rapids, Michigan: Zondervan Publishing House, 1997), 3:690.

38. Bowling, Andrew, '*pāḥad*,' *Theological Wordbook of the Old Testament* (Chicago: Moody Press, 1980), 2:721.

39. Delitzsch, 1:72.

40. Van Groningen, Gerhard, '*śānē*',' *Theological Wordbook of the Old Testament* (Chicago: Moody Press, 1980), 2:879-880.

41. Oswalt, John N., '*bāḥar*,' *Theological Wordbook of the Old Testament* (Chicago: Moody Press, 1980), 1:100.

42. Coppes, Leonard J., ''*ābâ*,' *Theological Wordbook of the Old Testament* (Chicago: Moody Press, 1980), 1:4.

43. Coppes, Leonard J., '*nā'aṣ*,' *Theological Wordbook of the Old Testament* (Chicago: Moody Press, 1980), 2:543.

44. Nel, Philip J., 'שלה,' *New International Dictionary of Old Testament Theology and Exegesis* (Grand Rapids, Michigan: Zondervan Publishing House, 1997), 4:117.

45. Oswalt, John N., '*bāṭah*,' *Theological Dictionary of the Old Testament*, (Chicago: Moody Press, 1980), 1:101.

46. Whybray, 49.

47. Oswalt, John N., 'שאן,' *New International Dictionary of Old Testament Exegesis and Theology* (Grand Rapids, Michigan: Zondervan Publishing House, 1997), 4:10.

Proverbs 2

2:1. My son, if you will receive my words And treasure my commandments within you,

The reader has heard the opposing invitations of wisdom (Prov. 1:20-33) and the young thugs (1:11-14). The one who has chosen the path of wisdom is now given more as to what he may expect along its way. The chapter begins with a series of conditional clauses. 'If' is found three times, but is implied eight times in verses 1-4. The corresponding 'then' is found in verse 5. We soon discover that wisdom is a product of both intense personal discipline (vv. 1-5) and God's grace (v. 6). God's wisdom comes only as a gift, but He does not give it if we will not seek it. When we seek God's wisdom and He extends it to us, we enjoy the benefit of protection from the evil way (vv. 7-11), protection from the evil man (vv. 12-15), protection from the evil woman (vv. 16-19), and the provision of God's goodness (vv. 20-22).

The first of a series of conditional statements is given here. These conditional statements lay out what is required of us if we are to discover 'the fear of the Lord' (v. 5). To possess the fear of the Lord is to operate with a Biblical worldview. The fool operates without an accurate view of the world in which he lives. He is trying to live in God's world without God. He is out of touch with reality.

The first steps toward embracing reality are laid out before us in these conditional statements. The first requirement is that we 'receive' the sayings of the wise. Here, the wise one is cast as parent and the learner as 'my son.' This surely applies to our familial relationships, but may also apply to other relationships among God's people as He directs His counsel to us through them. To 'receive' is to recognize that you do not possess something you need. Humility is what is called for here. Someone else knows something I do not know and that I need therefore, I must humble myself and receive it. This is the most basic posture required to begin to embrace reality. The humanistic notion that all I must do is look within myself is worse than nonsense; it is demonic (James 3:15). This first conditional statement teaches me who I am – I am a person who needs God's counsel (Prov. 10:8; 13:10).

In addition, we must 'treasure' the commandment of God if we are to discern the fear of the Lord. If the first conditional statement taught me who I am, this one teaches me what to value. 'Treasure' has the idea of hiding or concealing something of value for the purposes of protecting it.[1] The one who understands the hard realities of this life values God's word and treasures it away in his heart (Job 23:12; Ps. 119:11; Prov. 7:1). 'Wise men store up knowledge, But with the mouth of the foolish, ruin is at hand' (Prov. 10:14). The good news is that God reciprocates and stores up His wisdom for the one who values His word enough to store it away (Prov. 2:7a). This treasuring away of God's word implies advance preparation – a consistent study of God's word so that its wisdom is readily accessible when needed.

2:2. Make your ear attentive to wisdom, Incline your heart to understanding;

The two lines of this verse form a synonymous parallelism, the second line restating and emphasizing the first. To 'make your ear attentive' and to 'incline your heart' are figures employed to describe obedient attentiveness. To 'make ... attentive' your ear is to tune your ear to hear and obey God's commands. The ear is the pathway of ideas, it must be guarded cautiously. 'Take care what you listen to' (Mark 4:24). '... [Y]ou should listen and be careful to do it, that it may be well with you' (Deut. 6:3).

To 'incline' one's heart is to extend it, to bend it purposefully in a certain direction. The heart is the center of who we are. It describes our intellectual and reasoning abilities (Prov. 3:3; 6:18, 21; 7:3), our emotions (13:12; 15:15, 30), and our will (11:20; 14:14; 28:14). The result is a picture of stretching out your entire being to God and His word (Josh. 24:23; 1 Kings 8:58; Ps. 119:36).[2]

If I am to function wisely and successfully in God's world, it will require knowing who I am (v. 1a), what to value (v. 1b) and who to listen to (v. 2).

2:3. For if you cry for discernment, Lift your voice for understanding;

Wisdom only comes to those who seek it. Wisdom calls to us (Prov. 1:20; 8:1, 4). But, I also must call out to God for wisdom (James 1:5). This call is described with two verbs, 'cry' and 'lift your voice.' Both verbs describe the desperate pleading of one who understands their lack of resources to deal with their need (Prov. 21:13). Both imply that wisdom does not come quickly or easily. There will be times when wisdom seems far away. Discovery of wisdom takes sustained diligence and an expenditure of much energy.

The cry is for 'discernment' and 'understanding.' We met 'discernment' in 1:2 (cf. Prov. 3:5; 4:5, 7; 7:4; 8:14; 9:6, 10; 23:4), and 'understanding' was introduced only in the previous verse (3:13; 8:1; 15:21). These two terms are synonyms (not only of each other, but of 'wisdom'), but only in this verse do they appear in synonymous parallelism.³ A fourth requirement of a Biblical worldview is knowing what to ask for.

2:4. If you seek her as silver And search for her as for hidden treasures;
Notice how the writer piles one intense verb upon another in describing the quest for wisdom: 'receive,' 'treasure' (1), 'make ... attentive,' 'incline' (2), 'cry,' 'lift' (3). To these six he adds two more verbs in this verse: 'seek' and 'search.' These verbs speak of the passion of the search underway (note the intensive piel form of 'seek'). The metaphor only adds to the inherent strength of the verbs. The discovery of 'silver' and 'hidden treasure' is the goal. 'Hidden treasure' refers to something of such rare value that it is shielded from the public view.⁴

An instructive commentary on this verse can be found in Job 28:1-28. The promise of wisdom is 'I love those who love me; And those who diligently seek me will find me' (Prov. 8:17). For an expansion on this theme, see also Proverbs 3:14-15; 8:19; 16:16; Psalm 19:10; 119:14, 72, 127; Matthew 6:19-21; 13:44; 19:29. The fifth and final requirement for attaining a Biblical worldview is in knowing what to give my energies to.

2:5. Then you will discern the fear of the LORD And discover the knowledge of God.
The series of conditional clauses (vv. 1-4) now culminates with 'then,' here being given the result of fulfilling the conditions of diligent search. The outcome is 'the fear of the Lord' and 'the knowledge of God.' To possess 'the fear of the Lord' is to embrace reality. It describes a Biblical worldview. It defines the perspective of the person who has come to see that 'The earth is the LORD's, and all it contains, The world, and those who dwell in it' (Ps. 24:1). It describes an informed and appropriate perspective of who God is and who I am before Him. See also on Proverbs 1:7.

The 'knowledge of God' describes the great desire of God for His people (Hosea 4:1, 6; 6:6). The Hebrew word for 'knowledge' describes an intimate knowledge of the object involved; it is knowledge gained through personal and experiential relationship.[5] God desires, above all else, that we would know Him deeply and personally, more even than He desires our multiplied sacrifices (Hosea 6:6). This kind of intimacy with God is the end goal of God's redemptive plan for man (Hab. 2:14; Isa. 11:9). The 'fear of the Lord' and 'the knowledge of God' are often found as the twin towers of true religion (Isa. 11:2; 58:2), describing 'the poles of awe and intimacy' which God desires.[6]

Verses 5-8 form an interesting parallel with verses 9-11. Both begin with 'Then you will discern' (vv. 5, 9), the object of the first being 'the fear of the Lord' and of the second 'righteousness and justice.' Both then follow with an expression of motive signaled by the word 'for' (vv. 6, 10), the first motive being 'the Lord gives wisdom' and the second 'wisdom will enter your heart.' Two identical Hebrew words are used in both: 'guarding ... preserves' (v. 8) and 'will guard ... will watch over' (v. 11).[7] These parallels reveal that when one truly seeks wisdom he will find God and, when one seeks God, he will gain wisdom.

This pursuit will require 'discernment,' the ability to look at two things and distinguish the differences. See on Proverbs 1:2. The arrival at knowing God and acquiring wisdom requires choices, sometimes difficult choices. These choices, as we shall see in the next verse, must be based upon the revelation of God, not personal whim.

2:6. For the Lord gives wisdom; From His mouth come knowledge and understanding.

The reason one finds God when he seeks wisdom is that only God can dispense true wisdom. Notice that what verse 5 describes as being found is in fact given. Wisdom is a gift of grace. No amount of human effort can acquire it. Our diligent search is required, but is not efficient apart from God's grace: the grace both to seek and the grace to discover. That the Lord is the sole and only source of true wisdom is emphasized by the throwing of His name forward to lead the sentence.[8]

Not only is God the sole source of wisdom, but He only dispenses it in one way: the words of His mouth. 'All Scripture is God-breathed' (2 Tim. 3:16, niv). We must remember: 'Man shall not live on bread alone, but on every word that proceeds out of the mouth of God' (Matt. 4:4). Though Job's friend may not have understood all things, he was correct when he pleaded with Job, 'Please receive instruction

from His mouth, And establish His words in your heart' (Job 22:22).
Ultimately, wisdom is not a matter of discovery, but of revelation.

2:7. He stores up sound wisdom for the upright; He is a shield to those who walk in integrity,

The first line is complete in its thought, but the second continues to be developed by the two lines of verse 8. Not only does God dispense wisdom to the seeker, but He 'stores up' that wisdom for the hour in which we need it. When we store up ('treasure,' v. 1) what God says, He stores up His wisdom for us (v. 7). God has laid up in store for us His wisdom in His word (v. 6) and, then, when we dig and search for it (vv. 1-4), He lays it up in store within us (Ps. 119:11). The thing hidden is designated as 'sound wisdom,' a new Hebrew term being introduced here. The word carries the idea of 'sound judgment' and that which flows from it, i.e. abiding success in the practical affairs of life.[9] God's wisdom is not simply some esoteric philosophy. He has held in reserve for us all that we will need to prosper and advance in the world He has created for us. But, this wisdom is held in reserve only for 'the upright.' The root connotes the idea of straightness.[10] When we are straight with God, He is straight with us and leads us straight to His wealth of wisdom held for us.

Not only does God grant wisdom, He Himself is our 'shield.' The word describes the small round shield carried by the light infantry and officers. It was lighter, more mobile and moveable than the large rectangular shield which covered the entire body.[11] 'He is a shield to those who take refuge in Him' (Prov. 30:5). Again, God does not serve indiscriminately in this capacity, but only for those who 'walk in integrity' (or who are 'pilgrims of innocence').[12] 'Walk' is descriptive of the established and consistent way of life a person takes. 'Integrity' is 'whole, full submission, moral faultlessness, which chooses God with the whole heart, seeks good without exception....'[13] It does not denote moral perfection, but the full-orbed and whole-hearted submission of one's life to God.

2:8. Guarding the paths of justice, And He preserves the way of His godly ones.

The thought begun in the last line of verse 7 is continued here. It is important to allow the three lines to interpret one another. A 'shield,' 'guarding' and 'preserving' are parallel as are 'walk,' 'paths' and 'the way.' The meaning is less clear, however, when 'integrity,' 'justice' and 'His godly ones' are compared. While 'integrity' and 'justice' are not synonymous, they are complementary. The parallelism of 'integrity' and 'justice' with 'His godly ones' makes clear that the assurance is that, as we live justly, God promises to be our shield and guard (Prov. 2:11; 4:6; 13:6). There is no safety in folly and independence, but there is security in obedience and devotion to God. Indeed, 'godly ones' comes from the powerful Hebrew word *hesed* and connotes the loyalty of those who keep the terms of God's covenant.[14] God does the keeping, but He requires us to avail ourselves of His wisdom and enabling to stay in the paths He has promised to guard.

2:9. Then you will discern righteousness and justice And equity and every good course.

Compare vv. 9-11 with vv. 5-10 (see on v. 5). The second part of the parallel with those verses begins here. The 'fear of the Lord' and the 'knowledge of God' (v. 5) are paralleled here with four items. These are available only to those who 'discern' them, the same word being employed as in Proverbs 1:2, 5, 6 and 2:5.

What was described in verse 5 in terms of relationship to deity is here described in terms of the ethics of wisdom. 'Righteousness and justice and equity' form the ethical trio already found in Proverbs 1:3. 'Righteousness' refers to the ethical and moral measuring rod of God's own character.[15] 'Justice' makes reference to the perfect rule of God over His creation and is then used of correct judgment used in interpersonal human relationships.[16] Hence the idea of right choices comes through. 'Equity' first refers to the impartial and fair care of God over what He has made. Then it makes reference to a similar fairness in those who become like Him in their dealings with others.[17] These three terms are moral synonyms, but if any distinction is to be seen it might be that they refer to the character, choices and equity of God now incarnate in the man of wisdom.

These three terms are summarized by the phrase 'every good course.' 'Course' is related to the Hebrew verb 'to roll' and the noun 'cart,' thus rendering a literal meaning of 'the track of a wagon wheel.'[18] A path is formed when people, carts and animals repeatedly use it. The pursuit of God and His wisdom lead to habits of holiness. 'He guides me in the paths of righteousness' (Ps. 23:3).

2:10. For wisdom will enter your heart And knowledge will be pleasant to your soul;

In this extended parallelism, compare this verse with verse 6. Both 'heart' and 'soul' are words that encompass the entirety of a person's being. Wisdom and knowledge will penetrate to the very depths of who you are. The ways, thoughts, reasonings and choices of wisdom and knowledge are to captivate the mind, control the emotions, and conduct the will. Wisdom and knowledge are not appendages to one's life, but they become the very substance of who one is. They will make themselves at home in you ('enter') and, once there, they will bring joy.

The presence of wisdom and knowledge is 'pleasant.' Like the taste of bread to the hungry (Prov. 9:17), wisdom satisfies the appetite of the one who yearns for it (vv. 1-4). Like skilled music to the ears (Ps. 81:2), wisdom soothes and comforts the soul. Like a fortuitous inheritance of land (Ps. 16:6) to a wandering nomad, wisdom is a pleasing place to make your home. Like kind words to a wounded heart (Prov. 16:24), wisdom restores and heals our inner man. This pleasantness of wisdom is discovered by dwelling in the presence of God (Ps. 16:11). Indeed wisdom makes worshipers of us and causes us to find joy in His presence (Ps. 135:3; 147:1).

2:11. Discretion will guard you, Understanding will watch over you, This verse further develops what was set forth in the previous verse. The first verb, 'guard,' in its root means 'to exercise great care over.'[19] 'Watch over' echoes the assurance of verse 8, being the same verb there translated 'guarding.' This verb, meaning to guard by sitting over, is used both to describe another guarding us and our responsibility to guard over certain things. We are guarded by God (Prov. 2:8; 24:12), understanding (2:11), wisdom (4:6), and righteousness (13:6). On the other hand, we are to set watch over our parents' instruction (Prov. 3:1), wisdom and discretion (3:21), knowledge (5:2), our hearts (4:23), our mouths (13:3), our way (16:17), and the law (28:7). Thus, we discover that, ultimately, it is God who guards our lives (v. 8). But, as we walk in His ways, the discretion He permits us also acts as our shield (v. 11). We watch over our lives to keep His word and, in turn, He sets watch over us by His word. Walking in the ways and wisdom of God is a double wall of protection. The former verb, then, makes reference to the intensity of God's protection and the latter the superior vantage point from which He watches over us.

'Discretion' is the ability to consider wisely any action before it is taken. 'Understanding' is the capacity to examine two seemingly opposite lines of thinking and choose the correct one.[20] These two sentries post themselves over our lives as we pursue God's mind and walk in His ways. God guards our lives not by parapet and police, but by principle and precept.

2:12. To deliver you from the way of evil, From the man who speaks perverse things;
After speaking of the intensity of our search for wisdom (vv. 1-4), the gift of the fear of the Lord and the knowledge of God were presented (v. 5). These gifts of God guard our lives, as described in two parallel descriptions (vv. 5-8 and vv. 9-11). Now, the writer presents two specific areas in which God's wisdom protects us: from the evil man (vv. 12-15) and from the evil woman (vv. 16-19). Both are set off by the clause 'To deliver you' (vv. 12, 16).

'Deliver' in this verbal form (hiphil) means to rescue, to save, to snatch away, to pull out or to extricate.[21] 'Way' is often used in Proverbs to describe two alternative roads of life we may walk.[22] Already we have met the evil way (Prov. 1:15, 19, 31) as well as the good way (2:8). Here, the wrong path is designated as 'evil.' The word can range in meaning from moral wickedness to physical injury.[23] Poor moral choices lead us down the path to pain and destruction.

'The way of evil' is personified by 'the man who speaks perverse things.' The ways of wickedness find expression in the words of men. How often our words are the vehicle that crushes others. The words are 'perverse.' The word means to turn away from what is normal and right. The root occurs nine times in Proverbs (2:12, 14; 6:14; 8:13; 10:31, 32; 16:28, 30; 23:33) and only one other time in the Old Testament (Deut. 32:20). Often this turning away is expressed through the mouth (Prov. 2:12; 10:31, 32; 16:30), but only because it is already a condition of the heart (6:14) and mind (23:33), fed by what the eyes take in (16:30).[24]

2:13. From those who leave the paths of uprightness To walk in the ways of darkness;
This verse further develops the character of 'the evil man' (v. 12). Here, we find his design, in verse 14 we find his delight, and in verse 15 his demeanor. His design is to depart from the light and walk in the darkness, to throw off the restraints of wisdom. This departure appears to be premeditated. This one's brief walk in the light was not motivated by a true conversion, or else they would not have left the 'paths of uprightness' (1 John 2:19).

The paths left behind are characterized by 'uprightness.' The root idea is that of straightness. It is often used to describe the character of God (Deut. 32:4; Ps. 111:8; 119:137; Hosea 14:10). It comes, then, also to describe a moral quality of heart among those who honor Him (Deut. 9:5; 1 Kings 9:4); a moral quality that becomes visible

by the way they live their lives (Prov. 2:13; 4:11).[25] The straightness
of God's way is contrasted in the next verse by the 'perversity'
(i.e. crookedness) of the way of the evil. God promises He will
straighten the paths of those who look to Him (Prov. 3:6).

Here the contrast is with the newly chosen ways of 'darkness.'
About half the times this word is used it refers to literal darkness,
but often it also has, as here, a metaphorical meaning. John 3:19-21
is the perfect commentary on the ways of darkness (cf. Isa. 29:15;
Rom. 13:12-13). How different from the ways of the upright: 'The
path of the righteous is like the light of dawn, That shines brighter
and brighter until the full day. The way of the wicked is like
darkness; They do not know over what they stumble' (Prov. 4:18, 19;
cf. Eccles. 2:13).

2:14. Who delight in doing evil And rejoice in the perversity of evil;

God has created us with the capacity for 'delight,' but this one has
distorted God's intention by finding it in the wrong people, places
and things. 'Delight' describes a joyful gladness that emanates
from one's whole being. The Lord and the salvation He offers is the
most frequently cited source of this joy (e.g. Ps. 5:11; 9:2; 63:11).[26]
The root meaning of 'rejoice' is 'to circle around,' descriptive of the
enthusiastic physical expressions that joy evokes. The things that
Scripture most often identifies as producing this kind of joy are
God's works and attributes.[27]

Yet the one who has corrupted his conscience with sin finds his
deepest being resonating with the call of evil and he finds his feet
ready to dance down the path of wickedness. Indeed, his delight
is not simply in evil as a concept or philosophy, but in 'doing' it;
he strives to become a connoisseur of corruption. He rejoices in the
'perversity' of evil, the same word as in verse 12.

2:15. Whose paths are crooked, And who are devious in their ways;

'Paths' and 'ways,' denoting the course of one's life determined by
one's choices, show up often in this chapter (vv. 8, 9, 12, 13, 15,18-20)
and the rest of the book (e.g. Prov. 3:6, 17; 4:11, 26; 7:25; 8:32). The
evil man's ways are 'crooked' (found again in Prov. 8:8; 11:20; 17:20;
19:1; 22:5; 28:6, 18). The picture is of that which has been twisted and
distorted from its original design. The evil way may have a vestige
of morality remaining, but it has been deformed. What is evil may
be what was pure, but now slightly twisted – just enough of the

original remains to appear moral, but it is now distorted to serve the enemy's purposes. 'The perverse in heart are an abomination to the Lord' (Prov. 11:20a).

Similarly, these paths are 'devious.' In the niphal, as we have here, the word means to 'go the wrong way' (Prov. 3:32; 14:2; Isa. 30:12).[28] Such a person has taken the wrong path by trusting their own under-handed ways rather than obedience to the word of God (Isa. 30:12).

2:16. To deliver you from the strange woman, From the adulteress who flatters with her words;
The fear of the Lord delivers us not only from the evil man (vv. 12-15), but also from the evil woman (vv. 16-19). Here she is called first 'the strange woman' and, then, also 'the adulteress.' See Proverbs 7:5 for these terms in parallel again. 'Strange' can mean a non-Israelite (Ruth 2:10), but here means one who is outside the bounds of proper relationship for a given man (Prov. 5:3, 20; 7:5; 22:14; 23:33).[29] Similarly, 'adulteress' means, literally, 'foreigner' or 'alien' (Prov. 5:20; 6:24; 7:5; 23:27).[30] Because she resides outside a marriage covenant with you, she is to be 'foreign' to you. If you are single, there is no one on the face of this earth who may legitimately gratify your sexual desires. God will give you grace to joyfully keep your desires within His will. If you are married, there is only one who may legitimately gratify your sexual desires. That is your wife by covenant.

Yet, there are some who will seek to lure you from this safety zone of God's will. Her first method of allurement is words. 'Flatter' means to 'make smooth, make slippery.'[31] 'For the lips of an adulteress drip honey, And smoother than oil is her speech' (Prov. 5:3). For an example of her seductive ways, see Proverbs 7:14-20. 'With her many persuasions she entices him; With her flattering lips she seduces him' (Prov. 7:21). Discernment enables the wise man not only to recognize the evil and error of her pitch, but to immediately refuse to listen any longer. 'Flee from youthful lusts' (2 Tim. 2:22).

2:17. That leaves the companion of her youth And forgets the covenant of her God;
The description of the evil woman continues. Now, her unfaithfulness is emphasized. She leaves behind 'the companion of her youth,' i.e. her husband (cf. Prov. 5:18; Isa. 54:6). 'Companion' describes someone with whom you have shared an intimate friendship (Prov. 16:28; 17:9; Ps. 55:14; Jer. 3:4).[32] Longstanding relationships and enduring commitments mean nothing to her. They are easily

sacrificed for sensual fulfillment. Similarly, she forsakes 'the covenant of her God.' In the broadest sense, this could be a reference to her being a part of the covenant people of God, which included the seventh commandment (Exod. 20:14). More narrowly, it refers to her marriage covenant made before God (Gen. 2:24; Ezek. 16:8; Mal. 2:14). The parallel with the first line points to this more narrow understanding as the intended meaning, being understood within the context of the broader covenant with God.

This woman speaks smoothly (v. 16), but her words mean nothing. She uses people. Past promises are empty. Previous intimacies are soon forgotten. Fidelity is pointless to her. She finds no value in relationships, only in personal gratification.

2:18. For her house sinks down to death And her tracks lead to the dead;

Verses 18 and 19 go together and close the description of the evil woman. The phrase 'her house sinks down' is a difficult one, because the noun is masculine and the verb is feminine. There have been many attempts to untangle the challenges this poses for translation. The general meaning, however, is still clear – adultery brings a slow death. 'Her house is a highway to the grave' (Prov. 7:27, NIV). The path of adultery leads to death (Prov. 5:5; 9:18). The death may be a literal and sudden physical death (Prov. 29:1), or it will likely be a slow unfolding of the consequences of sin which end in death (5:23). It could describe the end brought on by sexually transmitted diseases, or it could describe the opposite of the prosperity, life and joy that comes from walking within wisdom (Prov. 4:8, 9; 8:18-21).

'The dead' translates a word that has Ugaritic origins. The Ugaritic word described 'the dead inhabitants of the netherworld.' Yet, the appearances of the Hebrew word are found in poetic settings (Prov. 9:18; 21:16; Job 26:5; Isa. 14:9; 26:14) and the word simply serves as a synonym for other more common Hebrew words, such as 'death' or 'Sheol,' as is the case here.[33]

'Tracks' is a Hebrew word that comes from a root word meaning 'calf.' The idea of 'tracks' comes from the well-worn trenches left by the regular movement of carts pulled by oxen.[34] The pathway this woman leaves comes from enduring habits of sin. What may seem like a onetime fling turns into an established pattern of life. What appears like a one-night-stand becomes a decade that becomes two, which then becomes a lifetime. Before one notices, life has passed her by. She has missed the joy of wisdom and has arrived at death's door.

2:19. None who go to her return again, Nor do they reach the paths of life.
What is true of the adulteress (v. 18) is now declared true for those who follow after her. The pursuit of immorality has a point of no return. 'Each one is tempted when he is carried away and enticed by his own lust. Then when lust has conceived, it gives birth to sin; and when sin is accomplished, it brings forth death' (James 1:14-15). The pull of immorality's vortex is nearly inescapable. When you walk through the door of sexual sin, it slams behind you and you soon discover that it is a door with a knob on only one side. While the possibility of repentance is always held out to the penitent, the nature of sexual sin is such that it blinds to that possibility.

The one who pursues this wanton lifestyle does not 'reach the paths of life.' What is rationalized as a youthful side trip on sin's path is soon discovered to be an addicting course of life that is more than difficult to leave. The addictive power of illicit sex, pornography, and voyeurism is nothing to be experimented with. 'I discovered more bitter than death the woman whose heart is snares and nets, whose hands are chains. One who is pleasing to God will escape from her, but the sinner will be captured by her' (Eccles. 7:26). To walk 'the paths of life' is to pursue a consistent pattern of godliness in thought and action. This path opens the way to ever increasing joy and life (Ps. 16:11; Prov. 10:17; 15:24). 'But the path of the righteous is like the light of dawn, That shines brighter and brighter until the full day' (Prov. 4:18). Yet, the adulteress and those like her, bent on immediate gratification, never give the disciplined paths of life a second thought (Prov. 5:6).

2:20. So you will walk in the way of good men And keep to the paths of the righteous.
'So you will walk' points not to the result, but to the purpose or intention of seeking wisdom (vv. 1-4).[35] Such a pursuit will bring one into a Biblical worldview (v. 5). It will also result in the avoidance of the evil man (vv. 12-15) and the evil woman (vv. 16-19). The primary intent of wisdom, however, is not simply avoiding evil, but seeking the good. The former must happen as an application of wisdom, but it is not the primary purpose. Wisdom is not first of all about refraining from bad things, but about pursuing God's best things. The orientation of wisdom is not primarily negative, but positive. The same Hebrew word for purpose is employed again in Proverbs 19:20: 'Listen to counsel and accept discipline, That you may be wise the rest of your days.'

2:21. For the upright will live in the land And the blameless will remain in it;
This verse and the next serve to conclude the chapter on the familiar tone of promise and warning. The promise is that those who walk in wisdom 'will live in the land.' This echoes the promise so often heard in Deuteronomy and elsewhere in the Old Testament that God would fulfill His promise to give Israel the land of Canaan (Gen. 17:8; Deut. 4:1; Ps. 37:3, 9, 11, 22, 29, 34).

Those to whom this assurance is given are 'the upright' and 'the blameless.' The former has been encountered already in verses 7 and 13. The root idea is that of 'straightness' and it represents, first, God's own character and, then, the character of the one who becomes like Him. 'The blameless' we have also met in the 'integrity' of verse 7. The word here means that which is complete, entire, and the same through and through.[36] It describes the character of one who has no hidden agendas and no cloaked sins. His heart and life are open to the Lord and therefore open to examination by all others as well.

While the promise of the land applies uniquely to the Jewish people, this verse broadens out to all who are followers of God. The promise, more broadly stated, is that the one who chooses to walk in the fear of the Lord and the knowledge of God (v. 5) may fully expect that God will honor all the promises of His word in his personal life. 'He has granted to us His precious and magnificent promises, in order that by them you might become partakers of the divine nature' (2 Pet. 1:4). 'For as many as may be the promises of God, in [Christ] they are yes' (2 Cor. 1:20).

2:22. But the wicked will be cut off from the land And the treacherous will be uprooted from it.
Here, we have the warning that balances the promise of verse 21. Deuteronomy promised the land of Canaan to the faithful, but also warned of judgment for those who rejected God's covenant. Our very word for 'uprooted' is found in the warning of Deuteronomy 28:63: '[Y]ou shall be torn from the land where you are entering to possess it.' To 'cut off' is an oft-used expression describing the sudden and irreversible judgment of God.

This judgment is for the 'wicked' and 'treacherous.' 'Wicked' is a noun used some 266 times in the Old Testament in parallel with every Hebrew word for sin, evil and iniquity.[37] The 'treacherous' is the one who does not honor his word. Unfaithfulness is his hallmark.[38] Such people cannot expect that God will follow through with the fulfillment of His promises of blessing, but rather that He must keep His promise of judgment for those who choose rebellion. The one who does not honor his covenant pledge to God can be certain that God will honor His covenant pledge of judgment for unfaithfulness. 'The righteous will never be shaken, But the wicked will not dwell in the land' (Prov. 10:30).

End Notes

1. Hill, Andrew E., 'צפן,' *New International Dictionary of Old Testament Theology and Exegesis* (Grand Rapids, Michigan: Zondervan Publishing House, 1997), 3:840.

2. Wilson, Marvin R., *'nāṭâ,' Theological Wordbook of the Old Testament* (Chicago: Moody Press, 1980), 2:574.

3. Goldberg, Louis, *'bîn,' Theological Wordbook of the Old Testament* (Chicago: Moody Press, 1980), 1:104.

4. Alexander, Ralph H., *'ṭāmēn,' Theological Wordbook of the Old Testament* (Chicago: Moody Press, 1980), 1:351.

5. Lewis, Jack P., *'yāda',' Theological Wordbook of the Old Testament* (Chicago: Moody Press, 1980), 1:366-367.

6. Kidner, Derek, *Proverbs* (Downers Grove, Illinois: InterVarsity Press, 1964), 61.

7. Whybray, R. N., *Proverbs* (Grand Rapids, Michigan: William B. Eerdmans Publishing Company, 1994), 51-52.

8. Whybray, 52.

9. Goldberg, Louis, *'yshh,' Theological Wordbook of the Old Testament* (Chicago: Moody Press, 1980), 1:413.

10. Adams, Jay E., *The Christian Counselor's Commentary: Proverbs* (Woodruff, South Carolina: Timeless Texts, 1997), 19.

11. Smith, James E., *'gānan,' Theological Wordbook of the Old Testament* (Chicago: Moody Press, 1980), 1:168-169.

12. Delitzsch, F., *Proverbs, Ecclesiastes, Song of Solomon* (three volumes in one) in C. F. Keil and F. Delitzsch, vol. 6, *Commentary on the Old Testament* (in ten volumes), (1872; rpt. Grand Rapids, Michigan: William B. Eerdmans Publishing Company, 1980), 1:78.

13. Ibid.

14. Kidner, 62.

15. Stigers, Harold G., *'ṣedeq,' Theological Wordbook of the Old Testament* (Chicago: Moody Press, 1980), 2:752.

16. Culver, Robert D., *'shāpaṭ,' Theological Wordbook of the Old Testament* (Chicago: Moody Press, 1980), 2:948.

17. Olivier, Hannes, 'ישר,' *New International Dictionary of Old Testament Theology and Exegesis* (Grand Rapids, Michigan: Zondervan Publishing House, 1997), 2:568.

18. Ross, Allen P., 'Proverbs,' *The Expositor's Bible Commentary* (Grand Rapids, Michigan: Zondervan Publishing House, 1991), 5:913.

19. Hartley, John E., *'shāmar,' Theological Wordbook of the Old Testament* (Chicago: Moody Press, 1980), 2:939.

20. Delitzsch, 1:79.

21. Hubbard, Robert L., Jr., 'נצל,' *New International Dictionary of Old Testament Theology and Exegesis* (Grand Rapids, Michigan: Zondervan Publishing House, 1997), 3:141.

22. Whybray, 53.

23. Livingston, G. Herbert, *'rā'â,' Theological Wordbook of the Old Testament* (Chicago: Moody Press, 1980), 2:853.

24. Hamilton, Victor P., 'hāpak,' Theological Wordbook of the Old Testament (Chicago: Moody Press, 1980), 1:222.

25. Wiseman, Donald J., 'yāshār,' Theological Wordbook of the Old Testament (Chicago: Moody Press, 1980), 1:417.

26. Waltke, Bruce W., 'śāmaḥ,' Theological Wordbook of the Old Testament (Chicago: Moody Press, 1980), 2:879.

27. Lewis, Jack P., 'gîl,' Theological Wordbook of the Old Testament (Chicago: Moody Press, 1980), 1:159.

28. Baker, David W., 'לוז,' New International Dictionary of Old Testament Theology and Exegesis (Grand Rapids, Michigan: Zondervan Publishing House, 1997), 2:770.

29. Buzzell, Sid S., 'Proverbs,' The Bible Knowledge Commentary (Wheaton: Victor Books, 1988), 1:910.

30. Konkel, A. H., 'נכר,' New International Dictionary of Old Testament Theology and Exegesis (Grand Rapids, Michigan: Zondervan Publishing House, 1997), 3:108.

31. Luc, Alex, 'חלק,' New International Dictionary of Old Testament Theology and Exegesis (Grand Rapids, Michigan: Zondervan Publishing House, 1997), 2:160.

32. Brown, Francis, S. R. Driver, Charles A. Briggs, A Hebrew and English Lexicon of the Old Testament (Oxford: Clarendon Press, n.d.), 48.

33. White, William, 'rāpâ,' Theological Wordbook of the Old Testament (Chicago: Moody Press, 1980), 2:858.

34. Brown, Driver, and Briggs, 722.

35. Whybray, 57.

36. Payne, J. Barton, 'tāmam,' Theological Wordbook of the Old Testament (Chicago: Moody Press, 1980), 2:974.

37. Livingston, G. Herbert, 'rāsha',' Theological Wordbook of the Old Testament (Chicago: Moody Press, 1980), 2:863.

38. Goldberg, Louis, 'bāgad,' Theological Wordbook of the Old Testament (Chicago: Moody Press, 1980), 1:89-90.

Proverbs 3

3:1. My son, do not forget my teaching, But let your heart keep my commandments;

This third chapter begins with the now familiar call of father to son (cf. Prov. 1:8, 10, 15; 2:1; 3:11, 21; 4:1, 10, 20, etc.). The opening section of this chapter (vv. 1-12) consists of a series of exhortations, each then followed by the promised reward given to those who heed it. The first exhortation is given here, the reason for heeding it in verse 2.

The objects of the solicited action are 'my teaching' and 'my commandments.' 'Teaching' is literally the Hebrew word *torah*, which most often refers to God's holy Law (e.g. Prov. 29:18) and can be a designation for the entire Pentateuch. However, here it refers specifically to what Solomon has given in these Proverbs as applications of the Law to daily living (Prov. 1:8; 4:2; 6:20, 23). We might also apply this more generally to what parents pass on to their children about how to apply God's law to life today, though it certainly would not carry the same authority as Solomon's inspired Scripture.[1] 'Commandments' is also used elsewhere to describe the Law handed down by Moses. But, in Proverbs, it often refers to the instruction passed on by parent or teacher from their position of authority.[2]

The exhortation is approached both negatively ('do not forget') and positively ('let your heart keep'). To forget God and His word is not simply to misplace a memory, but it is to disregard His commandments (Deut. 8:11), to go after other gods (Deut. 8:19), to live in fear and lack of faith (Isa. 51:13), and to challenge God (Ps. 106:13). This defiance usually grows from the comfort of having all one's need satisfied (Hosea 13:6).[3] To 'keep' something means to guard or watch over it. In this case, it is one's heart that is protected (cf. Prov. 4:23). The heart is the center and seat of one's inner life, including mind, emotions, and will. The word of God is to penetrate, subdue and rein in every cognition of our brain, every flame of passion and tongue of temper that leaps from the fire of our affections, and every choice both contemplated and embraced. Such unilateral submission of all I am to God's word requires that constant vigil be kept over my heart.

3:2. For length of days and years of life, And peace they will add to you.
The exhortation of verse 1 now finds its reason here. Long life and peaceful existence are promised to the one who will keep the commands of God. This book often emphasizes that obedience to God will lead to a long life (Prov. 3:16; 4:10; 9:11; 10:27; 11:4; 14:27; 15:24; 28:16). A long life is understood as an evidence of God's blessing (Exod. 20:12).

'Peace' will also be the lot of the one who esteems God's commands. The word *shalom* ('peace') here means more than absence of strife, but is a broad term with many nuances of meaning. It refers to well-being, prosperity, bodily health, and the internal condition of being at rest, contented or fulfilled. It is, in short, the state of blessedness one can expect when he lives his life within God's created design.[4]

God will 'add' these twin rewards of long life and peaceful prosperity to the lives of those who keep His word. God will make a point to give increased measures of days and years to all else that life may bring your way. These additional days and years will not be merely extensions of time, but they will be filled with the joy of seeing God's hand of peace and prosperity rest upon you.

This, as so many of the other proverbs, should be viewed as a general principle and not a unilateral promise. We all know of a godly person who has died while still young or of the person who conducted himself by God's word and yet bore great sorrows in this life. The basic pattern of life is that, if you keep God's commands, you will avoid the pitfalls and perils of seeking to walk out of step with Him and will instead enjoy the benefits of walking in step with the Creator and Sustainer of the universe.

3:3. Do not let kindness and truth leave you; Bind them around your neck, Write them on the tablet of your heart.
Again we meet an exhortation (v. 3) and promised reward (v. 4), except that, in this case, the exhortation is given in three lines rather than two. The first line is made up of a rather odd metaphor. 'Kindness' is actually the rich covenant term *hesed*, which so often represents the faithful covenant love of God to His people. Similarly 'truth' is also a standard Old Testament term for covenant keeping. The first has the idea of fidelity to the commitments of a relationship and the second the idea of that which is stable and can be relied upon.[5] While these are terms used of God's covenant keeping with

us, here the emphasis is on these qualities being true of us. One would expect that the 'son' would be exhorted not to leave these two qualities behind, but actually he is warned not to allow these two covenant terms to leave him. 'Kindness' and 'truth' are almost pictured as trying to escape from us. The principle is here presented as the reverse image of a photographic negative. It is not 'kindness' and 'truth' that leave us, but we who leave them. The metaphor is employed to heighten the intensity of our commitment to keeping covenant with God.

The second line also employs a vivid metaphor. Not only are we to do all within our power never to let these two qualities leave us, we are to 'bind' (Prov. 6:21; 7:3; 22:15) this 'kindness' and 'truth' around our necks. The first metaphor pictures not letting these qualities become distant from us, the second pictures keeping them as close as possible to us. Later Judaism misconstrued this and other similar Old Testament commands (Exod. 13:9; Deut. 6:8-9; 11:18) in a woodenly literal fashion, bringing on the use of phylacteries (Matt. 23:5). The idea here, however, is that we should make these covenant commitments so much a part of our lives that they adorn us like a beautiful necklace (Prov. 1:9; 3:22; 6:21). Count covenant keeping as your most precious jewel and most attractive feature! Wear faithfulness like a prize gem!

The third line makes the application even more powerful. Line one stressed not letting 'kindness' and 'truth' distance themselves from you. Line two brought them near to become the outward adornment of our lives. Line three, however, brings them closer still. Now, they are to be the very meditation of our inner being. We are to 'write them on the tablet' of our hearts (cf. Prov. 7:3).

The 'heart' is the comprehensive term for the inner person you are. It is the well-spring from which all of life flows (Prov. 4:23). For this reason, the commands of God must be indelibly written down in our minds through constant determined meditation and application. God promised that this deep, inner embracing of God's truth would become reality in His new covenant: 'But this is the covenant which I will make with the house of Israel after those days,' declares the LORD, 'I will put My law within them, and on their heart I will write it; and I will be their God, and they shall be My people' (Jer. 31:33; cf. Heb. 8:10; 10:16).

God is calling us to draw 'kindness' and 'truth' ever closer to ourselves until they become the fabric of our hearts, the substance of our thinking, and the first response of our wills.

3:4. So you will find favor and good repute In the sight of God and man.

The result of bringing near 'kindness' and 'truth' (v. 3) and internalizing them is given here. 'Favor' and 'good repute' are promised. 'Favor' means to be gracious or to show favor toward (for various translations of the noun see Prov. 3:34; 11:16; 13:15; 28:23; 31:30).[6] The difficulty comes in understanding its parallel: 'good repute.' The Hebrew word means shrewdness, insight or understanding. To many translators, this does not seem to be an appropriate reward. So, it is often translated by something like 'good repute' (NASB) or 'a good name' (NIV). But, there need be no conflict, because shrewdness need not be a negative trait. Indeed, it may lead one to success (cf. Prov. 10:5). This success would give one a reputation as one who wins at life.

These rewards are the more precious, because they are seen both by God and man. Can you imagine anything more wonderful than being deemed by God to be blessed and a winner? Add to this the secondary, but desirable, benefit of having the same pronouncement made by the significant people in your life. 'Jesus kept increasing in wisdom and stature, and in favor with God and man' (Luke 2:52). 'We have regard for what is honorable, not only in the sight of the Lord, but also in the sight of men' (2 Cor. 8:21).

3:5. Trust in the LORD with all your heart, And do not lean on your own understanding.

We come now to perhaps the most familiar and best loved verses in all of Proverbs. Here, too, we encounter an exhortation (vv. 5-6a) and, then, a promised reward (v. 6b). Like the last exhortation/ reward, the exhortation here is given in three lines. The first line calls us to 'trust' in the Lord with all our hearts. This 'trust' is the sense of security and safety that comes from being under the care of another more competent than ourselves.[7]

This trust is to be total: 'with all your heart' (cf. 'in all your ways,' v. 6). The heart represents the totality of one's inner being: mind, emotions and will. Everything we are and all we have must be rested upon the Lord as our security.

The second part of the exhortation is cast negatively: we are not to 'lean' on our own understanding. The root of the verb means to support yourself on something,[8] to lean with your entire weight upon something.[9] We are not to take our 'own understanding' as buttressing support. 'Understanding' is a word that is generally given a positive spin by Solomon (cf. Prov. 1:2; 2:3), but here is seen negatively. Here it is that human wisdom worked up from our natural selves as compared to the divine wisdom that God gives to those who seek Him (cf. James 3:15-18). This does not mean to imply that there is nothing to be trusted in 'common sense,' but simply that you don't use it as your sole, or even primary, support in life. Rather, we should bank our all on God and the wisdom of His ways. His ways are above ours (Isa. 55:8-9; Rom. 11:33-34), and must be chosen when they seem to contradict our earthly, human wisdom.

3:6. In all your ways acknowledge Him, And He will make your paths straight.

The third line of the exhortation is found here: 'In all your ways acknowledge Him.' The verb 'acknowledge' means simply 'to know.' Such knowledge is more than acquainting yourself with God, but describes a deep experiential knowledge. The fact that this is to be 'in all your ways' (cf. 'with all your heart,' v. 5) drives deeper still the level of intimacy intended.

Finally, the reward is stated: 'And He will make your paths straight.' The straight paths of the wise contrast with the crooked or perverse ways of the wicked (Prov. 2:13, 15; 3:17; 10:9). The reward is more than the promise of simple guidance. It includes the removal of obstacles (Isa. 40:3; 45:13) from the path of the wise and the surety of arriving at one's destination.[10]

When you abandon yourself to God in trusting obedience, finding your entire support in Him and striving in every avenue of your life to know Him more intimately, He guarantees that the path before you will be clearer and smoother than otherwise it would have been, and that He will keep you in His will.

3:7. Do not be wise in your own eyes; Fear the LORD and turn away from evil.

Again, we meet an exhortation and its reward in the next verse. Note the connection with the preceding verse: the one who is wise in his own eyes is the one who leans upon his own understanding. We are called to recognize that wisdom does not come from within, but from without – from God (Prov. 2:6). Fools says, 'Just let me think! I can figure this out if you'll just give me time!' God says, 'Do not be wise in your own estimation' (Rom. 12:16b). 'Do you see a man wise in his own eyes? There is more hope for a fool than for him' (Prov. 26:12). 'Woe to those who are wise in their own eyes, And clever in their own sight!' (Isa. 5:21). God honors and helps the one who admits he does not have the wisdom he needs and who seeks it from Him (James 1:5).

The opposite of being wise in one's own eyes is fearing the Lord. This is the theme of the book (see on Prov. 1:7). When we put God in His rightful place and reverence Him appropriately, we will 'turn away from evil.' 'A wise man is cautious and turns away from evil, But a fool is arrogant and careless' (Prov. 14:16). To love God is to hate what He hates (Ps. 97:10; 119:104, 128; 139:21). 'The fear of the Lord is to hate evil' (Prov. 8:13a). 'By the fear of the Lord one keeps away from evil' (Prov. 16:6b). You cannot love and fear God and turn toward evil. To turn toward evil is to belittle God and hate Him.

3:8. It will be healing to your body, And refreshment to your bones. 'It' refers to a lifestyle that reverences the Lord and turns away from evil. This lifestyle will bring 'healing to your body.' This should come as no surprise, since Scripture clearly reveals the negative effects of unconfessed sin on the human body: 'When I kept silent about my sin, my body wasted away Through my groaning all day long. For night and day Thy hand was heavy upon me; My vitality was drained away as with the fever heat of summer' (Ps. 32:3-4; cf. Ps. 38:3; 51:8; Lam. 3:4).

It should follow that righteous living will have a positive effect upon the body. The Hebrew term here translated 'body' literally refers to the umbilical cord. The only other uses of this word are found in Song of Solomon 7:2 and Ezekiel 16:4. Such language seems odd to us. How would righteous living bring healing to one's umbilical cord? It is possible that the navel is chosen because it harkens back to the original health of a newborn, when its first moments of independent life are experienced. It is more likely, however, that this is an example of synecdoche. This figure of speech employs a part of something to make reference to the whole of which it is a part. So, 'body' may not be a literal translation, but it captures the intent of the original language.

'Refreshment' comes from a root word that is often used to speak of giving drink to humans or animals. It is also used of irrigating or watering parched ground to make it fertile.[11] Here, the idea of 'moisture' to the bones gives that same sense of refreshment or renewal to the body (Job 21:24). 'Bones' are the framing structure of the entire body, so this also is a metaphorical reference to the whole of the body. The moisture for the health of the bones is contrasted by the consequences of sin on the bones: '... a broken spirit dries up the bones' (Prov. 17:22; cf. 12:4; 14:30; 15:30; 16:24).

All of this tells us that righteous living and a clean conscience is one of the avenues through which God brings good health to us. 'They are life to those who find them, And health to their whole body' (Prov. 4:22). Our spiritual well-being and our physical health are intimately connected. 'Beloved, I pray that in all respects you may prosper and be in good health, just as your soul prospers' (3 John 2).

3:9. Honor the Lord from your wealth, And from the first of all your produce;
Once again, we meet the exhortation here, then the reward awaiting us in the next verse. This verse represents the only time Proverbs advises making any of the sacrifices required by the books of Moses.[12] 'Honor' is a verb used occasionally – as here – in the sense of making sacrifice to the Lord (Ps. 50:23; Isa. 43:23; Dan. 11:38; Mal. 1:6-7). 'Wealth' refers to having enough of the goods of life for them to be considered riches or wealth.[13] Since what is sufficient is highly subjective, it probably refers to anything and everything beyond the basic daily requirement of food and clothing.

In Proverbs, such wealth is viewed both negatively and positively. Wealth is considered an insufficient security (Prov. 1:13; 11:4; 18:11; but see Prov. 10:15), but also as a reward for the wise (3:16; 8:18). Such wealth may not only be the reward of wisdom. But, when submitted to God, wealth may be transformed by wisdom into an opportunity to worship Him.

'First' is often a reference to 'first fruits.' Israel was called to sacrifice to God from the first portion gleaned from all their crops (Exod. 22:29; 23:19; Lev. 23:10; Num. 18:12-13; Deut. 18:4). This was a way of expressing thanks to God (Deut. 26:1-3, 9-11). Such offerings express our understanding of God's supremacy over all things (cf. 'In all your ways acknowledge Him,' v. 6). This offering of the first fruits makes clear our complete reliance upon God rather than the yield of our fields (cf. 'Trust in the Lord with all your heart,' v. 5a). Such sacrificial giving certainly requires that we 'do not lean on our own understanding' (v. 5b).

This principle of giving to God from our first fruits is an abiding principle for all God's people today (1 Cor. 16:2; Mark 12:44). We honor God when He gets the first check written after the deposit is made. We honor God when we calculate our giving off of the gross rather than the net. When we so honor God, He promises to honor us (v. 10).

3:10. So your barns will be filled with plenty, And your vats will overflow with new wine.

The reward for such giving is now stated. The giving enjoined by the Mosaic Law was to be done in recognition that God had redeemed them from slavery in Egypt (Deut. 26:1-10). They were not their own. They had been bought with a price. They possessed nothing, but managed everything. They had nothing but what had poured out of the hand of God to them.

Such giving cannot be viewed as taking some of 'mine' and giving it to God. Instead, it is selecting some of what is God's and trusting Him with it as He has trusted me with that which remains under my discretion. Such giving is a supreme act of faith. It evidences that we believe the God who gave us this is able and willing to give us more from where this came from. My part is but to evidence my belief that He is this kind of God by the sacrificial act of giving.

Thus, I am free from a miserly attitude that believes I must store up 'just in case' God doesn't come through in the future. Rather, I enjoy the freedom of knowing that One with infinitely greater resources than me is more committed to my good than I am. God promises that, in response to such faithful stewardship, He will fill and, indeed, 'overflow' our hands and houses with His blessings. 'Overflow' comes from a root word meaning to break through, break down, break over, or burst.[14] God is able to burst wide open any storehouse you can manufacture. God's ability to give exceeds your ability to receive and retain by as much greater a measure as infinity is than finitude. You cannot outgive God.

That God rewards those with such faith is an oft-repeated expression of Scripture: 'Bring the whole tithe into the storehouse, so that there may be food in My house, and test Me now in this,' says the LORD of hosts, 'if I will not open for you the windows of heaven, and pour out for you a blessing until it overflows' (Mal. 3:10). 'The LORD will command the blessing upon you in your barns and in all that you put your hand to, and He will bless you in the land which the LORD your God gives you' (Deut. 28:8). 'And God is able to make all grace abound to you, that always having all sufficiency in everything, you may have an abundance for every good deed' (2 Cor. 9:8). 'But seek first His kingdom and His righteousness; and all these things shall be added to you' (Matt. 6:33). 'Give, and it will be given to you; good measure, pressed down, shaken together, running over, they will pour into your lap. For by your standard of measure it will be measured to you in return' (Luke 6:38). See also Proverbs 11:24-25; 19:17; 22:9; Ecclesiastes 11:1-2; Philippians 4:19.

While such is the standard pattern of God's working with the faithful, He does not guarantee that He will not suspend this pattern in order to accomplish some higher purpose. If these assurances of Scripture were guarantees '... God would not be so much honoured, as invested in, by our gifts. Verses 11, 12 are therefore well placed to balance 8 and 10 (and to lead into 13ff), with the reminder of other divine methods and better prizes than prosperity.'[15] Let us guard our gifts from greediness and make them pure and holy offerings unto Him.

3:11. My son, do not reject the discipline of the LORD, Or loathe His reproof,

'My son' forms an inclusion with the same expression in verse 1 where this string of exhortations/rewards began. These two verses provide the sixth and final such combination.

Wisdom is not only gained by receiving rewards for faithfulness (vv. 9-10), but also by receiving discipline for unfaithfulness (vv. 11-12). Wisdom is learned not only by prosperity and blessing, but also through hardship and suffering. These verses are quoted in Hebrews 12:5-6, where they are then expounded upon. See also Proverbs 12:1; 6:23; and Psalm 119:71.

'Discipline' points first to an exhortation with a warning of consequences for disobedience, but it also then may refer to the physical punishment applied if the counsel is not followed.[16] 'Reproof' points more exclusively to verbal correction,[17] yet both terms are often found together (e.g. Prov. 5:12; 10:17; 12:1). Both are employed by God (through His word and through His providences) and ought to be a part of every godly parent's instruction as well.

The responses warned against are 'reject' and 'loathe.' The former refers to the action of pushing away counsel and discipline and walking away from it, refusing to learn anything from it.[18] The latter describes an emotional reaction to discipline. The purpose of the discipline is not perceived, so the emotions cannot abide with it and learn from it.[19] The first is an act of a rebellious will, the second a reaction of a misguided mind and emotions. The latter believes the discipline is capricious, and misses that God's discipline is one of the greatest evidences of His love (Heb. 12:7-11). It fails to see that 'He inflicts pain, and gives relief; He wounds, and His hands also heal' (Job 5:18). If these two misguided responses are avoided and the discipline embraced, rather than rejected, then 'afterwards it yields the peaceful fruit of righteousness' (Heb. 12:11b).

3:12. For whom the LORD loves He reproves, Even as a father, the son in whom he delights.
If we do not flee the correction and discipline of God, we will discover it to be a great sign of our sonship. God disciplines us, not because He does not love us, but in order to protect us. He allows difficult things to come our way, not because He delights in pain, but because He delights in us. 'It is for discipline that you endure; God deals with you as with sons; for what son is there whom his father does not discipline?' (Heb. 12:7). 'Behold, how happy is the man whom God reproves, So do not despise the discipline of the Almighty' (Job 5:17). 'Blessed is the man whom Thou dost chasten, O LORD, And dost teach out of Thy law' (Ps. 94:12). 'I know, O LORD, that Thy judgments are righteous, And that in faithfulness Thou hast afflicted me' (Ps. 119:75). 'Those whom I love, I reprove and discipline; be zealous therefore, and repent' (Rev. 3:19).

This is the only place in Proverbs where God is called 'Father.' In addition to lessons about our heavenly Father's love, we also have here instruction for those of us who are earthly fathers. Leniency is not love. Discipline does not signal displeasure.

3:13. How blessed is the man who finds wisdom, And the man who gains understanding.
This marks the beginning of a new section of the chapter, a portion in which the writer poetically extols the virtues of wisdom (vv. 13-18). This poem is set off as a separate section because its first and last words are from an identical root ('blessed,' v. 13 and 'happy,' v. 18). Between these two uses of the same word, we find a series of clauses intended to motivate the reader to pursue wisdom.

'How blessed is the man' echoes the psalmists' frequent cry of joy (Ps. 1:1; 32:2; 34:8; 40:4; 84:5, 12; 112:1; 127:5) and reminds one of Jesus' beatitudes (Matt. 5:3-12). See also Proverbs 28:14 and Isaiah 56:2. This blessedness describes a state of being that derives from walking rightly with God and having His seal of approval upon you.[20] It describes not so much a subjective condition of happiness as it does a state arising from having an objective verdict pronounced upon us by God. It is not so much emotional as it is factual, though the fact of God's blessing surely affects one's emotions.

No great distinction should be made here between 'wisdom' and 'understanding,' as they are used in poetic parallelism. To 'find' these jewels is a prized experience. 'The kingdom of heaven is like a treasure hidden in the field, which a man found and hid; and from joy over it he goes and sells all that he has, and buys that field'

(Matt. 13:44). To 'gain' such insight is precious indeed. 'Again, the kingdom of heaven is like a merchant seeking fine pearls, and upon finding one pearl of great value, he went and sold all that he had, and bought it' (Matt. 13:45, 46).[21]

3:14. For its profit is better than the profit of silver, And its gain than fine gold.

The benefits of wisdom are now enumerated. Wisdom is here counted of more worth than silver or gold. This same estimation is made elsewhere of the commands and precepts of God. 'The law of Thy mouth is better to me Than thousands of gold and silver pieces' (Ps. 119:72). 'Therefore I love Thy commandments Above gold, yes, above fine gold' (Ps. 119:127; cf. Ps. 19:10).

The profit and gain of wisdom is better than anything worldly wealth can afford. Solomon discovered that riches do not satisfy (Eccles. 5:10-15). Riches make an unstable foundation upon which to build one's life (1 Tim. 6:17), and the reckless pursuit of them opens one up to a world of evil influences (1 Tim. 6:6-10).

The words 'profit' and 'gain' ('a better return,' NIV) are descriptive of one who invests with a view to a good return. The best long-term investment one can make is the pursuit of God's wisdom and understanding. The dividends it yields far outweigh any gains made by the pursuit of gains in capital.

3:15. She is more precious than jewels; And nothing you desire compares with her.

The 'jewels' spoken of here were probably red corals of some kind (Lam. 4:7) and were regarded as extremely valuable in the ancient world.[22] But, more desirable than the finest gem is the wisdom of God (Job 28:18; Prov. 8:11; 20:15; cf. the value of an excellent wife, Prov. 31:10).

Surprisingly, we meet the second person 'you' in the second line of this verse. This is the only occurrence of the second person in this poem (vv. 13-18). Suddenly, the value of wisdom is pressed home and made personal. Nothing you can 'desire' will ever compare with the value of wisdom. The human capacity for desire is vast, but the exclusivity of wisdom's worth sets her apart as unique among all others. 'Whom have I in heaven but Thee? And besides Thee, I desire nothing on earth' (Ps. 73:25). 'Delight yourself in the LORD; And He will give you the desires of your heart' (Ps. 37:4). 'He satisfies my desires with good things, so that my youth is renewed like the eagle's' (Ps. 103:5, NIV).

3:16. Long life is in her right hand; In her left hand are riches and honor.
The mention of the right and left hand together signifies wisdom's generosity and readiness to give. Nothing held in wisdom's embrace is withheld from the one who will seek her. In her right hand, her hand of strength, comes the most precious gift of 'long life' (lit. 'length of days'). This gift has already been held forth in Proverbs 3:2 (see also 4:10). In her left hand, she holds forth the lesser, but still valuable, gifts of physical resources (cf. Prov. 8:18-21) and relational favor (cf. 3:35; 4:8; 8:18; 21:21). The one who embraces wisdom will live long, have plenty to sustain himself throughout his many years, and will be respected and praised by those in his network of relationships.

Solomon knew whereof he spoke. This was not mere instruction. It was personal testimony. When he asked God for wisdom, God promised it would be his. Yet, because Solomon asked for wisdom and not other more selfish prizes, God promised He would also give him what he had not asked for: riches and honor (1 Kings 3:12-13).

That these rewards are grace gifts and not guarantees in this world should be obvious. The wicked often prosper and live long lives (Ps. 37:1-2, 7; 49:16-20), but theirs is illegitimate pleasure and there is no peace with it. 'It is the blessing of the LORD that makes rich, And He adds no sorrow to it' (Prov. 10:22). Likewise, the righteous often die young, poor and in obscurity (Luke 16:19-31), yet they die well and the riches of eternity await them. 'The wicked is thrust down by his wrongdoing, But the righteous has a refuge when he dies' (Prov. 14:32).

3:17. Her ways are pleasant ways, And all her paths are peace.
Wisdom's virtues continue to be extolled. To understand 'ways' and 'paths,' see on Proverbs 2:13, 15. They describe the direction and substance of one's life as he makes his way through this world. Walking in the ways of wisdom is 'pleasant.' Ways which are 'pleasant' are those upon which one discovers what is 'agreeable to the inner and outer man, and which it does good to enjoy.'[23] In verbal form, it means to be pleasant, sweet, delightful and beautiful. As a noun, it is goodness, charm, loveliness.[24]

In addition, to tread the 'paths' of wisdom is in itself peace. This is the holistic Hebrew word *shalom* already met in verse 2. This peace is more than the absence of turmoil, but includes the broader condition of entire well-being, health, and being satisfied or fulfilled with one's lot.

It is a pernicious lie which says to walk the ways of wisdom is to be condemned to boredom, emotional restraint and a bland existence. Nothing could be further from the truth! Rather, these describe the character of earthly wisdom: 'These are matters which have, to be sure, the appearance of wisdom in self-made religion and self-abasement and severe treatment of the body' (Col. 2:23). It is true that God's ways may not be easy. They may not be frivolous. They certainly do not follow the path of least resistence. Yet, they are anything but bland. 'Thou wilt make known to me the path of life; In Thy presence is fulness of joy; In Thy right hand there are pleasures forever' (Ps. 16:11).

3:18. She is a tree of life to those who take hold of her, And happy are all who hold her fast.
'Tree of life' refers to wisdom personified as the source of life itself. The image of the tree of life began in Eden as the pages of Scripture opened (Gen. 2:9), and it continues through its pages until the closing picture of the new heavens and the new earth (Rev. 2:7; 22:2, 14). In addition, the image of the tree of life is not infrequent in Proverbs (Prov. 11:30; 13:12; 15:4). The tree symbolizes the long and fruitful life already spoken of in verse 16.

'Happy' is the promised outcome of those who embrace wisdom. 'Happy' also represents the closing of the inclusio begun with the same root word in verse 13 where it is translated 'blessed.' The verb here is in the intensive form, stressing that such a one will be made happy in the deepest understanding of the word. As it was in our ancestors' idyllic state, and as it will be in the eternal, perfect state, so even now, in measured portion, we may come to God's tree of life and eat of her fruit and be renewed and take of her leaves and discover healing for the ravages of sin and foolishness.

This reward does not come automatically, however. The tree of life is stationary. We must go to it. Wisdom may call to us (to employ a prior metaphor, cf. Prov. 1:20), yet she does not force her understanding upon anyone. We must 'take hold of her' and 'hold her fast.' The first expression comes from a verb whose root means to 'become strong,' but in this form (hiphil) means to 'take hold of' or 'seize' something.[25] The second expression refers to grasping something securely. It is most often used metaphorically of laying firm hold of moral matters or spiritual truths.[26] Entering into the joys of wisdom's blessedness requires our diligent pursuit and a firm grip upon her precepts. To 'take hold' and 'hold fast' are metaphorical expressions describing the determined obedience of the wise man or woman in the face of the ongoing enticements of foolishness and sin. We must be vigilant in our application of God's wisdom!

3:19. The LORD by wisdom founded the earth; By understanding He established the heavens.

Wisdom is basic to everything. God employed His wisdom, understanding, and knowledge (v. 20) in bringing forth all of creation (Ps. 104:24; 136:5; Jer. 10:12; 51:15). Wisdom predates all creation. It is an attribute of God – something He is – not something He possesses. See Proverbs 8:22-31 for greater development of the relationship between God, His wisdom and the creation.

The wisdom of God that guides us in life is the same wisdom that He employed in the formation of all things. This means that to walk in God's wisdom (as revealed in the Proverbs and the rest of the Scriptures) is to walk in harmony with the created order and all of God's world.[27] Indeed, this begins a new section (vv. 19-35) of the chapter. Verses 19-20 assert the basic place wisdom holds in relationship to all of creation. If wisdom is so foundational to the very creation itself (vv. 19-20), then it ought to be the foundation and fountain of our relationships (vv. 21-35). If God in His wisdom can establish the heavens, then His wisdom can establish our steps through this life (Prov. 4:26). 'And He shall be the stability of your times, A wealth of salvation, wisdom, and knowledge; The fear of the LORD is his treasure' (Isa. 33:6).

This sure foundation requires faith as its active agent. 'By faith we understand that the worlds were prepared by the word of God, so that what is seen was not made out of things which are visible' (Heb. 11:3). By faith we recognize and acknowledge what God in wisdom has done in the created order. No less faith is required as we encounter His foundational wisdom for our lives. The expressions of His wisdom in Proverbs often run contrary to our natural bents. Only faith-filled obedience can release the power of His divine wisdom into our lives and relationships.

3:20. By His knowledge the deeps were broken up, And the skies drip with dew.

The last verse spoke of the formation and foundation of the heavens and the earth. Now we hear of wisdom's part in the creation of the waters of the earth. This order lends itself well to the parallel of wisdom as both the foundation (Prov. 10:25) and the fountain of life (Prov. 4:23; 14:27; 16:22; 18:4).[28]

Exactly what is referred to here is not always immediately understood. The verb 'broken up' is used in Genesis 7:11 to describe the waters that sprang forth from the belly of the earth to join the waters that fell from the sky at the time of the great flood. However, the reference in these two verses seems to be to the time of creation. Perhaps this is a reference to the mist that God sent forth from the ground to irrigate the earth (Gen. 2:6). This may be so, since we are specifically told that God did not immediately send rain from the heavens (Gen. 2:5).

If the first line refers to God's bringing forth water from below the surface of the earth, the second line clearly makes reference to His bringing waters from above the earth. The first specific mention of rain we have in the Bible is at the time of the flood (Gen. 7:4), the same time the previous verb 'broken up' was used. It is possible, therefore, that verse 19 refers to the time of the creation and here we have a reference to the time of the flood. On the other hand, the verse could be written from the vantage point of one far distant from the days of creation and they simply report it as all having happened by God's creative wisdom, knowledge and understanding, without making fine distinctions about any intervals of time between.

However we fine-tune our understanding of this verse, the main point is clear: God's wisdom was operative at creation. Lift your eyes and look about you. If God's wisdom can hang the planets upon nothing and guide them in their courses, can His wisdom not also guide you aright? If God in His understanding can speak and, out of nothing, bring into existence this world, can His understanding not speak rightly as we live out our existence in this tangible reality? If His knowledge founded the heavens and the earth, can it not also make my feet to stand on solid ground? The answer is Yes. The implications of that answer will now be spelled out in the remainder of the chapter.

3:21. My son, let them not depart from your sight; Keep sound wisdom and discretion,

God used wisdom to found the creation. Now, the exhortation comes for us to found our lives and relationships upon His wisdom also. The call begins with the now familiar 'My son' (cf. Prov. 1:8, 10, 15; 2:1; 3:1, 11). The first line seems abrupt. The 'them' has no clear antecedent, leading critics to suppose that this is a unit carelessly dropped in by some editor from somewhere else, or to postulate some theory of inverting the lines of the Hebrew text in order to place 'sound wisdom' and 'discretion' before the first line and make them the antecedent. However, there need be no such frantic reconstruction. The general context of the entire book, as we have seen, is that of wisdom, understanding, and knowledge. These are the things understood by the original writer and his readers as the referent of the word 'them.'

The second line of the verse swiftly underscores this. We are warned against allowing this precious wisdom to 'slip from sight' (NEB). The verb means 'to turn aside' or, as here, 'to depart.'[29] See the same verb, though in a different form, in the nearly identical statement in Proverbs 4:21. The implication here is that wisdom once learned is not necessarily forever retained and appreciated (cf. even Solomon's defection from wisdom through sin, 1 Kings 11:1-13). Walking in wisdom today does not ensure we will pursue wisdom tomorrow. Every day, we must embrace wisdom afresh. At every turn, we must pursue her ways.

The second line continues this emphasis with the verb 'keep.' The word is used often of guarding treasured possessions such as a vineyard (Job 27:18), a fig tree (Prov. 27:18), a fortress (Nahum 2:1). It is used to describe the Lord's watching over His people (Deut. 32:10; Isa. 27:3; Prov. 24:12), as well as the personified wisdom watching over those who embrace her (Prov. 4:6). The word occurs often in Psalms and Proverbs in contexts relating to keeping covenant with God.[30] Our most prized possession in this life is a personal knowledge of God and the understanding of His ways. No price is too high to guard this relationship.

Specifically, we should guard 'sound wisdom' (see on Prov. 2:7). The idea is that of sound judgment and the success in life which flows from it.[31] Similarly, we should keep 'discretion.' This same noun is found in Proverbs 1:4. Its root idea is the practical ability to form a plan and work it to a successful end.[32] It is used in Proverbs to describe its ability to protect its possessor from the harm that comes from following an ill-advised plan (cf. Prov. 2:11).[33]

3:22. So they will be life to your soul, And adornment to your neck.
The exhortations of verse 21 are now followed by a series of benefits (vv. 22-26) that accrue to the account of the one who keeps them. The first is that wisdom, knowledge, understanding, and discretion 'will be life to your soul.' This imagery has already been brought before our mind's eye in verses 2, 16, 18. Note that the promise is not that wisdom will give life, but that it will itself be life to our souls (cf. Col. 3:4, 'Christ, who is our life'). Proverbs repeatedly declares the intimate relationship of wisdom and life (Prov. 4:10, 22; 7:2; 8:35; 9:11; 10:11, 16, 17; 11:19, 30; 12:28; 13:14; 14:27; 15:4, 24; 16:22; 19:23; 21:21; 22:4).[34]

The second line promises that wisdom and its synonyms will be 'adornment to your neck.' We have also previously encountered this word picture in Proverbs 1:9 and 3:3. Wisdom graces the life of the one who seeks her just as a beautiful necklace adorns the neck of its possessor. The moral and spiritual beauty of the wise is conspicuous and cannot remain unnoticed. These two metaphors, taken together, show that a life of wisdom is a life of vitality and beauty.

3:23. Then you will walk in your way securely, And your foot will not stumble.

The proverbs speak often of the 'way' as the course and direction of one's life, as determined by one's choices (Prov. 1:15, 31; 2:8, 12, 13, 20; 3:6, 17, etc.). The promise is that, when we are chasing after wisdom, our way will be secure. 'The law of his God is in his heart; His steps do not slip' (Ps. 37:31). This is a promise often reiterated both here and in the Psalms (Prov. 1:33; 2:7-8; Ps. 121:3). The assurance of God is that 'He who walks in integrity walks securely, But he who perverts his ways will be found out' (Prov. 10:9).

3:24. When you lie down, you will not be afraid; When you lie down, your sleep will be sweet.

How practical of God! Who does not need the reinvigoration of sweet sleep? Watchful wisdom during our waking hours leads to sweet slumber during our sleeping hours.

The verb 'be afraid' describes utter terror or extreme fear.[35] Here God speaks a word of assurance and promise to the one who suffers from 'night terrors.' We need to internalize these promises and claim them as the need arises. Even during an attempted coup, in which he had to flee for his life, David could say, 'I lay down and slept; I awoke, for the Lord sustains me' (Ps. 3:5). 'In peace I will both lie down and sleep, For Thou alone, O Lord, dost make me to dwell in safety' (Ps. 4:8). The teachings of David proved to provide this kind of rest for his son, Solomon, also (Prov. 6:22). See Leviticus 26:6 and Job 11:18-19 for similar assurances.

3:25. Do not be afraid of sudden fear, Nor of the onslaught of the wicked when it comes;

The theme of security continues. The 'sudden fear' is the 'dread' promised the wicked in Proverbs 1:27. It describes a paralyzing, overwhelming fear, as well as the person or thing that creates that terror.[36] What wisdom will laugh over in the case of the wicked (Prov. 1:26-27), she now promises need never be a concern of those who follow her.

There is some question about the second line. Does it describe the attack made by the wicked, or the calamity that comes upon the wicked as their judgment? The Hebrew text seems to give us the latter idea, while the LXX appears to favor the former. The NASB and NKJV here follow the LXX, while the NIV and RSV follow the Hebrew text. It seems best to stay with the Hebrew here and see it as descriptive of the fate of the wicked.[37] The confidence of wisdom, then, is that it will keep you from being numbered among the wicked when the day of their judgment comes.

Psalm 91:3-8 is a wonderful commentary on the security here promised to the one who walks in wisdom.

3:26. For the LORD will be your confidence, And will keep your foot from being caught.

The one who walks in wisdom has the confidence that God is with him. The word here translated 'confidence' in other contexts means to be at one's side.[38] God is with the one who walks in His wisdom. The confidence of God's presence is inestimable. 'The LORD is my light and my salvation; Whom shall I fear? The LORD is the defense of my life; Whom shall I dread?' (Ps. 27:1). 'If God is for us who is against us?' (Rom. 8:31). 'But the LORD is with me like a dread champion; Therefore my persecutors will stumble and not prevail' (Jer. 20:11).

Walking in God's wisdom not only assures us of God's presence, it also assures us that we will not be led into harm. Walking in God's ways will mean we never walk into the trap that foolishness brings. This same point was just made in verse 23. Here again, as elsewhere in Proverbs, life is pictured as a trek through this world that is filled with dangers and snares. The one who takes this journey with God is assured of safe passage.

3:27. Do not withhold good from those to whom it is due, When it is in your power to do it.

The chapter closes with a series of exhortations explaining how wisdom is to be fleshed out in our relationships. There are five exhortations cast in the negative by beginning with the words 'Do not' (vv. 27-31). These closing verses may be divided between exhortations about what it means to be a neighbor (vv. 27-30) and warnings to avoid wickedness (vv. 31-35).

Those referred to here seem to be those to whom one owes wages, because the good is 'due' them. Literally, it would read, 'Do not withhold good from its owners.' This describes not the gratuitous assistance of the unfortunate, but the just treatment of the worker.

The next verse will pick up on the former idea. The law required such justice (Lev. 19:13; Deut. 24:14-15) for laborers often lived hand to mouth, working for just enough money to purchase that day's bread. To delay their wages was to send them away hungry after a long day's work. 'Behold, the pay of the laborers who mowed your fields, and which has been withheld by you, cries out against you; and the outcry of those who did the harvesting has reached the ears of the Lord of Sabaoth' (James 5:4; cf. Jer. 22:13-17; 1 John 3:17-18).

By application, we are to pay debts and fulfill contractual obligations at the earliest possible time. This verse denies us the right to 'hold the check' for some selfish purpose, or in order to take advantage of an opportunity on another front. Those to whom you owe the money or service are to receive it as soon as 'it is in your power to do it.'

3:28. Do not say to your neighbor, 'Go, and come back, And tomorrow I will give it,' When you have it with you.

The point made in the previous verse is underscored here, but also advanced. Whereas verse 27 had to do with those to whom our good is 'due,' this verse seems to call for benevolence to all who are poor. We are warned about delaying acts of kindness until 'tomorrow.' In fact, 'Tomorrow' seldom comes for those whose expressions of mercy and goodness take second place to their concerns. The plea of 'tomorrow' is often only a cover-up for selfishness. We do well to heed the warning of Paul: 'Instruct those who are rich in this present world not to be conceited or to fix their hope on the uncertainty of riches, but on God, who richly supplies us with all things to enjoy. Instruct them to do good, to be rich in good works, to be generous and ready to share' (1 Tim. 6:17-18). James's warning is apropos as well: 'If a brother or sister is without clothing and in need of daily food, and one of you says to them, 'Go in peace, be warmed and be filled,' and yet you do not give them what is necessary for their body, what use is that?' (James 2:15-16; cf. also Luke 11:5-8; 1 John 3:17-18).

3:29. Do not devise harm against your neighbor, While he lives in security beside you.

The harm here described is intentional in nature. 'Devise' is often elsewhere translated as 'plow.'[39] As the farmer carefully cuts the rows into his field, so the wicked allows an injurious thought about his neighbor to cut a channel into his thinking and to plow a furrow of ill-will into the intentions of his heart. This same word is used elsewhere in Proverbs to describe the plotting of evil (Prov. 6:14, 18; 12:20; 14:22).

Such intentions and their outworkings are all the more wicked because they violate trust. The second line of the verse underscores the vulnerability of the neighbor, an exposure created by their presumption of your trustworthiness. The Scriptures make strong denunciations against such plotting: 'Woe to those who scheme iniquity, Who work out evil on their beds! When morning comes, they do it, For it is in the power of their hands. They covet fields and then seize them, And houses, and take them away. They rob a man and his house, A man and his inheritance' (Mic. 2:1-2; cf. also Prov. 16:29-30; Ps. 35:20; 55:20; 59:3; Jer. 18:18-20).

How meticulously we must guard every thought and buffer every offense with the grace of God! No relationship, however close it may be, is immune from the bitterness that can fester from a wrong done. We must take seriously the admonition of Romans 12:18: 'If possible, so far as it depends upon you, be at peace with all men.'

3:30. Do not contend with a man without cause, If he has done you no harm.

The word 'contend' generally describes strife and conflict between persons. That strife may be general and vague or specific and even violent. In legal contexts, it came to mean bringing charges against another. Repeatedly, the Proverbs admonish us to avoid such contention (Prov. 15:18; 17:1, 14; 18:6, 17; 20:3; 26:17, 21; 30:33).[40] The specific conflict denounced here is the one that is 'without cause.' Stirring up such discord is a violation of the ninth commandment (Exod. 20:16). It is the kind of thing the evil one does himself (Job 2:3) and inspires in others (1 Cor. 6:1-8).

In a society where frivolous lawsuits have created gridlock in the judicial system, this is a word we need to hear. 'I'm going to sue!' and 'You'll be hearing from my lawyer!' have become the battle cries of people too weak to personally resolve their interpersonal conflicts. Such taunts reveal not wisdom, but the folly of selfishness. In a conflict, the one devoid of wisdom has nothing left but to demand his 'rights.' A man of understanding, however, would rather be defrauded than violate this command (1 Cor. 6:7-8).

3:31. Do not envy a man of violence, And do not choose any of his ways.

Here we find the fifth in a series of exhortations that all begin with 'Do not' (vv. 27-31). This final exhortation introduces a key truth that the remaining verses of the chapter then explain. Verses 32-35 present four reasons why this truth should be embraced. Each of the reasons is stated in the form of a contrast.[41]

The first line of this verse tells us not to wish we were like the violent. The second tells us not to be like them. Scripture recognizes that it is easy to envy the wicked (Prov. 23:17; 24:1, 19; Ps. 73:3-5). It may appear that might is right and that power wins the day, but we ought not to be duped into thinking that crime pays. The Hebrew word used here for 'envy' describes a powerful emotion that all but takes possession of a person once initially entertained.[42] Such emotion, once stoked, can cloud the mind and impair judgment: '... [T]he anger of man does not achieve the righteousness of God' (James 1:20).

The word for 'violence' can mean wickedness of any kind, but is often used to describe physical brutality as it does here.[43] Such men have already been introduced to us in Proverbs 1:10-16. The connection of violence and envy is not incidental. Violent behavior might tip us off to an inner struggle with envy. Similarly, envy may warn us that violence may be among the next steps taken to satisfy that envy.[44] The second line warns us against putting the inner fantasy into action. We do well to remember that God's reason for destroying the world in Noah's day was its violence (Gen. 6:13). In the day of professional wrestling, increasing violence in professional sports, carjackings, gang violence, and increasing violent crime, what could be more timely than this exhortation? Note now the reasons why we ought to be counter-cultural in this regard.

3:32. For the crooked man is an abomination to the LORD; But He is intimate with the upright.
The first reason not to envy the violent or imitate his ways is the relational distance it creates between God and yourself. The point is here made by way of a contrast set off in two lines. The 'crooked man' is one who has twisted and perverted his ways so that they do not conform to the straight-edge of God's character and revealed will (Prov. 2:15; 14:2). He is contrasted with the 'upright.' The upright are not perfect, but have chosen to live in conformity to God's will.

The first man is 'an abomination' to the Lord. Proverbs speaks often of that which is an abomination to the Lord (Prov. 6:16; 11:1, 20; 12:22; 15:8, 9, 26; 16:5, 12; 17:15; 20:10, 23; 21:27; 24:9; 26:25; 28:9). An abomination is an attitude or action that is repugnant to the Lord and which He cannot endure.[45] Because God loathes these things, they come under His judgment. Things elsewhere listed as an abomination to the Lord include idolatry (Deut. 7:25), homosexuality and other sexual perversions (Lev. 18:22-30; 20:13), human sacrifice (Deut. 12:31), occult activity (Deut. 18:9-14), ritual prostitution (1 Kings 14:23f), dishonest business practices (Deut. 25:13-16), and sacrificing unclean or defective animals (Deut. 14:3-8; 17:1).[46]

The second man, however, finds himself on intimate terms with the Lord. Literally, the second line reads 'But with the upright [is] His intimacy,' the verb being understood. The word for 'intimacy' describes 'an intimate and confidential relationship, sometimes involving secret discussion of policy (15:22) and thus a position of trust.'[47] The Old Testament prophets were men to whom was granted this kind of intimacy with God (Jer. 23:18, 22; Amos 3:7). God promises to all who walk with Him an intimacy of relationship that includes the making known of His mind and will (Job 29:4; Ps. 25:14; John 15:15; 1 Cor. 2:16).

This is not tasteful to those who are fully immersed in our cultural worship of tolerance. Even the most morally stout among us often water the hatred of God down to a platitude about God hating the sin, but loving the sinner. Yet, that is not what this verse teaches. God hates the one who commits the sin and He loathes the one who turns from Him. We should let the extreme to which this truth goes on the one end inform our understanding of how far the promised intimacy of God with the upright projects in the other direction. Thoughtful reflection on the possibility of this level of relationship with God should create in us revulsion at the ways of the violent, rather than envy over the short-term outcome of their ways.

3:33. The curse of the Lord is on the house of the wicked, But He blesses the dwelling of the righteous.

Now, a second reason not to envy or imitate the violent is advanced. The reason is that the violent set themselves against God and, thus, His hand confounds their precarious prosperity. The Lord promises that His curse will rest upon the home of the wicked. How foolish the lie many a sinner tells himself: 'No one need know. This need not affect my family.' God Himself assures us that no sin remains hidden for long and that the effects of rebellion in one heart will be experienced by the whole family. Achan brought his trouble upon his entire household (Josh. 7:24-25).

But, as in all four of these reasons (vv. 32-35), there is a contrasting side. God's blessing rests upon the dwelling of the righteous. When God is honored in the heart of the home's head, the whole family resides under the sunshine of God's promises, providence and

peace. God makes sure that the entire family lives, and moves and has its being in the atmosphere of His grace when the head of the home seeks Him.

This contrasting blessing and cursing was woven into the very fiber of God's covenant with the nation of Israel: 'See, I am setting before you today a blessing and a curse: the blessing, if you listen to the commandments of the Lord your God, which I am commanding you today; and the curse, if you do not listen to the commandments of the Lord your God, but turn aside from the way which I am commanding you today, by following other gods which you have not known' (Deut. 11:26-28). This principle of cursing and blessing continues still today in the age of the New Covenant.

The blessing promised is surely not uninterrupted bliss and the removal of all problems, for many a godly family faces difficult days. Nor does the curse imply that all happiness will be obliterated, for often times the wicked do prosper materially. The blessing and the cursing here describe the fact that, by the choices of the family members, the entire household may find itself either cooperating with God and His providence and power in bringing about His will or they may set themselves against His will and struggle against His omnipotent hand. The former will, for the most part, find that life in this world goes well for them, while the later will, ultimately, find frustration as they struggle to impose their will upon God's world.

3:34. Though He scoffs at the scoffers, Yet He gives grace to the afflicted.
The third reason not to envy or imitate the violent is presented here. The principle of divine judgment is that you get what you give. The LXX has significantly softened the first line to 'The Lord resists the proud,' and James 4:6 and 1 Peter 5:5 seem to follow this.[48] But, the more extreme notion of the Hebrew is accurate. God will respond to us based upon our response to Him and others. Scoffing will draw not His indifference, but His scoffing at us (Prov. 1:22, 26). Even the strongest man who shakes his fist at heaven draws heaven's laughter and derision (Ps. 2:1-5).

On the other hand, God promises to extend grace to 'the afflicted.' Literally, the word means 'he who bends himself.'[49] Such bending low could be the result of inner humility or outward affliction. Either thought would provide a different, but valid, parallel to the violent man who started this section (v. 31).

The Scriptures consistently present God in this light. He gives us the first word, but, according to what we say, He finishes the conversation. 'With the kind Thou dost show Thyself kind; With the blameless Thou dost show Thyself blameless; With the pure Thou dost show Thyself pure; And with the crooked Thou dost show Thyself astute' (Ps. 18:25-26).

3:35. The wise will inherit honor, But fools display dishonor.
The fourth reason not to emulate or envy a violent man is now given. While the general sense of this proverb is clear, the meaning of 'display' is debated. The word means 'lift high' and then, by extension, 'exalt,' but that seems to make an awkward relationship to the first line. To complicate matters, this is a singular participle, while the subject is plural. Perhaps it is best to understand it in the sense of 'lift up and carry away' rather than 'lift up and exalt.'[50] In this way it parallels the first line in that the wise receive honor as their reward whereas the fool 'carries away as his only prize' the dishonor of a life wasted.

This contrast between the ultimate honor of the wise and the dishonor of the foolish is seen throughout the Scriptures: '... [T]hose who honor Me I will honor, and those who despise Me will be lightly esteemed' (1 Sam. 2:30; cf. also Prov. 3:16; 4:8; Dan. 12:2-3; 1 Tim. 5:24-25).

So then, the chapter concludes with an exhortation not to envy or emulate the violent. Four reasons are given: God will be far from you (v. 32); God will be against you (v. 33); God will scoff at you (v. 34); and God will dishonor you (v. 35). These reasons have been given in contrasts, so, positively stated, they are: God will draw near to you (v. 32); God will bless your home (v. 33); God will give grace to you (v. 34); and God will bestow honor upon you as the prize for a life well lived (v. 35). What powerful motivation to go against the grain of human nature and the current culture and live a life of godly wisdom!

End Notes

1. Kidner, Derek, *Proverbs* (Downers Grove, Illinois: InterVarsity Press, 1964), 63.

2.Whybray, R. N., *Proverbs* (Grand Rapids, Michigan: William B. Eerdmans Publishing Company, 1994), 51.

3. Hamilton, Victor P., '*shāḳaḥ*,' *Theological Wordbook of the Old Testament*, (Chicago: Moody Press, 1980), 2:922-923.

4. Nel, Philip J., 'שׁלם,' *New International Dictionary of Old Testament Theology and Exegesis* (Grand Rapids, Michigan: Zondervan Publishing Company, 1997), 4:131.

5. Ross, Allen P., 'Proverbs,' *The Expositor's Bible Commentary* (Grand Rapids, Michigan: Zondervan Publishing Company, 1991), 5:916.

6. Buzzell, Sid S., 'Proverbs,' *The Bible Knowledge Commentary* (Wheaton: Victor

Books, 1988), 1:911.

7. Oswalt, John N., *'bāṭaḥ,'* Theological Wordbook of the Old Testament (Chicago: Moody Press, 1980), 1:101.

8. Kidner, 63.

9. Delitzsch, F., *Proverbs, Ecclesiastes, Song of Solomon* (three volumes in one) in C. F. Keil and F. Delitzsch, vol. 6, *Commentary on the Old Testament* (in ten volumes), (1872; rpt. Grand Rapids, Michigan: William B. Eerdmans Publishing Company, 1980), 1:87.

10. Kidner, 64.

11. Austel, Hermann, J., *'shāqâ,'* Theological Wordbook of the Old Testament (Chicago: Moody Press, 1980), 2:952-953.

12. Whybray, 63.

13. Weber, Carl Philip, *'hûn,'* Theological Wordbook of the Old Testament (Chicago: Moody Press, 1980), 1:213.

14. Hamilton, Victor P., *'pāraṣ,'* Theological Wordbook of the Old Testament (Chicago: Moody Press, 1980), 2:737-738.

15. Kidner, 64.

16. Merrill, E. H., 'יסר,' New International Dictionary of Old Testament Theology and Exegesis (Grand Rapids, Michigan: Zondervan Publishing House, 1997), 2:480-481.

17. Hartley, John E., 'יכח,' New International Dictionary of Old Testament Theology and Exegesis (Grand Rapids, Michigan: Zondervan Publishing House, 1997), 2:444.

18. Kaiser, Walter C., *'mā'ēn,'* Theological Wordbook of the Old Testament (Chicago: Moody Press, 1980), 1:488.

19. Coppes, Leonard, J., *'qûs,'* Theological Wordbook of the Old Testament (Chicago: Moody Press, 1980), 2:794.

20. Ross, Allen P., 5:919.

21. Delitzsch, 1:91.

22. Whybray, 67.

23. Delitzsch, 1:93.

24. Wilson, Marvin R., *'nā'ēm,'* Theological Wordbook of the Old Testament (Chicago: Moody Press, 1980), 2:585.

25. Weber, Carl Philip, *'ḥāzaq,'* Theological Wordbook of the Old Testament (Chicago: Moody Press, 1980), 1:276.

26. Payne, J. Barton, *'tāmak,'* Theological Wordbook of the Old Testament (Chicago: Moody Press, 1980), 2:973.

27. Ross, 5:919.

28. Ibid.

29. Kaiser, Walter C., *'lûz,'* Theological Wordbook of the Old Testament (Chicago: Moody Press, 1980), 1:472.

30. Schoville, Keith N., 'נצר,' New International Dictionary of Old Testament Theology and Exegesis (Grand Rapids, Michigan: Zondervan Publishing House, 1997), 3:147-148.

31. Goldberg, Louis, *'yshh,'* Theological Wordbook of the Old Testament (Chicago: Moody Press, 1980), 1:413.

32. Wolf, Herbert, *'zāmam,'* Theological Wordbook of the Old Testament (Chicago: Moody Press, 1980), 1:244.

33. Whybray, 33.

34. MacArthur, John, *The MacArthur Study Bible* (Nashville: Word Publishing, 1997), p. 881.

35. Whybray, 71.

36. Bowling, Andres, *'pahad,'* Theological Wordbook of the Old Testament (Chicago: Moody Press, 1980), 2:721.

37. Delitzsch, 1:97.

38. Hamilton, Victor P., 'כְּסֶל,' New International Dictionary of Old Testament Theology

and Exegesis (Grand Rapids, Michigan: Zondervan Publishing House, 1997), 2:680.

39. Buzzell, 1:913.

40. Bracke, John M., 'רִיב,' *New International Dictionary of Old Testament Theology and Exegesis* (Grand Rapids, Michigan: Zondervan Publishing House, 1997), 3:1105.

41. Ross, 5:921.

42. Coppes, Leonard, J., *'qānâ,' Theological Wordbook of the Old Testament*, (Chicago: Moody Press, 1980), 2:802-803.

43. Whybray, 73.

44. Adams, 35.

45. Whybray, 73.

46. Youngblood, Ronald F., *'tôʿēbâ,' Theological Wordbook of the Old Testament* (Chicago: Moody Press, 1980), 2:976-977.

47. Whybray, 73.

48. Ross, 5:921.

49. Delitzsch, 1:103.

50. Delitzsch, 1:104.

Proverbs 4

4:1. Hear, O sons, the instruction of a father, And give attention that you may gain understanding,

This chapter falls out into three sections – each an exhortation to acquire wisdom and each marked off by a call to listen from father to son (vv. 1, 10, 20). The call we meet in this verse is very much like the other familial calls to wisdom we find in the book of Proverbs (e.g. Prov. 1:8; 3:1; 5:1, 7; 7:24), yet it is distinctive in that it is in the plural (but see also 5:7; 7:24; 8:32).

Debate has raged over this uniqueness, some suggesting that this refers in a metaphorical way to a teacher/disciple relationship rather than a literal father/son relationship. Such debate, however, is unnecessary, for many a father has more than one son. The mention of 'mother' in verse 3 also lends to an understanding of this in a familial sense (cf. Prov. 1:8; 6:20).[1] While the literal familial relationship of father and son is surely the meaning here, the wider application may extend to such teacher/disciple relationships and even to that of God the Father over us, His children.

There is not much new material presented in this verse. The 'instruction' and 'understanding' spoken of here have already been introduced in Proverbs 1:2. The call to 'give attention' is also familiar (Prov. 1:24; 2:2; 4:20; 7:24).

This repetition, however, is not useless in the least. This teaches us a basic principle of pedagogy: we learn best by repetition. The way of God with His children is still 'precept upon precept, precept upon precept; line upon line, line upon line' (Isa. 28:13, kjv). In an age that chases that which is new and different, we dare not lose the value of reminder (Rom. 15:15; 2 Tim. 1:6; 2 Pet. 1:12, 15).

4:2. For I give you sound teaching; Do not abandon my instruction.

The exhortation of verse 1 is buttressed here in the first line by a reason, then is reinforced in the second line by a prohibition against walking away from a father's wisdom.

The 'teaching' described implies the necessity of personally receiving the instruction.[2] The root of the word means to 'take' or to 'seize' (cf. Prov. 1:5). Maturity is evidenced as one gains an ever-

increasing ability to grasp with his mind the wisdom of God, as it
relates to his particular circumstances. He thus receives 'perception'
into the affairs of life.[3]

This teaching is further described as 'sound.' The term is the
broadest Hebrew word for good. Among its expansive connotations
are good, pleasant, beautiful, delightful, glad, joyful, precious,
correct, and righteous.[4] So, the teaching held out for us to lay hold
of is that which is desirous no matter what angle it is viewed from
or what light our circumstances may cast upon it.

The word 'instruction' is the familiar Hebrew word *torah*, which is
commonly translated as 'law.' Here, however, as in Proverbs 1:8; 3:1;
6:20; 13:14, it is correctly translated as 'instruction' (see on Prov. 3:1).
We are exhorted not to 'abandon' what our father lays down for us by
way of teaching. In its root, the idea is that of leaving, forsaking, and
loosing. It comes, then, to be the primary Hebrew word for apostasy.
Here in Proverbs, we are additionally warned against forsaking the
way of righteousness (Prov. 2:13; 15:10), wisdom (4:2, 6), reproof
(10:17), loyalty and faithfulness (3:3).[5] Sadly, perhaps the best
biblical illustration of this kind of apostasy is that of Solomon's own
son, Rehoboam. He turned away from the good wisdom of older
men and chose instead the foolish counsel of his younger advisors
(1 Kings 12:8, 13; 2 Chron. 10:8, 13). The result was a breach in the
kingdom of Israel and the desolation of the nation.

4:3. When I was a son to my father, Tender and the only son in the sight of my mother,

Solomon now speaks autobiographically, concurring with his father
David's assessment of him as 'tender' (1 Chron. 22:5; 29:1). Following
the death of David and Bathsheba's first child, Solomon was the first
of their four other sons (2 Sam. 12:24; 1 Chron. 3:5), making him
their only son for a time. This reference, however, may simply mean
that he felt loved as if he were the only son they had.

The Hebrew construction of 'I was a son to my father' carries
with it the emphasis that Solomon was under David's authority.[6]
He further describes himself as 'tender.' This adjective is used in
the sense of the tenderness or softness of few years (Gen. 18:7), of
soft words (Job 40:27), and in the sense of weakness (Gen. 29:17).[7]
Here, a loving father and mother see Solomon in the vulnerability
of young age. While youthfulness does not always appreciate such
a view by parents, the passing of time often brings the appropriate
appreciation, as it did for Solomon. It also demonstrates that parental
instruction can never begin too early.

Solomon's words here demonstrate that authority and affection need not be polar opposites. In a healthy parent/child relationship the two coexist as a helpful, but fallible, model of the perfect fatherhood of God.

4:4. Then he taught me and said to me, 'Let your heart hold fast my words; Keep my commandments and live;'
Verses 4b-9 quote David's instruction to his son. Solomon was passing this instruction on to his sons via this quotation. Solomon was stressing that he was once in the very position his sons now found themselves in: that of a learner. David and Solomon are both illustrating the fulfillment of the covenant obligation of parents to pass on the truth to the next generation. Deuteronomy 6:6-9 told of the transmission of truth across three generations (Moses, parents, children) just as we have pictured here. Similarly, in the New Testament, Paul called Timothy to transmit truth across generational lines in the church (2 Tim. 2:2), picturing four generations embracing the truth (Paul, Timothy, faithful men, others).

Teaching travels along lines of relationship and affection, making the home life the primary and most ideal place for instruction. The father is to take the initiative in this instruction, though certainly the mother is highly involved. Sometimes, under special circumstances, the weight of this responsibility must come upon the mother's shoulders only. In such cases, God will give grace (2 Tim. 1:5; 3:14-15), but this is no excuse for laziness and ineptitude by fathers.

David called Solomon to 'Let your heart hold fast my words,' a similar call to that already found in Proverbs 3:1, 5, where the call was to trust in God with all of one's heart (cf. 1 Chron. 28:9). The phrase 'Keep my commandments and live' is repeated in Proverbs 7:2a (cf. Isa. 55:3). This emphasis has already been met in Proverbs 3:1ff, giving ample evidence that Solomon had truly internalized his father's words.

The three discourses on wisdom that make up this chapter all contain a similar emphasis on the life-giving power of wisdom (Prov. 4:4, 10; 22-23). This emphasis, however, was not even original with David. As Moses stood with the children of Israel before they entered the land of promise he presented the law of God a second time in the book we call Deuteronomy. He concluded his sermons by declaring, 'See, I have set before you today life and prosperity, and death and adversity' (Deut. 30:15). Solomon got it from David. David, through his fathers, got it from Moses. And, of course, Moses got it from God. It is the duty of every father to so set before his children the wisdom of God, emphasizing the life-giving ways of God's wisdom. Proverbs will have much to say about how a father is to carry out this responsibility.

4:5. 'Acquire wisdom! Acquire understanding! Do not forget, nor turn away from the words of my mouth.'

The words of David still reverberate in Solomon's ears. Perhaps these very pleadings of David created within Solomon the desire to ask God for wisdom (1 Kings 3:5-14). His father pleaded with him to 'get' wisdom and understanding at any cost (cf. v. 7). The word 'acquire' in most contexts in the Old Testament refers to financial transactions to purchase land (Gen. 25:10) or slaves (Gen. 39:1). This led to the theological concept of God redeeming or buying back His people (Exod. 15:16; Ps. 74:2).

These usages inform the way the verb is used here in Proverbs to signify the necessity of gaining wisdom (Prov. 1:5; 4:7; 15:32; 16:16; 17:16; 18:15; 19:8; 23:23), though here the word is clearly not used in a literal commercial sense.[8] Here, the desired 'wisdom' and 'understanding' are clearly synonymous, as they are in other places throughout Proverbs, such as 2:2-3. There is no charge too high to pay for these priceless treasures (Matt. 13:45-46). Forget all else, but be certain to gain wisdom!

As strongly as David urged Solomon to gain the wisdom that he did not already possess, he also pressed him not to lose what wisdom he had already attained. To drive home this second point, he first exhorted him to 'not forget' his father's wisdom. The word warns against more than an absent-minded misfiling of information. It calls us to take personal action to recall what is important.

Often, it is a change in life-circumstances that creates the atmosphere in which one may forget previous experiences and instruction. But, just as often, the forgetfulness comes from personal neglect.[9] What parent does not worry that the distractions and enticements of this world will lure his child to forget what has been poured into his heart through many years of instruction in the home?

David stressed this exhortation by adding that Solomon was not to 'turn away from the words of my mouth.' The first exhortation in line two might be chalked up to distraction and enticement. This second command, however, implies willful turning away from his upbringing. The word can be variously translated by such words as extend, stretch out, turn, incline, divert, refuse, and disavow.[10] What begins as blind naïveté can quickly become willful rebellion.

The father confesses that his words are incomplete. His son needs to go even further in the pursuit of wisdom. A parent's job is never done. We will never feel we have sufficiently taught them all they need to know or that we wish to give to them. We are inevitably called to release our children to God in what we consider incomplete form. 'If I could only have them a few more years!'

4:6. 'Do not forsake her, and she will guard you; Love her, and she will watch over you.'
This succinct verse of only four words reinforces the last command given in verse 5; the first line does so negatively, the second positively. Wisdom, spoken of here in the third person, is again personified as a woman (1:20-35; 8:1-36).

'Forsake' and 'love' describe the same action from two different sides. These two verbs represent an oft-repeated call in Proverbs: to hold fast to wisdom and to passionately commit to her. The root word of 'forsake' is encountered ten other times in Proverbs (Prov. 2:13, 17; 3:3; 4:2; 9:6; 10:17; 15:10; 27:10; 28:4, 13). To 'love' wisdom is underscored especially in the eighth chapter. Those who love wisdom are loved by her (Prov. 8:17). To love wisdom is to succeed (Prov. 8:21). To hate wisdom is, on the other hand, to love death (Prov. 8:36). The son who loves wisdom gladdens the heart of his father (Prov. 29:3).

The words 'guard' and 'watch over' have already been encountered (Prov. 2:8, 11). The former carries the idea of exercising great care over something. The latter means to guard by sitting over something, and is used to describe both another watching over us and our responsibility to watch over certain things. See also Proverbs 3:21-23 for elaboration on the security that comes from embracing wisdom.

4:7. 'The beginning of wisdom is: Acquire wisdom; And with all your acquiring, get understanding.'
This verse is not found in the LXX, but this need not lead us to the extreme of removing it from our Bibles, as some kind of interruption to the thoughts of verses 8 and 9.[11]

The term 'The beginning' is the same as that we met in Proverbs 1:7, the theme verse for the entire book. There, the fear of the Lord is noted as the beginning of wisdom. Here, the beginning of wisdom is 'Acquire wisdom.' These are not contradictory statements, but complementary. The fear of the Lord creates a hunger to know His mind. You will never attain to what you do not ultimately want.

The first line of the verse is notoriously difficult to translate. A vital verb has been left out and it reads literally: 'beginning wisdom, get wisdom.' The two options most often chosen by translators are determined by where the verb is supplied. Some place 'is' between the first and second half of the first line and the result is 'The beginning of wisdom is: get wisdom' (NASB, RSV). Others, however, place the verb forward and the result is: 'Wisdom is the beginning [or primary thing]: get wisdom' (KJV, NIV).[12]

The second line adds emphasis to the first. In the business of life, we are actively working to acquire many things. As we are about all this acquiring, make certain that our highest priority is to acquire 'understanding,' which is here synonymous with 'wisdom.' The 'with' of this second line denotes price: 'No matter the price or the sacrifice, gain understanding!' (Matt. 13:44-46).[13]

The first line tells us what it takes to attain to wisdom: the desire and commitment to pursue it. The second line describes this desire and commitment: it must be our supreme desire and our ultimate commitment.

The attainment of wisdom is, in the final analysis, not a matter of I.Q. or G.P.A., but of desire and will.[14] Richard Baxter was right: 'You shall find this to be God's usual course: not to give his children the taste of his delights till they begin to sweat in seeking after them.'[15]

4:8. 'Prize her, and she will exalt you; She will honor you if you embrace her.'
Solomon continues to recount the teaching he received from his father. The simple principle here is that God honors those who honor Him (1 Sam. 2:30). The first line contends that, when you lift high wisdom, it pulls you up with it. When you attempt to lift yourself high, you will be brought low (Prov. 16:18). If, however, you concentrate not on exalting yourself, but placing wisdom high and to the forefront of all you do, then you also shall be lifted up and honored (James 4:10; 1 Pet. 5:6).

The second line changes the metaphor. Now, the picture is of holding wisdom close. If you embrace wisdom, she will 'honor you.' The root idea of 'honor' is that of weightiness or heaviness. It often has a negative connotation, but it can also, as here, have a positive meaning. The meaning of 'honor,' in this sense, is that you are weighty and heavy in that you are loaded with praise and good report. Proverbs often sounds the note that outward reputation comes through an inward embrace of wisdom (Prov. 21:21; 22:4; 26:1).[16] If you hold yourself close to wisdom, you will take on the weight of her honor as she is seen in you.

The first line speaks of distancing yourself from wisdom in the sense that you lift her up and are willing to stand back in the shadows while she receives the applause. The second line shifts the metaphor to picture us as pulling wisdom close through our embrace. When we hold her high and let her have the spotlight, we are brought higher ourselves. When we hold her close, the weightiness of her honor tips the scales in our favor when we are placed in the balance. Lift wisdom high and hold her close. This is the path to honor.

4:9. 'She will place on your head a garland of grace; She will present you with a crown of beauty.'
Solomon's remembrance of his father's words now comes to a close. For the 'garland of grace,' see Proverbs 1:9 and 3:22. Wisdom, it is promised, will award those who seek her, with a 'crown of beauty.' The same phrase is used in Proverbs 16:31 of a gray head as an award for righteous living. Note too that the wise are also crowned by a good wife (Prov. 12:4), riches (14:24), grandchildren (17:6), and, ultimately, the Lord Himself (Isa. 28:5). As it turns out, the path of wise living is actually the road to honor.

4:10. Hear, my son, and accept my sayings, And the years of your life will be many.
The second section of this chapter begins here (vv. 10-19), being signaled by the familial call 'my son' (cf. vv. 1, 20). The first section consisted primarily of Solomon's exhortation of his sons via recollections of his father David's exhortations to him concerning wisdom (vv. 1-9). Now, Solomon appears to exhort his own son directly. Solomon's exhortation extols the virtues of wisdom (vv. 10-13), as well as warns of the way of wickedness (vv. 14-17). Verses 18-19 then summarize the outcome of pursuing either path.[17]

The verb 'accept' is a common one used over one thousand times in the Old Testament. It is often translated as 'take,' 'get,' 'fetch,' 'lay hold of,' 'seize,' 'receive,' or 'acquire.'[18] Thus, we are reminded that it is not enough simply to 'hear' the truth, but that we must also 'accept' it as God sends it to us through parents or others.

If you will both hear and receive the wisdom taught, 'the years of your life will be many.' This is an echo of a familiar promise we often hear reverberating throughout the Proverbs (e.g. Prov. 3:2, 16; 9:11; 10:27; 14:27; 15:24).

4:11. I have directed you in the way of wisdom; I have led you in upright paths.

Solomon returns to the familiar metaphor of life as a path we walk (e.g. Prov. 1:15, 19; 2:7-9, 12-15, 18-19; 3:6, 23). Solomon reminds his son that he has 'directed' him in the way of wisdom. The verb, whose root idea means 'to throw' or 'to cast' in the hiphil form, as here, can have the idea of 'teaching.' There is a strong sense of control by the subject when these things are 'cast' forward. The verb is related to *torah*, the common noun for 'law.'[19] The sense seems to be that Solomon reminds his son that he has cast before him a clear path for wise living, guiding him and directing him in that path as he got his legs under him.

The way in which Solomon has directed his son is comprised of 'upright paths' (cf. Prov. 3:6). By the designation 'upright,' these paths are marked out as those which are right, both morally and practically.[20] More than guidance, however, is implied. It means that God makes the way smooth before you by removing all obstacles that might keep you from arriving at His desired goal for you (cf. Prov. 11:5; Isa. 45:13).[21] These upright paths should be contrasted with the crooked paths of the wicked (Prov. 2:15).

We observe here that a father can, and should, do all he can to make the way of wisdom obvious to, and achievable by, his children. In the end, however, each child must pick up his feet and keep them moving down the path of life his father has set before him. There is much anxiety and energy expended by the parent, but, in the end, the responsibility falls upon the child. Little wonder that, when the child walks in wisdom, he becomes a joy to his parents (Prov. 10:1; 15:20; 23:15; 23:24; 27:11).

4:12. When you walk, your steps will not be impeded; And if you run, you will not stumble.

The thought begun in verse 11 is embellished here. The pathway as a metaphor for life is encountered often in the Proverbs (see on v. 11). The assurance here is that the path of wisdom is one free from the obstacles and hindrances that slow or stop progress. Indeed, the path of wisdom provides firm footing, so that one may not only 'walk' through life securely, but may 'run' in God's way without concern for danger (Prov. 3:23; 10:9; Ps. 18:36; 37:31; 91:12; 119:32, 165). By contrast, the way of the wicked is crooked and full of stumbling blocks (vv. 14, 19; cf. Prov. 2:12-15; Job 18:7-8).

The obstacles are described by two verbs. The first, 'impeded,' describes a pressing, cramping, constricting action.[22] The idea is that you will not walk into situations which hem you in, narrow the path, or catch you between a rock and a hard place. The second verb is 'stumble.' The idea here is that of tangling the feet and falling headlong, whether from inner exhaustion and inability to continue on or from external obstacle that causes one to loose balance.[23] These two verbs combine to assure those who walk in God's paths that nothing will leap up before them, close in around them, or arise from within them so as to bring them low.

4:13. Take hold of instruction; do not let go. Guard her, for she is your life.

We have already been exhorted to lay hold of wisdom (vv. 5, 7). Now, having laid hold of wisdom, we are exhorted never to let go of her (Prov. 23:23). It requires great energy and commitment to attain wisdom. It requires as much or more of the same to remain in her ways, once attained. Solomon himself is perhaps the supreme example of this. He began his reign in wisdom, but ended in the shame of folly.

The reason to spend, and be expended, to gain and keep wisdom is that, it is not only the way to life, it is life itself (Prov. 3:18, 22; 8:35; Deut. 32:47; Eccles. 7:12). Compare this with the statements concerning Jesus, who is not only the way to life, but is life itself (John 14:6; Col. 3:4; 1 John 5:11-12).

4:14. Do not enter the path of the wicked, And do not proceed in the way of evil men.

The positive call to walk in paths of wisdom (vv. 10-13) now gives way to the negative command not to walk in wickedness (vv. 14-17). The two commands given in this verse are followed by four more given in rapid succession in the next to underscore the dangers of verses 16-17.

The first decision we must make with regard to sin is not even to enter its path or play at its gate. If we do not 'enter,' we cannot 'proceed.' Better to cut off temptation at its beginning, before its enticements gain momentum, than to attempt to stop the desires it has already aroused. 'But each one is tempted when he is carried away and enticed by his own lust. Then when lust has conceived, it gives birth to sin; and when sin is accomplished, it brings forth death' (James 1:14-15).

4:15. Avoid it, do not pass by it; Turn away from it and pass on.

The two commands of verse 14 are now quickly reinforced by four more similar imperatives given in rapid-fire succession. These four commands add a sense of urgent necessity to the matter.

The four verbs used here provide a wonderful strategy for fighting off temptation. First, we must 'avoid' temptation. When temptation is near, we must steer as wide a path away as possible. Do not make eye contact (Prov. 4:25; 6:13, 25; 10:10; 16:30). Cross the street and give it a wide berth (Prov. 5:8; Job 11:14).

Second, we must not 'pass by' temptation. While temptation may spring up and entice us unawares, there are also areas of temptation we know we are vulnerable to. We must calculate and construct our steps each day so as to stay as distant as possible from those temptations that we know may hound us.

Third, we must activate our will and immediately 'turn away' from the enticement of sin when confronted by it. To linger over temptation, to delay decision regarding it is to walk headlong into its trap (Ps. 119:60).

Fourth, we must 'pass on' once we have made the decision not to imbibe in the wanton pleasure of some allurement. Walk and keep walking. Do not contemplate the fleeting pleasure that might have been yours, if the decision had been different (Col. 3:1; Phil. 4:8). To look back after your hand has been put to the plow is to disqualify yourself (Luke 9:62; Rom. 6:21-23; Col. 3:5).

4:16. For they cannot sleep unless they do evil; And they are robbed of sleep unless they make someone stumble.
Solomon here adds one more reason to stay away from sin: its power to enslave. The vivid word picture holds before us the web of sin as its victim becomes ever more entangled in it. Now, they cannot even sleep until their evil plots are worked out. 'He plans wickedness upon his bed; He sets himself on a path that is not good; He does not despise evil' (Ps. 36:4). 'Woe to those who scheme iniquity, Who work out evil on their beds! When morning comes, they do it, For it is in the power of their hands' (Mic. 2:1). Darkness offers little opportunity for good. Beware of that which sprouts and blooms before the sun rises!

Contrast this fevered fight against sin with the sweet sleep of the righteous (Prov. 3:24). Also, contrast Psalm 132:3-5 and David's refusal to sleep until he provided a settled place for God's house.

Not content with their own misdeeds, they seek to 'make someone else stumble.' Oh, that we were as zealous in enlisting people for godliness as the wicked are in recruiting others for ruin! The word 'stumble' is used three times in this section (vv. 12, 19).

4:17. For they eat the bread of wickedness, And drink the wine of violence.

This verse both continues the thought introduced in verse 16 and concludes the exhortation not to walk in wickedness (vv. 14-17). The wicked cannot rest (v. 16) until they do evil, because satisfying their appetite for sin has become as powerful an urge as filling their stomach or quenching their thirst (Job 15:16). Contrast Jesus, who confessed: 'My food is to do the will of Him who sent Me, and to accomplish His work' (John 4:34). The wicked choose the short-term sweetness of stolen pleasures, not calculating the longer-term risks to their spiritual health (Prov. 9:17; 20:17).

The staples of their diet are 'wickedness' and 'violence.' The former is a broad term describing the life that is the opposite of that which God desires, often being contrasted with 'righteousness' in the wisdom literature.[24] We have already been introduced to those who employ 'violence' (Prov. 1:19; 3:31), and it will grow into a major theme of the book (10:6, 11; 13:2; 16:29; 21:7; 24:2; 26:6). A change in verb tenses takes the metaphor even further than is obvious in our English translations: The bread of 'wickedness' is gobbled up and then washed down with the wine of 'violence.'[25]

4:18. But the path of the righteous is like the light of dawn, That shines brighter and brighter until the full day.

This verse and the next summarize the arguments made for wisdom (vv. 10-13) and against wickedness (vv. 14-17), contrasting the outcome of both ways of life.

This verse sets forth what awaits those who walk the path of wisdom. The life of the righteous is one of progressive illumination, understanding and insight. The dawn begins with a faint glow on the horizon, progressively moves to that first brilliant moment when the sun peeks over the skyline, and, eventually, becomes the blazing midday sun. So also those who follow hard after God increasingly see and understand His wisdom as He leads them through life.

First, there comes the initial announcement of God's saving plan in Christ and the light of God's illumination begins to scatter the darkness of our hearts (Luke 1:78-79; John 3:19-21). Then, the 'sun of righteousness' dawns upon our hearts (Mal. 4:2) and we see Christ and ourselves more clearly (Isa. 60:1-2; John 8:12). Then, when we embrace Christ by faith (John 12:36, 46), we come into the fuller light of the revelation of God in Christ. As we continue in that faith relationship with Christ, we walk ever increasingly into the fuller light of His life (1 John 2:8).

Though we now see only dimly (1 Cor. 13:12), we keep our eyes on the brilliance of His glory and move stage by stage into that same image (2 Cor. 3:18). The Lord God Himself has promised that those who stay on this path will come to the place where 'there shall no longer be any night; and they shall not have need of the light of a lamp nor the light of the sun, because the Lord God shall illumine them; and they shall reign forever and ever' (Rev. 22:5).

What a powerful incentive to walk in wisdom! How convincing an argument to keep to the path of righteousness! Every step of obedience brings me into the fuller revelation of God's ways. Every day of faithfulness becomes another advancement in understanding God's purposes. Every move toward righteousness brings a greater measure of His light. There is a cumulative effect to the blessings of God: only those who keep to the path will enter in fully.

4:19. The way of the wicked is like darkness; They do not know over what they stumble.
In contrast to the progressive illumination that awaits those who walk the way of wisdom (v. 18), this verse holds forth the blinding darkness that encircles the path of wickedness.

Employing a simile, Solomon declares that the way of the wicked is 'like darkness.' The Hebrew word describes not simply that which is dark, but that which is utter darkness (cf. Prov. 7:9; Exod. 10:22). In the Old Testament, such darkness usually accompanies God's judgment. Such darkness comes upon those who seek occult knowledge (Isa. 8:22), who practice injustice (Isa. 58:10), and upon those who are unfaithful prophets and priests (Jer. 23:12). The day of the Lord will bring this kind of deep darkness (Joel 2:2; Zeph. 1:15).[26]

Those who reject God's wisdom and choose their own way end up confessing: 'We grope along the wall like blind men, We grope like those who have no eyes; We stumble at midday as in the twilight' (Isa. 59:10). Jesus said, '... [H]e who walks in the darkness does not know where he goes' (John 12:35). John agreed: 'And this is the judgment, that the light is come into the world, and men loved the darkness rather than the light; for their deeds were evil. For everyone who does evil hates the light, and does not come to the light, lest his deeds should be exposed. But he who practices the truth comes to the light, that his deeds may be manifested as having been wrought in God' (John 3:19-21).

Calamity is the experience of those who choose their own path, yet 'they do not know over what they stumble.' Those not walking in fellowship with Christ find their lives falling apart and have no clue as to why. They are bewildered by the continual frustration of their plans. They are lost as to the reason for their inability to get ahead and overcome. God has promised those who choose His way that, 'When you walk, your steps will not be impeded; And if you run, you will not stumble' (Prov. 4:12). He has also forewarned of the blindness of those who choose their own way.

4:20. My son, give attention to my words; Incline your ear to my sayings.

We now open the third exhortation of this chapter. Again, the call 'My son' opens the way for the flow of instruction to follow (vv. 1, 10). This section opens with a general call to hear wisdom (vv. 20-22) and, then, follows with a series of exhortations that are grouped around mention of various body parts (vv. 23-27). Solomon calls his son to guard his heart (v. 23), guard his mouth (v. 24), guard his eyes (v. 25), and guard his feet (vv. 26-27). This holistic caution will watch over every path of life and keep one in the way of wisdom.

The command to 'give attention' has already been met in Proverbs 1:24; 2:2; 4:1. The exhortation to 'incline' the ear is also common in Proverbs (Prov. 2:2; 5:1, 13; 22:17).

4:21. Do not let them depart from your sight; Keep them in the midst of your heart.

While the general introduction to this section continues here and into the next verse, the mention of 'sight' and 'heart' anticipates the imagery to come in verses 23, 25. The 'heart' has already been touched upon (Prov. 3:1, 3, 5). It most frequently points to what we would call the 'mind' (e.g. Prov. 3:3; 6:23a; 7:7b), but can also refer to the emotions (15:15, 30), the volition (11:20; 14:14) and, indeed, the entire inner being (3:5).[27] The heart is 'the inner you' or 'the real you.'

The commands of God through parents are to be treasured 'within you' (Prov. 2:1; Ps. 37:31; 40:8; 119:11). Thus, the command 'Do not let them depart' (3:21) is appropriate. Do not allow to escape that which has already been corralled.

The second line reinforces this imagery by calling us to keep parental instruction 'in the midst' of the heart. The centrifugal force of life has a tendency to move wisdom to the outer fringes of our conscious attention. Thus, transmitting wisdom from one generation to the next is not a one-time event. Wisdom requires constant maintenance. A heart once instructed in the ways of God's wisdom is not set for life. Reinforcement, repetition and reminder are tools all parents must carry on their belt. Due to the nature of our hearts, we must constantly learn, relearn and learn again the wisdom of God. How well God our Father knows our frame as He guides us, His children, into His wisdom!

4:22. For they are life to those who find them, And health to all their whole body.

The promise is that walking in wisdom gives 'life' and 'health.' For the first, consider Proverbs 4:4, 10, 13, 23; 8:35. For the second, this note has already been struck in Proverbs 3:8 and will be, again, in 16:24. Note that it is health 'to all their whole body.' The benefits of walking in wisdom accrue to every dimension of a man's life, i.e. physical, emotional, spiritual and psychological. This holistic health requires that our 'whole body' be consecrated to God and kept in obedience for Him (vv. 23-27).

This may sound silly to those blinded by the bias of our age toward a mechanistic understanding of the human body. Yet, who can calculate the physiological, emotional, and psychological devastations that sin brings? 'When I kept silent about my sin, my body wasted away Through my groaning all day long. For day and night Thy hand was heavy upon me; My vitality was drained away as with the fever heat of summer' (Ps. 32:3-4). Wisdom enables us to avoid these disastrous effects of foolishness and sin, with the benefits being real and lasting.

4:23. Watch over your heart with all diligence, For from it flow the springs of life.

Guard your heart! If there were one verse I could give to Christian young people, it would be this one. Nothing is more essential than guarding your heart.

The heart is more than simply the sentimental side of us. The Hebrew concept of the heart includes the mind and our ability to reason (Prov. 3:3; 6:23a; 7:7b), the volition and our ability to exercise our will (11:20; 14:14), and the emotions and our capacity for a broad range of feelings (15:15, 30). It is a term that reflects the totality of the inner person (Prov. 3:5).[28] Your heart is the real you.

The call is to 'watch over' the inner you. The verb can be translated as 'watch,' 'guard,' or 'keep.'[29] This vigil is to be undertaken 'with all diligence.' The word translated 'diligence' actually carries the idea of 'guard' or 'post.'[30] But this, in connection with the previous verb, has an intensifying effect. Indeed, as if this were not enough, in addition, it is 'all' diligence that is to be applied. The effect is the meaning that the heart is to be guarded above all other things put in your charge to watch over. It is to be protected as the supreme, and most valuable, possession of life.[31]

Why this great value placed upon the heart? The reason is because 'from it flow the springs of life.' Literally, the reading is 'for out of it the issues of life.' The word translated 'springs' is normally used to describe the farthest reaches of a geographical boundary or border (e.g. Josh. 16:3; 17:18).[32] The physical idea is here taken metaphorically, to describe the far reaches of where one's life will go. The goings forth, the end boundaries, the ultimate end of your life is a matter of the condition of your heart.

> The heart is the instrument of the thinking, willing, perceiving life of the spirit; it is the seat of the knowledge of self, of the knowledge of God, of the knowledge of our relation to God, and also of the law of God impressed on our moral nature; it is the workshop of our individual spiritual and ethical form of life brought about by self-activity – the life in its higher and in its lower sense goes out from it, and receives from it the impulse of the direction which it takes; and how earnestly, therefore, must we feel ourselves admonished, how sacredly bound to preserve the heart in purity....[33]

Jesus' own teaching reflected this same understanding of the heart: 'For the mouth speaks out of that which fills the heart. The good man out of his good treasure brings forth what is good; and the evil man out of his evil treasure brings forth what is evil' (Matt. 12:34b-35). 'For from within, out of the heart of men, proceed the evil thoughts, fornications, thefts, murders, adulteries, deeds of coveting and wickedness, as well as deceit, sensuality, envy, slander, pride and foolishness. All these evil things proceed from within and defile the man' (Mark 7:21-23). 'He who believes in Me, as the Scripture said, "From his innermost being shall flow rivers of living water"' (John 7:38).

There is nothing of greater value on this earth than the condition of your heart. There is no single action that will more directly affect the outcome and quality of your life than the guarding of your heart. There is not a more portentous predictor of your ultimate end than what you expose your heart to. Above all else, guard your heart!

4:24. Put away from you a deceitful mouth, And put devious lips far from you.

Also, guard your mouth! The quality of the heart is revealed in the contents of the speech. Jesus made a similar connection between heart (v. 23) and mouth (v. 24; cf. Luke 6:45).

Thus, we are warned to rid ourselves of a 'deceitful mouth.' The word 'deceitful' comes from a word meaning crooked (Prov. 2:15).[34] Thus, it refers to that which twists and distorts reality. Lies, half-truths, white-lies, deception and distortion of the truth reveal a heart problem. Such talk betrays one who has dropped the guard over his heart.

Similarly the second line demands we put way 'devious lips.' The word 'devious' describes perverted talk.[35] Unclean and course language are included here, as are swearing, cursing and minced oaths. 'Let no unwholesome word proceed from your mouth, but only such a word as is good for edification according to the need of the moment, that it may give grace to those who hear' (Eph. 4:29).

Proverbs will have much more to say about the use of the tongue (e.g. Prov. 2:12; 6:12; 8:13; 10:31-32; 17:20; 19:1, 28).

4:25. Let your eyes look directly ahead, And let your gaze be fixed straight in front of you.
Further, guard your eyes! The wise man knows where he is headed and maintains his focus on the goal. The fool gets distracted by allurements that call to him from off the path (Prov. 17:20). The eye is the lamp of the body (Matt. 6:22), projecting upon the screen of the soul the images before it. Godly instruction should be the center of our eye (Prov. 7:2). The eyes, once indulged, are never satisfied (Prov. 27:20). One peek, one lingering glance, will never assuage the appetite for more. It is not the first look that creates sin, but the second, lingering look of lust (Matt. 5:28). How wise, then, to make a covenant with our eyes about what we will and will not look upon (Job 31:1)? It is the lust for more that moves us to waste our energies upon that which will never last (Prov. 23:5).

Did not Jesus, in the fulfilling of His redemptive work, find it necessary to 'resolutely set His face to go to Jerusalem' (Luke 9:51)? How much more we in the matter of completing the Father's work for our lives?

4:26. Watch the path of your feet, And all your ways will be established.
Finally, guard your feet! The path the Lord guides us in is level and straight (vv. 11-12). The call is to keep our eyes upon it. But, what exactly does that mean? The verb in the first line is notoriously difficult to translate. The verb occurs infrequently in the Old Testament (Ps. 58:3; 78:50; Prov. 5:6, 21; Isa. 26:7). Translators struggle with whether the word primarily means 'to level' or 'to perceive'

(compare NIV and NASB). The former would indicate our need to employ our moral choices to make smooth the path of life before us. The latter would call us to be alert to, and step aside from, all encumbrances to proceeding down the path of God. The authorities are divided.[36] Its use in Proverbs 5:6 and 21 seems to clearly point to a meaning of 'to perceive.' It is probably best, then, to allow that meaning here to remain consistent within the same book.

The second line describes the outcome of taking heed to the first. The verb translated as 'will be established' in its root form means 'to bring something into being with the consequence that its existence is a certainty.'[37] The idea of 'be firm' seems best to describe its meaning here.[38] That is to say that, as you carefully watch over the path your feet take, you will find each step steady, safe and free of encumbrance.

4:27. Do not turn to the right nor to the left; Turn your foot from evil.

This verse continues the exhortation to guard our feet. The first line takes up the language of Moses when he exhorted the children of Israel as they were poised to enter the Promised Land (Deut. 5:32; 17:11, 20; 28:14). Here, as there, 'to the right nor to the left' views anything in these two directions as distractions from what lies directly ahead in the will of God. The call is to keep from becoming captivated by competing calls or entertaining options, but rather to stay focused on God's primary call and best course. '... [O]ne thing I do ... reaching forward to what lies ahead, I press on toward the goal' (Phil. 3:14). 'Let us run with endurance the race that is set before us, fixing our eyes on Jesus' (Heb. 12:1b-2a). Moral shortcuts always end in disaster.

The second line makes clear the evil nature of the distractions. The word translated 'evil' ranges in meaning from a passive sense of 'misfortune' or 'calamity' to an active idea of 'wickedness' or 'evil.'[39] Whether translated passively or actively, the options to either side are viewed as outside of God's will and, thus, dangerous. For similar exhortations, see Proverbs 1:15-16 and 3:7.

The LXX adds two more lines to this verse: 'God knows the ways on the right hand, but those on the left are crooked.'[40] These are, however, nearly universally considered not to be genuine. Indeed, they distort the meaning of 'right' and 'left' made in the Hebrew text. The Hebrew text makes 'right' and 'left' to be evil distractions, while this LXX addition makes the one to represent truth and, the other, error.[41]

End Notes

1. Ross, Allen P., 'Proverbs,' *The Expositor's Bible Commentary* (Grand Rapids, Michigan: Zondervan Publishing Company, 1991), 5:922.

2. Ibid.

3. Kaiser, Walter C., '*lāqaḥ*,' *Theological Wordbook of the Old Testament* (Chicago: Moody Press, 1980), 1:481-482.

4. Bowling, Andrew, '*tôb*,' *Theological Wordbook of the Old Testament* (Chicago: Moody Press, 1980), 1:345.

5. Schultz, Carl, "*āzab*,' *Theological Wordbook of the Old Testament* (Chicago: Moody Press, 1980), 2:658-659.

6. Whybray, R. N., *Proverbs* (Grand Rapids, Michigan: William B. Eerdmans Publishing Company, 1994), 76.

7. White, William, '*rākak*,' *Theological Wordbook of the Old Testament* (Chicago: Moody Press, 1980), 2:848.

8. Cornelius, Izak and Raymond C. Van Leeuwen, 'קנה,' *New International Dictionary of Old Testament Theology and Exegesis* (Grand Rapids, Michigan: Zondervan Publishing House, 1997), 3:940-941.

9. Allen, Leslie C., 'שׁכח,' *New International Dictionary of Old Testament Theology and Exegesis* (Grand Rapids, Michigan: Zondervan Publishing House, 1997), 4:103-105.

10. Hamilton, Victor P., 'נטה,' *New International Dictionary of Old Testament Theology and Exegesis* (Grand Rapids, Michigan: Zondervan Publishing House, 1997), 3:91.

11. Ross, 5:923.

12. Whybray, 77.

13. Delitzsch, F., *Proverbs, Ecclesiastes, Song of Solomon* (three volumes in one) in C. F. Keil and F. Delitzsch, vol. 6, *Commentary on the Old Testament* (in ten volumes), (1872; rpt. Grand Rapids, Michigan: William B. Eerdmans Publishing Company, 1980), 1:108.

14. Kidner, Derek, *Proverbs* (Downers Grove, Illinois: InterVarsity Press, 1964), 67.

15. Draper, Edythe, *Draper's Book of Quotations for the Christian World* (Wheaton, Illinois: Tyndale House Publishers, 1992), 496.

16. Oswalt, John N., '*kābēd*,' *Theological Wordbook of the Old Testament* (Chicago: Moody Press, 1980), 1:426-428.

17. Buzzell, Sid S., 'Proverbs,' *The Bible Knowledge Commentary* (Wheaton: Victor Books, 1988), 1:914.

18. Kaiser, Walter C., '*lāqah*,' *Theological Wordbook of the Old Testament* (Chicago: Moody Press, 1980), 1:481-482.

19. Hartley, John E., '*yārâ*,' *Theological Wordbook of the Old Testament* (Chicago: Moody Press, 1980), 1:403.

20. Olivier, Hannes, 'ישׁר,' *New International Dictionary of Old Testament Theology and Exegesis* (Grand Rapids, Michigan: Zondervan Publishing House, 1997), 2:567.

21. Buzzell, 1:911.

22. Swart, I. and Robin Wakely, 'צרר,' *New International Dictionary of Old Testament Theology and Exegesis* (Grand Rapids, Michigan: Zondervan Publishing House, 1997), 3:853f.

23. Harman, Allan M., 'כשׁל,' *New International Dictionary of Old Testament Theology and Exegesis* (Grand Rapids, Michigan: Zondervan Publishing House, 1997), 2:733-734.

24. Livingston, G. Herbert, '*rāshaʿ*,' *Theological Wordbook of the Old Testament* (Chicago: Moody Press, 1980), 2:863.

25. Delitzsch, 1:111.

26. Price, James D., 'אֹפֶל,' *The New International Dictionary of Old Testament Exegesis and Theology* (Grand Rapids, Michigan: Zondervan Publishing House, 1997), 1:479-481.

27. Kidner, 68.

28. Ibid.

29. Kaiser, Walter C., '*nāsar*,' *Theological Wordbook of the Old Testament* (Chicago: Moody Press, 1980), 2:594.

30. Hartley, John E., '*shāmar*,' *Theological Wordbook of the Old Testament* (Chicago: Moody Press, 1980), 2:939-940.

31. Delitzsch, 1:114-115.

32. Brown, Francis, S. R. Driver, Charles A. Briggs, *A Hebrew and English Lexicon of the Old Testament* (Oxford: Clarendon Press, n.d.), 426.

33. Delitzsch, 1:115.

34. Allen, Ronald B., ''*aqash*,' *Theological Wordbook of the Old Testament* (Chicago: Moody Press, 1980), 2:693.

35. Kaiser, Walter C., '*luz*,' *Theological Wordbook of the Old Testament* (Chicago: Moody Press, 1980), 1:472.

36. See Naude, Jackie A., "פלס,' *New International Dictionary of Old Testament Theology and Exegesis* (Grand Rapids, Michigan: Zondervan Publishing House, 1997), 3:628-629; Hamilton, Victor P., '*pālas*,' *Theological Wordbook of the Old Testament* (Chicago: Moody Press, 1980), 2:726; Brown, Francis, S. R. Driver, Charles A. Briggs, *A Hebrew and English Lexicon of the Old Testament* (Oxford: Clarendon Press, n.d.), 814.

37. Oswalt, John N., '*kûn*,' *Theological Wordbook of the Old Testament* (Chicago: Moody Press, 1980), 1:433.

38. Whybray, 83.

39. Livingston, G. Herbert, '*ra'â'*,' *Theological Wordbook of the Old Testament* (Chicago: Moody Press, 1980), 2:854.

40. Ibid.

41. Delitzsch, 1:117.

Proverbs 5

5:1. My son, give attention to my wisdom, Incline your ear to my understanding;
This fifth chapter contains warnings and instructions with regard to one's sexual life. Verses 1-6 warn of the wiles of an adulteress. Verses 7-14 provide motivation for steering a wide course around such a one by listing the disastrous outcomes of involvement with her. Finally, verses 15-23 call for enjoyment of a rich sexual relationship within the bonds of the marriage covenant. This entire chapter serves as an expansion on the theme already introduced somewhat more briefly (Prov. 2:16-19). One should also compare what we find here with Proverbs 6:24-35.

The opening series of warnings (vv. 1-6) begin with what has almost become a stock call to heed the instruction of the father (vv. 1-2). The familial call of 'my son' has already been met often (Prov. 1:8, 10, 15; 2:1; 3:1, 11, 21; 4:1, 10, 20). The commands to 'give attention' (Prov. 4:1, 20; 7:24) and to 'Incline' your ear are also frequent (2:2; 4:20; 22:17).

This verse calls us to give heed to 'wisdom' and 'understanding,' while the next verse adds 'discretion' and 'knowledge.' These are standard words used throughout Proverbs to describe the life of insight called for. Wisdom has already been encountered often (Prov. 1:2, 7; 2:6, 10; 3:13, 19; 4:5, 7, 11) and is a word that describes skillful living, which brings one to the place of success.[1] We have also met 'understanding' often (e.g. Prov. 2:2, 3, 6, 11; 3:13, 19). It describes intelligence, aptitude, and skill in living.[2]

5:2. That you may observe discretion, And your lips may reserve knowledge.
The general call to heed wisdom begun in verse 1 now continues before the exhortations become more specific (vv. 3-6). To 'wisdom' and 'understanding' (v. 1) are now added 'discretion' and 'knowledge.' The word translated 'discretion' is often elsewhere used with a negative connotation.[3] But, here in Proverbs (cf. Prov. 1:4), it describes wisdom's ability to protect its possessor from the harm brought on by foolishly proceeding with an ill-advised plan.[4] To 'observe' this discretion means that the possessor exercises the self-discipline necessary to stay in God's ways.

Here 'knowledge' is a deep intimate knowledge of the object known (Prov. 1:4, 7, 22, 29; 2:5, 6, 10; 3:20). This is knowledge that is gained through personal relationship to, and experience with, the object.[5] The possessor has gained this wisdom through personal application and experience. One is able to 'reserve' this knowledge when he guards and keeps it, not losing it in a momentary hormonal rush. This is especially understood when these lips that 'reserve knowledge' are contrasted with those of the adulteress that 'drip honey' (v. 3).

5:3. For the lips of an adulteress drip honey, And smoother than oil is her speech;

The 'adulteress' has already been introduced to us in Proverbs 2:16-19. The word means 'foreign' or 'alien' (e.g. Prov. 5:10, 17, 20; 6:1; 7:5; 22:14).[6] The meaning is metaphorical here, in the sense that, because she is outside of the marriage covenant with you, she is 'foreign' to you. Though her pleasures are alien, they are, nevertheless, alluring. Her 'lips' here refer to the enticing words she speaks rather than to her kisses (see Song of Sol. 4:11 for the same expression).[7] She seductively uses words that sound sweet ('drip honey') and are delivered in a fashion that is 'smoother than oil.'

The word selected for 'honey' refers to the honey as it drips directly from the comb before it is broken.[8] It is honey at its best, the sweetest substance known to ancient Israel. Similarly, well-pressed olive oil was the smoothest substance known to the ancient Hebrews.[9] With her words, she caresses your ego and, with her delivery of those words, she soothes, smoothes and softens every moral objection that may arise in opposition to her evil plan. Do not entertain her allurements for even a moment!

5:4. But in the end she is bitter as wormwood, Sharp as a two-edged sword.

The sweetness of the adulteress's compliments soon turns sour. The smoothness of her seductions 'in the end' cuts like a knife. The Hebrew word translated 'in the end' comes from a root meaning 'afterwards' or 'behind.' The word is best translated by 'that which comes after.'[10] There is always an 'afterward' in an illicit sexual relationship (e.g. Prov. 5:11; 16:25; 20:21; 23:32). When she is behind you – when the passing moments of pleasure are gone, there are consequences that linger and leave one wondering how he ever fell for the bait.

The promised sweetness (v. 3) is soon replaced by that which is 'bitter as wormwood.'

The bitterness of the wormwood plant is legendary (Deut. 29:18; Jer. 9:15; 23:15; Lam. 3:15, 19; Amos 5:7; 6:12; Rev. 8:11). Wormwood becomes a metaphor for sorrow, calamity and cruelty. The plant was placed between woolen garments to ward off maggots and moths.[11] It is so bitter that not even the lowest life forms could tolerate it! It perfectly describes the polar opposite of the drops of honey anticipated before the liaison (v. 3).

Similarly, the smooth flattery gives way to the unavoidable wounds of a 'two-edged sword.' The phrase is literally a 'sword of mouths,' but came to signify the sword with two cutting edges. The literal rendering preserves the imagery of her seductive words from verse 3, however. As with a two-edged sword, there is no escaping injury. There is no 'safe' or manageable side to immorality.

5:5. Her feet go down to death, Her steps lay hold of Sheol.

In this life, the consequences of immorality are bitter and sharp (v. 4). The consequences, however, are not merely temporal, they are also eternal. The words of this verse are paralleled both before and after this. 'For her house sinks down to death, And her tracks lead to the dead' (Prov. 2:18). 'Her house is the way to Sheol, Descending to the chambers of death' (Prov. 7:27; cf. also Prov. 9:18).

The words 'death' and 'Sheol' are in parallel. The KJV's 'hell,' where we have 'Sheol,' may be misleading. Sheol was the place where the dead were believed to dwell (Prov. 7:27). Sheol was certainly an actual place and a location of continued existence rather than annihilation. However, the more fully developed notion of hell, as the New Testament presents it, would have to await the progress of fuller revelation, when Christ 'brought life and immortality to light through the gospel' (2 Tim. 1:10).[12]

Little does the adulteress know (v. 6) that the party she throws is on the avenue leading to her destruction. Those who fall for her wiles never bother to look down the road to see what is coming. Not only does she entice others to play with her in the street, but her feet actually 'lay hold of' Sheol. Though she may not comprehend the process she is in, with every step she takes into immorality (and every step others take with her), she is grasping the grave and pulling herself and her partners closer and closer to their doom.[13]

5:6. She does not ponder the path of life; Her ways are unstable, she does not know it.

The verbs in both lines could be translated either as the third person feminine singular 'she does not' or as a second person masculine singular (a reference to the male who has fallen into her ways) 'you do not.'[14] It seems best to follow the majority of translations and see this as the third person singular feminine and thus a completion of the description of the adulteress, begun in verse 3.

The fact that she does not 'ponder' the paths of life reveals her willful rejection of God's ways. The verb 'ponder' has been met already in Proverbs 4:26 and will be again in 5:21. Her ways are 'unstable.' The word means to shake, reel, stagger or wander. At root, it pictures a repetitive motion which moves back and forth, whether on a small scale, like something swaying or shaking, or on a larger scale, where homeless vagabonds wander the earth.[15] Contrast the straight paths of God's wisdom in Proverbs 4:11.

The adulteress has no direction to her life. She lives for the moment. If pleasure calls to the left, to the left she goes. If something allures her to the right, she staggers after it. There is no thought for tomorrow. This moral myopia makes her unaware of the yawning abyss of death and destruction that lies down the winding path she takes.

5:7. Now then, my sons, listen to me, And do not depart from the words of my mouth.
Verses 7-14 now provide motivation for staying free of the entanglements of sexual immorality. There is much in this opening verse that is familiar to us by now. The call 'my sons' has been often encountered (Prov. 1:8, 10, 15; 2:1; 3:1, 11, 21; 4:1, 10, 20; 5:1). The exhortation to 'listen' is often heard in the Proverbs (e.g. Prov. 1:5, 8, 33; 4:1, 10; 5:13; 7:24; 8:6, 32, 33, 34; 13:1). The call 'do not depart' reminds us of Solomon's similar charge in Proverbs 3:21 and 4:21 (though a different Hebrew word is employed), both being general exhortations leading to more specific instructions as is the case here. Even the phrase 'the words of my mouth' has been met in Proverbs 4:5 (cf. 7:24).

These general exhortations, which appear at the head of sections of specific instruction found in chapters 1–9, should not be given less weight because of their frequency and broad appeal, but even more. These are the pleadings of a loving father who, because of the wisdom of God and the experience of years, sees what the blinded fancy of youth does not. Every child needs to learn early to take with utmost seriousness the warning cry of his parents rather than ignoring it and assuming they are just over reacting. The same is true of every child of the heavenly Father.

5:8. Keep your way far from her, And do not go near the door of her house,

There is more wisdom in never letting yourself be tested than in proving the strength of your convictions by flirting with temptation. 'Flee youthful lusts' is still the way of God's wisdom (2 Tim. 2:22). A man may say with his mouth, 'I would never …!', but all the while be titillating himself with how close he can come without entering into the physical act (Matt. 5:28, 29). 'Can a man take fire in his bosom, And his clothes not be burned? Or can a man walk on hot coals, And his feet not be scorched?' (Prov. 6:27). Does what we set our eyes upon in the printed page or computer or television screen draw us near her door (Prov. 7:25; Ps. 101:3)? Does what we open our ears to put us within the sound of her call (Prov. 9:14-17)?

5:9. Lest you give your vigor to others, And your years to the cruel one;

Now begins a recitation of the ruin that comes to the one who flirts with immorality.

First, you may end up giving your 'vigor' to others. The word is variously translated as splendor, majesty, vigor, glory and honor.[16] The word is often used of the glory, honor and majesty of God. What exactly it means here, however, is less clear. It seems best, in comparing it to line two, to understand it as referencing the strength and vitality of youthfulness.

The second line echoes the first and cautions about giving away your 'years' to someone else. The 'years' here represent not merely the chronological passing of time, but the productivity of those best years of strength and stamina. They represent all that could have been if only he had not entangled himself in an adulterous affair. Adultery impoverishes one, not only materially and financially, but it also robs one of his dreams and forces him to live with the 'if onlys!' and 'what ifs?'

Who exactly is referenced as 'the cruel one'? It is possible that it may refer to the enraged and jealous husband (Prov. 6:34-35) who, rather than having exacted the punishment of death (Lev. 20:10; Deut. 22:22), chooses to force you into financial restitution that encumbers you for years. It could be a judge who similarly renders a judgment of restitution or child support against you that handicaps you financially throughout the prime of your life. Possibly, it refers to one who has happened upon knowledge of your affair and then bilks you through extortion.[17] Perhaps, even the woman herself blackmails you. The one with whom the greatest human intimacy has been shared has become the cruel taskmaster demanding and controlling your life. Hell hath no fury like a woman scorned!

5:10. Lest strangers be filled with your strength, And your hard-earned goods go to the house of an alien;

The strain of thought carries through from verse 9. This verse makes the previous one clearer. The 'strangers' and 'alien' are probably members of the woman's family. These descriptive words may be chosen because most harlots were of other nations, since prostitution was illegal among the Hebrews. It is also possible that the words simply view her family as foreign because there is no legitimate connection with them, other than a momentary sexual liaison. The mention of 'the house' may mean that the man becomes their slave, if not in a literal sense, then perhaps in a metaphorical one, as he spends the rest of his days trying to meet their demands, so that their secret may be kept quiet. All his 'strength' is exerted on behalf of others to whom he is held in chains. All the 'hard-earned goods' he may produce with his best years are poured into someone else's cupboards.

The passing pleasure of sin carries a high price and long-lasting consequences that are seldom contemplated before the illicit rendezvous.

5:11. And you groan at your latter end, When your flesh and your body are consumed;

As the diving board appears disproportionately higher after having climbed to the top, so the cost of a diversion into illicit pleasure looks infinitely greater after the pleasure has passed.

The groaning of the 'flesh' and 'body' may refer to the ravages of a sexually transmitted disease. Little wonder Paul warned the Corinthian believers to 'Flee immorality.' For 'Every other sin that a man commits is outside the body, but the immoral man sins against his own body' (1 Cor. 6:18). On the other hand, it may simply refer to the advances of old age and how the perspective it grants causes one to lament what was done in younger years.

The fear of the Lord 'will be healing to your whole body, And refreshment to your bones' (Prov. 3:8). The precepts of God's word 'are life to those who find them, And health to all their whole body' (Prov. 4:22). How radically different the toll taken by sin on the human body! 'When I kept silent about my sin, my body wasted away Through my groaning all day long. For day and night Thy hand was heavy upon me; My vitality was drained away as with the fever heat of summer' (Ps. 32:3-4).

The word 'groan' describes the sorry state of the sinner, now become sufferer. The word describes the ravenous growl of an empty stomach seeking to fill its void (Isa. 5:29; Prov. 28:15), the hallow, repetitive crash of ocean waves upon the shore (Isa. 5:30), and the desperate echo of an inner emptiness from the poor and oppressed (Ezek. 24:23). It is 'an elemental, animal cry of anguish when the guilty finds himself destitute.'[18] Could this be a temporary and time-bound expression of what will become the unending 'weeping and gnashing of teeth' for the unrepentant (Matt. 8:12; 13:42, 50; 22:13; 24:51; 25:30)?

5:12. And you say, 'How I have hated instruction! And my heart spurned reproof!'

The outcome of sin is now viewed from the vantage point of old age. The conscience tormented for decades by its own irresponsibility now finds its voice (vv. 12-14). These laments are the cries of a heart that has awakened too late.

The verb 'hated' conveys an emotional attitude toward someone, or some thing, which you have come to detest, despise and hold as an enemy to you.[19] His problem is not that he hated something, but that he hated the wrong thing. He should have hated evil (Prov. 8:13), not the instruction of his parents. The verb 'spurned' conveys the idea of turning something away because you despise it (Prov. 1:30; 15:5).[20]

How sad to come to your latter end and realize that you have played the fool throughout your lifetime (Prov. 1:7, 22, 29-30). There is no comfort for that (Prov. 1:24-28)

5:13. 'And I have not listened to the voice of my teachers, Nor inclined my ear to my instructors!'

The sorry lament of the sinner continues. Though the call to 'Listen!' had come often (Prov. 5:7; 7:24; 8:6, 32; 19:20; 23:19, 22), it was not heeded. Now the consequences of spurning reproof have come to full fruition. So also the urging to incline the ear to wisdom had not been infrequent (Prov. 2:2; 4:20; 5:1; 22:17). Yet, other voices were found that were more pleasant to listen to than that of instruction.

Beware of listening only to that with which you already agree! Beware of listening only to him who compliments you! Beware of heeding only the advice that brings about your pleasure! Not every dissenting voice is wrong. It might be the voice of wisdom!

5:14. 'I was almost in utter ruin In the midst of the assembly and congregation.'

These laments close out the second section of the chapter (vv. 7-14), which has sought to provide motivation to steer a wide course around sexual immorality. The phrase 'utter ruin' is literally 'all evil.' What exactly the sinner is referring to has been debated. It is possible that capital punishment was nearly executed (Deut. 22:22). There certainly had been financial collapse (Prov. 5:9-10). There was also social embarrassment that would not go away (Prov. 6:33).

It would appear that, in all probability, the description includes all three of these elements. He had indeed had his bank account drained dry over the ordeal. Then, as he was found out, and the entire community ('the assembly and the congregation' doubles up the synonyms for emphasis) turned out to deal with his waywardness, he was afraid that they would stone him, as the Mosaic Law made provision for. They did indeed inflict blows upon him (Prov. 6:33), but, in the end, it was the public disclosure of his sin and the ongoing shame involved with it that lingered. Looking back, he recounts how close he came ('I was almost') to death. These are not, however, words of relief, but rather tears of sorrow over a life wasted.

5:15. Drink water from your own cistern, And fresh water from your own well.

We now embrace the closing section of the chapter (vv. 15-23). This portion continues the warning concerning sexual immorality, yet it does so from a positive standpoint, encouraging a rich sexual life within the bonds of the marriage covenant.

Note the robust imagery employed here: 'cistern,' 'well' (v. 15), 'springs,' 'streams' (v. 16), 'fountain' (v. 18). The metaphors refer to one's wife by covenant and the gratification found sexually in that relationship. A 'cistern' was a collection place for rainwater. It was, as such, a permanent fixture in the home and one dedicated to meeting the needs within that home. This is significant, because the LXX has substituted 'vessel' for 'cistern,' which may at first glance seem but a slight difference. But, as Ross has pointed out, 'the Hebrew imagery means that the wife is to be a source of pleasure, not a useful conveyance of pleasure.'[21] In addition, the wife is referred to as a 'well' (Song of Sol. 4:12, 15), making her a source of fulfillment, but not an object to be used.

To 'drink' is a euphemism for enjoying a healthy sexual relationship within the confines of marriage. That relationship is referred to as 'fresh water,' as opposed to that which runs through the gutters in the public square. Keeping our sexual expression within moral boundaries does not limit our pleasure, but actually enhances it. '... [L]et the marriage bed be undefiled ...' (Heb. 13:4).

We can now discover what may have been behind Paul's wise counsel to the Corinthians: 'But because of immoralities, let each man have his own wife, and let each woman have her own husband. Let the husband fulfill his duty to his wife, and likewise also the wife to her husband ... Stop depriving one another ... and come together again lest Satan tempt you because of your lack of self control' (1 Cor. 7:2-3, 5).

5:16. Should your springs be dispersed abroad, Streams of water in the streets?

While the imagery of 'springs' and 'Streams of water' clearly continues the metaphorical reference to sexual love begun in verse 15, this verse does contain some interpretational challenges. The first relates to whether this verse should be understood as a question (NASB, NIV, NKJV, ASV, RSV, Amplified), a prohibition (NEB, JB), or a command (KJV)? Whether the sentence is translated as a question or a prohibition, the effect is the same for the reader. There is nothing in the syntax of the Hebrew text to suggest we interpret this as a question, but it is not necessary that the interrogative particle be found if the context makes clear that this is the author's intention.[22] It seems clear that, whether constructed as a question or as a prohibition, the meaning of the author is that one ought not to undertake the action contemplated.

Another interpretational issue would be what exactly is being referred to by 'your springs' and 'Streams of water'? Is this a euphemistic reference to the male sexual act which wastes his seed upon numerous partners rather than keeping it for the sanctity and productivity of marital love? Or, is it a reference to the wife as the source of sexual pleasure? The first would warn the man that he may not only impoverish himself socially and materially (vv. 9-14) by means of immorality, but also in terms of raising up a godly heritage. The second is a warning that the man's infidelity may lead to the wife's marital unfaithfulness as well.

The imagery, as begun in verse 15, makes the wife the 'cistern' and the 'well,' i.e. the repository or source of the 'water.' The 'water' itself, then, is not used figuratively to speak of the wife herself, but of that which she, in the bonds of marriage, provides the husband – healthy, beautiful, sanctified sexual love. So, the 'springs' and 'Streams of water' here should not be seen as specifically referring to the male seed wasted upon multiple partners (though that would be the case in immorality), but rather a more general reference to his sexual passion and love.

What, then, is Solomon trying to say? It seems best to take the statement as a warning (whether by means of a rhetorical question or by a prohibition) against indiscriminate sexual activity outside of marriage, because it will waste upon what is common that which is to be sanctified to the holiness of the marriage bed (Heb. 13:4).

5:17. Let them be yours alone, And not for strangers with you.
The word 'them' refers to 'springs' and 'Streams of water' as their antecedent (v. 16). There, we found that these refer to the sexual passion that is healthy and blessed within the confines of marriage. Here, the thought concerns the exclusivity of married sexual love. This exclusivity is made emphatic by a more literal rendering of the first line: 'Let them be for you, you alone.'

The word 'strangers' is masculine in form. Those who would make verse 16 refer to the wife's reciprocal infidelity find support in this masculine form here. They contend that this verse then turns to her and tells her to keep her sexual activity confined to marriage. However, in accordance with the interpretation we have taken in verse 16, the masculine plural noun here may refer in a generic way to those who reside outside the marriage covenant, the issue of gender not being central, but rather the fact that they are alien to the covenant. It could also designate the husband of the woman with whom the man had sexual relations, referring in a loosely logical way to how the man gave his passions to a woman, and, thus, to a people, who are not his by covenant and the posterity of which he could not enjoy.

How many of the confusing and heart-rending child custody cases we encounter would be avoided if the marriage bed was kept holy? How many heart-aches would children be spared if only their parents would have maintained a godly reverence for the covenant of marriage?

5:18. Let your fountain be blessed, And rejoice in the wife of your youth.
The imagery continues as a healthy sexual relationship within marriage is pictured as a 'fountain.' Solomon calls for such sexual passion to be enjoyed within the confines of a monogamous marriage relationship. How remarkable, considering this is Solomon speaking. Despite having seven hundred wives and three hundred concubines

(1 Kings 11:3), Solomon counseled his sons to stay in a one man/ one woman relationship. When such boundaries are respected, the sexual relationship of husband and wife can expect to be 'blessed' by God. What a message for today's society: God wants to bless your sexual life and relationship! The best sex comes not through indiscriminate philandering, but through honored commitments within the divinely given covenant of marriage.

Do not let your heart wander, but determine to 'rejoice' in the one you are committed to by covenant. The word 'rejoice' is used here with overtones of sexual delight. Find your passion focused upon, and fulfilled in, your marriage partner. The phrase 'wife of your youth' refers to the woman you married while in your youth. The lifelong commitment of one man to one woman is God's pattern for marriage and family and is the union He will bless. The immoral abandon their marriage commitments after the initial thrill is gone (Prov. 2:17) and, in the end, find themselves empty and used. The godly continually recommit to the one God has given them in marriage and find that life, love, and romance continue to improve with the growth of their commitment.

5:19. As a loving hind and a graceful doe, Let her breasts satisfy you at all times; Be exhilarated always with her love.
We find here an unusual three line proverb. The first line continues the sexual imagery, this time turning to the animal world for its metaphor. The 'hind' (deer) and 'doe' (female mountain goat;[23] the romantic imagery is better maintained in English language by the translation 'doe'!) were considered graceful and beautiful animals with their delicate limbs. As such, they became apt metaphors for the grace and beauty of womanhood. Such imagery is found elsewhere in similar contexts (cf. a male pictured as a 'stag' in Song of Sol. 2:9).

The mention of 'breasts' is unusual in Hebrew writings, and was, undoubtedly, considered provocative in that culture (this Heb. word found only in Ezek. 23:3, 8, 21; but another similar word also found in Song of Sol. 1:13; 4:5; 7:3, 7, 8; 8:1, 8, 10 and elsewhere). The husband is exhorted to allow his wife's breasts to 'satisfy' him sexually. The word 'satisfy' means, literally, to 'saturate' or 'drench' and, thus, extends to the idea of 'satisfying' or 'satiating' something.[24] 'Drench yourself until satisfied in a healthy marital sexual relationship,' conveys the idea of Solomon.

The third line calls the man to always be 'exhilarated' with the sexual relationship with his wife. The word 'exhilarated' describes one who walks with staggering step. It can even imply that this wavering gait is due to intoxication.[25] The captivated husband is smitten by his wife's love. 'How much better is your love than wine' (Song of Sol. 4:10; cf. 7:9).

Note that the phrases 'Let ... satisfy' and 'Be exhilarated' both imply that we can make a choice about what satisfies and what exhilarates us. We are not powerless before our hormonal impulses. We, as moral and rational creatures made in the image of God, can determine what satisfies and, indeed, even captivates us. Sexual desires do not rule us. We rule them by the grace and power of God (1 Cor. 9:27).

5:20. For why should you, my son, be exhilarated with an adulteress, And embrace the bosom of a foreigner?

This verse provides reasoning for the commands of verse 19. The plea is to look objectively upon, and think rationally about, the matter of sexual desire. Considering the high and holy passion God grants within marriage and the disastrous results of infidelity, why would anyone stray from their marriage partner? The rhetorical questions make it a matter of common sense.

The verb 'exhilarated' is repeated from the previous verse. There it was used of the God-given, and intoxicating, passion of marital love. Here, however, it describes the blinding nature of illicit passion. Comparing the two reminds us that God does not seek to deny the highest expressions of sexual passion, only to direct which avenue they are experienced in. These boundaries serve both to safeguard us and to heighten the lasting pleasure of sexual fulfillment. The fool believes that forbidden fruit is the sweetest. The greatest heights of passion are not found outside marriage, but within it.

The second verb has already been used in Proverbs 4:8, where the young man is called to 'embrace' wisdom. Here he is to 'embrace' his wife. To hold exclusively to your wife is wisdom; to embrace wisdom is to hold exclusively to your wife.[26] A married man cannot have the one without the other. An unfaithful husband is a fool!

The designations 'adulteress' and 'foreigner' serve to remind us that the marriage covenant is sacred. Such women are not necessarily of different ethnic background, but are foreign in the sense that they reside outside the sacred bond created between man and wife. Thus they are foreign to the sexual exclusivity demanded by the marriage covenant.

5:21. For the ways of a man are before the eyes of the Lord, And He watches all his paths.

Sin is never secret. God knows all and sees all. 'For My eyes are on all their ways; they are not hidden from My face, nor is their iniquity concealed from My eyes' (Jer. 16:7). 'And there is no creature hidden from His sight, but all things are open and laid bare to the eyes of Him with whom we have to do' (Heb. 4:13; cf. Prov. 15:3; 2 Chron. 16:9; Job 31:4; 34:21; Ps. 11:4; 17:3; 139:1-12; Eccles. 12:14; Jer. 17:10; 23:24; 32:19; Hosea 7:2; Rev. 2:18, 23). How foolish, then, is the vain attempt to deceive God?

The word 'paths' refers literally to the ruts worn by repeated travel of wagons over a roadway.[27] When we bend our will toward temptation, we promise ourselves, 'Just this once!' Seldom do we calculate the addictive nature of sin, particularly sexual sin. God sees not only our individual acts of sin, but He sees also the destructive habits they will become.

5:22. His own iniquities will capture the wicked, And he will be held with the cords of his sin.

Those addictive habits foreseen by God are soon made actual in the adulterer's experience. We have already heard in general terms about the bondage that sin creates (Prov. 1:17-18, 31). The consequences of sin are often their own judgment (Num. 32:23; Ps. 7:15, 16; 57:6). Indeed, what we believe we do in unfettered freedom soon becomes 'the cords of ... sin'; this, again, is proof that God will not be mocked (Gal. 6:7, 8). When will we see that sin is not an expression of autonomy, but of bondage?

The nouns 'iniquities' and 'sin' are not found elsewhere in chapters 1–9, the former being found once (Prov. 16:6, in the singular) and the latter being found six additional times (10:16; 13:6; 14:34; 20:9; 21:4; 24:9) in chapters 10–31. Both terms have specifically religious connotations.[28] Far from implying that this verse is a later addition to the text, it simply proves the intensity and progression of Solomon's instruction to his sons. In a fervent attempt to press home to their hearts the vital nature of this instruction, he broadened his vocabulary.

5:23. He will die for lack of instruction, And in the greatness of his folly he will go astray.

The description of the devastating end of the adulterer continues. His final undoing will come about because he has spurned 'instruction.' We have met this word often already (Prov. 1:2, 3, 7, 8; 3:11; 4:1,

13; 5:12), and it will continue to play a prominent role in the book of Proverbs. A good alternate translation would be 'discipline,' for the word describes education through correction.[29] Rejecting the corrective instruction of parents and others in authority sets a man on a path whose end is death (Prov. 1:29-32; 2:18; 5:5; 7:21-25). In the end, he will bemoan his rejection of such counsel (Prov. 5:12).

We meet for the first time the word 'folly,' which will become a major theme in Proverbs (Prov. 12:23; 13:16; 14:1, 8, 17, 18, 24, 29; 15:2, 14, 21; 16:22; 17:12; 18:13; 19:3; 22:15; 24:9; 26:4, 5, 11; 27:22). 'Folly' is the opposite of 'knowledge' (Prov. 12:23; 13:16; 14:18; 15:2, 14), 'wisdom' (14:1, 8), 'understanding' (15:21), and 'prudence' (16:22).[30] 'Folly' is the outward manifestation that betrays one as a fool.[31]

It is this 'folly,' the acting out of inner foolishness, which leads one 'astray.' This word is the same one translated 'exhilarated' in verses 19 and 20, where it carried the idea of intoxication. When a man chooses not to be inebriated with the love of his wife (v. 19) and chooses rather to reel in lustful abandon after another woman (v. 20), it is, in fact, 'folly' which has taken control of his senses (v. 23) and is leading him, staggering, toward destruction.

End Notes

1. Goldberg, Louis, 'hākam,' *Theological Wordbook of the Old Testament* (Chicago: Moody Press, 1980), 1:282-284.

2. Fretheim, Terence E., 'בין,' *New International Dictionary of Old Testament Theology And Exegesis* (Grand Rapids, Michigan: Zondervan Publishing House, 1997), 1:652.

3. Ross, Allen P., 'Proverbs,' *The Expositor's Bible Commentary* (Grand Rapids, Michigan: Zondervan Publishing House, 1991), 5:927.

4. Wolf, Herbert, 'zāmam,' *Theological Wordbook of the Old Testament* (Chicago: Moody Press, 1980), 1:244.

5. Lewis, Jack P., 'yāda',' *Theological Wordbook of the Old Testament* (Chicago: Moody Press, 1980), 1:366-367.

6. Cohen, A., *Proverbs* (London: The Sconcino Press, 1946), 11.

7. Ross, 5:927.

8. Delitzsch, F., *Proverbs, Ecclesiastes, Song of Solomon* (three volumes in one) in C. F. Keil and F. Delitzsch, vol. 6, *Commentary on the Old Testament* (in ten volumes), (1872; rpt. Grand Rapids, Michigan: William B. Eerdmans Publishing Company, 1980), 1:119.

9. Buzzell, Sid S., 'Proverbs,' *The Bible Knowledge Commentary* (Wheaton: Victor Books, 1985), 1:914-915.

10. Hill, Andrew E., 'אַחֲרִית,' *The New International Dictionary of Old Testament Theology and Exegesis* (Grand Rapids, Michigan: Zondervan Publishing Company, 1997), 1:361-362.

11. Cooper-Shewell, W. E., 'Wormwood,' *The Zondervan Pictorial Encyclopedia of the Bible* (Grand Rapids, Michigan: Zondervan Publishing House, 1975, 1976), 5:969.

12. Buis, H., 'Sheol,' *The Zondervan Pictorial Encyclopedia of the Bible* (Grand Rapids, Michigan: Zondervan Publishing House, 1975, 1976), 5:395.

13. Whybray, 86.

14. Ibid.

15. Bowling, Andrew, 'nûaʻ,' *Theological Wordbook of the Old Testament* (Chicago: Moody Press, 1980), 2:564-565.

16. Hamilton, Victor P., 'hwd,' *Theological Wordbook of the Old Testament* (Chicago: Moody Press, 1980), 1:209.

17. Kidner, Derek, *Proverbs* (Downers Grove, Illinois: InterVarsity Press, 1964), 70.

18. Ross, 5:928.

19. Van Groningen, Gerard, 'sānēʼ,' *Theological Wordbook of the Old Testament* (Chicago: Moody Press, 1980), 2:879-880.

20. Delitzsch, 1:125.

21. Ross, 5:929.

22. Whybray, 89-90.

23. Gilchrist, Paul R., 'yʻl,' *Theological Wordbook of the Old Testament* (Chicago: Moody Press, 1980), 1:390.

24. Whybray, 91.

25. Ross, 5:930.

26. Murphy, Ronald E., *Proverbs* (Nashville: Thomas Nelson Publishers, 1998), 32-33.

27. Kidner, 71.

28. Whybray, 92.

29. Gilchrist, Paul R., 'yāsar,' *Theological Wordbook of the Old Testament* (Chicago: Moody Press, 1980), 1:386-387.

30. Pan, Chou-Wee, 'אֱוִיל,' *New International Dictionary of Old Testament Theology and Exegesis* (Grand Rapids, Michigan: Zondervan Publishing Company, 1997), 1:307-308.

31. Goldberg, Louis, ''wl,' *Theological Wordbook of the Old Testament* (Chicago: Moody Press, 1980), 1:20.

Proverbs 6

6:1. My son, if you have become surety for your neighbor, Have given a pledge for a stranger,
This sixth chapter addresses four topics, blending two new topics – both of which will be developed more fully in the coming chapters (surety, vv. 1-5 and laziness, vv. 6-11) – with a general description of the wicked (vv. 12-19) and a fourth topic already covered in some detail (adultery, vv. 20-35). The familiar call echoed so often in the first nine chapters is intoned again – 'My son' (Prov. 1:8, 10, 15; 2:1; 3:1, 11, 21; 4:10, 20; 5:1). A series of conditional clauses begins here and continues through the second verse, the resolution coming in verse 3.

The issue concerns having 'become surety.' Surety involved becoming responsible for the debt of another person, should they become unable to pay (Prov. 11:15; 17:18; 20:16; 22:26-27; 27:13). The person involved is described both as 'your neighbor' and 'a stranger.' The former is a general term that may mean something like 'anybody,' not referring necessarily to the person who lives next door.[1] The latter word refers to someone unknown to you.[2] Taken together, they seem to point to a rash financial decision made out of pity for one about whom you know very little. You do not know them, their financial standing or their ability to repay the loan they are asking you to guarantee. All the information you have is what they have told you. It is probable that, when working with such scanty information and under such time constraints, one would make a personally disastrous decision.

Does this preclude co-signing an auto loan for a young family member? Not necessarily. Yet, before entering into such an arrangement, one should always carefully study the person's character and survey their plan for repayment as well as one's own ability to take on the financial burden, if necessary. The Old Testament encouraged generosity (Deut. 15:1-15) and lending without interest. It was against the Mosaic Law to charge interest to a fellow Israelite (Exod. 22:25; Lev. 25:35-38), though it was permissible to charge reasonable interest to a non-Israelite. Even then, the charging of exorbitant interest was considered immoral (Neh. 5:7, 10; Prov. 28:8).

The phrase 'Have given a pledge' is literally 'struck your hands.' It is equivalent to our modern-day handshake to seal a transaction, though probably more binding than a handshake might be considered in our culture, where one's personal word has come to mean little. One should thus never give his word rashly, but only after careful understanding of the consequences.

6:2. If you have been snared with the words of your mouth, Have been caught with the words of your mouth,
The series of conditional clauses continue from verse 1 and await their resolution in verse 3. The conditional particle is not found in the Hebrew text, but is understood from the context of verse 1.[3]

The metaphor is that of an animal caught in a trap. The second verb ('caught') links this discussion with the previous discussion of adultery (Prov. 5:22). Both verbs prepare for the concluding verse of this section (v. 5). The metaphor is apt, given the overwhelming calamity, if suddenly faced with obligation for a debt one is not in a position to repay.

Twice the phrase 'the words of your mouth' is used. Far from being redundant, it underscores the power of a man's verbal agreement. Too often today, people reason, 'I didn't sign anything. They have no legal recourse over me. All they have is my word.' Sadly, they have forgotten that the man who wants to be near God 'swears to his own hurt, and does not change' (Ps. 15:4b). A wise person would not sign a legal document without reading the fine print. Likewise, the person of wisdom is careful not to rashly make a promise he might find difficult to keep at a later time.

6:3. Do this then, my son, and deliver yourself; Since you have come into the hand of your neighbor, Go, humble yourself, and importune your neighbor.
Now comes the resolution to the series of conditional statements made in verses 1-2. Making yourself responsible for the debt of another is of the utmost seriousness. You are trapped and need to 'deliver yourself.' You have 'come into the hand of your neighbor.' Your financial standing, security and future are no longer under your own control. You have become the slave of another and are at their mercy.

No time should be lost in seeking your freedom. The word 'then' implies that the action must be undertaken 'here and now.'[4] No personal pride should stand in the way of obtaining release from the obligation. To 'humble yourself' meant to crush, tread upon or demean yourself.[5] No social reserve should limit you in your attempt to free yourself. The word translated 'importune' ('press your plea,' NIV) is strong, and meant 'to storm at' another person[6] or to be boisterous, arrogant and even, perhaps, to bully the other until you get your way.[7] Perhaps the idea of making yourself obnoxious until they release you best represents the meaning. The call to such action points neither to acceptable social graces or God-honoring business practices, but to the serious nature of the bondage you have allowed yourself to slip into.

The 'neighbor' twice mentioned here could be either the debtor you pledged to cover or the creditor they owe the money to. Either one could ruin you, one by defaulting on the loan and the other by pressing you for payment in such a case. It is likely that the reference is to the debtor you have pledged to cover. On a purely practical level, however, a final decision about which is intended here is probably not necessary, since either one might be able to release you from the hasty obligation you entered into.

6:4. Do not give sleep to your eyes, Nor slumber to your eyelids;
No delay is acceptable. Hesitancy may spell ruin. No personal need is more urgent than the requirement to free yourself from this unwise commitment. Time will not cure this problem nor make it disappear, but can only hasten the potential destruction. Not one night should pass before you exhaust every attempt to extricate yourself from this pledge (Ps. 132:4).

6:5. Deliver yourself like a gazelle from the hunter's hand, And like a bird from the hand of the fowler.
Solomon now employs two similes ('like') to heighten the arguments made to this point. The imagery used here harkens back to the verbs of verse 2 and helps to bring closure to the matter.

Would not a gazelle caught in the hunter's hand exhaust every means to free itself? Would a bird grasped in the hand of the fowler sit quietly by as its life was weighed in the balance (Ps. 124:7)? Free yourself! Your life depends upon it!

6:6. Go to the ant, O sluggard, Observe her ways and be wise,
We are confronted with another path to destruction: laziness. Foolish business practices may ruin you (vv. 1-5), but so can sloth. The theme of the sluggard will surface again often (Prov. 6:9; 10:26; 13:4; 15:19; 19:24; 20:4; 21:25; 22:13; 24:30; 26:13-16). The word 'sluggard' describes one who is sluggish and lazy.[8] But, it is also set in contrast

to the 'upright' (Prov. 15:19) and the 'righteous' (21:25-26).[9] Solomon was probably not calling his sons sluggards, but was using the term rhetorically to speak to any, and all, of whom the description might be appropriate.

Such a one is to observe and reflect upon 'the ant.' The same imagery returns in Proverbs 30:25, when King Agur calls for a similar comparison. Such reflection will yield a new work ethic which prioritizes self-motivation, industry, diligence and planning (vv. 7-8). Embracing such a work ethic will cause one to 'be wise.' Wisdom is not some esoteric, other-worldly rhetoric. Wisdom is practical success in the real world. Hard work lies in its path.

6:7. Which, having no chief, Officer or ruler,

What is here stated as absolute fact is actually an observation derived from simple reflection. The ant appears to have no leader and no overt organization (cf. Prov. 30:27). Instinct compels them to work industriously, in order to lay up in store for lean times. They do not need an authority figure standing over them. The ant, by all appearances, is a self-starter. Even more than being a self-starter, the ant is a team player. While, to the human eye, there appears to be no leader among the ants, there is a well-ordered precision and coordination to all they do.

6:8. Prepares her food in the summer, And gathers her provision in the harvest.

Though, for all appearances, leaderless, the ant demonstrates a work ethic and team work beyond what many humans seem capable of. However, wisdom is found not simply in activity, but in the foresight of labor. The two lines of this verse are parallel, the second restating the point of the first in order to underscore its message. The timing is all-important, 'summer' and 'harvest' being terms which indicate the right time for gathering provision for more lean times. Foolishness only labors when the stomach growls. Wisdom labors because it knows the stomach will growl (Prov. 30:25).

The LXX adds a substantial section to the end of this verse: 'Or, go to the bee and learn how diligent she is and how seriously she does her work – her products kings and private persons use for health – she is desired and respected by all – though feeble in body, by honoring wisdom she obtains distinction.'[10] It would seem that this section was added by later editors to elaborate the point from more than one angle.

6:9. How long will you lie down, O sluggard? When will you arise from your sleep?
Once again, the 'sluggard' is addressed directly (v. 6). The goal of the two questions is to shame him into action and responsibility. The question 'How long ...?' reveals that his sloth has become an established pattern. All he can think of is how little he can get by with doing.

The second question asks when his appetite for sleep (vv. 6, 10) will be satisfied. Proverbs describes sleep as a blessing God gives to those who faithfully walk in wisdom (Prov. 3:24; 19:23). For the 'sluggard,' however, the blessing of God has become god. But, sleep makes a tyrannous ruler, for 'Laziness casts into a deep sleep' (Prov. 19:15). Thus, the wisdom of God is 'Do not love sleep, lest you become poor' (Prov. 20:13). A sluggard, however, has little time for such counsel – 'As the door turns on its hinges, So does the sluggard on his bed' (Prov. 26:14).

6:10. 'A little sleep, a little slumber, A little folding of the hands to rest' –
This verse appears to be a mocking quotation of the rationalization of the sluggard. The NASB and TEV set it off as such with quotation marks. The more the lazy man rests, the more rest he craves. Legitimate leisure becomes consuming laziness. His rationalization is thinly veiled as he hits the snooze button one more time. His delay and procrastination set him up for poverty and want (v. 11).

For the phrase 'folding of the hands,' see Ecclesiastes 4:4-8, where the polarized dangers of workaholism and laziness are set in contrast to responsible labor. The entirety of verses 10-11 are repeated almost verbatim in Proverbs 24:33-34, where again the sluggard's shame is set forth.

6:11. And your poverty will come in like a vagabond, And your need like an armed man.
The logical end of the reasoning espoused in verse 10 now comes into view. The demise of the sluggard is set forth under two similes set off in synonymous parallelism.

The problem is described both as 'poverty' and 'need.' The former becomes a familiar theme in Proverbs (Prov. 10:15; 13:18; 24:34; 28:19; 30:8; 31:7) and refers to being utterly destitute.[11] The latter refers simply to the lack of what is needed.[12]

The words 'vagabond' and 'armed man' personify such poverty. Both words are of uncertain derivation, but their general meaning is clear. The former ('vagabond') is variously seen as some kind of 'dangerous assailant' or bandit that waylays travelers unawares.[13] The ancient world was renowned for the bandits that would conceal themselves in the natural surroundings along a roadside and, with suddenness, attack, rob and sometimes kill unsuspecting travelers. The second term ('armed man') means literally 'a man of a shield.' It refers to a military man of the light infantry division.[14] The emphasis is on the fact that the man is well armed, but moves with swiftness and stealth.

The point of both similes is that poverty breaks suddenly upon the lazy man with overwhelming power, leaving him defenseless. Poverty does not happen overnight. The man has been lazy for some time. But, the realization of it is sudden. With arms folded, eyes closing in slumber, and mouth muttering rationalizations (v. 10), sudden economic destruction overtakes the sluggard unawares.

6:12. A worthless person, a wicked man, Is the one who walks with a false mouth,

Solomon now turns to a general description of the wicked (vv. 12-15). Every avenue of communication ('mouth,' v. 12; 'eyes,' 'feet,' 'fingers' v. 13) is employed in the service of the wicked, as they spread their guile.

Such a man is called 'worthless' and 'wicked.' Our word 'worthless' is a translation of the Hebrew word *belial*. It describes a man who is more than worthless. He is wicked. The word is of uncertain derivation, but may come from a word meaning 'a place from which none arises,' a euphemism for Sheol. The word is used twenty-seven times in the Old Testament and describes a person who has become so wicked and perverse that he is a liability to the community. Such a person tries to turn people from God (Deut. 13:14), is sexually deviant (Judg. 19:22; 20:13; 1 Sam 2:12), destructive in relationships (Deut. 15:19; 1 Sam. 30:22), rebellious toward authority (2 Sam. 20:1; 2 Chron. 13:7), and destructive with his lies (1 Kings 21:10; Prov. 19:28).[15] Eventually, 'Belial' became a name of the embodiment of all wickedness and worthlessness, Satan himself (2 Cor. 6:15).

The second descriptive word is 'wicked.' It denotes primarily one who abuses his power and position in order to harm or even kill those given over wholeheartedly to the worship of God.[16]

What power is it that the wicked and worthless use in an attempt to destroy the godly? It is the power they have to persuade others. The first avenue of communication they employ is that of their words. The precise expression for 'a false mouth' is found again only in Proverbs 4:24. The word for 'false' comes from the word meaning 'crooked' (cf. Prov. 2:15).[17] The wicked and worthless employ words that distort and twist reality through use of lies, half-truths, white-lies, deception and distortion. In this way they leverage themselves against the followers of God.

6:13. Who winks with his eyes, who signals with his feet, Who points with his fingers;

Not only is his mouth full of deceit (v. 12), but the wicked man employs all avenues of communication to shape his version of reality. He 'winks with his eyes.' Exactly the intent of such winking is not spelled out, but, from similar expressions used elsewhere, it is plain that it was a form of communication employed when devious plans were involved (Prov. 10:10; 16:30; Ps. 35:19).

Another means of communication is that the wicked man 'signals with his feet.' The word translated 'signals' is literally 'scrapes.'[18] By means of moving his feet back and forth along the floor or in the dirt, the devious one gives off prearranged signals that cue his partners in crime as to their next step.

The wicked also communicates as he 'points with his fingers.' Our word 'points' normally is translated as 'teaches,' but here likely means something like 'to point out.'[19] By means of previously agreed upon hand signals, the worthless man conducts his sinister symphony, unbeknownst to his victim.

Scripture is correct when it reminds us that 'the evil man out of the evil treasure brings forth what is evil; for his mouth speaks from that which fills his heart' (Luke 6:45). But, it is not only the lips which reveal the heart. It is the communication of all body language, sign language, and non-verbal cues as well. In this case, it is the perversity of the heart which is betrayed (v. 14). When pressed, the wicked man could testify, 'I never said that!' and feel justified in his strict accuracy. He may not have spoken the message that brought ruin, but he still communicated it clearly.

6:14. Who with perversity in his heart devises evil continually, Who spreads strife.

The man's problem is his heart. It is the repository from which all thinking and acting arise. It is the 'perversity' of his heart that creates the scheming and ill-will. The word 'perversity' describes that which has turned away from what is normal and right. It occurs nine times in Proverbs (Prov. 2:12, 14; 6:14; 8:13; 10:31, 32; 16:28, 30;

23:33), but only one other time in the Old Testament (Deut. 32:20).
Often, this turning away is expressed through the mouth (Prov. 2:12;
10:31, 32; 16:30), but only because it is already a condition of the
heart (6:14) and mind (23:33), being fed by what is taken in by the
eyes (16:30).[20]

Out of his own nature he then 'devises evil.' The word 'devises' has
been met already in Proverbs 3:29 and will be again in Proverbs 6:18
(cf. also Prov. 11:12; 12:20; 14:22; 17:28; 20:4). It means 'to plow.'[21] As a
farmer carefully plots out his field and plows accordingly, so the wicked, out of the perversity of his heart, devises a scheme of harm against
his neighbor. This has become habitual, for he does so 'continually.'

Such a heart, and such thinking, soon 'spreads strife' in the
community. The intentional spreading of dissension is a common
theme in Proverbs (Prov. 15:18; 16:28; 17:14; 18:18-19; 19:13; 21:9,
19; 22:10; 23:29; 25:24; 26:21; 27:15; 28:25; 29:22). The 'strife' being
described is of a domestic sort, which explodes with no one left to
arbitrate the dispute.[22]

Notice the progression: The heart is evil; from the evil heart spring
thoughts and plans; these plans then give rise to actions, which soon
draw others in as accomplices, and which bring destruction upon
the victim. Heart, thoughts, action – here is the pattern for human
activity. The only answer for sinful human activity is to transform
the heart, which will then lead to a new pattern of thinking, which
will produce a new kind of action. Thankfully, transformation of
heart is exactly what God promised us in the New Covenant enacted
through Jesus Christ (Ezek.11:19; 18:31; 36:26).

**6:15. Therefore his calamity will come suddenly; Instantly he will
be broken, and there will be no healing.**
The judgment of the wicked is deserved, swift, and final. The
judgment is designated as 'calamity.' The word can be variously
translated with words such as 'destruction,' 'ruin,' 'disaster,' and
'distress.' Often, it is combined with the Hebrew word for 'day,' to
describe 'the day of calamity,' an expression of divine judgment.
In such cases, it is parallel to 'doom' (Deut. 32:35), 'day of wrath,'
(Job 21:30) and 'time of their punishment' (Jer. 46:21).[23]

Such an end is deserved, as the 'Therefore' makes plain, by
logically connecting it to his unscrupulous ways described in verses
12-14. The very thing he plotted against others has now befallen him
(Prov. 1:18; 5:22; Job 4:8; Ps. 7:15-16; 9:16; 35:8; 57:6).

Such judgment will be swift. It comes 'suddenly' and 'Instantly.'
Both words come from the same root and carry the idea of both

suddenness and surprise. Of the twenty-five Old Testament uses
of the former word (cf. Prov. 3:25; 7:22; 24:22), all but one are used
in a context of disaster or judgment.[24] The latter appears again in
Proverbs 29:1. The two related words both also carry the sense of
splitting, opening, breaking out and breaking forth.[25] Suddenly, out
of nowhere, the judgment befalls them.

The calamity of the wicked is also final, for 'there will be no
healing.' Again, his calamity is further described as being 'broken.'
Like a shattered earthenware jar (Ps. 9:2; Isa. 30:14), whose pieces
cannot be restored, the wicked one will be swiftly broken in the midst
of his plot.[26] No explanation can restore him or clear his name.

6:16. There are six things which the LORD hates, Yes, seven which are an abomination to Him:

We have here (vv. 16-19) an example of a numerical proverb. While
specific sins are enumerated, the list is not intended as exhaustive.
The lists often build to the final item in the list. Such numerical
constructions are common (e.g. Prov. 30:15, 18, 21, 29; Job 5:19;
Eccles. 11:2; Amos 1:3, 6, 9, 13; 2:1, 4, 6; Mic. 5:5).

Here, the extended proverb builds upon the previous description
of the wicked man (vv. 12-15) and reinforces the Lord's attitude
toward such people. That this is an expansion on the previous section
is obvious from two lines of evidence. The first is the repetition of
similar themes: 'haughty eyes,' verse 17 (v. 13, 'winks with his eyes');
'a lying tongue,' verse 17 (v. 12, 'a false mouth'); 'hands,' verse 17
(v. 13, 'fingers'); 'heart,' verse 18 (v. 14, 'perversity of heart'); 'feet,'
verse 18 (v. 13, 'signals with his feet'); 'A false witness,' verse 19
(v. 12, 'a false mouth'). The second is the intentional repetition of the
Hebrew word for 'spreads strife' (vv. 14, 19).

The point made here is the Lord's attitude toward the ways of
the wicked: He 'hates' their conduct. The word describes the entire
spectrum of negative emotions humans are capable of. It may
include the most intense hatred as well as a more mild irritation.[27]
That Solomon had in mind the more intense end of this range is
clear from the description of these ways as 'an abomination' to
the Lord. This Hebrew word describes the most intense outrage
possible – hatred not toward evil in general, but toward a specific
expression of it.[28] The word describes God's hatred of pagan
practices (Deut. 18:9, 12), but also of unethical conduct (Prov. 3:32;
8:7; 11:1, 20; 12:22; 13:19; 15:8, 9, 26; 16:5, 12; 17:15; 20:10, 23; 21:27;
24:9; 26:25; 28:9; 29:27).

6:17. Haughty eyes, a lying tongue, And hands that shed innocent blood,

The list of hated sins now commences, the first three being given here. 'Haughty eyes' begins the list and is, literally, 'high eyes' (Prov. 8:13; 21:4; 30:13; Ps. 18:27; 101:5). The idea is that of a proud look which betrays an arrogant heart. The proud invader of Isaiah 10:12-14 is an illustration of 'haughty eyes.' The term translated as 'haughty' is used in Numbers 15:30 to describe willful, defiant sin. Such sin is done 'defiantly' or, literally, 'with a high hand.'[29]

Next is 'a lying tongue.' The phrase is found in Psalm 109:2, where David describes some nameless deceiver who has slandered him. The larger context of the psalm, however, is understood as Messianic, for verse 8 is quoted in Acts 1:20 as applying to Judas.[30] While deceit may win the day (Prov. 26:28), only a truthful tongue will endure (Prov. 12:19). Any advantages gained through deception will soon disappear (Prov. 21:6).

The third detestable thing is 'hands that shed innocent blood' (Prov. 1:11, 16; 28:17). King Manasseh was guilty of this sin (2 Kings 1:16) and left a legacy of judgment that the nation would bear even after he was off the scene (2 Kings 24:3-4). The Israelites were guilty of this as a whole people as well: 'They even sacrificed their sons and their daughters to the demons, And shed innocent blood, The blood of their sons and their daughters, Whom they sacrificed to the idols of Canaan; And the land was polluted with the blood' (Ps. 106:36-37). How descriptive of modern life, where thousands upon thousands of children are killed while yet in their mother's womb, and all because of some perceived right to make a 'choice!' God announces us an abomination and declares His hatred of our ways.

6:18. A heart that devises wicked plans, Feet that run rapidly to evil,

Items four and five of the list of seven hated sins are now before us. The Lord hates the 'heart that devises wicked plans.' For the word 'devises,' see on verse 14. For the word 'wicked,' see on verse 12. God was early on repulsed by this tendency in us: 'Then the Lord saw that the wickedness of man was great on the earth, and that every intent of the thoughts of his heart was only evil continually' (Gen. 6:5). Proverbs speaks in stern tones about such ones (Prov. 12:20; 14:22; 24:2), as do the rest of the Scriptures (Ps. 36:4; Mic. 2:1).

'Feet that run rapidly to evil' are also an abomination to the Lord. The 'feet' are a repeated emphasis from verse 12. All this repetition makes it clear that this section (vv. 16-19) is an expansion upon that which was introduced in the previous section (vv. 12-15).

The 'heart' describes the totality of the inner man, including his rational powers, emotions and volition. The 'feet' are what engage a man in what his heart has devised (Prov. 1:16; Isa. 59:7; Rom. 3:15). Together, they describe the inner man and his outward activities. The Lord hates the one whose nature is bent toward, and quick to pursue, that which is contrary to His nature.

6:19. A false witness who utters lies, And one who spreads strife among brothers.

The sixth abomination is that of a 'false witness who utters lies.' The word for 'false' is different than the one translated here by 'lies.' The former describes a distortion of the facts of a matter for personal advantage. The latter describes the manufacture of complete fiction.[31] When it says that such a person 'utters' lies, the literal meaning is 'breathes out.' Seven of this word's ten appearances in the Old Testament are found in Proverbs (12:17; 14:5, 25; 19:5, 9; 29:8). Most often, the word is associated with breathing out lies, as it is here (Prov. 14:5, 25; 19:5, 9). Only in Proverbs 12:17 is one said to breathe forth truth.[32] The one of wicked heart utters lies as naturally as he engages in the involuntary process of respiration.[33] Lies are the exhaust he puts off, having used people and circumstances to his ends. The first clause of this verse is identical with the last of Proverbs 14:5.

The seventh item brings the list to a crescendo and returns us to the theme of verse 14b. The Lord hates the one who 'spreads strife.' Note that it is not simply the strife that is an abhorrence to God, but the one who creates it and spreads it. The word strife has already been introduced in verse 14. God cherishes unity more than we know: 'Behold, how good and how pleasant it is For brothers to dwell together in unity!' (Ps. 133:1). David continues in that psalm to say that such unity is like the dew of heaven that descends upon the mountains of Zion. If such unity is a gentle, nourishing, refreshing, life-giving dew, then strife is a harsh, life-taking, discouraging blast of sulfurous breath from below. God despises the one who creates such division among brothers!

6:20. My son, observe the commandment of your father, And do not forsake the teaching of your mother;

The familiar call 'My son' is once again raised to arrest his attention and gain his ear. The section that begins here runs all the way through verse 35. The theme is avoidance of the adulteress, though the introduction is extended (vv. 20-23) and that theme does not come into evidence until verse 24. The warnings about the seductress will be expanded upon from previous instruction (Prov. 2:16-19; 5:1-23).

The opening call of verses 20-21 sounds very much like those issued previously by Solomon (Prov. 1:8-9; 3:1-3) and like what he will yet say in Proverbs 7:1-3. As in Proverbs 1:8, the mother's instruction is added to that of the father. This implies that a solid home life, with both father and mother contributing harmoniously to the training of the children, is a powerful deterrent to an immoral lifestyle.[34]

The father and mother are authorized by God to issue 'the commandment' and 'teaching' to their children. The parents have been vested with divine authority in the home to set the boundaries of behavior, thinking, and attitude for their children. The word 'commandment' describes the binding conditions of a contract (Jer. 32:11) and is used to describe the Ten Commandments (Exod. 24:12).[35] The word 'teaching' is the common word *torah*, which is often used for the Mosaic Law handed down by God. In a day of diminishing parental rights, where the state, the grandparents – even the child himself – are given ever expanding rights, this foundational and fundamental endowment from God to parents must be heard again. Parents, lead your homes!

6:21. Bind them continually on your heart; Tie them around your neck.

Proverbs often employs this imagery of binding and tying the instruction upon one's self (Prov. 3:3; 7:3a). In each instance, we find echoes of Moses' instruction in Deuteronomy 6:6-8 and 11:18-19. Kidner says that such expressions call us to glory in, meditate, and then act upon the instruction given.[36] It is impossible to miss the similarity between the expected response to the Mosaic Law (Deut. 6:6-8; 11:18-19) and the instruction of parents described here. Within the home, the instruction of parents ought to be 'law.' This is certainly not in the sense of God-breathed revelation, as in the Mosaic Law given us in Scripture, but in a respect and amenability of the children to the parents.

6:22. When you walk about, they will guide you; When you sleep, they will watch over you; And when you awake, they will talk to you.

Once again, we find traces of Deuteronomy 6:7 and 11:19 here. There the pattern is 'sit,' 'walk,' 'lie,' 'rise up.' Here we have 'walk,' 'sleep,' and 'awake.' There is never a place, nor a time, in your life in which the word of God taught by godly parents will not provide you the answers to guide you safely into His will. Untold sorrow can be avoided if parents will but teach their children the Scriptures and if children will but obey what they are taught.

The parents' instruction will 'guide,' 'watch over,' and 'talk' to the child. All these verbs are feminine and singular in form. There is no clear antecedent, though it seems best to connect them back to the 'them' of verse 21, which, in turn, looks back to 'commandment' of verse 20.

The words of parents, when thoroughly permeated with the word of God, move the feet and will of a child into the will of God. They become a personal guide through life. They also, then, are set as a sentry, keeping guard over the one who is thus guided.

When you rest yourself ('sleep') in the counsel of a godly parent, that counsel will protect you. Such instruction not only shows you the will of God, but protects you in it. And, while he is in the midst of walking in the will of God, the teachings of a wise parent will 'talk' to the child there. The word has the idea of inward, mental conversation. Perhaps the inward conversation of meditation is the best understanding.[37] As the child starts each new day, the instruction of his parents' will inwardly speak to him and whisper what direction his day should take.

Though it will not become evident until verse 24, the context in which these promises are made is in reference to the immoral woman. When lust screams your name, your parents' instruction will protect you from the wake of destruction that follows the fleeting pleasure of sin (cf. Prov. 3:23-24).

6:23. For the commandment is a lamp, and the teaching is light; And reproofs for discipline are the way of life,

The instruction of godly parents is further likened to the word of God. In an echo of the praise God's word receives in Psalm 119:105 (cf. also Ps. 19:8), the same words ('lamp' and 'light') are used here of the parents' teachings. More specifically, these teachings are called 'the commandment,' 'the teaching,' and 'discipline.' The word 'commandment' is used elsewhere in the Old Testament to describe the Law handed down from God through Moses. Most often in Proverbs, however, it describes the authoritative instruction of parent to child (Prov. 2:1; 3:1; 4:4; 6:20; 7:1, 2; cf. the more general usage in 10:8; 13:13; 19:16). The 'teaching' is the common Hebrew word *torah*, also often used for the Mosaic Law, but also of more general instruction, as here. The word 'discipline' has already defined one purpose of the Book of Proverbs (Prov. 1:2, 7). It describes instruction that comes through being corrected. A loving parent's counsel and command will sometimes step on your toes. But, there is much good to be learned and much sorrow to be avoided, if you will but embrace it.

A clear note is sounded for the authority of the parents to counsel, instruct, teach, guide, and set boundaries for their children. The benefit of wise parental discipline is both understanding and direction. It lights the path of life, so you see what God sees, and it steers the feet, so you experience what God desires for you.

This discipline is 'the way of life' (cf. 'the path[s] of life, Prov. 2:19; 5:6; 10:17; 15:24). The discipline consists of 'reproofs.' The word describes the correction, rebuke or chastisement that God gives to those whose steps leave the paths of His protection and will. The parent is often the audible voice and the tangible expression of such a divine rebuke. The fool finds such a reproof to be inhibiting and repulsive, while the wise man finds in its discomfort the opening of a trail to the joys of life, as God intended (Prov. 3:22; 4:22).

6:24. To keep you from the evil woman, From the smooth tongue of the adulteress.

The commandments, teaching and discipline of parents (vv. 20-23) all contribute to a balanced life that keeps one secure from the seductions of sensuality. Here the offending female is simply called 'the evil woman' and an 'adulteress.' Elsewhere, she is called 'the strange woman' (Prov. 2:16), 'the foreigner' (5:3), and a 'harlot' (6:26; 23:27). The exact description of her as 'the evil woman' is found nowhere else in the Old Testament. Some commentators suggest repointing the vowels so that it would read 'another man's wife.' Though this would provide better parallelism with the second line of the proverb, it seems an unnecessary violation of the text. It may be that she is the prostitute pointed to in verse 26 and that she is, indeed, not married at all. The second descriptive title is 'adulteress,' which simply means 'foreigner' or 'alien' (Prov. 2:16; 5:20; 7:5; 23:27). It is not her nationality that makes her 'foreign,' but the fact that she resides outside your covenant of marriage.

While, no doubt, her appearance is appealing, it is her words that hook the naïve young man. She possesses 'the smooth tongue.' That is to say, she 'flatters with her words' (Prov. 2:16; 7:5). The 'lips of an adulteress drip honey, And smoother than oil is her speech' (Prov. 5:3). See Proverbs 7:14-20 for an example of her alluring speech. 'With her many persuasions she entices him; With her flattering lips she seduces him' (Prov. 7:21). The frequency with which the Proverbs address the power of sexual talk should highlight its captivating power. Witness the explosion of phone businesses given exclusively to sexual talk. 'Flee from youthful lusts' (2 Tim. 2:22)!

6:25. Do not desire her beauty in your heart, Nor let her catch you with her eyelids.
In her arsenal of seductions are not only her words (v. 24), but also her physical appearance and her eye contact. One communicates in many ways. We are responsible before God for all of them.

While the seventh commandment forbade the physical act of adultery and, by implication, the thought of doing so as well, the tenth commandment plainly prohibited the desire (Exod. 20:14, 17). Jesus made plain that this was the intended meaning: 'You have heard that it was said, "You shall not commit adultery"; but I say to you that everyone who looks at a woman with lust for her has already committed adultery with her in his heart' (Matt. 5:27-28). The first line of our proverb is the Old Testament equivalent to these words of Jesus.

Notice that the danger lies in the heart. The heart describes the individual's powers of intellect, emotion and will. The heart is the core and substance of one's being. The heart represents who you are. The rest of the body, then, serves the heart and expresses its true nature. Little wonder Solomon has exhorted us to guard it above all else, 'For from it flow the springs of life' (Prov. 4:23). It is here that sin begins. Nip it in the bud (James 1:14-16)!

The second line of the proverb warns against letting the adulteress 'catch you with her eyelids.' The seductive glances and knowing looks cast intentionally by such a woman can have a powerful effect. 'You have made my heart beat faster with a single glance of your eyes' (Song of Sol. 4:9). The effect is said to be that she would 'catch you.' The verb has a broad range of possible translations, but the basic meaning is that of taking, seizing or laying hold of something. Though normally weaker in physical strength, the woman is often able to control a man in others ways (Prov. 5:20). It is the man's responsibility not to let such eye contact ever be made or to linger, if it does.

6:26. For on account of a harlot one is reduced to a loaf of bread, And an adulteress hunts for the precious life.
The translation of this verse is notoriously difficult. Part of the problem is the lack of a verb in the first line. The RSV has added a

verb and rendered it 'for a harlot may be hired for a loaf of bread, but an adulteress stalks a man's very life.' The issue of the first line seems to swing on the translation of the Hebrew word for 'on account of.' The RSV has chosen to take it to mean 'for the price of.'[38] The problem that creates is that this makes the proverb demand that, while adultery has very high cost (line 2), the services of a prostitute are much safer and less costly. This seems hardly to agree with the greater context and the teaching of the book of Proverbs or the Scriptures as a whole.

The gist of the proverb would seem rather to point to the high cost of immorality, whether that is with another man's wife or with a prostitute. Indeed, Proverbs teaches us that involvement with either a prostitute (Prov. 29:3) or an adulteress (5:10) will beggar a man. Involvement with a harlot will reduce a man's life to little more than a loaf of bread.

Likewise, an adulteress, for all of her self-justifying seductiveness, 'hunts' down the very life of the man. The word 'hunts' has the idea of stalking something and is often used of hunting or in contexts of persecution.[39] It implies intention and malice in the pursuit.

What she hunts is 'the precious life.' It is hard to get at what exactly is intended by the phrase. The Hebrew word translated 'life' is often translated 'soul,' 'life,' or even as 'person.'[40] The root of the word for 'precious' speaks of that which is heavy with honor or dignity. Thus, it describes that which is valuable, either because of its uniqueness or because of its inherent worth.[41]

The message of this proverb is simply: Immorality is costly! It may cost you all you have materially, and it may cost you everything your life is and has become. It can steal not only your material wealth, but also your integrity, fellowship with God, reputation, family, relationships, friends, and respect.

6:27. Can a man take fire in his bosom, And his clothes not be burned?

This verse must be taken with the following two, in order for its full intent to be seen and its full impact to be felt. Two absurd questions are asked (vv. 27-28), which both expect a resounding 'No!' for an answer. Then, in verse 29, the metaphors are linked with that to which they are to apply.

Sexual immorality is like playing with fire! There is a word play here between 'man' and 'fire,' the two sounding nearly identical in Hebrew. The verb translated 'take ... from' describes taking a burning coal from the fire by use of a tongs or shovel.[42] No man can nonchalantly place a glowing ember straight from the fire in his lap and not be burned! The negative consequences of adultery are unavoidable and certain.

6:28. Or can a man walk on hot coals, And his feet not be scorched?
This question builds upon the previous one (v. 27) and makes way for the searing application of verse 29. The verb translated as 'scorched' comes from a root word that describes a burn which leaves a scar.[43] The heat of immoral passion is never self-contained, but always rages out of control and burns those who dare to play with its fire. It will leave lasting scars upon the lives of all involved. No one who disobeys this warning will be spared.

Job also testifies to this fact. 'If my heart has been enticed by a woman, Or I have lurked at my neighbor's doorway, May my wife grind for another, And let others kneel down over her.... *For it would be fire that consumes* to Abaddon, And would uproot all my increase' (Job 31:9-10, 12, emphasis added).

6:29. So is the one who goes in to his neighbor's wife; Whoever touches her will not go unpunished.
The two rhetorical questions posed in verses 27-28 now find their answer here. The man who 'goes in to' his neighbor's wife will be burned! The phrase 'goes in to' is a euphemism for sexual intercourse.[44] Similarly, the word 'touches' is often used idiomatically for sensual touch designed to arouse sexual passion (Gen. 20:6; Ruth 2:9; 1 Cor. 7:1).[45]

Such immorality 'will not go unpunished.' The phrase is more literally 'will not be held innocent.' It is used often in Proverbs in connection with some kind of sinful action (Prov. 11:21; 16:5; 17:5; 19:5, 9; 28:20).[46] The punishment meted out is not specified, but it may include financial ruin, public disgrace, sexually transmitted disease, and physical harm from a jealous husband (Prov. 5:10-11, 14; 6:33-34).

6:30. Men do not despise a thief if he steals To satisfy himself when he is hungry;
A single lesson is woven into the fabric of vv. 30-35 as the chapter closes. Solomon compares the thief (vv. 30-31) and the adulterer (vv. 32-35). If a man steals because he is destitute and starving, many will privately understand, though socially they will be forced to condemn such action as wrong. Such a one will pay dearly with

all he has (vv. 31), but he will recover. Restitution is possible for the thief, as is restoration to the community. The adulterer, however, will be ruined socially (v. 33) and, perhaps, be in danger physically (vv. 34-35). Such a one 'destroys himself' (v. 32b). The adulterer has stolen something he can never restore. His shame will follow him for the rest of his life (v. 33).

It is significant to note that we have here two appetites held in contrast. One's appetite for food (vv. 30-31) is viewed as fundamental and necessary. One's sexual appetite (vv. 32-35) is seen as a powerful urge, but not as something all-controlling and necessary. We will die if we do not satisfy the one; not so the other. On the one hand, we must have food to live, but, on the other, sometimes indulging our sexual appetite will rob us of our life!

6:31. But when he is found, he must repay sevenfold; He must give all the substance of his house.
One who steals will pay a high price, but restitution is possible. In contrast, the one who commits adultery steals what cannot be returned or repaid.

Restitution is a Biblical teaching, though the highest mandatory compensation was five-fold (Exod. 22:1-9; Lev. 6:1-5; Num. 5:5-8). David's moral outrage over Nathan's illustration demanded only four-fold restitution (2 Sam. 12:6) and Zacchaeus's thorough repentance only evidenced the same degree of restitution (Luke 19:8). The number seven here appears to be symbolic, representing the fullness of the man's loss. This understanding parallels with 'all the substance of his house.'

6:32. The one who commits adultery with a woman is lacking sense; He who would destroy himself does it.
The personal leniency given to a thief will never be granted the adulterer. The one who commits adultery 'is lacking sense.' The phrase is, literally, 'lacks heart' and is equivalent to saying such a one is a fool (Prov. 7:7).

The foolishness of adultery is seen in that the one who so indulges 'destroys himself' (Prov. 2:18-19; 5:14; 7:22-23; 9:16-18). There is a sense of willful destruction through perversity. Surely the one does not intend to destroy himself, but personal, social, and spiritual suicide is the inevitable result. Solomon may be thinking of the capital punishment demanded by the jealous husband (Deut. 22:22) or, more likely, simply the spiritual death such sin incurs (1 Tim. 5:6). This is something Solomon would know well from personal experience (Eccles. 7:25-26).

6:33. Wounds and disgrace he will find, And his reproach will not be blotted out.

A jealous husband's rage may know no bounds. Physically, he will bring 'wounds' upon the man. The verbal form of the word describes the striking of someone with intent to injure or kill them.[47] The husband, in his pain, simply wants to bring pain upon the one who created his own. Rational thoughts do not measure his response, only revenge.

Socially, he will do everything within his power to bring 'disgrace' and 'reproach' upon the man. 'Disgrace' describes the opposite of pride and honor. Often, the disgrace arises from the unveiling of behavior that is a moral outrage to the community at large.[48] From this 'disgrace' grows 'reproach.' This word describes the taunting scorn of a community that has joined the offended husband in his outrage.[49]

The condemning jeers will never leave the adulterer's ears. They will never be 'blotted out.' The word is used to describe the ancient equivalent of erasures. A scroll of writing was 'erased' when water was used to wash or wipe away the ink already penned down. Thus, the word becomes a picture both of God's judgment and God's forgiveness.[50]

Significantly, the word is used in Numbers 5:23. There, the Law prescribed a test to determine whether a woman had been unfaithful to her husband. A priest was to take water mixed with dust from the floor of the Tabernacle and, having written the divine curses against an adulteress upon a scroll, he then washed the ink of these curses off into the water and dust mixture. The woman was then made to drink the water. If the 'water of bitterness' had no effect upon her, she was determined to be innocent. If, however, her stomach swelled and she became sick, she was determined to be guilty of the charge of adultery.

The guarantee here is that the curses of adultery will never be washed away, or without effect upon the one found guilty.

6:34. For jealousy enrages a man, And he will not spare in the day of vengeance.

An offended husband's jealousy smolders and bursts forth in a destructive, and uncontrollable, flame. The word 'enrages' refers to heat and wrath. It is also used to describe poison or venom.[51] Jealousy is a consuming conflagration. Jealousy is a bitter poison that consumes one's body and takes control of its every function. Such jealousy will not be extinguished by any attempt to appease or restore.

A man so enraged 'will not spare' the adulterer when his sin is uncovered. The verb points to holding back expected action or, even further, to the idea of pity or compassion.[52] A jealous husband will possess no emotional leniency for the one who has defiled his wife and marriage, nor will he, from some dispassionate perspective, withhold the full wrath of his anger. 'Wrath is fierce and anger is a flood, But who can stand before jealousy?' (Prov. 27:4). 'Jealousy is as severe as Sheol; Its flashes are flashes of fire, The very flame of the LORD.' (Song of Sol. 8:6).

6:35. He will not accept any ransom, Nor will he be content though you give many gifts.
There is no price to be paid for what has been taken. No monetary unit exists that can restore what the adulterer has stolen. No bribe can appease. No gift can turn back such anger.

The Mosaic Law called for capital punishment for the adulterer. Here such a penalty is not directly in view, though the husband's anger may be considered as that which would be prior to, and lead to, a civil trial and the exacting of punishment by the community. Bribes, while consistently condemned by the Scriptures (Exod. 23:8; Deut. 16:19; Ps. 15:5; Prov. 15:27; Eccles. 7:7), may represent a pathetic last-ditch attempt by the guilty man to keep the husband from making the matter known publicly.

End Notes

1. Kidner, Derek, *Proverbs* (Downers Grove, Illinois: InterVarsity Press, 1964), 72.

2. Murphy, Roland E., *Proverbs* (Nashville: Thomas Nelson Publishers, 1998), 36.

3. Whybray, R. N., *Proverbs* (Grand Rapids, Michigan: William B. Eerdmans Publishing Company, 1994), 95.

4. Ross, Allen P., 'Proverbs,' *The Expositor's Bible Commentary* (Grand Rapids, Michigan: Zondervan Publishing House, 1991), 5:932.

5. Buzzell, Sid S., 'Proverbs,' *The Bible Knowledge Commentary* (Wheaton: Victor Books, 1988), 1:916.

6. Whybray, 96.

7. Kidner, 72.

8. Ross, 5:932.

9. Buzzell, 1:916.

10. Ross, 5:932-933.

11. White, William, 'rûsh,' *Theological Wordbook of the Old Testament* (Chicago: Moody Press, 1980), 2:840.

12. Scott, Jack B., 'hāsēr,' *Theological Wordbook of the Old Testament* (Chicago: Moody Press, 1980), 1:309.

13. Ross, 5:933.

14. Smith, James E., 'gānan,' *Theological Wordbook of the Old Testament* (Chicago: Moody Press, 1980), 1:168-169.

15. Wegner, Paul D., 'בלה,' *New International Dictionary of Old Testament Theology and Exegesis* (Grand Rapids, Michigan: Zondervan Publishing House, 1997), 1:662.

16. Carpenter, Eugene and Michael A. Grisanti, 'אָוֶן,' *New International Dictionary of Old Testament Theology and Exegesis* (Grand Rapids, Michigan: Zondervan Publishing House, 1997), 1:310.

17. Allen, Ronald B., *"āqash,'* *Theological Wordbook of the Old Testament* (Chicago: Moody Press, 1980), 2:693.

18. Youngblood, Ronald, 'מלל,' *New International Dictionary of Old Testament Theology And Exegesis* (Grand Rapids, Michigan: Zondervan Publishing House, 1997), 2:968.

19. Whybray, 99.

20. Hamilton, Victor P., *'hāpak,'* *Theological Wordbook of the Old Testament* (Chicago: Moody Press, 1980), 1:221-222.

21. Buzzell, 1:913.

22. Schultz, Richard, 'רין,' *New International Dictionary of Old Testament Theology and Exegesis* (Grand Rapids, Michigan: Zondervan Publishing House, 1997), 1:938-942.

23. Alden, Robert L, *"wd,'* *Theological Wordbook of the Old Testament* (Chicago: Moody Press, 1980), 1:17.

24. Hamilton, Victor P., *'petaʿ,'* *Theological Wordbook of the Old Testament* (Chicago: Moody Press, 1980), 2:744.

25. Delitzsch, F., *Proverbs, Ecclesiastes, Song of Solomon* (three volumes in one) in C. F. Keil and F. Delitzsch, vol. 6, *Commentary on the Old Testament* (in ten volumes), (1872; rpt. Grand Rapids, Michigan: William B. Eerdmans Publishing Company, 1980), 1:145.

26. Ibid., 146.

27. Konkel, A. H., 'שׂנא,' *New International Dictionary of Old Testament Theology and Exegesis* (Grand Rapids, Michigan: Zondervan Publishing House, 1997), 3:1257.

28. Whybray, 100.

29. Ross, 5:935.

30. Ibid.

31. Delitzsch, 1:147.

32. Hamilton, Victor P., *'pûah,'* *Theological Wordbook of the Old Testament* (Chicago: Moody Press, 1980), 2:718-719.

33. Adams, Jay E., *The Christian Counselor's Commentary: Proverbs* (Woodruff, South Carolina: Timeless Texts, 1997), 52.

34. Ross, 5:936.

35. Hartley, John E., *'sāwâ,'* *Theological Wordbook of the Old Testament* (Chicago: Moody Press, 1980), 2:757.

36. Kidner, 63.

37. Ibid, 73.

38. Ross, 5:938.

39. Whybray, 106.

40. Waltke, Bruce K., *'nāpash,'* *Theological Wordbook of the Old Testament* (Chicago: Moody Press, 1980), 2:587-591

41. Hartley, John E., *'yāqar,'* *Theological Wordbook of the Old Testament* (Chicago: Moody Press, 1980), 1:398-399.

42. Delitzsch, 1:152.

43. Ibid., 153.

44. Martens, Elmer M., *'bô','* *Theological Wordbook of the Old Testament* (Chicago: Moody Press, 1980), 1:93-95.

45. Coppes, Leonard J., *'nāgaʿ,'* *Theological Wordbook of the Old Testament* (Chicago: Moody Press, 1980), 2:551-553.

46. Whybray, 106-107.

47. Harrison, R. K. and I. Swart, 'נגע,' *New International Dictionary of Old Testament*

Theology and Exegesis (Grand Rapids, Michigan: Zondervan Publishing House, 1997), 3:24.

48. Nel, Philip J., 'קלה,' *New International Dictionary of Old Testament Theology and Exegesis* (Grand Rapids, Michigan: Zondervan Publishing House, 1997), 3:924-925.

49. McComiskey, Thomas E., '*hārap*,' *Theological Wordbook of the Old Testament* (Chicago: Moody Press, 1980), 1:325-326.

50. Van Dam, Cornelius, 'מתה,' *New International Dictionary of Old Testament Theology And Exegesis* (Grand Rapids, Michigan: Zondervan Publishing House, 1997), 2:913-914.

51. Struthers, Gale B., 'חֵמָה' *New International Dictionary of Old Testament Theology and Exegesis* (Grand Rapids, Michigan: Zondervan Publishing House, 1997), 2:170-171.

52. Butterworth, Mike, 'תמל,' *New International Dictionary of Old Testament Theology and Exegesis* (Grand Rapids, Michigan: Zondervan Publishing House, 1997), 2:174.

Proverbs 7

7:1. My son, keep my words, And treasure my commandments within you.

Once again, warnings against the adulteress and prostitute are the subject of this chapter. As Proverbs 6:20-23 formed a general introduction that led to the specific instructions concerning sexual immorality in 6:24-35, so, here, 7:1-5 call in a general way for Solomon's son to heed these instructions and, then, in 7:6-27, he proceeds to the specific instructions. A similar strategy is employed in Proverbs 2:1-4 and 3:1-3. Warning against the adulteress and prostitute has been a recurrent theme thus far in the book (Prov. 2:16-19; 5:1-23; 6:20-35).

The chapter, then, is composed of a general call to heed a father's wise teaching (vv. 1-5), a dramatic narrative of one young man's seduction (vv. 6-23), and a closing plea to heed the warning sounded here (vv. 24-27).

The now familiar call 'My son' (Prov. 1:8, 10, 15; 2:1; 3:1, 11, 21; 4:10, 20; 5:1, 7, 20; 6:1, 3, 20; 7:24) is sounded again. This familiar plea will begin to fade, without completely passing away (Prov. 19:27; 23:15, 19, 26; 24:13, 21; 27:11; 31:2), throughout the rest of the book as a more general audience begins to be addressed.

As noted above, we encounter here much that is familiar. All the major terms in this opening verse have been met already: 'words' (e.g. Prov. 1:2, 21; 2:1, 16; 4:4, 5, 10, 20; 5:7; 6:2), 'commandments' (2:1; 3:1; 4:4; 6:20, 23), 'keep' (e.g. 2:8, 11, 20; 3:26; 4:4, 21), 'treasure' (1:11, 18; 2:1, 7). This sounds very much like the psalmist: 'Thy word I have treasured in my heart, That I might not sin against Thee' (Ps. 119:11).

7:2. Keep my commandments and live, And my teaching as the apple of your eye.

The general introduction continues to wind its way to the purpose toward which it points in verse 5. Once again, we meet words that we have met frequently already. The first line of the verse is identical to the end of Proverbs 4:4. The word 'commandments' is the same as in verse 1. The term 'teaching' has also been encountered often already (Prov. 1:8; 3:1; 4:2; 6:20, 23). The command to 'keep' such instruction echoes through the chapters of Proverbs (see on v. 1).

The term 'the apple of your eye' is, literally, 'the little man' in the eye, referring to the way the person gazed upon is reflected in the pupil of the eye.[1] The phrase comes to represent that which must be protected as precious above all else. God considers His own as being just this priceless and protects them as such (Deut. 32:10; Ps. 17:8; Zech. 2:8). Likewise, the son is so to value the teachings of his father. God's divine instruction should have no rival in our lives and be surrendered to no seduction.

7:3. Bind them on your fingers; Write them on the tablet of your heart.
Every good Jew would have recognized here a reflection of the command of Moses regarding the law of God: 'You shall bind them as a sign on your hand and they shall be as frontals on your forehead' (Deut. 6:8; cf. 11:18). The son is to treat his father's instruction in the same way, presumably because it is reflective of, and an application of, God's wisdom.

The imagery of binding the commands on the finger suggests placing them somewhere you will often be reminded of them. Today, we think of a person worried about forgetting some important task tying a string around their finger to remind them to take care of it. The picture of writing these instructions 'on the tablet of your heart' suggests the deep internalizing of the truths the father presses upon the son. Indeed, God promised that in the New Covenant: 'I will put My law within them, and on their heart I will write it' (Jer. 31:33). For both images, see Proverbs 3:3 and 6:21.

7:4. Say to wisdom, 'You are my sister,' And call understanding your intimate friend;
This verse stands in contrast with the entire rest of the chapter. Here wisdom is, once again, personified as a woman. The young man is urged to call her 'my sister.' It is true the term may simply refer to a female sibling, and, thus, the close tie of a blood relative. It is likely, however, that here it is used in the sense of 'bride.'

Such a usage is a legitimate understanding of the word, as the Song of Solomon reveals: 'You have made my heart beat faster, my sister, my bride ... How beautiful is your love, my sister, my bride! (4:9-10; see also 4:12; 5:1-2). In this sense the commitment is deeper yet, and the tie more intimate. Such a commitment to the Lady Wisdom stands over against the 'adulteress' of verse 5 and the rest of the chapter. A firm covenant relationship with wisdom will protect against the wiles of the loose woman.

Similarly, the young man is to call understanding his 'intimate friend.' The only other occurrence of the word is found in Ruth 2:1, where it refers to Boaz, who was the kinsman- redeemer of Ruth (see also Ruth 2:20; 3:2, 12; 4:3). As such, it refers to a blood relative of the closest order. It is a derivative of the Hebrew word 'to know,' which has overtones of deep intimacy.[2] It may be used in parallel with 'sister' to say that our relationship to the woman Wisdom should be intimate and closer than any other we have.

Here, as elsewhere, 'wisdom' and 'understanding' are held in parallel and seen as roughly synonymous (Prov. 1:2, etc.). They are not mentioned again in the chapter, nor is there found any reference to God. They are simply introduced here at the beginning and both, together, stand in contrast to the boisterous and lewd woman that dominates the remainder of the chapter. The implication is clear: a choice must be made between these two women (cf. Prov. 9:1-6, 13-18).

7:5. That they may keep you from an adulteress, From the foreigner who flatters with her words.

The end toward which the introductory call to wisdom has been directed is now revealed. I must protect wisdom's place in my life as my most valuable possession (v. 1b), my most sensitive organ (v. 2b), my most obvious adornment (v. 3), and my most intimate relationship (v. 4). If I adopt this stance toward wisdom, she will guard me against sexual immorality.

This verse is identical to Proverbs 2:16, except for the first word. There, the promise is to 'deliver' from the adulteress, here it is to 'keep' you from her.

The offending woman is called both an 'adulteress' and a 'foreigner.' The first word is actually two words in Hebrew: 'strange woman.' By 'strange' can be meant both a non-Israelite (Ruth 2:10) and also a person who is outside the bonds of your marriage covenant (Prov. 2:16; 5:3, 20; 22:14).[3] Similarly, 'foreigner' describes one who is an alien, in this case an alien to the exclusivity of the marriage covenant and is, thus, foreign to you.[4]

One of the seductions she uses is that she 'flatters with her words.' The word 'flatters' means to 'make smooth, make slippery.'[5] Elsewhere, we are reminded that 'the lips of an adulteress drip honey, And smoother than oil is her speech' (Prov. 5:3). Her seductive words are quoted here in Proverbs 7:14-20. 'With her many persuasions she entices him; With her flattering lips she seduces him' (Prov. 7:21).

7:6. For at the window of my house I looked out through my lattice,
Now the powerful dramatization of seduction begins, continuing
through verse 23. It is doubtful that this is an actual eye-witness
account, though it is related to us in that way. It would be unlikely,
for example, that, from the vantage point of a window above the
streets, Solomon could actually have heard all the woman's seductive
words in verses 14-20. Rather, this may be a dramatic teaching device
employed to drive home the point made often thus far in Proverbs
concerning the dangers of sexual promiscuity (Prov. 2:16-19; 5:1-23;
6:20-35). The details may have come from Solomon's own experience,
or that of his acquaintances, and been bound together via some
dramatic license to form this poignant narrative.

The point of view is presented first. The narrator describes the
scene from a lofty vantage point, high above the street. He looks
out his latticed window and down into a street being taken over
by encroaching darkness. There, a young man ambles along toward
destruction. From this elevated point of view, the narrator reports
the events from the perspective of God. From His objective position,
he sees our plans, movements, motives and their outcome clearly.
'The Lord looks from heaven; He sees all the sons of men; From His
dwelling place He looks out On all the inhabitants of the earth, He
who fashions the hearts of them all, He who understands all their
works' (Ps. 33:13-15).

**7:7. And I saw among the naïve, I discerned among the youths, A
young man lacking sense,**
From his lofty vantage point, Solomon saw a group of young
people. The entire group is described as 'naïve.' The 'naïve' are the
untaught and inexperienced. They are gullible and easily swayed.
They lack the discernment necessary to rightly evaluate people
and circumstances. Thus, they often unwisely open themselves to a
variety of people and influences. See on Proverbs 1:4 for more on the
'naïve.' They are also called 'the youths.' The term is literally 'sons.'
The word is used to describe 'the male offspring of human parents,'
but can also be used to speak of descendants more generally.[6] This
later sense is employed here, while the emphasis is still, no doubt,
upon the fact that these were young males.

Solomon's eyes were drawn to one young man milling among
this larger group. Whether in retrospect or because of immediate
evidence, it was noticed that this young man was 'lacking sense.'
The term, literally, means 'lacking heart.' Ignorance or low I.Q. is not
his problem, though. Inexperience and lack of discernment is. The

one who is 'lacking sense' does not count the cost of his impetuous actions (Prov. 6:32). His future holds only discipline and hardship, unless he learns wisdom (Prov. 10:13). He rashly says whatever is on his mind, thus ruining his relationships (Prov. 11:12). He wastes his time and talent upon vain pursuits, rather than diligent work (Prov. 12:11). His hasty decisions cost him dearly (Prov. 17:18). He is lazy (Prov. 24:30) and may seek to make gain through unjust and ruthless means (Prov. 28:16). Such a one must heed God's call to wisdom before it is too late (Prov. 9:4, 16).

7:8. Passing through the street near her corner; And he takes the way to her house,

The young man who is singled out for observation is nearing a danger point. Whether or not he intentionally headed toward 'her' house, or whether he stumbled unawares into her lair is not entirely clear. What is clear is that, from the higher vantage point of God's wisdom and some life experience, one can see what he either did not see or did not care to notice. The 'her' has no clear antecedent, but surely refers back to the 'adulteress' and 'foreigner' of verse 5.

Whether unwittingly or intentionally, the young man broke a fundamental principle of wisdom: 'Keep your way far from her, And do not go near the door of her house' (Prov. 5:8). 'Do not enter the path of the wicked, And do not proceed in the way of evil men. Avoid it, do not pass by it; Turn away from it and pass on' (Prov. 4:14-15). Before he is done, Solomon will end up pleading, 'Do not stray into her paths' (Prov. 7:25b).

The danger is doubled because, even if the naïve young man is unintentional in his actions, she is not: 'And she sits at the doorway of her house, On a seat by the high places of the city, Calling to those who pass by, Who are making their paths straight' (Prov. 9:14-15).

If we are to 'flee immorality' (1 Cor. 6:18; cf. 2 Tim. 2:22) then we must not flirt with temptation. We must not dawdle at the edges of what is permissible. We must not toy with the idea of sin, being titillated by the mere thought of indulging. Sadly, He who stops to play in the devil's neighborhood seldom ever leaves.

7:9. In the twilight, in the evening, In the middle of the night and in the darkness.

These two lines employ four expressions to note the time of the young man's folly and fall. The first, 'twilight,' refers to that time of day when darkness begins to encroach upon light. It is the transition time, as darkness progressively takes over everything.[7]

The second expression is 'in the evening.' It describes the time when the sun is setting on the western horizon.[8] As such, it parallels the first term and underscores the time that is indicated.

The third expression is 'In the middle of the night.' The word translated 'middle' is the same one translated as 'apple' in verse 2. The 'apple of the eye' is the pupil, the very center of the eye. Thus, this third expression describes not the onset of darkness, as do the first two, but a progression toward the complete cover of darkness found in the middle of the night.

The final expression is 'In the darkness.' This is a single word in Hebrew, a word that is sometimes translated 'thick darkness' (KJV, ASV, RSV). It is the term used to describe the three days of darkness that fell upon the land of Egypt as a plague from God (Exod. 10:21-22). The word is also used figuratively of calamity and the gloom of distress.[9]

This fourth term carries even further the progression of meaning in these four terms. The young man's fall begins at the transition point of light to night, when the sun is slipping behind the horizon. Instead of wisely running from the temptation zone, he lingers and protracts his sojourn in the growing cover of night. The darkness feeds his rationalization that no one will know or discover his passion-driven intentions or actions. Before he realizes it, he has frittered away the evening and is still on the prowl well into the night. His impending devastation looms on the dark horizon. 'The way of the wicked is like darkness, They do not know over what they stumble' (Prov. 4:19). How desperately we need wisdom! Only the fear of the Lord can 'deliver you ... from those ... who walk in the ways of darkness' (Prov. 2:13). The combination of location (v. 8) and time (v. 9) often proves to be a morally fatal combination![10]

7:10. And behold, a woman comes to meet him, Dressed as a harlot and cunning of heart.

As Solomon paints the narrative picture upon the canvas of the imagination, a new and pulse-quickening turn of events catches the attention. 'And behold' is the translation of a Hebrew particle employed to introduce a sudden change in the narrative and, thus, to arrest the attention.[11] Till now, Solomon has simply picked out one naïve young man among the pedestrians in the street. But, suddenly, in the same view, he can see not only this gullible youth, but also a worldly-wise and cunning woman who, unbeknownst to the young man, has him in her sights. He may be looking for her, but she already sees him. The full drama that is oblivious to the young man is obvious to the older and wiser Solomon, who watches from his lofty vantage point.

The woman comes out to meet the young man. She initiates the contact. He has put himself in the wrong place at the wrong time, no doubt with some unwise and sinful intent. But, she moves with intention and design. She is prepared for the encounter, for she comes 'dressed as a harlot.' What exactly that meant at the time is not clear. It may have included a particular kind of dress (Ezek. 16:16), veil (Gen. 38:14-15), facial makeup (2 Kings 9:22, 30; Jer. 4:30) and jewelry (Isa. 3:16-24).

Although her attire leaves little doubt about her intent, the designs of her heart are secretive. She is 'cunning of heart' or, more literally, 'guarded in heart.'[12] Her plans are not broadcast. Her designs are not made clear. She teases. She tempts. She lures and allures. Her seductions are all the sweeter because of the secrets hinted at in her dress, but not yet revealed by her words. 'Like a bandit she lies in wait' (Prov. 23:28).

7:11. She is boisterous and rebellious; Her feet do not remain at home;

Solomon, the narrator, turns from a description of the action to develop the main character: the adulteress. She is 'boisterous.' The word is difficult to translate uniformly in every context, but it means to cry out, to make a loud noise and to be turbulent. It is a vigorous word that speaks of 'unrest, commotion, strong feeling or noise.'[13] The same word is used of the Woman Folly in Proverbs 9:13.

The adulteress is also 'rebellious.' The idea of stubbornness is contained in the word.[14] This woman has an agenda of her own and has no time for those who might seek to restrain her. As such, she is not about to 'stay home,' just because social convention says she should or her husband expects her to. No, indeed! When night falls she hits the streets in pursuit of her prey. '... [T]hey go around from house to house; and not merely idle, but also gossips and busybodies, talking about things not proper to mention.' (1 Tim. 5:13).

7:12. She is now in the streets, now in the squares, And lurks by every corner.

Her place of preference is 'in the streets' and 'in the squares.' The first phrase simply implies that she prefers to be 'outside' or 'in the open air.' The second phrase describes the open spaces inside the city gate, where men gathered to do business.[15] She must be on the move. She despises domestic duties, which she believes confine and capture her.

When cover of darkness comes, she 'lurks' like a nocturnal predator seeking her prey. The connotation of 'lurks' is that of lying in wait, or setting an ambush with evil intent.[16] When she has sprung from her lair, her victim is like an ox being led to the slaughter or a captive held in chains (v. 22). While the naïve youth may be passing her way with curious intent, she stalks him from the cover of darkened doorways and concealed corners.

7:13. So she seizes him and kisses him, And with a brazen face she says to him:

To this point all progress toward their disastrous rendezvous has been silent and circumstantial. As they drew near one another on the street, his pulse rate may have quickened. But, then, his heart leapt as she made a sudden and bold move to spring her trap upon the smitten young man. She 'seizes him.' The word's root means to be strong, but in the hiphil form of the verb that we encounter here it means to take hold of or to seize.[17]

She, leaving convention and propriety behind, seizes control of the relationship and takes it where he would never have the nerve to take it on his own initiative. With two fists full of his tunic, she 'kisses him.' In a culture where the woman was not to let her hair hang loose or expose any part of her arm or ankle in public, this was, no doubt, a shock akin to a lighting strike (cf. Gen. 39:7, 12)! His personal, moral, and cultural limits were shattered in an instant and, if not for the rush of sensual arousal that shot through his body, he likely would have recoiled and run.

On the heels of her strong-armed seductions, she speaks for the first time to him. She does so 'with a brazen face.' The phrase is, literally, 'she hardens her face.' No doubt, the shock of their sudden first touch and her forceful kiss have left him stupefied. Eyes wide, like saucers, and jaw gone slack from the jolt, he is now stunned and helpless before her verbal seductions. His obvious amazement stands in stark contrast to her brazen and expressionless face. Sin has ceased to evoke pangs in her conscience. She knows her business. She is in control. He is nearly subdued and beyond protest and struggle. With her words, she will now tighten the noose around his neck.

7:14. 'I was due to offer peace offerings; Today I have paid my vows.'

Inwardly, a voice whispers to the mind of the paralyzed young man – is it that of his mother? His father? The priest? Is it the recollection of a memorized portion of Scripture? To answer the call of conscience, she hypocritically assures him all is well with God. After all, she has been to the temple and has offered her 'peace offerings.'

The background for such offerings is found in Leviticus 7:11-18. When an offering was made a part was offered up to God in worship, but the remaining portion of the animal was taken home by the worshipers. There, they gathered their family and friends for a great feast. Such a party was time sensitive, for the meat had to be consumed on the day of the sacrifice or the next, at the latest (Lev. 7:15-16). Even more convincing is the fact that this offering was made as a part of fulfilling a vow to God.

Does she not know that 'The sacrifice of the wicked is an abomination, How much more when he brings it with evil intent!' (Prov. 21:27; cf. 15:8)? Does she not realize that 'To obey is better than sacrifice' (1 Sam. 15:22)? Surely she does, but she does not care, for, in one fell swoop, she satisfied what remained of his Scriptural scruples and, at the same time, she urged him forward, for time was wasting and the party could not wait.

Justification of sin is only reinforced when it is done in the name of God! 'He will forgive me!' 'After all, God wants you to be happy!' 'If it feels so good, how could it be wrong?' 'Surely, this is God's will!'

But, God still says, 'I hate, I reject your festivals, Nor do I delight in your solemn assemblies. Even though you offer up to Me burnt offerings and your grain offerings, I will not accept them; And I will not even look at the peace offerings of your fatlings' (Amos 5:21-22).

7:15. 'Therefore I have come out to meet you, To seek your presence earnestly, and I have found you.'
The seducing words of the adulteress continue on through verse 20. She now employs flattery to further secure her victim. She tells him that he has been in her thoughts all along and that she has been combing the streets looking just for him. The expression 'to seek … earnestly' translates a word which can describe a search that is both early in the day and earnest in intent. The earnestness is seen in that the person rises early to start their search. Indeed, a form of the same word is the Hebrew expression for 'dawn.'[18] Thus, she tells him 'I arose this morning with you on my mind. I could find no rest until I found you. I have searched all day for you and, now, at last, have found the one I've been consumed with.' How gullible one must be to believe such a thinly veiled lie!

7:16. 'I have spread my couch with coverings, With colored linens of Egypt.'
She continues her allurements before she springs her direct invitation in verse 18. Now, she describes the inviting setting she has prepared in anticipation for their illicit rendezvous. She is a woman of means (ill-gotten, of course), for she owns a 'couch.' She has spread it with expensive and luxurious appointments. The word for 'spread' is used nowhere else in the Old Testament. But, in later Hebrew, it meant 'to join together' or 'to patch.'[19] Thus, she entices him with thoughts of her carefully laying each detail in place just for him. The 'colored linens' were items owned only by the wealthy (Prov. 31:22), and those imported from exotic Egypt were considered especially valuable (Isa. 19:9; Ezek. 27:7).

7:17. 'I have sprinkled my bed with myrrh, aloes and cinnamon.'
Not only does she have a bed carefully prepared just for him with fine linens. She has also perfumed it with exotic imported spices. Perhaps there was something considered particularly erotic about these three spices, for they are mentioned together in Song of Solomon 4:14, in a similar context (cf. also Ps. 45:8; Song of Sol. 1:3; 3:6; 5:5). Myrrh would have come from Arabia, aloes from India and the cinnamon from the east coast of Africa or Ceylon.[20] Thus imported, they would have been costly. She wants her young prey to know that, since no expense has been spared in alluring him, no protests should be made in refusing her.

What exactly is described by the verb 'sprinkled' is not certain. Perfumes were made in both powdered, as well as liquid, form. Perhaps she dusted her bed with these powdered spices. Perhaps she sprinkled the liquid perfume upon the sheets. It is possible it was even burnt as incense and waved over the area, allowing the scented smoke to settle upon the coverings of the bed. While what exactly is being described is not certain, what is certain is the intent of her words.

7:18. 'Come, let us drink our fill of love until morning; Let us delight ourselves with caresses.'
Having appropriately prepared the bait, the huntress now springs her trap. She directly invites him to enjoy the full extent of sexual pleasures with her throughout the night. Making love is often likened via metaphor to eating and drinking (Prov. 5:18; 9:17; 30:20; Song of Sol. 4:12, 15, 16; 5:1).

The invitation is twofold: complete sexual satisfaction and thorough emotional revelry. The first is communicated via the metaphor of drinking 'our fill.' The verb employed means to be satiated and completely satisfied.[21] Drawing out the metaphor, it means to drink to the dregs. The meaning of this intense verb is further heightened by the addition of the word 'until morning.' The second part of the invitation is seen in the words: 'Let us delight ourselves.' This verb is used only two other times in the Old Testament (Job 20:18; 39:13), and describes an enthusiastic celebration.[22] The harlot urges the young man to drop all his inhibitions for one night, to lay aside his scruples just this once, and to bring into the physical sphere what he has, heretofore, entertained only in his mind.

Two words are used to describe the kind of experience they are after: 'love' and 'caresses.' The former word is found only here in Proverbs, but is used over thirty times in the Song of Solomon in the context of sexual intimacy. The latter word is used elsewhere in the Old Testament only in Hosea 9:10, where it has illicit sexual nuances.

She invites the young man to stay with her throughout the night. True love lasts ('Love is patient ... bears all things ... endures all things. Love never fails,' 1 Cor. 13:4a, 7, 8a); lust is fleeting. True love is not subject to time limitations, but mere sexual gratification is. This is not love. This is merely raw sexual passion.

7:19. 'For the man is not at home, He has gone on a long journey;'
As the seductress closes her verbal appeal in this verse and the next, she does so by removing all fear of discovery. 'No one will ever have to know!' has been the foolish cry of many on their way to a destructive immoral relationship.

When she speaks of 'the man,' she is referring to her husband. The Septuagint actually interprets it this way, and so translates it. This is a rather unusual way of referring to one's husband. Thus, it may indicate some derision or disaffection in the marital relationship.[23] At least, she wishes the young man so to picture her marriage. He begins to think, 'She needs someone to really love her, like I could.'

The fact that her husband is on a long journey, and that he has taken 'a bag of money with him' (v. 20), may indicate that he is a merchant and that he is away on a business trip. Whatever the case, she seeks to reassure the nervous young man that no harm can befall them if he takes up her invitation. He had good sense to be nervous, for the dangerous jealousy of a husband has already been noted in these Proverbs (cf. 6:34-35).

7:20. 'He has taken a bag of money with him, At full moon he will come home.'

The husband is gone and is well-stocked for a lengthy trip. The word translated 'money' here is, literally, 'silver.' Not only were his pockets full, but the time was far distant for his return. It is not clear how far the 'full moon' was away. But, it must have been sufficiently distant to reassure the young man that no early arrival could interrupt their night of pleasure.

Here ends the verbal allurements of the woman. Now, it is time for a pregnant pause to see whether the trap has been sufficiently set. Will he go for the bait? Or, will wisdom win his heart? It is impossible to underestimate all that hangs in the balance at the moment of temptation. Blessed is the one who heeds the quiet, but steady, voice of wisdom at moments such as these!

7:21. With her many persuasions she entices him; With her flattering lips she seduces him.

Despite the cunning allurements of her dress and makeup (v. 10), her brazen manner (v. 11), and her aggressive physical seductions (v. 13), it is her words that pose the greatest threat to the young man (cf. 'who flatters with her words,' v. 5). It is with 'many persuasions' and 'flattering lips' that she lures and secures him. The former is a translation of a word found frequently in Proverbs (1:5; 4:2; 9:9; 16:21, 23). It can have the sense of taking hold of or fetching something.[24] Employing all the tools of her craft, she has sunk her hooks into the young man and, with her words, she now reels him in. The young man should have fled immediately, for her 'many' words piled up, then overwhelmed, him.

It is with 'flattering lips' that she entices him. The word translated 'flattering' is the word most often translated as 'share,' 'part,' 'territory' and usually refers to matters of dividing an inheritance. Thus, the word has the idea of dividing something.[25] Her lips are 'divided,' in the sense that she gives one impression, but yielding to her will produce something else. She promises pleasure, but entanglement with her brings only destruction.

The result of these words is that she 'entices' and 'seduces' him. The former is used twelve times in Proverbs and, most often, refers to inclining one's ear or heart to listen to wisdom (e.g. Prov. 2:2; 4:20; 5:1, 13; 22:17). The word carries the idea of 'extending,' 'stretching out,' or 'spreading out' toward something. Interestingly, we read, 'The king's heart is like channels of water in the hand of the LORD; He turns [the same word we have here] it wherever He wishes'

(Prov. 21:1). The Lord may not make a king choose a course of action, but He so influences his heart that he, by his own volition, makes the choice the Lord wanted all along. Similarly, though not as powerfully, the adulteress, through her words, inclines the lad's heart toward sin and destruction. He is not relieved of culpability for his sinful choice, but she has made it easier for him to choose that path.

She also 'seduces' him. The word describes forcibly driving or pushing something. The word is used of false shepherds who do not fail through neglect, but by willfully scattering the sheep (Ezek. 34:4). It is also used in a warning against false prophets who drive people from God (Deut. 13:5). The people of Israel are not, however, helpless sheep. They are people who are still able and responsible to employ the volition they were created with to choose God's way (Deut. 4:19).[26] So, the immoral woman with intention seeks, through her seductions and enticements, to do all in her power to force the young man to go her way. Yet, he remains capable of choosing the path of God's will. His capability implies his responsibility.

7:22. Suddenly he follows her, As an ox goes to the slaughter, Or as one in fetters to the discipline of a fool,
The bait is set. The trap is sprung. The victim is caught. The issue has been in doubt until now. But, 'suddenly,' his will is emasculated and his fate is sealed. All twenty-five uses of the term in the Old Testament are connected with disaster or judgment.[27]

Two metaphors are employed here (with more to follow in v. 23) to illustrate his unwitting compliance in his own destruction. The first metaphor is that of an ox stumbling willingly toward his own slaughter. Completely oblivious to the outcome of his decision, he follows whoever may pull at his halter.

The second metaphor is presented in the third line of the verse. This third line is notoriously difficult to translate. The Hebrew has 'fool,' whereas the LXX and Syriac has 'deer' or 'dog' (cf. NIV), and the Vulgate has 'lamb.'[28] The normal Hebrew parallelism would suggest that another comparison from the animal world is in order, thus the translation of the versions.

Whether technical discussions about text determine it is an animal or human illustration, the meaning is clear. At the moment of his yielding up his will, the fool who gives in to an adulteress has no idea of the high cost he will pay for doing so.

The death described may well not be the literal end of physical life (though it may, if the jealous husband has his way! cf. Prov. 6:33-35).

It may well be the death of moral and spiritual vitality that is in view. However, the death of integrity, purity and conscience is no small thing!

7:23. Until an arrow pierces through his liver; As a bird hastens to the snare, So he does not know that it will cost him his life.

The animal metaphors continue from the previous verse. As an unwitting animal does not know it stands in the crosshairs of the hunter until it feels the piercing pain of the arrow, so the foolish young man does not understand his fate until it is too late. As a bird hurries toward the bait unaware of the trap (cf. Prov. 1:17), so the adulterer chases what appears to be a fleeting encounter with pleasure, but ends up ruined.

Clearly, the young man does not calculate the ultimate price he will pay for his folly. 'That it will cost him his life' is literally 'That it is his soul (or life).' 'The one who commits adultery with a woman is lacking sense; He who would destroy himself does it' (Prov. 6:32). 'Moreover, man does not know his time: like fish caught in a treacherous net, and birds trapped in a snare, so the sons of men are ensnared at an evil time when it suddenly falls on them' (Eccles. 9:12).

7:24. Now therefore, my sons, listen to me, And pay attention to the words of my mouth.

The dramatic narrative of verses 6-23 has ended and, now, gives way to explicit applications, as the 'therefore' makes clear. Once again, there comes the oft-heard familial call to 'my sons' (for the plural form see Prov. 4:1; 5:7). The call to 'listen' has also been used often (Prov. 1:8; 4:1, 10; 5:7), as has the command to 'pay attention' (Prov. 2:2; 4:1, 20).

7:25. Do not let your heart turn aside to her ways, Do not stray into her paths.

Two more imperatives are added to those of verse 24. The first line employs a verb used only six times in the Old Testament ('turn aside'). In Proverbs 4:15, it is used in a positive sense of turning away from the path of the evil. But, its use in Numbers 5:12, 19-20, 29 is significant to our context here. Numbers 5 presents the test for marital unfaithfulness. Numbers holds this forth as a test for the woman. But, here, the word links it to the unfaithfulness of the man as well.

What is not to turn aside is the 'heart.' The word has already been used often, and with rich meaning, in Proverbs. It describes the whole of a person's inner life: mind, emotion and volition. The heart is to be bent toward wisdom (Prov. 2:2). It is to have a father's commandments written upon it (Prov. 3:3; 7:3) and bound to it (6:21). The heart is to hold fast to them (Prov. 4:4), with the intent of keeping them (3:1). The heart is to belong wholly to the Lord (Prov. 3:5) and, above all other things, is to be guarded (4:23).

The word for 'ways' has already been met some twenty times in Proverbs, often describing the ways of wisdom. Here, however, it is used in contrast, to reveal the competing, deadly 'ways' of the adulteress.

The second line is an affirmation of the first. The word 'stray' means to 'wander' and is, sometimes, used in connection with intoxication (Prov. 10:17; 12:26; 14:22; 21:16). The 'paths' are parallel to 'ways' and both, together, underscore a consistent theme held forth in Proverbs (cf. Prov. 2:8-20).

7:26. For many are the victims she has cast down, And numerous are all her slain.

This verse and the next contain the justification for the four imperatives found in verses 24-25. She has led the young man to believe she is interested only in him (v. 15). But, little does he know that long is the line of her paramours and countless the graves left in her wake ('many' and 'numerous').

She comes dressed seductively, but her allurements conceal her armor. She is pictured here as a warrior more intent on making blood flow than on letting the good times roll ('victims ... cast down' and 'all her slain'). The meaning may be metaphorical, but the imagery is intended to be more than simply startling. The outcome certainly is to the victim! 'He does not know that the dead are there, That her guests are in the depths of Sheol' (Prov. 9:18). Indeed, 'the waywardness of the naïve shall kill them' (Prov. 1:32a; cf. 24:11, Proverb's only two additional uses of the word here translated 'slain').

7:27. Her house is the way to Sheol, Descending to the chambers of death.

Now, with frightful finality, Solomon describes the end of such sensuality. The two lines of this verse hold forth the ultimate destination of those who dare tread the path of adultery. The 'way' of the adulteress stands in marked contrast to the way of wisdom so often held forth in the Proverbs. Wisdom's path is full of justice and safety (Prov. 2:8), deliverance (2:12), good and godly friends (2:20), pleasure and peace (3:17), security (3:23), longevity (4:26), and life (6:23). In contrast, the one who leaves these paths and walks the way of the adulteress ends up dead. In the Old Testament, 'Sheol' describes the abode of those who have passed from this life and into the shadowy, unknown existence of the next. Indeed, she is 'a highway to the grave' (NIV).

This contrast may be further emphasized by the reference to 'Her house.' This may, here, stand in contrast to the 'house' of the Lady Wisdom set forth in Proverbs 9:1, 14. If so, it emphasizes the greater unity of the entire first nine chapters of Proverbs. Perhaps this reveals that Solomon is about more than simply passing on random reflections on wisdom, but is trying to build a complete worldview regarding the way of life.

Not only does the adulteress's way lead to the doorway of death, but it leads downward 'to the chambers of death.' The word for 'chambers' usually describes a place where a person goes for privacy. It describes a place of seclusion, intimacy and secrecy. It often refers to one's bedroom.[29] The harlot has carefully prepared her bedroom with an air of plush seduction (vv. 16-17). The wise man, however, perceives that such adornments are but a thin veneer to disguise the dark walls of the grave itself. Consider, in this regard, Proverbs 2:18-19; 9:18; 14:12; 16:25; 22:14; 23:27.

End Notes

1. Ross, Allen P., 'Proverbs,' *The Expositor's Bible Commentary* (Grand Rapids, Michigan: Zondervan Publishing House, 1991), 5:939.

2. Lewis, Jack P., *'yāda','* Theological Wordbook of the Old Testament (Chicago: Moody Press, 1980), 1:366-367.

3. Buzzell, Sid S., 'Proverbs,' *The Bible Knowledge Commentary* (Wheaton: Victor Books, 1988), 1:910.

4. Konkel, A. H., 'נכר,' *New International Dictionary of Old Testament Theology and Exegesis* (Grand Rapids, Michigan: Zondervan Publishing House, 1997), 3:108-109.

5. Luc, Alex, 'חלק,' *New International Dictionary of Old Testament Theology and Exegesis* (Grand Rapids, Michigan: Zondervan Publishing House, 1997), 2:160.

6. Martens, Elmer A., *'bēn,'* Theological Wordbook of the Old Testament (Chicago: Moody Press, 1980), 1:113-116.

7. Delitzsch, F., *Proverbs, Ecclesiastes, Song of Solomon* (three volumes in one) in C. F. Keil and F. Delitzsch, vol. 6, *Commentary on the Old Testament* (in ten volumes), (1872; rpt. Grand Rapids, Michigan: William B. Eerdmans Publishing Company, 1980), 1:159-160.

8. Allen, Ronald B., *"ārab,'* Theological Wordbook of the Old Testament (Chicago: Moody Press, 1980), 2:694.

9. Feinberg, Charles L., *"pl,'* Theological Wordbook of the Old Testament (Chicago: Moody Press, 1980), 1:64-65.

10. Kidner, Derek, *Proverbs* (Downers Grove, Illinois: InterVarsity Press, 1964), 75.

11. Whybray, R. N., *Proverbs* (Grand Rapids, Michigan: William B. Eerdmans Publishing Company, 1994), 113.

12. Ross, 5:940.

13. Weber, Carl Philip, '*hāmâ,*' *Theological Wordbook of the Old Testament* (Chicago: Moody Press, 1980), 1:219.

14. Whybray, 114.

15. Ibid., 45.

16. Ross, 5:940.

17. Weber, Carl Philip, '*hāzaq,*' *Theological Wordbook of the Old Testament* (Chicago: Moody Press, 1980), 1:276.

18. Hamilton, Victor P., '*shāhar,*' *Theological Wordbook of the Old Testament* (Chicago: Moody Press, 1980), 2:917.

19. Whybray, 115.

20. Delitzsch, 1:166.

21. White, William, '*rāwâ,*' *Theological Wordbook of the Old Testament* (Chicago: Moody Press, 1980), 2:835-836.

22. Grisanti, Michael A., 'עלס,' *New International Dictionary of Old Testament Theology and Exegesis* (Grand Rapids, Michigan: Zondervan Publishing House, 1997), 3:427-428.

23. Whybray, 116.

24. Kaiser, Walter C., '*lāqaḥ,*' *Theological Wordbook of the Old Testament* (Chicago: Moody Press, 1980), 1:481-482.

25. Wiseman, Donald J., '*hālaq,*' *Theological Wordbook of the Old Testament* (Chicago: Moody Press, 1980), 1:292-293.

26. Coppes, Leonard J., '*nādah,*' *Theological Wordbook of the Old Testament* (Chicago: Moody Press, 1980), 2:556.

27. Hamilton, Victor P., '*peta',*' *Theological Wordbook of the Old Testament* (Chicago: Moody Press, 1980), 2:744.

28. Kidner, 76.

29. Weber, Carl Philip, '*hādar,*' *Theological Wordbook of the Old Testament* (Chicago: Moody Press, 1980), 1:265.

Proverbs 8

8:1. Does not wisdom call, And understanding lift up her voice?
Once again, wisdom is personified as a woman, as it was in both
Proverbs 1:20-33 and 3:14-18, and as it will continue to be in 9:1-6. This
chapter begins with a personal introduction (vv. 1-3) and ends with a
fitting hortatory conclusion (vv. 32-36). The introduction is clearly set
forth in the third person, while the body of the speech is given in the
first person. The substance of the speech is comprised of statements
organized in three general ways: the attributes of wisdom (vv. 4-11), the
benefits of wisdom (vv. 12-21) and the origin of wisdom (vv. 22-31). These
first-person statements of wisdom build toward, and culminate in, the
applicational conclusion, which begins with 'Now therefore' (v. 32).

As before, wisdom issues her 'call' and lifts 'her voice'
(cf. Prov. 1:20-21). Once again, 'wisdom' and 'understanding'
appear and are roughly synonymous (cf. Prov. 2:2, 10-11; 3:13, 19;
5:1). This call of the woman wisdom is in stark contrast to the verbal
enticements of the adulteress (Prov. 7:14-21). The immoral woman
asked for the love of the young man (Prov. 7:18), but the end was
death (7:26-27). The Woman Wisdom also calls for the love of the
naïve (Prov. 8:21), but the end of walking with her is life (8:35). The
woman of chapter 7 is a woman of immoral character (Prov. 7:10-11),
while the Woman Wisdom is virtuous (8:4-11). The harlot is a liar
(Prov. 7:13-15; 21), while Wisdom is full of truth (8:7).

Many have attempted to identify the personified wisdom of this
chapter with the preincarnate Christ. The chapter presents wisdom
as active in creation (vv. 22-31). Wisdom appears to predate creation
(v. 23). Yet, it is inappropriate to make this personification identical
with the person of Christ. Christ, as the revelation of God's nature,
both embodied and revealed God's wisdom (Matt. 11:19; 12:42;
Luke 11:49; 1 Cor. 1:24, 30; Col. 1:15-20; 2:3). Thus, this personification
of wisdom bears striking resemblance to our Savior. Yet, wisdom,
despite the literary use of personification, is something God is, not
a being in and of itself. That which is truly an attribute of God must
itself be eternal, since God is a singular Being and no attribute stands
alone, but is one with all God's other attributes.[1]

Let us not miss the fact stated here: wisdom is ever speaking,
calling, seeking, inviting, and demanding our attention! God is not

silent. He does not sit by quietly, letting the world pass by until someone stops and gives Him attention. He calls to us in creation, in Christ, by the Spirit through the Word of God, through our conscience, and in His providence. Our failure and foolishness is not for lack of His voice, but for lack of our listening.

8:2. On top of the heights beside the way, Where the paths meet, she takes her stand;

We are not required to cloister ourselves away in some monastic setting to hear God speak His wisdom. This verse and the next use four phrases to indicate that wisdom is not only useful in, but can be discovered amidst, the busy rush of this world's activities. Wisdom is for the board room as surely as it is for the Sunday School room. It is on 'top of the heights beside the way' and 'Where the paths meet' that wisdom functions and can be found. The 'top of the heights' is, more literally, 'at the top of the high places' and, thus, refers to places of public interchange. Similarly, 'Where the paths meet' is the crossroads of busy thoroughfares. Where traffic is busiest, wisdom wishes to be most active.

Kidner insightfully says, 'A chapter which is to soar beyond time and space, opens at street-level, to make it clear, first, that the wisdom of God is as relevant to the shopping-centre (2, 3) as to heaven itself (22).'[2]

8:3. Beside the gates, at the opening to the city, At the entrance of the doors, she cries out:

Two more phrases are added to the two used in verse 2, all describing wisdom's practicality and public call. Wisdom calls 'Beside the gates, at the opening to the city.' This was the place of commerce and a place where public authorities sat to make official decisions. God's wisdom belongs in the marketplace and in the judicial system. Similarly, wisdom calls at 'the entrance of the doors' – the place through which people must funnel to get to where they are going. Wherever people are found, the wisdom of God longs to have a voice.

Wisdom works in the real world. God is practical. The ways of God are contemporary, current, and culturally significant. You need not park your commitment to God with your auto when you go to work. You need not leave it at home when you head off to school. The wisdom of God is to be introduced into the discourse of public debate and life. One's relationship to God is not merely a private matter, but must affect every avenue of one's life. To try to compartmentalize life into the spiritual and secular is to shut your ears to wisdom's cry.

8:4. 'To you, O men, I call, And my voice is to the sons of men.'
Now, wisdom, for the first time since Proverbs 1:20-33, clears her voice and begins to speak in the first person. Her personal call will continue through verse 36. Her cry is to all men. The references 'O men' and 'the sons of men' sound the tone of a universal appeal. This bidding to all 'men' and 'the sons of men' is echoed in verse 31. Nevertheless, verse 5 will specify the call to the 'naïve ones' and 'fools.'

There is not a person who does not desperately need the wisdom of God. The believer and the unbeliever, the religious and the irreligious, the wealthy and the poor, the cultured and the barbarian, the educated and the illiterate – to them all wisdom lifts her voice and invites them to come. Wisdom's call crosses all racial, national, cultural, educational and sociological barriers. The appeal is universal because the need is universal. 'Hear this, all peoples; Give ear, all inhabitants of the world, Both low and high, Rich and poor together. My mouth will speak wisdom; And the meditation of my heart will be understanding' (Ps. 49:1-3).

8:5. 'O naïve ones, discern prudence; And, O fools, discern wisdom.'
While this call is universal, it is most needed by a particular class of people – the 'naïve ones' and the 'fools.' The 'naïve ones' are those who are vulnerable to any, and every, wind of influence that may blow their way. They are open to every sales pitch. They are gullible, silly and easily convinced. They are, thus, unstable. For more on the 'naïve ones,' see on Proverbs 1:4, 22, 32; 7:7.

The 'fools' are a harder lot than the naïve. This most common word in Proverbs for the fool describes one who is thick-headed and stubborn. He is not intellectually deficient, but morally and spiritually inept. Both words appear in combination also in Proverbs 1:22, 32.[3]

What such ones need, and what they may find, is 'prudence' and 'wisdom.' The word translated 'prudence' may be used both negatively ('guile,' Exod. 21:14) or positively, as here.[4] The command is directed toward the 'naïve ones.' Wisdom can make the gullible to see and avoid the pitfalls of life. The 'naïve ones' can find good judgment, if they seek and heed wisdom's voice.

The command of the second line appears a bit odd to the English reader. Why would wisdom (v. 1) be calling people to find 'wisdom?'

In the Hebrew text, the two words, however, are not the same. The word we have here translated as 'wisdom' is literally 'heart.' In the Hebrew understanding, the 'heart' is the seat of the whole of life. It represents variously the intellectual, emotional and volitional elements of life. Perhaps the call is to 'have a heart' inclined toward wisdom. Or, maybe the sense is that, if you 'have a mind to' learn wisdom, you will. The wisdom of God can bring all the elements of the heart (mind, emotions and will) into perfect balance with one another and into perfect alignment with God, thus enabling one to see what God sees. Indeed, the call is to 'discern' both of these things. The word is frequent in Proverbs (e.g. Prov. 1:2, 5, 6; 2:5, 9; 7:7; 8:9). It describes the ability to look at two things and distinguish the differences.[5] It is the capacity to observe any situation, circumstance, person or option and see what God sees. What more valuable treasure could one enjoy than this God-sent gift?

8:6. 'Listen, for I shall speak noble things; And the opening of my lips will produce right things.'
The imperative 'Listen' has become a frequent exhortation in this Wisdom Literature (Prov. 4:1; 5:7; 7:24; 8:32, 33). The exhortation is justified, as the virtues of wisdom are now expounded upon (vv. 6-11).

Wisdom claims her words contain 'noble things.' More literally, the translation might be 'princely things.' The word is unusual in this context and normally refers to a ruler, prince or even military leader.[6] It is used one other time in Proverbs (Prov. 28:16). The emphasis intended is difficult to state exactly. Perhaps it emphasizes the excellence of what wisdom speaks. Or, maybe it refers to the authority of what she says. Whatever the exact translation settled upon, the notion is that what wisdom speaks is of the utmost importance and deserves our highest respect and obedience.

Similarly, when wisdom speaks, 'right things' come forth. This Hebrew word is found nineteen times in the Old Testament with a range of meaning which includes notions of a level way, order, justly, uprightness, straightness, equity, justice and integrity.[7] The words of wisdom conform to reality. They are in line with what God is. For this reason, wisdom must not only be trusted, but fully embraced.

There are eight virtues of wisdom listed in verses 6-9. Interestingly, there are eight descriptions in Philippians 4:8 of the virtues we are to make our minds dwell upon: 'Finally, brethren, whatever is true, whatever is honorable, whatever is right, whatever is pure, whatever is lovely, whatever is of good repute, if there is any excellence and if anything worthy of praise, let your mind dwell on these things.'

8:7. 'For my mouth will utter truth; And wickedness is an abomination to my lips.'
The basis of the exhortation to 'Listen' in verse 6 continues here as the virtues of wisdom are set forth. Wisdom speaks only 'truth.' The word is a standard one in Old Testament covenant terminology. It describes that which is firm, stable and reliable.[8] Only such words will wisdom 'utter.' The word is a colorful one, most often referring to a barely audible sound that is peculiar to the dove (Isa. 38:14; 59:11) or the throaty rumble of a lion over its victim (Isa. 31:4). It comes also to describe, however, the inward thoughts and plans of the heart.[9] Note Proverbs 15:28 in this regard: 'The heart of the righteous ponders [our same word] how to answer, But the mouth of the wicked pours out evil things.' Thus, wisdom not only will not audibly speak anything but truth, it will not ponder or contemplate anything else. Do we ponder only truth? Do we think the thoughts of God after Him?

The reverse is also descriptive of wisdom – 'wickedness is an abomination.' The term 'wickedness' always denotes the devising of evil and injustice against God or others.[10] The phrase 'an abomination to my lips' is a somewhat unusual one. The usual expression refers to 'an abomination to the Lord' (e.g. Prov. 3:32; 11:1, 20; 12:22; 15:8, 9, 26). Yet, here, such wicked notions or actions are an 'abomination' to wisdom. This implies an intense hatred toward that which is set up against God and His people.[11] The 'lips' of wisdom hold this attitude toward all such wickedness. The metaphor all but pictures wisdom spitting, or spewing, forth any tepid, distasteful wickedness that would ever encroach upon the pallet. Are we offended over that which offends the Lord? Do we hate what God hates? Do we hate as God hates?

8:8. 'All the utterances of my mouth are in righteousness; There is nothing crooked or perverted in them.'
To the previous four virtues of wisdom (vv. 6-7), two more are now added. The first is stated positively and the second negatively. The utterances of wisdom are 'in righteousness.' This translates a standard Old Testament word whose root refers to that which is 'straight,' in the sense that it conforms to an ethical or moral standard. In this case, the standard of measure is the very nature of God.[12] The word is used in Proverbs 1:3; 2:9; 8:15, 18; 12:17; 16:13; 17:15; 25:5; 31:9. Here, it is prefixed with a term pointing to the essence or inherent quality of a thing and how it is expressed. Thus, the words of wisdom have woven into the warp and woof of their very essence the quality of

righteousness.[13] The righteousness of wisdom is inseparable from the words of wisdom, for they express its very nature.

In contrast to this 'righteousness,' and stated in the negative, is the assertion 'There is nothing crooked or perverted in them.' The first word, 'crooked,' is not used elsewhere in Proverbs. It describes that which is radically skewed from its original design, retaining only a vestige of its earliest appearance or purpose. The root of the word can describe the threads of a rope being twisted together, in and out, until one cannot tell where one thread begins and where the other ends. Thus, it can come to describe the crafty and deceitful words of a huckster.[14] The deceptive words of the adulteress offer an illustration of her gaudy, misshapen character. Here, in chapter 8, the pure words of Lady Wisdom stand in bold contrast (cf. the contrasting words of wisdom and 'the woman of folly' in Prov. 9:4-6, 16-17).

The word for 'perverted' is used elsewhere in Proverbs 2:15; 11:20; 17:20; 19:1; 22:5; 28:6, 18. The word pictures that which has been twisted or distorted from its original design. It has become a parody or caricature of the original.[15] Words are not intended to be used in 'crooked' ways, that is, to mislead. Wisdom's words, thus, are pure and in accord with God's original design. They do not mislead.

8:9. 'They are all straightforward to him who understands, And right to those who find knowledge.'

To the previous six (vv. 6-8), two additional virtues of wisdom are now added to complete the justification for the exhortation 'Listen' (v. 6). The first is that all that wisdom speaks is 'straightforward.' The word is used only eight times in the Old Testament (2 Sam. 15:3; Prov. 8:9; 24:26; Isa. 26:10; 30:10; 57:2; 59:14; Amos 3:10). It generally is used as an adjective meaning something like straight, right, or plain.[16] Here, it stands in contrast to 'crooked or perverted' (see above on v. 8). This points to the idea that there is nothing hidden in the ways or words of wisdom. What she means, she says. What she says, she means. There are not hidden nuances that are only for the few. There are no loopholes in the fine print.

The second virtue listed here is that the words of wisdom are 'right.' The Hebrew word is one of the key Old Testament terms for describing justice and integrity. It describes that which is straight, level, right, just and righteous.[17] This also stands in contrast to that which is 'crooked and perverted' (v. 8). The ways of wisdom, rather than taking a winding way of decision, cut straight to the heart.

When you walk in wisdom, there is no fear of what lies around the next bend or what might rise up and trip you. There is security and confidence in listening to, and walking with, wisdom.

Both lines contain disclaimers. The virtues of wisdom are 'to him who understands' and 'to those who find knowledge.' The word behind the translation 'understands' describes 'to discern between' two things. The idea is the ability to distinguish that which leads to understanding.[18] The disclaimer of the second line speaks of finding 'knowledge.' In Proverbs 2:5, the fear of the Lord and the knowledge of God are intimately tied together. This is where wisdom starts: with a clear, accurate view of who God is and a resulting healthy and holy awe of Him.

The ways of wisdom may not appear so wise to the uninitiated and unbelieving (1 Cor. 1:18-25). But, to the one who trusts in the revelation of God imparted by the Holy Spirit to the heart, the virtues of wisdom become obvious. The Jews questioned Jesus about His teaching, as to how they could know it was from God. Jesus replied, 'If any man is willing to do His [the Father's] will, he shall know of the teaching, whether it is of God, or whether I speak from Myself' (John 7:17). Discerning the inherent wisdom of Jesus' teaching is dependent upon a prior bowing of the will to obey God, no matter what He may reveal. First, the will must bow in submission and trust to God, then He awards deeper insight into the inherent wisdom of His ways.

8:10. 'Take my instruction, and not silver, And knowledge rather than choicest gold.'

Matching the command to 'Listen' (v. 6) we now find a second imperative to 'take.' This command is followed by justification for its instruction (v. 11), as was the first (vv. 6-9). The command is not simply a passive 'receive,' but the more active 'take.' There is personal responsibility here.

Proverbs and other Scriptures are filled with comparisons of the superior value of wisdom to riches (Job 28:12-28; Ps. 19:10; 119:72, 127; Prov. 2:4; 3:14, 15; 8:19-21; 16:16). This, however, is not merely a comparison, but a command.[19] No option is left for the one who wants the life afforded by wisdom.

The specific comparison is that of 'instruction' and 'knowledge.' The first is found some thirty times in Proverbs (e.g. Prov. 1:2, 3, 7, 8) and describes education through discipline or correction.[20] The second is also frequent in Proverbs, appearing thirty-nine times (e.g. Prov. 1:4, 7), and describes input gained through the senses.[21]

True wealth is measured not in dollars and cents, but in the not-so-common sense arising from the impartation of God's truth.

8:11. 'For wisdom is better than jewels; And all desirable things can not compare with her.'

Now, wisdom provides reason for her command to 'Take instruction' (v. 10). Her justification here is nearly identical with Proverbs 3:15. Note that, suddenly, there is a break from the first person reference to wisdom, as this verse is set in the third person. Here 'wisdom' is seen in parallelism with the 'instruction' and 'knowledge' of verse 10. The distinctions cannot be pressed too far, but our word, here, seems to point toward the skill of living successfully in God's world.[22]

We meet here one of Proverbs' many 'better than' comparisons. They were introduced to us in Proverbs 3:14 and occur a total of twenty-one times (Prov. 3:14; 8:11, 19; 12:9; 15:16, 17; 16:8, 16, 19, 32; 17:1; 19:1, 22; 21:9, 19; 22:1; 25:7, 24; 27:5, 10; 28:6).

The variables in this 'better than' comparison are 'jewels' and 'all desirable things.' As for 'jewels,' they were probably some kind of red corals (Lam. 4:7) that were regarded as extremely valuable in the ancient world.[23] The latter of the two describes that which a person desires passionately to have.[24] Coupled with the word 'all,' it is moved to the extreme and refers to that which is the utmost among the things one might long for. Better than your wildest dreams is the wisdom necessary to live skillfully and successfully in God's world! Nothing can 'compare' with her.

8:12. 'I, wisdom, dwell with prudence, And I find knowledge and discretion.'

Having extolled her virtues personally (vv. 4-11), now wisdom describes the many benefits that come to those who embrace her (vv. 12-21). This section is made up of two sections, each beginning with the first person singular pronoun 'I' (vv. 12-16; 17-21).

Pursue wisdom and you also come into the company of a trio of other riches: 'prudence,' 'knowledge' and 'discretion.' All three terms are familiar by now to the reader of Proverbs (all being found together in Prov. 1:4). Wisdom has made herself at home with prudence. She has pitched her tent with prudence. To dwell in wisdom is to live with prudence also. The word translated 'prudence' may be used either negatively ('guile,' Exod. 21:14) or positively, as here and throughout Proverbs.[25] It describes a person who sees where the course of life is headed and is able to anticipate and deal with obstacles and dangers.[26]

Similarly, wisdom boasts that she can 'find' knowledge and discretion. This verb is used approximately 450 times in the Old Testament and can have a variety of nuances of meaning. Generally, it describes a process of seeking and finding something.[27] Walk with wisdom and you too will find 'knowledge' and 'discretion.' The latter describes the ability to look at life attentively and formulate objectives, goals, and strategies that will be successful. The former describes the knowledge that is able to make this happen.[28]

8:13. 'The fear of the LORD is to hate evil; Pride and arrogance and the evil way, And the perverted mouth, I hate.'
In describing the benefits which come with wisdom, we now have set before us by way of negative statement that which must be left behind. We have seen that the 'fear of the Lord' is the theme of the entire book of Proverbs (Prov. 1:7, 29; 2:5; 8:13; 9:10; 10:27; 14:26, 27; 15:16, 33; 16:6; 19:23; 22:4; 23:17). We are told, on the positive side, that the fear of the Lord is the beginning of wisdom and knowledge (Prov. 1:7, 29; 2:5; 9:10; 15:33). On the negative side, the fear of the Lord is the beginning of a resolute hatred of all that is evil. The word translated 'hate' '... expresses an emotional attitude toward persons and things which are opposed, detested, despised and with which one wishes to have no contact or relationship. It is therefore the opposite of love. Whereas love draws and unites, hate separates and keeps distant. The hated and hating persons are considered foes or enemies and are considered odious, utterly unappealing.'[29]

Such strong statements catch off guard those raised to believe you must never hate anything or anyone. Yet, the Scriptures are clear. If I am to be remade in the likeness of God, then I must hate as He hates. The broader context of Scripture tells us God hates empty religious ritual (Amos 5:21-23), the works of those who fall away from His way (Ps. 101:3), the double-minded (Ps. 119:113), and falsehood (Ps. 119:163). Specifically, here, the things which repulse God are four: 'pride and arrogance and the evil way, And the perverted mouth.'

The word translated 'pride' is found only here in the Old Testament. That which stands behind our translation 'arrogance' comes from the same root word, but is found more often in the pages of Scripture (e.g. Ps. 47:5; 59:13; Prov. 16:18). The root meaning behind both means 'to rise.'[30] Here, the idea is that of rising up in self-will, self-promotion, and self-congratulation, as opposed to bowing low before God's majesty.

The theme of 'the evil way' has already been fully developed in Proverbs (Prov. 2:12; 3:31; 4:14, 19). Wisdom also hates the 'perverted mouth.' We have read of a 'deceitful mouth' (Prov. 4:24) and a 'false mouth' (6:12). But this is not the first time the word 'perverted' has been combined with the organs of speech (Prov. 2:12; see comments there).

Comparing the first and third lines of the verse reveals that what God hates (line one), wisdom also hates (line three). There is no conflict between wisdom and godliness. Any wisdom that does not honor and fear God is vain philosophy. True godliness is the path to wisdom. True wisdom leads to godliness.

8:14. 'Counsel is mine and sound wisdom; I am understanding, power is mine.'

That which is not, and must not be, allowed in the presence of wisdom has been set forth (v. 13) and, now, we return to that which positively accompanies wisdom. The personal pronouns employed in verses 14-17a are emphatic and set wisdom itself on center stage, not just the advantages she brings.[31]

Four benefits of wisdom are enumerated. The first is 'Counsel.' Such counsel stands in contrast to the plans of one's own heart (Prov. 19:20-21). Indeed, following one's own way and rejecting counsel is dangerous (Prov. 1:25, 30). The counsel of the Lord is found in His word (Ps. 119:24) and it stands forever (Ps. 33:11a). The word is used often in military and political contexts.[32]

Wisdom also brings 'sound wisdom.' This word describes the solid judgment that enables one to experience abiding success in the practical affairs of life (Prov. 2:7; 3:21; 18:1).[33]

There is also 'understanding.' The term is used often in Proverbs (e.g. Prov. 1:2; 2:3; 3:5; 4:1, 5, 7). It describes not only knowledge of something, but also the ability to come into that knowledge.[34]

The fourth benefit of wisdom is 'power.' The word is often used of the political or military power of kings (2 Kings 18:20; Isa. 11:2; 36:5).[35] But, ultimate 'power' rests in the Lord's hands (1 Chron. 29:11-12; 2 Chron. 20:6; Ps. 65:6; 66:6-7; 80:3; 106:8; Jer. 10:6).

This verse finds a parallel in two key Old Testament passages. The first is Job 12:13, where several of the terms used here to describe wisdom are there used to enunciate the attributes of God. The second is Isaiah 11:2, where three of the four terms are used to describe the coming Messiah: 'And the Spirit of the Lord will rest on Him, The spirit of wisdom and understanding, The spirit of counsel and strength, The spirit of knowledge and the fear of the Lord.' While, as noted above, this does not equate wisdom with the second Person of the Trinity, it does indicate that wisdom, as one of His attributes, is inseparable from His being. Jesus came as the embodiment of wisdom. This part of His nature He graciously shares with those who seek and trust Him.

8:15. 'By me kings reign, And rulers decree justice.'

Indeed, this power to rule is in the forefront of Solomon's mind as he writes to prepare his sons to be 'kings,' 'rulers,' (v. 15), 'princes' and 'nobles' (v. 16). After all, he had prayed for wisdom to rule (1 Kings 3:9; 2 Chron. 1:10) and God had given it (1 Kings 3:28; 2 Chron. 1:11-12).

Wisdom will bring the rulers of the world the ability to establish justice and rule in fairness. This justice has been promised as a product of studying and observing this Book of Proverbs (Prov. 1:3) and of seeking the Lord (2:9). Such a ruler will speak truth (Prov. 12:17; 16:13) and surround himself with counselors of wisdom and godliness (25:5). Wisdom guides such leaders to defend the helpless and to render just verdicts for the needy (Prov. 31:9). The promise is that 'The king gives stability to the land by justice' (Prov. 29:4).

8:16. 'By me princes rule, and nobles, All who judge rightly.'

How vast and wide is the influence of wisdom! Scripture is clear: God establishes the rulers of the kingdoms and nations of the world. 'There is no authority except from God, and those which exist are established by God' (Rom. 13:1b). Each is, indeed, 'a minister of God' (Rom. 13:4), divinely appointed as a delegated authority to administer a measure of God's program in this world. How the leaders of the nations should cry out to God for the wisdom to fulfill their God-given calling! How sad that, too often, they 'take counsel together Against the Lord and against His Anointed' (Ps. 2:2).

There is some dispute about the last line, between the Masoretic Text (which the NASB follows here) and other Hebrew manuscripts and some versions. Some substitute 'the earth' instead of 'rightly.' But, there appears no good reason to abandon the Masoretic Text. It is true that the word 'rulers' is often linked with 'of the earth' (Ps. 2:10; 148:11; Isa. 40:23).[36] But, 'rightly' holds this verse in parallel with the previous one.

8:17. 'I love those who love me; And those who diligently seek me will find me.'

Wisdom continues in her first-person discourse. This second 'I' section (cf. vv. 12-16) is set off by the use of the word 'love' (vv. 17, 21).[37]

The promise of wisdom is that she will love the one who loves her. The matter is set in absolute terms. To love wisdom is to hate evil (v. 13). To fail to love wisdom is to forsake or hate her (Prov. 4:6) and, instead, love death (3:36). But, in giving this ultimate loyalty and allegiance to wisdom is found all the benefits she can bestow (vv. 18, 21)! The matter of love is made a reciprocal affair. The principle of reciprocity reminds us that we are just as wise as we want to be (James 1:5; 4:8). Love is, after all, ultimately a matter of obedience (John 14:21).

The second part of the promise is that those who seek wisdom will find her. It is true that wisdom has already said that some will seek her and fail to find her (Prov. 1:28), but that is because they have waited too long. The day of her invitation came and they greeted her with scorn (Prov. 1:24). They sought her not for her own sake, but for relief from the hardships of folly. Our search must be both well-timed and all-consuming (Prov. 2:1-5). 'Seek the Lord while He may be found; Call upon Him *while He is near*' (Isa. 55:6, emphasis added).

8:18. 'Riches and honor are with me, Enduring wealth and righteousness.'

Wisdom continues to announce the benefits that accompany her. In this verse, these benefits are enumerated in sets of two. The first is 'Riches and honor.' Proverbs does not hesitate to name tangible wealth as one of the rewards of walking in wisdom. The one lacking wisdom makes many foolish and self-destructive choices. These can become life-style patterns which are financially unwise and are counter-productive to financial success. Yet, the rewards of wisdom are not monetary and physical only, for coupled with 'riches' is 'honor.' Solomon reminds us in another place: 'A good name is to be more desired than great riches, Favor is better than silver and gold' (Prov. 22:1). Indeed, Solomon ended his life with much wealth (1 Kings 3:12-14; 10:14-29), but with a reputation for a lack of self-control (1 Kings 11:1, 4-9, 14)! More than once, Solomon mentions these contrasting but corresponding traits (Prov. 3:16; 22:4).

The second pair of benefits are 'Enduring wealth and righteousness.' A pattern similar to that discovered in the first pair is, again, found here. One benefit of wisdom is 'wealth.' Yet, notice that it is 'enduring' wealth. The word translated 'enduring' is found nowhere else in the Old Testament. The root meaning of the word is somewhat difficult to discern, given its scant usage. Yet, that which is old or lasting seems to be the idea.[38] The word may describe durable wealth that is enduring, in the sense that it is perpetually passed on from parents to children.[39] In our day, we might call it 'old money,' describing wealth that has become hereditary and is passed down from one generation to the next. Of course, this tangible wealth is coupled again, as in the first pair, with the more intangible, and vastly more valuable, 'righteousness.' The NIV translates with 'prosperity,' a meaning that may be possible, but which seems to work against the intended contrast of tangible/intangible wealth. The only place the word is found in Proverbs 1–9 is here and in verse 20. Thereafter it is frequent (Prov. 10:2; 11:4, 5, 6, 18, 19; 12:28; 13:6; 14:34; 15:9; 16:8, 12, 31; 21:3, 21). The use in verse 20 clearly calls for the ethical and moral sense of 'righteousness,' rather than 'prosperity,' and, thus, it seems here also. Enduring monetary riches are a boon, if held by a righteous heart. They become a bane, if the heart goes astray.

8:19. 'My fruit is better than gold, even pure gold, And my yield than choicest silver.'

Here, again, we meet a 'better than' comparison (cf. v. 11). And, again, the comparison is between the value of the products of wisdom and that of gold and silver. It is true that one of the by-products of wisdom can be wealth (v. 18), but that is only a part of the greater harvest that comes to the one who walks in wisdom.

Notice the introduction of 'fruit' and 'yield' to the comparison. Wisdom is a 'tree of life' (Prov. 3:18), a living thing, that, when planted, grows and bears fruit. When wisdom comes to your life, you begin to experience just the outer fringes of its potential blessings. A bountiful and untold harvest awaits the one who cultivates his relationship with wisdom. Gold and silver are, however, only inanimate objects, not living things. They are valuable (in this world) and attractive, to be sure. Yet, they cannot yield more than they are. Their value is static (in eternity's view). 'How much better it is to get wisdom than gold! And to get understanding is to be chosen above silver' (Prov. 16:16; cf. 3:14).

8:20. 'I walk in the way of righteousness, In the midst of the paths of justice,'

Verse 18 has reminded us that wisdom is bound to morality. This connection becomes even more explicit here. The theme of 'way ... paths' is, as we have seen, frequent in the Proverbs (Prov. 1:15; 2:8, 13, 15, 20; 3:6, 17; 4:11, 14, 26; 5:6, 21; 7:25; 8:2; 12:28; 15:19). Wisdom is found in the way, or along the paths of, 'righteousness' and 'justice.'

We have already encountered the first term in verse 18. The second term has been seen in Proverbs 1:3; 2:8, 9. The word 'justice' described the judicial procedures which were rightly undertaken and executed in order to provide a fair trial, and to make certain that what came of the proceedings was right. The word translated 'righteousness,' on the other hand, described the character and behavior of the one whose job it was to make certain these proceedings achieved this end.[40]

The form of the Hebrew verb translated 'walk' points to action that is steady or continuous.[41] Wisdom does not promise a get-rich-quick scheme, but a grow-wise-steadily program that also yields tangible benefits, in most cases.

8:21. 'To endow those who love me with wealth, That I may fill their treasuries.'

This second section of the chapter (vv. 12-21), which has set forth the tangible, this-worldly benefits of wisdom, now draws to a close. Again, the familiar theme of reward through possessions or property is in view.

The verb translated 'endow' describes the giving or receiving of property that comes about as a result of being handed down and which becomes a permanent possession.[42] Thus, the picture here is not simply wealth, but lasting, family wealth of tangible, enduring (at least from the perspective of this world) value. The word translated 'wealth' is only here found as a noun in the Old Testament. It normally functions as a particle which points to 'the existence or presence of an object or a quality.'[43] It would seem, then, that the promise is that those who love wisdom are able to obtain wealth and live in such a way as to hold on to it, passing it on from generation to generation. Not only do they hand down the property or possessions. They apparently are able to hand off the love for wisdom that enables them to retain the family's wealth (cf. v. 18).

So generous is wisdom that she will 'fill their treasuries' to overflowing (Prov. 3:10; 24:4; Mal. 3:10; Deut. 28:8, 12). Compare this with the cry of the hoodlum gangs of Proverbs 1:13, who entice the wayward youth with the promise 'We shall fill our houses with spoil,' but whose end is sudden and definite (Prov. 1:16-19). Or, compare this blessed outcome for the lover of wisdom with that of the adulterer who 'must give all the substance of his house' (Prov. 6:31) for his fleeting moments of pleasure.

8:22. 'The LORD possessed me at the beginning of His way, Before His works of old.'

The third section of the chapter now begins and continues through verse 31. Whereas verses 12-21 extolled the this-worldly benefits of wisdom, the present section lifts us, as it were, from the terra firma to the heavenlies as wisdom's role in the formation of the cosmos is set forth. As noted under verse 1, it is best not to take these words as a description of the pre-incarnate Christ per se. What is set forth here is developed by New Testament writers to help describe Christ (John 1:1-3; 1 Cor. 1:24, 30; Col. 2:3).

Wisdom is personified throughout this chapter, as it has been in other places in Proverbs (cf. Prov. 1:20-33; 3:14-18). Yet, what is described is best understood as an attribute of Christ that was actively a part of His work before the world began. Indeed, wisdom confesses, 'The Lord possessed me at the beginning of His way.' It would seem inappropriate for one member of the Trinity to speak of possessing another member of the Trinity (worse yet if the NIV's translation be adopted: 'The Lord brought me forth as the first of his works'!). However, if what is spoken of is an attribute of God, something that is true of Him, the language would be appropriate.

There has been widespread division over the translation of the verb standing behind our word 'possessed.' In its frequent use in the Old Testament, it almost universally has the sense of 'get' and, thus, 'possess.' In just a handful of instances can it mean 'create,' and, even there, the contexts do not require such a translation. Some have even suggested the meaning 'beget.'

The debate is long and heated, yet there appears here no reason to depart from the common meaning of the verb: 'possess.' Yet, this does not end the discussion. If one pushes for the root meaning 'to get,' one is left with the question of how God, who is before all things, might 'get' something which He did not either first create or which predated Him? Such discussion, while making for lively theological debate, nevertheless pushes the language of the present passage beyond its intent.[44]

Wisdom, as portrayed here, clearly predates all that is created. As such, she must be eternal, for she stands before the creation of time itself. She is eternal, however, not in some independent type of existence, but as one attribute of the eternal Godhead. Wisdom predates all we know in this world, and was fundamental to the creation of all we know (Prov. 3:19-20). How essential, then, to embrace God's wisdom, if we desire to live in God's world? How foolish to attempt to live in God's world without pursuing at all costs His fundamental principle of creating this world? 'O LORD, how many are Thy works! In wisdom Thou hast made them all' (Ps. 104:24).

8:23. 'From everlasting I was established, From the beginning, from the earliest times of the earth.'
Again, the eternality of wisdom is set forth. Note the piling up of words and concepts: 'everlasting,' 'the beginning,' 'the earliest times.' Wisdom predates history. It was in these far-reaching distances of eternity past that wisdom 'was established.' The verb is difficult and commentators have debated over its meaning. It appears to be used much as it is used in Psalm 2:6: 'But as for Me, I have installed My King Upon Zion, My holy mountain.' Interestingly, the second psalm is prophetic of Jesus Christ. The verb, then, does not have the idea of 'create,' but rather of divine appointment.

Wisdom is one of the attributes of God. One attribute of God is His simplicity; that is, that all God's attributes are one in Him. Wisdom is what God is. Eternal is what God is. Thus, it must be that wisdom has always resided in coexistive relationship with eternity. When employed, as here and other places in Proverbs, as a part of a personification, the attribute, which is truly indivisible from God since it is a description of His being, can begin to sound as though it has taken on a life all its own. The attribute can begin to sound like it is an independent being. Thus, the similarity of speech regarding wisdom and the Messiah (cf. John 1:1; Mic. 5:2; John 17:5) causes some to leap to conclusions that make the two identical. When we come to a faith relationship with Christ, the fullness of wisdom indwells us (Col. 2:3). But, to confuse the Being and the attribute is like confusing the silver with its luster or the gold with its gleam.

Rather than being drawn into debates about identifying wisdom with Jesus Christ, we ought to behold the wonder of God's wisdom. We ought to contemplate the intrinsic need for wisdom, if we are to reside in harmony with God in His creation. We ought to hunger and thirst to possess this wisdom, or, perhaps better, be possessed by this wisdom of God.

8:24. 'When there were no depths I was brought forth, When there were no springs abounding with water.'
What was stated succinctly in verse 22 is now developed at length (vv. 23-31): wisdom predates all creation. Verse 23 recounts the creation events of the first day: earth (Gen. 1:1-5). Here, it is the separation of the waters on the second day that is spoken

of (Gen. 1:6-8). The creation of land on day three is spoken of in verses 25-26 (Gen. 1:9-13).[45]

Wisdom speaks of her being 'Brought forth.' The verb is also used of the origin of the seas (Job 38:8-9), mountains (Prov. 8:25) and earth (Ps. 90:2). The literal meaning is 'born,' though it is, obviously, a figurative expression here.

In what sense can we speak of 'wisdom,' an attribute of God, being born? If it is truly an attribute of God, it must, of necessity, share in His eternal essence. An attribute is not something God takes to Himself. It is something He is in His fundamental nature. Perhaps we could speak of wisdom being 'born' not in an ontological sense, but in a functional sense. What would 'wisdom' have been called before the creation, before there was anything other than the eternal Triune Godhead? Is 'wisdom' simply one of God's other attributes viewed from the vantage point of the creation? Is it perhaps His intelligence, as it interacts with all He has created? This does not diminish wisdom or make it less than a true attribute of God. But, it does mean that, whatever particular attribute it is, it has been and only could be known as 'wisdom' from the vantage point of God's interaction with the created order. In this sense, it could be said that wisdom was 'born.'

8:25. 'Before the mountains were settled, Before the hills I was brought forth;'

Wisdom predates the events of the third day of creation as well. Here, we are told that 'the mountains were settled.' The verb means 'to sink.'[46] Today, we speak of 'sinking' the footings for a new building. Similarly, the notion here is that, when God created the earth, He settled the mountains upon a solid, seemingly immovable base (Job 38:6). This base (or pillars, Job 9:6; Ps. 75:3), presumably, extends under the oceans (Prov. 8:24; Jonah 2:6).

The key, however, is the repetition of the verb 'brought forth' from verse 24. Again, wisdom is seen as older than, and fundamental to, all that we know as reality. How desperately, therefore, do we need to acquire wisdom?

8:26. 'While He had not yet made the earth and the fields, Nor the first dust of the world.'

The 'mountains' and 'hills' of verse 25 are here paralleled with 'the earth and the fields' and 'the first dust of the world.' The emphasis is still upon the creation of terra firma. The words 'earth' and 'fields' are again found together in Job 5:10. The word translated 'dust' is in the plural, probably indicating each and every speck of dust that makes up the earth as we know it.[47] One can almost picture wisdom stooping and scooping up a handful of dry earth and, as the dust particles slip between her fingers, reminding us how she predates everything we know and depend upon for physical life here.

8:27. 'When He established the heavens, I was there, When He inscribed a circle on the face of the deep,'

Verses 24-26 emphasize wisdom's presence *before* the creation. Now, in verses 27-29, the stress is on her presence at creation.[48] Verses 27-28 return to the second day of creation and God's work at dividing the atmosphere and the oceans (Gen. 1:6-8). Note that, with her own mouth, wisdom confesses that 'He [God] established the heavens' and 'He [God] inscribed a circle on the face of the deep.' That is to say, the literary personification distinguishes herself from the One of whom she is an attribute.

The verb translated 'established' means 'to give a firm position or a definite direction.'[49] And the second verb translated 'inscribed' means to prescribe, measure off, consign and directly mark something out. The action is taken by the firm impressions made by an engraver's tool.[50]

The word 'circle' is found only two other times in the Old Testament, both of which are also in contexts describing the origin of the cosmos (Job 22:14; Isa. 40:22, but note the related form of the word in Job 26:10). The word can describe either that God established a boundary for the waters far in the distance, at some indefinable point, or at the line of the horizon. We who have been so trained to think in categories defined by the process of scientific investigation often try to press the language of the writers of Scripture beyond their intent. 'The poets of the OT describe their universe phenomenologically, i.e. as it appears to them standing on the earth and looking above and about. This perspective differs from that of modern scientific thought, which assumes a perspective beyond the earth. Both are accurate and useful according to their own perspectives.'[51]

8:28. 'When He made firm the skies above, When the springs of the deep became fixed,'

Wisdom continues to describe her role in creation, moving with downward references to individual parts of the creation event. Verses 28-29 move from the heavens to the seas, emphasizing wisdom's presence for the creation spectacle.

There is some struggle over the understanding of the verb in line one. The translation of the NASB is somewhat vague (what exactly does 'made firm' mean?), but gives the general sense of God's commanding craftsmanship over the atmospheric heavens. The second line reminds us that God commanded water to spring from the earth (Gen. 7:11; Prov. 3:20) and that wisdom was there as an eyewitness and participant.

8:29. 'When He set for the sea its boundary, So that the water should not transgress His command, When He marked out the foundations of the earth;'
Here, and in the next verse, we encounter unusual three line proverbs. Here, the first and second lines work together to make a complete thought, and the third stands more independently of the first two. God sat at the potter's wheel with the earth spinning before Him. He molded the earth so that the water and the land were separated, establishing shorelines for the oceans (Gen. 1:9; 7:11; 8:2; Job 38:8-11; Ps. 33:7; 104:9). Through the prophet Jeremiah, God asked: '"Do you not fear Me?" declares the LORD. "Do you not tremble in My presence? For I have placed the sand as a boundary for the sea, An eternal decree, so it cannot cross over it. Though the waves toss, yet they cannot prevail; Though they roar, yet they cannot cross over it"' (Jer. 5:22). Wisdom makes one, thus, fear the Lord, for she was there as an observer at this remarkable stage of creation!

The third line repeats the same line of thought, though it is in regard to the 'foundations of the earth.' Here God's questions to Job are the best commentary: 'Where were you when I laid the foundation of the earth? Tell Me, if you have understanding, Who set its measurements, since you know? Or who stretched the line on it? On what were its bases sunk? Or who laid its cornerstone, When the morning stars sang together, And all the sons of God shouted for joy?' (Job 38:4-7; cf. Prov. 3:19; Ps. 24:2). Wisdom humbles us before our Creator!

8:30. 'Then I was beside Him, as a master workman; And I was daily His delight, Rejoicing always before Him,'
Whereas verses 24-26 spoke of wisdom's presence before creation and verses 27-29 spoke of her presence at creation, now verses 30-31 tell us of her rejoicing over creation.[52] Wisdom's joy over God's creation is stated three times (v. 30, lines two and three, and v. 31). In the second line of this verse, the NASB's translation makes it sound as if God was delighting in wisdom ('I was daily His delight),

a meaning adopted by the LXX. This would seem to be an intrusive new idea, contrary to the focus of the context. One should note that 'His' is an interpretational addition of the translators. More literally, the Hebrew reads 'and I was delights.' Kidner and Murphy alike point out that the meaning may be 'I was happiness itself.'[53] We read elsewhere of God Himself rejoicing over His creation (Gen. 1:31). The angels of God rejoiced over the created order (Job 38:7). The attribute of wisdom, now personified, is added to the list. This joy was 'daily,' something that sounds like an echo of God's daily pronouncements of 'good' over His creation (Gen. 1:10, 12, 18, 21, 25, 31).[54]

A great deal of paper has been consumed in the debate as to the meaning of the expression 'a master workman.' Does this singular, and rare, Hebrew word mean something like 'workman' or 'craftsman' (NASB, NIV, RSV), or something more like 'nursling' or 'baby' (KJV, NEB)? Does it refer to wisdom at all, or could it be a reference to God Himself ('I was beside Him, the Craftsman)? These are the central questions, and they are old ones. While the arguments are lengthy on both sides, it appears best to go with the majority of translators and, on the weight of the use of the word in Song of Solomon 7:1 and Jeremiah 52:15, favor the translation 'workman' or 'craftsman.'[55] The suggestion that the word may describe God and not wisdom is a relatively new one in the history of the verse's interpretation. The argument is made that nowhere else is wisdom described as taking an active role in the creation.[56] But, read Proverbs 3:19: 'The LORD by wisdom founded the earth; By understanding He established the heavens.' It seems best to see the word as describing the nature of the attribute of God's wisdom in the creation.

Murphy notes that twice in this verse we are met by a startling 'I am' ('I was' here).[57] This sends one's mind streaming back to Exodus 3:14 where God revealed Himself as Yahweh – 'I am.' This sacred, ineffable Name was so to be revered that copyists refrained from writing it and no pious Jew would articulate the name, for fear of mispronouncing it. This untouchable Name is here echoed from wisdom's lips. But, it is not just echoed. She dares to speak of herself in the same phrases. The self-existent, covenant-making, and keeping, God of Israel is all wisdom!

8:31. 'Rejoicing in the world, His earth, And having my delight in the sons of men.'

The words translated 'Rejoicing' and 'delight' are the same ones used in verse 30. Their order is reversed, however, creating a chiastic pattern. When verse 30 is translated by something like 'baby' instead of 'workman,' some try to see these words as meaning 'play.' This, however, is a stretch, motivated more by an unfortunate translation of verse 30 than the meaning of these two Hebrew words.[58] 'Rejoicing,' in the piel form as here, describes someone's extreme rejoicing or playing musical instruments in jubilation. It is a word of celebration.[59] The word translated 'delight' simply describes something over which someone finds intense joy or bliss.[60]

Note that, here, the object of this intense delight and rejoicing is man. Man is the pinnacle of creation, sharing in the very image of God (Gen. 1:26-28). Thus, the highest joy is evoked by the highest creation. As the only one of God's created beings made in His own image, man is unique in his ability to understand, share in, and appreciate God's wisdom. Thus there is a reciprocal rejoicing – wisdom in man, man in wisdom.

8:32. 'Now therefore, O sons, listen to me, For blessed are they who keep my ways.'

Wisdom's first person address that has been underway since verse 4 is now being brought to a conclusion (vv. 32-36). That these applications are based on what has preceded is clearly seen by the 'Now therefore' that heads this verse. This verse and the next contain exhortations. The justification for these commands is then given in verses 34-36.

Wisdom here takes up themes already familiar in the Proverbs and normally used by Solomon. The call 'O sons' has been echoed often thus far, normally from Solomon's mouth (cf. Prov. 1:8, 10, 15, etc.). Similarly, the command to 'listen' is not unfamiliar (cf. Prov. 1:8; 4:1, 10, etc.). Often, we have heard of the 'ways' of wisdom (Prov. 2:8, 20; 3:17, 23, etc.). Nor is the exhortation to 'keep' the ways of wisdom new (Prov. 1:15; 2:20; 4:4, etc.).

The promise is that those who fully embrace the woman wisdom will be 'blessed.' The word sends one's mind racing to similar promises in Scriptures such as Psalm 1:1; 32:2; 34:8; 40:4; Proverbs 28:14; Isaiah 56:2, and even Jesus' own beatitudes (Matt. 5:3-12). The blessing is not so much a subjective state of euphoric emotion, but the objective state of walking rightly before God and thus having His smile upon you.[61] The state of 'blessedness' is not so much emotional as it is factual, but the true recognition of these facts surely evokes much emotion.

8:33. 'Heed instruction and be wise, And do not neglect it.'

The Hebrew word translated 'Heed' is the same as that rendered 'listen' in verse 32. The word for 'instruction' has also become stock language in these proverbs (Prov. 1:2, 3, 7, 8; 3:11; 4:1, 13, etc.). The root of the word rendered 'neglect' has the meaning of 'to let loose' and can refer to the unbraiding or cutting of long hair. It also can refer to allowing something to run wild. Yet, the meaning here, as in several other places in Proverbs (Prov. 1:25; 13:18; 15:32), is to let something slip through your fingers by way of neglect.[62]

8:34. 'Blessed is the man who listens to me, Watching daily at my gates, Waiting at my doorposts.'

This verse has much in common with verse 32. The pronouncement 'Blessed' is again intoned over the one faithful to Lady Wisdom, and the words 'listen' and 'waiting' ('keep,' v. 32) are repeated also. In fact, what we discover is an alternation of terms from verses 32 through 34: 'Listen' (v. 32), 'blessed' (v. 32), 'listen' (v. 33), 'Blessed' (v. 34), 'listens' (v. 34).[63] The wise quickly understand that paying close attention to and obeying God's ways leads to a life full of joy, peace and the favor of God. Conversely, what is implicit here, and becomes explicit in verse 35, is that a life of disregard toward and distraction from God's ways leads to pain, struggle and frustration.

The second and third lines of this verse are virtually synonymous. Here, the picture is of a lover anxiously waiting at the door of his beloved, anticipating her return (cf. Song of Sol. 2:8-10). Contrast the exhortation to stay far away from the door of the adulteress (Prov. 5:8). We must pursue wisdom, seeking her company and her companionship.

8:35. 'For he who finds me finds life, And obtains favor from the LORD.'

As verses 32-34 hang together thematically, so verses 35-36 cohere around contrasting themes: 'life' and 'favor' (v. 35), on the one hand, and 'injures' and 'death' (v. 36), on the other hand. The theme of 'life' is a common one in Proverbs (Prov. 3:2, 18; 4:4, 13, 22-23; 7:2; 9:11; 10:17; 19:23; 21:21) as is 'favor' (Prov. 3:4; 12:2; 18:22). The word for 'favor' means 'pleasure,' 'delight,' and 'favor.' This noun and its companion verb have a wide range of meaning, but find their primary importance as the most common expressions for God's preceptive will.[64]

How can one who reads Proverbs fail to see this life or death summons? 'I call heaven and earth to witness against you today, that I have set before you life and death, the blessing and the curse. So choose life in order that you may live, you and your descendants' (Deut. 30:19).

8:36. 'But he who sins against me injures himself; All those who hate me love death.'

The dark side of the contrast with verse 35 is now presented. Note the contrast of 'finds' (v. 35) and 'sins' (or 'misses,' v. 36). The translation 'sins' is accurate, for that is its most frequent meaning in the Old Testament. Yet, its root idea is that of missing something after which you run, seek or shoot.[65] Thus, sin is often described as 'missing the mark.' Here the older notion is clearly in view as the contrast with 'finds' (v. 35) reveals. The RSV represents this last antithesis well: 'he who finds me ... he who misses me.'

We also find here the negative side of the 'love' (v. 35) and 'hate' (v. 36) antithesis. These words may carry great emotional overtones in our language which they did not necessarily convey in the Hebrew of the time. The notion is more one of willful choice rather than emotional response.[66] We have been told that wisdom 'is a tree of life' (Prov. 3:18). Thus, to choose another path is to choose death. At the hour of decision, one may not consciously think he is opting for death, but that is where the pathway opposite of wisdom leads (Prov. 1:28-33; 5:12, 23; 7:27). Truly, such a one 'injures himself.'

What claims Wisdom has made for herself in this eighth chapter! Breathe deeply and think again of all she has laid credit to for herself. How seriously one must take Wisdom's invitation to draw near her! How carefully one must choose his path! Everything is at stake in our choice!

End Notes

1. Ross, Allen P., 'Proverbs,' *The Expositor's Bible Commentary* (Grand Rapids, Michigan: Zondervan Publishing House, 1991), 5:943.

2. Kidner, Derek, *Proverbs* (Downers Grove, Illinois: InterVarsity Press, 1964), 76-77.

3. Ibid., 40-41.

4. Ross, 5:906.

5. Goldberg, Louis, 'bîn,' *Theological Wordbook of the Old Testament* (Chicago: Moody Press, 1980), 1:103-104.

6. Aitken, Kenneth T., 'נָגִיד,' *New International Dictionary of Old Testament Theology and Exegesis* (Grand Rapids, Michigan: Zondervan Publishing House, 1997), 3:20.

7. Olivier, Hannes, 'ישׁר' *New International Dictionary of Old Testament Theology and Exegesis* (Grand Rapids, Michigan: Zondervan Publishing House, 1997), 2:567.

8. Ross, 5:916.

9. Wolf, Herbert, 'hāgâ,' *Theological Wordbook of the Old Testament* (Chicago: Moody Press, 1980), 1:205.

10. Carpenter, Eugene and Michael A. Grisanti, 'רשׁע,' *New International Dictionary of Old Testament Theology and Exegesis* (Grand Rapids, Michigan: Zondervan Publishing House, 1997), 3:1201.

11. Whybray, 100.

12. Stigers, Harold G., 'ṣādēq,' *Theological Wordbook of the Old Testament* (Chicago: Moody Press, 1980), 2:752-755.

13. Whybray, 71.

14. Delitzsch, F., *Proverbs, Ecclesiastes, Song of Solomon* (three volumes in one) in C. F. Keil and F. Delitzsch, vol. 6, *Commentary on the Old Testament* (in ten volumes), (1872; rpt. Grand Rapids, Michigan: William B. Eerdmans Publishing Company, 1980), 1:176.

15. Ibid.

16. Wilson, Marvin R., 'nkh,' *Theological Wordbook of the Old Testament* (Chicago: Moody Press, 1980), 2:579.

17. Olivier, Hannes, 'יֹשֶׁר,' *New International Dictionary of Old Testament Theology and Exegesis* (Grand Rapids, Michigan: Zondervan Publishing House, 1997), 2:563.

18. Goldberg, Louis, 'bîn,' *Theological Wordbook of the Old Testament* (Chicago: Moody Press, 1980), 1:103-104.

19. Murphy, Roland E., *Proverbs* (Nashville: Thomas Nelson Publishers, 1998), 50.

20. Gilchrist, Paul R., 'yāsar,' *Theological Wordbook of the Old Testament* (Chicago: Moody Press, 1980), 1:386-387.

21. Ross, 5:907.

22. Goldberg, Louis, 'ḥākam,' *Theological Wordbook of the Old Testament* (Chicago: Moody Press, 1980), 1:282-284.

23. Whybray, 67.

24. Wood, Leon J., 'ḥāpēṣ,' *Theological Wordbook of the Old Testament* (Chicago: Moody Press, 1980), 1:310-311.

25. Ross, 5:907.

26. Luc, A., 'עָרַם,' *New International Dictionary of Old Testament Theology and Exegesis* (Grand Rapids, Michigan: Zondervan Publishing House, 1997), 3:539-541.

27. Grisanti, Michael A., 'מצא,' *New International Dictionary of Old Testament Theology and Exegesis* (Grand Rapids, Michigan: Zondervan Publishing House, 1997), 2:1061-1063.

28. Delitzsch, 1:177.

29. Van Groningen, Gerard, 'śānē',' *Theological Wordbook of the Old Testament* (Chicago: Moody Press, 1980), 2:879-880.

30. Hamilton, Victor P., 'gā'â,' *Theological Wordbook of the Old Testament* (Chicago: Moody Press, 1980), 1:143-144.

31. Kidner, 78.

32. Whybray, 125.

33. Goldberg, Louis, 'yshh,' *Theological Wordbook of the Old Testament* (Chicago: Moody Press, 1980), 1:413.

34. Brown, Driver and Briggs, 108.

35. Whybray, 125.

36. Whybray, 126.

37. Murphy, 51.

38. Smith, Gary V. and Paul D. Wegner, 'עתק,' *New International Dictionary of Old Testament Theology and Exegesis* (Grand Rapids, Michigan: Zondervan Publishing House, 1997), 3:570.

39. Allen, Ronald B., '"atēq,' *Theological Wordbook of the Old Testament* (Chicago: Moody Press, 1980), 2:708.

40. Sunukjian, Donald R., 'Amos,' *The Bible Knowledge Commentary* (Victor Books, 1985), 1:1439.

41. Buzzell, Sid S., 'Proverbs,' *The Bible Knowledge Commentary* (Wheaton: Victor Books, 1985), 1:922.

42. Leonard J. Coppes, 'nāhal,' *Theological Wordbook of the Old Testament* (Chicago:

Moody Press, 1980), 2:569-570.

43. Hartley, John E., '*yēsh*,' *Theological Wordbook of the Old Testament* (Chicago: Moody Press, 1980), 1:411.

44. Whybray, 129-130.

45. MacArthur, John, ed., *The MacArthur Study Bible* (Nashville: Word Bibles, 1997), 888.

46. Whybray, 132.

47. Whybray, 133.

48. Ross, 5:946.

49. Delitzsch, 188.

50. Ibid.

51. Yamauchi, Edwin, '*hûg*,' *Theological Wordbook of the Old Testament* (Chicago: Moody Press, 1980), 1:266-267.

52. Ross, 5:946.

53. Kidner, 81 and Murphy, 53.

54. Ross, 5:946.

55. Cornelius, I., 'אָמַן,' *New International Dictionary of Old Testament Theology and Exegesis* (Grand Rapids, Michigan: Zondervan Publishing House, 1997), 1:433-434.

56. Whybray, 134-136.

57. Murphy, 52-53.

58. Ibid., 136.

59. Payne, J. Barton, '*sāhaq*,' *Theological Wordbook of the Old Testament* (Chicago: Moody Press, 1980), 2:763-764.

60. Carew, Douglas and James D. Price, 'שׁעע,' *New International Dictionary of Old Testament Theology and Exegesis* (Grand Rapids, Michigan: Zondervan Publishing House, 1997), 4:204-208.

61. Ross, 5:919.

62. Hamilton, Victor P., '*pāra',*' *Theological Wordbook of the Old Testament* (Chicago: Moody Press, 1980), 2:736-737.

63. Buzzell, 1:923.

64. White, William, '*rāsâ*,' *Theological Wordbook of the Old Testament* (Chicago: Moody Press, 1980), 2:859-860.

65. Delitzsch, 1:195.

66. Murphy, 54.

Proverbs 9

9:1. Wisdom has built her house, She has hewn out her seven pillars;

This ninth chapter forms a fitting conclusion to the first eight chapters of Proverbs by contrastingly presenting both the Woman Wisdom (vv. 1-6) and the Woman Folly (vv. 13-18). The two vignettes are highly symmetrical. The general invitation of both is quoted (vv. 4-6, 16-17) and the contrasting ends of life (v. 6) and death (v. 18) are offered in conclusion. In addition, both have prepared a meal (vv. 2, 17), both call from a high point to attract attention (vv. 3, 14) and their opening invitations in verses 4 and 16 are nearly identical. Both wisdom and folly are pictured as having homes (vv. 1, 14). Wisdom 'has built' her house (cf. Prov. 14:1), while folly is pictured as merely sitting (v. 14). Both invite men to enter their house (vv. 4, 16; cf. 7:8; 8:34).

Verses 7-12 remind the reader that the difference between listening to wisdom or folly is found in one's response to reproof.

Wisdom is here in the plural form with a singular verb. This unusual plural is probably used in some intensive way to present the fullness, pre-eminence or honorableness of wisdom. This plural form is found only here and in Proverbs 1:20; 24:7 and Psalm 49:3.[1]

The reference to 'seven pillars' has provoked many varied and highly creative interpretations. It likely designates it as a house large enough to welcome all who will turn in or, to treat it symbolically, it may point to the perfection of the environment wisdom builds.

9:2. She has prepared her food, she has mixed her wine; She has also set her table;

Within her home, Lady Wisdom has set a banquet table to which she will invite all who will come (vv. 3, 4). With vivid metaphor, Solomon pictures the banquet hall set for those who will take up wisdom's offer. The first picture is that she 'has prepared her food.' Literally, the Hebrew says she 'has slaughtered her slaughter.' In other words, she has slain the best among her herds and offers it now to those who will come. The slaughter of animals and offer of meat marks the occasion as one considered especially noteworthy.

The second picture is that 'she has mixed her wi~ ' Th~~ i debate about what she mixes the wine with and wh, the wine was mixed with water (as much as eight parts v. part wine, or more) in order to make it palatable. Wine was reg~ mixed with water as a means of purifying it for human consumption.~ It also cut the intoxicating qualities, for unmixed wine was considered strong drink among the Hebrews, and that was an abomination (Prov. 20:1; 31:4, 6; Isa. 5:11, 22; 24:9). It is also possible that the wine was mixed with spices to add flavoring and make it a more festive drink (Song of Sol 8:2). Whatever the conclusion about what 'mixed wine' means, it obviously involved work and extensive preparation.

The third picture of wisdom's banquet is seen in that she 'has also set her table.' The phrase is used to describe unrolling a tablecloth, bringing out the dishes and arranging the table so as to be presentable for those invited to eat the meal.[3]

These metaphors are employed to picture the rich nourishment of soul and life that wisdom offers freely to all who will seek her and live by her. It is a royal treat to live a life of wisdom. The supply of practical, daily help will never run dry. A life of wisdom leads to a life rich in God's blessing.

9:3. She has sent out her maidens, she calls From the tops of the heights of the city:

Wisdom again lifts her voice and calls to those who will hear. She has royal servants to carry her invitation (cf. Matt 22:2-3). While she dispatches her couriers with the party announcements, they know well whom they serve. The Hebrew text clearly declares that 'she calls,' the form being the feminine singular. Although she sends multiple maidens out, it is her invitation that is sounded. They speak on her behalf and with her authority. None other than wisdom herself is calling the undeserving to her banquet table of rich understanding and knowledge.

This is no exclusive, highbrow party, however. The invitation to come find wisdom is given publicly and indiscriminately. We have already seen that the wisdom of God is not afraid to weigh in on public discourse or roll up her sleeves and get to work in the streets, homes and workplaces of everyday life (cf. Prov. 1:20-21; 8:1-3). The Woman Folly is not reticent about making her call open and public (v. 14), and wisdom finds no need to be ashamed to do so either (Matt. 22:9; John 18:20).

Could it be that you and I serve, on occasion, as one of wisdom's 'maidens'? 'For this reason also the wisdom of God said, "I will send

to them prophets and apostles ..."' (Luke 11:49). Is God calling you
to sound the invitation to come to Him to find the wisdom, insight
and knowledge necessary to survive and thrive in the world He has
created? If so, it is God Himself who speaks through you!

9:4. 'Whoever is naïve, let him turn in here!' To him who lacks understanding she says,

Now, once again, we hear from wisdom herself. She clears her
throat and issues her invitation, running through verse 6. Of note
immediately is that those invited stand in contrast to the fastidious
preparations made. The invitation is to the 'naïve' and 'him who lacks
understanding.' The 'naïve' are those who are open and vulnerable
to any and all influences because they lack life experience. They
are not hardened fools or confirmed rebels. They simply lack good
judgment and are not observant of signs for caution (cf. Prov. 1:4).
The words 'him who lacks understanding' are, literally, 'one lacking
heart' (see comments on Prov. 7:7). The phrase is equivalent to calling
such a one a 'fool.'

The invitation for this banquet is not prepared based upon what
a person has, but on what a person lacks. You do not have to possess
superior intelligence to be wise, simply awareness that you do not
yet possess it and a hunger to discover it. Note that virtually an
identical invitation is given by the Woman Folly in verse 16.

9:5. 'Come, eat of my food, And drink of the wine I have mixed.'

The metaphor continues as the banquet table is set and the
invitation is received. Such invitation imagery has always been
appropriate to reflect God's offer to man (Isa. 55:1-3; Luke 14:16-24;
Rev. 22:17). The picture of eating and drinking reflects the nature
of appropriating or internalizing God's wisdom. One must
so completely take in God's wisdom that it becomes the very
substance of who and what one is. While the imagery is simple,
the implications are searching. Jesus made similar such claims
about Himself (John 6:27, 35, 51, 55). The result was that 'Many
therefore of His disciples, when they heard this said, "This is a
difficult statement; who can listen to it?"' (John 6:60). Blessed is
the one who understands and enters in.

The food and wine here stand in contrast to the stolen water and
secret bread folly offers in verse 17 (cf. Prov. 4:17). The first (wisdom)
nourishes the inner man, bringing life (v. 6); the second (folly) brings
death (v. 18).

9:6. 'Forsake your folly and live, And proceed in the way of understanding.'

Now, so there is no misunderstanding the metaphorical intent of the banquet scene, the writer makes clear the purpose of this word picture.

The demand is to 'Forsake your folly.' The word 'folly' is an unusual plural of the word 'naïve' found in verse 4. There, the invitation is to come to wisdom's banquet of life. Here, the invitation is turned into a life or death imperative. In this context, the word is often translated 'simple ways' (NIV) or, as some suggest and is possible, 'simple ones.' The first would suggest the naïve patterns of living and habits of life the simple have adopted and which are counter-productive to a pursuit of wisdom. The latter would suggest that the naïve must break off from their companions in silliness lest they be dragged down to ever-increasing foolishness (Prov. 1:22). Both notions are taught elsewhere in Scripture and either would be appropriate here. However, the translation 'simple ways' is probably best, since it maintains the parallelism with the second line of the verse: 'the way of understanding.'

The call of wisdom brings each of us to a fork in the road of life. Will we 'forsake' the way of the simple and 'proceed' in the way of understanding? Whose voice will we listen to: the Woman Wisdom (vv. 4-6) or the Woman Folly (vv. 16-17)? The choice is ours to make. The consequences are ours to bear.

The desirable option is to choose wisdom and 'live' (cf. Prov. 3:2, 18; 4:4; 7:2; 8:35; 9:11; 19:23). To continue the metaphor, such a one will indeed 'live,' for the meal has been prepared from a tree of life (Prov. 3:18; 11:30; 13:12; 15:4).

9:7. He who corrects a scoffer gets dishonor for himself, And he who reproves a wicked man gets insults for himself.

A clear transition takes place at this verse. The function of verses 7-12 have been much debated, leading to many fanciful theories concerning the authenticity of this section. The major concern is over its relation to the two, clearly parallel, sections in verses 1-6 and verses 13-18. But it is much ado about nothing. The chapter opens with the call of the woman Wisdom (vv. 1-6) and closes with the contrasting call of the woman Folly (vv. 13-18). What we find sandwiched between those two invitations is an example of the kind of response each invitation finds: verses 7-8a describes the scoffer's response to correction, while verses 8b-9 describes the wise man's response to a rebuke. The following verses of the section (vv. 10-12) highlight the theme of the entire book (v. 10) and the benefits of choosing wisdom (vv. 11-12). This section, then, is no interruption, but a necessary and integral part of the entire chapter.

We have already met the 'scoffer' in Proverbs 1:22. The 'scoffer' is a simpleton (v. 6) that has been confirmed in his foolishness. The 'scoffer' cannot stomach the correction and discipline that is so much a part of the way of instruction in wisdom (Prov. 1:30; 13:1: 15:12). He is independent and wants no restraint on his thinking or actions. God will one day scoff at the scoffer (Prov. 3:34). The 'simple' must beware, for it is a slippery slope that descends through the degrees of foolishness recounted in Proverbs. The final end is described as 'the scoffer.' Indeed, a 'scoffer' is synonymous with 'a wicked man.'

The one who would dare to reprove such a one gets 'dishonor' and 'insults' in return. The word for 'dishonor' describes the derisive contempt and disregard with which the 'scoffer' treats the well-intentioned efforts of the reprover.[4] It is, however, not simply personal rebuff that is the price of rebuking such a one. You will also gather to yourself 'insults.' The word, literally, describes a blotch, defect, or stain.[5] The 'scoffer' will turn like a wild animal upon the one trying to rescue it from a snare. He will seek to ruin you socially, as well as wound you personally. He may denounce you publicly, initiate a ruinous rumor concerning you or spread blatant lies about you – but you will end with a blotch or stain upon your public persona. And that is the price for trying to rescue one caught in the vortex of foolishness.

9:8. Do not reprove a scoffer, lest he hate you, Reprove a wise man, and he will love you.
To 'reprove' someone is a powerful thing. The word has strong judicial and forensic connections. It can mean to decide, judge and prove. It is a word found often in courtroom contexts. This same word is then used to describe the action of reproving, rebuking or correcting one that has gone astray.[6] Little wonder, then, that the 'scoffer' has no time for the person who takes this tack with him. In fact, the scoffer will 'hate' you for such righteous judgments. This 'hate' can have the sense of deep-seated negative emotions, but the idea is more clearly that of flat rejection of a person or thing. Note Proverbs 5:12, where hate is made synonymous with turning away reproof: 'And you say, "How I have hated instruction! And my heart spurned reproof!"' A similar contrast is seen in Proverbs 1:29: 'Because they hated knowledge, And did not choose the fear of the Lord.' Here, hate is the opposite of choosing or embracing the fear of the Lord. Thus, a scoffer may say,

'I don't hate you' (meaning they don't hold a deep emotional dislike toward you) and mean it. But, their rejection of God's reproof through you is 'hate' in this biblical sense (cf. 1 Kings 22:8).

On the other hand, the same action of reproof will draw a markedly different response from one who possesses some kernel of wisdom. When confronted, exposed and judged by your rebuke, the wise man will 'love' you. This, too, may not necessarily speak of overflowing positive emotion, but has more to do with accepting, embracing and learning from the truth as you have presented it. Indeed, a rebuke will likely unsettle the emotions and make one uncomfortable in your presence, but the wise one will hear the truth and recognize in it the gift of life from God. Frequently, this notion of 'love' and 'hate' as acceptance and rejection are set over against one another (Prov. 1:22; 8:36; 12:1; 13:24; 14:20).

What was a general principle in verse 7 has now become a clear prohibition in verse 8. It is not only a waste of time and an opportunity for personal heartache to reprove a scoffer, it is wrong. 'Do not give what is holy to dogs, and do not throw your pearls before swine, lest they trample them under their feet, and turn and tear you to pieces' (Matt. 7:6).

9:9. Give instruction to a wise man, and he will be still wiser, Teach a righteous man, and he will increase his learning.
The first line is, literally, 'Give to a wise man and he will be more wise.' What is given is clearly 'instruction' (added interpretively by the NASB). This is clear from the context and the fact that 'Teach' is held in parallel in line two.

It is a teachable spirit that makes the difference between wisdom and foolishness. 'The wise of heart will receive commands ... knowledge is easy to him who has understanding ... he who listens to reproof acquires understanding' (Prov. 10:8a; 14:6b; 15:32b). 'When the scoffer is punished, the naïve becomes wise; But when the wise is instructed, he receives knowledge' (Prov. 21:11).

It is significant to note that 'a wise man' and 'a righteous man' are paralleled in the two lines of this verse. Wisdom is more than esoteric philosophy. It transforms the moral nature and conforms one's conduct to that new nature. Likewise, righteousness is far more than moralisms and legalistic rules. It involves the ability to insightfully weigh every option from God's vantage point (cf. 'the fear of the Lord' in the next verse). Often, these Proverbs hold righteousness and wisdom together as inseparable (Prov. 1:3; 10:31; 11:30; 23:24).

The one who is wise will ever advance in that direction. The storehouse of God's wisdom is inexhaustible. God's promise still stands: 'For whoever has, to him shall more be given, and he shall have an abundance; but whoever does not have, even what he has shall be taken away from him' (Matt. 13:12; cf. 25:29). The wise will become rich in wisdom. The scoffer will only become more beggared in what really matters.

9:10. The fear of the LORD is the beginning of wisdom, And the knowledge of the Holy One is understanding.
Here, again, the main theme of the book is sounded. Proverbs 1:7 and 9:10 form an inclusio. Serving as bookends on either side of the first nine chapters, these two statements set off this section as a distinct and complete unit.

The 'fear of the Lord' is an oft-repeated refrain in Proverbs (Prov. 1:7, 29; 2:5; 8:13; 10:27; 14:26, 27; 15:16, 33; 16:6; 19:23; 22:4; 23:17). To the unredeemed, this 'fear' is the terror of having fallen into the hands of the living God (Heb. 10:31). To the child of God, this 'fear' is not terror, but a reverential awe that holds his heavenly Father in highest honor. At its heart is an attitude of submissive worship. This heart attitude is 'the beginning of wisdom.' The word translated 'beginning' here is a different one from that found in Proverbs 1:7. There, 'beginning' signified the starting point and controlling principle of all spiritual knowledge. Here, 'beginning' has the idea of that which is the first of a series of events or ideas.[7] It might even have the notion of being the prerequisite to all true wisdom.[8]

Wisdom will not be had without knowing God (Job 28:28; Ps. 111:10; Prov. 2:4-6; Eccles. 12:13). The second line echoes this same thought. Here, 'the Holy One' is actually a plural form without the article, eliciting a translation of 'holy ones' by some. This, however, appears to be the so-called 'plural of majesty,' in which the plural is employed to express the fullness of the idea being set forth. That this is a reference to God is clear from the parallel in line one ('LORD'), and that this is emphasizing His complete holiness is seen in the plural form. The same meaning results from this form in Proverbs 30:3 and Hosea 11:12.

9:11. For by me your days will be multiplied, And years of life will be added to you.
One supporting reason is given to back up the veracity of the propositions of verse 10. Note that we return to the first-person

address of Lady Wisdom. Perhaps it should be treated as a supporting quotation from what she has already promised earlier in the book (cf. Prov. 3:2, 16, 18; 4:10, 13; 8:35; 9:6; cf. also 10:27; 14:27; 15:24; 19:23). A life of obedience brings one under Divine protection and ensures life and strength to fulfill all of His will (cf. Deut. 6:2).

Note the mathematical words employed. To us, 'multiplied' and 'added' do not mean the same thing. Things grow more slowly by simple addition, but exponential growth comes when things are multiplied. It is, however, doubtful that such twenty-first-century Western precision was intended by Solomon. He simply means that, all things being equal, a person who seeks and lives by God's wisdom will live significantly longer than they would have if they pursued a life of selfish sin.

9:12. If you are wise, you are wise for yourself, And if you scoff, you alone will bear it.

A stronger statement of individual responsibility would be hard to find. Each one must choose for or against wisdom and each one will bear the burden of his choice. This is not to deny the clear teaching of Scripture that our sin affects others and that theirs affects us. Nor does it deny that there are residual effects of walking in wisdom that accrue to one's companions (1 Cor. 7:14). But, in the final analysis, each man stands alone before God. Each person accrues interest to himself for what he has done (2 Cor. 5:10; Prov. 14:10). 'But let each one examine his own work, and then he will have reason for boasting in regard to himself alone, and not in regard to another. For each one shall bear his own load' (Gal. 6:4, 5). 'The person who sins will die. The son will not bear the punishment for the father's iniquity, nor will the father bear the punishment for the son's iniquity; the righteousness of the righteous will be upon himself, and the wickedness of the wicked will be upon himself' (Ezek. 18:20).

This NASB translation is highly literal, the NIV has chosen a more interpretive paraphrase of the first line: 'If you are wise, your wisdom will reward you.' This, of course, builds on the idea of reward that is inherent in the verse, but it obscures the parallelism between 'for yourself' and 'you alone.'

9:13. The woman of folly is boisterous, She is naïve, and knows nothing.

The 'woman of folly' of verses 13-18 stands in bold contrast to Lady Wisdom (vv. 1-6). Both women have prepared a feast and are inviting people to it. That is where the similarities end. The word 'folly' is found only here, but is the feminine form of the more common masculine form usually translated as 'fool' (cf. Prov. 1:7, 29; 10:1; 14:8, etc.).[9]

Three things are said to describe this woman. To begin with she is 'boisterous.' The word has already been used, in Proverbs 1:21, to describe the streets of the city and, in 7:11, to describe the harlot. The word describes that which is loud, turbulent, full of unrest and commotion.[10]

Secondly, she is 'naïve.' This, too, is the only time this word is found in Proverbs, but it comes from the more common root most often translated 'naïve.' It describes one who is simple-minded, gullible, silly and open to any, and all, influences. The 'woman of folly' is no better off than those she solicits (cf. Prov. 9:16). Both Lady Wisdom and the 'woman of folly' call to the 'naïve' (vv. 4, 16), but Lady Wisdom promises to take them forward into understanding (v. 6) while the 'woman of folly' leaves them mired in their foolishness.

Thirdly, it is said that she 'knows nothing.' This phrase has proven notoriously difficult to translate. Literally, the Hebrew reads 'and she knows not what,' a somewhat vague and unclear statement. Most older translations have taken 'what' to mean 'anything' or, as here in the NASB, 'nothing.' Thus it signifies complete ignorance. The RSV has emended it to a word meaning 'shame.' But, this seems unnecessary and the sense of complete ignorance should stand.[11]

This personification of foolishness invites her victims to a loud life of riotous partying, without thought of the consequences and without ability to calculate what it will cost them.

9:14. And she sits at the doorway of her house, On a seat by the high places of the city,

Compare the demeanor and tactics of the 'woman of folly' (vv. 13-18) with that of Lady Wisdom (vv. 1-6). Folly, like wisdom, has a prominent place at 'the high places of the city' (cf. Prov. 8:2; 9:3). She intends to stake her claim on public life and discourse. Folly wants to win the day in markets, streets and homes. Unlike wisdom, however, folly merely 'sits at the doorway of her house.' Wisdom is active, building her house (v. 1), making meticulous preparations for those who will come to her (v. 2). Wisdom has proactively commissioned messengers to penetrate the work-a-day world of people with her invitation (Prov. 9:3-4).

Folly's inactivity smacks of laziness. She is not about to serve, but intends only on garnering servants for herself. Indeed, the word translated 'a seat' is found 136 times in the Old Testament, all but seven of which are translated 'throne' (cf. Prov. 16:12; 20:8, 28; 25:5; 29:14).[12] She wants to establish a tyrannical rule of foolishness over the lives of the unsuspecting and naïve.

Already we have been warned often of the dangers of drawing near the 'house' of the adulteress and harlot (Prov. 2:18; 5:8; 7:8, 11, 19, 20, 27). Now, we must beware of the abode of folly personified.

9:15. Calling to those who pass by, Who are making their paths straight:

Folly raises her raucous voice to turn aside those who are on the path of life. The concept of a call going out from wisdom has been prominent in these opening chapters of Proverbs (Prov. 1:21, 24, 28; 8:1, 4; 9:3). But, now, it is Folly who raises her voice to woo, whistle, and allure unsuspecting travelers. They are merely 'those who pass by.' They are on their way, carrying out life's responsibilities and pursuing life's joys. Not all are so pure in their objectives – some seek her out (Prov. 7:8). 'Avoid it, do not pass by it; Turn away from it and pass on' (Prov. 4:15), is still God's counsel regarding the ways of wickedness.

Yet, Folly has a sinister plan that involves also these more innocent ones. Now, she seeks to recruit them. They are those who 'are making their paths straight.' That can mean either that they are living in an upright way, or that they simply have an objective in mind and are intent on pursuing and achieving it. Either way there lies a foe named Folly along their path and they must be wary of her. 'Folly is joy to him who lacks sense, But a man of understanding walks straight' (Prov. 15:21).

9:16. 'Whoever is naïve, let him turn in here,' And to him who lacks understanding she says,

The appeal of folly, like that of wisdom, goes to 'Whoever is naïve' and 'him who lacks understanding' (cf. v. 4, which see for explanation of the terms). The content of her invitation awaits the next verse.

That the entreaty of wisdom and folly are nearly identical ought not arouse concern. Men have always wanted the shell of sophistication without the substance. The world has its vain philosophies and inverted wisdom (1 Cor. 3:19; Col. 2:8) in order to pacify the hunger wrought for true wisdom by the Creator. Where the wisdom of God is rejected, the appeal of folly is taken up unexamined because it appeals to pride and independence. The fool can maintain a facade of spirituality, because his folly is often dressed in the guise of divine wisdom.

9:17. 'Stolen water is sweet; And bread eaten in secret is pleasant.'
Here, now, is the actual verbal enticement of folly. It is strange that her enticement includes not only the promise of sensual pleasures fulfilled, but also an admission of the illicit nature of the way they will be obtained.

The fare at the banquet of folly seems to pale in comparison to that offered at the table of wisdom (cf. v. 2). The 'water' of folly momentarily tastes sweeter than the 'wine' of wisdom, but only because it is stolen. The pleasure of sin procured at the risk of being caught is more intense simply because of the gamble of being found out. The greater the risk, the more intense the momentary thrill, but also the more damaging the long-term effects.

Proverbs has already used the drinking of water as a euphemism for the marital sexual relationship (Prov. 5:15-20). For this reason, 'Stolen water' and 'bread eaten in secret' may be metaphorical references to immoral sexual behavior (Prov. 7:18; 30:20). The same word here translated 'secret' is used of David's immoral relationship with Bathsheba (2 Sam. 12:12).

'And the eyes of the adulterer waits for the twilight, Saying, "No eye will see me."' (Job 24:15). Yet, 'His eyes are on their ways' (Job 24:23b). Nothing is truly hidden from God (Heb. 4:13). Indeed, the fleeting sweetness of illicit pleasures will soon turn to enduring bitterness. 'Though evil is sweet in his mouth, And he hides it under his tongue, Though he desires it and will not let it go, But holds it in his mouth, Yet his food in his stomach is changed To the venom of cobras within him' (Job 20:12-14). 'Bread obtained by falsehood is sweet to a man, But afterward his mouth will be filled with gravel' (Prov. 20:17; cf. Isa. 5:20).

9:18. But he does not know that the dead are there, That her guests are in the depths of Sheol.
Here, all the warnings of wisdom throughout chapters 1–9, as well as the contrast set forth here in Proverbs 9:1-6 and 13-18, are brought to a fitting climax. The invitation of folly has been intoned (vv. 16-17). Out in the street, her promises of pleasures untold bind and draw the simple. Despite the risks, all seems safe. Only unfettered indulgence has captured the imagination.

But, beyond her seductive lines in the street lies the inner chamber of her banquet hall. Once entered, there is no exit. There, one finds company only with the dead. The path that appeared strewn with sensual pleasures has become the wide avenue leading to death.

The ones who thought to consume sensual delicacies discover that it is they who are being consumed by death and descending into the very throat of hell itself. The contrast of the 'way' of wisdom and the 'way' of folly, developed throughout these first nine chapters, is now laid bare to be seen in all its hideous reality.

Death is the reward for the one foolish enough to pursue folly, just as it is of the one who embraces the adulteress (Prov. 2:18, 19; 5:5, 6; 7:21-23, 26, 27). The outcome of the fool stands in stark contrast to the 'life' awarded to the one who follows wisdom (v. 11). 'The dead' is a word often translated as 'shades,' referring to the shadowy existence of the souls of the dead in the grave. It has already been used in Proverbs 2:18.

Thus, Solomon concludes this opening section of Proverbs (1–9), in which he develops at length the 'way' of wisdom and foolishness, the exhortations to his 'sons,' and the contrasting invitations of the women 'wisdom' and 'folly' (or the adulteress or harlot). These extended discourses will give way now to the more individualized nuggets of truth that we have come to know as proverbs. But, as the style changes, the emphasis does not. The foundation that has been laid in chapters 1–9 will now be built upon in the following chapters.

End Notes

1. Whybray, R. N., *Proverbs* (Grand Rapids, Michigan: William B. Eerdmans Publishing Company, 1994), 45.

2. Geisler, Norman L., 'A Christian Perspective on Wine Drinking,' *Bibliotheca Sacra* (January-March, 1982), 46-55.

3. Delitzsch, F., *Proverbs, Ecclesiastes, Song of Solomon* (three volumes in one) in C. F. Keil and F. Delitzsch, vol. 6, *Commentary on the Old Testament* (in ten volumes), (1872; rpt. Grand Rapids, Michigan: William B. Eerdmans Publishing Company, 1980), 1:198.

4. Whybray, 145.

5. Buzzell, Sid S., 'Proverbs,' *The Bible Knowledge Commentary* (Wheaton: Victor Books, 1985), 1:924.

6. Gilchrist, Paul R., '*yākah*,' *Theological Wordbook of the Old Testament* (Chicago: Moody Press, 1980), 1:376-377.

7. Arnold, Bill T., 'תְחִלָּה,' *New International Dictionary of Old Testament Theology and Exegesis* (Grand Rapids, Michigan: Zondervan Publishing House, 1997), 4:286.

8. Buzzell, 1:924.

9. Ibid.

10. Weber, Carl Philip, *hāmâ*,' *Theological Wordbook of the Old Testament* (Chicago: Moody Press, 1980), 1:219-220.

11. Whybray, 148.

12. Oswalt, John N., '*kissē*',' *Theological Wordbook of the Old Testament* (Chicago: Moody Press, 1980), 1:448.

Proverbs 10

10:1. The proverbs of Solomon. A wise son makes a father glad, But a foolish son is a grief to his mother.
The tenth chapter begins a new section of the book, which is set off here by the words 'The proverbs of Solomon' (cf. Prov. 1:1; 25:1; Eccles. 12:9). This series of short, pithy nuggets of wisdom continues through Proverbs 22:16.

The numerical value of the Hebrew consonants in the name Solomon equals 375. Interestingly, this is the exact number of proverbs found in Proverbs 10:1–22:16. Perhaps this is intentional, given the fact that these appear to be selected from a larger body of proverbs written by Solomon (1 Kings 4:32).[1] If the number 3,000 is to be taken woodenly in 1 Kings 4:32, then the proverbs of Proverbs 10:1–22:16 would represent only about 12.5 percent of all the proverbs Solomon wrote. We do, however, find another collection of his proverbs in Proverbs 25:1–29:27.

The arrangement of the proverbs in this section initially appears to follow no particular pattern. Upon further study, however, we begin to observe certain proverbs grouping together and creating a context helpful to understanding the others. Some of these would be Proverbs 10:4-5, both discussing laziness and diligence; Proverbs 10:11-14, 18-21, 31-32, addressing the tongue; Proverbs 16:1-7, all mentioning 'Lord'; Proverbs 16:12-15, all mentioning 'king'; Proverbs 15:16-17, both beginning with 'better'; Proverbs 12:9-11, all discussing domestic scenes; and Proverbs 11:9-12, all beginning will the same Hebrew letter.[2]

The majority of the proverbs found in this tenth chapter are antithetical in nature. That is to say that the first and second lines are in contrast, to point out a difference between the wise and the foolish.

The actual proverb here declares that family ties make certain that one is never completely independent. One's actions always affect the others in the family. Here, the contrast is between a 'wise son' and a 'foolish son.' These two characterizations find much press in Proverbs. The 'wise son' is mentioned elsewhere in Proverbs 13:1; 15:20; 23:24 (cf. also Prov. 23:15, 19; 27:11; 29:3). The 'foolish son' is met in Proverbs 17:25; 19:13; (cf. also Prov. 29:15). The 'wise son' is also contrasted with 'a scoffer' (Prov. 13:1), 'a foolish man' (15:20) and 'he who keeps company with harlots' (29:3). The word 'foolish' here comes from the Hebrew word so commonly used in these Proverbs to describe the thick-headed, stubborn individual who refuses to listen to others.

The effect of the 'wise son' is that he makes his father 'glad.' The word describes a joy that affects the whole of a person: heart (Exod. 4:14; Ps. 19:8; 104:15), soul (Ps. 86:4), and eyes (Prov. 15:30).[3] The effect of the 'foolish son' is that he brings his mother 'grief.' Such a son brings much hardship upon his parents (Prov. 17:21, 25; 19:13). Indeed, he not only hurts them; he personally 'despises' them (Prov. 15:20)!

The father and mother are mentioned separately, not because one is more susceptible to hurt and the other more prone toward joy, but as a literary device to indicate that the whole of the family shares in the follies and triumphs of other family members. No child can avoid bringing either joy or pain to his parent's lives (Prov. 17:21, 25; 23:24-25; 28:7; 29:3). While an age of greater independence is desired by all, one never outgrows one's responsibility to, or effect upon, one's family. What capacity for pain we take on when we hold our first child in our arms! But, oh, how our opportunities for joys untold are expanded at the same time!

10:2. Ill-gotten gains do not profit, But righteousness delivers from death.

This antithetical proverb sets forth the futility of getting rich by unjust means, a common theme in Proverbs (Prov. 1:11-14, 18-19; 10:16; 13:11; 16:8; 21:6; 28:16). 'Ill-gotten gains' is, literally, 'treasures of wickedness' (cf. Mic. 6:10). 'Ill-gotten' describes, generally, the kind of life that is the opposite of God's character.[4] In Proverbs, 'treasures' can be a blessing from God (Prov. 8:21), but, if they become the goal of one's life, they become the end of one's life (15:16; 21:6, 20).[5] The word translated 'profit' has a decidedly negative tone in the Old Testament. It is used to describe the yield of pursuing idols (Isa. 44:10), security through foreign alliances (Isa. 30:5), and, as here, wealth.[6] Clearly, Solomon is not denying that there is some temporal and fleeting benefit to gaining wealth. Even riches acquired unjustly meet a need momentarily. But, such things cannot lastingly satisfy or fulfill.

Why is this certain? Because there is a sovereign God watching over the affairs of this life, Who will make certain that such gains eventually end up in the debit column. '... [T]heir silver and their gold shall not be able to deliver them in the day of the wrath of the LORD. They cannot satisfy their appetite, nor can they fill their stomachs, for their iniquity has become an occasion of stumbling' (Ezek. 7:19).

It is just this sovereign Lordship that makes the second and contrasting line of the proverb stand as true. No doubt, 'righteousness' here has a more specific meaning of 'honesty' or 'uprightness' in this context.[7] Such honesty God has promised to honor. The exact nature of the 'death' that is delivered from is not specified. This could mean literal, physical death, spiritual death or eternal death of punishment away from God's presence. It is likely that, while not denying the last two, it is the first that is primarily in view here. One who lives in 'righteousness' avoids the many places, people and circumstances that can lead to physical harm and even death. This second line of the proverb is identical with Proverbs 11:4b. As with the first, the emphasis of this second line is also echoed often in Proverbs (Prov. 2:16-19; 3:2; 13:21).

10:3. The LORD will not allow the righteous to hunger, But He will thrust aside the craving of the wicked.

In another antithetical proverb, the general direction of the Israelite understanding of justice is set forth. This is not a set of tracks from which God cannot jump, as it may agree with His sovereign purposes, but a general principle deduced from His dealings with man.

The first line is, more literally, 'The Lord does not allow to hunger the soul of the righteous.' Here, 'the soul' is not to be set over against the body, but, rather, represents the whole of the immaterial life. It can be used to designate one's inner appetite (Prov. 23:2) and may have that meaning here.[8] Such appetite, however, should be understood as more comprehensive than simply the physical appetite of hunger. It includes the entire passion and longing of one's life, as one presses toward the righteousness of God.

The second line, then, sets forth the contrasting commitment of God toward the wicked. The word 'craving' clearly is not limited to the physical cravings of hunger (Prov. 11:6 and Mic. 7:3). The inner purpose, passion and direction of the wicked will not, ultimately, be attained. This is because God will 'thrust aside' their cravings. This verb often carries a violent and negative connotation. Indeed, this is the verb used to describe how God 'thrust out' the nations of the land of Canaan before the conquering Israelites (Deut. 6:19; 9:4; Josh. 23:5).[9] All the divine omnipotence stands ready to assure that those who stand opposed to Him will never ultimately fulfill their wicked plot of autonomous pleasure.

Again, it is obvious that this is a general rule regarding God's dealings with men (Ps. 34:9-10; 37:19, 25; Prov. 12:21; 13:25; 28:25). Scripture acknowledges, however, that the opposite is also sometimes true. 'For I was envious of the arrogant, As I saw the prosperity of the wicked... . Behold, these are the wicked; And always at ease, they have increased in wealth' (Ps. 73:3, 12). Such seeming injustice vexes the heart of the faithful, but only for a time. 'Until I came into the sanctuary of God; Then I perceived their end. Surely Thou dost set them in slippery places; Thou dost cast them down to destruction. How they are destroyed in a moment! They are utterly swept away by sudden terrors!' (Ps. 73:17-19).

10:4. Poor is he who works with a negligent hand, But the hand of the diligent makes rich.
Proverbs often contrasts the outcomes of the lazy and the diligent (Prov. 6:6-11; 12:11, 24, 27; 13:4; 14:23; 18:9; 27:23-27; 28:19). Here, the emphasis expands upon the promise of verse 3. The Lord may 'not allow the righteous to hunger,' but He usually employs the means of hard work to make this actual in their experience.

Proverbs speaks frequently of the 'poor,' this being the first of thirty-three times (employing three different Hebrew words). The term 'a negligent hand' can have the idea of that which is slack, loose, deceitful or slothful.[10] The term is used three other times in Proverbs (Prov. 12:24, 27; 19:15). It describes not necessarily the person who is completely inactive, but, rather, one who only half-heartedly does his job. He has a poor work ethic. He does not care about the quality of his work. Such laziness leads to financial leanness.

The phrase 'the hand of the diligent' uses a word that describes that which is pointed or sharp. It is used, literally, to describe the sharpened edge of a threshing sledge (Isa. 28:27; 41:15; Amos 1:3; Job 41:30). It is also used metaphorically, as here, to describe action that is 'sharp' and 'keen,' in the sense that it is skillful, efficient and useful.[11] Solomon here portrays not the workaholic, but one who takes seriously his employment and gives it his best effort. In the normal course of things, such diligence is met with financial reward.

Lack of effort is not the only cause of poverty, nor is diligence the only ingredient in the formula for success. In the providence of God, other factors may be calculated in as well. Yet, all things being equal, diligence dramatically improves the likelihood of being financially secure and able to provide for yourself and your family.

10:5. He who gathers in summer is a son who acts wisely, But he who sleeps in harvest is a son who acts shamefully.
In another antithetical parallelism, the lesson of diligence (v. 4) is repeated and applied more specifically. The contrast is between response to opportunity ('gathers' and 'sleeps') as well as outcome ('a son who acts wisely' and 'a son who acts shamefully'). Diligence is 'to make hay while the sun shines.' The wise one is he who thinks first of opportunity and only secondarily of desirability. Most of the truly significant things ever accomplished in the world were done by people who did not feel well – who could have given a list of excuses why they should do other than what they did.

Regarding the outcome, the meaning of 'acts wisely' comes from a Hebrew word found nineteen times in Proverbs, but only twice thus far (Prov. 1:3; 3:4; 10:5, 19; 12:8; 13:15; 14:35; 15:24; 16:20, 22, 24; 17:2, 8; 19:11, 14; 21:11, 12, 16; 23:9). Its primary meaning is 'prudent,' and it describes an intelligent thought process wherein one reasons through the complexities of each issue and arrives at the wisest and most successful course of action.[12] The idea of 'acts shamefully' is either that he brings disgrace upon those associated with him (i.e. his family, cf. v. 1) or that he himself is considered to be worthless.[13]

Proverbs often condemns sloth when opportunity for laying up provisions for the future is at hand (Prov. 6:9-11; 13:4; 15:19; 19:15; 20:13; 24:30-34; 28:19, 20).

10:6. Blessings are on the head of the righteous, But the mouth of the wicked conceals violence.
This antithetical proverb, at first glance, appears incoherent. The first line would lead one to expect something different from what we seem to find in the second line. The intended contrast is not immediately clear. However, with a bit of digging and reflection, the meaning becomes clear enough.

The first line echoes the standard Hebrew practice of placing the hands upon the head of another and pronouncing blessings upon them (cf. Gen. 48:14-22).[14] Such a blessing was considered 'official' and its contents prophetic and binding. All would soon become aware that such a blessing rested upon a person.

The second line does not immediately seem to stand in contrast to this, though it begins with the adversative 'but.' Certainly, 'the righteous' and 'the wicked' stand in contrast, but it is the rest of the line that is difficult. The word 'conceals' is part of our challenge. The word can mean simply 'to cover' and, then, also 'to conceal by covering.'[15] The same word is used in verse 12b: 'love covers all transgressions.'

The translation of the NASB makes it sound as if it is what comes out of the mouth of the wicked that covers up their violent plans (i.e. their deceitful words conceal their true goal and motives). This may be, but it does not seem to preserve the contrast intended between the two lines. It would seem more consistent to see the 'violence' as covering over the things that are coming from the mouth of the wicked (cf. NIV). The blessing that rests upon the head of the righteous is obvious, public, clear to all. In contrast, the wicked will inherit violent judgment. They will reap what they have sown. They have sown to the wind and they will reap the whirlwind. Such judgment will be so obvious, so overwhelming, so public that their verbal protests and excuses will be 'covered' and 'concealed' by the obvious fact of the outcome of their wicked way of life (cf. Hab. 2:17). Their well-deserved judgment, as we might say, will be written all over their faces – so much so that their words of opposition are drowned out.

One should note that our second line here is identical to the second line of verse 11. At first glance, it may not appear that our understanding of its phrase here would be appropriate with the meaning of that verse. Normal hermeneutical protocol would demand that the same thing repeated within such close proximity would require the same interpretation. We will show in our discussion of verse 11 that this principle does hold true here.

10:7. The memory of the righteous is blessed, But the name of the wicked will rot.

This verse continues the broad theme of verse 6, as is evidenced by the repetition of the words 'righteous,' 'wicked' and 'blessed.' The theme, however, is developed somewhat differently here. The word 'memory,' as we might expect, describes the mental act of recollection. It is also used to describe specific acts taken so as to remember someone or some thing.[16] This word and the one for 'name' are often found as synonyms.

The 'memory' of the righteous is their fame, renown or legacy. Such a mental legacy of the 'righteous' is a blessing. That is to say, to think about, reflect upon, study and contemplate the life of a righteous man yields great benefit to the one who expends the energy to do so. History is a treasure chest of blessing to the one who studies it with eyes of faith. The biography of the righteous is a boon. 'Remember those who led you, who spoke the word of God to you; and considering the result of their conduct, imitate their faith' (Heb. 13:7).

Such is the advantage of the one who will set his eyes upon the 'righteous' and discern a likeness to God. What incentive, therefore, to live righteously! We can leave a legacy of lasting influence simply by living our lives in sacrificial service to God. 'A good name is to be more desired than great riches, Favor is better than silver and gold' (Prov. 22:1). 'A good name is better than a good ointment' (Eccles. 7:1a).

The heights of blessing to which the memory of the righteous might take us are balanced here by the depths of shame to which the recollection of the wicked plunge us. Their name 'will rot.' The Hebrew word comes from a root meaning of to become thin or to dissolve into fine parts.[17] Once dead, the memory of the wicked man's life will rot like his corpse. The wicked will simply disappear off the scene of human events and slip from the thoughts of all those who remain. When they do come to mind, their name will be the stench of death to those who recall them. Having lived to promote self in this life, their identity will slip into obscurity and all they worked for will be lost eternally.

10:8. The wise of heart will receive commands, But a babbling fool will be thrown down.

This proverb heads a whole series of wise sayings about the use of the tongue in this chapter (Prov. 10:10, 11, 13, 14, 18-21, 31, 32). Wisdom is demonstrated in one's response to authority. The one with understanding 'will receive commands.' The word 'receive' is used over 1,000 times in the Old Testament and has a broad range of meaning, such as 'take,' 'get,' 'fetch,' 'lay hold of,' 'seize,' 'receive,' and 'acquire.'[18] The Hebrew word for 'commands' has been used already (Prov. 2:1; 3:1; 4:4; 6:20, 23; 7:1, 2). It is used elsewhere to describe the law handed down by God through Moses, but in Proverbs it normally refers to instruction passed on by parent, teacher or one in another position of authority.[19] Wisdom is found in the humility of living under authority and in cultivating a teachable spirit (Prov. 1:5; 9:8-9).

The fool stands in contrast as one who is unteachable and reveals as much through his speech. The phrase 'a babbling fool' is, literally, 'a fool of lips.' Though the meaning is not perfectly clear, it appears that the phrase describes one who rattles on, talking when he should be listening. Their verbal responses prove they are prideful, unteachable, and hard of heart. The word for 'fool' describes one who is morally insolent. Such a one refuses counsel (Prov. 1:7; 10:8; 12:15; 15:5) and mocks at sin (14:9). In his folly, he has nearly passed the point of no return (Prov. 10:21; 27:22).

Such 'a chattering fool' (NIV) will 'be thrown down.' This rare verb is found elsewhere only in verse 10 (where the second line is identical with v. 8b) and in Hosea 4:14. The translation 'thrown down' comes closer to the literal meaning of the verb than does the NIV's 'comes to ruin.' But the idea is that of defeat. Whereas the one who has learned to hold his tongue, listen and learn comes to success, the one who is quick to speak and slow to learn (cf. James 1:19) soon defeats himself by his attitude and actions (cf. Prov. 10:14, 18; 13:3).

10:9. He who walks in integrity walks securely, But he who perverts his ways will be found out.

One who 'walks in integrity' is one whose inmost desire is to bring all of life into harmony with God and the others in his life. It describes one whose disposition and conduct is blameless and innocent.[20] He is not sinless, but has brought the whole of his life into submission to God. The outcome of such a life is that one 'walks securely.' There is freedom from anxiety. Worry does not nip at one's heels. Past sins do not trail behind, plaguing the mind with 'what if?' questions. The word for 'securely' describes the sense of well-being and security that is afforded one who has another they can trust to watch over and care for them.[21] It describes a state of mind that is at peace and free from anxiety.[22] 'He is a shield to those who walk in integrity' (Prov. 2:7b). 'Then you will walk in your way securely, And your foot will not stumble' (Prov. 3:23; cf. 13:6; 18:10; 28:18; Ps. 25:21; Isa. 33:15-16).

The security of the upright stands in contrast to the instability and insecurity of the one who 'perverts his ways.' The phrase is, more literally, 'makes his ways crooked.' The crookedness of his ways is in direct contrast to the straightness of the ways the man of integrity takes (cf. Prov. 2:15). Focusing upon the expediency of the moment rather than the fixed point of God's Person and truth, he plows a crooked furrow through life. Before long, he 'will be found out,' or, more literally, 'shall be known.' Certainly, God already knows all about him and his ways (Prov. 16:2; 21:2). But, the self-destructive nature of his ways will soon become obvious to all (Prov. 26:26; 1 Tim. 5:24-25; 2 Tim. 3:9). To the inherent instability of his ways, God will add His judgment (Prov. 24:12; Luke 8:17). 'He who walks blamelessly will be delivered, But he who is crooked will fall all at once' (Prov. 28:18). '... be sure your sin will find you out' (Num. 32:23b).

10:10. He who winks the eye causes trouble, And a babbling fool will be thrown down.

For the first time in this chapter, we encounter a proverb that is not antithetical. These two lines are in the form of a comparison. The first line speaks of one who covertly seeks to communicate a message to one person that is different from the message being sent to another. The wink of the eye may be an agreed upon cue for springing a trap upon someone, it may be a part of deception as one signals the majority that he really doesn't mean what he has communicated to another, or it could even be considered magical/demonic as 'the evil eye' (Ps. 35:19; Prov. 6:13, 14; 16:30)[23]

Whatever the intent, the result is that it 'causes trouble.' The word for 'trouble' is used only four other times in the Old Testament (Job 9:28; Ps. 16:4; 147:3; Prov. 15:13). It describes both physical pain and emotional sorrow.[24] Does the winker bring this upon himself or foist it upon those who are the victims of his gestures? The Hebrew word translated 'causes' can describe getting something for oneself[25], but the vast majority of its over 2,000 uses in the Old Testament describe giving something to another.[26] Of course, in the long run, inflicting pain upon others will come around to be a pain in one's own life.

The question becomes how this first line relates to the second. This second line is an exact duplicate of what we encountered in verse 8b. The first line describes the hurtful nature of our actions upon others. The second line describes the destructive nature of our actions upon ourselves. The first line describes one who communicates without words, the second line one who spoils all communication by too many words. The first line describes one who seems to know more than others in the situation, the second line describes one who, because of incessant talking, does not see the reality of the situation he finds himself in. The first line describes the painful physical and emotional results of sinful communication, the second line goes further and describes the calamitous result of not listening to anyone but yourself.

Many commentators abandon the Hebrew text and go with the vastly different LXX rendering. This is often done on the basis of the claim that the two lines as we have them here are unintelligible. This, however, is unnecessary. The proverb begins with careful, but deceitful communication and shows its hurtful result. The second line extends, and takes further, the lesson about communication, underscoring the utterly self-destructive nature of listening only to one's own speech and never taking time to listen to others.

10:11. The mouth of the righteous is a fountain of life, But the mouth of the wicked conceals violence.
Another antithetical proverb continues the theme of speech and communication. The 'mouth of the righteous' (cf. Prov. 10:31) is elsewhere called 'the mouth of the upright' (12:6). It stands in contrast to the 'perverted mouth' (Prov. 8:13), 'false mouth' (6:12), 'deceitful mouth' (4:24), 'flattering mouth' (26:28), 'the fool's mouth' (18:7; cf. 10:14; 14:3; 15:2, 14; 26:7, 9), the 'mouth of the wicked' (10:6, 32; 11:11; 15:28; 19:28), the mouth of the 'godless' (11:9) and the 'mouth of the adulteress' (22:14). 'The mouth of the righteous' is the mouth that has been taught before it speaks and, then, communicates the life-giving wisdom of God.

The metaphor of 'a fountain of life' was apt in a culture given to periodic and devastating drought (Prov. 18:4). To become such 'a fountain of life' one must go to the source, for God Himself is that fountain (Ps. 36:9). Indeed, 'the fear of the Lord is a fountain of life' (Prov. 14:27; cf. 1:7). Having thus learned of God, 'the teaching of the wise is a fountain of life' (Prov. 13:14), not only for those to whom we speak, but 'to the one who has it' (Prov. 16:22).

The New Testament takes this even further, for we in the church are able to be indwelt by the Spirit of God Himself. Thus, Jesus promised, 'He who believes in Me, as the Scripture said, "From his innermost being shall flow rivers of living water"' (John 7:38) and 'whoever drinks of this water that I shall give him shall never thirst; but the water that I shall give him shall become in him a well of water springing up to eternal life' (John 4:14).

The question then becomes: How does the second line stand in contrast and complete the meaning of the proverb? The second line is identical to the second line in verse 6. At verse 6 we determined that violence is the obvious judgment that covers over the protestations and defenses of the wicked. That interpretation agreed well with the first line in verse 6 and also makes good sense here. The first line here in verse 11 emphasizes the resulting effect of the words of the righteous: lasting life to others. The second line stands in contrast, in that the product of 'the mouth of the wicked' yields no good, not even to himself. The 'mouth of the righteous' has lasting, far-reaching benefits. The 'mouth of the wicked,' however, can neither hold back the violent judgment that breaks upon his head, nor offer a convincing excuse before it.

10:12. Hatred stirs up strife, But love covers all transgressions.
This is another antithetical proverb dealing with interpersonal relationships. The word translated 'hatred' is an intensified form of

the word describing an emotional attitude of detesting, opposing, or despising things or people. It stands as the opposite of love – love draws in and unites whereas hatred divides, separates and distances.[27]

This attitude of hatred 'stirs up' trouble in our relationships. This word means to arouse someone to activity they would not otherwise have undertaken. The action to which they are incited requires extra effort, which they would not have put in had it not been for the one who stirred them up.[28] The word 'strife' describes interpersonal or domestic disputes, as opposed to national or legal troubles, and is used almost exclusively here in Proverbs.[29] Though wrong was committed and hurt inflicted no interpersonal explosion would have ensued, if it were not for the hateful response of the 'innocent' party. Harmony could have been maintained, if not for someone's perceived 'right' to get even.

In contrast, the response of love 'covers' the wrongs done to us. This is the same word translated 'conceals' in verses 6b, 11b. There, violence covered over the protestations of the wicked as they were swept away by the judgment of their sins. Here, just the opposite happens, the righteous man covers over and hides from view the personal offenses committed against him. Rather than pulling these wrongs out to public view and responding in kind, the righteous throws a wet blanket over the flame of another's sin against him. Rather than calling down judgment on the one who wrongs us, we are to personally absorb the wrong in the cushion of our love.

This verse is picked up by James 5:20 and 1 Peter 4:8, showing, through repetition, how necessary such enduring, patient love is to our relationships. Indeed, 'A man's discretion makes him slow to anger, And it is his glory to overlook a transgression' (Prov. 19:11). 'He who covers a transgression seeks love, But he who repeats a matter separates intimate friends' (Prov. 17:9). Truly love 'is not provoked, does not take into account a wrong suffered' and it 'bears all things, believes all things, hopes all things, endures all things' (1 Cor. 13:5, 7).

10:13. On the lips of the discerning, wisdom is found, But a rod is for the back of him who lacks understanding.
This antithetical proverb concerns what it takes to steer a person's life. The first character is 'the discerning.' He has come to the place where he can look at two things and see what God sees in them. He can distinguish wrong from right, good from bad, better from best. He has, through practice in applying God's word, learned to discern

God's way in this world (Heb. 5:14). What a word for we who live in an age of relativism! We are told today that such discernment is not only useless, but evil. Rather, we must just accept any, and every, voice as equally true. But, that is not the way of wisdom, it is the way of folly.

The person who has learned to so distinguish God's way is a person worth listening to, for wisdom is found on his lips. He has been teachable, now he can teach. He has taken the path of learning, now we can follow and learn from him.

The wise have listened to God and learned, and now they are teachers. However, he 'who lacks understanding' can be steered only by one means: sheer force. Indeed, only 'the rod' will move him. Even then, it is doubtful that he learns anything, for the same is needed over and over again (Prov. 14:3; 19:29). Like a dumb animal, he responds not to revelation, wisdom, understanding or discernment, but only the immediate pain of the rod (Prov. 26:3; Ps. 32:8, 9).

This is the first of many references to 'the rod.' Often, it is for the child (Prov. 13:24 22:15; 23:13, 14; 29:15), but it is also for the fool (Prov. 14:3; 26:3). Here, it awaits 'him who lacks understanding' and proves it by opening his mouth (cf. Prov. 18:2, 6-8). The discernment he could have gained through God's word has been lost and he is void of any sense of reality (Prov. 5:23; 6:32; 7:7; 9:4, 16; 10:21; 11:12; 12:11; 15:21; 17:18; 24:30; 28:16).

10:14. Wise men store up knowledge, But with the mouth of the foolish, ruin is at hand.
The wise 'store up' what they are learning. The verb means to cover up something with a specific objective in mind. That objective might be protection or it might be for illegitimate purposes.[30] This can be taken to mean to hide, to treasure or to lay in store. Here the notion is, as the translators of the NASB make plain, 'store up.' The wise man does not rest upon wisdom already gained, but he keeps seeking, digging, yearning to acquire more wisdom (cf. Prov. 2:1-5). To taste of wisdom is to desire more. To be satisfied with God's understanding is to instantly become hungry for more insight into His ways.

The wise do not flaunt their wisdom. They are not reticent to share it when it will be helpful, but they do not feel constrained to spout it off in a demonstration of their understanding. That is the way of the fool. He runs off at the mouth, spouting the pseudo-wisdom he has stumbled across (cf. Prov. 10:8, 10). Cliches, platitudes, truisms roll from his lips, but they gain him only 'ruin' (cf. Prov. 13:3). The word can describe physical ruins (Ps. 89:40), destruction as an abstract concept (Prov. 18:7), and an external object of terror (Jer. 7:17; 48:39). Here, it is 'ruin' still in the abstract.[31] The door is left open for all manner of destruction to break upon the head of the one who runs off at the mouth with his self-proclaimed wisdom. Such is said to be 'at hand.' The word can describe nearness in a variety of ways – space, time, family ties, interest and spiritually.[32] Here, the notion is rather general: 'ruin' is not far off from one who reveals his foolishness with his running mouth.

The New Testament affirms the same lesson: 'If anyone thinks himself to be religious, and yet does not bridle his tongue but deceives his own heart, this man's religion is worthless' (James 1:26; cf. 3:1-12).

10:15. The rich man's wealth is his fortress, The ruin of the poor is their poverty.

This verse presents good evidence for why no one proverb must be taken alone, but balanced with the whole of the book's teaching. The author simply states the facts as they appear from the human plane: the rich are far more secure in this life than are the poor. There is no moralizing about the evils of riches. Nor does he wax eloquent about the blessedness of the poor. Neither of these two lines must be taken as the ultimate conclusion of the outcome of either state. For surely God blesses and protects the poor (Prov. 22:22-23; Ps. 12:5) and He lays low those who trust in their riches rather than Him (Prov. 11:4, 28).

Nevertheless, the fact is that riches insulate a person's life with many friends (Prov. 14:20; 19:4). How long those friendships will last or how deep their commitment runs is not in view at present. In this world, wealth postures one well and puts one in a position of power (Prov. 18:23; 22:7). These are, to borrow a phrase from Ecclesiastes, the facts as they appear 'under the sun.' Ultimately, though, security is found only in the Lord (Ps. 20:7; 52:7; Prov. 11:4, 28; 18:10-12). This first line is virtually synonymous with the first line of Proverbs 18:11. Comparison of the two proverbs, however, rounds out the fuller perspective of God. The first line of each proverb describes the rich man in terms of a walled and, therefore, impregnable and invulnerable city. But, the second line of Proverbs 18:11 makes clear that this security may only be in his 'imagination!' Indeed, only 'The name of the Lord is a strong tower' and 'the righteous runs into it and is safe' (Prov. 18:10). Closer to this chapter, one can find balance by comparing with verses 2 and 16. Certainly, the one who puts ultimate trust in riches will be sorely disappointed (Prov. 11:4; 23:5).

The second line is also a simple observation of facts as they play
out on the human plane, without God's perspective. Scripture does
not romanticize about poverty. The fact is that poverty leaves you
lonely (Prov. 14:20; 19:4, 7) and often powerless in the currency of
this world (Prov. 18:23; 22:7). They come to 'ruin'; the same word is
found in verse 14.

Certainly, God takes up the case of the poor when they trust in
Him (Prov. 22:22-23; Ps. 12:5). But, a bald fact of life in this world
is that riches have some built-in advantages and poverty has some
built-in disadvantages. One can offer some manner of temporary
and frail security. The other leaves little flesh on the bones to fight
off the cold, hard realities of this life.

10:16. The wages of the righteous is life, The income of the wicked, punishment.

This verse connects loosely with the previous one, in that it continues
the broad topic of 'wealth' through the use of the words 'wages'
and 'income.' The verse also prepares for verse 17, in that the word
translated 'life' is found in both.

The two lines of the proverb contrast with one another. The words
'wages' and 'income' provide the common link. The word translated
'wages' is used fourteen times in the Old Testament. It can describe
the wages of a man hired for labor (Lev. 19:13). It can also be used
to designate the broader idea of reward from God, either because of
good (Isa. 40:10; 49:4; Jer. 31:16) or evil (Ps. 109:20).[33] The latter word
comes from the agricultural world and denotes the crop or yield
that is gained in the harvest.[34]

Thus, living as either one of 'The righteous' or one of 'the wicked'
is a decision that has implications beyond just the moment. Either
lifestyle yields lingering consequences. Choices sow seeds; seeds
germinate, grow and, eventually, bring forth a crop. It is interesting
that the yield is not described in terms of wealth or poverty, but as
'life' or 'sin.' The Hebrew word describes 'sin' and, only by extension,
its 'punishment.'[35]

What exactly did Solomon intend to communicate about these
opposite outcomes? Are 'life' and 'sin' the wages that are received?
Or, is their exact identity left unspecified and general, noting only
what those undesignated wages are spent on (i.e. the wages of the
righteous are spent on those things that make for life and the income
of the wicked is squandered on that which is, or leads to, sin)?

In favor of the first view is the way the New Testament picks
up on this theme. 'The wages of sin is death, but the free gift of

God is eternal life in Christ Jesus our Lord' (Rom. 6:23). 'Do not be deceived, God is not mocked; for whatever a man sows, this he will also reap' (Gal. 6:7). The teaching of Proverbs prepared the way for such teaching (Prov. 1:31; 3:2, 16, 18, 21-22; 4:4, 22; 7:2).

But, in support of the second option is the more literal reading of the Hebrew text. A rather wooden reading would be something like this: 'The wages of the righteous for life; the harvest of the wicked for sin.' This would leave the 'wages' and 'income' unspecified, but regard them as the literal money or advantages gained in this world through either lifestyle. These real-world wages are, then, viewed as being spent either on that which makes for 'life' or that which is, or leads to, 'sin.' In this case, 'life' would not take on the nuance of spiritual or eternal life, but rather the tangible, real-world support of family and fulfillment of responsibilities. The word seems to be used in this way in Proverbs 27:27 where it takes on a meaning something like 'sustenance' or 'maintenance.'[36]

Both options describe Biblical truth. God is a just rewarder and will give to each one that which his actions deserve. It is also true, however, that how we spend our resources goes a long way in revealing the reality of our heart's condition spiritually. It is more likely that, in this context, the latter of the two is the intended meaning.

10:17. He is on the path of life who heeds instruction, But he who forsakes reproof goes astray.
This verse is linked to the previous one by sharing the Hebrew word for 'life.' Our proverb here is capable of two basic interpretations. The first is represented by our NASB translation. It sees the results of either listening, and holding to, instruction or turning back reproof as falling upon the individual himself. Because of their own decisions, they are either on the path of life or not. The second interpretation is represented by the NIV, which sees the person as one who shows forth to others what the path of life is by holding to instruction. The opposite is also true: that, if they reject reproof, they lead others astray.

The NIV's interpretation is supported by the fact that the Hebrew text reads, most literally: 'A path of life [is] one keeping instruction.' This would make the one who holds to instruction to be the path of life (or a guide on or to the path of life) to those watching him. The NASB's interpretation, however, requires repointing the Hebrew word in order to make it mean something like 'is traveling towards' or 'is on the way to.'[37] Also, in support of the NIV's interpretation is the fact that the verb 'goes astray' is in the hiphil form. This, normally, would yield a causative meaning, something like 'causes to go astray.' If the first line is left as the Hebrew text has it, this verb in the second line would, then, seem most naturally to point to causing others to go astray. The NASB's interpretation would require taking the verb as an intransitive, a form it seems to hold in Isaiah 63:17, but which is more unusual.[38]

Overall, it would seem the NIV's rendering is probably closest to the idea of the original. However, it should be noted that neither interpretation excludes the understanding of the other. One cannot be a guide on the path of life, if he is not first walking on it himself. And if he is walking himself in the path of life, inevitably someone will see and follow him.

The verb 'heeds' is strong and describes holding fast to something.[39] Walking the way of wisdom is not a passive enterprise. It requires great concentration and a tremendous outlay of energy. Similarly, the word 'forsakes' is also quite descriptive. Its basic root carries three connotations: to depart, to abandon, and to loose. It would seem that 'forsakes' is closer to the idea than 'ignores' (NIV). It is the Hebrew word that describes apostasy.[40] The words for 'instruction' and 'reproof' are favorites of chapters 1–9. See the comments on Proverbs 1:2 for 'instruction' and, on 1:25, for 'reproof.'

Whether simply for one's self or also for those who see and follow you, it must be understood that 'reproofs for discipline are the way of life' (Prov. 6:23b) and 'He who hates reproof will die' (15:10b; cf. 5:12).

10:18. He who conceals hatred has lying lips, And he who spreads slander is a fool.

The string of antithetical proverbs is here broken by the inclusion of this proverb which is synonymous in its parallelism. The second line does not stand in contrast to the first, but, rather, continues in the same vein and brings the thought to a climatic conclusion. The two lines, taken together, reveal two equal errors in dealing with hatred. The first line decries the strategy of cover-up; the second line holds forth the stupidity of catharsis. The one who harbors hatred in his heart toward another will, if he chooses the path of cover-up, inevitably, be forced into a lie (Prov. 26:24, 26, 28). The one who determines to give free expression to his feelings will destroy that relationship and others along with it (Prov. 16:28; 20:19; 25:9-10; 26:20, 22). The best answer to hatred is not held forth here, only the equal foolishness of these two erroneous strategies. The correct answer for the problem of hatred is found in the forgiveness of verse 12.

10:19. When there are many words, transgression is unavoidable, But he who restrains his lips is wise.
This proverb contrasts the outcome of speaking many or few words. The person who rattles on and chatters incessantly will not be able to avoid sinning with those words. They will promise something they cannot keep; they will offend someone; they will embarrass themselves; they will reveal their ignorance; they will bore someone; they will selfishly reveal their pride by speaking on and on about their own affairs – the possibilities are endless, for the tongue 'is a fire, the very world of iniquity; the tongue is set among our members as that which defiles the entire body, and sets on fire the course of our life' (James 3:6). 'The one who guards his mouth preserves his life; The one who opens wide his lips comes to ruin' (Prov. 13:3). 'Do you see a man who is hasty in his words? There is more hope for a fool than for him' (Prov. 29:20). 'A babbling fool will be thrown down' (Prov. 10:8b, 10b).

How wise, then, is the one who 'restrains his lips'! True religion, says James, goes right to the tongue (James 1:26). 'A man of understanding keeps silent' (Prov. 11:12b). 'He who restrains his words has knowledge' (Prov. 17:27). 'Even a fool, when he keeps silent, is considered wise; When he closes his lips, he is counted prudent' (Prov. 17:28). How wise the one who prays as the psalmist did: 'Set a guard, O LORD, over my mouth; Keep watch over the door of my lips' (Ps. 141:3; cf. Ps. 39:1).

10:20. The tongue of the righteous is as choice silver, The heart of the wicked is worth little.
Continuing the theme of the power of one's speech, this proverb holds in parallel one's 'tongue' and one's 'heart.' The 'heart,' in the Hebrew understanding, describes one's powers of rational thought, emotion and volition. It is the seat of the entire personality. The heart, therefore, represents what a person is.

The heart is man's most fundamental problem (Jer. 17:9; Matt. 15:18, 19). The tongue simply lets everyone else in on that fact. The contents of the heart are soon revealed by the product of the mouth: 'For the mouth speaks out of that which fills the heart. The good man out of his good treasure brings forth what is good; and the evil man out of his evil treasure brings forth what is evil' (Matt. 12:34b-35).

When the heart belongs to Christ, and He has transformed it, the worth of that which proceeds from the mouth is inestimable (Prov. 3:14; 8:10, 19; 15:23; 25:11). If the heart is precious, so too are the words. But, if the heart is worthless, how foul the odor of the communication it puts off!

10:21. The lips of the righteous feed many, But fools die for lack of understanding.

Several words link these verses together. The word 'lips' ties this verse to verses 18 and 20 where it is also found. The designation 'the righteous' is also found in verse 20a and stands in contrast to 'the wicked' (v. 20b). The word 'heart' found in verse 20 is also found here, though it is translated here as 'understanding.' Thus, the theme of the tongue and its fruit carries through into this verse.

The word 'feed' is used of the activity of a shepherd with his sheep, often being translated with words such as 'pasture,' 'tend,' 'graze,' or 'shepherd.'[41] In the Old Testament, the imagery of the shepherd is often applied to kings and to God Himself, but only here is it applied to 'the righteous.'[42]

Think of it! As you search out the wisdom of God, and as He nourishes your soul on His truth, the very words you speak, though few in number (v. 19), become precious (v. 20) to those around you, because they find through them their souls being shepherded, fed, protected and nourished (cf. v. 11). What a high privilege! What an awesome responsibility!

In contrast, the fool discovers not only that his thoughts and words are worthless to help others (v. 20), but they cannot even sustain his own life. His problem is that he has a 'lack of understanding.' Literally, it reads 'lack of heart' (cf. Prov. 7:7; 9:16). He lacks divine life at the core of his being. The place from which his thoughts arise is corrupt. The seat of his emotions is sick. The base from which his choices are launched is tottering and unstable. He is dying from the inside out (Prov. 1:29-32; 5:23).

10:22. It is the blessing of the Lord that makes rich, And He adds no sorrow to it.

We are confronted now with a rarity in this chapter: a non-antithetical proverb (but see also vv. 10, 15, 16, 18, 20). The first line employs an emphatic pronoun to make its point abundantly clear. A literal reading would be: 'The blessing of the Lord, it makes rich.'[43] This is both a reminder of the limitations of human scheming and plotting and an affirmation of what true wealth is. All the human effort in the world cannot produce wealth, if the Lord has not determined to grant it. All the wealth in the world cannot make one truly rich, if

God has not also granted His blessing to it. One may have none of this world's goods, yet be rich because he possesses 'it'!

There is division among the scholars as to the appropriate translation of line two. One camp is represented by the translators of the NASB and the NIV. In this view, the point is the lack of anxiety and trouble brought on by the blessings God bestows as opposed to the worries produced by ill-gotten gain. The other opinion believes the point to be that only the Lord can make one rich (line one), and that no amount of human labor can produce wealth, if God is not inclined to grant it (line two). Thus, the RSV's marginal translation says 'and toil adds nothing to it.' Similarly, the JB renders it 'to this hard toil has nothing to offer.' The noun here translated as 'sorrow' is also in other contexts translated as 'labor' or 'toil' (Ps. 127:2; Prov. 5:10; 14:23).

The Scriptures seem to support both views. Wealth wrongly obtained carries many troubles (Prov. 10:2; 15:6; 16:19; 21:6), but the rewards of godly living are enjoyable (Prov. 10:16). Yet, neither can hard work alone produce anxiety-free wealth (Ps. 127:1-2). With this understanding, there would appear to be no good reason to abandon the translation of the NASB.

10:23. Doing wickedness is like sport to a fool; And so is wisdom to a man of understanding.

The ways of the wicked and the way of the righteous are contrasted here, as in the proverbs extending to the end of the chapter. The word translated 'wickedness' is a Hebrew word reserved to describe the most heinous of wrongs: incest, adultery, idolatry and the like. The exact phrase is found only one other time in the Old Testament, where it describes gang rape and is called a 'lewd ... act in Israel' (Judg. 20:6).[44]

To a fool, this kind of sin is 'like sport.' The word, literally, refers to laughter. They get their pleasure from using others. Their consciences having been seared (1 Tim. 4:2), the path of least resistance for them is abominable and grievous sin. They cheer their partners. It becomes their relaxation. Sin has become recreational. Note that this person is called 'a fool,' the thick-headed and stubborn individual so often decried in these proverbs.

Standing in contrast to such abomination is 'a man of understanding.' He is an individual characterized by his ability to discern right from wrong, good from evil, truth from falsehood, and the holy from the profane.

This second line has no verb and thus reads, literally, 'so wisdom to the man of understanding.' Translators and commentators have generally carried over the verb from the first line, resulting in a translation like that of the NASB or NIV.[45] Thus, the meaning is that the pursuit of wisdom is what brings pleasure to the one with understanding. It is not that the prudent have no fun. They simply find it in wholesome, life-giving pursuits. Pleasure is not taboo; it is the constant companion of the one who pursues God and His ways. It is, however, true that one's heart is revealed by what one takes pleasure in. Our laughter betrays our true character.

10:24. What the wicked fears will come upon him, And the desire of the righteous will be granted.
The contrast here is between the opposite anticipations of the wicked and the righteous. The assurance is that what both anticipate or desire will come upon them in the end. The simple fact that the wicked live in fear should not be missed. The first, and most fundamental, consequence of sin to human emotions was the introduction of fear (Gen. 3:10). While such fear is often redirected and remains unidentified, it nevertheless lingers (Heb. 2:15). There is, in every human, 'a certain terrifying expectation of judgment' (Heb. 10:27). This, Solomon assures us, will eventually befall the wicked. True, the wicked often prosper for a time (Ps. 73:3ff). This may cause the righteous to nearly stumble (Ps. 73:1-2), but 'Then I perceived their end. How they are destroyed in a moment! They are utterly swept away by sudden terrors!' (Ps. 73:17b-19).

The wicked eventually get what they are afraid of: the judgment of God. What the righteous most desire they also get (Ps. 37:4; 145:19). Their heart's cry is 'Thou wilt make known to me the path of life; In Thy presence is fulness of joy; In Thy right hand there are pleasures forever' (Ps. 16:11). True, the immediate reward of the righteous often appears to be only pain and toil, but, in the end, God Himself guarantees that the thing they have most longed for they will have: the conscious enjoyment of His full presence. 'Blessed are those who hunger and thirst for righteousness, for they shall be satisfied' (Matt. 5:6).

10:25. When the whirlwind passes, the wicked is no more, But the righteous has an everlasting foundation.
This proverb continues the thought raised in the previous verse and makes more exact the nature of the dread of the wicked. The best commentary on this proverb is Jesus' description of the wise and foolish builders in Matthew 7:24-27.

The judgment of God is often pictured as a whirlwind (Job 27:19-21; Ps. 58:9; Prov. 1:27; Isa. 5:28; 29:6; 66:15; Jer. 4:13).

The figure aptly describes the sudden and overwhelming nature of God's wrath when finally released (Prov. 3:25). God has warned that we will reap what we sow: 'Whatever a man sows, that will he also reap' (Gal. 6:7). He has also promised that we will reap more than we sow: 'For they sow the wind, And they reap the whirlwind' (Hosea 8:7). When harvest time comes, the wicked will not stand.

Unlike the wicked, the righteous has a firm foundation that stands after the judgment of God has passed over the land. Proverbs often sounds the note of the security of the righteous in the day of calamity (Prov. 10:9, 30; 12:3; 14:11). 'Yet a little while and the wicked man will be no more; And you will look carefully for his place, and he will not be there. But the humble will inherit the land, And will delight themselves in abundant prosperity' (Ps. 37:10-11).

10:26. Like vinegar to the teeth and smoke to the eyes, So is the lazy one to those who send him.
This proverb functions off of a comparison revealed by the formula 'Like ... so.' The first line provides two similes. The first builds off the negative reaction brought on by vinegar to the teeth. The bitter, acidic taste brings instant recoil from the one unfortunate enough to ingest the biting liquid (Ps. 69:21; Prov. 25:20). Similarly, the second simile works off the blinding reaction to smoke in one's eyes: eyelids lock down, tears pour, hands begin to rub the eyes. Corresponding to this is the reaction a lazy servant brings to the one who has banked on his trustworthiness. The 'lazy man' is the translation of the Hebrew word so often translated 'sluggard' in the Book of Proverbs (cf. Prov. 26:13-16). The word is found fourteen times in this book, revealing the importance of diligent hard work.

The untrustworthy messenger or servant is a bane to his master (Prov. 13:17; 26:6). The faithful servant is a rare jewel: 'Like the cold of snow in the time of harvest Is a faithful messenger to those who send him' (Prov. 25:13). Wise is the one who carefully evaluates a man's character before he employs his services.

10:27. The fear of the LORD prolongs life, But the years of the wicked will be shortened.
These closing six verses of the chapter are closely related to one another. They are all antithetical in nature and, in every case, the positive side of the contrast is set forth first. The name of God ('LORD') forms the basis for the contrasts (vv. 27, 29).

The contrasts deal more with righteousness/wickedness than wisdom/foolishness. Note that the word 'righteous' occurs four times

(vv. 28, 30, 31, 32) and some expression for wickedness or sin appears in every verse (vv. 27, 28, 29, 30, 31, 32).[46] The way of righteousness produces length of life (v. 27), quality of life (v. 28), security for life (v. 29, 30), and wisdom for life (v. 31, 32). In contrast, the way of wickedness leads to shortened life (v. 27), unfulfilled dreams (v. 28), insecurity (v. 29, 30), and a foolish philosophy of life.

The truth set forth in this particular proverb is general in application, rather than unalterable. As a general rule, those who live in the fear of the Lord live longer (Prov. 3:2, 16; 9:11; 10:2; 14:27; 19:23; 22:4). Generally, the wicked find their lives cut short (Prov. 10:25; 11:10; 13:9; 19:9, 16; 20:20; 21:28). That such is not always the case, and thus of great consternation to the righteous, is obvious both from observation and the teaching of Scripture (Ps. 73). God, in His sovereignty, may achieve higher purposes by reversing this rule in particular situations, but that does not destroy the general pattern of His dealings with us (Ps. 49).

For the first time in this second section of Proverbs, the main theme of the book is mentioned. The fear of the Lord served as bookends for the opening nine chapters (cf. Prov. 1:7; 9:10), as it does for the whole of the book (1:7; 31:30). It is found often in the rest of the book as well (14:26-27; 15:16, 33; 16:6; 19:23; 22:4; 23:17).

10:28. The hope of the righteous is gladness, But the expectation of the wicked perishes.
This proverb continues the general theme of the future of the righteous and the wicked introduced in the previous verse in general fashion. It finds an even more specific echo in verse 24. The words translated 'hope' and 'expectation' both describe an earnest, searching, concentrated gaze for something.[47] Both the righteous and the wicked hopefully anticipate the fulfillment of their desires. The contrast is found in the difference of what comes of those expectations. As a general rule, God makes certain that the righteous experience the joyful fulfillment of their godly desires (Ps. 37:4; 145:19). The wicked, however, find that their expectations perish, in the sense that their desires simply never become reality (Ps. 9:17). They die with their dreams unfulfilled (Prov. 11:7).

10:29. The way of the Lord is a stronghold to the upright, But ruin to the workers of iniquity.
The phrase 'The way of the Lord' is found frequently in the Scriptures, particularly the Old Testament. It can refer either to the ethical, moral paths that God prescribes in His word (Gen. 18:19;

Judg. 2:22; 2 Sam. 22:22; 2 Kings 21:22; 2 Chron. 17:6; Ps. 18:21;) or the path on which God takes the course of history as He deals with individuals and all of mankind (Isa. 40:3; Ezek. 18:25, 29; 33:17, 20; Matt. 3:3; Mark 1:3; Luke 3:4; John 1:23).

Note that there is a single subject for both lines: what is 'a stronghold' to one is 'ruin' to another. Some have objected that a 'way' cannot be a 'stronghold.' Therefore, they stress that it is the word 'LORD' which must be the subject. Yet it is not any, and every, 'way' that is deemed 'a stronghold,' but it is precisely 'the way of the LORD.' He is the one that makes His way a place of refuge. Chapters 1–9 have built a strong theology of 'the way.' The metaphor is often used to describe one of two alternate roads of life that people may walk: the evil way (Prov. 1:15, 19, 31, etc.) or the good way (2:8; 8:20, etc.).[48]

So, which sense of 'the way of the Lord' should we understand here? Given the contrast in this second line, it is probably better to understand it as God's providential dealings with man and men, rather than strictly referring to His moral and ethical standards. It would be difficult to understand how 'workers of iniquity' could be described as walking in the ethical and moral standards of God. Nor how, if they did, these would be their 'ruin' rather than their salvation. It is easier to see how the dealings of God with men in the flow of history can be, at the same time, a 'stronghold' to some and a 'ruin' to others.

The two usages of 'the way of the LORD' should not, however, be considered mutually exclusive. One catches stride with God as He advances His purposes in this world by actively obeying His revealed will in the Scriptures. Conversely, disobedience puts one at odds with God and His purposes in this world (cf. Hosea 14:9; John 15:22; 2 Pet. 2:21).

Note that the second line of the proverb is identical with Proverbs 21:15b.

10:30. The righteous will never be shaken, But the wicked will not dwell in the land.
This proverb echoes a principle articulated earlier in the chapter (Prov. 10:9, 25) and to be heard again (12:3). The first line remains rather general, while the second becomes more specific. At root is the divine promise regarding the land of Israel (cf. Gen. 15:18; 17:8). Actual and lasting possession of the Promised Land was promised only to the righteous (Lev. 26; Prov. 2:21). In fact, God sternly warned that flaunting His statutes would result in expulsion from the land

of promise (Prov. 2:22). 'For evildoers will be cut off, But those who wait for the LORD, they will inherit the land. Yet a little while and the wicked man will be no more; And you will look carefully for his place, and he will not be there. But the humble will inherit the land, And will delight themselves in abundant prosperity' (Ps. 37:9-11, cf. also vv. 3, 18, 22, 28, 29, 34).

The enduring principle for today is that God guarantees the fulfillment of His promises to those who walk faithfully in His ways. Presumption upon the divine promises ends in spiritual and personal poverty.

10:31. The mouth of the righteous flows with wisdom, But the perverted tongue will be cut out.

Solomon returns, again, to the theme of the tongue of the righteous and the wicked (vv. 11-14, 18-21). The primary metaphor employed here is that of a fruit-bearing tree. The word translated 'flows with' is, more literally, 'bears fruit.'[49] And the term 'cut off' is used both of cutting trees or fruit (Num. 13:23, 24) and as a metaphor for God's judgment (Num. 15:30, 31).[50]

The words produced from a righteous heart (Luke 6:43-45) yield the fruit of wisdom (Prov. 12:14; 13:2; 18:20). They grow. They learn. They confer life to those who hear them (Prov. 13:14). How unlike the 'perverted tongue' (cf. Prov. 2:12). The word describes that which is turned, twisted or crooked. From the overflow of their twisted heart, flow twisted words that confuse, confound, and, ultimately, die. Their words do not live, they are cut off and thrust aside like the barren, dry branches of a tree whose day has come and gone (Ps. 12:3).

Our words can outlive us and confer life to others, or they can die before they reach the end of our tongues and produce nothing!

10:32. The lips of the righteous bring forth what is acceptable, But the mouth of the wicked, what is perverted.

The theme is still the tongue. The words 'righteous,' 'mouth,' and 'perverted' were all found in the previous verse as well. The words of the 'righteous' and the 'wicked' differ not only in the matter of wisdom and foolishness, but also in 'what is acceptable' and 'what is perverted.'

The verb 'bring forth' may get at the basic idea, but could be a bit misleading, since the word is literally 'know.' The word describes a deep, experiential knowledge of something. What the lips of the righteous 'know' is described as 'what is acceptable.' The word describes that which gives satisfaction, either to God or man. Cohen contends that, in Proverbs, wherever the satisfaction of God is intended, His name is also found (Prov. 8:35; 11:1, etc.).[51] Therefore, it probably refers to what people, in general, receive, welcome and deem acceptable. The tongue of the righteous helps him in his relationships. Conversely, what the wicked 'know' is 'what is perverted' (Prov. 8:13). The word describes that which is twisted, crooked or skewed from what is accepted as normal. The mouth of the wicked makes his relationships more difficult.

Perhaps Solomon had been taught to pray by his father: 'Let the words of my mouth and the meditation of my heart Be acceptable in Thy sight, O LORD, my rock and my Redeemer' (Ps. 19:14).

End Notes

1. Murphy, Roland E., *Proverbs* (Nashville: Thomas Nelson Publishers, 1998), 64.

2. Buzzell, Sid S., 'Proverbs,' *The Bible Knowledge Commentary* (Wheaton: Victor Books, 1985), 1:925.

3. Waltke, Bruce K., '*śāmaḥ*,' *Theological Wordbook of the Old Testament* (Chicago: Moody Press, 1980), 2:879.

4. Livingston, G. Herbert, '*rāsha*',' *Theological Wordbook of the Old Testament* (Chicago: Moody Press, 1980), 2:863.

5. Hamilton, Victor P., '*'ôṣār*,' *Theological Wordbook of the Old Testament* (Chicago: Moody Press, 1980), 1:68.

6. Gilchrist, Paul R., '*yā'al*,' *Theological Wordbook of the Old Testament* (Chicago: Moody Press, 1980), 1:389.

7. Ross, Allen P., 'Proverbs,' *The Expositor's Bible Commentary* (Grand Rapids, Michigan: Zondervan Publishing House, 1991), 5:953.

8. Kidner, Derek, *Proverbs* (Downer's Grove, Illinois: InterVarsity Press, 1964), 85.

9. Klingbeil, Martin G., 'הדף,' *New International Dictionary of Old Testament Theology and Exegesis* (Grand Rapids, Michigan: Zondervan Publishing House, 1997), 1:1012.

10. White, William, '*rāmâ*,' *Theological Wordbook of the Old Testament* (Chicago: Moody Press, 1980), 2:849.

11. Coppes, Leonard J., '*ḥāraṣ*,' *Theological Wordbook of the Old Testament* (Chicago: Moody Press, 1980), 1:326.

12. Goldberg, Louis, '*śākal*,' *Theological Wordbook of the Old Testament* (Chicago: Moody Press, 1980), 2:877.

13. Whybray, R. N., *Proverbs* (Grand Rapids, Michigan: William B. Eerdmans Publishing Company, 1994), 158.

14. Ibid., 160.

15. Domeris, W. R., 'כסה,' *New International Dictionary of Old Testament Theology and Exegesis* (Grand Rapids, Michigan: Zondervan Publishing House, 1997), 2:674-678.

16. Bowling, Andrew, '*zākar*,' *Theological Wordbook of the Old Testament* (Chicago: Moody Press, 1980), 1:241-243.

17. Delitzsch, F., *Proverbs, Ecclesiastes, Song of Solomon* (three volumes in one) in C. F. Keil and F. Delitzsch, vol. 6, *Commentary on the Old Testament* (in ten volumes), (1872; rpt. Grand Rapids, Michigan: William B. Eerdmans Publishing Company, 1980), 1:213.

18. Kaiser, Walter C., '*lāqaḥ*,' *Theological Wordbook of the Old Testament* (Chicago: Moody Press, 1980), 1:481.

19. Whybray, 51.

20. Olivier, J. P. J., 'תמם,' *New International Dictionary of Old Testament Theology and Exegesis* (Grand Rapids, Michigan: Zondervan Publishing House, 1997), 4:306-308.

21. Oswalt, John N., '*bāṭaḥ*,' *Theological Wordbook of the Old Testament* (Chicago: Moody Press, 1980), 1:101-102.

22. Kidner, 86.

23. Murphy, 73.

24. Allen, Ronald B., "*āṣab*,' *Theological Wordbook of the Old Testament* (Chicago: Moody Press, 1980), 2:687-688.

25. Whybray, 162.

26. Fisher, Milton C., '*nātan*,' *Theological Wordbook of the Old Testament* (Chicago: Moody Press, 1980), 2:608-609.

27. Van Groningen, Gerard, '*śāne*',' *Theological Wordbook of the Old Testament* (Chicago: Moody Press, 1980), 2:879-880.

28. Hamilton, Victor P., 'עור,' *New International Dictionary of Old Testament Theology and Exegesis* (Grand Rapids, Michigan: Zondervan Publishing House, 1997), 3:357-360.

29. Schultz, Richard, 'רין,' *New International Dictionary of Old Testament Theology and Exegesis* (Grand Rapids, Michigan: Zondervan Publishing House, 1997), 1:941.

30. Hartley, John E., '*ṣāpan*,' *Theological Wordbook of the Old Testament* (Chicago: Moody Press, 1980), 2:774-775.

31. Bowling, Andrew, '*ḥātat*,' *Theological Wordbook of the Old Testament* (Chicago: Moody Press, 1980), 1:336-337.

32. Coppes, Leonard J., '*qārab*,' *Theological Wordbook of the Old Testament* (Chicago: Moody Press, 1980), 2:811-813.

33. Carpenter, Eugene, 'פעל,' *New International Dictionary of Old Testament Theology and Exegesis* (Grand Rapids, Michigan: Zondervan Publishing House, 1997), 3:646-649.

34. Cornelius, I., 'יבול,' *New International Dictionary of Old Testament Theology and Exegesis* (Grand Rapids, Michigan: Zondervan Publishing House, 1997), 2:389-390.

35. Livingston, G. Herbert, '*ḥāṭā*',' *Theological Wordbook of the Old Testament* (Chicago: Moody Press, 1980), 1:277-279.

36. Cohen, A., *Proverbs* (London: The Soncino Press, 1946), 60.

37. Whybray, 166.

38. Ibid.

39. Ross, 5:955.

40. Schultz, Carl, "*āzab*,' *Theological Wordbook of the Old Testament* (Chicago: Moody Press, 1980), 2:658-659.

41. White, William, '*rā*'â,' *Theological Wordbook of the Old Testament* (Chicago: Moody Press, 1980), 2:852-853.

42. Murphy, 75.

43. Cohen, 61-62.

44. Whybray, 170.

45. Kidner, 88-89.

46. Whybray, 171-172.

47. Delitzsch, 1:226-227.

48. Whybray, 53.

49. Coppes, Leonard J., '*nûb*,' *Theological Wordbook of the Old Testament* (Chicago: Moody Press, 1980), 2:560.

50. Carpenter, Eugene, 'כרה,' *New International Dictionary of Old Testament Theology and Exegesis* (Grand Rapids, Michigan: Zondervan Publishing House, 1997), 2:729-731.

51. Cohen, 64.

Proverbs 11

11:1. A false balance is an abomination to the Lord, But a just weight is His delight.
This chapter opens with a theme that is familiar throughout the whole of the Old Testament: God has no tolerance for false business practices. Such activity is condemned in the Law (Lev. 19:35-36; Deut. 25:13-16), the Prophets (Ezek. 45:10; Amos 8:5; Mic. 6:10) and, here, in the Wisdom Literature (Prov. 16:11; 20:10, 23).

The term 'false balance' could well be translated 'scales of deceit' and the term 'a just weight' is, literally, 'a perfect stone.' In the absence of coinage, merchants conducted trade by using balances and weighted stones with labels indicating their mass. Businessmen were known to use two sets of weights – both falsely labeled. One set was weighted less than the indicated amount and were used when making a sale. The other set was weighted more than the indicated amount and were used when making a purchase.[1]

This kind of business conduct is 'an abomination to the Lord.' Twelve times, Proverbs speak of that which is 'an abomination' to the Lord (e.g. 3:32; 6:16; 11:1, 20; 12:22; 15:9). An abomination is an attitude or action that is repugnant to the Lord and which He cannot endure.[2] Because God loathes these things, they come under His judgment. Other things listed as 'an abomination' to the Lord include idolatry (Deut. 7:25), homosexuality and other sexual perversions (Lev. 18:22-30; 20:13), human sacrifice (Deut. 12:31), occult activity (Deut. 18:9-14), ritual prostitution (1 Kings 14:23f), and sacrificing unclean or defective animals (Deut. 14:3-8; 17:1).[3]

The 'just weight,' on the other hand, is God's 'delight.' The word here translated is the same as 'acceptable' in the last verse of the previous chapter. It refers to the pleasure God finds in one whose character and conduct is according to His will.

The introduction of the divine name ('Lord') to this verse should alert us to perhaps its greatest lesson: the world of business and commerce is a world in which God is actively involved and in which He desires uprightness. The Bible allows for no dichotomy between the secular and the sacred.

11:2. When pride comes, then comes dishonor, But with the humble is wisdom.
The contrast of pride and humility is one that is drawn frequently in these proverbs (Prov. 6:17; 13:10; 16:18; 18:12). The word 'pride' comes from a word meaning 'to boil,' and thus describes arrogant insubordination.[4] It pictures one whose view of life and its circumstances is full of himself and his abilities, rather than God and His divine capacity.[5] Instead of the personal triumph he pictures, such a one encounters 'dishonor.' Instead of acclaim, he finds that he remains unnoticed. Rather than being considered a heavyweight to be contended with, he is lightly esteemed. Instead of being valued, he is disdained (Isa. 10:12; 14:13-15).[6]

The word translated 'the humble' occurs only here. The verbal form is used in Micah 6:8 ('To walk humbly with your God'). It describes one with a submissive, modest spirit before both God and man.[7] Such a one comes into the possession of 'wisdom.' Humility has its rewards: '... [B]efore honor comes humility' (Prov. 15:33; cf. Prov. 18:12). 'It is better to be of a humble spirit with the lowly, Than to divide the spoil with the proud' (Prov. 16:19). 'The reward of humility and the fear of the LORD Are riches, honor and life' (Prov. 22:4).

11:3. The integrity of the upright will guide them, But the falseness of the treacherous will destroy them.
How can one find his way through this world? This proverb promises that the 'integrity' of the upright will move them safely through life. The word translated 'integrity' is found five times in the Old Testament, the rest of them in Job (2:3, 9; 27:5; 31:6).[8] The word describes moral wholeness or completeness. One who possesses integrity is upright, no matter where you examine him; uprightness has permeated and controlled every part of his life. The promise is that this thorough integration of uprightness will 'guide them.' The same verb is found in Proverbs 6:22, where it refers to the instruction of father and mother. Parents do their best to guide their children in God's path. The day comes, however, when they release the child and he must make his own decisions. Their prayer is that their instruction in uprightness has permeated every part of their child's life and that this 'integrity' will continue to guide them through life.

In contrast to this stands the end of those who choose wily ways. The word 'falseness' describes crookedness or perverseness in one's conduct. Those who employ these means are labeled as 'the treacherous.' This word describes one who is unfaithful and deceitful in his relationships. This might include one's marriage relationship (Exod. 21:8; Mal. 2:14), friendships (Job 6:15), official contractual or covenantal agreements (Judg. 9:23), disputes over legal matters (Jer. 12:6), and even one's relationship with God (Jer. 9:2).[9] In contrast to the outcome of the 'upright,' such scheming 'will destroy' the treacherous and deceitful.

Two Old Testament characters lend powerful illustrative help in understanding this verse. Joseph was a man of integrity, and that integrity did indeed guide him. He suffered greatly, but, in the end, he could testify 'God meant it for good in order to bring about this present result' (Gen. 50:20). Job, likewise, was a man of integrity. His suffering is legendary. Yet, God brought him through the suffering and, in the end, 'the Lord restored the fortunes of Job' (Job 42:10). This proverb must not be seen as a promise of trouble-free living, but of ultimate vindication for the person of uprightness and integrity.

11:4. Riches do not profit in the day of wrath, But righteousness delivers from death.

This proverb finds a close parallel with Proverbs 10:2, where the second line is identical to the second line here. The major difference between the two proverbs is that the 'Ill-gotten gains' of Proverbs 10:2 are replaced here with simply 'Riches.' The contrast of 'Riches' and 'righteousness,' by itself, may imply that the riches were gained unrighteously, but the parallel with Proverbs 10:2 makes that idea explicit.

The exact phrase 'day of wrath' is found also in Ezekiel 7:19 and Zephaniah 1:18 (cf. Isa. 10:3) and, no doubt, carries the same idea. See Proverbs 11:23 for the same word: 'wrath.' When that day of divine wrath arrives, no amount of earthly wealth will be of any benefit. 'Their thought is, that their houses are forever ... But man in his pomp will not endure' (Ps. 49:11a, 12a). 'And the kings of the earth and the great men and the commanders and the rich and the strong and every slave and free man, hid themselves in the caves and among the rocks of the mountains; and they said to the mountains and to the rocks, "Fall on us and hide us from the presence of Him who sits on the throne, and from the wrath of the Lamb; for the great day of their wrath has come; and who is able to stand"' (Rev. 6:15-17).

The notion that living uprightly before God and man lengthens life is a familiar one in these proverbs (e.g. Prov. 3:2; 9:11; 10:27). That righteousness delivers is also a repeated theme of this chapter (Prov. 11:6, 8).

11:5. The righteousness of the blameless will smooth his way, But the wicked will fall by his own wickedness.

The way one lives his life either complicates it or simplifies it. If we walk in God's way, we will discover that the pathway we tread is much less complicated – not void of conflicts, but easier than it would have been otherwise. God's standard is that we be 'blameless.' The word does not describe complete moral perfection, but, rather, comes from the negative angle of an absence of moral blot.[10] The word is used of animals suitable for sacrifice, because they do not possess any defect. To live blameless does not mean that we are perfect in every dimension, but that we have, by God's grace, avoided the staining of our soul through choosing unrighteousness. This word is related to the word 'integrity' in verse 3.

Such living 'will smooth his way.' The word is the same one used in the famous promise of Proverbs 3:5-6. It is found elsewhere in relation to the leveling of the path of the one who walks in trust of God (Prov. 9:15; 15:19, 21). It describes more the leveling of the path than it does the precision of its straightness.[11] This is a note that is sounded often in the Proverbs (Prov. 10:9; 11:3, 8). The metaphor of the 'way' is one carried over from the first nine chapters (Prov. 1:15, 31; 2:8, 12, 13, 20; 4:11-19, etc.).

In contrast to the security and stability of the 'blameless,' the 'wicked,' by their own 'wickedness,' will complicate their walk through this life and needlessly place before themselves the objects of their own ruin. An ungodly lifestyle is often its own judgment.

11:6. The righteousness of the upright will deliver them, But the treacherous will be caught by their own greed.

In an echo of the previous verse, this proverb underscores the self-destructive nature of lust and the inherent security found in walking with God. All the key terms of the first line are repeats from the surrounding context. The term for 'righteousness' is the same one as in verses 4, 5. The word 'upright' was met in verse 3 and the verb 'deliver' was encountered in verse 4.

The second line is also quite familiar in emphasis. The word translated 'treacherous' is the same as in verse 3. The verb 'capture' is not unfamiliar (e.g. Prov. 5:22; 6:2; 16:32), but is new to the immediate context here. The majority of its 120 uses in the Old Testament describe men capturing towns, men and spoils. It can be used with the sense of entrapment in a snare.[12] That which ensnares the 'treacherous' is their own 'greed.' The word ranges in meaning from calamity to wickedness, evil desire, craving and lust.[13] Whereas, in verse 5, the thing that created trouble for the wicked was their own acts of wickedness, here the problem is seen as being deeper. It is not just the things that the wicked do, but the desires that drive what they do, that lead them into judgment. Living by the standard of 'if it feels good do it' destroys one's life. Just doing 'what feels right' is, in the end, self-destructive (Ps. 7:16; 9:15; 59:12; Prov. 5:22).

11:7. When a wicked man dies, his expectation will perish, And the hope of strong men perishes.
We encounter here a momentary interruption of the antithetical proverbs and face one of synonymous parallelism. The point is not a new one (cf. Prov. 10:28), but is more fully developed here. The one who does not know or honor God eventually sees all his hopes and dreams die. He lives only for this life. He has lived for himself and, when the object of his desire passes, there is no more dream.

The words 'expectation' and 'hope' together describe the longing of the ungodly man's heart. The first comes from a root meaning to wait or look for with eager expectation.[14] The second brings in the eternal element of hope.[15] No such prospect awaits the one who turns from God. No amount of 'wicked' scheming, and no matter how 'strong' he may have built himself or his earthly assets, they and he cannot withstand the certainty of death (cf. v. 23; Prov. 24:20). But, how different the anticipation of the righteous (Prov. 23:18; 24:14)!

11:8. The righteous is delivered from trouble, But the wicked takes his place.
This antithetical proverb assures the reality of retribution. The first line is similar to the note already sounded in verses 3, 5-6, but here it is carried further (cf. also Prov. 12:13). While the picture is not painted with great detail, it appears that the righteous man has become the object of the schemes of the wicked. These plots appear nearly successful, for the righteous must be 'delivered' from them.[16] In this verbal form, it is used to speak of divine deliverance.[17]

The second line does not mention God as the one who intervenes, but surely it is He who sees to it that the disaster designed by the wicked for the righteous ends up being turned back upon their own heads. 'He has dug a pit and hollowed it out, And has fallen into the hole which he made' (Ps. 7:15; cf. also Ps. 9:16; 35:8; 57:6). 'He who leads the upright astray in an evil way Will himself fall into his own pit, But the blameless will inherit good' (Prov. 28:10; cf. 1:28; 5:22; 26:27).

No time-frame is given for the fulfillment of the guaranteed retribution. It may occur in this life, but certainly, at least, in the next. No better illustration of this kind of judgment exists than that of Haman, whose wicked plot against Mordecai backfired and became his own undoing (Esther 5:14; 6:4; 7:9-10).

11:9. With his mouth the godless man destroys his neighbor, But through knowledge the righteous will be delivered.
The intended contrast in this antithetical proverb is not immediately clear. The contrast between the 'godless man' and the 'righteous' is clear enough. The first is related to a verb that describes defilement and that which is polluted, profaned or corrupted.[18] The former is the same word encountered in the previous verse and over sixty other times throughout these proverbs. Neither is it difficult to imagine how the 'mouth' of the godless man can destroy those close to him. Slander, gossip and backbiting are potent weapons in an offensive against one's reputation. We are all only one rumor away from being thus destroyed.

What is not so clear is how the righteous man 'will be delivered' by 'knowledge.' Does the deliverance happen after the slander has taken place, or before? How does 'knowledge' bring about such a deliverance? The only place the word translated 'delivered' is found in Proverbs is here and in verse 8. There, too, it described deliverance from the plots of the wicked, the schemes being turned back upon their own heads.

If the deliverance is preventative, it is probably that 'knowledge' prevents the righteous person from having anything to do with these godless individuals. No relationship is built, and, thus, no intimacies are shared. It does not prevent a rumor from starting, but it gives no foundation for them to be launched either. If, on the other hand, the deliverance is to be seen as taking place after the release of the slander, the 'knowledge' is probably best seen as being that which sees through the emotion, shame and confusion, and discerns the schemes of the wicked neighbor. Thus, 'through knowledge,' the evil plot is uncovered. See Proverbs 2:10-16 for a lengthy description of the protecting power of such 'knowledge.'

11:10. When it goes well with the righteous, the city rejoices, And when the wicked perish, there is glad shouting.
This verse and the next stand together, verse 11 providing the basis for this one. Like so many other of the proverbs in this chapter, this too contains a contrast. The antithesis exists not in the reaction

of the people, for 'rejoices' and 'glad shouting' describe the same jubilance. The contrast is seen in what creates this joy. In the first line, the rejoicing is the result of the good fortune of those who are righteous. In the second line, the jubilation is over the destruction of the wicked.

Similar sentiments are sounded elsewhere in Proverbs. 'When the righteous triumph there is great glory, But when the wicked rise, men hide themselves' (Prov. 28:12). 'When the righteous increase, the people rejoice, But when a wicked man rules, people groan' (Prov. 29:2).

An example of rejoicing over the blessing of the righteous is seen in Mordecai's vindication: 'Then Mordecai went out from the presence of the king in royal robes of blue and white, with a large crown of gold and a garment of fine linen and purple; and the city of Susa shouted and rejoiced. For the Jews there was light and gladness and joy and honor' (Esther 8:15). An example of joy over the wicked's departure is see in the response to Athaliah's death: 'So all the people of the land rejoiced and the city was quiet. For they had put Athaliah to death with the sword at the king's house' (2 Kings 11:20, cf. also Isa. 30:32; Nah. 3:19; 2 Chron. 21:20).

11:11. By the blessing of the upright a city is exalted, But by the mouth of the wicked it is torn down.
The previous verse left us uncertain as to exactly why the people would rejoice over the blessing of the righteous and the destruction of the wicked. We now discover the answer to that question. The residents of the city have come to appreciate the upright because, by their 'blessing,' the city has been exalted. This 'blessing' could be their verbal pronouncement over the city or it could be that their very presence and their righteously produced prosperity bring residual benefits to the other residents. In view of the contrast with 'the mouth of the wicked,' it would seem most natural to understand 'the blessing' as verbal in line one as well. The notion of their presence and prosperity being a blessing should not, however, be completely forgotten. 'Righteousness exalts a nation, But sin is a disgrace to any people' (Prov. 14:34).

The contrasting joy over the destruction of the wicked is produced because, by his mouth, the wicked has 'torn down' the greater community in which he resides. After all, 'With his mouth the godless man destroys his neighbor' (v. 9). 'A worthless person, a wicked man, Is the one who walks with a false mouth, Who winks with his eyes, who signals with his feet, Who points with his fingers;

Who with perversity in his heart devises evil continually, Who spreads strife' (Prov. 6:12-14; cf. 28:12, 28).

For a contemporary illustration of the truth of this proverb, contrast the difference in the people's reaction to the deaths of ex-dictaror Nicolae Ceausescu in Romania and Princess Diana of the United Kingdom.

11:12. He who despises his neighbor lacks sense, But a man of understanding keeps silent.

This verse continues and advances the theme of speech beginning in verses 9-11. The first line announces the foolishness of the one 'who despises his neighbor.' By itself, this line might sound as if it refers to simply an inward attitude of disdain. The word, however, describes outward, expressed and vocalized contempt.[19] In Proverbs, it describes contempt for 'wisdom and instruction' (Prov. 1:7; 23:9), 'a thief' (6:30), God's 'word' (13:13), parents (23:22; 30:17), and a neighbor as here (14:21). That this disdain is expressed is clear from the contrast of 'keeps silent' in line two.

One who gives uncontrolled expression to such feelings 'lacks sense.' Literally, the text reads 'lacks heart' (Prov. 6:32; 7:7; 9:4; 10:13; 12:11; 17:18; 24:30). Such a one lacks the inner discernment to see that a relationship with a neighbor is a valuable thing, not something to be wasted over a few needless comments made rashly. Indeed, it is more than foolish; it is sinful (Prov. 14:21). No doubt, this spite, at various times, takes the form of gossip (Prov. 11:13; 20:19), slander (10:18), false witness (12:17), boasting (25:14) and quarreling (15:18).

In contrast to the rash words of the fool is the silence of 'a man of understanding.' That is to say, he possesses discernment (Prov. 2:2, 3). Such discernment often keeps itself quiet, rather than flaunting its insight. 'When there are many words, transgression is unavoidable, But he who restrains his lips is wise' (Prov. 10:19; cf. 13:3; 17:27).

11:13. He who goes about as a talebearer reveals secrets, But he who is trustworthy conceals a matter.

Solomon continues to illustrate how powerful an influence the tongue is. The word 'talebearer' is a translation of a rare Hebrew noun found only six times in the Old Testament (Lev. 19:16; Jer. 6:28; 9:4; Ezek. 22:9; Prov. 20:19). It refers not simply to one who, without thinking, unwittingly reveals a confidence, but to one who maliciously uses privileged information to his advantage.[20] The word 'secrets' refers to confidential conversation, thus it is often translated as 'counsel.' It may refer either to divine or human information.[21]

The Scriptures repeatedly denounce one who betrays a confidence and uses it to his own advantage (Lev. 19:16; Prov. 16:28; 18:8; 20:19; 26:20, 22; Ezek. 22:9).

In contrast to such a treacherous companion is 'he who is trustworthy.' The phrase is literally 'the faithful of spirit.' The basic root of the word means that which is firm or certain.[22] With such a one, you know what and who you are dealing with. You are never uncertain as to their motives, nor their dependability. There is no concern that they might not keep in confidence what is shared with them. Such a one 'conceals a matter.' The word means 'to cover' and 'to conceal.'[23] They 'keep a lid on it,' as we might say. Whether the information is gained through a personal confidence or they stumble across such knowledge, your well-being is safe with this neighbor (cf. v. 12b; 25:9).

11:14. Where there is no guidance, the people fall, But in abundance of counselors there is victory.
Whether applied to corporate settings (such as a nation or grouping of people like a church or organization) or to the individual's life, this proverb underscores the essential nature of soliciting and listening carefully to the advice of wise counselors (Prov. 1:5; 15:22; 20:18; 24:6). Vision is absolutely essential to a healthy nation, church or organization, not to mention the individual's life. The word 'guidance' is a rare word (Job 37:12; Prov. 1:5; 12:5; 20:18; 24:6) that comes from a root having to do with the tackle necessary for the steering of a ship. People need to know how to steer a wise course through life and its multitude of opportunities.[24] They need to 'learn the ropes' of their particular circumstance and find God's charted course through it.[25]

For this to happen, they need an 'abundance of counselors.' The verbal form of the word describes giving counsel, deliberating, determining purpose and making a decision. We first meet the word in Exodus 18:19 when Jethro, Moses's father-in-law, gives him wise counsel about how to handle his workload. Men like Rehoboam (1 Kings 12:8, 13) and Absalom (2 Sam. 17) illustrate the danger of rejecting good counsel and following bad advice. It is not only folly to fail to listen to good counsel, but also to seek out and heed bad counsel. One error is often as devastating as the other. It is, of course, ultimately, the 'counsel of the Lord' (Ps. 33:11) which one wants most to determine. He only is the 'Wonderful Counselor' (Isa. 9:6).[26] Yet, the proverb here tells us that, to determine His counsel, we must often seek out those around us who possess wisdom and insight.

With such counsel, there is 'victory.' The word often carries the connotation of 'salvation' or 'deliverance' from danger.[27] One can be delivered from the consequences of an otherwise devastating choice if he will seek wise counsel. Finding such wise counsel comes not just from seeking one source, but an 'abundance of counselors.' Through the diversity of their insights, one may begin to detect a pattern of common agreement. The proclivities of one and the opinions of the few are balanced by the collective wisdom of the many.

Solomon's father, David, provides an excellent example of one humble enough to seek and heed the advice of others (2 Sam. 15:30–17:23). 'And the advice of Ahithophel, which he gave in those days, was as if one inquired of the word of God; so was all the advice of Ahithophel regarded by both David and Absalom' (2 Sam. 16:23).

11:15. He who is surety for a stranger will surely suffer for it, But he who hates going surety is safe.
The issue of 'surety' has been encountered already in Proverbs 6:1-5. Turn there for more insight. This, basically, involves guaranteeing repayment of another person's debt, should they become unable to pay. Proverbs repeatedly warns against such a decision (Prov. 17:18; 20:16; 22:26-27; 27:13). And, it is all the riskier here because it is for 'a stranger.' The reference is to one that you do not know. They might have been, in the original context, from another nation or they may have simply been an Israelite with whom one was personally unfamiliar. In either case, the danger is entrusting your financial stability into the hands of one whose character is unknown. Solomon states the outcomes as a settled matter: you will 'suffer for it.'

On the other hand, one who refuses 'going surety' avoids such personally disastrous consequences. The phrase 'going surety' is literally 'shakers [of hands],' something akin to our modern handshake, though no doubt more binding. This path of wisdom leaves you 'safe'; that is to say, free from the anxiety and concern of potential financial ruin.

11:16. A gracious woman attains honor, And violent men attain riches.
This verse presents several unusual contrasts. It is a contrast between a 'woman' and 'men,' the only time such a contrast occurs in Proverbs.[28] The contrast is, even more specifically, between one who is 'gracious' and one who is 'violent.' Additionally, it is between 'honor' and 'riches.' The one constant is that the verb in both lines is identical.

The word 'gracious' can be variously translated as 'favor,'
'grace,' or 'charm.' The emphasis is not upon the giver, but upon
the recipient of what is given. The word appears thirteen times in
Proverbs, usually with the idea of aesthetic charm or beauty.[29] Such
is not measured merely physically, but inwardly (Prov. 11:22). In
contrast stands 'violent men.' The word describes one who instills
terror because of his extremely wicked and ruthless ways.[30]

The contrast also includes the outcome of such living. The one
receives 'honor,' the other 'wealth.' To some, the antithesis does not
seem appropriate. The emphasis, however, seems to be that violent
oppression may gain one a measure of tangible, worldly wealth, but
that, by gracious living, one may achieve the far more lasting and
valuable treasure of 'honor' in the sight of men and God (Prov. 22:1;
31:28, 30). Violence pays only in this life, if at all (Prov. 1:18-19; 10:2;
11:4), while a life tempered by grace pays dividends not only in this
life, but also in the next.

11:17. The merciful man does himself good, But the cruel man does himself harm.

This entire antithetical proverb is a contrast. The English translation
does not evidence it, but 'himself' in the first line is 'his own soul,'
and the same English word in the second line is 'his own flesh.' Both
represent the individual in question, thus the English translation is
acceptable.

Also standing in contrast to one another is the 'merciful man' and
the 'cruel man.' The outcomes of their particular dispositions and
actions are also contrasted: 'does himself good' and 'does himself
harm.'

The 'gracious woman' of verse 16 finds her counterpart here in
the 'merciful man.' The operative word here is the richly theological
word *hesed*, which so often describes the covenant lovingkindness
of God. The 'cruel man' is one who is void of all compassion, mercy
or kindness.[31]

The main point of the proverb is that we often create our own
rewards or punishments by our dealings with others. The judgment
for our own sins often comes simply by committing them. The
uncaring, unsympathetic man does himself 'harm' (also used in
Prov. 11:29; 15:6, 27). The word is the one used to describe Achan,
who 'troubled' the nation and his own house (Josh. 7:25, 26). Ahab
accused Elijah of being such a 'troubler,' but it was, in fact, the ungodly
king himself who brought such agony to his nation (1 Kings 18:17,
18). On the other hand, the one who shows mercy will be shown

mercy himself (Matt. 5:7; Luke 6:38). There is a divinely ordained reciprocating nature to our disposition and deeds.

11:18. The wicked earns deceptive wages, But he who sows righteousness gets a true reward.

This antithetical proverb plays off of the similar sound of the Hebrew words translated 'deceptive' and 'reward.' This highlights the contrast between the empty promises of ill-gotten wealth and the enduring benefit of a life of righteousness.

It is quite true that 'violent men attain riches' (v. 16b), but these are 'deceptive wages.' Literally, the phrase is 'a wage of falsehood.' The promise of personal benefit through unrighteously obtained wealth is a lie. The benefit is soon gone and one is left empty in this life (Hag. 1:6) and the next (Prov. 10:2, 16).

In contrast to 'a wage of falsehood' is 'a reward of truth.' Such a solid, enduring reward comes to one 'who sows righteousness.' The imagery of a farmer sowing his seed probably speaks of the pattern of how one lives his life (Gal. 6:8-9). Certainly, as here, one may 'sow righteousness,' but there is also one who 'sows iniquity' (Prov. 22:8). The 'true reward' awaits the one who chooses righteousness. The imagery of sowing also intimates that it is not just that one is careful to act righteously personally, but that they also seek to broadcast that influence and lead others to a life of righteousness as well. 'And the seed whose fruit is righteousness is sown in peace by those who make peace' (James 3:18). 'Now this I say, he who sows sparingly shall also reap sparingly; and he who sows bountifully shall also reap bountifully' (2 Cor. 9:6). 'Sow with a view to righteousness' (Hosea 10:12a).

11:19. He who is steadfast in righteousness will attain to life, And he who pursues evil will bring about his own death.

Continuing on the theme of the previous verse, this proverb contrasts the outcome ('life' or 'death') of those who pursue either 'righteousness' or 'evil.' The themes are familiar to Proverbs (Prov. 10:16; 12:28; 19:23; 21:16, 21): 'life' being offered to the righteous and 'death' to the unrighteous (Rom. 6:23; James 1:15).

The opening expression is problematical for many commentators. The Hebrew text points toward the NASB translation of 'steadfast in righteousness,' while the emendation of the LXX, one manuscript and the Syriac point toward 'a son of righteousness.'[32] It seems best to take the term as adjectival ('steadfast in righteousness,' NASB) or as a participle ('truly righteous,' NIV), rather than substantival ('son of righteousness').[33]

11:20. The perverse in heart are an abomination to the Lord, But the blameless in their walk are His delight.
Solomon continues on the theme of the wicked and the just (vv. 18-19), though this time choosing different words. The word 'perverse' describes that which is 'twisted' or 'crooked,' while 'blameless' describes that which is 'without blemish,' 'whole' or 'upright.' The crookedness of the one is a matter of the 'heart,' the word in Hebrew that describes the very core of a person, encompassing the mind, emotions and the will. At their basic core, they are twisted and turned away from God. Thus, they are 'an abomination' to Him. Proverbs speaks often of that which is an abomination to the Lord (e.g. Prov. 3:32; 6:16; 11:1; 12:22; 15:8, 9, 26; 16:5; 17:15; 20:23). It is an attitude or action that is repugnant to the Lord and which He cannot endure.[34]

While God detests the one who is bent away from Him at his core, He delights in the one who walks blamelessly (Prov. 2:7, 21; 11:3). This speaks not of moral perfection, for who could measure up to that? Rather it considers the wholeness or integrity of one's heart and behavior.

11:21. Assuredly, the evil man will not go unpunished, But the descendants of the righteous will be delivered.
Continuing the theme of the fate of the wicked and righteous this proverb begins in an unusual way. The word 'Assuredly' is, literally, 'hand to hand.' This was probably an idiomatic way of speaking of the certainty of a thing. It may have harkened back to the practice of sealing a deal with a handshake and, thus, testifying to the certainty that each party will hold to the agreement (cf. Prov. 6:1).[35] The phrase is also used in Proverbs 16:5, where it is also followed by 'will not go unpunished.' Additionally, both times the phrase is used in Proverbs, it is in close connection with talk of that which is 'an abomination to the Lord' (Prov. 11:20; 16:5a).[36]

What is so certain is that the evil 'will not go unpunished.' This phrase is found often in Proverbs (Prov. 6:29; 16:5; 17:5; 19:5, 9; 28:20). The certainty of God's retribution against evil is one of the steady themes of this book (Prov. 1:26ff; 2:22).

In contrast stands the fate of those who are God's. Such folk are here referred to as 'the descendants of the righteous,' which is, literally, 'the seed of the righteous.' While the word 'seed,' generally, is used to describe descendants, it is also used on occasion to refer to the present generation (Isa. 1:4; 65:23).[37] Kidner believes that the expression refers to a particular class of people.[38] The point, then, may well not be so much about what the offspring of the righteous get, but rather what all those who are righteous themselves may expect from God. The certainty for these folks is that they 'will be delivered.' The word may describe any number of kinds of escape, but, most often, it is used to refer to rescue from death, whether that be inflicted by a personal enemy (1 Sam. 19:11; 23:13), a national one (2 Sam. 19:10), or by sickness (Ps. 107:20). Such help cannot be had from the strength of a horse (Ps. 33:17), a nation (Isa. 21:6) or riches (Job 20:20), but only from the hand of God.[39]

11:22. As a ring of gold in a swine's snout, So is a beautiful woman who lacks discretion.
This is the first example of emblematic parallelism, in which 'like,' 'as' or 'so' is used to make a comparison.[40] It is noteworthy, however, that the Hebrew text contains no word paralleling our 'So.' The comparison is left stark and unexplained. This adds to the force of the point being made.

Rings of gold were worn by women in their noses (Gen. 24:22, 47; Isa. 3:21; Ezek. 16:12) as symbols of beauty. While such a practice may not sound attractive to many of us today, the notion would have been much like our earrings, bracelets or necklaces. How foolish to place a valuable and beautiful piece of jewelry on a pig? Pigs were condemned as ceremonially unclean and unfit for sacrifice. In addition, they were considered among the most filthy of animals. No amount of jewelry can make a pig beautiful.

In comparison stands the beautiful woman who lacks 'discretion.' The word is, literally, 'taste,' and can describe the taste of food (Exod. 16:31), wise insight (1 Sam. 25:33), or moral judgment (Ps. 119:66).[41] Probably, here, the idea is that this woman lacks sound moral judgment. No amount of physical, outward beauty can disguise the inherent deficiency of her inner person. As a gold ring is a waste in a pig's snout, so physical beauty is wasted upon a woman without character. Contrast this with the 'gracious woman' of Proverbs 11:16! 'Charm is deceitful and beauty is vain, But a woman who fears the LORD, she shall be praised' (Prov. 31:30). There is nothing inherently superior in homeliness, but beauty without character is a waste.

11:23. The desire of the righteous is only good, But the expectation of the wicked is wrath.
At first glance, the import of the first line is not abundantly clear. However, the second line explains what is meant by 'is only good.' There is no verb in the Hebrew, so it, literally, reads: 'The desire of

the righteous only good.' Is it that the righteous only finds his heart going after that which is morally upright? Not exactly. The second line reveals that 'desire' is parallel to 'expectation.' The anticipated outcome of one's actions is in view. The end product of what the righteous pursue turns out to be, from God's ultimate perspective, good.

In contrast, the anticipated outcome of the pursuits of the wicked is 'wrath.' What exactly is meant by that? The word translated 'wrath' does indeed carry that connotation in the Old Testament when referring to God. It signifies the overflowing anger of God. When the divine wrath is kindled, it is abundant, unrestrainable and no one stands before it. However, in relation to man, it most often has the notion of 'arrogance,' or 'pride.' The verbal root means 'to pass over' or 'to overflow.'[42] Compared with the first line, the idea is that this arrogance, mixed with anger, brings nothing in the end to 'the wicked.' His arrogance leads him to desire that which he cannot have, even at the price of wrath and anger. In the end, it is ultimately self-defeating. The desire of the righteous ends eventually in what God pronounces as good (Prov. 13:4). The desire of the wicked ends in want and emptiness, no matter how hard he fights for it (Prov. 10:24, 28; 11:4, 7).

We are reminded here that, ultimately, one's desires, and the character with which he seeks their fulfillment, determine the outcome of his life.

11:24. There is one who scatters, yet increases all the more, And there is one who withholds what is justly due, but it results only in want.
Solomon now takes up the theme of generosity (vv. 24-28). In doing so, he uses a form that states simple, observable fact: 'There is one ... And there is one ... .' He does not necessarily commit to this as an unalterable, infallible pattern, but simply that, if one looks after these patterns of dealing with things, he will discover that this is generally true.

What is true is that the one who gives, gets and the one who hangs on, loses that which he clutches. That the generous increase their store by giving is a theme that is taught often elsewhere in Scripture (Ps. 112:9; Prov. 3:9-10; Eccles. 11:1-2; John 12:24-25; Luke 6:38; 2 Cor. 9:6-9). Similarly, the stingy, selfish man ends up, by his hoarding, with less than he started with (Prov. 21:13; 28:22).

Because the verb 'who scatters' is found also in Psalm 112:9, in a context of philanthropy to the poor, this verse is often also understood this way. But, the context here does not make clear what it is that 'is justly due'? Nor is it immediately clear to whom it is due. Both Cohen and Delitzch take the view that what is referred to here is a man withholding from himself that which is justly due to himself (i.e. what any normal human being would allow himself to spend his money on).[43] Thus, what is spoken against in the second line is not a lack of generosity to others (though that would also, no doubt, be true), but rather a person who is so bent on hoarding his money that he won't even spend a dime on himself. Such a person does not win by hoarding, but rather ends up with less than if he had not compulsively clutched to his wealth at all costs.

11:25. The generous man will be prosperous, And he who waters will himself be watered.

The theme of generosity continues. This proverb is built upon a synonymous parallelism in which the second line repeats and underscores the first (as in v. 29). The basic thought has already been sounded in verses 17, 24a, and will be heard again (Prov. 22:9).

The first line is, literally, 'The soul of blessing will be made fat.' The 'soul' represents the person, the inner drive and passion expressed in their actions. From their inward person, and out through their physical body, flows 'blessing' to others. Such a one will be 'made fat.' This is a metaphorical way of describing their prosperity and health. The expression was powerful in a part of the world prone to drought and inconsistent crops (Prov. 13:4; 28:25).

The picture in the second line may be from the agricultural world (Deut. 29:18; Ps. 65:10; Isa. 55:10; 58:11; Jer. 31:12), or it may simply picture the personal satisfaction of a drink of water (Ps. 36:9). The one who pours out a cup of cool water in the name of the Lord will find that his Lord makes certain the action is reciprocated in some way (Jer. 31:25). 'For whoever gives you a cup of water to drink because of your name as followers of Christ, truly I say to you, he shall not lose his reward' (Mark 9:41).

The same imagery continues in the New Testament in similar agricultural metaphors. 'Now this I say, he who sows sparingly shall also reap sparingly; and he who sows bountifully shall also reap bountifully' (2 Cor. 9:6). 'Give, and it will be given to you; good measure, pressed down, shaken together, running over, they will pour into your lap. For by your standard of measure it will be measured to you in return' (Luke 6:38).

11:26. He who withholds grain, the people will curse him, But blessing will be on the head of him who sells it.
Solomon continues on the theme of generosity. Yet, this time, the proverb has a more definitive reference to commerce. The word 'withholds' is different from the word so translated in verse 24. The word there implies the power of the one who holds back what he has.[44] Here the word describes what only God or His designated authority has the right to withhold.[45] Thus, it appears that the idea here is of one who possesses a storehouse of grain in a time of famine or want. With neighbors in need and asking to buy from his store, he refuses, because he calculates that, if he waits, the price he may charge will skyrocket. Such a one will be cursed by the people. He is a profiteer, not a neighbor. Thus, he has become an unethical speculator in grain futures. It is not wrong for him not to sell the grain. Consider the example of Joseph in Egypt who purposefully stored up grain to relieve human hardship, rather than exploit it (Gen. 41). It is, however, wrong for one in such a position to purposely not sell for the express purpose of exploiting his neighbors at a later time. Natural disaster or personal misfortune is a time for generosity and fairness, not profiteering.

The 'blessings ... on the head' (cf. Prov. 10:6) are probably more than good wishes, but probably also entail a more tangible reward.[46] Thus, if one is generous and works to 'meet pressing needs' (Titus 3:14), God will see to it that, through those to whom he has been a blessing, a tangible blessing will return.

11:27. He who diligently seeks good seeks favor, But he who searches after evil, it will come to him.
The general theme of generosity continues (vv. 24-26), but with a twist. We meet here three different terms for seeking. The first, 'diligently seeks,' has the notion of seeking something earnestly or early. It comes from a root related to the word for 'dawn,' thus the notion is of seeking something the first thing in the morning.[47] It is a word that describes a person's priorities. The second word translated 'seeks' was used only one time in the prologue (Prov. 2:4), but will be used a great deal in the anthologies of proverbs (14:6; 15:14; 17:9, 11, 19; 18:1, 15; 21:6; 23:35; 28:5; 29:10, 26). This, too, describes an earnest search. This, however, does not include a mental or cognitive searching.[48] The third word is translated 'searches' and is a rough synonym of the second term, though it differs in that it can describe a cognitive search that aims to end in knowing something.

What does this tell us? The one who seeks good (here it probably refers not so much to a moral goodness of God, but the welfare of the community) does so as first priority. The one who puts others first is, ultimately, seeking his own good as well, though he is not cognitively setting out to arrive at that point. In other words, his motives are not bent on pleasing himself by pleasing others. That is, it is a heavenly by-product that they unwittingly discover themselves to have been pursuing by their good will (cf. Prov. 11:17a).

On the other side of the adversative, we find, however, one who is bent on seeking the evil (harm, downfall) of his neighbor(s). His intention from the beginning has been to use and abuse those around him. Such a one will discover that, what he seeks for others, he has acquired for himself (cf. Prov. 11:8, 17b).

11:28. He who trusts in his riches will fall, But the righteous will flourish like the green leaf.

The theme of generosity continues as this antithetical proverb highlights the way one relates to his worldly wealth. The possession of wealth is not evil; rather, it may actually put one in a position to help those in need (Prov. 19:17; 22:9) and, in this way, it becomes a means to performing righteousness. Wealth is evil when it becomes the object of our trust. It is not only evil, but it is not worthy as an object of faith, for it will prove unreliable and bring one down (Ps. 9:6; 62:10; Prov. 11:4; 23:4, 5; 1 Tim. 6:17).

Here, 'the righteous' probably has in view not those without wealth, for there is no inherent righteousness in poverty. Rather, it pictures those who possess wealth and, yet, hold it with an open hand, freely giving to the needy (1 Tim. 6:17-19). The promise comes in the form of a familiar image, that of a flourishing, healthy plant that brings forth fruit (Ps. 1:3; 92:12-15; Prov. 11:30; Jer. 17:7-8).

The contrasting images of 'fall' and 'green leaf' are not perfectly parallel, and, for this reason, some have tried to emend the Hebrew text and change 'fall' to 'wither.'[49] This is unnecessary, as 'fall' in Hebrew was an oft-used way of describing one's ruin, while the 'green leaf' was a picture of prosperity and fruitfulness.[50]

11:29. He who troubles his own house will inherit wind, And the foolish will be servant to the wisehearted.

This proverb uses synonymous parallelism to make its point. Precisely what that point is can be rather hard to say. The general intention is clear, but the specifics are more elusive. The one 'who troubles his own house' may be the master of the house, or it could be a child who brings hardship and pain upon his parents. If it is the former, the notion may be that he is inept (thus 'foolish') at managing the assets that God has entrusted to him. If it is the latter, it could mean that the family's inheritance might go to another or that his rebellion might beggar the family. In either case, he 'will inherit the wind.' The 'wind' is used elsewhere (Prov. 27:16; Eccles. 1:14, 17; 2:11, 17, 26; 4:4, 6, 16; 6:9) to describe that which is without substance, elusive and impossible to control or keep. The verb 'troubles' has been met already in verse 17.

The second line reaffirms and extends the point made by the first. If the first line refers to the father of a home, then the idea here is that he will end up being an indentured slave to his creditors. If it refers to a son who brings the whole family down, he will, in his indigence, also be forced to submit himself to another to provide food and housing for himself. In Proverbs, the foolish inevitably end up serving the wise, regardless of how the assets are distributed at the start (Prov. 14:19; 17:2).

11:30. The fruit of the righteous is a tree of life, And he who is wise wins souls.
In contrast to the foolish man who troubles his own family (v. 29), we meet here the wise man whose life and influence become a boon to those who know him. The first line, admittedly, seems to mix its metaphors. How does 'fruit' become 'a tree of life'? But, this is to miss the point the author is seeking to make. By the 'fruit of the righteous' is meant not simply, nor primarily, the results in one's own life. Rather, it is the outcome of one's relationships and the results born in others because of one's presence and influence. These changed lives (one's 'fruit'), in turn, become 'a tree of life' to others. Is that not, after all, what fruit does? It falls from the tree, deposits seeds in the earth, which then grow to become another tree? Does not this transference continue on in one tree giving life to another tree (or many trees!)?

This thrust is affirmed by the second line, when it, too, is rightly understood. There has been much debate over the expression 'wins souls.' The reading could be, literally rendered, 'one taking lives.' The verb is used in Psalm 31:13 in the sense of murder. Indeed, the word means to 'lay hold of, seize, conquer.'[51] Some have followed the LXX and Syriac and chosen to emend the Hebrew text and arrive at a translation like 'lawlessness takes away lives' (RSV). Such an emendation is unnecessary, however. If the first line is understood correctly, then the second functions not in antithetical parallelism, but in synonymous parallelism. The second line takes up the thought of the first and recasts it in powerful terminology. One who is truly wise uses all his means of influence to draw others to wisdom, for herein is life (Prov. 3:2, 16, 18, 22; etc.)!

While not exactly the same, the gist of the verse is very close to being an Old Testament version of the New Testament call to be fishers of men (Dan. 12:3; Luke 5:10; 1 Cor. 9:19-22; James 5:20). That is especially so, when we note that the imagery of 'tree of life' is first met in the garden (Gen. 2:9) and continues until the close of the Scriptures and of history in the new heavens and the new earth (Rev. 2:7; 22:2, 14). The image is frequent here in Proverbs (Prov. 3:18; 13:12; 15:4). Note also the connection to the 'leaf' that will 'flourish' in Proverbs 11:28.

11:31. If the righteous will be rewarded in the earth, How much more the wicked and the sinner!

We meet here the first of four 'how much more' proverbs (15:11; 19:7; 21:27). Consider also the 'how much less' logic found in Proverbs 17:7 and 19:10.

Many have protested that the blanket assurances made in the Proverbs are nearly too good to be true. They seem, in some people's eyes, to be overly simplistic and the promises overstated. This proverb, however, tells us that the promises of Proverbs cannot be entirely spiritualized or cast only in some distant future. Indeed, the outcome is said to be 'in the earth.'

What is the relationship of the two lines of this proverb? What is the nature of the reward promised in each line? It is possible that the first line might have in view the reward for righteous living and the second the repayment for a wicked lifestyle. The verb 'rewarded' can be used both in a positive and negative sense.[52] On the other hand, it seems wiser, in view of the 'how much more' argumentation, to view the two lines in the same way. Thus, the meaning appears to be 'If the righteous find that even for their comparatively minor sinful actions God repays them in this life, then how much more should the wicked sinner be assured he will not escape this life without his sins coming to bear upon him?'

Elsewhere in the Wisdom Literature, we are reminded 'Indeed, there is not a righteous man on earth who continually does good and who never sins' (Eccles. 7:20). One of Job's friends reminded him, 'What is man, that he should be pure, Or he who is born of a woman, that he should be righteous? Behold, He puts no trust in His holy ones, And the heavens are not pure in His sight; How much less one who is detestable and corrupt, Man, who drinks iniquity like water!' (Job 15:14-16).

The LXX has changed the sense of the verse to read 'If the righteous be scarcely saved,' and this is reflected in 1 Peter 4:18. The difference appears to have arisen over a confusion of letters, which change 'in the earth' to a word meaning 'deficiency' or 'want,' or even perhaps to a word meaning 'to cut off' or 'shorten.' It would be a stretch to make the verb 'rewarded' mean 'saved.'[53]

End Notes

1. Buzzell, Sid S., 'Proverbs,' *The Bible Knowledge Commentary* (Wheaton: Victor Books, 1985), 1:928.

2. Whybray, R. N., *Proverbs* (Grand Rapids, Michigan: William B. Eerdmans Publishing Company, 1994), 73.

3. Youngblood, Ronald F., '*tô'ēbâ*,' *Theological Wordbook of the Old Testament* (Chicago: Moody Press, 1980), 2:976-297.

4. Ross, Allen P., 'Proverbs,' *The Expositor's Bible Commentary* (Grand Rapids, Michigan: Zondervan Publishing House, 1991), 5:959.

5. Wood, Leon J., '*zîd*,' *Theological Wordbook of the Old Testament* (Chicago: Moody Press, 1980), 1:239.

6. Nel, Philip J., 'קלה,' *New International Dictionary of Old Testament Theology and Exegesis* (Grand Rapids, Michigan: Zondervan Publishing House, 1997), 3:924-925.

7. Buzzell, 1:928.

8. Payne, J. Barton, '*tāmam*,' *Theological Wordbook of the Old Testament* (Chicago: Moody Press, 1980), 2:973-974.

9. Goldberg, Louis, '*bāgad*,' *Theological Wordbook of the Old Testament* (Chicago: Moody Press, 1980), 1:89-90.

10. Delitzsch, F., *Proverbs, Ecclesiastes, Song of Solomon* (three volumes in one) in C. F. Keil and F. Delitzsch, vol. 6, *Commentary on the Old Testament* (in ten volumes), (1872; rpt. Grand Rapids, Michigan: William B. Eerdmans Publishing Company, 1980), 1:232.

11. Ibid.

12. Kaiser, Walter C., '*lysh*,' *Theological Wordbook of the Old Testament* (Chicago: Moody Press, 1980), 1:479-480.

13. Payne, J. Barton, '*hāwâ*,' *Theological Wordbook of the Old Testament* (Chicago: Moody Press, 1980), 1:209-210.

14. Hartely, John E., '*qāwâ*,' *Theological Wordbook of the Old Testament* (Chicago: Moody Press, 1980), 2:791.

15. Gilchrist, Paul R., '*yāhal*,' *Theological Wordbook of the Old Testament* (Chicago: Moody Press, 1980), 1:373-374.

16. Whybray, 179.

17. Els, P. J. J. S., 'חלץ,' *New International Dictionary of Old Testament Theology and Exegesis* (Grand Rapids, Michigan: Zondervan Publishing House, 1997), 2:157-159.

18. Goldberg, Louis, '*hānēp*,' *Theological Wordbook of the Old Testament* (Chicago: Moody Press, 1980), 1:304-305.

19. Grisanti, Michael A., 'בוז,' *New International Dictionary of Old Testament Theology and Exegesis* (Grand Rapids, Michigan: Zondervan Publishing House, 1997), 1:618-619.

20. White, William, '*rākal*,' *Theological Wordbook of the Old Testament* (Chicago: Moody Press, 1980), 2:848.

21. Patterson, R. D., 'swd,' *Theological Wordbook of the Old Testament* (Chicago: Moody Press, 1980), 2:619.

22. Scott, Jack B., ''*āman*,' *Theological Wordbook of the Old Testament* (Chicago: Moody Press, 1980), 1:51.

23. Harris, R. Laird, '*kāsâ*,' *Theological Wordbook of the Old Testament* (Chicago: Moody Press, 1980), 1:448-449.

24. Kidner, Derek, *Proverbs* (Downers Grove, Illinois: InterVarsity Press, 1964), 92.

25. Ibid., 37.

26. Gilchrist, Paul R., '*yā'as*,' *Theological Wordbook of the Old Testament* (Chicago: Moody Press, 1980), 1:390-391.

27. Hartley, John E., '*yāsha'*,' *Theological Wordbook of the Old Testament* (Chicago: Moody Press, 1980), 1:414-416.

28. Cohen, A., *Proverbs* (London: The Soncino Press, 1946), 68.

29. Yamauchi, Edwin, '*hānan*,' *Theological Wordbook of the Old Testament* (Chicago: Moody Press, 1980), 1:302-304.

30. Buzzell, 1:929.

31. Baker, David W., 'אָכַר,' *New International Dictionary of Old Testament Theology and Exegesis* (Grand Rapids, Michigan: Zondervan Publishing House, 1997), 1:392-393.

32. Ross, 5:963.

33. Whybray, 184.

34. Ibid., 73.

35. Cohen, 69-70.

36. Whybray, 184.

37. Cohen, 70.

38. Kidner, 93.

39. Carr, G. Lloyd, '*mālat*,' *Theological Wordbook of the Old Testament* (Chicago: Moody Press, 1980), 1:507.

40. Buzzell, 2:930.

41. Ross, 5:964.

42. Van Groningen, Gerard, ''*ābar*,' *Theological Wordbook of the Old Testament* (Chicago: Moody Press, 1980), 2:641-644.

43. Cohen, 71; and Delitzch, 1:245.

44. Coppes, Leonard J., '*hāśak*,' *Theological Wordbook of the Old Testament* (Chicago: Moody Press, 1980), 1:329.

45. Carr, G. Lloyd, '*māna'*,' *Theological Wordbook of the Old Testament* (Chicago: Moody Press, 1980), 1:515.

46. Whybray, 186-187.

47. Kidner, 61.

48. Coppes, Leonard J., '*bāqash*,' *Theological Wordbook of the Old Testament* (Chicago: Moody Press, 1980), 1:126.

49. Murphy, 84.

50. Ross, 5:965.

51. Ibid., 5:966.

52. Delitzsch, 1:249-250.

53. Ross, 5:967.

Proverbs 12

12:1. Whoever loves discipline loves knowledge, But he who hates reproof is stupid.
This chapter is made up almost exclusively of antithetical proverbs (except see vv. 9, 14, 28), and primarily of contrasts between the wicked and the righteous, rather than the wise and the foolish (though see vv. 15, 16, 23).

Two identical participles in the first line ('loves') help state the matter plainly. The Hebrew concepts of 'love' and 'hate' are not filled with as much emotion as we associate with the words, but focus on the priority of choice. The one who would embrace 'knowledge' must also, by logical extension, embrace 'discipline.' This 'knowledge' is introduced early in the book (Prov. 1:4) and is met often throughout its pages. It is nearly synonymous with wisdom. If one wants this all-important, life-giving knowledge, one must also embrace 'discipline.' This 'discipline' (cf. Prov. 1:2) is instruction with a sense of chastening. To arrive at the one, you must not only endure the other, but embrace it and appreciate it for its life-giving benefits (Prov. 6:23; 10:17), despite the personal pain it brings.

The second line also makes its point boldly. The sterner side of 'discipline' in line one is affirmed by the word 'reproof' in the second line. This word conveys the idea of correction or rebuke, and is often found in tandem with 'discipline.'[1]

Though it is unpleasant, the one who refuses such correction is declared to be 'stupid.' The word for 'stupid' is found five times in the Old Testament (Ps. 49:11; 73:22; 92:7; Prov. 12:1; 30:2). It carries the idea of the denseness of a dumb animal. Psalm 73:22 gives the idea: 'Then I was senseless and ignorant; I was like a beast before Thee.' The word refers to the brutish man who does not possess the rational capacity that marks the distinction between humans and animals.[2]

If one refuses correction and difficult counsel, he makes himself no better than an animal who can be moved only by sheer power and never improves because of it (Prov. 1:22, 29-30; 5:12; 15:10, 12). The one who willingly receives correction ascends the ladder of learning and comes into possession of the 'knowledge' needed to excel in life (Prov. 12:15; 13:1, 13, 18; 15:5, 31-32). Such an arrangement should not surprise us, for Solomon has declared from the beginning that this 'knowledge' only comes through 'the fear of the Lord' (1:7).

12:2. A good man will obtain favor from the LORD, But He will condemn a man who devises evil.

The 'good man' is, according to Delitzsch, the one who operates from a fundamentally self-sacrificing motive of love.[3] The opposite of such a man is one 'who devises evil.' The verb is used throughout Proverbs. In the first nine chapters, it is used positively (Prov. 1:4; 3:21; 5:2; 8:12), in the second half negatively (Prov. 14:17; 24:8).[4] Positively, it describes the 'discretion' which wisely thinks through each venture and each encounter. The negative connotation is that of 'scheming' evil.[5] Here, the negative idea is in view.

The 'good man' comes to possess the 'favor' of the Lord (Prov. 3:4; 8:35). Heaven smiles upon him; the seal of God's approval is affixed to his life. The second man, however, God 'will condemn.' The word has a judicial flavor, indicating that the verdict of God will be cast against such a one.[6] 'He captures the wise by their own shrewdness And the advice of the cunning is quickly thwarted' (Job 5:13; cf. 1 Cor. 3:19).

12:3. A man will not be established by wickedness, But the root of the righteous will not be moved.

While the previous verse focused upon what a man receives from God, this verse views the man from the vantage point of the stability of his foundation. The words 'not be established' and 'not be moved' stand in antithesis. The basic root of the former carries the idea of firmness and, then, extends to that which is settled and established.[7] The latter, without the negative, describes that which is profoundly unstable, but, with its negation and relation to God, it speaks of that which is dependable and solid.[8]

Solidity of life can never be found through fleeing God's path and choosing one's own ways (Prov. 10:7; 11:5). The contrast to 'wickedness' is 'the root of the righteous' (cf. Ps. 1; Jer. 17:7, 8). The phrase is used again in verse 12. Here, the notion is that the one who sinks the roots of his choices, allegiance and commitment deep into God and His ways will find security and longevity (Prov. 10:25, 30). In verse 12, the one who so establishes himself in God will find his life yields what he needs for the fulfillment of God's will. Living God's way brings stability and fruitfulness.

What is true for individuals is also true for nations, as the prophets reveal (e.g. Isa. 54:14).[9]

12:4. An excellent wife is the crown of her husband, But she who shames him is as rottenness in his bones.
The description of an 'excellent wife' is also taken up at length in Proverbs 31:10-31 and the phrase is used as a descriptive title for Ruth (Ruth 3:11). In the Hebrew arrangement of the Scriptures, the Book of Ruth immediately follows the Book of Proverbs, thus putting her as the next literary piece, immediately following that exalted description of the perfect wife. That description and her example become, then, the best commentary on this verse.

The well-known translation, 'virtuous woman' (KJV), can be somewhat misleading in today's world. When translated, the word 'virtuous' came from the Latin virtus, the word for 'manly excellence.' Thus, the idea of 'virtuous woman' then was 'the manly woman,' something rather distant from what the modern reader understands by the term 'virtuous'! The notion Solomon is attempting to communicate is that of strength and military prowess. In fact, a study of Proverbs 31:10-31 will reveal a number of military terms used to describe the activities of the 'excellent wife.' This is why he opts for the title 'valiant wife.'[10] The idea is of a woman with both strength of character and significant competency in dealing with life.

Such a woman is 'the crown of her husband.' The metaphor of a crown conveys the idea of rulership, esteem, honor and community recognition (Prov. 4:9; 14:24; 16:31; 17:6).[11] Such a wife enables her husband to gain the applause and respect of their community, perhaps for his many successes, but not the least of which is having the good sense to marry such a wonderful woman. Proverbs has a great deal to say about the value of a godly wife (Prov. 11:16; 18:22).

In contrast, there is also 'she who shames' her husband. Such a wife lowers the community's evaluation of her husband. He may achieve other successes, but he is never able to rise above the community's evaluation of his wife. She becomes 'as rottenness in his bones.' This describes the eating away of his life and honor from the inside out. The word is used in Job 13:28 of a moth-eaten garment. She is, in modern terms, a 'cancer' to her husband.[12] Corresponding to its many descriptions of a good wife, Proverbs also takes its time to underscore the harm of a bad wife (Prov. 19:13; 21:9, 19; 25:24; 27:15).

12:5. The thoughts of the righteous are just, But the counsels of the wicked are deceitful.
This antithetical proverb contrasts the plans of the just and the wicked. The word 'thoughts' describes a person's plans, thoughts and intentions (Prov. 6:18; 15:22, 26; 16:3; 19:21; 20:18; 21:5).[13] These inner

calculations and projections are 'just.' In contrast stand the 'counsels of the wicked.' The word 'counsels' is related to a word for 'rope' or 'cord.' A word picture emerges from the world of sea travel. Sailors steered their ships by skillfully pulling these ropes to keep the ship on a true course (cf. Prov. 1:5; 11:14; 20:18; 24:6).[14] The word 'deceitful' describes that which fundamentally functions as betrayal and fraud.[15]

The 'righteous' are concerned first, and foremost, in all of their plans with what is right in the eyes of God and men. The 'wicked' begin all considerations from the vantage point of what benefits them. The thoughts, plans and choices of each then proceed from those starting points.

12:6. The words of the wicked lie in wait for blood, But the mouth of the upright will deliver them.

What were mere plots and plans (v. 5) have now become words and arguments (v. 6). The wicked use their words to ambush the innocent. The phrase 'lie in wait for blood' is a graphic one. A similar idea was used in Proverbs 1:11 to describe the vocalized plots of gang members. 'But,' as became clear there, 'they lie in wait for their own blood; They ambush their own lives' (Prov. 1:18). Perhaps the setting is judicial and the idea is that of false testimony. Maybe a more general idea of slander is in view. Either way, the wicked are bent on destruction through their words.

In contrast stand the upright, who use their wisdom-come-to-words to 'deliver.' What is not clear is whether 'them' refers to the upright themselves who have been verbally attacked or whether it refers to some innocent third party who has become the target of the wicked's venom. The commentators appear divided over the matter. If it is the former that is in view, Samson would provide a good illustration (Judg. 14). If it is the latter, then David's rebuttal of his men's counsel to kill Saul is a good picture (1 Sam. 26:1-12).

One of the stated objectives of seeking wisdom is 'To deliver you from the way of evil, From the man who speaks perverse things ... To deliver you from the strange woman, From the adulteress who flatters with her words' (Prov. 2:12, 16). 'With his mouth the godless man destroys his neighbor, But through knowledge the righteous will be delivered' (Prov. 11:9).

12:7. The wicked are overthrown and are no more, But the house of the righteous will stand.

Thoughts (v. 5) became words (v. 6) and, now, what the wicked have plotted for others (vv. 5-6) has come back upon them. The disaster they wished for others is now their lot. The verse is nearly identical to the thought of Proverbs 10:25.

The verb 'overthrown' is often used in connection with God's judgment upon unrepentant Sodom and Gomorrah (Gen. 19:21, 25, 29; Deut. 29:23; Jer. 20:16; Lam. 4:6; Amos 4:11). The overthrow of these infamous cities is the warning of God for all who rebel against Him, whether that be Jerusalem (2 Kings 21:13), Nineveh (Jonah 3:4), the unbelieving nations (Hag. 2:22) or, as here, 'the wicked' more generally.[16]

When disaster strikes, the wicked 'are no more' (cf. Ps. 37:10). They live on the edge constantly. They exist on the brink of ruin, recognized or not. They have no backup, no reserve, nothing and no one to fall back on.

How markedly different is 'the house of the righteous.' The imagery probably includes not simply the physical structure in which the righteous dwell, but the family and all that they deem of ultimate worth. The verse does not promise that disaster will not befall the righteous, only that, when it does, they will survive, endure and remain. The certainty of this is the nearness of God. He makes certain that the righteous will survive and thrive again (Prov. 3:25-26; 12:3; 14:11; Matt. 7:24-27).

12:8. A man will be praised according to his insight, But one of perverse mind will be despised.
This verse and the next concern a person's reputation in the community. Here the appreciation of the community rides on one's common sense. The word for 'insight' describes the practical ability to think clearly. It includes, but is not limited to, the realm of moral discernment and extends to an ability to think straight about all that one encounters.[17] A man's praise is measured 'according to' the measure of his common sense. The phrase 'according to' is, literally, 'by the mouth of.' The picture seems to be that his common sense 'makes a statement' about the kind of man he is. In this measure, the community responds with respect.

In contrast to such a clear-headed thinker is the 'one of perverse mind.' Again, 'perverse' here speaks of that which is crooked and twisted. The phrase reads, literally, 'one crooked of heart.' The heart, as we have so often seen in Proverbs, represents the totality of one's inner being: mind, emotions and will. When a man is fundamentally twisted within, he will see all of life with skewed vision. He will, thus, lack the ability to respond wisely to life and all it delivers. The result will be that he will be 'despised' by the community at large.

Proverbs 13:15 offers a good parallel: 'Good understanding produces favor, But the way of the treacherous is hard.' Old Testament illustrations of such individuals might include Joseph (Gen. 41:39), David (1 Sam. 18:30), and Abigail (1 Sam. 25:3).

12:9. Better is he who is lightly esteemed and has a servant, Than he who honors himself and lacks bread.
The antithesis of this proverb is expressed through the words 'Better ... than' rather than 'but.' This is the first of many such proverbial sayings: Proverbs 15:16, 17; 16:8, 19, 32; 17:1; 19:1, 22; 21:9, 19; 22:1; 25:7, 24; 27:5, 10; 28:6.

The first line of the contrast presents us with two options for translation. The traditional reading is 'and has a servant.' The suggestion of the LXX and Syriac is 'and serves himself.' Either is possible using the same Hebrew consonants. The first describes the person who does not put on airs, but, at least, has enough cash flow to sustain a personal servant. The second points to a person who may not have much, but at least is self-employed. The difference hinges on whether a preposition is viewed as a possessive ('have a servant') or an indirect object ('servant for himself').[18] Either option is possible, and either makes the same basic point: humility, with at least moderate means, is to be preferred to image without daily sustenance.

Repeatedly, these proverbs remind us to be content with what we have (Prov. 15:16, 17; 16:8; 17:1; 19:1; 28:6).[19] The second line exhorts us to consider the folly of acting like a big shot when you have nothing. 'There is one who pretends to be rich, but has nothing; Another pretends to be poor, but has great wealth' (Prov. 13:7).

12:10. A righteous man has regard for the life of his beast, But the compassion of the wicked is cruel.
Here the considerate gentleness of the righteous is contrasted with the brute selfishness of the wicked. The first line may be translated, more literally, 'knows the soul of his beast.' The Hebrew verb for 'has regard' is the rich word usually translated 'know.' It speaks of a deeply intimate and personal knowledge. We have here a beautiful picture of the inherent gentleness and compassion that the Spirit of God engenders in the heart of anyone who gives Him control of his life. Elsewhere, we are exhorted to 'know well the condition of your flocks and pay attention to your herds' (Prov. 27:23). The law of God recognized this as well (Deut. 25:4).

In contrast are the brutal ways of the wicked. The description in the second line involves an apparent oxymoron: 'The compassion of the compassionless.'[20] By nature, the wicked are self-serving and ruthless. The word 'cruel' pictures the merciless attitude of those who are bent only on self-protection and promotion (Prov. 5:9; 11:17; 17:11; Isa. 13:9; Jer. 6:23; 30:14; 50:42).[21]

The character of a man is seen in the way he treats those under his care or at his mercy, even when they are animals. This verse demonstrates that we are responsible to have dominion over the animals, while doing so in a way that reflects the tenderness of our Creator (Ps. 104:14, 27; 145:16; 147:8-9). The often out-of-balance animals rights movement may find here a general concession that animals should be treated with understanding, but no affirmation of their elevation of animals to a place of better treatment than even we who are made in God's image.

12:11. He who tills his land will have plenty of bread, But he who pursues vain things lacks sense.
This antithetical proverb contrasts the fruitfulness of hard work with the foolishness of get-rich-quick schemes. The first line promises that the one who works diligently, applying consistent effort to his fields, will find he always has enough. The second line speaks of the one who seeks an easier way. The noun 'vain things' has the idea of 'delusions' or 'fantasies.'[22] These appear to be schemes bent on quick, easy money. It is not that such a man does not work hard, for the participle 'who pursues' is in the intensive form ('who pursues diligently'). It is simply that he believes his yield will be higher if he pursues his racket.

These proverbs resolutely deny this notion. Proverbs 28:19 is nearly identical: 'He who tills his land will have plenty of food, But he who follows empty pursuits will have poverty in plenty.' 'In all labor there is profit, But mere talk leads only to poverty' (Prov. 14:23; cf. 6:6-11; 20:4; 24:30-34). The proverb should not be read to elevate either farming, in particular, or manual labor, in general, above other less strenuous forms of employment today. Rather, it is pointing to one's motivation, attempting to get something for nearly nothing.

12:12. The wicked desires the booty of evil men, But the root of the righteous yields fruit.
The exact text is difficult to determine, as the Masoretic Text, LXX, Syriac and Latin all have slightly different renderings for the first line. Instead of 'booty,' the Masoretic Text has 'net.'[23] By 'net' may be implied that which is caught in one's net – thus, by extension, 'booty.' One certainty in the text is the contrast of 'the root of the

righteous,' a repetition from verse 3. The translation 'yields fruit' is an interpretation of the verb which simply means 'gives.' The point of this simple verb appears indecipherable to some. Yet, the point seems to be that the 'wicked' long after what seems an inexhaustible store of wealth that belongs to the 'evil men.' But, the truly unending supply of all we need is found in 'the root of the righteous.' The one who does justice and maintains his integrity will find that such a path pays better than the unscrupulous who lust after ill-gotten gain.

An alternative is to understand the Hebrew word 'net' (NASB, 'booty') as coming not from that root, but one meaning 'stronghold.'[24] Then, following the LXX for the second line, the verb 'gives' (NASB, 'yields fruit') becomes 'endures.'[25] This understanding of the second line would preserve the similar emphasis given to 'the root of the righteous' in verse 4. In this case, the meaning would be that the 'wicked' long for the apparent security of the 'evil men,' while that which truly, and finally, endures is the security of the just man who keeps his integrity and casts his lot with God.

Whichever translation is finally chosen, the difference is merely a matter of emphasis, for the same basic point is made. Crime does not pay and, even when it appears to, its rewards are fleeting. Righteousness, on the other hand, yields a great and lasting reward.

12:13. An evil man is ensnared by the transgression of his lips, But the righteous will escape from trouble.

We come now to a series of proverbs that all deal with speech (vv. 13-25, except vv. 21, 24). The first line teaches us that an evil man ends up perilously tangled in the web of his own words. Proverbs often speaks of the danger of a snare (Prov. 13:14; 14:27; 18:7; 20:25; 22:25; 29:6, 25). The most perilous trap is often the one an evil heart has devised against another (Prov. 1:18). 'A fool's mouth is his ruin, And his lips are the snare of his soul' (Prov. 18:7). This hazard is constant, because our words betray the reality of our hearts (Luke 6:45). Even if an evil person wiggles out of the trap his words unwittingly have set for himself, he will give an account before God (Matt. 12:36-37).

The righteous man stands in contrast. His words are few (Prov. 21:23). What words he does speak are measured and knowledgeable (Prov. 11:8-9). In this way, he 'will escape' from the snares of rash and unwise words. The word 'escape' is the common verb for 'to go out.' Thus, the idea is not only that he will not get into trouble in the first place, but that, when trouble does befall him, he will emerge from it unscathed.[26] He will not fall into needless troubles because of rashly spoken words, and, when in a tight place ('trouble'), he will find a way out by his words. The word for 'trouble' is a powerful one that describes intense inner turmoil, anguish, terror and pain.[27] It is not that the righteous never experience such panic, but that it is not their words that put them there and it is their words that help free them from such a trap.

12:14. A man will be satisfied with good by the fruit of his words, And the deeds of a man's hands will return to him.
The theme of speech continues. Here, speech is not that which extracts one from trouble (v. 13), but that which yields a rich reward. The first line is echoed in Proverbs 13:2 and 18:20, though the second lines in each case are quite different than what we find here.[28] The fruit of one's lips pays a wage as surely as the labor of one's hands. Here, it is viewed as a positive reward, though certainly the reverse may be true as well (Prov. 1:31; 15:4; 18:4). Let us, therefore, give ourselves as diligently to measured words as to hard work. 'Death and life are in the power of the tongue, And those who love it will eat its fruit' (Prov. 18:21).

12:15. The way of a fool is right in his own eyes, But a wise man is he who listens to counsel.
A man who resolutely demands he is right and all others are wrong, even trusted friends, proves himself a fool. The word for fool speaks of a man resolute and stubborn in his refusal to receive counsel (Prov. 1:7; 10:8; 15:15). He mocks at sin (Prov. 14:9), and will hear no one who speaks to dissuade him from his self-destructive course (1:25, 30). In the end, he will destroy himself, for he has shut himself up to a view of the world limited to his own perspective (Prov. 3:7; 26:12). 'There is a way which seems right to a man, But its end is the way of death' (Prov. 14:12; 16:25). Only God knows the heart and truly understands our motives (Prov. 16:2; 21:2).

For these reasons, the man who 'listens to counsel' proves himself wise (Prov. 13:10). While correction may be painful in the short term, it yields life when followed (Prov. 10:17). Even a man's good ideas may be sharpened by others in such a way that he will become even more successful (Prov. 11:14; 15:22). The wise man sees the value of supportive friends who are brave enough to contradict him graciously (Prov. 25:12). Proverbs consistently proves that the ability to listen is as important to being wise as the ability to speak wise words (Prov. 1:5; 9:9; 19:20). 'A poor, yet wise lad is better than an old and foolish king who no longer knows how to receive instruction' (Eccles. 4:13).

12:16. A fool's vexation is known at once, But a prudent man conceals dishonor.

Our wisdom or foolishness is proven the instant an insult comes our way. The fool immediately reveals his true heart condition through his unrestrained anger. The word 'vexation' describes an agitated, provoked, stirred up, emotionally volatile state of heart.[29] The fact that a man feels this way in the face of an insult is not what is condemned here. His problem is that such a response to injury 'is known at once.' The phrase, literally, is 'known in a day,' meaning immediately and without a buffer for cooling off or collecting one's thoughts and emotions.

That this surge of emotion arises from an affront is clear from the second line. The word 'dishonor' is a general one, but is often linked with some kind of public insult or even physical injury (Prov. 6:33; 9:7; 13:18). The 'prudent man' is quite different in his response to such a rebuff. He 'conceals' the emotion that arises. This does not mean he represses or suppresses his emotion, living in denial. Rather, it means that he does not give immediate expression to it, bringing his emotions under the control of his thinking and will. The same verb is found in Proverbs 10:12: 'Hatred stirs up strife, But love covers all transgressions.' Such a one is deemed a 'prudent man.' The adjective translated 'prudent' is used both positively and negatively. The negative meaning betrays a crafty, sinister side (Gen. 3:1; Job 5:12; 15:5). The positive usage, as we find here, describes one who handles a situation shrewdly, with wisdom and care.[30] 'A fool always loses his temper, But a wise man holds it back' (Prov. 29:11).

12:17. He who speaks truth tells what is right, But a false witness, deceit.

We are here ushered into a courtroom, as the vocabulary shows us. The word 'witness' is often found in legal settings and the word 'speaks' is used in Proverbs in such contexts (Prov. 6:19; 14:5, 25; 19:5, 9).[31] The verb in the first line is, literally, 'breathes,' which shows us that a faithful witness finds telling the truth as natural as breathing. It is part of his nature. It is an involuntary response; he does not have to think twice about it.[32] A contrasting character is found in the second line of the proverb. The grammar is abrupt and casts this liar almost as 'deceit incarnate.'[33]

The outcome of speaking the truth is not simply 'what is right,' but is a revelation of justice – for so the word must be understood in this forensic setting. Our system of justice, ultimately, depends upon the basic character and honesty of those who give testimony. A witness's calling is not to put 'spin' on an issue or event, but to simply state as plainly as possible the facts as they relate to the questions asked. Justice will never be known apart from this. Thus, 'a lying tongue' is an abomination to the Lord (Prov. 6:17, 19; cf. 14:5, 25; 19:5, 9; 21:28).

12:18. There is one who speaks rashly like the thrusts of a sword, But the tongue of the wise brings healing.
This is the second in a series of proverbs beginning with 'There is' (Prov. 11:24; 13:7; 14:12; 16:25; 20:15). The law made provision for vows rashly taken (Lev. 5:4; Num. 30:7, 9), but here the idea is of one who unlocks the door of their lips and lets flow whatever the moment may evoke. There is no thought, no weighing of one's words, only reaction. When we speak like this, we wound, and even kill, relationships. 'Death and life are in the power of the tongue, And those who love it will eat its fruit' (Prov. 18:21). Moses paid a dear price for his rashly spoken words (Ps. 106:33). The effect is likened to that of 'the thrusts of a sword' (Ps. 52:2; 57:4; 59:7; 64:3). Like a mad man flailing away with a sword in a crowd of innocent people, so the person who does not measure and control his words wounds many innocent people.

In contrast, there is the one whose words bring healing. Such are the wise words of a father (Prov. 4:22). But, anyone with wisdom and self-control can be used of God to bring such words of soothing and restoration (Prov. 10:21; 13:17; 15:4; 16:24). Ephesians 4:29 may be the best guide for our words: 'Let no unwholesome word proceed from your mouth, but only such a word as is good for edification according to the need of the moment, that it may give grace to those who hear.'

12:19. Truthful lips will be established forever, But a lying tongue is only for a moment.
The contrast in this proverb is in the tenure of words of truth and falsehood. The lines are arranged after a chiastic scheme, which highlights the contrast in the Hebrew by placing 'will be established forever' immediately up against 'only for a moment.'[34] 'Truthful' carries not only the idea of veracity and accuracy, but also of durability, permanence and reliability.[35] Indeed, they 'will be

established forever.' The verb is used in Proverbs to describe God's creation of the earth (Prov. 3:19) and the heavens (8:27). It is used metaphorically of the building of a house that will last (Prov. 24:3) and the enduring reign of a righteous king (16:12; 29:14). This stands in contrast with false words that last 'only for a moment.'[36] That little phrase is, literally, 'until I move (my eyelid)' or, in our vernacular, 'the wink of an eye.'

Elsewhere, Proverbs promises that a false witness will not go unpunished (Prov. 19:5, 9). Perhaps the justice of this world is what is in view, though so many examples of the temporal triumph of lies seem to mitigate against it. More likely, it is divine justice, in this world or the next, that is in view. 'You love all words that devour, O deceitful tongue. But God will break you down forever; He will snatch you up, and tear you away from your tent, And uproot you from the land of the living' (Ps. 52:4-5).

12:20. Deceit is in the heart of those who devise evil, But counselors of peace have joy.

While the form of this proverb is antithetical ('But'), the contrast intended is not immediately clear. The contrast between 'Deceit' and 'joy' seems awkward. The first line appears, at first glance, to be nothing more than a cliché – of course the plotting of evil involves deceit. The contrast comes into focus, however, when we understand the deceit not to be primarily toward others, though obviously it does not exclude it. Rather, this is self-deception at work. The point of the proverb is that what we seek for others we, unwittingly, bring upon ourselves. This is clearest in the second line. If we pursue peace for the larger society within which we live, we will discover a residual joy that is ours through the pursuit. On the other hand, if we think that we can pursue the downfall of another and not reap the negative personal consequences in our inner life, we are deceiving ourselves.

Indeed, the word translated 'evil' has not only that ethical, moral connotation, but it also carries the idea of pain with it.[37] Pursuing evil inherently includes seeking pain, for those whose harm we seek and for ourselves. In contrast is the 'peace' that is sought for the larger society and its individual members. This is the word *shalom*, which describes not just personal, inner tranquility, but the wholeness and completeness of that entity for which it is sought. The one who seeks such wholeness for those around him is also, by so doing, seeking his own welfare. Any other understanding of the inter-connectedness of our lives and relationships is self-deception. The word 'counselors' carries not simply the idea of giving good suggestions, but also that of mentally devising, resolving or decreeing that which will affect others.[38] This more directive sense of 'counsel' is echoed in the word 'devise.' The word is often translated elsewhere as 'plow.' As the farmer carefully cuts the rows in the field, so one can, through thoughts and plans, carve and cut intentions of ill-will toward others (cf. Prov. 3:29).[39]

Is this not the point of Jesus in the Beatitudes? 'Blessed are the peacemakers, for they shall be called sons of God' (Matt. 5:9). Those who seek the wholeness of the larger community, in which they live find themselves benefiting indirectly from that pursuit – they gain a name as being like their heavenly Father!

12:21. No harm befalls the righteous, But the wicked are filled with trouble.

This proverb appears to break the pattern of speech related to words of wisdom (vv. 13-25) and makes a statement about life in general. The proverb, taken alone, seems to be not much more than a platitude. In far too many instances, it simply does not seem in accord with reality.

The promise that 'No harm befalls the righteous' seems almost naïve. But, by examining closely what it actually says, and allowing the context to inform our reading of the proverb, its meaning becomes clearer. The word 'harm' can be translated 'evil' in the ethical sense, or it can describe 'calamity,' 'misfortune,' or, as the translators of the NASB have chosen, 'harm.' Even where the latter seems the best translation, it is nevertheless calamity that is the product of some sin that is in view.[40] Therefore, this is not a general proverb about whether or not life will dish out evil, in general, or calamity, specifically, to the righteous, but it is about whether or not some calamitous event culminating from evil intents and actions will break upon the head of the righteous.

Add to this the fact that the verb 'befalls' carries the idea of that which is allowed or sent and the verse's meaning starts to come clear.[41] No misfortune that is the product of evil plots will be allowed to come upon the righteous. Yet, that still sounds too good to be true. It raises the question: Who won't allow this to happen? God certainly seems to allow this too often! But, now, factor in the context. All the surrounding verses speak of the tongue and the dangers of its misuse. It is not God who is viewed as not allowing this misfortune to come upon the righteous, but it is the righteous man himself that will not allow this to happen. How? By the restrained and wise use of his tongue. The circumspect man curbs his speech and trains it for righteousness. In so doing, he does not create by his words those situations that can backfire and end up wounding himself.

Now, we are ready for the second line – 'but the wicked are filled with trouble.' Is that not the point made over and over in these verses (vv. 13a, 14, 19b, 20a)? Unwise speech makes life harder for the speaker of those words.

12:22. Lying lips are an abomination to the Lord, But those who deal faithfully are His delight.
We now return to explicit comment on the use of the tongue. This proverb provides the fundamental base upon which the others of this section rest (especially vv. 17, 19, 20). The form 'are an abomination ... are His delight' is familiar from Proverbs 11:1, 20. See the comment on these verses for other things that God identifies as 'an abomination' to Him. These proverbs repeatedly denounce the one who speaks untruthfully (Prov. 6:16-17, 19; 12:17, 19; 21:6; 26:28). 'The Lord abhors the man of ... deceit' (Ps. 5:6). He will be excluded from the New Jerusalem (Rev. 21:27) and God will finally, and forever, shut him out from His presence (Rev. 22:15).

In contrast are those 'who deal faithfully.' The word is the same as that translated 'truth' in verse 17. The term is used to describe the total dependability of God (Deut. 32:4) and is used to describe one of the attributes of God (1 Sam. 26:23; Ps. 36:5; 40:10; Lam. 3:23). It is, thus, characteristic of what God does (Ps. 33:4) and what God says (Ps. 119:86; 143:1). Because God is this way, He expects that those who follow Him will take on this same characteristic (2 Chron. 19:9). The person who has placed his faith in God will demonstrate this quality as one of the sure evidences of that faith (Hab. 2:4).[42] This steadfastness is not only the basis from which such words arise, but is the result and outcome of these kinds of words (Prov. 12:19).

12:23. A prudent man conceals knowledge, But the heart of fools proclaims folly.
The theme of speech continues, here the contrast being between the wisdom of selective silence and the folly of untimely chatter. Proverbs speaks often about the wisdom of one who restrains his words (Prov. 10:14; 11:13; 17:27; 29:11). 'When there are many words, transgression is unavoidable, But he who restrains his lips is wise' (Prov. 10:19). One who heeds this counsel is called a 'prudent man.' The word is the same as that met in verse 16 and is found often through the Book of Proverbs (Prov. 13:16; 14:8, 15, 18; 22:3; 27:12).

It can have a negative connotation, pointing to a dark, diabolical motive. It can, however, be used positively, as it is here and so often throughout Proverbs. In these cases, it refers to one who is shrewd, cunning and wise. Such a person is one who understands a situation and what will best serve to achieve a desired end, in this case God's end. Thus a 'prudent man' knows that more often than not rushing in with one's opinion is counter-productive. A bit of reserve sets the stage for his opinion to be counted as more weighty and for it to eventually have more influence.

The second line describes the fool who proves his folly by speaking before he thinks. He is sure his word will end the discussion. He is quick to display what little knowledge he does possess. In so doing, he ends up not looking wise, but 'proclaiming folly.' His words do not wow, but betray the basic foolishness of his heart. Proverbs again warns repeatedly of being quick to speak (Prov. 13:16; 15:2; 29:11). 'A fool's vexation is known at once' (Prov. 12:16a).

Generally, the more likely one is to speak, the less likely it is to be worth much and, conversely, the less likely one is to speak, the more likely it is to be worth hearing when he does.

12:24. The hand of the diligent will rule, But the slack hand will be put to forced labor.
This proverb interrupts the series of statements about the use of the tongue (vv. 13-25), but leads us to the topic of diligence and laziness. Diligence leads to freedom and a self-directed life, while laziness ends in 'forced labor.' This latter term does not refer to regular slavery, but rather to the oppressive and, often, cruel form of compulsory servitude. This was what the Israelites were to bring the inhabitants of Canaan into (Deut. 20:11; Josh. 16:10; 17:13; Judg. 1:28). It characterized Solomon's dealings with his own people (1 Kings 5:13; 11:28). Sometimes, it takes on almost the notion of imprisoned chain-gangs.[43] The contrasting verb 'will rule' carries the idea of wielding absolute power and fills out the strength of the proverb's metaphor.[44] This vigorous word picture is not intended to necessarily be taken literally (all laziness ends in literal 'forced labor'), but points to the opposite extremes of where consistent diligence and consistent laziness can lead.

Proverbs often draws out this contrast. The diligent are extolled (Prov. 10:4; 12:27; 13:4; 17:2; 21:5), while the lazy are denounced (Prov. 6:6-11; 19:15; 21:25, 26; 24:30-34; 26:13-16). The one who works steadily and vigorously becomes his own boss (in a limited sense, of course), but the lazy one is forever taking orders from someone else.

12:25. Anxiety in the heart of a man weighs it down, But a good word makes it glad.

The second line of this proverb returns us to the theme of speech. The proverb gives remarkable insight into the psychology of depression. The word translated 'weighs it down' probably carries the idea of being depressed (cf. NKJV). That which produces the depression is anxiety. The anxiety spoken of is worry mingled with fear. For example, the word is used to describe the fear of the tribes of Israel which settled on the east of Jordan. They feared that, when cut off from the tabernacle and its sacrifices, their children would forget the Lord. For this reason, out of their anxiety, they set up an alternative altar (Josh. 22:24; cf. Jer. 49:23; Ezek. 4:16; 12:18-19).[45] Under the weight of some anticipated calamity, the heart can begin to be bowed down, the thoughts can be consumed, and perspective can be lost. 'A joyful heart makes a cheerful face, But when the heart is sad, the spirit is broken' (Prov. 15:13). 'A joyful heart is good medicine, But a broken spirit dries up the bones' (Prov. 17:22).

The remedy is 'a good word' from a supportive friend. The word is 'good' in that it is timely, measured according to the need of the moment and confers grace (Eph. 4:29). Such a word brings 'hope.' The anticipated tragedy is not perceived to be as likely. The character of God comes again into view and, with it, other more pleasant possibilities. 'A man has joy in an apt answer, And how delightful is a timely word!' (Prov. 15:23). '... the tongue of the wise brings healing' (Prov. 12:18b).

12:26. The righteous is a guide to his neighbor, But the way of the wicked leads them astray.

The first line of this proverb is notoriously difficult to translate. The basic options can be seen in the various translations: 'A righteous man is cautious in friendship' (NIV; cf. NKJV). 'A righteous man turns away from evil' (RSV; cf. NEB). 'The righteous is more excellent than his neighbor' (KJV). 'An impartial arbiter is his own best friend' (JB).

Many commentators toss it aside as undecipherable. This is too radical. The Hebrew seems to read, literally, as 'the righteous [verb, variously understood] his friend.' Basically, the implied verb is understood as either 'investigates' or 'guides.' The authorities seem to back the view that the verb means something like 'investigates,' 'spies out,' 'searches out.'[46] This would seem to provide an excellent contrast to the second line and, for this reason, is to be preferred. The gist, then, is that a righteous man is one who cautiously moves into new relationships, knowing how powerful the influence of close associates are in one's own life. In contrast, the wicked rush headlong into relationships without thinking. This course leads to their ruin (Prov. 18:24; 22:24-25).

All in all, the NIV seems to capture the idea of the proverb: 'A righteous man is cautious in friendship, but the way of the wicked leads them astray.' This is echoed by Paul in the New Testament: 'Do not be deceived: "Bad company corrupts good morals"' (1 Cor. 15:33).

12:27. A slothful man does not roast his prey, But the precious possession of a man is diligence.

The virtues of diligence and the demerits of sloth are compared. Both lines are somewhat difficult to translate as the variety of translations attest. The difficulty in the first line is that the verb is found only here in the Old Testament. The LXX, Targum, and Syriac all translate with a meaning of 'catch' (cf. RSV). Whereas the latter Rabbinic writers, working from Aramaic and Arabic root words, give it a meaning of 'roast' (NASB, NIV, NKJV, NRSV).[47] Most modern translators and scholars adopt the meaning 'roast.'[48]

The idea, then, appears to be that the lazy person may start his projects, but never finishes them. He thinks about hunting and providing food for his family, but it never ends up on the table. He is full of good plans and good intentions, but short on follow-through. He only roasts his game in his head. He only tastes roast game in his imagination. Even if he gets up off of the couch and actually bags his prize, he lacks the discipline to skin it out and cook it.

The second line presents a contrasting character. This line also has proven difficult for translators, but it is because of the word order. It is difficult to tell if it means that a diligent man holds his hard-earned wealth to be precious (KJV, NIV), that the man's diligence is his most prized possession (NASB, NKJV), or that a diligent man eventually possesses what other, less diligent, men consider precious (ASV, NRSV).

The debate is long, but the basic point is clear. In contrast to the slothful man of line one, the diligent man of line two ends up with what he sets out after. He is a finisher. He has the discipline to obtain what he dreams. In this way, the contrast is between the dreamer who lacks the diligence to see his dreams become reality (Prov. 19:24) and the dreamer who pursues and keeps pursuing his dream until it is reality (Prov. 12:11, 24; Eccles. 5:19). The latter becomes 'a have' and the former ends up 'a have not,' and the difference is largely a matter of personal discipline and drive.

12:28. In the way of righteousness is life, And in its pathway there is no death.

We are surprised to meet here a proverb of synonymous, not antithetical, parallelism (though some try to reconstruct it to conform it to the latter pattern).[49] The contrast between two competing ways was frequent in the first nine chapters (Prov. 1:15, 31; 2:8, 12, 20; 4:11, 14, 19, etc.), and, though found less often thereafter, it is not absent (10:29; 11:5; 12:15, 26, etc.). Here the focus is on 'the way of righteousness' and the outcome of taking its path. The first line promises 'life,' a not infrequent guarantee of these proverbs (Prov. 2:19; 3:16, 18, 22; 4:10, etc.). The meaning here is probably extended and prosperous existence on this earth (Prov. 3:2; 11:4).[50] The second line, however, seems to look beyond this world and into the next. Certainly, a promise that one will never die (in this life) would be farfetched. But, the promise of immortality (see NIV) can be expected. Though it is true that the doctrine of immortality is not as fully developed in the Old Testament, it is found there (Job 19:25-27; Ps. 16:9-11; 17:15; 49:15; Isa. 25:8). It is even found here in the Proverbs: 'The wicked is thrust down by his wrongdoing, but the righteous has a refuge when he dies' (Prov. 14:32).[51]

End Notes

1. Gilchrist, Paul R., '*yākah,*' *Theological Wordbook of the Old Testament* (Chicago: Moody Press, 1980), 1:376-377.

2. Pan, Chou-Wee, 'בער,' *New International Dictionary of Old Testament Theology and Exegesis* (Grand Rapids, Michigan: Zondervan Publishing House, 1997), 1:690-691.

3. Delitzsch, F., *Proverbs, Ecclesiastes, Song of Solomon* (three volumes in one) in C. F. Keil and F. Delitzsch, vol. 6, *Commentary on the Old Testament* (in ten volumes), (1872; rpt. Grand Rapids, Michigan: William B. Eerdmans Publishing Company, 1980), 1:251.

4. Cohen, A., *Proverbs* (London: The Soncino Press, 1946), 73.

5. Wolf, Herbert, '*zāmam,*' *Theological Wordbook of the Old Testament* (Chicago: Moody Press, 1980), 1:244-245.

6. Carpenter, Eugene and Michael A. Grisanti, 'דשע,' *New International Dictionary of Old Testament Theology and Exegesis* (Grand Rapids, Michigan: Zondervan Publishing Company, 1997), 3:1201.

7. Oswalt, John N., '*kûn,*' *Theological Wordbook of the Old Testament* (Chicago: Moody Press, 1980), 1:433.

8. Kaiser, Walter C., '*môt,*' *Theological Wordbook of the Old Testament* (Chicago: Moody Press, 1980), 1:493.

9. Cohen, 73.

10. Waltke, Bruce K., 'The Role of the 'Valiant Wife' in the Marketplace,' *CRUX* (September 1999, Vol. XXXV, No.3), 23-34.

11. Whybray, R. N., *Proverbs* (Grand Rapids, Michigan: William B. Eerdmans Publishing Company, 1994), 191.

12. Ibid.

13. Hartley, John E., 'שׁב,' *New International Dictionary of Old Testament Theology and Exegesis* (Grand Rapids, Michigan: Zondervan Publishing House, 1997), 2:303-310.

14. Ross, Allen P., 'Proverbs,' *The Expositor's Bible Commentary* (Grand Rapids, Michigan: Zondervan Publishing House, 1991), 5:906.

15. Carpenter, Eugene and Michael A. Grisanti, 'רמה,' *New International Dictionary of Old Testament Theology and Exegesis* (Grand Rapids, Michigan: Zondervan Publishing Company, 1997), 3:1122-1124.

16. Hamilton, Victor P., 'hāpak,' *Theological Wordbook of the Old Testament* (Chicago: Moody Press, 1980), 1:221.

17. Cohen, 74.

18. Ross, 5:969.

19. Whybray, 193.

20. Murphy, Roland E, *Proverbs* (Nashville: Thomas Nelson Publishers, 1998), 90.

21. Oswalt, John N., 'kzr,' *Theological Wordbook of the Old Testament* (Chicago: Moody Press, 1980), 1:436.

22. Shepherd, Jerry, 'דיק,' *New International Dictionary of Old Testament Theology and Exegesis* (Grand Rapids, Michigan: Zondervan Publishing House, 1997), 3:1106-1109.

23. Ross, 5:970.

24. Cohen, 76.

25. Whybray, 194.

26. Gilchrist, Paul R., 'yāsā',' *Theological Wordbook of the Old Testament* (Chicago: Moody Press, 1980), 1:393-394.

27. Hartley, John E., 'sārar,' *Theological Wordbook of the Old Testament* (Chicago: Moody Press, 1980), 2:778-779.

28. Whybray, 195.

29. Van Groningen, Gerard, 'kā'as,' *Theological Wordbook of the Old Testament* (Chicago: Moody Press, 1980), 1:451.

30. Allen, Roland B., ''ārōm,' *Theological Wordbook of the Old Testament* (Chicago: Moody Press, 1980), 2:697-698.

31. Whybray, 196.

32. Murphy, 91.

33. Ibid.

34. Ibid.

35. Whybray, 197.

36. Cohen, 77.

37. Ross, 5:972.

38. Delitzsch, 1:263.

39. Buzzell, Sid S., 'Proverbs,' *The Bible Knowledge Commentary* (Wheaton: Victor Books, 1985), 1:913.

40. Delitzsch, 1:264.

41. Kidner, Derek, *Proverbs* (Downer's Grove, Illinois: InterVarsity Press, 1964), 98.

42. Scott, Jack B., ''āman,' *Theological Wordbook of the Old Testament* (Chicago: Moody Press, 1980), 1:51-53.

43. Klingbeil, Gerald A., 'מַס,' *New International Dictionary of Old Testament Theology and Exegesis* (Grand Rapids, Michigan: Zondervan Publishing House, 1997), 2:992-995.

44. Whybray, 197.

45. Stigers, Harold G., 'dā'ag,' *Theological Wordbook of the Old Testament* (Chicago: Moody Press, 1980), 1:177.

46. Gesenius, William, trans. Francis Brown, S. R. Driver, and Charles A. Briggs, *A Hebrew and English Lexicon of the Old Testament* (Oxford: Clarendon Press, n.d.), 1064; and Youngblood, Ronald F., 'tûr,' *Theological Wordbook of the Old Testament* (Chicago: Moody Press, 1980), 2:967; and Matties, Gordon H. and J. A. Thompson, 'תור,' *New*

International Dictionary of Old Testament Theology and Exegesis (Grand Rapids, Michigan: Zondervan Publishing House, 1997), 4:283-284.

47. Kidner, 99.

48. Naude, Jackie A., 'חרם,' *New International Dictionary of Old Testament Theology and Exegesis* (Grand Rapids, Michigan: Zondervan Publishing House, 1997), 2:276.

49. Murphy, 88.

50. Ross, 5:974.

51. Delitzsch, 1:268-270.

Proverbs 13

13:1. A wise son accepts his father's discipline, But a scoffer does not listen to rebuke.

This first verse begins the chapter on the theme of the instruction of the home as an antidote to foolishness and sets up an inclusio upon this theme (v. 24). It also serves to introduce the general theme of the wisdom of listening to counsel and instruction (vv. 10, 13-14, 18).[1]

The first line of the proverb lacks a verb. The juxtaposition is, however, powerful in making its point: 'A wise son – his father's discipline.' The absence of the verb serves to make the point more effectively than if the verb was present. To make good sense for the average English reader, however, translators must supply a verb. Generally, two options have been followed. Some see a similarity with Proverbs 12:1, and borrow the verb 'loves' from there, so that the translation becomes 'A wise son loves his father's discipline.' The second option is to understand the verb from line two of this verse, so that the translation becomes 'A wise son listens to ("obeys") his father's discipline.' All in all, it seems best to stay with the immediate context and follow the suggestion of the second line of the proverb.

The theme of a father's instruction to his son was a frequent feature of the first nine chapters (Prov. 1:1, 8, 10, 15; 2:1; 3:1, 11, 12, 21; etc.), and is not absent from the collection of proverbs in chapters 10–31 (10:1, 5; 13:24; etc.). The word 'discipline' has also been used often (Prov. 1:2, 3, 7, 8; 3:11; 4:1, 13; 5:12, 23; 6:23; 7:22; 8:10, 33; 10:17; 12:1). The word is sometimes translated 'instruction' and carries the notion of education through correction.[2] Fundamental to all that Proverbs teaches is the notion that we do not in and of ourselves think correctly about life and that we each need the corrective instruction of God (Prov. 3:11), His word (1:2, 3), our parents (1:8; 4:1; 13:24), and God's people (10:17; 13:18; 19:20). To reject this discipline is to reject the fundamental principle of wisdom: the fear of the Lord (Prov. 1:7).

The 'scoffer' is a fool sunk to his lowest level of folly (Prov. 1:22; 3:34; 9:7-8, 12; 14:6, 9; 15:12; 19:25, 28, 29; 20:1, 11; 21:11, 24; 22:10; 24:9). He rejects all authority, instruction, counsel and rebuke. He despises God and His strictures. The word 'rebuke' is stronger than 'discipline.' It is used to describe God's command to dry up the sea

(Isa. 50:2), to make the heavens shake (Job 26:11), and to defeat the solider (Ps. 76:6).[3] Proverbs counsels against even trying to correct a scoffer (Prov. 9:7-8).

13:2. From the fruit of a man's mouth he enjoys good, But the desire of the treacherous is violence.

This verse and the next re-introduce us to the repeated theme of the tongue. The 'fruit of a man's mouth' is a figurative way of referring to the words he speaks. Our words are perhaps the single most influential determiner of whether or not our lives are pleasant or not. A man of measured and gracious words finds that 'good' returns to him (Prov. 12:14, 18).

On the other hand, the second line reminds us that those who do not harness their words find their lives to be unpleasant and unnecessarily difficult. The thought here is not that the treacherous desire either to dish out or receive violence. Rather, the notion is that their insatiable craving leads them to words and actions that end up bringing a violent response from others. Because the end result of their longing is so clearly set, and because the vantage point of wisdom sees this, the 'desire' and the 'violence' are made nearly to be one.

The word 'desire' is found again in verse 4 and is, literally, 'soul' or 'breath.' The word can, in certain contexts, describe the inner desires and cravings of both humans and animals. This meaning may arise from the idea of panting breath being associated with deep desire. This desire can range from the sexual drive of a donkey in heat (Jer. 2:24), to physical hunger (Prov. 23:2; Eccles. 6:7), to the holy longings of those who love God with all their 'heart ... soul and ... strength' (Deut. 6:5).[4] In this case the 'desire' is obviously bad for it arises out of 'the treacherous.' Such men are the kind that plot evil designs in order to bring the downfall of others.[5]

13:3. The one who guards his mouth preserves his life; The one who opens wide his lips comes to ruin.

This verse and the next hang together with verse 2, due to their common use of the Hebrew word translated 'craving' in verse 2, 'life' here in verse 3, and 'soul' in verse 4. The word most commonly is translated 'soul' and comes from a root meaning 'breath.' It is the essence of who and what you are; it is your very life. The nuance of meaning is clearly distinct here from verses 2 and 4, though the commonality can quickly be seen.

The emphasis here is that one who holds his tongue retains his life. Setting watch over one's speech is setting a sentry over one's life. So powerful is the tongue considered in Proverbs! 'Death and life are in the power of the tongue, And those who love it will eat its fruit' (Prov. 18:21). 'He who guards his mouth and his tongue, Guards his soul from troubles' (Prov. 21:23; cf. 10:10, 19, 21; 14:3; 17:28; James 3:1-12).

The converse is also true. Such a one 'opens wide his lips' in unexamined promises, revelations, curses, or statements. The ruinous possibilities for such unfiltered speech are legion, spanning the social, financial, physical and spiritual arenas of life.[6] The tongue's powerful potential for self-inflicted ruin is a frequent part of these proverbs (Prov. 10:8, 14; 12:18; 18:7; Eccles. 10:12-14).

13:4. The soul of the sluggard craves and gets nothing, But the soul of the diligent is made fat.

The thematic relation of verses 2-4 continues with the word translated here twice as 'soul.' The first line is abrupt in making its point: 'The soul of the sluggard craving, but nothing.' This terseness helps make the point of the barrenness of the slacker. In contrast the diligent man is 'made fat' in his soul, a common expression for prosperity and blessing (Prov. 11:25).

The use of 'soul' here should be linked with its translation 'craving' in verse 2. Clearly, that is what is in view here. The deepest, inner longings of the lazy remain only vaporous dreams, for they lack the willingness to apply themselves to a course that will see those dreams become reality (Prov. 6:6, 11; 21:25-26). The longings of the 'diligent,' however, are destined to become concrete, for they will take any legitimate, and moral, step to see that their dreams become reality (Prov. 10:4, 24; 12:24).

13:5. A righteous man hates falsehood, But a wicked man acts disgustingly and shamefully.

The contrasting ways of the 'righteous' and 'wicked' are set forth. Part of loving God is hating what He hates. Because God hates lying (Prov. 6:16-17; 8:13; 12:22), so does the one who conforms to His character (Ps. 119:163). Our word 'falsehood' is, literally, 'a word of falsehood.' It refers not only to overt lying, but also to any deception in communication with or without words.

The 'wicked man' sees no revulsion in falsehood, but rather an opportunity. When, however, he tries to seize upon the occasion he invites disaster. The twin verbs used here speak of the odious nature of his dealings. The verb for 'acts disgustingly' means, literally, 'creates a stink.'[7] Some want to emend it to a verb meaning 'to be ashamed.' This is attractive to some translators, because this new verb is found in tandem with the second verb listed here in other contexts (Prov. 19:26).[8] The second verb, translated here as 'shamefully,' describes losing face by being humiliated, embarrassed, or through some kind of mix-up. In fourteen of its seventeen usages, it is found in conjunction with the verb translators attempt to create by emending the first verb.[9] There appears, however, no good reason to resort to emendation of the first Hebrew verb.

As far as the righteous are concerned, deception stinks. As for the wicked, the stench of their sin has attached itself to them, and everyone (but them) can smell it – what a shame!

13:6. Righteousness guards the one whose way is blameless, But wickedness subverts the sinner.
This antithetical proverb again contrasts the righteous and the wicked. Here, 'Righteousness' and 'wickedness' are each personified. They watch over and protect or undermine and overthrow.

The word translated 'Righteousness' describes conformity to the law and order of God.[10] This, then, is the path over which God watches and upon which He guarantees success. This security is for 'the one whose way is blameless.' The word for 'blameless' is used eight times in Proverbs (Prov. 2:7; 10:9, 29; 13:6; 19:1; 20:7; 28:6; 29:10) and often is translated 'integrity.' The idea is not that of moral perfection, but consistent and thorough conformity to God's ways. When we walk in conformity to God's ways, He guarantees us success and safety (Prov. 2:11; 4:6).

On the other hand, when we go the way of 'wickedness' we are assured of disaster. That path is self-defeating. It 'subverts' the plans and efforts of the one who chooses it. The word means to twist, distort or pervert.[11] From this basic meaning comes the notion of turning upside down (i.e. ruining) the plans of a man (Prov. 19:3; 22:12). Since sin itself is a perversion and a twisting of God's way, it is little wonder that, when one chooses that course, his plans and efforts get twisted and overturned.

This contrast between the successful and secure way of the righteous and the self-destructive way of the wicked is a recurring theme in Proverbs (Prov. 2:21, 22; 10:9; 11:3, 5, 6; 12:21; 13:3).

13:7. There is one who pretends to be rich, but has nothing; Another pretends to be poor, but has great wealth.
God despises deception (Prov. 6:16-17; 8:13; 12:22), as does the man who conforms to His character (Prov. 13:5). This proverb unmasks

two equally erroneous types of deception. On the one hand, there are some people who deceive by making themselves look better than they are, perhaps in hopes of some social advantage (Prov. 12:9). On the other hand, there are some who make themselves appear poor, when in fact they are rich. Again, the reason may be for some economic leverage, perhaps in the negotiation of a financial transaction (Prov. 20:14). We are not privy to the exact application intended. What we are warned of is that all is not as it seems. One can deceive (or be deceived!) on both ends of the truth.

What do we make of the Apostle Paul's strategy for ministry: '... as poor yet making many rich, as having nothing yet possessing all things' (2 Cor. 6:10)? At first glance, it would appear he is describing deception. In actuality, however, he is describing a self-imposed poverty for the sake of the gospel. He, in Christ, possessed all things, yet he did not demand these things. He did not grasp after all that was his right. He, rather, lived a life of sacrifice and service so that others might know Jesus Christ. This sacrificial life-style is the opposite of the deception Solomon warns of here.

13:8. The ransom of a man's life is his riches, But the poor hears no rebuke.

The exact point of this antithetical proverb is not immediately evident. The comparison made in the two lines is not obvious. The first line seems to be clear enough. A person of means is in the position to use his wealth to buy his way out of trouble, even in the face of a death threat, if necessary (though cf. Prov. 6:35). What is not clear is whether the extortion or blackmail is because the person is rich or if their wealth is seen as simply an advantage in a more unspecified threat.

The second line is less clear. The Hebrew text of line two is identical to the text of the second line of Proverbs 13:1, except that 'the poor' has been substituted for 'a scoffer.' Most commentators take 'rebuke' here to mean something like 'threat.' The idea is, then, that while the rich, because of their wealth, are a target for the unscrupulous threats of blackmailers and thieves, the poor, because of their lack of material wealth, have nothing to make them a target for such thugs. This may well be the contrast intended, but it is unclear that 'rebuke' can have the idea of an underhanded, evil 'threat.' This certainly would require a meaning quite different from what the identical words require in verse 1. Nevertheless, it would appear that the semantic range of the Hebrew word can tolerate this stretch.[12]

Thus, the meaning does seem to be that the poor are in at least a slightly better position than the rich, in that they are less likely to become the target of those who would simply like to get their hands on their money (2 Kings 24:14; 25:12; Jer. 39:10; 41:8). The one who has nothing to lose is more secure than the one who has much to protect. Riches don't bring security; contentment does.

This verse stands, then, as an effective counterbalance to Proverbs 10:15: 'The rich man's wealth is his fortress, The ruin of the poor is their poverty' (cf. Job 2:4).

13:9. The light of the righteous rejoices, But the lamp of the wicked goes out.

Here, an understanding of the metaphorical use of 'light' and 'lamp' are essential if the point of the proverb is to be identified. The two nouns are often used as pictures of life, vitality, and joy (Job 3:20; Esther 8:16; Prov. 4:18; 6:23). Conversely, the imagery of darkness (implied here in 'goes out') pictures death, defeat and finality (Job 18:5, 6; Prov. 20:20; 21:4; 24:20).

There is debate over whether 'rejoices' is the correct translation for the verb in line one. Some commentators demand that the verb means 'shines brightly' (cf. NIV).[13] They argue that the verb had either Ugaritic or Arabic origins that demand this translation.[14] They contend that the resulting contrast between 'rejoices' and 'goes out' is strained.[15] Additionally, they believe that the personification required by 'rejoices' is too strong to be credible.[16]

There are others, however, who find sufficient reason to overcome these obstacles. While it may be possible that the roots of the verb point to the meaning 'shines brightly,' one can see how the word's evolution of usage could lend itself to the idea of 'rejoicing.'

The contrast seems to be between the joyous vitality of life enjoyed by those who pursue a course of righteousness and the self-defeating and self-destructive path of those who pursue their own course (Prov. 21:17).

13:10. Through presumption comes nothing but strife, But with those who receive counsel is wisdom.

The contrast here is between a pride that refuses to listen to others and a humility that is open to the input of trusted friends. The word 'presumption' describes pride and arrogance (Prov. 11:2; 12:24). The translation 'presumption' can, at first, be misleading, but should be understood as an arrogant demand that one is correct in his view of things and, therefore, needs no input from others.[17] This 'strife' is not just occasional, but constant: 'nothing but strife.' Quarreling is the only thing that can, or will, result from such arrogant self-reliance.

How different is the result if one is willing to listen! Instead of broken relationships and wounded friends, one gains 'wisdom.' The key is an inward willingness to 'receive counsel.' It is born of an understanding that one does not see the world clearly by himself, but must be aided by the perspective given by others who look at life from a different vantage point. Blind spots are unveiled and potential hazards are avoided. 'Listen to counsel and accept discipline, That you may be wise the rest of your days' (Prov. 19:20; cf. 12:15; 20:18).

13:11. Wealth obtained by fraud dwindles, But the one who gathers by labor increases it.

Wealth is often viewed in these proverbs as a sign of God's blessing. Here, the way in which wealth is obtained is in view. The end does not justify the means. The contrast is between wealth that is 'obtained by fraud' and the one who 'gathers by labor.' The first phrase is, more literally, 'from vanity.' The LXX and Vulgate have changed it to 'haste,' since 'vanity' does not seem to provide a suitable antithesis to 'by labor.' The more difficult reading of the Hebrew text is the more likely and its meaning becomes clear enough. The word means vapor, breath, vanity and thirty-six of its seventy-one usages are in Ecclesiastes.[18] What Solomon has in view is the gaining of wealth through get-rich-quick schemes, which are founded on nothing but vaporous speculations (cf. Prov. 20:21; 28:20, 22). The lottery, casinos, para-mutual betting and the like are modern counterparts. The idea might be extended, by way of application, to unscrupulous and unethical methods of becoming rich ('fraud,' NASB; cf. Prov. 10:2; 11:18; 21:6).

The second, and contrasting, means of gaining wealth is 'by labor.' The phrase is, literally, 'by hand.' From this comes the notion of manual labor. In post-Biblical Hebrew, the phrase becomes a figure of speech for 'gradually.'[19] The idea is that which is gained through diligent, consistent, measured, accumulation (Prov. 10:4; 6:6-11; 12:11, 24, 27; 13:4; 14:23; 28:19), perhaps not to be limited only to manual labor.

Not only are the means of gaining the wealth contrasted, but also the longevity of the wealth that is gained. That which is gathered through vain speculations 'dwindles.' The word describes that which is small and insignificant, as well as that which decreases.[20] The idea could be either that the wealth gained through such means will never amount to much in the first place or that what is gained will not last long (Prov. 23:5; Jer. 17:11). The contrast is with that which 'increases,' a word describing abundance and that which is great and numerous.[21] That which is gathered 'little by little' (NIV), whether through manual labor or through incremental investment, will grow.

13:12. Hope deferred makes the heart sick, But desire fulfilled is a tree of life.

This proverb contrasts the psychological reaction between getting what one longs for and seeing a longing prolonged in fulfillment. The first line speaks of the disappointment of waiting. The verb 'deferred,' basically, means to 'draw,' 'drag,' or 'seize.'[22] When applied to the concept of time, as here, it describes a prolonging of the expected length of time necessary for something to take place. One has come to anticipate a certain thing to happen at a particular time. But, when the time comes and the desire remains unfulfilled it 'makes the heart sick.' The word 'sick' describes that which is weak, tired, ill or exhausted, and thus, sick.[23] The Hebrew word for 'heart' describes the whole of the inner person: mind, emotions and will. Thus, when a long anticipated desire is left unfulfilled, a person's thoughts may become confused, the emotions tend toward depression and discouragement, and the will becomes weak and exhausted. Unclear thinking, feelings of discouragement and an anemic will make a person want to give up (Prov. 13:4).

On the other hand, 'a desire fulfilled is a tree of life.' The word 'desire' is a broad one which can describe either ungodly or godly longings. Here no moral verdict is given, but we may assume that the desire in view is at least a morally neutral one. However, the psychological observation is accurate of both the godly and the ungodly. When such a desire becomes reality, it is like eating from 'a tree of life.' The imagery of 'a tree of life' is frequent in Proverbs (3:18; 11:30; 15:4). The 'tree of life' imagery spans the whole of the Bible's revelation and forms an inclusion, beginning in Genesis 2:9 and ending in Revelation 2:7 and 22:2, 14, 19.

The stark contrast is not lost. The pendulum swing from the discouragement of a 'hope deferred' to the vitality and energy associated with 'a tree of life' is dramatic. When one's long-awaited desire comes true, the mind's rational abilities are sharpened, the emotions are lightened and the will is energized and quick to forge ahead (Gen. 21:6-7). 'The hope of the righteous is gladness' (Prov. 10:28a). 'Desire realized is sweet to the soul' (Prov. 13:19a).

13:13. The one who despises the word will be in debt to it, But the one who fears the commandment will be rewarded.

This antithetical proverb contrasts the outcome of one's response to the revelation of God. The terms 'the word' and 'the commandment' often refer to Scripture, the former being the more general term and the latter the more forceful.[24] The words are also used in Proverbs as the instruction that conforms with written revelation and the will of God.

The contrasting responses are seen in the 'one who despises' and 'the one who fears.' The first describes a contemptuous response to what God says, the second a reverential obedience. Depending upon our response to God's revelation, we either 'will be in debt to it' or 'will be rewarded.' The former phrase translates a Hebrew word over which there is some debate. The choice seems to be between whether this is a more general word meaning 'destroy' or a word meaning 'be in debt to.' The NASB translates the latter, while the NIV the former. The idea of 'be in debt to' is that of entering into a debt and putting down a deposit of some kind that will be held in deposit/pledge, awaiting the satisfaction of the debt. In the case of default, the pledge will be forfeited.[25] Here, the exact nature of the deposit/pledge is not specified, though it may be the person's life that is in view. Thus, the notion would be that, in a vain attempt to express one's autonomy from God's revelation, one actually enslaves one's self more. The only path to freedom is obedience, not rebellion. Liberty is had only through service, not self-expression. This understanding is not lost with either choice of verb, but it is made more forcefully with the choice of the NASB.

13:14. The teaching of the wise is a fountain of life, To turn aside from the snares of death.

The pattern of antithetical parallelism is broken now by the introduction of a proverb of synonymous parallelism. The Hebrew word translated 'teaching' is *torah*, the word normally associated with the Law of God and the Pentateuch. Here, it has its more general sense of 'teaching,' but such teaching arises from, and is in conformity with, the written revelation of God. Note the close connection with the idea of such revelation in verse 13. Such instruction is 'wise,' first because it is in conformity to God's law, but also because it arises from a life trained, disciplined, rebuked and shaped by that law. Such a one approaches life in submission to God's revelation and can, thus, be called 'wise.' But, such a one is 'wise,' not simply because he can spout off Bible verses, but because the Spirit of God guides him into appropriate and timely application of the truth of God's written revelation.

When you find a person who instructs you out of, and in conformity to, God's written revelation, out of a personal conformity to that revelation and with a skillful sense of application, you have discovered 'a fountain of life.' The imagery is used elsewhere in Proverbs and is there associated with 'the mouth of the righteous' (Prov. 10:11), 'The fear of the Lord' (14:27), and 'Understanding' (16:22). Note the similar metaphor of a 'tree of life' in verse 12 (cf. Prov. 3:18; 11:30; 15:4). But, here, instead of luscious fruit, the picture is that of pure, cool, revitalizing water that bubbles up in a never-ending stream. People gladly return, again and again, to such teaching.

While the first line sets forth what the 'teaching of the wise' provides us, the second line holds out what it keeps us from. Wise instruction enables one to avoid the 'snares of death.' The notion of an evil trap has been seen before (Prov. 1:17; 5:22; 7:23; 12:13) and will be again (14:27; 18:7; 20:25; 22:25; 29:6, 25). Proverbs reminds us that, generally, life is longer and more pleasant when lived in wisdom (Prov. 1:32-33; 2:11; 3:13-18; 4:4, 10, 20-22; 8:35-36).

Those who despise the power of consistent, quality Bible teaching do not know what they do. The wise teacher keeps on holding forth the truth in the hope that 'God may grant them repentance leading to the knowledge of the truth, and they may come to their senses and escape from the snare of the devil, having been held captive by him to do his will' (2 Tim. 2:24-26).

13:15. Good understanding produces favor, But the way of the treacherous is hard.
This first line of the proverb is clear enough. The expression translated 'Good understanding' has been met already in Proverbs 3:4, where it is translated 'good repute.' It seems to describe 'the capacity for good sense, sound judgment, and wise opinions.'[26] When one possesses such qualities, he is destined to possess much more than simply this, for such character 'produces favor.' Wisdom, character and integrity rarely abide alone. They draw other virtues and blessings like a magnet.

This second line has been much debated. The verb 'is hard' is the major stumbling block. The meaning 'hard' is questionable. The verb normally has the idea of 'enduring' or 'perennial.' It is used to describe the ever-flowing, ongoing rush of a stream that never dries up (Ps. 74:15; Amos 5:24). It also describes an 'enduring' nation

(Jer. 5:15) or 'long established' leaders (Job 12:19).[27] This does not, in most commentators' minds, make good sense here. For this reason, many look at the Hebrew text as corrupted. Some have opted to see an error in transmission of the text that yields a meaning of 'is not lasting.'[28] Others have followed the LXX and translated with 'ruin.'[29]

These emendations, or an abandoning of the Hebrew text, are not necessary, however. The verb makes good sense as it is. The 'good understanding' of a wise man includes the ability to listen to rebuke, change course, repent, grow and change. In contrast, the way of the 'treacherous' never changes. He is always the same. Reproof brings no repentance. He is destined to always be what he is. He has no hope of growth, change, improvement. He has, by his unwillingness to listen, shut himself up to a perpetual state of sameness. Thus, he finds his way 'hard,' because it is immovable and unalterable. In this sense, it accords with the general sentiments expressed in verse 13.

13:16. Every prudent man acts with knowledge, But a fool displays folly.

The substance of a man's character is soon shown through his actions. This antithetical proverb contrasts the 'prudent man' and 'a fool.' The word 'prudent' is often negative in connotation, meaning something like 'crafty' or 'shrewd' (Gen. 3:1). It also, however, has a positive side that is evident here and in these instances it has the idea of 'to be skillful' or 'wise' (Prov. 12:16, 23; 14:8, 15, 18; 22:3; 27:12).[30] The prudent man acts 'with knowledge.' The word is a frequent synonym for 'wisdom' in Proverbs.[31]

In contrast is the 'fool.' He 'displays' his folly. The word is, more literally, 'spreads out' [for display] his folly.[32] The picture may well be that of a merchant arraying his products before potential customers, with hopes of making a sale.[33]

Thus, the basic message of this proverb is that a man's wisdom or folly is often seen in how he behaves and speaks. A fool cannot but parade his folly to those around him. A prudent man reveals his true nature through his actions, also.

This appears to stand in contrast with Proverbs 12:23 (where the same word for 'prudent' is found): 'A prudent man conceals knowledge, But the heart of fools proclaims folly.' In Proverbs 12:23, a prudent man 'conceals' what he knows, while here he 'acts with knowledge.' The two are not in opposition, however. The act that may reveal a man's wisdom is the self-restraint exercised in not saying all he knows. In both proverbs, the fool cannot contain his folly (Prov. 10:14; 12:16; 15:2; 29:11).

13:17. A wicked messenger falls into adversity, But a faithful envoy brings healing.
In the age of technology and instant communications, we have lost sight of the importance of trusted envoys. They were trusted to accurately convey a message and, perhaps, even to undertake important diplomatic or economic negotiations for the one sending them.[34] Thus, their character was of the utmost importance. Here, the messenger is 'wicked.' It means more than simply inept (Prov. 10:26); it implies purposeful evil. He misuses his trust for personal gain.

There is some debate as to whether the Hebrew text of the first line should stand as is. The verb, as we have it, means that the messenger himself 'falls into adversity.' Some have suggested the verb should be re-pointed to make it causative, and, thus, more parallel with the second line (cf. RSV). Thus, the translation would be 'plunges [the one who sent him] into trouble.' Both are, no doubt, true (Prov. 26:6), but the Hebrew text should stand. The unfaithful envoy will bring reprisal upon himself, because he has caused calamity for his superior.

What a contrast the faithful messenger is! He 'brings healing.' The word is almost always used figuratively.[35] Here it describes the *shalom* that is fostered when he acts both as an accurate conduit for information and as an agent for reconciliation (Prov. 12:18; 15:4). 'Like the cold of snow in the time of harvest Is a faithful messenger to those who send him, For he refreshes the soul of his masters' (Prov. 25:13).

13:18. Poverty and shame will come to him who neglects discipline, But he who regards reproof will be honored.
One's economic and social standing depends, in large measure, on how one responds to the input of others (Prov. 3:16-18). The two keys are 'discipline' and 'reproof.' The former refers to instruction through correction.[36] The latter describes the correction, rebuke or chastisement that comes to one when he goes astray. Whether or not one sees such input as negative or positive, and whether or not one listens and responds to it will largely determine his success in life. Here, the primary consideration is the social and business realm of one's life. Anyone who wants to be a success, or even just 'make it' in life, must come to appreciate and learn from the contrary opinions and input of others (Prov. 12:1; 13:1, 13).

The contrasting outcomes are heightened in two ways. The original word order is such that it highlights the differences in outcome. The words describing the results are set at opposite ends of the verse to call attention to them: 'Poverty and shame [shall come to] one ignoring discipline, But one keeping correction shall be honored.'[37] In addition, the words 'shame' and 'honored' involve a word play in Hebrew. The word 'shame' means 'lightness' and the word 'honored' means 'made heavy.'[38] The one who rebuffs input, in an attempt to look like an intellectual 'heavyweight,' will, in the end, be perceived as a 'lightweight' when it comes to wisdom.

13:19. Desire realized is sweet to the soul, But it is an abomination to fools to depart from evil.

Some commentators try to set aside this proverb as hopelessly disjointed, without a coherent relationship between the first and second lines. This is unnecessary. The first line is an echo of verse 12: 'Hope deferred makes the heart sick, But desire realized is a tree of life.' The word 'desire' is used a number of times in Proverbs. It can refer to selfish desires (Prov. 18:1) and to cravings never attained because of laziness (Prov. 21:25-26). Here, however, the desires are good. The righteous are granted their 'desires' (Prov. 10:24), because they conform to God's character and desires (Prov. 11:23). When this happens, the whole inner person is delighted (Prov. 13:12).

As the righteous have longings they seek to have fulfilled, so also 'fools.' Their desires are wicked and selfish and their hearts are captivated by a lust for satisfaction. All they can see is the object of their craving. They reject all counsel to 'depart from evil,' for that is the only path they see to the satisfaction of their cravings. In fact, such wise counsel 'is an abomination.' This is an interesting use of the word, because it is normally used to describe the response of God to evil.[39] Here, wise counsel evokes a deep, intense revulsion in the fool. Since the satisfaction of their lust is the fool's highest good, anything that threatens that goal is deemed by him to be evil (Prov. 29:27). 'Woe to those who call evil good, and good evil; Who substitute darkness for light and light for darkness; Who substitute bitter for sweet, and sweet for bitter!' (Isa. 5:20; cf. Mal. 2:17). Such a fool is himself an abomination to the Lord (Prov. 17:15). One can only hope that he sees the futility of his ways before it is too late (Eccles. 2:10-11).

When we desire what God desires as much as God desires it, He will make certain we are satisfied. Our quest is not to get what we want, but to conform our desires to God's character and purposes. 'Praise the Lord, O my soul, and forget not all his benefits ... who satisfies your desires with good things so that your youth is renewed like the eagle's' (Ps. 103:2, 5, NIV).

13:20. He who walks with wise men will be wise, But the companion of fools will suffer harm.

The difference between wisdom and foolishness rests not merely upon formal training, but also upon the informal relationships of life. Wisdom and foolishness are not simply taught, but caught. For this reason, one must guard carefully who influences him.

The first line demands that constant exposure to those who are wise will have a residual effect upon one's life. You cannot remain the same, if you have a wise man or woman as your friend. It also implies the necessity of having good, godly, wise role models, particularly in our teen and young adult years, for companionship with 'fools' brings destruction and folly to one's life.

The Hebrew of this second line contains a play on words. The Hebrew words translated 'companion' and 'will suffer harm' sound very much alike.[40] Knox attempted to convey this in English: 'Fool he ends that fool befriends.'[41] The proverbs often echo this theme of the danger of association with the foolish (Prov. 1:10; 2:12; 4:14-17; 16:29; 22:24-25; 23:20-21; 28:7).

13:21. Adversity pursues sinners, But the righteous will be rewarded with prosperity.

Commentators often demand that this proverb states the case as it is generally, but not necessarily universally, found. They liken this to the problem with Job's counselors, who demanded that, since he experienced 'evil,' then 'evil' must be present in him (i.e. he had sinned and was being judged for it). While Job's counselors were wrong (cf. Acts 28:4), it would be a misreading of this proverb to connect it with them. This proverb does not read backward from calamity to sin, but from sin forward to judgment and righteousness forward to blessing. The reasoning is flawless and unalterable when it moves forward in this way, but is flawed and erroneous when reversed. What is not stated, and not certain, is just when this outworking of sin or righteousness will take place, but rest assured, it will, whether in this life or the next.

The first line personifies 'Adversity' as one who 'pursues' sinners. The verb 'pursues' is, most often, used to describe an enemy or an entire army in pursuit of their enemy.[42] The irony of a life of rebellion is that we begin by pursuing sin (Prov. 11:19) and end up being pursued by it! Just what the outcome of the hunt is, we are not told in specific terms. However, verse 22 describes it as including a loss of worldly goods and verse 25 as perpetual hunger. As God reminded Cain: 'if you do not do well, sin is crouching at the door;

and its desire is for you, but you must master it' (Gen. 4:7). The lesson here is that you can 'be sure your sin will find you out' (Num. 32:23; cf. Ps. 140:11).

The reverse is also true: that those who pursue a course of righteousness will find in the end that they will 'be rewarded with prosperity.' The word 'prosperity' is the general term for 'good,' as also the word 'Adversity' in line one is the basic word for 'evil.' Here, the context helps determine the exact nuance of their meaning. This idea of 'reward' to the righteous is a steady stream running through the landscape of Proverbs (cf. v. 13; see also Prov. 3:2, 16-18; 8:18; 10:6, 22; 21:21; 28:25).

The imagery of this verse is powerful! The rebel is hunted down and set apart for destruction, while the righteous man is ushered into the King's presence and conferred with rewards for faithful service.

13:22. A good man leaves an inheritance to his children's children, And the wealth of the sinner is stored up for the righteous.
That this verse should be connected to the proceeding one is clear from their shared vocabulary. Both verses contain the Hebrew words translated 'prosperity/good,' 'sinner(s),' and 'righteous.'[43]

To the Hebrew mind, one's legacy in children and material goods was of the utmost importance. The statement made here is clearly a general principle, as was the one made in the previous verse. Of course, there are good people who do not have children at all, and, even if they do, they may not have grandchildren. There are good people who lose their worldly wealth in calamity.[44] But, generally speaking, the principle that the righteous pass on a good inheritance to their children's children holds true. The Scriptures view this more as an expectation than an exception (Ps. 25:12-13; 102:28; 112:1-2; 128:6).

The reverse is also true: those who gather goods while defying God will not ultimately hold on to them. God so works that what the sinner has accumulated can actually be accrued to the benefit of the righteous (Job 27:16-17; Ps. 49:10, 17; Prov. 28:8; Eccles. 2:26). God may choose to work differently for the outworking of His purposes (Ps. 17:13-14), but this is, generally, the pattern for the one who trusts and obeys Him. This certainly was the case for Jacob who, in the end, enjoyed Laban's wealth (Gen. 31:1, 9, 16). It was proved true as the people of Israel came to possess the wealth of Egypt (Exod. 12:35-36) and Canaan (Josh. 11:14; Ps. 105:44). Also, Haman's wealth eventually went to Esther and Mordecai (Esther 8:1-2).[45]

13:23. Abundant food is in the fallow ground of the poor, But it is swept away by injustice.

Again, many commentators pronounce this proverb hopelessly corrupt and beyond understanding.[46] While translational challenges remain, the basic sense of the verse seems clear. The first line stresses that, even among the poorest of people, if there is diligence and wisdom applied to their work, they can produce what is necessary to sustain life (Prov. 12:11a; 27:18a; 28:19). Their 'ground' – or, by way of application, whatever their field of endeavor for making a living – is, generally, sufficient to provide for themselves and their families, if they will simply work wisely and diligently.

The second line presents, however, one obstacle to their sustenance: injustice. It is not clear exactly who perpetrates the injustice described. Is it committed by 'the poor' themselves and then, by way of judgment, God sweeps away what they may have produced by their labors? Or, is it committed by others, perhaps the rich and powerful, who crush these simple, hardworking folks and leave them destitute? If the latter, the proverb is a call for those with position to cease their unjust treatment of 'the poor.' If the former, it is a summons for 'the poor' to wake up and see that they are only hurting themselves by their injustice to others.

13:24. He who spares his rod hates his son, But he who loves him disciplines him diligently.

This is the first of a number of proverbs relating to the 'rod' as a means of disciplining a child (Prov. 22:15; 23:13-14; 29:15). The 'rod' is also referred to more generally in Proverbs (Prov. 10:13; 22:8; 26:3; also 14:3 though using a different Hebrew word). The notion of corporal punishment flies in the face of much popular psychology, but is a clear part of God's program for parenting a child to maturity. To withhold corporal punishment is not a sign of advanced learning, wisdom, or even greater love for the child. Far from it, it proves that a parent 'hates his son'! The contrast between 'hates' and 'loves' is intentionally strong. The notion conveyed by these words is often that of comparative love, rather that emotional revulsion over someone (Gen. 29:31; Deut. 21:15; Mal. 1:2f; Rom. 9:13).[47] Thus, withholding appropriate spankings is not a sign of superior love for one's children, but rather a signal that one loves something, or someone, more than his child. Perhaps the parent loves himself (avoiding the personal pain or self-discipline that comes with disciplining his child) more than his child, or perhaps he loves the affirmation and approval of others (who may disapprove of corporal punishment) more than he desires his child's welfare. Certainly, such a one loves someone more than he loves God, since he yields his obedience to them in this matter, rather than following God's word.

The true signal that parents love their child is their willingness to do the painful work of discipline. Here, 'discipline' certainly includes corporal punishment, but Proverbs also demands other forms of 'discipline,' which include verbal instruction, reproof and correction (Prov. 15:5), as well as action.

The word translated 'diligently' can mean either 'earnestly' (as the translators of the NASB have understood it here) or 'early' (cf. Prov. 1:28).[48] This second possibility would stress the need to begin early in the child's life to curb his folly through parental discipline. This does not call for the 'rod' at the earliest stages of a child's life, but the full-orbed perspective of parental training and discipline described in Proverbs.

Our heavenly Father disciplines His children (Prov. 3:12; Deut. 8:5; Heb. 12:5-11). Earthly fathers reflect His perfect love when they follow His lead and lovingly discipline their children. Such discipline is always measured and controlled (Eph. 6:4), but it is also consistent.

Note that this second to the last verse of the chapter answers to the opening verse, rounding out the chapter and completing the inclusio.[49]

13:25. The righteous has enough to satisfy his appetite, But the stomach of the wicked is in want.

The chapter has prepared the way for this proverb by more general statements along the same theme (vv. 13, 18, 21). The Scriptures, generally, teach that the righteous will have enough for their needs, while the wicked will never be satisfied. Though some might doubt this holds true in every case, the Scripture is not so hesitant. 'O fear the LORD, you His saints; For to those who fear Him, there is no want. The young lions do lack and suffer hunger; But they who seek the LORD shall not be in want of any good thing' (Ps. 34:9-10; cf. Prov. 28:25). Though this, too, is tempered at times, 'Better is the little of the righteous Than the abundance of many wicked' (Ps. 37:16). Yet, it can be immediately followed up by more confident assertions: 'They will not be ashamed in the time of evil; And in the days of famine they will have abundance.... I have been young, and now I am old; Yet I have not seen the righteous forsaken, Or his descendants begging bread' (vv. 19, 25).

Here, 'appetite' is, literally, 'soul.' The word represents the whole of one's immaterial life. It is sometimes used to designate one's inner appetites (Prov. 10:3; 23:2).[50]

The opposite is also consistently set forth in Scripture: that the wicked will consistently lack what they need (Deut. 28:48; 32:24; Prov. 6:11; 24:34; Isa. 65:13-14).

End Notes

1. Whybray, R. N., *Proverbs* (Grand Rapids, Michigan: William B. Eerdmans Publishing Company, 1994), 199.

2. Gilchrist, Paul R., '*yāsar*,' *Theological Wordbook of the Old Testament* (Chicago: Moody Press, 1980), 1:386.

3. Stigers, Harold G., '*gāʿar*,' *Theological Wordbook of the Old Testament* (Chicago: Moody Press, 1980), 1:170.

4. Fredericks, D. C., 'נֶפֶשׁ,' *New International Dictionary of Old Testament Theology and Exegesis* (Grand Rapids, Michigan: Zondervan Publishing House, 1997), 3:133.

5. Cohen, A., *Proverbs* (London: The Soncino Press, 1973), 80.

6. Kidner, Derek, *Proverbs* (Downers Grove, Illinois: InterVarsity Press, 1964), 101.

7. Cohen, 81.

8. Murphy, Roland E., *Proverbs* (Nashville: Thomas Nelson Publishers, 1988), 94.

9. Wood, Leon J., '*hāpēr*,' *Theological Wordbook of the Old Testament* (Chicago: Moody Press, 1980), 1:311.

10. Ross, Allen P., 'Proverbs' in *The Expositor's Bible Commentary* (Grand Rapids, Michigan: Zondervan Publishing House, 1991), 5:976.

11. Patterson, R. D., '*sālap*,' *Theological Wordbook of the Old Testament* (Chicago: Moody Press, 1980), 2:627.

12. Stigers, Harold G., '*gāʿar*,' *Theological Wordbook of the Old Testament* (Chicago: Moody Press, 1980), 1:170 and Hartley, John E., 'גער,' *New International Dictionary of Old Testament Theology and Exegesis* (Grand Rapids, Michigan: Zondervan Publishing House, 1997), 1:884-887.

13. Ross, 5:997.

14. Grisanti, Michael A., 'שׂמח,' *New International Dictionary of Old Testament Theology and Exegesis* (Grand Rapids, Michigan: Zondervan Publishing House, 1997), 3:1251.

15. Cohen, 82.

16. Whybray, 203.

17. Smith, Gary, V., 'זיד,' *New International Dictionary of Old Testament Theology and Exegesis* (Grand Rapids, Michigan: Zondervan Publishing House, 1997), 1:1075, 1094-1096.

18. Hamilton, Victor P., '*hābal*,' *Theological Wordbook of the Old Testament* (Chicago: Moody Press, 1980), 1:204-205.

19. Cohen, 82.

20. Carroll R., M. Daniel, 'מעט,' *New International Dictionary of Old Testament Theology and Exegesis* (Grand Rapids, Michigan: Zondervan Publishing House, 1997), 2:1016-1017.

21. White, William, '*rābâ*,' *Theological Wordbook of the Old Testament* (Chicago: Moody Press, 1980), 2:828-289.

22. Hamilton, Victor P., '*māshak*,' *Theological Wordbook of the Old Testament* (Chicago: Moody Press, 1980), 1:532-533.

23. Harrison, R. K., 'חלה,' *New International Dictionary of Old Testament Theology and Exegesis* (Grand Rapids, Michigan: Zondervan Publishing House, 1997), 2:140-143.

24. Ross, 5:978.
25. Cohen, 83.
26. Ross, 5:979.
27. Buzzell, Sid S., 'Proverbs,' *The Bible Knowledge Commentary* (Wheaton: Victor Books, 1985), 1:933.
28. Kidner, 103.
29. Murphy, 94-95.
30. Allen, Ronald B., ''*ārōm*,' *Theological Wordbook of the Old Testament* (Chicago: Moody Press, 1980), 2:697-698.
31. Whybray, 206.
32. Hamilton, Victor P., 'פרשׁ,' *New International Dictionary of Old Testament Theology and Exegesis* (Grand Rapids, Michigan: Zondervan Publishing House, 1997), 3:699-700.
33. Delitzsch, F., *Proverbs, Ecclesiastes, Song of Solomon* (three volumes in one) in C. F. Keil and F. Delitzsch, vol. 6, *Commentary on the Old Testament* (in ten volumes), (1872; rpt. Grand Rapids, Michigan: William B. Eerdmans Publishing Company, 1980), 1:281.
34. Bowling, Andrew, '*l'k*,' *Theological Wordbook of the Old Testament* (Chicago: Moody Press, 1980), 1:464-465.
35. Whybray, 207.
36. Gilchrist, Paul R., '*yāsar*,' *Theological Wordbook of the Old Testament* (Chicago: Moody Press, 1980), 1:386.
37. Murphy, 98.
38. Ross, 5:980.
39. Murphy, 98.
40. Whybray, 208.
41. Kidner, 104.
42. White, William, '*rādap*,' *Theological Wordbook of the Old Testament* (Chicago: Moody Press, 1980), 2:834.
43. Whybray, 208.
44. Bridges, Charles, *Proverbs* (Edinburgh: The Banner of Truth Trust, 1846, reprint 1998), 166.
45. Ibid., 167.
46. Whybray, 209-210.
47. Cohen, 85.
48. Ross, 5:982.
49. Whybray, 210.
50. Kidner, 85.

Proverbs 14

14:1. The wise woman builds her house, But the foolish tears it down with her own hands.
This proverb provides a concrete example of the personification of wisdom and folly provided in Proverbs 1:20-33; 8:1-36; 9:1-6, 13-18. Commentators have wrestled with the Hebrew text, attempting to conform it perfectly to Proverbs 9:1.[1] One of the primary troubles seems to be that the first line has a concrete noun 'The wise woman,' while the second line has an abstraction, literally, 'folly.' The likeness is close enough as it stands, however, to make clear that the two passages are connected in the original author's mind.

By 'builds her house' one should not picture a carpenter erecting a physical structure for the family to dwell in. Rather, the notion is that of the many other components that go into making a house a home and that are often supplied by the woman (Prov. 24:3-4). Women were clearly involved in commerce (Prov. 31:15, 24). The woman provided the daily needs of her family (Prov. 31:13-15). She is actively involved in the training and discipline of the children (Prov. 6:20). She tirelessly works for the good of her husband (Prov. 12:4) and children (Prov. 31:18). She leads in ministry to the needy (Prov. 31:20). Her labors free her husband to be a community leader (Prov. 31:23). All of these things, and the innumerable other ways a wife and mother serves her family, are in view here.

The industrious and conscientious ways of the Woman of Wisdom are contrasted with the lazy, self-serving ways of 'the foolish.' By her actions ('with her own hands'), she 'tears ... down' those entrusted to her care by God.

Compare Woman Wisdom: 'Wisdom has built her house, She has hewn out her seven pillars; She has prepared her food, she has mixed her wine; She has also set her table; She has sent out her maidens, she calls From the tops of the heights of the city: "Whoever is naïve, let him turn in here!" To him who lacks understanding she says, "Come, eat of my food, And drink of the wine I have mixed. Forsake your folly and live, And proceed in the way of understanding"' (Prov. 9:1-6). Note the way the Woman Folly destroys her life and the lives of those with her: 'The woman of folly is boisterous, She is naïve, and knows nothing. And she sits at the doorway of her house, On a seat by the high places of the city, Calling to those who pass by, Who are making their paths straight: "Whoever is naïve, let him turn in here," And to him who lacks understanding she says, "Stolen water is sweet; And bread eaten in secret is pleasant." But he does not know that the dead are there, That her guests are in the depths of Sheol' (Prov. 9:13-18).

Contrast the difference between the wise and godly Lois and Eunice (2 Tim. 1:5; 3:15), and the disastrous results of those 'weak women weighed down with sins, led on by various impulses, always learning and never able to come to the knowledge of the truth' (2 Tim. 3:6-7). No doubt, the most detailed commentary on this proverb is found in Proverbs 31:10-31.

14:2. He who walks in his uprightness fears the Lord, But he who is crooked in his ways despises Him.

The fear of the Lord, the main theme of Proverbs (Prov. 1:7; 9:10; 31:30), resurfaces three times in this chapter (vv. 2, 26, 27). One's basic attitude toward God is evidenced in his actions (Prov. 8:13; 16:6). Here, Solomon reasons backward from action to attitude. If one walks 'in his uprightness' (e.g. Prov. 2:13; 4:11; 11:24; 17:26), it is proof that he reverences God in his heart. If, however, his steps are 'crooked' (e.g. Prov. 2:15; 3:32; 10:19), it proves that he 'despises' God. The Apostle John uses this same logic in the New Testament (1 John 3:8; 4:7).

Determine, then, to live in reverence of God! Fear of the Lord is a choice (Prov. 1:29). 'Do not let your heart envy sinners, But live in the fear of the Lord always' (Prov. 23:17).

14:3. In the mouth of the foolish is a rod for his back, But the lips of the wise will preserve them.

This antithetical proverb compares the speech of the foolish and the wise. In light of Proverbs 13:24, we might be quick to assume that this 'rod' is a tool of punishment (Prov. 10:13; 26:3). However, the word translated 'rod' here is a different Hebrew word, one being found elsewhere only in Isaiah 11:1. There, it clearly refers to a shoot or branch that grows up out of a tree stump. There is no reason, then, to leap to the conclusion that the 'rod' here has chastisement in view. The phrase 'a rod for his back' is, literally, 'a rod of pride.' Most translations have opted for an emendation of the noun 'pride' and thus supplied (as the nasb and niv have done) the noun 'back' (cf. Prov. 19:29). Most believe this brings the two lines into better parallelism.[2] However, there is no warrant for this from the ancient versions and no compelling reason for it translationally.[3]

The meaning would seem to be this: The mouth of the foolish becomes a branch, a shoot, a sprig that shoots forth, expressing the essence of his inner life: his pride. He is arrogant; His words cannot help but express that pride. As a branch can only be what the tree is, so our words can be only what our hearts are.[4] Did not Jesus teach this? 'The good man out of the good treasure of his heart brings forth what is good; and the evil man out of the evil treasure brings forth what is evil; for his mouth speaks from that which fills his heart' (Luke 6:45).

In contrast, the wise discover that their 'lips' (i.e. words) 'will preserve them.' Because their hearts are wise, their words (or lack of words) will be also. A heart of wisdom within us is one of the greatest shields God sets around us (Prov. 13:3). The arrogant fool's pride will show in his words and, eventually, bring him down (Prov. 11:2; 16:18; 29:23). The wise man's heart will find expression in his words and he will, thus, avoid much unnecessary harm. The 'shoot' of prideful words brings down the fool, but 'the root of the righteous will not be moved' (Prov. 12:3).

14:4. Where no oxen are, the manger is clean, But much increase comes by the strength of the ox.
Productivity has a price. One may grow tired of the mess of life. One may conclude that the answer is to get rid of the things, people and circumstances that make life a mess. A farmer may grow weary of cleaning up after his oxen. If he makes the decision to rid himself of the oxen, he will have a clean manger. He should, however, also calculate what he will lose when that ox leaves. He will have no mess, but he will also have no income. No oxen, no mess. No oxen, no way to work the fields. No way to work the fields, no crop. No crop, hunger. The path to prosperity is messy. Perhaps Charles Ryrie has stated it most succinctly, 'There is no milk without some manure.'[5] Choose which you would rather have.

The word translated 'clean' is also used by the psalmists (Ps. 24:4; 73:1) to describe those who are single-minded toward God (i.e. 'pure heart') and to refer to the 'pure' words of God (Ps. 19:8).[6] Here, it refers to the absence of that which is not wanted: the manure and mess of cattle.

14:5. A faithful witness will not lie, But a false witness speaks lies.
The proverb seems to state the obvious. The first line states the matter bluntly. A 'faithful witness' simply will not lie. They won't be moved by bribes, pressure, threats, intimidation or manipulation.

Their basic nature is bent toward truthfulness. When the pressure is on they will continue to be what they are: faithful to the truth.

The second line stands as a stark contrast. The 'false witness' brings forth lies. The root of the verb translated 'speaks' means 'breathe.' It is often used in a negative way to speak of 'uttering lies' (Prov. 6:19; 14:25; 19:5, 9).[7] That which arises from the deepest recesses of a person – his breath – is the vehicle for the expression of his nature. In this case, it is the basic deceitfulness of his character that is exposed by his words. Under the pressure of the witness stand, no amount of pretending will help. He will be what he is: false.

Indeed, there is a contrast here, yet there is also a remarkable similarity. Both witnesses act according to their nature. While the 'faithful witness' cannot help but be what he is ('faithful'), so too the 'false witness' acts according to his nature and his very breath is false.

Truthfulness is one of the most basic building blocks of all human communication and, thus, of human society as a whole. Apart from honesty, there can be no meaningful relationships and no significant progress made as a society (Exod. 20:16). Thus, Proverbs repeatedly pleads for truthfulness in speech (Prov. 6:19; 12:17; 14:25; 16:10; 19:5, 9; 21:28; 24:28; 25:18).

14:6. A scoffer seeks wisdom, and finds none, But knowledge is easy to him who has understanding.
It is a shock to hear of a 'scoffer' who 'seeks wisdom.' The 'scoffer' represents folly at its lowest ebb. A 'scoffer' is one who is confirmed in his foolishness. He will not endure the correction and discipline that is required to walk the way of wisdom (Prov. 1:30; 13:1; 15:12). He is independent and flees all restraints upon his thinking or actions. He is confirmed in his rebellion (Prov. 21:24; 22:10; 29:8). He scoffs at God and His ways; God will one day scoff at him (Prov. 3:34).

Why, then, would such a one seek after wisdom? Perhaps it is because it brings social standing (Prov. 3:16), or maybe because he has seen the practical kind of success that is the regular experience of those with wisdom. Whatever the motivation, the 'scoffer' will never attain to wisdom. The expression is terse and pointed in the Hebrew text: 'A scoffer seeks wisdom, but it [is] not.'[8]

The basic reason the attainment of wisdom is impossible for the 'scoffer' is that he refuses the most basic building block of understanding: the fear of the Lord (Prov. 1:7; 9:10).

How different it is for 'him who has understanding'! He is one who has discernment. He is able to see and differentiate between things. The fear of the Lord has given him the lenses necessary to perceive reality. With these resources, 'knowledge is easy' for him. The word translated 'easy' basically means 'slightness.' It can be used negatively to describe one who is considered a 'lightweight' and, thus, of low esteem (Gen. 16:4-5).[9] But, in our context, it probably means either something like 'swift' (wisdom comes quickly) or 'easily' (all hindrances removed or at least minimized). The major obstacle to wisdom and understanding is humility and attitude. Clear that hurdle and all other major impediments to wisdom are overcome as well.

14:7. Leave the presence of a fool, Or you will not discern words of knowledge.

The parallelism in this proverb is synthetic. The second line explains or expands upon the first line. The imperative is the first in the collection of proverbs that began in Proverbs 10:1.[10]

Proverbs often emphasizes the significance of choosing wisely one's friends. Here, Solomon demands that one waste no time in 'the presence of a fool.' Don't debate it. Don't prolong it. Leave.

What is the reason for such an abrupt, and seemingly 'cold,' response? You 'will not discern words of knowledge' in their presence. Remember, from Proverbs' perspective, wisdom and knowledge are all-important. Only those who provide or reinforce the ways of wisdom are worthy of our intimate relationships. This is not a proverb about evangelism, but about who becomes our confidant. We must guard carefully who influences us. A fool is dangerous to our spiritual well-being (Prov. 17:12). 'He who walks with wise men will be wise, But the companion of fools will suffer harm' (Prov. 13:20). The New Testament echoes this warning (1 Cor. 5:11; 1 Tim. 6:3-5).

14:8. The wisdom of the prudent is to understand his way, But the folly of fools is deceit.

This antithetical proverb hails the value of self-examination and self-understanding. The word for 'prudent' is used both negatively, with a sinister, evil connotation (Gen. 3:1; Job 5:12; 15:5), and positively, with the emphasis on the shrewdness and caution of wisdom (Prov. 12:16, 23; 13:16; 14:15, 18). The 'wisdom' possessed by such a man is 'to understand his way.' The verb 'to understand' means to discern between two options. It is the innate ability to look at two options and see what God sees in them. Such a one can look at his conduct ('his way'), and his motives and accurately identify them for what they are.

In contrast, the 'folly of fools is deceit.' Upon whom is the deception of the fool worked: others or himself? The word employed here is used elsewhere of deceiving others, but never of deceiving self.[11] The parallelism, however, would seem to point to self-deception. In the end, the immediate context would seem to push toward an understanding of self-deception. After all, the line of demarcation between deception of others (1 John 1:6) and self-deception (1 John 1:8) is not always distinct. The 'folly' (vv. 18, 24, 29) of it all is that soon such a one calls God a liar (1 John 1:10), demanding that His evaluation of their conduct is in error!

The proverbs repeatedly hail the one who can objectively evaluate himself and trim his actions accordingly (Prov. 4:26; 14:15; 15:28; 21:29). Conversely, 'The way of a fool is right in his own eyes' (Prov. 12:15) and 'There is a way which seems right to a man, But its end is the way of death' (Prov. 14:12; 16:25).

14:9. Fools mock at sin, But among the upright there is good will.
The first line of this proverb is difficult to translate. One of the chief difficulties is in deciding what the subject is. The NASB has chosen 'Fools' as the subject, but some object to this, noting that the verb is singular. To rectify this, some offer an emendation of 'sin,' so that it becomes 'sin-offering.' The meaning, then, becomes something like 'A sin-offering mocks at fools' (i.e. there will be no remission for their sin). The translation of the NASB can stand, however. Kidner has demonstrated that a plural subject can take the singular verb, if the meaning desired is 'every last one.' Thus, the idea would be that 'All fools mock at sin.'[12]

The word translated 'sin' is one that basically refers to 'the guilt, responsibility, or culpability that a person must bear for some offense.'[13] It does not describe the subjective feelings of guilt, but the fact of standing condemned for one's actions. A fool scornfully laughs off all talk of personal accountability. They do not perceive the reality that their attitudes and actions are done before a holy God and that He will hold them accountable.

The root of the verb 'scoffs' is found often in Proverb (Prov. 1:22; 3:34; 9:7, 8, 12; 13:1; 14:6, etc.). Being impervious to God's watchful, authoritative gaze is not wise. The one who laughs at God and His ways will find that one day He will mock him in his judgment. 'I will even laugh at your calamity; I will mock when your dread comes' (Prov. 1:26).

In contrast, 'the upright' find that among their number there is 'good will.' The word translated 'good will' is used frequently in

Proverbs and refers to one's acceptance or approval before another (Prov 8:35; 10:32; 11:1, 20, 27; 12:2, 22; 15:8; 16:15; 18:12; 19:12).[14] The one who takes God's holiness and his accountability to Him seriously finds favor and harmony in his relationships, whether it be with God Himself (Prov. 3:34; 11:20) or with his fellow man (Prov. 11:27). Was this not the testimony of Jesus, even in His childhood? 'And Jesus kept increasing in wisdom and stature, and in favor with God and men' (Luke 2:52).

14:10. The heart knows its own bitterness, And a stranger does not share its joy.

This synthetic proverb underscores the individuality of the human heart. No one can know perfectly the inner anguish or exhilaration of a person's emotions (1 Cor. 2:11a). This was certainly true for Hannah (1 Sam. 1:10), Peter (Matt. 26:75), the Shunammite woman (2 Kings 4:27) and Jesus (Matt. 26:39-46). The depths and quality of the emotions are the individual's alone (1 Kings 8:38). Ultimately, we cannot even understand our own hearts (Prov. 21:2; Jer. 17:9).

Only God sees and knows the depths of our hearts (Ps. 44:21; Prov. 15:11; Jer. 17:10). This is true because of God's omniscience, but is even more personal because of Jesus' incarnation and sufferings (Isa. 53:3-4; Heb. 4:15-16). It is true that God 'comforts us in all our affliction so that we may be able to comfort those who are in any affliction with the comfort with which we ourselves are comforted by God' (2 Cor. 1:4). Yet, we must be cautious about ever saying, 'I know exactly how you feel!' No one knows exactly how another person feels. The good news is that God does know and every ache in our hearts evokes an equal, and, indeed, magnified, ache in the heart of God. He bottles and records our every tear (Ps. 56:8). The anxiety (Prov. 12:25), disappointment (Prov. 13:12), fulfillment (Prov. 13:19) and myriad other emotions God has made the human heart capable of experiencing, can be shared perfectly only by God and the individual. Larry Crabb is correct, 'The route to knowing God eventually passes directly through the valley of profound loneliness.'[15]

14:11. The house of the wicked will be destroyed, But the tent of the upright will flourish.

This proverb of antithetical parallelism points to final outcomes. Character and integrity, we discover, contribute in large portion to security and prosperity. The first line echoes the counsel of Bildad to Job in his suffering (Job 8:15; 18:14-15). The proverb here is true – ultimately, the 'house of the wicked will be destroyed.' Bildad, however, was in error to assert that, every time a house was destroyed, it was because of wickedness. God has other reasons, in His sovereignty, for allowing such things to happen to the righteous.

The second line employs an unusual metaphor. The verb 'will flourish' is the one used to speak of a tree blossoming or budding.[16] An odd picture – a tent blooming! This points to the fact that, ultimately, 'house' and 'tent' are references, as often, to the inhabitants of those homes (e.g. 2 Tim. 1:16; 4:19). Proverbs often contrasts these opposing outcomes of the 'wicked' and the 'upright' (Prov. 10:25; 11:28; 12:7; 15:25).

An additional contrast that has commentators divided is between the more substantive and permanent structure of a 'house' and the more flimsy makeup of a 'tent.'[17] It is possible that these are simply poetic ways of contrasting the people and possessions of a man. It is also possible that Solomon intends a more subtle message as well. For the evil man to have a 'house' may mean that he has built it with funds obtained by illegitimate means. His life appears stable, but, in the end, it will be brought down. The righteous man, however, has lived in his integrity. Though his 'tent' appears vulnerable and unstable, with God's blessing it will not only stand, but grow and expand! Appearances mean little; it is the blessing of the Lord that makes for stability and security.

14:12. There is a way which seems right to a man, But its end is the way of death.

This antithetical proverb demands that presumption is deadly. The use of 'way' sends one's mind back to its frequent usages in Proverbs 1–9 and, in particular, the 'way' of the temptress in Proverbs 7:21-27. But, the thought here, while not excluding that of open rebellion and sin, may be that of prideful assumption that one's unexamined thinking is correct (Prov. 12:15). The word 'right' is the same one translated 'upright' in the previous verse. It often carries overtones of moral rightness.[18] One may choose a path, genuinely believing it to be the best one (even God's path!), but notwithstanding the sincerity, such a path still ends in death. Sincerity has never been the final test of truth. The word 'right' may here also refer merely to the fact that, from the trail head, the way ahead may appear passable, level and unobstructed; in a word: safe.

Having started so well, such a one will discover that 'its end is the way of death.' Literally, the Hebrew reads, 'But its end [is] the ways of death.' What was originally discerned to be the singular best way, now has opened into a plethora (note the plural) of possible death traps (Prov. 9:18; 11:19; 21:25). Pride, presumption and autonomy begin with promise, but they cannot sustain that hope into the future.

Proverbs 16:25 provides an exact repetition of this vitally important proverb. Jesus echoed the same warning: 'Enter by the narrow gate; for the gate is wide, and the way is broad that leads to destruction, and many are those who enter by it. For the gate is small, and the way is narrow that leads to life, and few are those who find it' (Matt. 7:13-14).

14:13. Even in laughter the heart may be in pain, And the end of joy may be grief.

This proverb of synthetic parallelism is at first glance a bit depressing. The meaning may run along several lines of thought. The point may be that even in the height of pleasure, we are never completely removed from pain (Ezra 3:11-12). This life offers no pure form of joy. Or, the point may be that this life offers no permanent pleasures. While seasons of delight may come, they are not the guarantee of a continuing life of ease. Laughter may temporarily force the awareness of hardship from our minds, but, before long, experience will remind us of reality (Eccles. 7:6).

Who has not laughed along with the crowd when he did not truly feel the joy? Did some tragedy or worry unknown to your friends make the smile on your face feel hollow or hypocritical (Prov. 14:10)? It is but a short distance from laughter to tears, from hilarity to hysteria. Not all who laugh are truly joyful.

14:14. The backslider in heart will have his fill of his own ways, But a good man will be satisfied with his.

This proverb of antithetical structure contrasts 'The backslider in heart' with 'a good man.' The former describes one of willful rebellion. The root of the word for 'backslider' means to 'turn back.' It is, normally, used in a negative sense of those who turn away from God, His truth and His people. They are apostates. The same root yields the word 'dross,' that which is skimmed off the top and taken away as worthless during the refining process of metals.[19] Ironically, the 'backslider' turns himself away from God and His ways, thinking them to be valueless, but, in so doing, proves himself to be worthless.

But the primary contrast of this proverb is not just the character of these two men, but the outcomes of their ways of life. The 'backslider' is going to 'have his fill of his own ways.' Most often, the word for 'have his fill' describes the nourishing satisfaction of sufficiency.[20] However, here it is used in a mocking sense – he will have 'had it up to here' with his ways and their consequences.[21] The natural outcome of one's actions is often one's own worst judgment in this life. 'So they shall eat of the fruit of their own way, And be satisfied with their own devices' (Prov. 1:31; cf. 11:5; 12:21; 18:20; 22:8).

The second line of the proverb has no verb, but the verb from the first line should probably be read into this second one. Thus, the understood verb in the second line would be used in its more natural sense of nourishing satisfaction, i.e. the good man will find that blessing comes from his ethical, moral and virtuous ways (Prov. 12:11, 14). 'Do not be deceived, God is not mocked; for whatever a man sows, this he will also reap. For the one who sows to his own flesh shall from the flesh reap corruption, but the one who sows to the Spirit shall from the Spirit reap eternal life' (Gal. 6:7-8).

14:15. The naïve believes everything, But the prudent man considers his steps.

Verses 15-18 form a subsection. The words 'naïve' and 'prudent' form an inclusio, acting like bookends to hold the verses together. The theme seems to be various ways in which foolishness can manifest itself. One may be foolish by being gullibly naïve (v. 15), arrogantly rash (v. 16), or emotionally impetuous (v. 17). The contrast to all these forms of folly is to be 'prudent' (vv. 15, 18).[22] Note also that verse 15b restates the general thought of verse 8a.

The 'naïve' are open-minded to a fault. They believe anything, and everything, they hear. They are blown wherever the wind of popular opinion may take them. They lack sound judgment (Prov. 1:4, 22, 32; 7:7; 8:5; 9:4, 6, 16; 14:18; 19:25; 21:11; 22:3; 27:12).

How different the 'prudent man!' The word for 'prudent' is used both negatively, with a sinister, evil connotation (Gen. 3:1; Job 5:12; 15:5), and positively, with the emphasis on the shrewdness and caution of wisdom (Prov. 12:16, 23; 13:16; 14:8, 18; 22:3; 27:12). The 'wisdom' possessed by such a man is 'to understand his way' (Prov. 14:8). The man is 'prudent' because he can discern the truth about events, people, enticements and promises. He is 'prudent' because he has taken seriously the warning of his father: 'Watch the path of your feet, And all your ways will be established' (Prov. 4:26). He does not try to prove his strength in the face of temptation, he flees: 'The prudent sees the evil and hides himself, But the naïve go on, and are punished for it' (Prov. 22:3; cf. 27:12).

A similar warning is sounded in the New Testament: 'Beloved, do not believe every spirit, but test the spirits to see whether they are from God; because many false prophets have gone out into the world' (1 John 4:1).

14:16. A wise man is cautious and turns away from evil, But a fool is arrogant and careless.

The contrast here, as so often, is between a 'wise man' and 'a fool.' The former, in this case, is 'wise' because of timidity. The word 'cautious,' most often, describes fear. The full first line is literally 'A wise man fears and turns from evil.' The NIV has supplied the words 'the Lord' after 'fears,' but this is interpretational. While this 'fear' may refer remotely to the fear of the Lord, it, in all likelihood, speaks of an inherent alarm over the potential negative consequences of a given course of action. The word 'evil' can refer to either ethical evil or personal calamity, or both. Perhaps here the emphasis is on an impending sense of personal calamity if a given course of action is taken (Prov. 22:3).

In contrast, 'a fool' is said to be 'arrogant and careless.' The first of these two descriptive terms is difficult to translate. It carries both the idea of arrogance and overwhelming anger.[23] Perhaps, the contrast with 'fear' would tip the scales in favor of the notion of 'arrogance.' Whereas the wise man has a natural, humble aversion to that which carries potential for harm, the arrogant man proudly and angrily dismisses all warnings as personal affronts to his sufficiency (Prov. 21:24).

The latter word ('careless') is a basic word for godly trust. It describes a confident reliance upon someone or something that is firm and solid. If, however, the thing trusted is not worthy of that confidence, the trust is misplaced and, thus, 'careless.'[24] In this case, the arrogant man wrongly places his confidence in his own ability to accurately discern a situation. When he finds himself in error, it is too late to reverse course and avoid calamity.

14:17. A quick-tempered man acts foolishly, And a man of evil devices is hated.

This is a proverb of synthetic parallelism, the second line repeating and intensifying the first. The RSV has tried to make it an antithetical proverb. To do so has required emending the verb in the second line, perhaps following the lead of the LXX. While not set as a contrast, there is a sense of progression in these lines. The first is the undisciplined man who is 'quick-tempered' and unable to control his feelings and his reactions. The second is 'a man of evil.' Generally, the word here translated is elsewhere used in Proverbs in the positive sense of prudence, discretion or shrewdness (Prov. 1:4; 3:21; 5:2; 8:12). It also has a more sinister side, though, and Solomon is not afraid to use it in this sense, as here and Proverbs 12:2. The progression is between the bumbler who unthinkingly stumbles along, creating havoc, and the schemer, who thoughtfully charts a course of evil.

There is also progression of how people receive these two men. The former 'acts foolishly.' People watch, shake their heads with embarrassment and walk away. He 'exalts folly' (Prov. 14:29). The latter incites active hatred toward himself. In the end, he will 'go astray' (Prov. 14:22).

The RSV tries to make this an antithetical proverb, because it feels compelled to take the word translated 'an evil man' in a positive sense, as it is usually employed in Proverbs. Because of this, they are forced into an emendation of the verb in the second line, changing it from 'is hated' to 'is patient' (probably following a similar thought pattern of the LXX translators). This is unnecessary, for the Hebrew makes good sense.[25]

14:18. The naïve inherit folly, But the prudent are crowned with knowledge.
Together with verse 15, this verse forms an inclusion, by repeating 'naïve' and 'prudent.' The theme of how foolishness reveals itself (vv. 15-17) is now summarized. The 'naïve' are the silly and immature, who are mindlessly open to all kinds of influences. See on verse 15 for more development on this word. The verb 'inherit' seems to have an active sense of 'acquire,' as opposed to the more passive sense of receiving an inheritance. Those who are open to anything, and everything (cf. v. 15a), gather more of the 'folly' they already possess. Bits and pieces of pop wisdom are worked together into a pragmatic mosaic of madness. The 'naïve' end up wasting their lives, for they end up with what they already had.

How different is the lot of the 'prudent.' The 'prudent' man is he who is discerning and displays spiritual savvy. The word is often negative ('guile,' 'cunning'), but is also used often in Proverbs in a positive sense of 'shrewdness.' See on verses 8 and 15 for further development of the word. This man's end is the honor of being 'crowned with knowledge.' Proverbs has already used the imagery of the wise man being 'crowned' (Prov. 4:9; 12:4) and will again (14:24; 17:6; 27:24). But, the Hebrew word employed here is different. As a verb, it means 'to surround.' When used in the context of a lament, it refers to being surrounded by one's enemies (e.g. Ps. 22:12).[26] Here, however, it is used positively to picture the knowledge of God surrounding 'the prudent' man as a shield. The discerning man who carefully guards what influences him (cf. v. 15b), at the end of the day, is found wearing honor and encircled by the safety of wise and godly choices.

14:19. The evil will bow down before the good, And the wicked at the gates of the righteous.
This proverb employs synonymous parallelism to develop its point. Here, the emphasis shifts from the 'naïve' vs. the 'prudent' (vv. 15-18) and moves to the 'evil/wicked' vs. the 'good/righteous.'

The case is stated in absolute terms, as it so often is in Proverbs (Prov. 11:29; 17:2). This can be a disconcerting fact, considering that reality seems so seldom to conform to this. This empirical 'fact' moves us to look for the complete fulfillment of this proverb in a future age. Exegetically, it is helpful to note that the form of the verb 'will bow down' has the sense of 'have bowed down.' The reversal of fortunes is so sure that it is presented as though it has already happened. Far too often in this life, righteous Lazarus bows at the gate of the wicked man (Luke 16:19-20). But, how their fortunes are reversed in the end (Luke 16:23-26)! On occasion, God even allows it to take place in this life (Gen. 42:6; 43:28; Exod. 11:8; Esther 7:7-8; Acts 16:39). But, often, it remains a hopeful prophetic promise held for future fulfillment (Isa. 60:14; Rev. 3:9).

14:20. The poor is hated even by his neighbor, But those who love the rich are many.
This antithetical proverb states a sad fact of life: what one possesses often determines one's popularity.[27] Those who find themselves without the daily provisions they need will find that neighbors, and even family (Prov. 19:7), turn away from them. The 'rich' man, on the other hand, has more than a few 'friends'! Woe unto the man who, in days of plenty, believes that all his friends are true! And woe to the man who loses those riches, for he will soon discover the true commitment of those who have gathered around him!

'Wealth adds many friends, But a poor man is separated from his friend.... Many will entreat the favor of a generous man, And every man is a friend to him who gives gifts. All the brothers of a poor man hate him; How much more do his friends go far from him! He pursues them with words, but they are gone' (Prov. 19:4, 6-7; cf. 10:15).

The verbs 'hated' and 'loves' are not highly emotional words, but describe the determination of choice and rejection.[28]

14:21. He who despises his neighbor sins, But happy is he who is gracious to the poor.

What was stated as a fact in verse 20 is now given a moral judgment. The contrast in this antithetical proverb seems to address both the action and outcome of reacting to the needy. The one who 'despises' them sins. The verb has the idea of holding one in contempt and belittling or ridiculing him.[29] The contrasting response is to be 'gracious,' i.e. giving, meeting his needs.

The contrasting outcomes are seen in that one 'sins' and the other is left 'happy.' The parallel between the two is not perfect. One seems to be a moral verdict about the act and the other a state or condition personally experienced. It is assumed that the one who finds himself in sin is not left ultimately happy.

Proverbs describes a variety of ways one can be 'gracious' to the needy: listening to their woes (Prov. 21:13), lending money (19:17), defending the rights of the powerless (31:9), sharing from one's material resources (28:8). In such actions, one finds that he is, ultimately, being gracious to the Lord Himself (Prov. 19:17). This honors the Lord (Prov. 14:31). Such a man will be rewarded (Prov. 19:17) and lack nothing (28:27).

Proverbs also offers a strong warning to the one who 'despises his neighbor': 'He who shuts his ear to the cry of the poor Will also cry himself and not be answered' (21:13).

14:22. Will they not go astray who devise evil? But kindness and truth will be to those who devise good.

Here, we meet the first question used since this anthology began at Proverbs 10:1.[30] The emphasis in these two contrasting lines is on the planning of one's actions: 'devise.' The word is used elsewhere of both the artisan and the farmer who plows his fields (cf. Prov. 20:4).[31] They plot out their work. They formulate a plan of action and, then, carry it to completion. So, too, we think through our actions to one degree or another – whether they be 'good' or 'evil.'

Premeditated evil causes one to 'go astray.' The verb has the idea of turning down the wrong road.[32] Such a person misses God's will and blessing upon his life. God hates such a man (Prov. 6:14-18). He resides under God's condemnation (Prov. 12:2). On the other hand, premeditated 'good' enables one to experience 'kindness and truth.' These come, ultimately, from God Himself, but are often channeled through other people. See the contrasting schemes displayed in Isaiah 32:7-8.

14:23. In all labor there is profit, But mere talk leads only to poverty.

This antithetical proverb is built around a contrast of both action and outcome. The contrasted action is between 'labor' and 'mere talk.' The former refers to toil that is laborious and painful.[33] Compare its use in Genesis 3:16 and Proverbs 10:22.[34] The phrase 'mere talk' is, literally, 'the word of lips' and refers to empty, boastful talk that seems to never lead to action.[35] The contrast of outcomes is seen in the words 'profit' and 'poverty.' The contrast is pronounced in the original, where the two Hebrew words have similar sounds and are the final words in each line.[36]

These contrasts between toil and talk and profit and poverty point to the simple lesson that one should not unceasingly verbally dream about what they would like to do, but rather do it, expending the hard work necessary to make the dream reality. 'For the dream comes through much effort, and the voice of a fool through many words' (Eccles. 5:3). The Scriptures repeatedly denounce the idle talker and approve the diligent worker (Prov. 10:4, 10; 12:11, 24; 28:19; 2 Thess. 3:10-12; 2 Tim. 2:15).

14:24. The crown of the wise is their riches, But the folly of fools is foolishness.

Some make radical emendations to this proverb in an attempt to craft the text to say what they expect it to say. Instead of 'their riches' in line one, some substitute a word for 'wisdom.' In the second line, 'folly' is changed to read 'wreath,' so that it parallels the first line better.[37] This reconstruction is unnecessary, however, as the proverb makes good sense as it is.

The antithesis of this proverb speaks to the gains made by 'the wise' and 'fools.' The gains of 'the wise' include 'riches.' This, no doubt, includes additional growth in additional wisdom (cf. the emendation made by some[38]). But, here, the emphasis is also on the reward of tangible wealth in this world (Prov. 3:16; 8:18). These gains are worn like a 'crown,' a symbol in Proverbs of honor and esteem (Prov. 4:9; 12:4; 16:31; 17:6).[39] The fool, on the other hand, gains only more of what he already has: 'folly' (Prov. 14:18). The words 'folly' and 'foolishness' are the same in the Hebrew text. The second line is, literally, 'The folly of fools [is] folly.' The wise wear a crown of honor, through gaining more of what they already have (wisdom), and, in addition, that which they did not previously have ('riches'). The fool, however, gains only more of the very thing that already makes him a fool: folly. He is confirmed in his foolishness, while the wise man continues to grow inwardly and materially.

14:25. A truthful witness saves lives, But he who speaks lies is treacherous.

This proverb ushers us into the judicial world of the courtroom. The entire process of justice depends upon the veracity of the witnesses. Should a person be falsely accused, his only human hope is that those brought forth to testify will love the truth more than the proposed benefits of lying. Such a witness 'saves lives.' The word for 'lives' is, literally, 'souls.' Here, 'souls' refers to persons and all their lives stand for – physical life, career, reputation, etc. See verse 5 for an expansion upon what is meant here.

The same expression for 'speaks lies' is used there. It means 'breathes lies.' One's breath arises from the deepest recesses of his person. As such, it is the vehicle for the expression of his nature. In this case, it is the basic deceitfulness of his character that is exposed by his words. Under the pressure of the witness stand, no amount of pretending will help; they will be what they are: false. The word 'treacherous' is a translation of the same word in verse 8 where it is translated 'deceit.' The word is abstract, but should be understood to refer to someone concrete: 'the deceiver.'[40]

Proverbs, like all of Scripture, underscores the necessity of truthful witnesses to the outworking of justice on earth (Prov. 6:19; 12:17; 14:5; 19:5, 9).

14:26. In the fear of the Lord there is strong confidence, And his children will have refuge.

This verse and the next are linked by the common thread of 'the fear of the Lord' (cf. also v. 2). As we have noted, this is the key theme to the entire book (Prov. 1:7; 9:10; 31:30). The 'fear of the Lord' is the most basic and elemental building block of a life that pleases and proves God. Without it, one cannot come into possession of the wisdom and knowledge of God (Prov. 1:7; 9:10). Without the wisdom and knowledge of God, one cannot live joyfully successful in the world God created and sovereignly rules. The 'fear of the Lord' is developed by exposure to the revelation of God (Ps. 19:7-9). But, the reality of the 'fear of the Lord' is proved in our lives only by our obedience to God. Talk means nothing. Only a humble, obedient response to God's voice proves we truly fear the Lord.

When we gain the 'fear of the Lord,' we also come into possession of a 'strong confidence.' Obedience is often frightening, but the very thing that prompts obedience is what grants us the courage to follow Him. The question becomes 'Who or what do you fear most? Do you fear the potential consequences of obedience? Or do you fear disobedience to God?'

Once you are certain of God's call, you may move forward with bold confidence because you view God as bigger than any obstacle or potential consequence of following His leading. Such confidence has a great reward (Prov. 3:7, 25, 26; 29:25). 'Therefore, do not throw away your confidence, which has a great reward' (Heb. 10:35).

The rewards of the 'fear of the Lord' pass from one generation to the next. The children of the one who conducts his life in the fear of the Lord will 'have refuge' (Prov. 18:10; 19:23). The children of such people have 'a fortress or place of protection, a refuge in every time of need.'[41] Scripture promises that practical benefits accrue to one's children when one walks in the obedient fear of the Lord (Ps. 115:13-14; Prov. 20:7). We each must ask ourselves, 'Do I want to simply tell my children about the Lord and teach them His ways? Or do I want to also demonstrate what obedient fear of the Lord looks like and prove the promises of His word to them?'

'The angel of the Lord encamps around those who fear Him, And rescues them. O taste and see that the Lord is good; How blessed is the man who takes refuge in Him! O fear the Lord, you His saints; For to those who fear Him, there is no want. The young lions do lack and suffer hunger; But they who seek the Lord shall not be in want of any good thing. Come, you children, listen to me; I will teach you the fear of the Lord' (Ps. 34:7-11).

14:27. The fear of the Lord is a fountain of life, That one may avoid the snares of death.
Continuing the theme of the 'fear of the Lord' from the previous verse, it is now seen as 'a fountain of life.' Taking the two verses together reveals that the 'fear of the Lord' is both our secure fortress and our fountain of supply.[42] This verse is a repetition of Proverbs 13:14, except that here, the 'fear of the Lord' has been substituted for the 'teaching of the wise.' This exchange reveals that true wisdom belongs only to Yahweh and that, apart from living in reverent, submissive awe of Him, one can never truly gain wisdom. Indeed 'The fear of the Lord is the instruction for wisdom' (Prov. 15:33a).

The imagery of 'a fountain of life' is found elsewhere, where the subject is variously the 'teaching of the wise' (Prov. 13:14), the 'mouth

of the righteous' (Prov. 10:11) and 'understanding' (Prov. 16:22). The
metaphor of 'a fountain of life' was appropriate in a culture given to
recurrent and calamitous drought. Whatever else may be going on
around you, when you fear the Lord, He, who is the very fountain
of life, bubbles forth from within you (Ps. 36:9; John 7:37-38). But,
how sad the man who turns back from such fear of the Lord! 'Like
a trampled spring and a polluted well Is a righteous man who gives
way before the wicked' (Prov. 25:26).

One only avoids 'the snares of death' by drinking from 'the
fountain of life.' Paradoxically, studying the snare does not deliver
from it, but only entangles one. Rather, we must fix our eyes upon
and drink from the 'fountain of life' and, by so doing, we will
automatically avoid the 'snares of death.' The imagery of the 'snare'
is frequent in Proverbs (Prov. 12:13; 13:14; 18:7; 20:25; 22:25; 29:6,
25). The specific imagery of the 'snares of death' is found also in
Proverbs 13:14.

14:28. In a multitude of people is a king's glory, But in the dearth of people is a prince's ruin.

This is the first of what some call the 'royal proverbs,' which are
simply proverbs that speak of kings and rulers (cf. v. 35; 16:15; 17:7;
19:10, 12; 21:1; 25:7; 28:2).[43] The point of this proverb is simple enough:
numbers equal renown in the world of politics. When the people are
many, the ruler of those people is highly esteemed. 'There are three
things which are stately in their march, Even four which are stately
when they walk ... a king when his army is with him' (Prov. 30:29,
31). When, however, the number of citizens is comparatively small,
the leader has proportionately less respect.

This proverb also teaches a general principle of leadership:
official position means little when people are not following you.
A post without people is pointless. Titles without influence are
worthless. The king is ultimately expendable (Prov. 30:27), or at least
replaceable (1 Sam. 16:1), but not the people (2 Sam. 19:7).

14:29. He who is slow to anger has great understanding, But he who is quick-tempered exalts folly.

Proverbs speaks frequently of the wisdom of self-control (Prov. 15:18;
16:32; 19:11). The one who is 'slow to anger' (lit., 'long to anger')
proves that he possesses 'great understanding.' In the flash of the
moment, the wisdom of reserve may not seem evident as one is
rebuffed, but time proves that such a man saw more than the others
standing around. The word 'understanding' describes the ability to

examine two seemingly opposite lines of thinking and choose the correct one.[44] The light of a new day reveals that, in the heat of rising emotions, this man has chosen wisely.

The contrast is the 'quick-tempered' (lit., 'short of spirit') man. His fuse is short and he is quick to prove it at the slightest snub. Time reveals that this man 'exalts folly.' The word 'exalts' may mean to 'display to public view' or to 'promote' (cf. Prov. 3:35).[45] Before long, the apparent wisdom of defending one's honor proves to have been a foolhardy plunge into foolishness. Such a man proves the stupidity of emotional outbursts. 'A quick-tempered man acts foolishly, and a man of evil devices is hated' (v. 17). Thus the New Testament echoes this warning of Proverbs: 'But let everyone be quick to hear, slow to speak and slow to anger; for the anger of man does not achieve the righteousness of God' (James 1:19b-20).

14:30. A tranquil heart is life to the body, But passion is rottenness to the bones.
This antithetical proverb reveals the intimate connection between a person's inner state and his physical condition. The 'heart' is the innermost you. It is the seat of all your thoughts, the center of all your emotions and the place from which all your choices arise. As such, it affects every dimension of your life. When it is 'tranquil,' the body thus enjoys the effects. The word 'tranquil' is, more literally, 'healing' or 'health' (cf. Prov. 4:22; 16:24).[46] Thus, health in every dimension of one's inner life brings 'life to the body.' The physical bears the marks of the spiritual (Prov. 3:8; 4:22).

The opposite is also true, as experience has taught us and the second line reveals. The word 'passion' translates a word that describes an extremely powerful emotion, wherein some object or some quality of the object is desired by the subject. The term can be both negative ('envy,' 'jealousy') or positive ('zeal'), the difference being determined by the immediate context. The particular form we find here describes a condition wherein a person is dominated and controlled by such emotion.[47] Here, the emotion is clearly negative; a passionate yearning after something illegitimate that remains unfulfilled. When one's heart is thus under the sway of such emotion, it is 'rottenness to the bones.' The term has already been met at Proverbs 12:4. It describes the eating away of a person's life from the inside out. In modern terms, such passion eats away at a person like a cancer. One's 'bones' are often used in Proverbs to describe one's core physical condition (Prov. 3:8; 15:30; 16:24; 17:22).

14:31. He who oppresses the poor reproaches his Maker, But he who is gracious to the needy honors Him.

How one treats the poor reveals one's true heart toward God. The word 'oppresses' is frequently employed to describe the contemptuous attitude and actions of those rich in money and power. It also is used of ordinary stealing or swindling of a neighbor.[48] Such action is a reproach directed toward God. The word 'reproaches' has the idea of taunting or casting sharp words toward.

The 'sin' (Prov. 14:20-21) enters in when one discovers that, what one does to the poor, one does to God (Matt. 25:40). It is done to 'his Maker.' Technically, the pronoun 'his' could refer to either the oppressor or the oppressed. There is good warrant to take it as referring to the poor man and, thus, his Creator (Prov. 20:12; 22:2; 29:13; Job 31:15; James 3:9). In this case, the rich oppressor is not actually any better than the poor man. They are, in fact, brothers on a common plane. 'He who mocks the poor reproaches his maker' (Prov. 17:5). 'Do not rob the poor because he is poor, Or crush the afflicted at the gate; For the Lord will plead their case, And take the life of those who rob them' (Prov. 22:22-23).

The second line presents the opposite of this contempt. The actual word order is: 'But one honoring Him favors the needy.' Instead of leading with the action to the poor and concluding with the attitude that it reveals about God, the word order begins with the attitude toward God and shows that such an attitude cannot but be revealed in one's attitude toward those who are disadvantaged. 'Happy is he who is gracious to the poor' (Prov. 14:21). 'He who is gracious to a poor man lends to the Lord, And He will repay him for his good deed' (Prov. 19:17; cf. 28:27). The law required benevolence toward the poor (Deut. 15:1-11) and Jesus (Matt. 25:31-45) and the New Testament writers affirmed the same (1 John 3:17-21).

14:32. The wicked is thrust down by his wrongdoing, But the righteous has a refuge when he dies.

This antithetical proverb contrasts the final state of the 'wicked' and the 'righteous.' The former is eventually 'thrust down' by the course of his sin. Proverbs repeatedly underscores the inevitable downfall of those who choose a path other than God's (Prov. 1:26-27; 6:15; 11:5; 24:16).

In contrast is the 'righteous' man who 'has a refuge when he dies' (Prov. 12:28). Many commentators and translators (rsv) are quick to emend the Hebrew text and change 'when he dies' to 'in his integrity.' In so doing, they claim the support of the LXX, but it seems to have more to do with their refusal to believe that Proverbs can even hint at a doctrine of immortality.[49] As so often in the Old Testament, the doctrines that are found in full bloom in the New Testament are here in only seed form. There is no need to reject the notion that, even in Solomon's day, as one died with his faith in the God who promised a deliverer and Savior, they found a refuge.

14:33. Wisdom rests in the heart of one who has understanding, But in the bosom of fools it is made known.
The first line of this antithetical proverb is clear enough. The second line, however, is what translators and commentators struggle with. It appears to have two possible meanings. The Hebrew text simply reports that wisdom 'is made known' in the fool. This does not provide the contrast anticipated by the first line. Possibly for this reason, the LXX has inserted the negative particle and translated it with 'is not made known.' This provides exactly the opposite meaning of the Hebrew text, yet the one anticipated by the first line (Prov. 12:23; 13:16; 15:2, 14). The KJV, NKJV and ASV have all followed the Hebrew text, but have inserted the words 'that which is,' so as to divert the meaning from 'wisdom' to the folly that is presumed to reside in the fool's heart. The RSV, NRSV and JB have all followed the LXX by inserting 'not.' NIV attempts to solve the problem by inserting the word 'even' to emphasize how remarkable it is that even a bit of wisdom might be found in the fool.

The notion that wisdom, in any form, may be found in the heart of a fool (the meaning of the Hebrew text) goes against the whole direction of Proverbs. The idea that the fool does not possess wisdom and is quick to reveal his lack (the meaning of the LXX) is repeatedly taught in these proverbs (Prov. 12:16, 23; 13:16; 15:2, 14, 28; 29:11). This, however, may very well have provided rationale for the translators of the LXX to attempt to 'improve' the Hebrew text.

Perhaps the issue is solved by emphasizing the word 'rests' in line one. In the heart of the understanding, 'wisdom' is at rest or feels free to abide and remain.[50] Wisdom is at home in the heart of one who possesses understanding. It stays put, spreads out, and makes its influence felt there. With this emphasis in the first line, then perhaps the point of the second line is that, while wisdom, at some early stage of the fool's life, makes itself known to him, it finds no rest there and is never able to settle in, stay put, feel at home, remain or abide. What is a life-giving, lifelong relationship with 'one who has understanding' is a fleeting encounter which breaks off quickly with 'fools.'

14:34. Righteousness exalts a nation, But sin is a disgrace to any people.
The generations and ages have repeatedly proved the truth of this proverb. A nation which conducts itself in righteousness 'exalts' itself. The word 'exalts' describes the lifting up, or elevating, of the people's collective life.[51] It is more of a moral term than descriptive of material benefits.[52] This has already been stated in regards to a 'city' (Prov. 11:11) and it applies to 'kings' (Prov. 16:12; 14:28).

In contrast, the people who tolerate and promote sin find it, in the end, to be 'a disgrace.' The word here is rare and unusual. It is rare in that it is found elsewhere only in Leviticus 20:17 (the verbal form is also found in Prov. 25:10) and unusual in that it has precisely the same Hebrew consonants as the cherished and rich word for God's covenant love: *ḥesed*. How different the meaning of this word, however! It describes a deep and disgraceful shame of almost unspeakable proportions (Lev. 20:17).[53]

This truth applies to any nation and to all peoples (Lev. 18:24-25), but has been perhaps most notably illustrated by the nation of Israel (Deut. 28:1-68; Judg. 2:6-14).

14:35. The king's favor is toward a servant who acts wisely, But his anger is toward him who acts shamefully.
This 'royal proverb' (cf. Prov. 14:28; 16:10, 12-15) focuses on issues of competence and incompetence in service. The one in authority ('king's') finds delight in rewarding one who serves him 'wisely.' The Hebrew word is often translated with the English word 'prudent.' It describes someone who intelligently works through the many complexities of an issue and then arrives at the wisest and most successful course of action.[54] 'Do you see a man skilled in his work? He will stand before kings; He will not stand before obscure men' (Prov. 22:29).

How different the response to an incompetent servant! Such a one 'acts shamefully.' This may mean that he brings disgrace upon his superior or that he is considered to be worthless in himself (Prov. 10:5; 12:4; 19:26; 29:15).[55] The response evoked is 'anger' (Prov. 16:14; 19:12). The Hebrew word often describes a justified outbreak of judgmental fury.[56]

The atmosphere of one's workplace is most often a product of one's own work ethic. The attitude of one's superiors is generally shaped by one's attitude toward his work.

End Notes

1. Whybray, R. N., *Proverbs* (Grand Rapids, Michigan: William B. Eerdmans Publishing Company, 1994), 211.

2. Ross, Allen P., 'Proverbs,' *The Expositor's Bible Commentary* (Grand Rapids, Michigan: Zondervan Publishing House, 1991), 5:983.

3. Murphy, Roland E., *Proverbs* (Nashville: Thomas Nelson Publishers, 1998), 101.

4. Kidner, Derek, *Proverbs* (Downers Grove, Illinois: InterVarsity Press, 1964), 106.

5. Ryrie, Charles C., *The Ryrie Study Bible* (Chicago: Moody Press, 1978), 956.

6. Kalland, Earl S., *'bārar,'* *Theological Wordbook of the Old Testament* (Chicago: Moody Press, 1980), 1:134-135.

7. Hamilton, Victor P., *'pûah,'* *Theological Wordbook of the Old Testament* (Chicago: Moody Press, 1980), 2:718-719.

8. Murphy, 104.

9. Coppes, Leonard J., *'qālal,'* *Theological Wordbook of the Old Testament* (Chicago: Moody Press, 1980), 2:800-801.

10. Buzzell, Sid S., 'Proverbs,' *The Bible Knowledge Commentary* (Wheaton: Victor Books, 1985), 1:935.

11. Delitzsch, F., *Proverbs, Ecclesiastes, Song of Solomon* (three volumes in one) in C. F. Keil and F. Delitzsch, vol. 6, *Commentary on the Old Testament* (in ten volumes), (1872; rpt. Grand Rapids, Michigan: William B. Eerdmans Publishing Company, 1980), 1:295.

12. Kidner, 107.

13. Carpenter, Eugene and Michael A. Grisanti, 'אשׁם,' *New International Dictionary of Old Testament Theology and Exegesis* (Grand Rapids, Michigan: Zondervan Publishing House, 1997), 1:554.

14. Buzzell, 1:923.

15. Crabb, Lawrence J., Jr. and Dan B. Allender, *Encouragement: The Key to Caring* (Grand Rapids, Michigan: Zondervan Publishing House, 1984), 58-59.

16. Hostetter, Edwin C., 'פרה,' *New International Dictionary of Old Testament Theology and Exegesis* (Grand Rapids, Michigan: Zondervan Publishing House, 1997), 3:683-685.

17. Cohen, A., *Proverbs* (London: The Soncino Press, 1946), 88.

18. Kidner, 108.

19. Patterson, R. D., *'sûg,'* *Theological Wordbook of the Old Testament* (Chicago: Moody Press, 1980), 2:619.

20. Waltke, Bruce K., *'śābēaʻ,'* *Theological Wordbook of the Old Testament* (Chicago: Moody Press, 1980), 2:869-870.

21. Adams, Jay E., *Proverbs* (Woodruff, South Carolina: Timeless Texts, 1997), 108.

22. Whybray, 216-217.

23. Struthers, Gail B., 'עבר,' *New International Dictionary of Old Testament Theology and Exegesis* (Grand Rapids, Michigan: Zondervan Publishing House, 1997), 3:316-318.

24. Oswalt, John N., *'bātah,'* *Theological Wordbook of the Old Testament* (Chicago: Moody Press, 1980), 1:101.

25. Whybray, 217-218.

26. Allen, Leslie C., 'כהה,' *New International Dictionary of Old Testament Theology and Exegesis* (Grand Rapids, Michigan: Zondervan Publishing House, 1997), 2:744-745.

27. Ross, 5:988.

28. Murphy, 106.

29. Buzzell, 1:936.

30. Ibid.

31. Delitzsch, 1:305.

32. Whybray, 219.

33. Cohen, 91.

34. Whybray, 220.

35. Delitzsch, 1:306.

36. Whybray, 219.

37. Ross, 5:989.

38. Ibid.

39. Whybray, 220.

40. Murphy, 106.

41. Delitzsch, 1:308.

42. Kidner, 110.

43. Whybray, 222.

44. Delitzsch, 1:79.

45. Kidner, 111.

46. White, William, '*rāpā''*,' *Theological Wordbook of the Old Testament* (Chicago: Moody Press, 1980), 2:857.

47. Coppes, Leonard J., '*qānā*',' *Theological Wordbook of the Old Testament* (Chicago: Moody Press, 1980), 2:802-803.

48. Whybray, 223.

49. Murphy, 102, 107.

50. Delitzsch, 1:313.

51. Buzzell, 1:936.

52. Kidner, 112.

53. Nel, Philip J., 'חסד,' *New International Dictionary of Old Testament Theology and Exegesis* (Grand Rapids, Michigan: Zondervan Publishing House, 1997), 2:210-211.

54. Goldberg, Louis, '*śākal*,' *Theological Wordbook of the Old Testament* (Chicago: Moody Press, 1980), 2:877.

55. Whybray, 158.

56. Struthers, Gale B., 'עבד,,' *New International Dictionary of Old Testament Theology and Exegesis* (Grand Rapids, Michigan: Zondervan Publishing House, 1997), 3:316-318.

Proverbs 15

15:1. A gentle answer turns away wrath, But a harsh word stirs up anger.
This chapter displays several distinctive features. Verses 1, 2, 4, 7, 14, 23, 26, and 28 all deal with the tongue. Nine out of the thirty-three verses of this chapter speak of Yahweh (vv. 3, 8, 9, 11, 16, 25, 26, 29, 33).[1] The antithetical form of the proverbs grows less frequent beginning in this chapter (only in vv. 3, 10-11, 12, 23-24, 30-31, 33).[2]

Speech has the potential to quiet a riot or to fan the embers of anger (Prov. 12:18; 15:18; 25:15). A 'gentle' word is the way to respond to a threatening situation. The word 'gentle' means soft, tender or delicate.[3] Here the idea is probably that of a conciliatory tone.[4] We should be 'gentle' in tone of voice, terms chosen and non-verbal communications that accompany our speech.

Unguarded words escalate any ill will that may be already present. A 'harsh word' is not simply one spoken with abrasiveness or out of irritation, but it is one designed to wound the other person.[5] Note also that it is one single 'word' that wields such power.[6] How many arguments, rifts and fights could have been avoided by simply refraining from a single word!

Note well the two words describing the negative emotions. The first, 'wrath,' speaks of anger at its hottest. The second, 'anger,' is the most common word for anger and comes from a root that means to breathe through the nostrils.[7] Thus, we see that a 'gentle answer' may quench even white-hot anger, while a single poorly timed word may fan a little huff into a raging fire. What power lies in the tongue!

An example of the peacemaking power of speech is seen in Gideon's response to the Ephraimites in Judges 8:1-3. An illustration of the capacity of the tongue to escalate an argument is seen in Nabal's response to David's men (1 Sam. 25:10-13) and Jephthah's response to the Ephraimites (Judg. 12:1-6).

15:2. The tongue of the wise makes knowledge acceptable, But the mouth of fools spouts folly.
Continuing the theme of speech, this antithetical proverb does not merely contrast wise and foolish speech. Rather, it compares the presentation of each. The 'tongue of the wise' is not simply found in

what it says, but how it says it. It 'makes knowledge acceptable.' The verb means to make something pleasing[8] or to do something well.[9] It is used elsewhere of well-groomed hair (2 Kings 9:30), walking in a stately manner (Prov. 30:29), and playing an instrument so as to soothe and please others (Ezek. 33:32). The person of wisdom skillfully employs his words, so as to win others over to wisdom's side (Prov. 15:7; 16:21). This involves prudence in when to speak (Prov. 15:23), selection of the words used (Prov. 15:28), and the tone of voice (Prov. 15:1).

The 'mouth of fools,' as one might guess, performs in exactly the opposite manner. It 'spouts folly.' The metaphor pictures a bubbling brook (cf. the same word in Prov. 18:4). Unlike the discretion of the one wise in speech, the fool simply opens wide his mouth and lets flow whatever comes to his lips. The same verb is seen in verse 28: 'the mouth of the wicked pours out evil things.' There are no standards for speech. Nothing is off-limits. If he thinks it, he says it (Prov. 12:23; 13:16; 14:33). He speaks whatever comes to his mind and cares not for those who don't like it. Such speech is abrasive; it separates and divides.

The notion is not so much that the wise are slick-talkers and the foolish are more plain-spoken. The contrast is also not so much in their intention, though that cannot be dismissed completely. Rather, the comparison is between the natural and effectual attraction or repulsion of each kind of speech.

15:3. The eyes of the LORD are in every place, Watching the evil and the good.

The two lines of this proverb are arranged in a synthetic parallelism, the second line expanding and explaining the first.

The wording 'eyes of the LORD' is found also in Proverbs 5:21 and 22:12. Its introduction here is surprising, given the theme of speech that began in verses 1-2 and continues hereafter (vv. 4, 7, etc.). The 'eyes of the LORD' speak of the omniscience of God. Perhaps the particular emphasis here is that He 'sees' all that one 'says,' a strange mixing of metaphors, but, nevertheless, true to the context. We should not, however, limit the knowledge of God to simply what is said in any place. The knowledge here attributed to God is universal. God knows all that we do (v. 3b) and even why we do what we do (Prov. 16:2). Even Sheol and all it contains is open to the Lord's scrutiny (Prov. 15:11).

The Scriptures repeatedly underscore the completeness of God's knowledge (Job 31:4; 34:21; Ps. 11:4; Jer. 16:17; 17:10; Zech. 4:10).

Such knowledge is at one and the same time a terror to 'the evil' and a comfort to 'the good.' To the one contemplating an independent course, the Scriptures warn: 'And there is no creature hidden from His sight, but all things are open and laid bare to the eyes of Him with whom we have to do' (Heb. 4:13). To those who choose God's path, the Scriptures promise 'the eyes of the Lord move to and fro throughout the earth that He may strongly support those whose heart is completely His' (2 Chron. 16:9).

15:4. A soothing tongue is a tree of life, But perversion in it crushes the spirit.
We return now to the theme of speech (cf. vv. 1, 2). This antithetical proverb contrasts the effects of our words. The differing types of speech are a 'soothing tongue' and a tongue with 'perversion in it.' The word 'soothing' comes from a root word meaning to heal or make healthful (cf. Jer. 8:15).[10] The phrase is literally 'a healing tongue.' Words have the ability to bring health to the physical body (Prov. 4:22; 12:18). They can be 'Sweet to the soul and healing to the bones' (Prov. 16:24). As such they are like 'a tree of life,' an image introduced early (Gen. 2:9) and that continues to the very end of the Scriptures (Rev. 2:7; 22:2, 14). It is also a metaphor found repeatedly in Proverbs. Sometimes, it is wisdom that is so pictured (Prov. 3:18), but at other times it is the products of a righteous life (Prov. 11:30) or the fulfillment of a longtime desire (Prov. 13:12). Here, it is our words that may be the source of life for another.

In contrast, there is speech with 'perversion in it.' The word translated 'perversion' is found only here and Proverbs 11:3. It describes that which is twisted or false.[11] Twisting words so that they serve our own evil intent 'crushes the spirit' of those we are in relationship with. A nearly identical expression in Isaiah 65:14 contrasts 'a glad heart' with this kind of 'broken spirit' or 'heavy heart.'[12] This seems to point to a mood of devastation or a spirit of despair (Prov. 15:13; 18:14). Such a state of mind can also affect the physical body (Prov. 17:22).

What potential lies within our words! We are endowed by our Creator with the capacity to bring either genuine, substantive help to those around us or to inflict incalculable lasting harm upon them – all of that by simply opening our mouths!

15:5. A fool rejects his father's discipline, But he who regards reproof is prudent.
A common theme in Proverbs is one's response to correction, in general, and a child's response to his father's discipline, in

particular. To reject paternal discipline identifies one as a 'fool.' The word used here was introduced in Proverbs 1:7 and has been used often since. Such a person is thick-headed and stubborn. He is not mentally deficient, but spiritually impaired. In his rejection of all authority, he has developed a resolute outlook on life. He does not fear the Lord and is not interested in truth. He refuses the counsel of others (Prov. 1:7; 10:8; 12:15). He mocks at sin (Prov. 14:9). Apart from the grace of God, he is almost certainly headed toward ruin (Prov. 27:22).[13]

What such a person is said to reject is paternal 'discipline.' The word describes a process of instruction that takes place through correction.[14] A fool leaves no room for learning by failure. He refuses to believe that anyone else may see things more clearly than he. He is determined to prove to the world he needs no one.

In contrast, 'he who regards reproof is prudent.' The word translated 'prudent' can mean 'shrewdness' in a negative sense (1 Sam. 23:22), but is used in Proverbs positively (Prov. 19:25).[15] It is related to a noun so used in Proverbs 1:4; 8:5, 12 and an adjective used similarly in Proverbs 12:23; 13:16; 14:8, 15, 18; 22:3; 27:12.[16] The verb may be translated either 'is prudent' (1 Sam. 23:22) or 'becomes prudent' (Prov. 19:25).[17] It seems more likely that the latter is the point being made here. Not that listening to parental correction reveals a heart of shrewdness, but, rather, it helps to create such a heart.

For further teaching along this line, see Proverbs 6:23; 10:1, 17; 12:1; 13:1, 18; 15:10, 31, 32; 19:20; 25:12.

15:6. Much wealth is in the house of the righteous, But trouble is in the income of the wicked.
This antithetical proverb contrasts the treasure of 'the righteous' with the trouble of 'the wicked.' The first line demands that, for those who walk the way of righteousness, God will provide joy in the physical abundance He gives them. The root of the word translated 'wealth' has the idea of a store or the laying up of valued goods.[18] The idea is that the house of the righteous becomes a great storehouse.[19] That house becomes a repository for untold treasures (both material and non-material) from which the righteous may draw as he follows God's path. Proverbs often speaks of the physical and material blessings that God sends the way of those who walk in wisdom or righteousness (Prov. 3:10, 16; 8:18, 21; 10:22; 14:24; 22:4; 24:4). It is true that, on occasion, as it may serve God's higher purposes, He may allow the righteous to suffer deprivation, but it is not the norm that Proverbs would lead them to expect.

In contrast, the second line demands that 'trouble is in the income of the wicked.' Note the contrast is not that the righteous become rich and the wicked become poor. Income comes to both the evil and the just. It is the effect of those riches that are contrasted. It is the ability to enjoy what is accumulated that is the point here. The word 'trouble' usually describes the trouble brought upon one from another person.[20] The word is quite similar to the name Achan, the 'troubler' of Israel (1 Chron. 2:7).[21] His story of ill-gotten gain in Joshua 7 provides an excellent historical illustration of the truth of this second line. The same word is found in Proverbs 15:27: 'He who profits illicitly troubles his own house, But he who hates bribes will live.' Proverbs often declares the ultimate inability of the wicked to enjoy the wealth they have schemed to acquire (Prov. 1:19; 10:2, 16; 11:17).

15:7. The lips of the wise spread knowledge, But the hearts of fools are not so.
A contrast between 'the wise' and fools' is not unexpected in an antithetical proverb. What is startling is the contrast between their 'lips' and their 'hearts.' Some commentators demand emendation of the Hebrew text in a needless attempt to 'make sense' of the text.[22] But, the text makes good sense already. The heart and lips have already been connected in Proverbs 4:23-24.[23] Did not Jesus affirm that the mouth speaks out of the overflow of the heart (Luke 6:45)? The point is that the hearts of the wise are full of knowledge, understanding and wisdom. Naturally, then, they leave a trail of learning behind them. The hearts of fools are devoid of such valuable commodities. They are, thus, left without such influence.

The verb used for 'spread' is rather unusual. It is almost always used in a somewhat negative way. It describes the winnowing of grain to remove the chaff.[24] Perhaps the best understanding is that, in the discourse of this world, the breath of the wise carries far and wide their understanding, while the hearts of fools yield only vacuous wind.

15:8. The sacrifice of the wicked is an abomination to the LORD, But the prayer of the upright is His delight.
The first line of this antithetical proverb is virtually identical to the first line of Proverbs 21:27, where it is found in a synthetic parallelism. Mere ritualism is not only worthless to move God, but He responds to it with the most vehement rejection possible. An 'abomination' is an attitude or an action which the Lord refuses to endure.[25] Proverbs

speaks of a number of things which are thus repulsive to the Lord (Prov. 3:32; 6:16; 11:1, 9; 12:22; 15:9, 26; 16:5). The issue is not sacrifice generally, but sacrifice brought insincerely (1 Sam. 15:22; Prov. 21:3; Isa. 1:11; Jer. 6:20; Mic. 6:7).

In stark contrast to His reaction to the manipulative efforts of the wicked to move Him through their sacrifices, God finds 'delight' in the prayer of those whose hearts are right before Him. God distances Himself from the wicked when they call, but 'He hears the prayer of the righteous' (Prov. 15:29b). It is not simply the ritual of insincere sacrifice that God rejects, but even their prayer is an abomination (Prov. 28:9). Likewise, it is not just the prayer of the righteous that God delights in, but also their sacrifices (Ps. 4:5). The point is not the rightness of prayer over sacrifice. Rather, it is Divine distaste for hypocrisy and manipulation and His pleasure in the worship of those who are truly His.

15:9. The way of the wicked is an abomination to the LORD, But He loves him who pursues righteousness.

This antithetical proverb complements the preceding verse, clarifying what was intended there. The primary link is the word translated in both verses as 'an abomination' (Prov. 6:16-19; 11:20). What was the 'sacrifice' of the wicked (v. 8) is here described as their 'way.' It is, ultimately, not even just the specifics of their lives that repulse God, but it is the entire direction they are headed. Conversely, the Lord finds delight in the one who 'pursues' righteousness (Prov. 21:21; 1 Tim. 6:11). It is not the perfection of every detail upon which God's pleasure hangs, but a consistent, steady, intense, purposeful, set direction toward His righteousness. The verb form of 'pursues' signifies the intensity of the search.

The responses of God also stand in contrast: 'an abomination' and 'loves.' Both are necessary. To posit the love of God without also affirming the wrath of God is a logical absurdity. One demands the other. The answer to our discomfort with the doctrine of the wrath of God is not ignoring it, but in the pursuit of His righteousness. In the course of that pursuit, we will come to exist in the atmosphere of His pleasure, and, with the way opened for the flow of His grace, He can then make us to understand the truth of His holy wrath.

15:10. Stern discipline is for him who forsakes the way; He who hates reproof will die.

Translators and commentators are divided over how to understand this proverb. There is no verb provided in the first line of the Hebrew text. Is the word translated 'stern' to describe the manner or severity

of the 'discipline' (NASB, NIV, etc.)? Or, is it to describe the perception
of the correction (KJV, NEB, JB)? Either translation is possible.[26] The
NASB suggests that it is the discipline itself that carries the quality of
sternness. The KJV suggests that it is only as the correction is rejected
that it is considered 'grievous' in the heart of the rebel. The former
seems to view the proverb as synonymous in parallelism, equating
'Stern discipline' with 'will die' as two ways of referring to the same
thing. The latter appears to understand the proverb as synthetic in
parallelism, the first line being more fully developed in the second.
If the discipline is rejected and considered grievous to the rebel, then
it will become more difficult yet, ending eventually in death.

The majority of modern commentators and translators side with
the NASB and the first option. The word translated 'stern' basically
describes that which is evil or bad. It can describe something as
morally wicked (Prov. 15:3) or as calamitous and unfortunate
(Prov. 15:15).[27] Which meaning does it carry here? Probably the
latter notion is in mind.[28] The discipline itself is bitter, difficult, stern,
severe and heavy. Such discipline awaits the one who 'forsakes the
way.' The 'way' is the path of wisdom and righteousness so often
set forth in Proverbs, particularly in chapters 1–9 (Prov. 2:13, 19, 20,
etc.), but also in the collections (10:17; 12:28).

This severest form of discipline is held for those who are
confirmed in their rebellion, for him who 'hates reproof' (Prov. 10:17;
12:1; 15:5, 12). An illustration would be Ahab's attitude toward
the prophesying of Micaiah (1 Kings 22:8-28). Confirmed in his
direction, his path can only lead to death (Prov. 1:31, 32; 5:11, 12, 23;
1 Kings 22:34-38). The New Testament assures us that the severest
form of church discipline involves delivering 'such a one to Satan
for the destruction of his flesh, that his spirit may be saved in the
day of the Lord Jesus' (1 Cor. 5:5; cf. 1 Cor. 11:28-30; 1 Tim. 1:20;
James 5:19-20; 1 John 5:16).

15:11. Sheol and Abaddon lie open before the LORD, How much more the hearts of men!

This verse serves as a pivot point (that which looks backward and
forward) – God's complete knowledge of the human heart looks
back to verse 3, while the word 'hearts' is repeated in verses 13, 14,
15. The argument from the lesser to the greater ('How much more')
is used also in Proverbs 11:31; 19:7; 21:27.

The word 'Sheol' describes the realm of the dead, generally. The
word 'Abaddon' is used six times in the Old Testament, all in the
Wisdom Literature (Job 26:6; 28:22; 31:12; Ps. 88:11; Prov. 15:11; 27:20).

It seems to refer to the condition of punishment and ruin, coming from a word meaning 'to perish' or 'to destroy,'[29] or it may refer to the deepest, darkest recesses of the realm of the dead.[30] Interestingly, later in Scripture, the word is transliterated and becomes a name for the leader of demons (Rev. 9:11).

In the Hebrew mind, nothing could be farther removed from God's presence than the grave. The point here is that such places are completely open before the Lord. The phrase 'lie open before the LORD' points to God's 'irresistible omniscience.'[31] He knows everything about these places and conditions. 'If I ascend to heaven, Thou art there; If I make my bed in Sheol, behold, Thou art there' (Ps. 139:8). His knowledge is immediate. He does not learn. He is not informed by someone. He knows perfectly, and instantly, all that actually is and all that could possibly be. Even the deepest darkness is arrayed before Him and scrutinized in its every part.

If God knows such far-reaching places, then surely the human heart is not shrouded to Him. I may be deceived about the condition of my own heart (Jer. 17:9-10), but God is not (1 Sam. 16:7; 2 Chron. 6:30; Ps. 44:21; Acts 1:24). He knows my thoughts. He sees clearly my motives. He scrutinizes my desires and longings. My feelings are plain to Him. He knows me – which is both a fright and a comfort, depending upon what I know He sees in me.

15:12. A scoffer does not love one who reproves him, He will not go to the wise.
This proverb is developed through synthetic parallelism – the second line affirms and advances the thought of the first. The first line re-introduces the 'scoffer,' one who despises being corrected (Prov. 9:7, 8; 13:1). His autonomous bent makes it impossible for him to find wisdom (Prov. 14:6). A 'scoffer' is the lowest level of the class of fools presented in Proverbs. He is hardened and confirmed in his folly and rejection of authority (Prov. 21:24; 22:10; 29:8).

Solomon used the literary device known as litotes to make his point. He states the negative to make a more powerful positive statement. Such a one 'does not love one who reproves him.' What he actually points to is not so much the absence of love, but the presence of active, and vociferous, hatred.

This active abhorrence of wisdom is extended in the second line, for here we discover that the 'scoffer' will not even seek out one who is wiser than he. The LXX has changed the notion to 'will not go with' the wise, but the NASB appropriately follows the Hebrew text and emphasizes that the scoffer 'will not go to' (i.e. seek out) another person for wisdom.[32]

This general theme is repeated in verses 5, 10, 31. As in the comments on verse 10, the example of Ahab and Michaiah (1 Kings 22:8-28) is apropos here as well.

15:13. A joyful heart makes a cheerful face, But when the heart is sad, the spirit is broken.
Verses 13-15 are all linked by the Hebrew word for 'heart.' Here, we have the 'joyful heart,' in verse 14 we find the discerning heart, and in verse 15 the 'cheerful heart.'[33]

This antithetical proverb contrasts the emotional states of being 'joyful' and 'sad.' The primary point is that the inner disposition determines the outward expression (Prov. 14:30; 17:22). We are controlled from the inside out, rather than from the outside in. There is no denying that outward circumstances affect us emotionally, but it is inner response to those outward events that determines our emotional, psychological and social response to them. Inner strength breeds outer confidence and courage.

The parallelism appears imperfect to us. The first line demonstrates the inner state controlling the outward expression. The second line shows that the emotional state can be allowed to control self-image as well (Prov. 15:4; 18:14). Delitzsch says that the word 'spirit' here describes one's 'power of self-consciousness and self-determination.'[34]

The proverb, as a whole, would then teach us that it is not so much what happens to you, but your attitude toward what happens to you that determines your view of yourself and your life. Attitude is everything!

15:14. The mind of the intelligent seeks knowledge, But the mouth of fools feeds on folly.
This antithetical proverb contrasts the preoccupation of the wise and foolish. The word 'mind' is the same word translated 'heart' in verses 13, 15. As verse 7 contrasted the 'heart' and the 'lips,' so here it is the heart and the 'mouth' that stand in opposition.[35]

The contrast is most noticeable in the verbs. The first verb 'seeks' points to a quest characterized by passionate intention.[36] The second verb 'feeds' describes the arbitrary munching of domesticated animals.[37]

The wise are said to already possess the 'mind of the intelligent.' The word 'intelligent' has the idea discernment, the ability to look at two things and see what God sees.[38] The wise are said to already possess such insight, but they, nevertheless, yearn, seek after and pursue more of that which they already possess (Prov. 14:33; 18:15; 19:25; 21:11). The fool, however, contentedly reclines in his folly and ruminates upon the silliness and naïveté he has fed his heart and mind upon already.

To have tasted of God's wisdom is to desire it all the more. To have numbed one's mind on folly is to ruin its taste for anything higher and better (Prov. 15:2, 21). Beware what you satisfy your heart on!

15:15. All the days of the afflicted are bad, But a cheerful heart has a continual feast.

This completes the trilogy of the heart that began in verse 13. And, as in verse 13, this proverb underscores that it is not so much one's circumstances as one's attitude that determines the quality of life enjoyed. Again, attitude is everything!

The first group, 'the afflicted,' are literally the 'poor.' They may or may not be 'poor' materially. Their lack may also be in the generous benefits of life in other realms as well. Whatever the lot that makes them 'afflicted,' their verdict on their experience is that it is 'bad.' The word is the one most often translated 'evil.' It is his disposition, not his predicament, that prevents him from finding joy amid his hardship (Ruth 1:20-21).

How different the experience of the one with 'a cheerful heart.' The attitude controls the experience, rather than vice versa (Prov. 14:30; 17:22; Hab. 3:17-18). Whatever his lot, he has 'a continual feast.' Feasts were momentary times of celebration. This man, however, because of his temperament, basks in the perpetual joy of celebrating life and its wonders.[39]

15:16. Better is a little with the fear of the LORD, Than great treasure and turmoil with it.

This is another of Proverbs' many 'Better ... than' bits of wisdom (Prov. 12:9; 15:16, 17; 16:8, 16, 19, 32; 17:1; 19:1, 22; 21:9, 19; 22:1; 25:7, 24; 27:5, 10; 28:6). Clearly, this proverb builds off of the cue of the 'continual feast' in the previous verse, yet that connection is only loose compared to the link with verse 17.

The point here seems to be the comparative quality of contentment and covetousness, worry and wealth, treasure and turmoil. The 'little' of line one is not specified. It does not require that we picture abject poverty; the contrast is with 'great treasure.' This comparative 'little' is not, in itself, to be preferred over 'great treasure.' It is 'little' when accompanied with 'the fear of the LORD,' which is of far greater worth.

The contrast between 'the fear of the LORD' and 'turmoil' does not, at first glance, appear to be clear. The word 'turmoil' describes 'wild, confused disorder, extreme discord.'[40] It is a word often associated with holy war and describes the confused and frantic state of the enemies of God when faced with His holy presence and power (Deut. 7:23; 28:20; 1 Sam. 5:9, 11; 14:20; 2 Chron. 15:5; Isa. 22:5; Amos 3:9).[41] This helps us understand that the 'great treasure' is that which is acquired outside the bounds of God's will (Ps. 37:16; Prov. 10:2; 16:8). Better to trust God with your investment portfolio than to throw aside the boundaries of His revealed will and attempt to gain security through your own frantic attempts to amass a financial sanctuary. 'But godliness actually is a means of great gain, when accompanied by contentment' (1 Tim. 6:6).

15:17. Better is a dish of vegetables where love is, Than a fattened ox and hatred with it.
Here we have another 'Better ... than' proverb (see v. 16). Like the preceding proverb, the contrast is between comparative wealth ('a fattened ox') and poverty ('a dish of vegetables'). A 'dish of vegetables' would have been the normal, daily fare for the average worker. It does not indicate destitution. The 'fattened ox' was a meal reserved for special occasions (Matt. 22:4; Luke 15:23). It was certainly the more desirable of the two meals.

The contrast also extends to the relational atmosphere in which the meals are shared: 'love' and 'hatred.' The contrast is not uncommon in Proverbs (Prov. 1:22; 8:36; 9:8; 10:12; 12:1; 13:24; 14:20). Relationships are more important than wealth. Any calculation of success must factor in the quality of relationships before material wealth and its luxuries (Prov. 17:1; 21:19). The latter without the former is, ultimately, worthless and unsatisfying.

Note that, whereas verses 13-15 form a trilogy of the heart (see on v. 13), verses 15-17 also seem to form a trio as well. Verse 15 points to a man at peace with himself ('a cheerful heart'), verse 16 speaks of being at peace with God ('fear of the LORD') and verse 17 extols being at peace with others ('love'). All three verses are linked by a common Hebrew word ('cheerful,' v. 15; 'Better,' vv. 16, 17).[42]

Recognize that this proverb does not extol vegetarianism above eating meat. If anything, it does precisely the opposite. All things being equal, the proverb points to the desirability of the meal where meat is served.[43]

15:18. A hot-tempered man stirs up strife, But the slow to anger pacifies contention.

Continuing on the theme of personal relationships, this antithetical proverb contrasts the effects of anger and patience. The word translated 'hot-tempered' comes from the verb to 'be hot.' It describes heat, hot displeasure, indignation, anger or wrath.[44] A man with a propensity toward this uncontrollable emotion 'stirs up strife.' The precise phrase is found in Proverbs 28:25 and 29:22. The word 'stirs up' is most often used in Scripture in contexts of warfare.[45] If there is any ember of contention still smoldering beneath the surface of formal social conventions, then this man can find it and fan it to flame once again (Prov. 14:17, 29; 19:19; 22:24).

How different 'the slow to anger'! The word for 'slow' in its most basic form describes something that becomes long, lengthened or extended.[46] Such a one forbearingly draws out all inducements to quarrel (Prov. 14:29; 16:32; 19:11; James 1:19). They are, literally, longsuffering. The presence of such a one 'pacifies contention.' Every flaming missile is extinguished in the depth of his character (Prov. 15:1). His mere presence is a blanket that suffocates all embers of anger seeking the oxygen necessary to thrive. The sheer magnanimity of his demeanor stills all strife. 'Blessed are the peacemakers' (Matt. 5:9)!

15:19. The way of the sluggard is as a hedge of thorns, But the path of the upright is a highway.

This antithetical proverb sets the way of the lazy man over against the path of one who lives uprightly. The 'sluggard' has been met already (Prov. 6:6, 9; 13:4), and will be again. His laziness has now caught up with him. Because he has lacked diligence, the pathway before him has become overgrown with thorns (Prov. 22:5; 24:30-31). A 'hedge of thorns' could be used as fencing – making the way impassible and directing travelers along another route (Hosea 2:6).[47] This man has failed to tend to the hedge of thorns along the path near his house. It has become overgrown. Now, he is cut off from progress. He is landlocked. He can only sit idly by and complain that he can do nothing else.

How different the path of the 'upright'! It is like 'a highway' (Prov. 16:17). The word has the idea of building, or throwing up, dirt to make a level and easily passable roadway.[48] The contrast between the 'sluggard' and the 'upright' is unusual. This has led to calls for emendation. This is unnecessary, however. The contrast reminds us that there is something unethical and unholy about laziness.[49] In the case of

the 'sluggard,' his sin has now found him out. He is stuck. He cannot
go forward in life. The word 'upright' is perfect in this context for, in its
root, it has the idea of that which is straight.[50] Is that not precisely the
point made here? Because, in his uprightness, he has lived diligently,
when the time comes for him to make a new move and travel down
the path, the way is clear and unobstructed (Prov. 3:6; 4:26).

**15:20. A wise son makes a father glad, But a foolish man despises
his mother.**
This antithetical proverb is nearly identical to the lead proverb of
this entire collection (Prov. 10:1ff). The first line is precisely the same.
The second line of Proverbs 10:1 speaks of the result of the wayward
son's actions upon the mother – 'is a grief.' Here, the second line
focuses upon the attitude of the son – 'despises his mother.' Not only
is the son a pain to his parents, but He couldn't care less what effect
he has upon them.

Such a son is called, literally, 'a fool of a man.' He is 'Exhibit A' of
a fool. He is the poster child of the folly so often described in these
proverbs. He is the fool par excellence.[51]

To become a parent is to place your emotional well-being in
jeopardy (Prov. 17:21, 25). A child holds in his hands the power to
inflict untold pain or joy upon his parents (Prov. 29:3). The whole
person is wrapped up in loving a child.

The callousness of this fool's attitude toward his parents will be
fleshed out through his actions. He may curse (Prov. 20:20; 30:11),
mock (Prov. 30:17), rob (Prov. 28:24) and even assault and drive away
his parents (Prov. 19:26). Such a fool will be judged (Prov. 20:20) in
the severest of fashions (Prov. 30:17).

**15:21. Folly is joy to him who lacks sense, But a man of under-
standing walks straight.**
We meet another antithetical proverb, this time contrasting the
mindless pursuit of the fool with the intentionality of the wise man.
The words 'lacks sense' are, more literally, 'lacks heart.' The phrase
has been met before (Prov. 6:32; 10:13; 12:11) and is another way of
identifying a fool. He is so completely devoid of understanding, it
is like someone has cut his heart (the seat of thinking, feeling and
choosing) out. He seems to have lost all ability to think correctly,
choose the right path and process his jumbled emotions. Little
wonder, then, that such a one finds 'joy' (cf. Prov. 15:13, 23, 30) in
folly. His thinking is skewed, which leads to poor choices and, in
turn, ends up in a confused sense of pleasure.

The 'man of understanding,' on the other hand, 'walks straight.' The word 'understanding' is one of the frequently used synonyms of wisdom. Proverbs has frequently used the imagery of the 'way' or 'path' to speak of how one travels through life. That imagery is reintroduced here. The idea is that, while the fool gleefully stumbles headlong toward destruction as he chases every fleeting pleasure, the 'man of understanding' chooses his course carefully, weighing each choice by what is right before God and man. 'Let your eyes look directly ahead, And let your gaze be fixed straight in front of you. Watch the path of your feet, And all your ways will be established. Do not turn to the right nor to the left; Turn your foot from evil' (Prov. 4:24-27). 'The path of the upright is a highway' (Prov. 15:19b).

15:22. Without consultation, plans are frustrated, But with many counselors they succeed.

This proverb echoes a consistent theme of the book: plans go better when we seek input from others (Prov. 11:14; 20:18; 24:6). The lack in the first line is 'consultation.' The emphasis is upon the confidentiality of the communication. The advice should be sought from a trusted circle of intimate friends. These need to be people whom you can trust to keep the secret (Prov. 11:13; 20:19; 25:9).[52] Without such input from trusted friends, 'plans are frustrated.' The word 'plans' can describe thought patterns (Gen. 6:5), a specific independent plan of action (Jer. 18:12) or a skilled worker who can put into physical expression any invention pictured in the mind (2 Chron. 2:14).[53] Such independence, when not curbed by the counsel of wise confidants, inevitably will be 'frustrated.' The verb describes a fracture.[54] Such independently conceived, and stubbornly clung to, plans will shatter and come apart in the end. Pride may be one of the key reasons people avoid such counsel (Prov. 13:10).

This defeat is unnecessary, however. With 'many counselors,' a man's plans may 'succeed.' The word 'many' implies that multiplied counselors is a safeguard. As one surveys trusted individuals, he may see a pattern of advice develop. Ultimately, it is not human counsel one wants, though, but the counsel of the Lord, for it alone will stand (Prov. 19:21). Yet, it may be through such friends that blind spots are laid bare, miscalculations are uncovered and unforeseen obstacles are brought into view.

With the humility of seeking other's input (v. 22) and the personal discernment of identifying God's ways (v. 21), the eventual form of the plan will 'succeed.' Note that the verb is in the singular, pointing to each individual plan as coming to fulfillment.[55]

Begin now to watch for people who display God's wisdom. Cultivate friendships with them. Seek their input when you face important decisions.

15:23. A man has joy in an apt answer, And how delightful is a timely word!

This proverb of synonymous parallelism brings us back to a repeated theme of the book: wise speech (Prov. 15:1). The 'joy' spoken of here could be experienced either by the one speaking it (pleased with himself) or by the one receiving the good word (pleased in the counsel he receives). It is more likely the latter, however, because of its proximity to the word about counsel in verse 22.

The first line literally reads, 'Joy [is] to a man by the answer of his mouth.' The word translated 'answer' is used to describe a verbal answer or response.[56] The emphasis seems to be on the correctness or accurateness of the response (Prov. 24:26). It is the right answer which brings joy.

The second line points to the timing of the answer. The word 'timely' relates the whole matter to an opportunity or to a particular season.[57] 'Like apples of gold in settings of silver Is a word spoken in right circumstances' (Prov. 25:11). 'Let no unwholesome word proceed from your mouth, but only such a word as is good for edification *according to the need of the moment*, that it may give grace to those who hear' (Eph. 4:29, emphasis added).

A wrong answer given when a correct answer is sought is misleading. A right answer given at the wrong time may be well-intentioned and technically correct, but damaging. The right answer at the right time is priceless!

15:24. The path of life leads upward for the wise, That he may keep away from Sheol below.

This proverb employs synthetic parallelism to make its point, the second line expanding upon and explaining the first. The contrast of the 'path of life' and 'Sheol below' helps achieve the point. As so often in chapters 1–9, and still occasionally in the collections (Prov. 10:17; 12:15, 26, 28; 15:19), life is described as walking a path. Here, it is the paths of 'life' and death ('Sheol') that are in view. The 'path of life' picks up on this chapter's notion of a 'highway' (v. 19) and he who 'walks straight' (v. 21).

Certainly, the proverb points to the oft-repeated fact that walking in God's ways brings health and longer life (Prov. 3:2, 16; 4:10; 9:11), while walking in the way of sin will cut one's days short (Prov. 2:18;

5:4-14). But, does it also point to a hope of immortality? Many commentators rush to deny any such doctrine in Proverbs. Some cite the fact that the words here translated as 'upward' and 'Sheol' are missing in the LXX. This, they say, is a significant signal that these words were probably added at a latter time by those who had come to believe in the hope of life after death.[58] The LXX, however, has been seen to offer free, and often radical, departures from the Hebrew text, as we have it.

'Sheol' normally seems to speak of the realm of the dead in general. We have seen, however, that Proverbs is not afraid to point to the hope of immortality (Prov. 14:32). It would seem that the doctrine of life after death, which we find in full flower in the New Testament, is found in at least seed form here.

15:25. The Lord will tear down the house of the proud, But He will establish the boundary of the widow.

The inclusion of the divine name Yahweh ('Lord') is the introduction of a theme, the name being found here and in verses 26, 29, 33 and eight more times in the first nine verses of the next chapter. This serves to further underscore the moral and spiritual underpinnings of wisdom.

In ancient Israel, the ownership of land was a person's link to family, the nation and the divine covenant promises. To lose the family allotment of land was a tragedy beyond comprehension and, often, spelled material and social ruin. For this reason, the law (Deut. 19:14; 27:17) denounced in the strongest terms anyone who would deceitfully move a boundary stone. The Prophets (Hosea 5:10) and Wisdom Literature (Job 24:2; Prov. 22:28; 23:10) joined in this universal condemnation of such underhanded theft. The most vulnerable to this kind of trickery was the 'widow,' for women had little judicial recourse, and the widow had no one else to naturally come to her defense. For this reason, God vowed to put all His divine power behind defending her (Ps. 68:5; 146:9) and those like her (Prov. 23:10-11).

The most likely to undertake such deception would be 'the proud' (Prov. 16:19). They are just brash enough to assume they can get away with it. God, however, pledges to tear down whatever they build through deception (Prov. 12:7; 14:11). Ahab's unethical acquisition of Naboth's land serves as a picture of such a man (1 Kings 21).

In contrast, the Lord will 'establish' the boundary of the defenseless. The word means to set, station, erect, fix or establish something.[59]

15:26. Evil plans are an abomination to the LORD, But pleasant words are pure.
This antithetical proverb presents a powerful contrast between the two lines. The second line is somewhat difficult to translate. Equally perplexing is its purpose in relationship to the first line. The first line underscores that, while God finds the ways and worship of the wicked abominable (vv. 8-9), His revulsion goes much deeper – all the way back to their basic way of thinking. It is not a method or a manner that is fundamentally their problem. It is that their entire way of reasoning is not in line with God's way of thinking. The word 'plans' refers to scheming and evil plotting (Prov. 6:18).[60]

The second line literally says 'pure [are] the words of pleasantness.' The 'pleasant words' are a contrast to the 'evil plans' of line one. The thoughts are now considered at the level where they have come to expression. In what sense are these words 'pleasant' and who finds them to be so? They are apparently 'pleasant,' ultimately, to God, since the aforementioned 'plans' were weighed in relationship to Him. They are 'pleasant' to God, and because they please Him, they, ultimately, turn out to be pleasing for all those He governs.

The words are deemed to be 'pleasant' because they are determined to be 'pure.' The word 'pure' stands in contrast to 'an abomination to the LORD' in line one – not the contrast one might have expected. The word translated 'pure' is almost a technical term for the ritual purity of sacrifices. It can also, however, carry a sense of ethical purity.[61] The NIV inverts the line, following the LXX, and seeks to maintain a cleaner parallelism by translating 'pleasant words' as 'those of the pure.' They, then, editorially add 'to him' to the line in an attempt to make sense out of the inversion. All this is unnecessary, for the NASB's more literal rendering of the Hebrew text makes good sense, as explained above.

15:27. He who profits illicitly troubles his own house, But he who hates bribes will live.
This antithetical proverb warns of the self-destructive nature of an illicit longing after wealth. The words 'profits illicitly' were already used in Proverbs 1:19, where it was translated as 'gains by violence.' The emphasis here seems to be not so much on the means, but the motive, of the gain.[62] Such avarice inevitably 'troubles' (Prov. 11:29; 15:6) the family of the one who possesses it, or rather is possessed by it. Achan's destruction of his family serves as a powerful illustration (Josh. 7:24-26). Such a pursuit of gain inevitably ends up as a catastrophic loss.

The second line displays one kind of illicit profit: bribery. The word 'bribes' is literally 'gifts.'[63] It can be used in a generic sense (Prov. 19:6), but often is used of a 'gift' given with a specific selfish intent. The law strongly denounced bribery (Exod. 23:8; Deut. 16:19) as does the Wisdom Literature (Prov. 17:8, 23; 29:4; Eccles. 7:7) and the Prophets (Isa. 1:23; 33:15). Proverbs can display a more neutral tone toward the practice as well, however (Prov. 6:35; 21:14).

For contrasting illustrations of response to bribery, see Elisha and Gehazi's responses (2 Kings 5). Abraham provides another godly response (Gen. 14:22-24).

15:28. The heart of the righteous ponders how to answer, But the mouth of the wicked pours out evil things.

Here the 'heart' and the 'mouth' stand in contrast – 'the wicked' awards 'the mouth' with the controlling influence due only to the 'heart.' The filter of wisdom and morality should strain one's words well before they arrive at the lips. The contrast is between 'the righteous' and 'the wicked.' There is a similarity with verse 2 (where the contrast was between 'the wise' and the foolish), where it underscores the moral foundations of wisdom. Yet, without question, this antithetical proverb's primary contrast is between well-thought-through speech and rash, off-the-cuff responses.

The heart of the righteous 'ponders' how he ought to respond to a question or a comment. The word originally described a low sound, like muttering under one's breath. From this origin, the word became descriptive of meditation, picturing one mulling something over in his head. As one thinks about something over and over, the lips might be muttering to one's self under the breath.[64] The idea here is that a righteous man does not respond quickly to a question or a rebuff. Rather, he takes the comment or question in. He considers it. He weighs his answer. He responds from the strength of contemplation, rather than from the weakness of immediate emotion. In this way, his speech can be the timely, needed word the situation calls for (Prov. 15:23).

How different 'the wicked' are! His mouth 'pours out evil things.' The verb is used in Proverbs 15:2 and 18:4. It is descriptive of the bubbling of a brook. There is no restraint. There is no guard set upon the lips. Nothing is off limits. Whatever 'the wicked' thinks or feels at the moment is what finds expression in his words. After all, as the modern defense goes, 'I'm just being honest!' Such an approach to speech results in 'evil' rather than honesty.

15:29. The Lord is far from the wicked, But He hears the prayer of the righteous.

The quality of one's living affects the effectiveness of one's praying. That the Lord 'is far from' those who do not know Him is often attested to in Scripture (Ps. 18:41; 66:18-19; 138:6; John 9:31). The worship of the 'wicked' is an abomination to God (Prov. 15:8, 9, 26). Until they repent, they will not be heard by God (Prov. 1:28). Unconfessed sin is clearly an obstacle, even to a true believer (1 Pet. 3:7).

On the other hand, God 'hears the prayer of the righteous.' The word 'hear' is found also in verses 31, 32. The Lord finds great pleasure in the prayer of those whose goal is to conform their hearts to His, rather than to change His mind to theirs (Prov. 15:8). 'The Lord is near to all who call upon Him, To all who call upon Him in truth. He will fulfill the desire of those who fear Him; He will also hear their cry and will save them' (Ps. 145:18-19). 'The effective prayer of a righteous man can accomplish much' (James 5:16b).

15:30. Bright eyes gladden the heart; Good news puts fat on the bones.

This proverb is constructed in synonymous parallelism, the second line restating the point of the first. Just what is meant by 'Bright eyes' is found in its parallel expression 'Good news.' The first line, by itself, might appear to be a comment about personal joy and its benefits to one's physical health. However, the parallel with 'Good news' makes it clear that the 'Bright eyes' are not in us, but in those we meet. Someone comes to us with 'Good news' and it brings refreshing to us, even physically ('puts fat on the bones'). Likewise, when we encounter a person whose eyes are gleaming over some good news they have encountered or that they have to share, we too find our hearts lifted (Prov. 25:25). The word for 'bright' is the word for a lamp or source of life.[65] It describes light being given off by another's eyes. When you find a person that delighted, contented and satisfied, it is a pleasing thing personally.

Joy is contagious! 'A joyful heart makes a cheerful face' (Prov. 15:13a; cf. 16:15). The root of 'gladdens' is also found in Proverbs 15:20, 21, 23. The expression 'fat on the bones' is a figure used to describe physical refreshing, health and reviving (Prov. 3:8; 12:4; 14:30; 16:24; 17:22). A good illustration of the truth of this proverb is found in Jacob's response to the news that his son, Joseph, was still alive (Gen. 45:27-28).

15:31. He whose ear listens to the life-giving reproof Will dwell among the wise.
While this proverb contains two distinct lines, they do not form the traditional two-part parallel we have become accustomed to. Rather, the two parts form one sentence. While the form may be unconventional, the point is not: teachability is the path to wisdom. This is a repeated theme of Proverbs.

The counsel to receive 'reproof' is by now familiar (Prov. 1:23, 25, 30; 3:11; 5:12; 6:23; 10:17; 12:1; 13:18; 15:5, 10, 32; 27:5; 29:1, 15). Here, the rebuke is made specific: 'the life-giving reproof.' 'For the commandment is a lamp, and the teaching is a light; And reproofs for discipline are the way of life' (Prov. 6:23). 'He is on the path of life who heeds instruction, But he who forsakes reproof goes astray' (Prov. 10:17). 'He who hates reproof will die' (Prov. 15:10). Those who are wise will listen and become wiser still (Prov. 9:9). Those who refuse to listen further confirm their hardness (Prov. 15:12).

Hearing, and heeding, such reproof will enable one to 'dwell among the wise.' It is not abundantly clear whether the content of the rebuke is to check one's companions and make certain to 'dwell among the wise' or if simply heeding the reproof entitles one to stand among such folk. Either way, the end result is the same. Proverbs can state the matter both positively, as here, or negatively: 'Whoever loves discipline loves knowledge, But he who hates reproof is stupid' (Prov. 12:1).

No one likes reproof; it cuts against our natural pride. Yet, it is precisely at this point that we reveal the true condition of our hearts. Do not light-heartedly pass off a reproof! It is easy to explain it away. It is so satisfying to believe 'They just don't understand.' Yet, the way you respond at this point places you squarely in one of two camps (Prov. 9:7-9).

15:32. He who neglects discipline despises himself, But he who listens to reproof acquires understanding.
This proverb, through antithesis, makes the same point as verse 31.[66] The root of the word 'neglects' means 'to loosen.' Here, it has the idea of a willful ignoring of available instruction (Prov. 1:25; 8:33; 13:18).[67] Such willful neglect may appear to arise because one disagrees with the one doing the correcting, but it often has more to do with personal pride (Prov. 1:7). The rejection of such counsel is, in fact, not so much a rejection of the counsel, but of one's own self (Prov. 8:36)! Such a one 'despises' himself. The word is a powerful one, describing wicked men's rejection of God (Num. 11:20; 1 Sam. 8:7; 10:19) and

God's rejection of them (Hosea 4:6). The trouble is not the action, but its object. We reject that which we should embrace (Hosea 4:6), and we embrace that which we should reject (Ps. 36:4).[68]

The contrast is seen in 'he who listens to reproof.' Such a one 'acquires understanding.' The word translated 'understanding' is the Hebrew word for 'heart.' The word has already been used in this metaphorical way in Proverbs 6:32; 7:7; 9:4, 16; 10:13, 21; 11:12; 12:11; 15:21 (cf. also 8:5). The heart describes the complex from which the thoughts, emotions and choices arise. The heart is who you are. Reproofs are a vital part of shaping who we are. We can never be all God wants us to be without remaining open to correction and teachable in spirit (Prov. 15:5, 10, 31).

15:33. The fear of the Lord is the instruction for wisdom, And before honor comes humility.
This proverb of synthetic parallelism begins with the theme of the book: the 'fear of the Lord.' In this regard, compare it with Proverbs 1:7; 9:10. There it was the beginning, most elemental and fundamental part of a life of wisdom. Here, it is 'the instruction' for wisdom. The word is used often throughout Proverbs (Prov. 1:2, 3, 7, 8; 3:11, etc.). It points to correction that brings about learning.[69] The 'fear of the Lord' will bring one into a relationship to God in which He will lay bare things about us that need to be changed. These changes, when made, result in wisdom. In light of who He is, we see who we are and, for those with courage enough to change, we can become increasingly more like Him.

The second line, at first glance, seems somewhat detached from the first. The keynote is 'humility,' however. The humility engendered from being in God's presence is the path to not only wisdom, but also honor. Humility and the fear of the Lord are also connected in Proverbs 22:4. The 'fear of the Lord' is elsewhere associated with hatred of pride and arrogance (Prov. 8:13). Proverbs 18:12b is nearly identical with this second line. This notion of humility before honor is oft repeated here (Prov. 16:18; 25:6-7; 29:23), as well as in the New Testament (Matt. 23:12; Luke 14:11; 18:14; Phil. 2:5-11; James 4:10; 1 Pet. 5:6).

End Notes

1. Whybray, R. N., *Proverbs* (Grand Rapids, Michigan: William B. Eerdmans Publishing Company, 1994), 225.

2. Murphy, Roland E., *Proverbs* (Nashville: Thomas Nelson Publishers, 1998), 111.

3. White, William, '*rākak*,' *Theological Wordbook of the Old Testament* (Chicago: Moody Press, 1980), 2:848.

4. Ross, Allen P., 'Proverbs,' *The Expositor's Bible Commentary* (Grand Rapids, Michigan: Zondervan Publishing House, 1991), 5:992.

5. Cohen, A., *Proverbs* (London: The Soncino Press, 1946), 95.

6. Kidner, Derek, *Proverbs* (Downers Grove, Illinois: InterVarsity Press, 1964), 112.

7. Delitzsch, F., *Proverbs, Ecclesiastes, Song of Solomon* (three volumes in one) in C. F. Keil and F. Delitzsch, vol. 6, *Commentary on the Old Testament* (in ten volumes), (1872; rpt. Grand Rapids, Michigan: William B. Eerdmans Publishing Company, 1980), 1:315-316.

8. Brown, Francis, S. R. Driver and Charles L. Briggs, *A Hebrew and English Lexicon of the Old Testament* (Oxford: Clarendon Press, n.d.), 405.

9. Gordon, Robert P., 'טוב,' *New International Dictionary of Old Testament Theology and Exegesis* (Grand Rapids, Michigan: Zondervan Publishing House, 1997), 2:353.

10. White, William, '*rāpā*',' *Theological Wordbook of the Old Testament* (Chicago: Moody Press, 1980), 2:857.

11. Whybray, 226.

12. Kidner, 113.

13. Ibid., 41.

14. Gilchrist, Paul R., '*yāsar*,' *Theological Wordbook of the Old Testament* (Chicago: Moody Press, 1980), 1:386-387.

15. Allen, Ronald B., "*ārōm*,' *Theological Wordbook of the Old Testament* (Chicago: Moody Press, 1980), 2:697-698.

16. Buzzell, Sid S., 'Proverbs,' *The Bible Knowledge Commentary* (Wheaton: Victor Books, 1988), 1:937.

17. Kidner, 113.

18. Delitzsch, 1:318-319.

19. Cohen, 96.

20. Kidner, 113.

21. Ross, 5:993-994.

22. Ibid., 994.

23. Buzzell, 1:937.

24. Carroll, M. Daniel, and Mark D. Futato, 'זרה,' *New International Dictionary of Old Testament Theology and Exegesis* (Grand Rapids, Michigan: Zondervan Publishing House, 1997), 1:1144-1145.

25. Whybray, 73.

26. Kidner, 114.

27. Livingston, G. Herbert, '*rā'a*',' *Theological Wordbook of the Old Testament* (Chicago: Moody Press, 1980), 2:854-856.

28. Brown, Driver and Briggs, 949.

29. Harris, R. Laird, "*ābad*,' *Theological Wordbook of the Old Testament* (Chicago: Moody Press, 1980), 1:3-4.

30. Delitzch, 1:322.

31. Ross, 5:995.

32. Ibid.

33. Buzzell, 1:938.

34. Delitzsch, 1:323.

35. Murphy, 113.

36. Chhetri, Chitra, 'בקש,' *New International Dictionary of Old Testament Theology and Exegesis* (Grand Rapids, Michigan: Zondervan Publishing Company, 1997), 1:720-726.

37. Kidner, 115.

38. Goldberg, Louis, '*bîn*,' *Theological Wordbook of the Old Testament* (Chicago: Moody Press, 1980), 1:103.

39. Adams, Jay E., *Proverbs* (Woodruff, South Carolina: Timeless Texts), 118-119.

40. Delitzsch, 1:325.

41. van Rooy, Harry F., 'הום,' *New International Dictionary of Old Testament Theology and Exegesis* (Grand Rapids, Michigan: Zondervan Publishing House, 1997), 1:1018-1020.

42. Murphy, 113.

43. Adams, 119.

44. Van Groningen, Gerard, '*yāham*,' *Theological Wordbook of the Old Testament* (Chicago: Moody Press, 1980), 1:374-375.

45. Waltke, Bruce K., '*gārâ*,' *Theological Wordbook of the Old Testament* (Chicago: Moody Press, 1980), 1:171.

46. Thompson, J. A. and Elmer A. Martens, 'ארך,' *New International Dictionary of Old Testament Theology and Exegesis* (Grand Rapids, Michigan: Zondervan Publishing House, 1997), 1:517-518.

47. Delitzsch, 1:326.

48. Harman, Allan M., 'סלל,' *New International Dictionary of Old Testament Theology and Exegesis* (Grand Rapids, Michigan: Zondervan Publishing House, 1997), 3:264-266.

49. Kidner, 115.

50. Murphy, 113.

51. Delitzsch, 1:327.

52. Patterson, R. D., '*swd*,' *Theological Wordbook of the Old Testament* (Chicago: Moody Press, 1980), 2:619.

53. Wood, Leon J., '*hāshab*,' *Theological Wordbook of the Old Testament* (Chicago: Moody Press, 1980), 1:329-330.

54. Delitzsch, 1:328.

55. Cohen, 100.

56. Beck, John A., 'ענה,' *New International Dictionary of Old Testament Theology and Exegesis* (Grand Rapids, Michigan: Zondervan Publishing House, 1997), 3:447-449.

57. Coppes, Leonard, J., ''*ānâ*,' *Theological Wordbook of the Old Testament* (Chicago: Moody Press, 1980), 2:679-680.

58. Whybray, 234.

59. Fisher, Milton C., '*nāsab*,' *Theological Wordbook of the Old Testament* (Chicago: Moody Press, 1980), 2:591-592.

60. Cohen, 101.

61. Whybray, 236.

62. Ibid.

63. Ross, 5:1000.

64. Wolf, Herbert, '*hegeh*,' *Theological Wordbook of the Old Testament* (Chicago: Moody Press, 1980), 1:205.

65. Whybray, 237.

66. Ibid.

67. Taylor, Richard A., 'פרע,' *New International Dictionary of Old Testament Theology and Exegesis* (Grand Rapids, Michigan: Zondervan Publishing House, 1997), 3:690-691.

68. Kaiser, Walter C., '*mā'as*,' *Theological Wordbook of the Old Testament* (Chicago: Moody Press, 1980), 1:488.

69. Gilchrist, Paul R., '*yāsar*,' *Theological Wordbook of the Old Testament* (Chicago: Moody Press, 1), 1:386-387.

Proverbs 16

16:1. The plans of the heart belong to man, But the answer of the tongue is from the LORD.

The name of the 'LORD' is prominent throughout this section, being used eight times in verses 1-9. It had begun to be used thematically in Proverbs 15:25, but here the use is even more concentrated. That these nine verses form a distinct section is clear, not only from the thematic use of the divine name, but because of the similarity of the first and ninth verse. These two serve as an inclusion, marking off a pericope dealing with the relationship of God's sovereignty and man's activity. Similarly, on a larger scale, the first and last verses of the chapter also form an inclusio, both containing the name 'LORD' and emphasizing His sovereignty. The word 'king' dominates verses 10-15, being used in every verse but verse 11. It seems likely that these dual themes are intentionally found at the mid-point of the book, the central verse being Proverbs 16:17.[1]

It has been often noted that chapters 10–15 are dominated by proverbs of antithetic parallelism, while chapters 16:1–22:16 are dominated by proverbs of synonymous or synthetic parallelism. While this observation is astute, there is nothing in the text to signal a major transition between chapters 15 and 16. The continuation of the Yahweh proverbs begun in chapter 15 has been pointed out. Proverbs 15:33, then, serves as a transitional verse.[2]

The root of 'plans' describes arranging something in an orderly manner. Related forms can describe setting forth an army in battle array (Gen. 14:8), the priest's orderly arrangement of items before the altar (Lev. 1:8; 24:8), or even the logical and ordered presentation of a legal case (Job 13:18).[3] Thus the first line of the proverb emphasizes man's ability, as one made in God's image, to think, reason and plan. This is a God-given, and God-glorifying, ability. It must, however, be undertaken with humility and dependence upon God.

The second line offers a contrast to the freedom of man to make his plans. While the thought and designs 'belong to man,' the truly effective response to the immediate need 'is from the LORD.' The word translated 'answer' describes more than a mere reply. It is the correct and perfect response to the immediate situation. It 'hits the nail on the head.'[4] While man may plan what he thinks is best, only

God, Who knows all, can put the perfect and effective answer in man's mouth.

The emphasis upon God's sovereignty will continue in the next two verses, revealing His control, not only over our words (v. 1) and our 'works' (v. 3), but also His all-inclusive knowledge of the motives behind both (v. 2). God is completely sovereign (Prov. 21:1, 30-31), yet that should never provide a theological cop-out for inactivity on man's part.

Do you need to make a decision? Does a response to an offer need to be made? God has warned us not to 'lean on your own understanding' (Prov. 3:5), but He has not told us to abandon it either (Prov. 16:1a). Plan. Think. Reason it through. But, do so in complete dependence upon the Lord! We do not know tomorrow or what it may hold (Prov. 27:1; James 4:13-16). Only He can give you the right response to the decision or offer before you (Prov. 16:33; 19:21; 20:24).

16:2. All the ways of a man are clean in his own sight, But the LORD weighs the motives.

This antithetical proverb continues the theme of the sovereignty of God over the ways of men. Here the inward 'plans' (v. 1) of a man have become his outward actions ('ways'). The point of the proverb is that God is far better positioned to make a true judgment as to our motives than we are. Even the wisest are capable of self-deception.

The natural human tendency is to justify one's self. Thus, Proverbs often speaks of one's ability to rationalize (Prov. 12:15; 14:12; 16:25). We tend to see our ways as 'clean.' The word is used elsewhere to describe undiluted oils or liquids.[5] We look at ourselves and see unalloyed motives. The ultimate answer to our subjective self-examination is constant awareness of God's objective test of our motives (Prov. 17:3; 21:2; 1 Sam. 16:7). 'If you say, "See, we did not know this," Does He not consider it who weighs the hearts? And does He not know it who keeps your soul? And will He not render to man according to his work?' (Prov. 24:12).

Are we left to wonder about God's evaluation until we stand before Him? No, the word of God is His tool to examine and weigh us even now (Heb. 4:12-13). We would be wise to humble ourselves before God and ask for Him to expose to us, through His word, that which He sees about us that we may be missing (Ps. 139:23-24). Yet, any final evaluation must await the last day! Paul declared 'I am conscious of nothing against myself, yet I am not by this acquitted; but the one who examines me is the Lord' (1 Cor. 4:4). He said, ultimately, 'I do not even examine myself' (1 Cor. 4:3b). This, of course, does not mean he did as he pleased, without thinking about it, but that any personal evaluation he made of his own motives and actions was only preliminary. The ultimate judgment is not by self or others, but the Lord – 'Therefore do not go on passing judgment before the time, but wait until the Lord comes who will both bring to light the things hidden in the darkness and disclose the motives of men's hearts; and then each man's praise will come to him from God' (1 Cor. 4:5).

16:3. Commit your works to the LORD, And your plans will be established.

This third verse continues the theme of verses 1-2 and uses synthetic parallelism to advance its point. The first line calls upon us to 'Commit' our endeavors to God. The verb is, more literally, 'roll,' and is used to describe rolling a large stone from the mouth of a well (Gen. 29:3, 8, 10). The idea here seems to be rolling one's planned, and proposed, 'works' over onto the Lord. Through prayer, we roll the anxiety of whether or not our hopes and plans will come true over onto God (Ps. 22:8; 37:5; 55:22). '... [C]asting all your anxiety upon Him, because He cares for you' (1 Pet. 5:7).

The second line takes up 'your plans' (Prov. 16:1, 9), revealing that the parallel 'works' of line one were not yet completed, but merely projected. When we do put the burden of seeing our dreams come true upon the Lord, He promises they 'will be established.' The verb is one used to describe God's work in creation (Prov. 8:27-29). God 'established' the heavens and the earth. So, we too are given the privilege of seeing our hopes, dreams and aspirations become a part of His-story for the world![6]

God does not guarantee any, and every, plan we may conjure up, but those which the Lord has had a part in (v. 1) and which He has been allowed to scrutinize (v. 2). When our plans are in line with His plan, our plan becomes a part of the story of God's redemptive plan for this world. If we plan and undertake our dreams with utter dependence upon the Lord for their fulfillment (v. 1), and if we humbly acknowledge our accountability to Him (v. 2), He delights to mold our plans to conform to His and thus 'establish' them (Prov. 4:26; Ps. 90:17).

16:4. The LORD has made everything for its own purpose, Even the wicked for the day of evil.

The thematic divine name 'LORD' continues to bind this verse to the previous three and the following five. This proverb is developed by a synthetic parallelism. The point it stated in the first line and, then, expanded and expounded in the second.

The first line asserts that the Lord has crafted everything 'for its own purpose.' The phrase is a tricky one for translators. The word for 'purpose' is literally 'answer.' Is it stating that God has so constructed the created order that everything within it must, ultimately, 'answer' to something? Is the 'answer' to God? Is it to the purpose for which the thing itself was made?

The vast majority or translators and commentators opt for the translation 'purpose.' The point seems to be that God makes everything answer to its divinely appointed purpose. No one acts with impunity. Consequences will always correspond to actions. God has created a moral order to the universe. This brings great comfort to the righteous. This should be a great fear to the ungodly.

Everything is under God's sovereign control. He has made everything to serve His purposes, indeed 'even the wicked'! The problem of evil has long perplexed mankind. God asserts here, in simple terms, that His plan is so all-encompassing that even the rebellion of man will in the end be made to serve His purposes. 'For the wrath of man shall praise Thee' (Ps. 76:10a). In the end, those who have freely chosen evil will find that this choice has not set them over God's plan, but that, through their choice, they have chosen 'the day of evil.' Even here, in the day of retribution and wrath, God's purposes will be served. 'What if God, although willing to demonstrate His wrath and to make His power known, endured with much patience vessels of wrath prepared for destruction?' (Rom. 9:22). Through Pharaoh and his hardness of heart, God demonstrated to the world that, no matter what the condition of an individual's heart, God will use them to serve His purposes (Exod. 9:16; Rom. 9:17). In the end, we will all proclaim 'For from Him and through Him and to Him are all things. To Him be the glory forever. Amen' (Rom. 11:36).

16:5. Everyone who is proud in heart is an abomination to the LORD; Assuredly, he will not be unpunished.
The writer has been probing the mysteries of God's sovereignty. In verse 4, he extended that sovereignty to even 'the wicked.' That claim is made even more specific now in verse 5. Here, it is the 'proud in heart' who are more specifically in view. The phrase is, more literally, 'lifted up in heart.'[7] Such a condition is a direct affront to God Himself, an attack on the very sovereignty that is being set forth in these verses. Compare Satan's five 'I will' statements in Isaiah 14:12-14.

Such people are 'an abomination to the LORD' (Prov. 3:32; 6:16; 11:1, 20; 12:22; 15:8, 9, 26). He utterly reviles them. He cannot stand their presence, and they will not stand in His. They stand against and in defiance of all that God is (Prov. 6:16-17). The 'fear of the Lord is to hate evil; Pride and arrogance and the evil way' (Prov. 8:13).

The second line echoes the first, but advances it by making more specific what is meant by their being 'an abomination.' 'Assuredly' represents the literal phrase 'hand in hand' (Prov. 11:21). It probably points to the certainty of the matter. It may look back to the sealing of a transaction with a handshake, testifying to the certainty that each party will hold to the agreement (Prov. 6:1).[8] The guarantee is that the proud 'will not be unpunished.' The word means to be free or to be exempt from guilt or responsibility.[9] God, the judge of all, will make certain that, for all their arrogance and pomp in this life, the proud will not be acquitted in the end.

Refer to Proverbs 11:20-21 to observe some remarkable parallels to the construction of this verse. See Proverbs 16:18, 19 for further development of this same theme within this chapter.

16:6. By lovingkindness and truth iniquity is atoned for, And by the fear of the LORD one keeps away from evil.

This proverb of synonymous parallelism is difficult. The first line seems to teach salvation by works. Does the 'lovingkindness and truth' refer to qualities in God which moved Him to make provision for sin in Christ? Or, do they refer to qualities to be found in the man who would find forgiveness from God? Despite a sincere attempt by some to protect grace,[10] the context demands that these be seen as qualities of the man. They are often used to describe God's character, but they are also used elsewhere of man (Prov. 3:3; 20:28; Isa. 39:8). The parallel with 'the fear of the LORD' (a quality found in the man) in line two indicates that these qualities are likewise those found in the man.

What then does the verse teach? Is this a denial of salvation by grace? No. The word translated 'atoned' is a technical term used of the provision for sin provided in the sacrificial system (Lev. 1:4, 4:20, 26, 31, 35, etc.). It is also used, however, in another way. Later in the chapter, the same word is used to describe a 'covering' of sin, not in a redemptive way, but in a relational way: 'The wrath of a king is as messengers of death, But a wise man will appease [cover] it' (Prov. 16:14). For a similar thought, note Proverbs 10:12: 'Hatred stirs up strife, But love covers all transgressions.' In this way, it is pointing not to redemptive peace with God, but relational peace between men. Verse 7 affirms that this is the direction the writer is thinking.

The first line understood thus, the second line then also speaks about how one avoids undue calamity in personal relationships: through 'the fear of the LORD.' The word 'evil' can mean moral evil, or it can refer to calamity. Either one might match the context here. It is through the 'fear of the LORD' that one avoids behaving sinfully in relationships. It is also through the same reverent fear that one avoids creating disaster in those relationships. Behaving sinfully leads to relational disaster! A proper view of, and relationship to, God provides a solid base from which to conduct our relationships. 'The fear of the LORD is to hate evil; pride and arrogance and the evil way' (Prov. 8:13).

16:7. When a man's ways are pleasing to the LORD, He makes even his enemies to be at peace with him.
The present verse now affirms that our understanding of verse 6 was accurate. The phrase 'a man's ways' is duplicated from verse 2. There, the notion was that his 'ways' are under the scrutiny of the Lord. Here, assuming he passes the test, his 'ways' are said to be 'pleasing to the LORD.'

The second line affirms that, when we please God, we will also please men, even our enemies. Certainly, this cannot be understood as a universally true maxim, without exception. For the Scriptures often remind us of the hostility of the world (2 Tim. 3:12). Jesus faced the opposition of the world (John 7:7), and, thus, we will as His followers (John 15:18-20). Scripture does exhort us to do our best to live at peace with all men (Rom. 12:18; Heb. 12:14). This, however, is achieved, not by concentrating on our enemy's pleasure, but upon God's. This verse is not a call to compromise, but to godly courage and fearlessness. God can take care of our enemies, if we please Him!

There is debate about the subject of the 'he' in this second line. Is it referring to God or the man? Commentators seem to be divided, some asserting that it is a reference to God[11] and others to the man.[12] The reference is probably to the man, but the conclusion is that both God and the man are involved. Ultimately, God is the governor of men's hearts and responses, but He will only do so (in the limited sense spoken of in this proverb) through us, as we walk with Him.

Scripture offers ample illustrations of the truth of this bit of wisdom: Abraham and Abimelech (Gen. 20:15), Isaac and Abimelech (Gen. 26:27-31), Jacob and Esau (Gen. 33:4), Asa and his enemies (2 Chron. 14:6, 7), and Jehoshaphat and his enemies (2 Chron. 17:10).

16:8. Better is a little with righteousness Than great income with injustice.

This verse seems to break the theme, for the divine name is not found for the first time in verses 1-9. However, the current verse may occur as an expansion upon what verse 7 means when it speaks of 'a man's ways ... pleasing to the LORD.' Indeed, when the near parallel in Proverbs 15:16-17 is examined, the theme does seem to be carried through, because, in Proverbs 15:16, 'the fear of the LORD' is used instead of 'righteousness' here.[13]

This is another example of the 'Better ... Than' proverbs (Prov. 12:9; 15:16, 17; 16:19, 32; 17:1; 19:1, 22; 21:9, 19; 22:1; 25:7, 24; 27:5, 10; 28:6). The point being made here is not the relative moral worth of poverty over riches, but the unilateral value of justice over injustice. Not even 'great income' can transform injustice into a worthy thing. See James 5:1-5 for a New Testament equivalent.

16:9. The mind of man plans his way, But the LORD directs his steps.

With the first verse of the chapter, this one completes an inclusio that emphasizes the sovereignty of God over the ways of man. Again, the human heart is in view in the first line. Here the emphasis is upon his 'plans.' The word describes not so much an understanding or insight, but the generating of new ideas. The notion of planning and devising is in view.[14] We are adept at dreaming of what we would like to do. We chart our course. We set forth a plan. We pursue our goals. 'Many are the plans in a man's heart' (Prov. 19:21a).

The second line, however, sets forth the antithesis that each man must bear in mind. It is the sovereign Lord who 'directs his steps' (Prov. 20:24). The verb is the same one found in verse 3. It is a word used to describe God establishing the heavens and the earth in creation.[15] The idea is not just that the Lord 'directs' one's steps, but that He is the only one who can take our flighty dreams and plans and make them reality. When we entrust our aspirations to God, (v. 3) and seek to bring our lives in line with His sovereign will, He will establish, as a part of settled reality, His divine will for our individual lives. When we stubbornly push our agenda over God's, there is no guarantee He will bring our plans to reality, not even if we are the king (Prov. 16:12, same verb). This is not a note of fatalism, but of freedom through submission to God (Ps. 37:23; Jer. 10:23). Our prayer should be 'Establish my footsteps in Thy word' (Ps. 119:133a).

16:10. A divine decision is in the lips of the king; His mouth should not err in judgment.

Now, the subject matter changes from 'Lord' to 'king' (found five times in vv. 10-15). The two sections, however, are not unconnected. We find here a delightful interplay between the absolute sovereignty of God and the measured sovereignty of Israel's (or any earthly) king. The point is that God upholds His moral order of the universe through His divinely appointed king on earth.[16] These royal proverbs find their ultimate fulfillment only in the King of kings, Jesus Christ.

We must seek to understand these proverbs along three lines: their historical understanding among the historical kings of Israel, their prophetic fulfillment in Jesus Christ, and their application to earthly rulers in our day. The kings of Israel were viewed as being under divine commission (Deut. 17:18-20). They were to make a personal copy of God's law and study it thoroughly and regularly. Every aspect of their rule was to conform to God's revealed will. In such a divine appointment, God had delegated a measured portion of His absolute authority to the earthly king. God would use the king to accomplish His will. The kings were certainly not perfect. Their decisions were never flawless. This did not serve to elevate them to some kind of divine status, but to place upon them the heavy burden of submission to God and the call to justly rule over men. It should cause them to call out to God for His wisdom, as Solomon had in 1 Kings 3:9. Only then could the people find in the earthly king the security and representation of God's ways (1 Kings 3:28; 2 Sam. 14:17, 20; 19:27).

The words 'divine decision' are a translation of a word that always elsewhere refers to sinful, occult divination (e.g. Deut. 18:10, 14), and is strictly prohibited under divine law. Here, however, the word is used in a rare positive light. God will make His will known through the earthly king. 'The king's heart is like channels of water in the hand of the Lord; He turns it wherever He wishes' (Prov. 21:1). This assures that God works in His world in an ordered way. He has established governments and individual kings (Rom. 13:1-7). The individual king may be corrupt, sinful, unbelieving and depraved. God, however, is sovereignly in control and can even use such rulers to accomplish His ends (e.g. Cyrus, Isa. 44:28; 45:1; Nebuchadnezzar, Jer. 25:9; 27:6). On a rare occasion, refusal to obey a sinful command of an earthly ruler may be necessary (Acts 4:19-20; 5:29). But, generally, God's purposes are worked out through the thoughtful and intentional submission of His people to the governing authorities.

The ruler may speak better than he knows (e.g. John 11:49-52), yet it is a 'divine decision.' This does not elevate sinful rulers, but it affirms again their accountability to God. It should drive them, in holy fear, to humble themselves before God, for 'His mouth should not err in judgment'! The verse does not guarantee the king will not err, but warns him to guard against it. Ultimately, only Jesus Christ Himself can fulfill this Divine responsibility perfectly (Isa. 11:1-5).

16:11. A just balance and scales belong to the LORD; All the weights of the bag are His concern.

This proverb underscores the Lord's desire for justice from the king (v. 10). The keyword 'just' is found in both verses ('judgment,' v. 10). Note the crossover of the 'LORD' theme (vv. 1-9) into this section devoted to the 'king' (vv. 10-15).

The word translated 'weights' is literally 'stones.' Merchants used scales and a set of pre-weighed stones to measure out silver in payment for goods and services. Unscrupulous businessmen would carry a set of stones that were lighter than labeled and also a set that were heavier that labeled. His choice of which set was used was determined by who was paying whom. Official weights and measures were established by the king. '... [H]e weighed the hair of his head at 200 shekels *by the king's weight*' (2 Sam. 14:26, emphasis added).[17]

Proverbs has already sounded a warning in light of God's concern for justice in commerce (Prov. 11:1), and will do so again (Prov. 20:10, 23). The Law joins in that warning (Lev. 19:35-36) as do the prophets (Amos 8:5; Mic. 6:11).

This proverb is startling, however, in that it goes beyond simply warning of God's interest in justice in commerce. The word translated 'concern' is literally, 'work.' God is intimately involved in establishing what justice in the business world looks like. The standard of ethics for business is divinely established! Unethical business practices are not only in defiance of the king, but of God Himself. There is more to be considered in business than mere pragmatics.

Let every businessman take heed, for, ultimately, the Lord weighs the hearts of all men (Prov. 21:2; 24:12)!

16:12. It is an abomination for kings to commit wickedness, For a throne is established on righteousness.

This proverb continues the royal theme intermingled with Divine overtones. The second line gives an explanation of the first.

Just who considers 'wickedness' an 'abomination' is not stated. This word of revulsion is, most often, descriptive of God's response

to sin (Prov. 3:32; 6:16; 11:1, 20; 12:22; 15:8, 9, 26; 16:5). We have seen
that the king is under divine commission; he answers to the Lord.
Therefore, the king should react to sin as the Lord does. It should be
to him 'an abomination,' also.

Though the most ideal reason for this should be that the king
shares God's heart, yet God recognizes a more pragmatic reason. The
wise king understands that his rule is 'established on righteousness.'
The term 'established' is the same one used in verse 3. Here, it is
descriptive of the stability and solidity of the king's rule. Scripture
affirms that God sets rulers in place (Rom. 13:1). So, too, God keeps
rulers in their place. He delegates to earthly authorities a measured
portion of His own absolute authority, and they are responsible to
use it in His ways. He lifts up and brings down whom He wishes.
The ruler with understanding knows that to choose the way of
righteousness is to choose the way of lasting rule (Prov. 14:34;
Rom. 13:3). It must be remembered that 'righteousness and justice
are the foundation of [God's] throne' also (Ps. 89:14; 97:2).

Practically, then, a king can help establish his throne in
righteousness by ridding himself of ungodly counselors (Prov. 25:5),
treating the poor with equity (Prov. 29:14) and rejecting all attempts
at bribery (Prov. 29:4).

**16:13. Righteous lips are the delight of kings, And he who speaks
right is loved.**
This proverb employs synonymous parallelism to reveal that what
the king values in himself ('righteousness,' v. 12), he also values in
those who serve him. The wise king understands that 'righteousness'
establishes his rule under God (v. 12). He expects this of himself, and
so he expects it of all those who help administrate his reign.

Any leader's stability is, in large measure, determined by the quality
of those he gathers around himself. Some advisors employ a 'flattering
mouth' (Prov. 26:28) in an attempt to tell the king what he wants to
hear. A ruler of understanding discerns their self-serving motives and
rightly rejects their counsel and banishes them from his cabinet. But,
when one whose lips respectfully speak the truth is found, he is 'the
delight of kings' (cf. Prov. 14:35). The subject is plural ('kings'), but the
verb in the second line is singular. 'He who loves purity of heart And
whose speech is gracious, the king is his friend' (Prov. 22:11).

We know that 'Lying lips are an abomination to the LORD, But
those who deal faithfully are His delight' (Prov. 12:22). Here, what is
true of the Lord, is also said to be true of the ruler who understands
His divine commission in this world.

16:14. The wrath of a king is as messengers of death, But a wise man will appease it.

Because of the critical role advisors play in a king's administration, and because of a ruler's intense desire for faithfulness in such advisors (v. 13), his 'wrath' may be quickly aroused toward a devious servant. The 'wrath of a king' is elsewhere likened to the roar of a lion (Prov. 19:12; 20:2). Here it is called 'messengers of death.' When an unfaithful advisor is found out, the expression upon the king's face may announce the verdict of guilt and the sentence of execution.

Illustrations of this may be found throughout the Old Testament. Pharaoh dealt wrathfully with his cupbearer and chief baker (Gen. 40). Saul responded to Ahimelech similarly, though unjustly (1 Sam. 22:16-19). Solomon similarly dealt with Adonijah (1 Kings 2:25), Joab (1 Kings 2:29-34) and Shimei (1 Kings 2:46). Wicked Haman discovered King Ahasuerus's wrath (Esther 7:7-10).

In view of this kind of royal authority and power, 'a wise man will appease' the king's wrath. The word 'appease' serves to further link the 'Lord' section of verses 1-9 to the 'king' section here in verses 10-15. The same root word was used in verse 6 to describe how one gets his sins 'atoned for.'[18] The Lord punishes those who raise themselves up against His rule (v. 5), yet there is the possibility of forgiveness. So it is with the king. He will deal swiftly with any threat to his administration (v. 14a), but one with understanding will know how to either avoid or turn back such royal anger. 'By forbearance a ruler may be persuaded, And a soft answer breaks the bone' (Prov. 25:15; cf. Prov. 15:1, 4; 29:8). 'If the ruler's temper rises against you, do not abandon your position, because composure allays great offenses' (Eccles. 10:4).

Daniel's wisdom in dealing with Nebuchadnezzar serves as an example of the wisdom spoken of in this second line (Dan. 2:5, 12-16).

16:15. In the light of a king's face is life, And his favor is like a cloud with the spring rain.

This proverb uses synonymous parallelism to make exactly the opposite point of that made in verse 14. If the king's wrath is 'as messengers of death' (v. 14), then his favor 'is life.' When the king smiles, one may be at peace. The expression 'the light of a king's face' is a powerful metaphor, most often used of the favor of God (Ps. 4:6; 44:3; 89:15). That it is ascribed to the king here is a further indication of the intricate literary entwinement of the themes of 'Lord' (vv. 1-9) and 'king' (vv. 10-15). The expression may be best known from the blessing of Aaron (Num. 6:25).

The second line likens the king's favor to 'a cloud with the spring rain.' The spring rain usually fell in March or April, and was essential to the complete ripening of the crop. Being thus so essential to life, the sight of clouds in the spring was taken as an indication of divine favor. Elsewhere, the favor of the king is compared to 'dew on the grass' (Prov. 19:12). Psalm 72, designated 'A Psalm of Solomon,' also likens the king to the 'showers that water the earth' (vv. 6, 15-17).

When one is in the favor of those who hold authority over him, life is good. When one has fallen into disfavor with those in authority, life is in danger. Strive to live under authority!

16:16. How much better it is to get wisdom than gold! And to get understanding is to be chosen above silver.

The previous interplay between the themes of 'LORD' (vv. 1-9) and 'king' (vv. 10-15) is now complete. This verse is, however, the perfect next breath. Considering the absolute authority of God and His delegated authority to the governing ruler, how precious it is to gain the wisdom and understanding necessary to live with both!

Solomon has already spoken of the comparative value of wisdom and gold, understanding and silver (Prov. 3:14; 8:10-11, 19). Having wealth is not sinful in itself. It is simply that there is at least one pursuit more worthy. If a choice must be made, let it be for wisdom over wealth! Solomon had more of both assets than any other man. Comparing them both, he chose wisdom. 'Because you have asked this thing and have not asked for yourself ... riches ... but have asked for yourself discernment to understand justice, behold, I have done according to your words. Behold, I have given you a wise and discerning heart, so that there has been no one like you before you, nor shall one like you arise after you. And I have also given you what you have not asked, both riches and honor, so that there will not be any among the kings like you all your days' (1 Kings 3:11-13).

How much more true for those of us who stand on this side of the Cross, knowing that in Christ 'are hidden all the treasures of wisdom and knowledge' (Col. 2:3)!

16:17. The highway of the upright is to depart from evil; He who watches his way preserves his life.

This proverb of synonymous parallelism is the middle verse of the entire book in the Hebrew text.[19] It is appropriate, therefore, to return to a ubiquitous theme – that of the way or path. Here it is described as a 'highway.' The word describes a raised roadway that has been carefully groomed, graded and maintained. Flood waters are not likely to overwhelm it. Obstacles have been removed. The upright make for themselves such a path through life as they 'depart from evil.' By 'evil' is probably meant moral wrong, rather than calamity and misfortune. They choose the path that is 'upright' and, thus, they bear its name. In such a course of conduct, many of the obstacles that lie in the path of sin are avoided (Prov. 15:19; 22:5).

The word translated 'depart' means basically 'to turn aside.'[20] Thus, it can mean either departing from something already encountered (NASB), or avoiding something, so as not to meet it in the first place (NIV).

The second line makes the same point. The verb 'watches over' has the idea of guarding that which is valuable.[21] The thing that is thus valued is 'his way' – that is to say, his course and conduct through life. The residual effect is that he 'preserves his life.' The way we live our lives is not a matter of 'alternative lifestyles,' but of life and death! The fear of the Lord steers one into the path of life (Prov. 3:7; 8:13; 16:6). 'And a highway will be there, a roadway, And it will be called the Highway of Holiness. The unclean will not travel on it, But it will be for him who walks that way, And fools will not wander on it.' (Isa. 35:8).

16:18. Pride goes before destruction, And a haughty spirit before stumbling.

This proverb makes its point through synonymous parallelism. Proverbs often warns of the dangers of arrogance (Prov. 6:17; 11:2; 13:10; 18:12; 29:23). Verse 5 has already named it as 'an abomination to the LORD.' Such a divine revulsion at all forms of pride comes because it is the exact opposite of the most fundamental element of wisdom: 'the fear of the LORD.'[22]

The warning of 'destruction' for pride should be taken seriously. The word is descriptive of the shattering of a bone.[23] Thus, one's dreams, indeed, one's very self, will be shattered. The warning of the second line is of 'stumbling.' It is descriptive of a tottering that leads to a fall.[24]

Thus, whether through sudden, shattering destruction or through a tottering stumble to a fall, God in His providence has so ordered the world that the proud will be defeated (Ps.18:27).

16:19. It is better to be of a humble spirit with the lowly, Than to divide the spoil with the proud.

This proverb uses the comparative 'better ... than' formula to make its point, a strategy used some twenty-one times in Proverbs (Prov. 3:14;

8:11, 19; 12:9; 15:6, 7; 16:8, 16, 19, 32; 17:1; 19:1, 22; 21:9, 19; 22:1; 25:7, 24; 27:5, 10; 28:6). The 'better' is a 'humble spirit' (rather than 'the spoil') and 'the lowly' (rather than the 'proud').

The person of 'humble spirit' is one who is economically disadvantaged. Without the second line, one would not see this, but the parallel is the one who divides 'the spoil.' The term is often used in military contexts. But, here, it describes one who has entered into wealth in one way or another.

The term 'lowly' refers to a humility of attitude in contrast to 'the proud,' who are arrogant and brash. The term ('the proud') is also found in Proverbs 15:25. This points to the fact that they have, no doubt, come upon 'the spoils' through unethical and immoral means (Prov. 1:13-14).

Better an empty belly than a swelled head! Better a right attitude than a well-dressed sense of superiority. Better to rightly evaluate one's self than to luxuriantly provide for one's self.

16:20. He who gives attention to the word shall find good, And blessed is he who trusts in the Lord.

This proverb uses synonymous parallelism to make its point. The exact translation of the first line is debated. The primary issue seems to be the translation of 'the word.' The word can describe a matter, a word or instruction more generally. The niv translates as 'Whoever gives heed to instruction prospers,' an obvious contrast to the nasb. The writer's point is best arrived at by comparing the parallel expression in the second line. The one who 'gives attention to the word' is paralleled with 'he who trusts in the Lord.' A translation of 'matter' or 'instruction' would not seem appropriate, while 'the word' (the Divine word of God) conforms to the parallelism. The same expression in Proverbs 13:13 clearly refers to a word from God.

So 'good' (prosperity, blessing, good fortune) comes to the one who responds in a particular way to the word of God. That response is described as one 'who gives attention.' The word is a common one in Proverbs. It describes not only distinguishing between two things, but also understanding the reason why the distinction must be made.[25] Thus, thoughtful reflection upon, and purposeful response to, God's word is the key to blessing.

Obedience to the divine word is then tantamount to trust in the Lord. Such faith-filled obedience is guaranteed the blessing of heaven (Prov. 19:8). It will not go unrewarded (Prov. 3:5-6; 28:25). Perhaps, then, the old hymn is not so trite after all: 'Trust and obey, for there's no other way, to be happy in Jesus, but to trust and obey'!

16:21. The wise in heart will be called discerning, And sweetness of speech increases persuasiveness.
Through synonymous parallelism, this problem gets at the issue of leadership and influence. The first line uses roughly synonymous terms ('wise' and 'discerning') to make its point. That one is 'wise in heart' is good. Soon, such a one will 'be called' for what he is – 'discerning.' The wisdom in his heart will not long be silent nor hidden. He will, if truly wise, soon gain a public reputation for his understanding. How will this take place? His wisdom will show itself in perhaps many ways, but, primarily, it will come to light through his speech.

The second line states that the wise in heart will use 'sweetness of speech.' Verses 23-24 will enlarge upon just what is meant by 'sweetness of speech.' The word for 'sweetness' does not refer to slick, sugary words of manipulation. Rather, it points to words that are measured in selection, tone and presentation. They are unselfish, understanding and timely (Eph. 4:29). The wise man knows how to communicate! The result is that he 'increases persuasiveness.' The word 'persuasiveness' occurs nine times in the Old Testament, four of which are in combination with our word for 'increases' (Prov. 1:5; 9:9; 16:21, 23). The root of the word speaks of taking or seizing something. Here, the apprehending is with one's mind. In Proverbs 7:21, it is used negatively of the persuasiveness of a prostitute. But, here it is the ability of the wise to convince.[26]

16:22. Understanding is a fountain of life to him who has it, But the discipline of fools is folly.
Antithetical parallelism here reveals the difference between the fool and the man of understanding. The word translated 'Understanding' describes a shrewd prudence or insight into matters at hand. It is descriptive of a negative trait ('cunning'), but is often used in Proverbs in a positive sense, as it is here. Such insight is 'a fountain of life' to the one who possesses it. The metaphor is common in Proverbs. From the heart 'flow the springs of life' (Prov. 4:23). When the fear of the Lord has captured that heart (Prov. 14:27), it becomes a 'fountain of life,' not only to the one who possesses it (Prov. 16:22), but to those who are willing to hear what it has to say (Prov. 10:11; 13:14; 18:4). Wisdom is not merely situation specific, but pays compounding dividends to one's self and to one's friends and family.

It is possible to understand the second line in a number of ways. Does it mean that a fool's folly is his own worst discipline? Or, does it mean hat they are only destroying their own lives? Or, does it mean that an attempt to teach a fool is folly? Or, that the only place a fool can learn anything is through the outworking of the folly of his actions?

The understanding of the verse seems to rest largely upon identifying the subject and defining what is meant by 'discipline.' The subject could be either 'folly' (NIV) or 'discipline' (NASB). Either is possible, but the word order seems to point to 'discipline' as being the appropriate choice. That leaves us to define what is meant by 'discipline.' The word can also mean instruction, correction, chastisement or punishment.[27] The general sense is that of instruction through correction. Here, the word does not point to self-discipline, but to the attempt to educate a fool through correction of some kind. While the understanding of the first line points to something that a person possesses within his own heart (though it often arrives there through submission to outward correction), this points to something that is brought to the fool from outside of himself. Such attempts are wasted upon a true fool. They come to nothing. He learns from no one. Don't waste your time or God's resources. To do so is to lower yourself to his level and participate in his 'folly.'

16:23. The heart of the wise teaches his mouth, And adds persuasiveness to his lips.

The parallelism of this proverb is synthetic, the second line expanding upon and extending the first. The first line demands that inner character ('The heart') will be known through outward expression ('his mouth'). The mouth speaks what is in the heart. 'For the mouth speaks out of that which fills the heart. The good man out of his good treasure brings forth what is good; and the evil man out of his evil treasure brings forth what is evil' (Matt. 12:34-35). The 'heart' is the seat of thinking, feeling and choosing. As such, it cannot but find expression in our communication.

The second line is a close parallel to verse 21 (which see). The heart, having been possessed by wisdom, then controls the tongue. The tongue then finds that its work is easier because of the wisdom that it spreads. The next verse helps understand exactly what kind of words are lauded here.

16:24. Pleasant words are a honeycomb, Sweet to the soul and healing to the bones.

The 'sweet talk' continues here from verses 21 and 23. The word translated 'Pleasant' is not the same as the one used in verse 21, but the meaning is not demonstrably different (cf. Prov. 15:26). It describes that which is beautiful, kind and full of favor.[28] The word 'honeycomb' harkens to imagery of a comb so loaded with honey that it drips from its cells.[29] Accordingly, 'Pleasant words' fall from a heart overflowing with wisdom (v. 23a; Prov. 24:13-14; Ps. 19:10).

The second line extends the first and takes it further. Such words are not only 'Pleasant,' but also 'Sweet' and 'healing.' See verse 21 for what is meant by 'Sweet' words. Such words are of benefit not only to the 'soul,' but also to the 'bones.' A careful differentiation between the physical and non-physical components of man is not the point. Rather, the author is pointing to the all-encompassing benefits of careful and wise speech. It is profitable to every part of a man. That wise words are good for a man's emotional and psychological well-being goes without saying, but Proverbs speaks often of the benefits of wisdom that are felt even in the physical body (Prov. 3:8; 4:22; 14:30; 17:22), especially as that wisdom controls one's tongue (Prov. 12:18; 15:30).

16:25. There is a way which seems right to a man, But its end is the way of death.

This proverb of antithetical parallelism is identical to Proverb 14:12. The contrast is between 'a way which seems right' and 'the way of death.' The second line, while set in contrast to the first, extends and explains the first line also.[30] See the comments on Proverbs 14:12 for an explanation and exposition.

Many have wondered at why there is an exact repetition of a previous proverb? Is it merely to underscore the importance of its truth? That, no doubt, it true, but why is it repeated here? This chapter began with a strong emphasis on the sovereign control of the Lord over all things (vv. 1-9). This verse about man's attempted autonomy provides a perfect warning in such a chapter.

16:26. A worker's appetite works for him, For his hunger urges him on.

This proverb of synthetic parallelism states a simple fact about human motivation. The first line observes, by way of a word play, that while a 'worker' labors for another man, his 'appetite' works for him.[31] The word 'appetite' is literally 'soul.' As in Proverbs 10:3 and 23:2, the Hebrew word for 'soul' is descriptive of the immaterial and intangible cravings and needs of the physical body.

How is it that one's 'appetite works for him'? The second line explains – 'his hunger urges him on.' The word 'hunger' is, literally, 'mouth.' The 'mouth' here represents not the organ of speech, as it so often does in Proverbs, but the appetite that is satisfied through the mouth. The verb has the idea of pressing hard.[32] If for no other reason, when work becomes toilsome and boring, the need of food for one's self and one's family will keep a man's hand to the task.

Indeed, the word translated 'worker's' is descriptive of laborious work that is often misery to the one engaged in it.[33] There are higher motivations for our work, such as philanthropy (Eph. 4:28), worship (Eph. 6:7) and social responsibility (2 Thess. 3:10-12). That is to say that there are other 'hungers' inherent to the human heart. They, too, will drive a man forward in hard work. Yet, if for no other reason, satisfaction of one's own physical appetite is a worthy prod to keep us on task. Left to itself, however, such a motivation soon produces discontent: 'All a man's labor is for his mouth and yet the appetite is not satisfied' (Eccles. 6:7).

16:27. A worthless man digs up evil, While his words are as a scorching fire.

This begins a series of four proverbs describing evil people who destroy relationships. These verses have an affinity with Proverbs 6:12-19, both thematically and in terms of the vocabulary used. 'A worthless man' is paralleled in Proverbs 6:12. The word translated 'perverse' (vv. 28, 30) is also found in Proverbs 6:14. Here, Solomon denounces the man who 'digs up evil' and, in Proverbs 6:18, he similarly denounces the one who 'devises wicked plans.' The verb 'compresses' (v. 30) is also found in Proverbs 6:13, where it describes the winking of the eye, similar to the expression found here in verse 30a.[34]

The subject here is 'A worthless man,' literally 'a man of belial.' The word became descriptive of the deepest levels of depravity (Deut. 13:13; 1 Sam. 10:27; 30:22; 1 Kings 21:10, 13). Between the testaments, the word began to be used as a proper name of Satan (2 Cor. 6:15).[35] The particular wickedness here is that he 'digs up evil.' Some take this to mean he digs a trap for his enemies, others that he digs up 'dirt' in order to ruin those he dislikes. The psalmists often speak in the former sense (Ps. 7:16; 57:6; 94:13; 119:85), and Proverbs will also (Prov. 26:27). Here, however, it seems that he is digging up news about a person, in order that it might be used with evil intent against him.

Indeed, his 'words are as a scorching fire.' When he is through with his victim, his life is like burned-over earth – nothing is left. It is barren, fruitless, worthless. Even if the 'research' into the person's affairs begins as 'a quest for the truth,' it all too often ends up as personal vendetta. The infernal nature of such gossip and slander is affirmed in the New Testament: 'And the tongue is a fire, the very world of iniquity; the tongue is set among our members as that which defiles the entire body, and sets on fire the course of our life, and is set on fire by hell' (James 3:6).

16:28. A perverse man spreads strife, And a slanderer separates intimate friends.
The description of the troublemaker continues. He is called first 'A perverse man.' The word 'perverse' describes turning away from what is normal and right. Its root appears nine times in this book (Prov. 2:12, 14; 6:14; 8:13; 10:31, 32; 16:28, 30; 23:33), and only one other time in the Old Testament (Deut. 32:20). Often, this turning way is expressed through the mouth (Prov. 2:12; 10:31, 32).[36] The idea is, literally, that of one who turns things upside down by his words.[37] Through this verbal departure, he 'spreads strife.' Intentionally creating dissension is a common theme in Proverbs (6:14; 15:18; 16:28; 17:14; 18:18-19; 19:13; 21:9, 19; 22:10; 23:29; 25:24; 26:21; 27:15; 28:25; 29:22). The 'strife' being described is of a domestic sort which explodes with no one left to arbitrate the dispute.[38] The root of the verb 'spreads' is used in Judges 15:4, 5 to describe the release of foxes with flaming torches tied to them into the fields of the Philistines.[39] Given the connection with the imagery of 'scorching fire' in verse 27, this may provide a telling metaphor of the danger of wrong speech.

The second line affirms and makes more specific the assertion of the first line. The individual is now called 'a slanderer' (Prov. 18:8; 26:20, 22). The word describes one who whispers or murmurs. Here, it is behind someone's back, spoken in soft tones. 'Did you hear about?' Such gossip soon 'separates intimate friends' (cf. Prov. 17:9). By 'intimate friends' is meant one who is known well (Ps. 55:13). In Proverbs 2:17, it describes one's own marriage partner, the person to whom you are closer than any other.[40] Gossip soon drives a wedge where no wedge should ever be allowed to enter.

16:29. A man of violence entices his neighbor, And leads him in a way that is not good.
The corrupt man is here again described. Note that each of verses 27-29 begin with some form of 'A man of ... .' Here, the notable quality is 'violence.' The word is used in the Old Testament of sinful violence, often extreme wickedness. It can have broader societal implications like in Genesis 6:11, 13, where it is named as the cause of the flood.[41]

Here, the particular 'violence' is that he 'entices' those he comes in contact with. The word was introduced in Proverbs 1:10, and the nine verses which follow there develop this personality. In its root, it describes that which is open, spacious and wide. A derivative is the oft-used word in Proverbs for the 'naïve' or 'simple.'[42] They are gullible, open to any influence. The 'man of violence' preys upon such gullibility and seduces the naïve into sin (Prov. 12:26).

Now, by synthetic parallelism, the second line extends and makes more complete the first. The expression 'a way that is not good' is simply a backward expression for 'a wicked way.' Note that we have returned to a discussion of the 'way,' a frequent theme of Proverbs 1-9. Read Proverbs 4:14-17 for an excellent commentary on this path.

16:30. He who winks his eyes does so to devise perverse things; He who compresses his lips brings evil to pass.

This proverb seems to indicate that both verbal and non-verbal communication, ultimately, are still both communication. Much can be learned by not only listening, but by observing. Here the winking of the eyes and the pursing of the lips are said to indicate evil intent. Whether or not these are universal signals that communicate the same message in every culture and in any generation is not the point. Solomon often speaks of the danger of speech (e.g. vv. 27-29). Here, he points to non-verbal communication as being just as dangerous. Consult Proverbs 6:13-14 for a fuller treatment of non-verbal communication (cf. Prov. 10:10; Ps. 35:19).

The plea 'I didn't say a word!' does not hold up, for non-verbal cues can accomplish 'perverse things' the same as speech (same word in v. 28). Our actions are able to bring 'evil to pass' as surely as our words (same word in v. 27). It is not just what one says with his 'lips' (same word in v. 27), but all he communicates with them (v. 30b) for which he will be held accountable.

Some commentators feel that the perfect tense verb in the second line ('brings ...to pass') points to action that is already completed or at least as good as done.[43] If this is correct, it may point not only to the inability to hide one's plans toward evil, but also the impossibility of perfectly covering one's trail.

16:31. A gray head is a crown of glory; It is found in the way of righteousness.

This proverb of synthetic parallelism strikes a chord familiar in Proverbs; namely, that the righteous are rewarded with long life

(Prov. 3:1-2, 16; 9:6; 10:27; 12:28; 16:17). In such cases, one's 'crown of glory' is his gray hair. How our culture needs to learn this lesson! The elderly are not a bane, but a boon. Today, we worship young, firm bodies instead of honoring gray heads of wisdom found in 'the way of righteousness.' 'The glory of young men is their strength, And the honor of old men is their gray hair' (Prov. 20:29).

The Hebrew Law called for respect for the elderly. 'You shall rise up before the grayheaded, and honor the aged, and you shall revere your God; I am the LORD' (Lev. 19:32). Of course, Solomon was not guaranteeing that gray hair indicated either wisdom or righteousness, nor that youthfulness required naïveté. He well knew that the exact opposite could be true: 'A poor, yet wise lad is better than an old and foolish king who no longer knows how to receive instruction' (Eccles. 4:13).

16:32. He who is slow to anger is better than the mighty, And he who rules his spirit, than he who captures a city.
Another 'better than' proverb (e.g. Prov. 3:14; 8:11, 19; 12:9; 15:16, 17) uses synonymous parallelism to make its point – mature patience over military prowess; self-control over self-expression.

The first line exalts one 'who is slow to anger.' The expression is most often used of God (e.g. Exod. 34:6; Num. 14:18; Ps. 86:15).[44] But, here, it is a quality He will share with those willing to receive, and exercise, it (Prov. 14:29; 15:18; Eccles. 7:8). The expression is, literally, 'long of nostril.' The nose turns red when angry. Such a person, thus, takes a long time before allowing his nose to become inflamed with anger.[45] Such a one is superior to 'the mighty.' The word refers to recognized military heroes or champions of the armed forces.[46] The society at large is better served by one patient man who, consistently, is slow to provocation than it is by a great military hero who, in the flash of a moment, achieves some great victory.

The same point is made in the second line. By 'rules his spirit' is meant that he is in control of his emotional state (Prov. 14:17, 29; 15:1, 18; 17:27; 19:11; 29:11). Such a one is to be preferred to the valiant man who can take on a whole city and win (Eccles. 9:18a). Indeed, the man who cannot so control himself is already defeated: 'Like a city that is broken into and without walls Is a man who has no control over his spirit' (Prov. 25:28).

'But let everyone be quick to hear, slow to speak and slow to anger; for the anger of man does not achieve the righteousness of God' (James 1:19-20).

16:33. The lot is cast into the lap, But its every decision is from the LORD.

The chapter ends where it began, with the theme of God's sovereignty (vv. 1-4, 9). This time His control is said to extend even over the 'lot' (Prov. 18:18). In both Testaments, the Bible speaks of the use of the 'lot' by both believers and unbelievers (Lev. 16:7-10, 21, 22; Josh. 14:2; 1 Sam. 14:41; 1 Chron. 25:7, 8; 26:13ff; Neh. 10:34ff; Jonah 1:7; Matt. 27:35; Acts 1:26). Some believe that the high priest's use of the Urim and Thummim (Exod. 28:30; Deut. 33:8) was a form of casting lots. Here, the reference, as often in the rest of Scripture, is to the more general population.[47]

The exact form and mechanics of using the lot is not entirely clear. Here, it was 'cast into the lap.' That is to say, into the fold of the garment created as one sat down.[48] Presumably, it provided some kind of 'Yes' or 'No' answer to the dispute in question and was, thus, akin to our practice of drawing straws or flipping a coin.

It is worth noting that the Bible does not command us to use the lot in making decisions. In fact, it is significant that the final use of the lot (Acts 1:26) came just prior to Pentecost and the coming of the Holy Spirit. While not prohibiting its use, this does remind us that we are privileged, above all other generations, to possess both the completed written revelation of God and the indwelling Spirit of God who authored it.

Nevertheless, there may be rare occasions when the use of some form of lot is not unwarranted. When might that be? 'There is a lazy, superstitious use of the lot and other such means that is not recommended here. The use of the lot ... ought never to supersede biblical commandments and the application of scriptural principles .... When, having followed biblical injunctions to their limit you are left with several options, all of which are acceptable to God, the lot may be used to decide among them .... But where there is biblical direction, the lot should never replace obedience to it.'[49]

What is robustly affirmed here is that, in such legitimate situations, God is in absolute control, even over what may appear to be mere chance events. God's providence extends even to the tumble of the dice. We should look to this God for our direction (Prov. 29:26).

End Notes

1. Whybray, R. N., *Proverbs* (Grand Rapids, Michigan: William B. Eerdmans Publishing Company, 1994), 238.

2. Ibid., 238-239.

3. Allen, Ronald B., *"ārak,'* *Theological Wordbook of the Old Testament* (Chicago: Moody Press, 1980), 2:695-696.

4. Waltke, Bruce K., 'The Dance Between God and Humanity,' in *Doing Theology for the People of God: Studies in Honor of J. I. Packer,* ed. Donald Lewis and Alister McGrath, (Downers Grove, Illinois: InterVarsity Press, 1996), 96.

5. Ross, Allen P., 'Proverbs,' *The Expositor's Bible Commentary* (Grand Rapids, Michigan: Zondervan Publishing House, 1991), 5:1002.

6. Waltke, 99.

7. Whybray, 241.

8. Cohen, A., *Proverbs* (London: The Soncino Press, 1946), 69-70.

9. Olivier, J. P. J., 'נקה,' *New International Dictionary of Old Testament Theology and Exegesis* (Grand Rapids, Michigan: Zondervan Publishing House, 1997), 3:152.

10. Buzzell, Sid S., 'Proverbs,' *The Bible Knowledge Commentary* (Wheaton: Victor Books, 1988), 1:940.

11. Kidner, Derek, *Proverbs* (Downers Grove, Illinois: InterVarsity Press, 1964), 119. and Murphy, Roland E., *Proverbs* (Nashville: Thomas Nelson Publishers, 1998), 121.

12. Cohen, 104; and Ross, 5:1004.

13. Whybray, 242.

14. Wood, Leon J., *'hāshab,'* *Theological Wordbook of the Old Testament* (Chicago: Moody Press, 1980), 1:329-330.

15. Martens, Elmer A., 'בון,' *New International Dictionary of Old Testament Theology and Exegesis* (Grand Rapids, Michigan: Zondervan Publishing House, 1997), 2:615-617.

16. Waltke, 100.

17. Kidner, 119.

18. Whybray, 245.

19. Murphy, 122.

20. Patterson, R. D., *'sûr,'* *Theological Wordbook of the Old Testament* (Chicago: Moody Press, 1980), 2:620-621.

21. Schoville, Keith N., 'שמר,' *New International Dictionary of Old Testament Theology and Exegesis* (Grand Rapids, Michigan: Zondervan Publishing House, 1997), 4:182-184.

22. Kidner, 120.

23. Delitzsch, F., *Proverbs, Ecclesiastes, Song of Solomon* (three volumes in one) in C. F. Keil and F. Delitzsch, vol. 6, *Commentary on the Old Testament* (in ten volumes), (1872; rpt. Grand Rapids, Michigan: William B. Eerdmans Publishing Company, 1980), 1:345.

24. Ibid., 346.

25. Goldberg, Louis, *'śākal,'* *Theological Wordbook of the Old Testament* (Chicago: Moody Press, 1980), 2:877.

26. Kaiser, Walter C., *'lāqaḥ,'* *Theological Wordbook of the Old Testament* (Chicago: Moody Press, 1980), 1:481-482.

27. Merrill, E. H., 'יסר,' *New International Dictionary of Old Testament Theology and Exegesis* (Grand Rapids, Michigan: Zondervan Publishing House, 1997), 2:480-481.

28. Wilson, Marvin R., *'nā'ēm,'* *Theological Wordbook of the Old Testament* (Chicago: Moody Press, 1980), 2:585.

29. Delitzsch, 1:348.

30. Ross, 5:1010.

31. Buzzell, 1:941.

32. Carroll R., M. Daniel, 'אכף,' *New International Dictionary of Old Testament Theology and Exegesis* (Grand Rapids, Michigan: Zondervan Publishing House, 1997), 1:397.

33. Allen, Ronald B., *"āmal,'* *Theological Wordbook of the Old Testament* (Chicago: Moody Press, 1980), 2:675.

34. Whybray, 249-250.

35. Kaiser, Walter C., '*bālâ*,' *Theological Wordbook of the Old Testament* (Chicago: Moody Press, 1980), 1:110-111.

36. Hamilton, Victor P., '*hāpak*,' *Theological Wordbook of the Old Testament* (Chicago: Moody Press, 1980), 1:221-222.

37. Cohen, 109.

38. Schultz, Richard, 'רין,' *New International Dictionary of Old Testament Theology and Exegesis* (Grand Rapids, Michigan: Zondervan Publishing House, 1997), 1:938-942.

39. MacArthur, John, *The MacArthur Study Bible* (Nashville: Word Bibles, 1997), 900.

40. Merrill, E. H., 'אלף,' *New International Dictionary of Old Testament Theology and Exegesis* (Grand Rapids, Michigan: Zondervan Publishing House, 1997), 1:415-416.

41. Harris, R. Laird, '*hāmas*,' *Theological Wordbook of the Old Testament* (Chicago: Moody Press, 1980), 1:297.

42. Goldberg, Louis, '*pātâ*,' *Theological Wordbook of the Old Testament* (Chicago: Moody Press, 1980), 2:742-743.

43. Delitzsch, 1:350; and Whybray, 251.

44. Hamilton, Victor P., ''*ārak*,' *Theological Wordbook of the Old Testament* (Chicago: Moody Press, 1980), 1:71-72.

45. Ibid.

46. Oswalt, John N., '*gābar*,' *Theological Wordbook of the Old Testament* (Chicago: Moody Press, 1980), 1:148-149.

47. Hamilton, F. E., 'Lots,' *The Zondervan Pictorial Encyclopedia of the Bible* (Grand Rapids, Michigan: Zondervan Publishing House, 1975, 1976), 3:988.

48. Murphy, 124.

49. Adams, Jay E., *Proverbs* (Woodruff, South Carolina: Timeless Texts, 1997), 134.

Proverbs 17

17:1. Better is a dry morsel and quietness with it Than a house full of feasting with strife.
This 'Better ... Than' proverb makes a point similar to those in Proverbs 15:16, 17 and 16:8. Poverty, with its meager rewards, is better than prosperity with its sumptuous banquets. The primary contrast is between 'quietness' and 'strife,' though the 'dry morsel' and 'feasting' help to make the point.

The 'dry morsel' would be a leftover corner of bread, dried from the heat and arid conditions, and unaccompanied by anything in which it might be dipped.[1] The expression 'feasting with strife' is, more literally, 'sacrifices of strife.' The 'sacrifices' probably refers to the so-called peace offering of Hebrew Temple worship (Lev. 7:11-17). Only a portion of the peace offering was actually consumed on the altar. The rest was to be eaten that day and made a reason for a grand celebration with family and friends (cf. 1 Sam. 9:12-13; 20:6; Prov. 7:14). If so, it makes for a mocking parody of the reason for celebration and the actual state of affairs within the home. Better the peaceful and honest integrity of a meager meal than the clamorous hypocrisy of religious sham.

One possible reason for the infighting mentioned here is the squabbling over the family estate mentioned in the next verse.

17:2. A servant who acts wisely will rule over a son who acts shamefully, And will share in the inheritance among brothers.
The two lines of this proverb produce one continuous thought, though there is parallelism found in 'will rule' and 'share in the inheritance.'[2] The point is that production is more worthy than privilege. A lazy son (Prov. 10:5; 12:24) will lose out, while a diligent servant may come to have a share in the harvest. Faithfulness is thicker than blood. The 'son who acts shamefully' may do so by disrespect and violence (Prov. 19:26), indulgent living (Prov. 28:7) or willfulness (Prov. 29:15).

The words 'acts wisely' are a translation of a word describing one who is observant and careful in difficult conditions. Such a person has discernment into how to solve the problem at hand and the ability to apply the solution and produce results. Such skill will be rewarded wherever it is found, inside or outside of family lines.[3]

The Bible is replete with examples. Eliezer, though a slave, would have become Abraham's heir had no son been born (Gen. 15:3). Ziba became heir of Mephibosheth (2 Sam. 16:1-4; 19:24-30). Jarha, though a servant, was allowed to marry into the family (1 Chron. 2:35). Even in Solomon's own experience, Jeroboam came to possess much of what could have been Rehoboam's (1 Kings 11-12). God says that what is true physically may also be true spiritually (Matt. 8:11-12).

Such a result was out of the norm, but not unheard of (Eccles. 10:7). Thus, this proverb was meant to shock a slothful son into action and faithfulness (Prov. 11:29; 12:24; 30:22).

17:3. The refining pot is for silver and the furnace for gold, But the Lord tests hearts.

This antithetical proverb compares the assaying of precious metals with God's work in the heart of a man. The heart, while notoriously deceitful (Jer. 17:9; Prov. 16:2), is laid bare before the Lord (Jer. 17:10; Prov. 15:11).

The first line employs the oft-used metaphor of the testing and purifying of silver and gold (Ps. 66:10; Isa. 1:25; 48:10; Jer. 6:29; Ezek. 22:17-22; Mal. 3:3). This first line is repeated verbatim in Proverbs 27:21, though the second line varies significantly. Precious, but impure, metals were fired until they became liquid. The impurities rose to the top as dross and were skimmed away. Thus, the process was both for testing (line two) and improving (line one) the quality of the metal.

God as a tester of the hearts of men is a common theme in Scripture (1 Chron. 29:17; Ps. 7:9; 17:3; 26:2; 139:23; Jer. 17:10). In a slightly different metaphor, but emphasizing the same truth, God is said to 'weigh' the heart (Prov. 21:2; 24:12) and its motives (Prov. 16:2).

For the believer, the fire which both tests and refines is generally understood to be the trials of life God sovereignly allows (James 1:2-4; 1 Pet. 1:7). But, the pleasantries of life, such as congratulations and praise, can also reveal the contents and quality of the heart (Prov. 27:21).

17:4. An evildoer listens to wicked lips, A liar pays attention to a destructive tongue.

Through synonymous parallelism, the proverb makes its point that what we listen to says something about us. My inner character is revealed not just by what I say (Luke 6:45), but by what I willingly listen to others say. Proverbs warns about listening to wrong influences (Prov. 1:10-16). This proverb, however, takes the matter a step farther – it's not simply that what I listen to may corrupt me, but that it reveals the corruption already in my heart. Tabloid readers beware! Readers of the gossip column beware! Scandalmongers beware!

17:5. He who mocks the poor reproaches his Maker; He who rejoices at calamity will not go unpunished.
How one responds to others is an indication of His true response to the Lord Himself. The ridicule, even inwardly, of one less fortunate than oneself is a theological statement. It is tantamount to a reproach upon God. For God made both the poor and the rich (Prov. 22:2) and He made them to reside in the condition in which you found them (1 Sam. 2:7). The Lord gives light to the eyes of both the poor and his oppressor (Prov. 29:13). Thus, how one treats the poor is how one treats the Lord (Prov. 19:17). Jesus made the same point: 'Truly I say to you, to the extent that you did it to one of these brothers of Mine, even the least of them, you did it to Me.... Truly I say to you, to the extent that you did not do it to one of the least of these, you did not do it to Me' (Matt. 24:40, 45). The attitude is as despicable as the act (Prov. 14:21, 31).

The second line appears to provide an imperfect parallel. But, what this second line adds is the indication that the poverty of line one is a result of 'calamity.' Scripture leaves no doubt about its condemnation of those who rejoice over the hardship of another (Job 31:29; Prov. 24:17). God Himself vows to bring punishment upon such folk. Historical examples include Amon (Ezek. 25:3-7) and Edom (Ezek. 35:12-15; Obad. 12) in their response to the hardship of God's people.

17:6. Grandchildren are the crown of old men, And the glory of sons is their fathers.
This proverb pictures the ideal relationship between three succeeding generations. The elderly man (Prov. 16:31) finds a 'crown' of reward and honor in being surrounded by grandchildren (Gen. 48:11; Ps. 128:5-6). His life has mattered, it continues on, in a sense, through the succeeding generations. He has not only raised up godly sons and daughters, but he has raised them to raise up the same kind of children. There is hope for the future!

While line one witnesses the pride running from the elderly to the youth, the second line pictures it flowing the opposite direction. Children find great honor in having an honorable father. True, the commandment requires children to honor their father and mother

(Exod. 20:12), but it is also incumbent upon the father to give his children reason to do so. What greater earthly incentive could there be to live honorably as a man, than to have your children be proud of you and long to model your character?

Proverbs is not shy about unveiling the opposite kind of family relationships (Prov. 17:21, 25). The kind of relationships pictured in this proverb are expected (Mal. 1:6), but they will not be reality without God's supernatural intervention and enabling (Mal. 4:6). Lord, make me a man who is worthy of the admiration and honor of my children!

17:7. Excellent speech is not fitting for a fool; Much less are lying lips to a prince.

This proverb introduces some new elements of form not encountered before. The comparison is between opposites and what is acceptable in each. The same 'not fitting ... Much less' form is found in Proverbs 19:10 (cf. 26:1).

The contrast is between 'a fool' and 'a prince' and what is acceptable for each. The word for 'fool' here is *nābāl*, a different word than any we have encountered to this point in Proverbs. Indeed, it is found elsewhere in Proverbs only in verse 21 and 30:22 (cf. 30:32). It describes one who is completely godless and beyond the reach of wisdom. He is confirmed in his folly and resolute in his outlook. He even denies that there is a God to whom he must answer (Ps. 14:1). The character Nabal is the model for such a person (1 Sam. 25:25).

On the other hand, the 'prince' is one of noble character. It does not so much describe a political ruler as it does one of excellent character, one who is generous, giving and magnanimous.[4] The two words are found together again in Isaiah 32:5-8, which provides further insight into their differences.

There are particulars about each that are contrasted here. It is unfitting to find 'Excellent speech' in the mouth of a fool. The root meaning of the word translated 'Excellent' is that of excess. This has been interpreted to mean excellent, arrogant or heightened.[5] Here, the idea could be either that of eloquence (in form or character) or arrogance. Taking it as 'arrogant talk' would not provide a contrast, for that is exactly what one would expect from a fool (Prov. 24:7). For this reason, it seems best to see it as speech that is 'excellent' in its moral makeup and in its conformity to wisdom. Such would never come from the mouth of a *nābāl*.

The contrast of the second line is that of deception ('lying lips'). What is completely out of character for 'a prince' (translated 'noble' in v. 26) of such great magnanimity would be the holding back of information for the sake of personal gain. Lying simply would not be anticipated from such a man of character (Prov. 12:22). A noble must not act like a *nābāl*!

17:8. A bribe is a charm in the sight of its owner; Wherever he turns, he prospers.
This proverb appears at first glance to approve of bribery. However, it is a simple observation of fact; as things are in this world, bribes often work. It is not a commendation, even if it does fall short of a condemnation. The word 'bribe' can mean 'gift,' but it has been shown that the word never describes a gift without some expected return.[6] Such a 'gift' is tantamount to a magic 'charm' to the one who gives it. The word 'charm' is actually 'a stone of grace.'

As we say, the bribe 'works like a charm.'[7] More often than not, in this world, it gains one what he is after (Prov. 18:16; 21:14; Eccles. 10:19). The pragmatics of the matter are stated in the second line: 'Wherever he turns, he prospers.' That this is a simple observation of fact and not an endorsement is witnessed by the fact that, elsewhere in Scripture, bribes are universally condemned; in the Law (Exod. 23:8; Deut. 16:19; 27:25), the Historical Books (1 Sam. 12:3), Wisdom Literature (Ps. 15:5; Eccles. 7:7) and the Prophets (Isa. 1:23; Amos 5:12). Elsewhere, the Proverbs also condemn their use (Prov. 15:27; 28:16), even here in this chapter (v. 23).

17:9. He who covers a transgression seeks love, But he who repeats a matter separates intimate friends.
By means of a contrast, this proverb lays down a fundamental principle of godly relationships: forgiveness. The first line pictures either a person who has been wronged by another or who, at least, has discovered the wrong of another person. The answer, in either case, is to seek to dispose of the matter quietly. Some sins need to be confronted (Matt. 18:15-17), and, if necessary, brought before the church. A good many sins that strain relationships can simply be absorbed in the grace of the person offended (Prov. 10:12; 1 Pet. 4:8). It does not mean that an unrepentant person is left to compound the consequences of his sin in his life and the lives of those around him (James 5:20). This proverb presupposes remorse and repentance on the offender's part. The word translated 'covers' means not only to cover, but to conceal (Prov. 10:18) or overwhelm (Prov. 10:6, 11, NIV). Ultimately, the word gets at the idea of forgiveness (see Ps. 32:1; 85:2 where it is paralleled by 'forgiveness.')[8] Because of the love

and forgiveness we have found in Christ, we are able to absorb the consequences of another's sin for the glory of God and the good of all.

The second line presents the opposite. The picture is either of a wounded person who refuses to let go of his pain, even though the person has sought forgiveness, or of a person who gossips around about the sin they've discovered in another. In either case, the result is the same: the dividing of friendships. The words 'intimate friends' are a translation of a Hebrew word already introduced in Proverbs 2:17 and 16:28. It describes friendship of the most intimate kind.[9] Indeed, in Proverbs 2:17, it is descriptive of the relationship of husband and wife. No relationship, no matter how close and strong, can bear up under the strain of a petty person's refusal to absorb the consequences of someone else's sin. But, such a one is more than merely petty; he is a 'perverse man' and a 'slanderer' (Prov. 16:28).

17:10. A rebuke goes deeper into one who has understanding Than a hundred blows into a fool.

This proverb concerns one's receptivity to correction. A stern word does more for a wise person than extreme physical punishment for an unteachable one. The 'rebuke goes deeper' into the person. The verb means 'to descend.' In the verbal form found here, it means to penetrate or sink into (Ps. 38:2).[10] It points to the fact that a simple verbal correction is able to penetrate past a wise man's pride and get down into his heart and effect change. 'Do not reprove a scoffer, lest he hate you, Reprove a wise man, and he will love you. Give instruction to a wise man, and he will be wiser still, Teach a righteous man, and he will increase his learning' (Prov. 9:8-9).

How different is the 'fool'! Not only will verbal reprove deflect off of him, but you won't even be able to 'beat it into his head'! The Law allowed no more than forty blows to be inflicted upon a man, thus the 'hundred blows' are no doubt an exaggeration.[11] But 'blows' were not out of the question for a fool (Prov. 10:13; 19:25, 29; 26:3).

17:11. A rebellious man seeks only evil, So a cruel messenger will be sent against him.

Translation of the first line of the proverb has been a matter of debate. Commentators are divided over whether 'rebellious' should be the subject and 'evil' the object, or vice versa. While not unimportant, it ultimately makes little difference for the understanding of the proverb. Rebellion is evil, and the essence of evil is rebellion against proper authority.

What is important is the consequence spelled out in the second line. A 'cruel messenger' will be appointed to hunt down the rebel. Debate rages over whether this should be understood politically (2 Sam. 20:1-22; 1 Kings 2:25, 29, 34, 46) or spiritually. Again, the matter is more fundamental than that. God is ultimate authority. He delegates measured portions of His authority within the state, church and home for the administration of the world He has created. Wherever authority is resisted, whether directly against God or indirectly by resistance to a delegated authority, there will be consequences. God delegates His authority to promote His glory and maintain peace. Where such authority is defied, the delegated authority is responsible to deal with it. Ultimately, God Himself will deal with rebellion (Ps. 35:5-8; 78:49). The 'cruel messenger' has, no doubt, been left intentionally vague so as to heighten the sense of foreboding.

17:12. Let a man meet a bear robbed of her cubs, Rather than a fool in his folly.

The ferocity of the bear seems to have been legendary (2 Kings 2:23-24; Prov. 28:15; Lam. 3:10; Amos 5:19), especially a mother bear bereft of her cubs (2 Sam. 17:8; Hosea 13:8). But, one might rather meet up with her than with 'a fool in his folly.' The word translated 'fool' describes a thick-headed and obstinate individual. His problem, however, is not mental slowness, but a resolutely immoral and unspiritual outlook on life.[12] His 'folly' is simply the outward proof of his inward state (Prov. 13:16). His 'folly' may be evidenced in deceitfulness (Prov. 14:8), but, more often, the word is associated with uncontrolled anger (Prov. 14:17, 29). He is his own undoing (Prov. 19:3).[13]

Encountering such a man in his time of anger is dangerous! 'A stone is heavy and the sand weighty, But the provocation of a fool is heavier than both of them' (Prov. 27:3). 'When a wise man has a controversy with a foolish man, The foolish man either rages or laughs, and there is no rest' (Prov. 29:9).

Better is the man who watchfully observes the fool and steers a wide berth around him. There may be a more advantageous time to approach him, or, perhaps, total avoidance will be the wisest choice. Carefully determine whether it is your responsibility to bring discipline to bear upon him before you engage him (Prov. 22:15).

17:13. He who returns evil for good, Evil will not depart from his house.

This proverb makes its point by means of a double use of the word 'evil.' In the first line, the word describes intentional harm, in the second it describes calamity. The source of the calamity is not stated.

It may be directly from the hand of God or, more indirectly, arise from
the natural outcome of one's evil actions. Either way, the one man's
choice redounds to his entire family ('house'). The consequences of
our sin are seldom, if ever, ours alone to bear.

The particular sin in view is that of returning 'evil for good.'
Animals return evil for evil; it is the way of survival. God, however,
condemns it (Prov. 20:22; 24:29; Rom. 12:17-20; 1 Thess. 5:15). To return
'evil for good' is sub-human (cf. Ps. 35:12; 38:20; 109:5; Jer. 18:20).
That is, however, how Saul responded to David (1 Sam. 19:4), how
David responded to Uriah (2 Sam. 11–12), and how Nabal responded
to David (1 Sam. 25:21). God, therefore, promised David 'the sword
shall never depart from your house' (2 Sam. 12:10). Both returning evil
for evil and evil for good misses God's ideal. God's way is to return
good for evil (Prov. 25:21; Matt. 5:43-48; Rom. 12:21; 1 Pet. 3:9).

**17:14. The beginning of strife is like letting out water, So abandon
the quarrel before it breaks out.**
A destructive flood begins with but a tiny leak in the dam. Wise
is the man who sees that leak, not for the trickle of water it is at
the time, but for the raging torrent it will soon become and then
flees from it. So it is with bickering and quarreling. What begins as a
barbed comment soon becomes a biting accusation. That accusation,
fueled by pride, quickly breaks out into arguments. The arguments
give rise to bitter anger. The anger divides relationships, breaks up
friendships, splits churches and produces icy homes.

Oh, how much trouble could be avoided if only someone would
walk away from that barbed comment! 'So abandon the quarrel
before it breaks out.' 'Keeping away from strife is an honor for a
man, But any fool will quarrel' (Prov. 20:3). Scripture everywhere
exhorts us to avoid quarrels at all cost (Prov. 14:29; 15:1; 16:32; 19:11;
25:8; Matt. 5:25-26). The Apostle Paul exhorted us 'If possible, so far
as it depends on you, be at peace with all men' (Rom. 12:18). It is
not always possible, but we must exhaust the possibilities before
any contention is entered into! 'But refuse foolish and ignorant
speculations, knowing that they produce quarrels. And the Lord's
bond-servant must not be quarrelsome, but be kind to all, able to
teach, patient when wronged' (2 Tim. 2:23-24).

**17:15. He who justifies the wicked, and he who condemns the
righteous, Both of them alike are an abomination to the Lord.**
Fundamentally, this proverb addresses the need for true justice in
our civil courts. It does not, however, rule out application to the
judgments we each are required to make in the course of life.

God had laid out specifically in the constitution of the nation that justice must prevail (Exod. 23:7; Deut. 16:18-20; 25:1) and this continued to be stressed by the Prophets (Isa. 5:23) and in other Old Testament Writings (Ps. 94:21). God is equally displeased with the one 'who justifies the wicked' (cf. Prov. 18:5; 24:23-24) and the one 'who condemns the righteous' (cf. James 5:6). One may err on either side and both are equally odious to the Lord. 'Woe to those who call evil good, and good evil; Who substitute darkness for light and light for darkness; Who substitute bitter for sweet, and sweet for bitter!' (Isa. 5:20).

The reason injustice is so repulsive to the Lord is that it is a violation of His just character. For this reason, both errors 'are an abomination to the LORD.' The word describes the most intense outrage possible to holy God.[14] To God, unethical behavior and judgments are on a par with pagan practices (Deut. 18:9, 12) and both are repulsive to Him (Prov. 3:32; 6:16; 11:1, 20; 12:22; 15:8, 9, 26; 16:5; 20:10, 23; 21:27; 28:9).

God delegates measured portions of his authority to the civil rulers (Rom. 13:1-7). They are called to be 'a minister of God, an avenger who brings wrath upon the one who practices evil' (Rom. 13:4). They also serve to commend those who do good (Rom. 13:3). Such rulers represent God in a tangible way. When they render unjust verdicts, they do not represent accurately God's holy character.

Additionally, as Kidner points out, the truth of this proverb underlies the gospel itself. God took pains, through Christ, to provide sufficient legal satisfaction for our sins. For this reason, 'He might be just and the justifier of the one who has faith in Jesus' (Rom. 3:26b).[15]

17:16. Why is there a price in the hand of a fool to buy wisdom, When he has no sense?

The two lines of this proverb make up one continuous sentence. The question is rhetorical. The point is made with a taste of sarcasm. Wisdom is not for sale. It is there for the taking for anyone with an appetite for it. The 'fool' only proves his classification as such (cf. vv. 10, 12) by his attempt to purchase what can only be had at the price of the right heart condition. The word translated 'sense' is, literally, 'heart.'

Some will note Proverb 23:23 in contrast: 'Buy truth, and do not sell it, Get wisdom and instruction and understanding.' This is not instruction to literally attempt to purchase wisdom. It is metaphorical language designed to get at the way one values wisdom (Prov. 3:15-18; 4:7; 8:10-11, 19). Our desire for, and pursuit of, wisdom should be greater than anything else. Though it cost you everything else in life, gain wisdom!

One is reminded of wicked Simon in the city of Samaria. 'Now when Simon saw that the Spirit was bestowed through the laying on of the apostles' hands, he offered them money, saying, "Give this authority to me as well, so that everyone on whom I lay my hands may receive the Holy Spirit"' (Acts 8:18-19). In his response, Peter echoes the sentiment of this proverb: 'May your silver perish with you, because you thought you could obtain the gift of God with money!' (v. 20). Simon's problem was not a matter of finances, but of heart condition – '"You have no part or portion in this matter, for your heart is not right before God"' (v. 21). Only humble repentance could obtain the change of heart needed (v. 22).

17:17. A friend loves at all times, And a brother is born for adversity.
This proverb has created a division of opinion among commentators. The question is whether the parallelism is antithetical or synonymous. The connective translated 'And' can also mean 'but.'[16] If the two lines are set off in antithesis, then a contrast is intended between the love of a 'friend' and a 'brother.' Even here there is division, for some see the point being that the love of the brother is superior and others that the love of the friend is being exalted (Prov. 27:10). If, however, the two lines are set in synonymous parallelism, then the two are not contrasted. But, the point is simply to highlight the importance of strong human relationships.

It seems preferable to see a synonymous parallelism here. A friend 'loves at all times.' No matter what your circumstances, a true friend will always stand with you. A brother 'is born for adversity.' Even when family tensions have created relational distance, often, in calamity, the ties of blood bring that family member rushing back to your side. They were indeed 'born for' this. Adversity is often a revelation of who your true friends are (John 15:13). 'A man of many friends comes to ruin, But there is a friend who sticks closer than a brother' (Prov. 18:24). The Bible holds up Ruth (Ruth 1:16) and Jonathan (2 Sam. 1:26) as marvelous examples of genuine friends.

17:18. A man lacking in sense pledges, And becomes surety in the presence of his neighbor.
This proverb sounds a familiar warning against becoming 'surety' for another. The topic is taken on in depth in Proverbs 6:1-5. See our comments there. Such a one is 'lacking in sense,' or, literally, 'lacking

in heart.' The expression is roughly synonymous with calling one a fool. In Proverbs 7:7, it is applied to the naïve young man who lacks the experience and insight of years. A person 'lacking heart' does not count the cost of his impetuous actions (Prov. 6:32). His future holds only discipline and hardship (Prov. 10:32). He rashly says whatever is on his mind, thus ruining relationships (Prov. 11:12). He chases what is vain (Prov. 12:11) and is lazy (Prov. 24:30). He may seek to gain through unjust and ruthless means (Prov. 28:16).

His naïveté is revealed here by his willingness to make 'pledges.' The phrase is, more literally, 'strikes the hand' (Prov. 6:1; 11:15). It describes a practice that is roughly comparable with our modern-day handshake to seal a transaction. The ancient custom was, no doubt, more binding than a handshake might be considered today in a culture where one's personal word has come to mean little. Here a man's word is considered binding. One should not give it, or any other kind of guarantee, without serious thought.

The first line has presented the folly of giving your word rashly. Now, through synthetic parallelism, the second line advances the idea, making it more specifically address the problem of 'surety' (Prov. 6:1; 11:15; 20:16; 22:26; 27:13). The expression is, literally, 'pledges a pledge' or 'guaranteeing a guarantee.'[17] The issue is becoming responsible for the debt of another person should he become unable to pay. The counsel here is to never do so. This does not contradict the wisdom of the previous verse. On the contrary, a man who 'becomes surety' not only endangers the financial health of his own family, but also often encourages his 'friend' to make a rash decision that could ruin his. Sometimes being a good 'friend' means not doing what your 'friend' asks of you.

The expression 'in the presence of his neighbor' could mean that he is becoming surety for his neighbor, or he is willing to become surety for someone else who is taking a loan from his neighbor. Either case is foolish.

17:19. He who loves transgression loves strife; He who raises his door seeks destruction.

The entire verse is somewhat problematic for interpreters. The challenge of the first line is to figure out what should be understood as subject and predicate. The NASB agrees with the KJV, NKJV, RSV, and NRSV, while the NIV reverses them. The Hebrew word order seems to slightly favor the NASB and those who side with it.[18] The point is that the one who loves to sin also loves to cause trouble between people (Prov. 10:12; 11:9; 12:6; 16:27; 17:14; 29:22).

It is the second line, however, that creates the most controversy. What exactly does 'raises his door' mean? Many commentators take it as a metaphorical reference to one's mouth, not unlike our modern way of speaking of a man's mouth as his 'trap.'[19] If this is the meaning, then the problem is one of arrogant talk. Others take the reference to be more literal, and see it as an ostentatious and elaborate entrance to one's home (Jer. 22:13-17). This, they say, invites trouble as others will break in to steal what they believe such an ornate house must hold. The fact is, we are not certain which of these two is closer to the original intention.

What is clear is that this seems to be a proverb of synonymous parallelism and, thus, the attempt in the second line (whether by arrogant talk or gaudy living) is to elevate one's self above others.[20] Fueled by such motives, actions of any kind are asking for trouble and will surely find it (Prov. 16:18; 29:23).

17:20. He who has a crooked mind finds no good, And he who is perverted in his language falls into evil.

This verse continues the theme of the ill-fortunes reserved for the wicked. The character in the first line is the man of 'crooked mind.' The word 'crooked' describes the twisting, distorting nature of sin.[21] It is his 'mind' or, more literally, 'heart' that is the center of this distortion. His thoughts are distorted and turned away from a true view of reality. His emotions are all over the map. His choices may coincide with the fanciful views of his twisted mind, but they have little to do with reality. Such a man 'finds no good.' Contrast his fate with that of the faithful man: 'He who gives attention to the word shall find good' (Prov. 16:20a; cf. 24:20). The difference is found in that people of 'crooked mind' are 'an abomination to the Lord' (Prov. 11:20, same phrase).

What is in the heart inevitably finds expression through one's mouth (Luke 6:45). Thus, also, the one of 'crooked mind' becomes known as 'he who is perverted in his language.' The word 'perverted' means basically to turn or to overturn. This is a man who uses his speech to turn circumstances to his advantage (i.e. by lying). Through his words, he 'turns things upside down,' creating chaos and confusion.[22] Such a one inevitably 'falls into evil.' How unlike the words of Lady Wisdom: 'All the utterances of my mouth are in righteousness; There is nothing crooked or perverted in them' (Prov. 8:8). Eventually, 'the perverted tongue will be cut out' (Prov. 10:31), because the Lord hates such a mouth (Prov. 8:13). Little wonder he 'falls into evil' (i.e. calamity).

17:21. He who begets a fool does so to his sorrow, And the father of a fool has no joy.

While the parents carry God-delegated authority for leadership in the home and the training of the children, the children hold a *de facto* power over the joy their parents will experience in this life. Not all parents are glad to be such. The grief of having a foolish son is a well-worn theme in these proverbs (Prov. 10:1; 15:20; 17:25; 19:13, 26).

The two lines make up a synonymous parallelism. The two words translated 'fool,' however, are slightly distinct. The first line uses the word *kᵉsîl*, which describes the thickheaded 'dimwit.' The second line uses the more extreme word, *nābāl*. It is used in Proverbs only in verse 7 and 30:22 (cf. 30:32). The *nābāl* is completely godless and beyond the reach of wisdom. He is established in his folly and fixed in his viewpoint. He even denies that there is a God to whom he must answer (Ps. 14:1). Abigail's husband, Nabal, is the poster child for such folly (1 Sam. 25:25).

17:22. A joyful heart is good medicine, But a broken spirit dries up the bones.

This proverb, along with many others from this book, remind us of the intimate and complex connection between the body and the spirit. One's inner state of mind and heart seriously affects one's health and physical vitality. The 'joyful heart' not only 'makes a cheerful face' (Prov. 15:13), but 'good medicine.' The word translated 'medicine' is used only here in the Old Testament. It is, however, related to the word found in Hosea 5:13b: 'But he is unable to heal [our related word] you, Or to cure you of your wound.' Here, too, it appears to refer to 'healing' in some sense.[23] One's peace of mind, or lack thereof, seriously affects one's ability to maintain good health and to recover from ill health (Prov. 12:25; 14:30; 15:13, 30).

The contrast of the first line is seen in the second. A 'broken spirit' is descriptive of a depressed state of mind (Prov. 18:14). The dried up bones (Ps. 22:15; 32:3; 37:7-8; Prov. 3:8) are the opposite of 'fat on the bones' spoken of positively in other proverbs (Prov. 15:30). A similar expression is 'rottenness to the bones' (Prov. 12:4; 14:30).

17:23. A wicked man receives a bribe from the bosom To pervert the ways of justice.

This verse adds to the thoughts expressed in Proverbs 15:27 and 17:8 about bribery. In verse 8, the focus was the pragmatics of bribery, not its morality. Here, however, the purpose clause squarely unveils the motive as evil. It is described as coming 'from the bosom.' The expression implies secretive gestures and covert transfer, in order to hide the evil nature of the transaction (cf. Prov. 6:27; 16:33; 21:14).

The second line gets directly to the motive: 'To pervert the ways of justice.' Since God is fundamentally just, any departure from justice is not only a violation of social order, but an affront to His personal holiness. Both the Law (Exod. 23:8) and the Prophets (Mic. 3:11; 7:3) echo these sentiments.

17:24. Wisdom is in the presence of the one who has understanding, But the eyes of a fool are on the ends of the earth.
Concentration and focus are two keys that unlock the treasure trove of wisdom. The first line is, most literally, 'In the face of the wise [is] wisdom.' The nasb has taken 'in the face of' to mean 'in the presence of,' while the niv has 'in view.' The point seems to be that 'the one who has understanding' is ever focusing intently upon wisdom. That this is the point of the first line is made clear through the contrast of the second. Unlike the wise man, who has set his goal upon wisdom, ever keeping it in his view, the eyes of the fool flit to and fro from one thing to the other, never able to consistently keep his interest and focus set upon one thing, let alone that which matters most of all. The 'ends of the earth' is a metaphorical way of referring to all the far-flung fancies of a mind that is never at rest. His attention never settles on one thing.

Mary's 'one thing' set her apart from Martha, who was 'worried and bothered by so many things' (Luke 10:41-42). Jesus demanded focused allegiance when He announced, 'No one, after putting his hand to the plow and looking back, is fit for the kingdom of God' (Luke 9:62). Paul narrowed his interests until He could say, 'this one thing I do' (Phil. 3:13). We are to be 'fixing our eyes on Jesus' (Heb. 12:2).

Such focus makes the pursuit and discovery of wisdom achievable. 'A scoffer seeks wisdom, and finds none, But knowledge is easy to him who has understanding' (Prov. 14:6).

17:25. A foolish son is a grief to his father, And bitterness to her who bore him.
This proverb corresponds to that of verse 21 (see also Prov. 15:20; 19:13). Here, however, both parents are specifically named for their sorrow (cf. Prov. 10:1). The 'grief' here is a different and stronger word than that of verse 21. The word here describes vexation, provocation, anger or wrath produced in the father by the attitudes and actions of the son.[24] Note that which is attributed to the father and that which is attributed to the mother in regards to response to

the child. The father is provoked to anger; the mother experiences 'bitterness.' The word is used only here, but is akin to that found in Proverbs 14:10: 'The heart knows its own bitterness, And a stranger does not share its joy.' Truly, no one but a mother can understand the grief a wayward child causes! The authority of the father is defied; thus, there is provocation to anger. The tender care of the mother is tossed aside; thus, there is bitter sorrow in her soul.

17:26. It is also not good to fine the righteous, Nor to strike the noble for their uprightness.
This 'is ... not good' proverb is the first of a number to use that negative formula to make its point (Prov. 18:5; 19:2; 20:23; 24:23; 25:27; 28:21).

The first word, a seemingly disconnected conjunction ('also'), has aroused much discussion. Is it evidence that this proverb has been severed from a companion proverb, now located elsewhere? That is highly doubtful. It is more likely that it is used, much like it is in Proverbs 19:2, to introduce a comparison of the lesser to the greater seen in the two lines.[25] If it is 'not good to fine the righteous' (and it has already been proven that punishing the innocent is clearly a violation of justice, Prov. 17:15, 23; 18:5), then how much worse is it 'to strike the noble for their uprightness'?

The 'strike' (probably flogging, Deut. 25:2, 3) of line two is viewed as more serious than the 'fine' of the first. The individual in the first line, 'the righteous,' is guiltless. He is wrongly accused and condemned. The word 'noble' of the second line normally refers to those of nobility class (cf. v. 7 where it is translated 'prince'), but may also point to one of noble character.[26] Not all corporal punishment is condemned (Prov. 17:10), only that which is unjustly handed down and administered. Jeremiah's wrongful flogging is a classic example of such a miscarriage of justice (Jer. 20:2).

17:27. He who restrains his words has knowledge, And he who has a cool spirit is a man of understanding.
Self-control pays high dividends! Wise is the one 'who restrains his words.' The verb can mean refrain, withhold, keep in check, prevent, spare and even hoard something.[27] In this case, it is one's thoughts, feelings and ideas expressed in words. When a person practices this kind of self-control in his speech, he proves that he 'has knowledge,' or, more literally, 'knows knowledge.' The verb is the familiar Hebrew word for deep, personal, experiential knowledge. One sure way to prove that you have truly embraced the knowledge of God

is to hold your tongue when tempted to make a retort. 'When there are many words, transgression is unavoidable, But he who restrains his lips is wise' (Prov. 10:19). 'He who despises his neighbor lacks sense, But a man of understanding keeps silent' (Prov. 11:12). The same notion is often stated negatively in the Proverbs. 'The one who opens wide his lips comes to ruin' (Prov. 13:3b). 'Do you see a man who is hasty in his words? There is more hope for a fool than for him' (Prov. 29:20). While silence may be a mark of wisdom, the next proverb reminds us that it may also conceal the exact opposite.

That the first line has primary reference to the temptation to retort when tempers start to flare is made obvious by the second line. A 'cool spirit' rather than being a hot-head proves that one has come to possess 'understanding.' To make a point, to put someone in their place or to get the last word may feel like the 'right' thing to do, but it is seldom anything more than a foolish indulgence of one's pride. 'He who is slow to anger has great understanding, But he who is quick-tempered exalts folly' (Prov. 14:29). 'A hot-tempered man stirs up strife, But the slow to anger pacifies contention' (Prov. 15:18). 'He who is slow to anger is better than the mighty, And he who rules his spirit, than he who captures a city' (Prov. 16:32). 'A man's discretion makes him slow to anger, And it is his glory to overlook a transgression' (Prov. 19:11). 'But let everyone be quick to hear, slow to speak and slow to anger; for the anger of man does not achieve the righteousness of God' (James 1:19-20).

17:28. Even a fool, when he keeps silent, is considered wise; When he closes his lips, he is counted prudent.
Read this proverb in connection with the previous one. There, restraint of one's words is evidence of wisdom. Here, it is merely a cover for folly, though an effective one. Two warnings emerge. First, that not all who appear silent and thoughtful are in fact just that. Second, measured words are best, no matter what your proximity to wisdom. Even Job's friends appeared caring and wise while they remained silent (Job 2:13). Once their mouths were opened, however, Job sarcastically lamented: 'O that you would be completely silent, And that it would become your wisdom!' (Job 13:5).

The problem is that 'A fool does not delight in understanding, But only in revealing his own mind' (Prov. 18:2). 'Yet the fool multiplies words' (Eccles. 10:14a). 'A prudent man conceals knowledge, But the heart of fools proclaims folly' (Prov. 12:23). 'When there are many words, transgression is unavoidable, But he who restrains his lips is wise' (Prov. 10:19).

End Notes

1. Ross, Allen P., 'Proverbs,' *The Expositor's Bible Commentary* (Grand Rapids, Michigan: Zondervan Publishing House, 1991), 5:1013.

2. Ibid.

3. Waltke, Bruce, Course notes, *Proverbs OT 698* (Deerfield, Illinois: Trinity Evangelical Divinity School, 2000), 5.

4. Carpenter, Eugene, and Michael A. Grisanti, 'נרב,' *New International Dictionary of Old Testament Theology and Exegesis* (Grand Rapids, Michigan: Zondervan Publishing House, 1997), 3:31.

5. Ross, 5:115.

6. Kidner, Derek, *Proverbs* (Downers Grove, Illinois: InterVarsity Press, 1964), 124.

7. Buzzell, Sid S., 'Proverbs,' *The Bible Knowledge Commentary* (Wheaton: Victor Books, 1985), 1:942.

8. Harris, R. Laird, 'kāsâ,' *Theological Wordbook of the Old Testament* (Chicago: Moody Press, 1980), 1:448-449.

9. Brown, Francis, S. R. Driver, Charles R. Briggs, *A Hebrew and English Lexicon of the Old Testament* (Oxford: Clarendon Press, n.d.), 48.

10. Hamilton, Victor P., 'נחז,' *New International Dictionary of Old Testament Theology and Exegesis*, 1997), 3:90-91.

11. Buzzell, 1:942.

12. Kidner, 40.

13. Goldberg, Louis, ''wl,' *Theological Wordbook of the Old Testament* (Chicago: Moody Press, 1980), 1:19-20.

14. Whybray, R. N., *Proverbs* (Grand Rapids, Michigan: William B. Eerdmans Publishing Company, 1994), 100.

15. Kidner, 125.

16. Murphy, 130.

17. Cohen, A., *Proverbs* (London: The Soncino Press, 1946), 115.

18. Kidner, 126.

19. Ross, 5:1019.

20. Murphy, 131.

21. Allen, Ronald B., ''āqash,' *Theological Wordbook of the Old Testament* (Chicago: Moody Press, 1980), 2:693.

22. Hamilton, Victor P., 'hāpak,' *Theological Wordbook of the Old Testament* (Chicago: Moody Press, 1980), 1:221-222.

23. Chan, Alan Kam-Yau, 'גהו,' *New International Dictionary of Old Testament Theology and Exegesis* (Grand Rapids, Michigan: Zondervan Publishing House, 1997), 1:831-832.

24. Gerard, Van Groningen, 'kā'as,' *Theological Wordbook of the Old Testament* (Chicago: Moody Press, 1980), 1:451.

25. Cohen, 117.

26. Whybray, 262.

27. Martens, Elmer A., 'חשׁך,,' *New International Dictionary of Old Testament Theology and Exegesis* (Grand Rapids, Michigan: Zondervan Publishing House, 1997), 2:301-302.

Proverbs 18

18:1. He who separates himself seeks his own desire, He quarrels against all sound wisdom.
At first glance, the point of this proverb is difficult to discern. What is meant by one 'who separates himself'? What is it he distances himself from? The word so translated refers to dividing things, often people. In the verbal form we have here, it can describe dividing peoples into nations (Gen. 10:5, 32; 25:23), individuals or groups from one another (Gen. 13:9, 11, 14; 2 Sam. 1:13), or a person from his tribe (Judg. 4:11).[1] Here, the individual takes the initiative and separates himself from the community at large. Within the context of Proverbs, the group he separates himself from would, no doubt, be the faithful, wise community of God's people. In our context, we might refer it to the family or church (whether local or at large). Solomon is describing the renegade, the lone ranger, the anti-social individualist, who will not listen to others. He finds his identity in his non-conformity and obstinately sets himself apart, independently, from the body of those to whom he should belong and who could offer wise counsel.

Such a person 'seeks his own desire.' In simple terms, he is selfish. All his thoughts lead to himself. He measures everything by his thoughts, his wishes, his comfort, his perspective – assuming that they are supreme.

Such a person 'quarrels against all sound wisdom.' The word translated 'sound wisdom' has the idea of 'sound judgment' and that which flows from it, i.e. abiding success in the practical affairs of life (Prov. 2:7).[2] God's wisdom is not some esoteric philosophy. But, He has held in reserve for us all that we will need to prosper and advance in the world He has created us for. Such success cannot be had through stubborn independence. It is found in humble relationship with the believing community of God's people and is worked out in all the frustrating quirks of human relationships.

The one who feels he does not need others 'quarrels against' such wisdom. The word is of uncertain derivation, but may come from a root meaning 'to show one's teeth' or perhaps 'to break forth in hostilities.'[3] It is found only three times in Proverbs (Prov. 17:14; 18:1; 20:3), and always appears to have to do with quarreling. Fierce independence snarls and growls at all attempts from others to counsel or guide. In the end, the doggedly self-willed person may indeed get his 'desire,' but lose 'sound wisdom.' Such a man has forfeited his treasure.

18:2. A fool does not delight in understanding, But only in revealing his own mind.

This antithetical proverb (a form rare to this chapter, cf. vv. 12, 14, 23, 24) lays bare the unteachable, and arrogant, spirit of the fool. The first line makes its point by stating its opposite – 'A fool does not delight in understanding,' (i.e. he despises understanding).[4] He has no interest in listening or learning. Rather, as the second line reveals, his only thought is to expose what is on his own mind. The root of the verb 'revealing' can mean to uncover, to reveal, to be away or to go away.[5] The particular form employed here is found only one other time in the Old Testament: in Genesis 9:21, where Noah got drunk and uncovered himself, sleeping naked in his tent.[6] Thus, it would not be a stretch to understand this as a description of a man with a bit of an exhibitionist tendency. The fool, to his own shame, has only a perverse interest in exposing himself – in this case, his thoughts, feelings, opinions, musings and vaunted insights. He is oblivious to both the divine and public evaluation of him – 'A fool.' He lives in a delusional world, where he always has the key insight and always inspires and informs others.

Proverbs has often underscored the inability of the fool to constrain his speech and, thus, his tendency to make public display of his folly (Prov. 12:23; 13:16; 15:2). In the previous verse, Solomon warned of the man who is so arrogant as to see no need for influence from others (Prov. 18:1). At least, there, he kept his arrogance to himself. Here, he parades it before the community. 'He who restrains his words has knowledge ... Even a fool when he keeps silent, is considered wise; When he closes his lips, he is counted prudent' (Prov. 17:27a, 28).

18:3. When a wicked man comes, contempt also comes, And with dishonor comes reproach.

Wickedness keeps miserable company! The two lines of the proverb are arranged synthetically, the three terms ('contempt,' 'dishonor,' and 'reproach') telescoping out in a description of the ever-increasing ignominy that befalls the 'wicked man.'

Do these three terms, however, really refer to what befalls the 'wicked man,' or do they (or, at least, some of them) refer to what comes to those who come into contact with him or dare relate to him? In this latter understanding, the first line would mean that, when a wicked man comes your way, contempt for you comes along with him and, soon, dishonor and reproach follow.

Even if all three terms are taken as descriptive of what comes to the 'wicked man,' it is not difficult to see how they also come to the one who associates with him. In the end, the debate may be moot. It seems best to view these three derisions as that which befalls the 'wicked man.' In that case the point is that a life of sin inevitably ends in reproach. The choice to pursue temptation and live in sin is the choice to destroy your life. There is no alternative outcome possible once the path has been chosen.

Though the terms are not always clearly distinct, they may indicate some kind of progression into degradation. The first thing to befall the man who chooses sin is 'contempt.' It is, primarily, an inner disposition that others come to after observing the attitudes and actions of the 'wicked man.' Growing out of this 'contempt' comes 'dishonor.' The word has the notion of that which is 'light,' as opposed to that which is 'heavy.'[7] Thus, 'dishonor' (that which is lightly esteemed) is the opposite of 'glory' (that which is 'heavy'). This appears to be a more abiding reputation. The final extension of the telescope, 'reproach,' describes the casting of blame or scorn on another. It is an outward, objective act.[8]

Some commentators require an emendation of the Hebrew, so that, instead of the concrete 'wicked man,' it reads 'wickedness' instead. While some commentators follow this emendation, by no means is it universally accepted. It seems an unnecessary reconstruction of the text.

18:4. The words of a man's mouth are deep waters; The fountain of wisdom is a bubbling brook.

The challenge of this proverb is to accurately identify the kind of parallelism employed. Is it antithetical, contrasting the first and the second lines? Or is it synonymous, the second line simply restating the point of the first for emphasis?

The notion of antithetical parallelism depends upon interpreting 'deep waters' as meaning obscure, concealed or unreachable except by the greatest of efforts. In support, some cite the same phrase in Proverbs 20:5, where this seems to be the intent. If this be the case, then the person speaking those 'words' is in his natural, unenlightened state. The second line, then, would contrast the easily accessibly 'bubbling brook' and flowing 'fountain' of wisdom with the obscure and inaccessible comprehension of the natural man's thoughts, which lie behind his words.

If taken as a synonymous parallelism, 'deep waters' must mean something like profound or weighty. In this case, the person who possesses these words is considered to be a wise man. The descriptions of line two then, simply, go on to further expound upon the value of what lies within him. The man's words are not only sage, but accessible and useful.

On the whole, it seems too much to demand that 'deep waters' requires understanding it as a negative reference. While it is possible to understand it as such, neither this proverb nor the one in Proverbs 20:5 demands it. Thus, it seems preferable to understand this as a synonymous parallelism. The first line points out the profundity of the thoughts expressed in words by the person of wisdom. The second line reveals that, while their words are deep and thus valuable, they are also accessible, life-giving and practical. The imagery of a 'fountain' of wisdom has been seen often, though more frequently it is a 'fountain of life.' The difference is not significant, however, because the 'fountain of life' is never disconnected from wisdom (Prov. 13:14), understanding (Prov. 16:22), righteousness (Prov. 10:11) and the fear of the Lord (Prov. 14:27). The words of such a person are a delight to listen to. They stretch you. They make you think. They shed light on your situation. They are never trite, canned or easy clichés. One has the inescapable sense that they are only the bubbling forth of a vast supply of wisdom that lies much deeper within.

18:5. To show partiality to the wicked is not good, Nor to thrust aside the righteous in judgment.
This proverb attacks the injustice of favoritism. In this regard, it echoes a frequent tenet of the Law (Lev. 19:15; Deut. 1:17; 16:19) that is just as frequently affirmed by these proverbs (Prov. 17:15, 23, 26; 24:23-25; 28:21; 31:5). The two lines form one continuous sentence, rather than two lines in synonymous parallelism.[9]

The first line follows the 'not good' formula previously encountered in Proverbs 16:29 and 17:26, and which will be met again (Prov. 19:2; 20:23; 24:23; 25:27; 28:21). What is 'not good' is to 'show partiality to the wicked.' The word for 'show partiality' is, literally, 'lift up the face of.' It pictures one who is bowed down before the judge, head rightfully hanging in shame over his crime. The partiality is that the judge reaches down and lifts the face that, because of guilt, could not otherwise look him in the eye. It was an idiom for expressing favor to a person (Ps. 3:3).

But the story does not end there, for, if the person is genuinely guilty, as this proverb supposes, then the injustice is seen not just in showing favor to the individual, but in a slighting of the rights of the one who was wronged. The second line addresses the other edge of the sword of injustice. The problem is that, in his leniency toward the guilty, the judge also moves 'to thrust aside the righteous' in his judgment. The word for 'to thrust aside' vividly pictures the gentle hand of the judge lifting the guilt-heavy face of the culpable, while forcefully using the other to push aside the innocent victim and his rights under the law.

A society is only as stable as its judicial system. Any society's judicial system is only as just as the individual judges who make it up. How weighty a responsibility is laid upon their shoulders! Even a well-intentioned compassion toward the guilty inevitably cuts the other way, depriving the victim(s) of the rights they should expect under the law.

We are also reminded that, at the price of His own Son's life, our Father remained both 'just and the justifier of the one who has faith in Jesus' (Rom. 3:26). The penalty for our sin was exacted from Jesus, that God might set us free from the condemnation we deserved. Only in Jesus is there both perfect justice and perfect love!

18:6. A fool's lips bring strife, And his mouth calls for blows.
This verse coupled with the next reveals the fool's primary downfall: his speech. In fact, the two verses, taken together, reveal a chiastic arrangement: 'lips ... mouth ... mouth ... lips.'[10] The two lines are synonymous in parallelism, but hold the cause ('strife') and its result ('blows') in parallel as well.[11]

The talk of a fool will 'bring strife' to his relationships (Prov. 17:14, 19; 20:3). The word translated 'strife' may refer either to simple relational tension or to official legal action.[12] Either is possible as a translation, and either is possible in the realm of personal relations. If the 'strife' is understood as fractured human relationships, then the 'blows' of line two may be understood as coming either from his father, or perhaps because of bloody fisticuffs that result from some foolish statement. If the 'strife' comes to the point of legal action, then the 'blows' may be an officially sanctioned scourging (Prov. 19:29).[13]

18:7. A fool's mouth is his ruin, And his lips are the snare of his soul.
Read this proverb and these comments in conjunction with the previous one. Together, they remind us that the consequences of a

fool's speech not only compound upon others, but also upon the fool himself.

The fool's unexamined words, hasty counsel, uninvited information, unwise promises and other drivel bring about his own 'ruin.' The word can describe physical ruins (Ps. 89:40), destruction metaphorically (Prov. 10:14), or some external object that evokes extreme fear (Jer. 17:17; 48:39).[14] Here, it is used in the sense of some unspecified destruction that will overtake him because of his foolish speech. Frequently, the Scriptures attribute this outcome to the unguarded tongue (Ps. 64:8; 140:9; Prov. 12:13; 13:3; Eccles. 10:12).

The 'ruin' comes because his words become a 'snare' to him (Prov. 5:22; 6:2). Hasty promises and rash vows have trapped many who should have known better, such as Jephthah (Judg. 11:30-35), Saul (1 Sam. 14:24-30, 36-45), and certain Jewish men (Acts 23:14). Indeed, as we will learn later in this chapter: 'With the fruit of a man's mouth his stomach will be satisfied; He will be satisfied with the product of his lips. Death and life are in the power of the tongue, And those who love it will eat its fruit' (Prov. 18:20-21).

18:8. The words of a whisperer are like dainty morsels, And they go down into the innermost parts of the body.

This proverb is repeated, verbatim, in Proverbs 26:22. The problem is the 'words of a whisperer.' The word for 'whisperer' is used only here and in Proverbs 16:28 and 26:20, 22. It makes reference to one who murmurs and whispers about others behind their backs. Such a person is a gossip. What they have to share is 'like dainty morsels.' The word occurs only here and in Proverbs 26:22. It comes from a root meaning to devour, swallow or gobble up.[15] Listening to gossip is as easy as eating candy. Stopping a gossip who is about to share some tasty tidbit of news with you is harder than pushing away from a delicious dessert. They are 'dainty morsels,' in that they are something special, something you believe not everyone has the privilege of enjoying.

The trouble is that, once the gossip is shared, it goes 'down into the innermost parts of the body.' The expression 'innermost parts of the body' is found again only in Proverbs 20:27, 30. It is, more literally, 'inner chambers [rooms] of the belly' (i.e. farthest depths of a man). Once gossip is shared and heard, one cannot help but be influenced by it. It settles deep within you. You never look at the person of whom the gossip spoke in the same way again, even if you tell yourself the gossip was probably not true. Gossip irrepressibly shapes our view of people.

A wise man's words are also pleasant (Prov. 16:21, 24), but their consumption yields a very different outcome. They are life and health to the whole body (Prov. 4:22), while gossip warps a man's mind, distorts his perception and destroys his relationships.

18:9. He also who is slack in his work Is brother to him who destroys.
The two lines of this proverb form one continuous sentence that makes its point via a comparison. The word 'brother' forms the hinge of the comparative statement, holding two characters from a common stock. The first line presents him 'who is slack in his work.' The word in this form means to show oneself to be lazy, indolent, idle or disheartened.[16] Proverbs speaks often of the dangers of laziness (Prov. 6:6-11; 10:4; 12:11, 24, 27; 13:4; 14:23; 27:23-27; 28:19). This indolence shows itself 'in his work.' The expression describes that which you are commissioned by another to perform on his behalf. As a king may deploy a messenger or ambassador on royal business, so all of us are put under a charge at one time or another.[17]

The one who proves negligent in such a stewardship is 'brother to' a man whose intent, from the beginning, is to destroy that royal work. Though the lazy man would distance himself from the destroyer, the fact is that he comes from the same moral gene pool. Jesus later would point out that the angry man and the murderer were of the same master, and would incur similar sentences (Matt. 5:21-22), and that the lustful man and the adulterer were together guilty of the same sin before God (Matt. 5:27-28). Solomon, long before Jesus' time, similarly affirms that, in terms of social outcome and life-effect, the lazy man and the social 'demolition expert'[18] are no different. The idle are consorting with the enemy of their King!

The expression 'him who destroys' is, more literally, 'lord of destruction.' The first word is one which does double duty as both the proper name of the false god Baal and a more common noun meaning 'lord,' 'possessor,' or 'owner.'[19] The root of the second word is used to describe the destruction of cities, a dynasty (2 Chron. 21:7), nations who oppose God's own (Jer. 51:11), and God's own wayward people and that which they have acquired.[20] The similar phrase is used again in Proverbs 28:24.

Indolent neglect, as much as wicked intent, is culpable before God. Let us, therefore, be careful to keep the charge committed to us, not until we are satisfied, but until our King who laid it upon us releases us from it!

18:10. The name of the Lord is a strong tower; The righteous runs into it and is safe.

We find here the only occurrence in Proverbs of the phrase the 'name of the Lord,' though see 'the name of my God' in Proverbs 30:9. The 'name of the Lord' stands for the Lord Himself. His name is the revelation of who He is; it is His attributes making themselves known to man. Thus, the expression does not speak about something belonging to the Lord, but who the Lord is in Himself. As such, it becomes a common way of speaking of one's confidence that God will be God in one's own experience. 'Some boast in chariots, and some in horses; But we will boast in the name of the Lord, our God' (Ps. 20:7). 'I will wait on Thy name, for it is good, in the presence of Thy godly ones' (Ps. 52:9b). 'Our help is in the name of the Lord, Who made heaven and earth' (Ps. 124:8). Here the specific 'name' is Yahweh, the covenant name of God (Exod. 3:14-15).

This self-revealing God is said to be 'a strong tower.' That trust in the 'name' of the Lord is tantamount to trust in the Lord Himself is clear, in that elsewhere the Lord Himself is spoken of in similar terms. 'For Thou has been a refuge for me, A tower of strength against the enemy' (Ps. 61:3). 'The way of the Lord is a stronghold to the upright' (Prov. 10:29a).

Ancient cities often included a tall tower built as a place of escape for the citizens, should they come under attack. When the enemy came, they would flee to this place of security and refuge. 'Then Abimelech went to Thebez, and he camped against Thebez and captured it. But there was a strong tower in the center of the city, and all the men and women with all the leaders of the city fled there and shut themselves in; and they went up on the roof of the tower' (Judg. 9:50-51).

The righteous are said to 'run' into the tower which the Lord is for them. The verb is used in a metaphorical sense to describe the confident faith a righteous person places in God's ability to keep and protect him. When one so trusts in the Lord, he finds that he is 'safe.' The word translated here as 'safe' is a military term which means, literally, 'set on high' or 'exalted' (i.e. they are kept above the threats of the enemy).[21] The same expression is used in Proverbs 29:25b: 'he who trusts in the Lord will be exalted.' For similar expressions by Solomon's father David, see Psalm 27:4-5 and 91:14. Solomon apparently had learned well from his father (Prov. 14:26).

Such confidence in God as our shelter, refuge and fortress is expressed many times throughout the Scriptures, especially in poetic writings (2 Sam. 22:2-3, 33, 51; Ps. 18:2; 27:1, 4-5; 61:3; 91:1-2; 144:2).

This secure confidence in our God of such sterling character is now to be contrasted with the fool who trusts in the fleeting nature of his wealth (v. 11).

18:11. A rich man's wealth is his strong city, And like a high wall in his own imagination.

This proverb must be understood in relation to several others. The first line here is identical to that in Proverbs 10:15: 'The rich man's wealth is his fortress, The ruin of the poor is their poverty.' In Proverbs 10:15, the point is that there is some actual earthly security in wealth, measured as it is. There are certain things in this world that wealth can protect you from while poverty leaves you vulnerable to them.

This proverb, however, must also be taken in relationship to verse 10. The two are connected by the repetition of the Hebrew words here translated as 'strong' (same in v. 10) and 'high' ('save' in v. 10). Taken together, one proverb emphasizes absolute security (v. 10) and the other imaginary security (v. 11). There is no contradiction between Proverbs 10:15 and 18:11, however. The first looks at security from an earthly perspective, the second from a heavenly one. Trusting wealth may seem to pay for a while, but, eventually, in the end, its inability to protect and deliver is uncovered. Woe to the one who rests his hopes in riches! Read Psalm 49 for a vivid expression of the fragile nature of hope in earthly wealth.

18:12. Before destruction the heart of man is haughty, But humility goes before honor.

The thought of the previous two verses is carried through to this one as well. The word translated 'haughty,' literally, means 'high.' Compare this with 'safe' (v. 10b) and 'high wall' (v. 11b). In verse 10, the safety is actual, since it involves the name of the Lord. In verse 11, the security is illusionary, since it is based in financial considerations. Here, there is again an imagined security, but now it is false, for the 'high' thing is one's own self – the arrogant self-confidence which holds resolute even while being swept away 'Before destruction.'

The truth of this proverb should sound familiar, for the first line is nearly the same as Proverbs 16:18a and the second line is identical to Proverbs 15:33b. Additionally, Proverbs often remind us that pride inevitably precedes calamity (Prov. 11:2; 16:18; 17:19; 29:23).

As self-elevation precedes being brought low, so also humbling one's self precedes being honored. These are axioms which God has set as fixed laws of His creation. Again, Proverbs often states this law (e.g. Prov. 15:33; 25:6-7), as do the rest of the Scriptures (Matt. 23:12; Luke 14:11; 18:14; 1 Pet. 5:6). Jesus' own experience exemplifies the unfaltering nature of this God-given rule (Isa. 52:13- 53:12; Phil. 2:5-10).

18:13. He who gives an answer before he hears, It is folly and shame to him.

This proverb takes up a theme already introduced in verses 2 and 7 and continued on in verse 17. Some folk think it a mark of wit and intelligence to always have a quick retort to any question or a hasty answer to settle any dispute. This proverb declares that such quick wittiness is, in fact, a sign of dimwittedness. It is a sign of a man's 'folly and shame,' not his cleverness. He reveals that his great preoccupation is not in hearing and understanding, but in showing off his own supposed insight (Prov. 18:2). Because of this propensity, he is vulnerable to the loudest and quickest to speak their mind (Prov. 18:17). He proves to be his own worst enemy (Prov. 18:7; 20:25).

Generally speaking, Job's friends erred in this way. Nicodemus, however, appealed to the law to take a stand against such a spirit when dealing with Christ (John 7:51; Deut. 13:12-15).

18:14. The spirit of a man can endure his sickness, But a broken spirit who can bear?

This proverb makes its point by means of an antithetical parallelism. The first line describes that which is unfortunate and unwanted, but endurable, the second line describes that which is catastrophic and unbearable. The first deals with concrete suffering, that is to say ailments that are experienced in the body. While physical sufferings certainly can affect one's inward attitude, they need not. A man 'can endure' such suffering, as intense as it may be. The root of the verb describes containing something inside a vessel of some sort. At times, it is used, as here, metaphorically to describe the human inability to endure something (Joel 2:11; Amos 7:10; Mal. 3:2).[22] What can 'contain' or make bearable even the afflictions of one's body? It is the 'spirit of a man.' As long as there is inward resolve, a survival instinct or a will to live, a person can face overwhelming physical suffering or sickness. His 'spirit' wraps itself around the trouble and contains, smothers and subdues it – not necessarily defeating it, but keeping it from overwhelming him.

The second line, however, wonders out loud what will become of the man who loses that inward resiliency of spirit. The truly overwhelming thing comes when a person's spirit is 'broken.' The phrase 'broken spirit' is found again in the Old Testament only in Proverbs 15:13 and 17:22. In both of these cases, the 'broken spirit' is contrasted with 'a joyful heart.' It describes a man who has come to the end of himself. There are no mental, emotional or spiritual reserves to draw upon. The well is dry. Troubles overwhelm. Pain chokes. Trials bury him.

When a man is cut adrift in a sea of pain, his spirit can hold him up. But, if the spirit loses its buoyancy, what becomes of him?

18:15. The mind of the prudent acquires knowledge, And the ear of the wise seeks knowledge.

The synonymous parallelism of this proverb points out that the truly wise one is the one who understands his lack of wisdom and seeks, at all cost, to find the wisdom he lacks. The repetition of the word 'knowledge' ties the two lines together, as do the verbs of initiative – 'acquires' and 'seeks.' The 'mind' (lit., 'heart') and 'ear' are found together elsewhere (Prov. 2:2; 23:12) as the dual organs for the reception of wisdom and knowledge. The first line is identical to Proverbs 15:14a, except that the verb is different.[23]

Proverbs repeatedly stresses that wisdom resides in the attitude of having never actually arrived at wisdom and in the constant search for it. 'A wise man will hear and increase in learning, And a man of understanding will acquire wise counsel' (Prov. 1:5). 'Acquire wisdom! Acquire understanding! Do not forget, nor turn away from the words of my mouth' (Prov. 4:5). 'The beginning of wisdom is: Acquire wisdom; And with all your acquiring, get understanding' (Prov. 4:7).

18:16. A man's gift makes room for him, And brings him before great men.

Here again we encounter teaching about the taking of a bribe. The word here is different and more general than the word rendered 'bribe' in Proverbs 17:8, 23. It is, however, found in parallelism with that word (Prov. 21:14), so the distinction between the two, if any, is minor.

The point here is made via a synthetic parallelism. The first line states the matter in general terms – a 'gift' enlarges the way before a man. Exactly what this means is left unstated until the second line – it 'brings him before great men.' For most people, the pathway to the presence of a person of power and influence is narrow, if not completely closed off. But, a well-timed and well-thought-out 'gift' may be just the ticket to a personal meeting with him.

The line of demarcation between a 'bribe' and a legitimate 'gift' is often difficult to discern. The 'bribe' generally 'works' (Prov. 17:8), but it encourages the wicked in their ways and usually corrupts justice (Prov. 17:23). The 'gift' also pragmatically achieves its purpose (Prov. 19:6; 21:14), but the repercussions are felt even in one's own family (Prov. 15:27). Some examples of such 'innocent gifts' are found in Jacob's gifts to Esau (Gen. 32:13-20) and Joseph (Gen. 43:11); Abigail's gift to David (1 Sam. 25:27) and Jesse's gift to the army commander of his sons (1 Sam. 17:18).

We must never 'bribe' anyone and must approach with the greatest caution the giving or receiving of anything that may even approach such a perversion of justice. In certain social situations, a 'gift' may be legitimate, though not always completely disinterested. Walk carefully here!

18:17. The first to plead his case seems just, Until another comes and examines him.

The first evidence always sounds like the only evidence until further investigation takes place. The two lines of this proverb form one continuous sentence. The context appears to be that of a court of law, yet the principle of the proverb applies far more widely. The law demanded that judges impartially hear both sides of a dispute (Deut. 1:16). This is also essential for a parent, counselor or pastor – anyone who deals with people. Listening before forming a fixed opinion is mandatory, if justice is to be done (Prov. 18:2, 13).

The difference between hasty judgment and the right judgment comes when one 'examines' that which seems so obvious. The verb means to search, investigate or to examine. It describes an intensive, searching probe for the truth.[24] In relationships, a ponderous question is often more useful than a quick answer.

18:18. The lot puts an end to contentions, And decides between the mighty.

The topic of casting lots has already been introduced in Proverbs 16:33. Read our comments there for elaboration on the background and use of the lot. The point made there is that God's sovereignty extends over all things, even the outcome of casting lots. In His providence, and given the parameters discussed under Proverbs 16:33, God may use such a method to communicate His will.

Here, the point seems to be the social implications of using the lot. Where bitterly divided opponents have reached an impasse, and where both parties mutually subscribed to the divine use of the casting of lots, it could be an effective way to end a dispute. The problem is 'contentions.' People are at odds with one another and fighting. The extent to which the lot may be useful is seen in that it even works among 'the mighty.'

The lot 'decides' between such factions. The word, more literally, means 'to separate.' It is used five times in Proverbs (16:28; 17:9; 18:1, 18; 19:4). It can describe a wedge driven between people whose relationship should be well established. Proverbs 16:28 describes the man of loose tongue dividing good friends. It can describe a person who willfully sets himself apart from others (Prov. 18:1).[25] Here, the warring factions can be peacefully separated, pulled apart and put at peace with one another.

Today, this side of the Cross and Pentecost, when God's people reach a relational impasse, they should turn to the principles of God's written word and the guidance of the Holy Spirit, mediated through mature and spiritually minded believers (1 Cor. 6:1-8). But, even here and now, both parties must believe that God will work through these means or no peace will be found.

18:19. A brother offended is harder to be won than a strong city, And contentions are like the bars of a castle.
This proverb logically follows upon the previous two. The most exceedingly difficult cases to resolve are those among family. The word 'brother' may mean either a blood relative or a very close non-relative.[26] Both may be in view here, but the illustrative power of the proverb is built on the notion of the closest human relationships possible.

The first line is difficult to translate, being, literally, 'A brother offended a city of strength.' Part of the struggle in translation is that the LXX has changed 'offended' to 'helped,' which changes the entire import of the proverb and transforms it into an antithetical proverb, rather than a synonymous or synthetic one. The Syriac, Targum and Vulgate all follow the LXX, as does the RSV. However, the similar imagery of 'a strong city' and 'a castle' in both lines seems to point to the validity and accuracy of the Hebrew text.[27]

Scripture abounds with illustrations of the bitter animosity that is born when conflict between close relatives is not soon settled: Cain and Abel (Gen. 4), Joseph and his brothers (Gen. 37:3-5, 18-27), Benjamin and his brothers (Judg. 20), Eliab and David (1 Sam. 17:28), Absalom and Amnon (2 Sam. 13:22), and Judah and Israel (2 Chron. 13:16-17).[28]

Seldom do we find illustrations of such bitter rivalries settled. We do have Esau and Jacob, who became bitter enemies (Gen. 27:41-45;

32:6-11), but who seem to have settled their dispute (Gen. 33:5-11). However, the ongoing bitterness between their families brings into doubt the depth of their reconciliation (Num. 20:14-21; Ezek. 35:5; Obad. 10–14).[29] We do, however, find Paul and Barnabas bitterly divided over Mark (Acts 15:39), but later Paul's praise of Mark (2 Tim. 4:11).

We are reminded of the division possible when people look at themselves and their own desires, rather than those of others (Prov. 18:1). Likewise, we are reminded of the wisdom of nipping strife in the bud: 'The beginning of strife is like letting out water, So abandon the quarrel before it breaks out' (Prov. 17:14). If 'contentions are like the bars of a castle,' how much wiser is the man 'who rules his spirit, than he who captures a city' (Prov. 16:32b).

18:20. With the fruit of a man's mouth his stomach will be satisfied; He will be satisfied with the product of his lips.

This proverb and the one following provide a healthy balance for each other. The two lines here are arranged synonymously. The 'fruit of a man's mouth' is a poetic expression to describe the words he says, as is also 'the product of his lips.' The word 'fruit' ties this proverb with the next. One's words make him 'satisfied,' the word being found in both lines here. The word can mean either 'satisfied' in a good sense (Prov. 12:11; 20:13; 28:19) or 'sated' in a bad sense (Prov. 1:31; 14:14; 25:16, 17).[30] Here, it is intended in a good sense, but the next verse will show that the bad consequences of one's speech are not far off, if the tongue is not guarded.

Many have spoken of the fractured metaphor used here – one's belly being satisfied by what comes out of the mouth rather than what goes into it.[31] Even Jesus, however, used such imagery to make a point (Matt. 15:11). The point is that what is inside a man defines him more than that which he might acquire and take into his life.

Proverbs often speaks of the positive benefits of wise speech, both for others (Prov. 13:14) and even for one's self, as here. How wise the man who prays daily, 'Set a guard, O LORD, over my mouth; Keep watch over the door of my lips' (Ps. 141:3).

We are, because of our own blunders, all too aware of the negative consequences of unwise words, but we need to remember both the consequences and benefits of our speech! 'A man will be satisfied with good by the fruit of his words, And the deeds of a man's hands will return to him' (Prov. 12:14). 'From the fruit of a man's mouth he enjoys good' (Prov. 13:2a).

18:21. Death and life are in the power of the tongue, And those who love it will eat its fruit.
This proverb follows on the previous one, being tied together by the common word 'fruit' and the common theme of speech. Here, 'Death and life' are said to lie in the 'power of the tongue.' The reference to 'Death and life' reminds one of Moses' plea in Deuteronomy 30: 'See, I have set before you today life and prosperity, and death and adversity ... I call heaven and earth to witness against you today, that I have set before you life and death, the blessing and the curse. So choose life ...' (vv. 15, 19). There, the reference was to obedience to God's law, here it is the outcome of what one says.

Indeed, one's tongue is attributed with 'power.' The word 'power' is, literally, 'hand' in the Hebrew. The expression reads 'Death and life are in the hand of the tongue.' The 'hand' is often used as a metaphorical expression for coming into the grasp of or under the power of another.[32] The particular power attributed to the 'tongue' is the ability to bring 'life' or to bring 'death.' Are these benefits or liabilities seen as coming to the speaker of the words or those to whom he speaks? If a choice must be made, it is probably the former that is in view here. However, they cannot truly be separated. Part of the 'life' that well-spoken words bring to the speaker is their life-giving effect upon his listeners. Part of the 'death' they bring is the destruction wreaked upon the relationships of the speaker as his words come to others.

Proverbs stresses the life-giving effects of wise speech. 'The tongue of the righteous is as choice silver' (Prov. 10:20a). 'The lips of the righteous feed many' (Prov. 10:21a). 'The mouth of the righteous flows with wisdom' (Prov. 10:31a). The reverse is also true, however, and one's words may destroy. 'Words from the mouth of a wise man are gracious, while the lips of a fool consume him; the beginning of his talking is folly, and the end of it is wicked madness. Yet the fool multiplies words. No man knows what will happen, and who can tell him what will come after him?' (Eccles. 10:12-14).

While the exact effect of one's speech may not be determined exactly, the fact that 'those who love it will eat its fruit' is a given. We will reap the benefits or endure the pains of what we say. The word 'its' refers to one's speech, the product of one's tongue. Our words are seeds sown in the soil of other people's lives. Those words never remain neutral. They yield a harvest either to 'life' or to 'death' for them and for us. The one who loves to talk (Prov. 10:19; 18:2; 20:19) will live or die by his speech.

James wisely warned us: 'Let not many of you become teachers, my brethren, knowing that as such we shall incur a stricter judgment' (James 3:1). The context of this warning is the dangers of speech (vv. 2-12; cf. 3:6-10). Jesus also warned us, 'And I say to you, that every careless word that men shall speak, they shall render account for it in the day of judgment. For by your words you shall be justified, and by your words you shall be condemned' (Matt. 12:36-37).

18:22. He who finds a wife finds a good thing, And obtains favor from the LORD.

How blessed is the man with a good, and godly, wife! This proverb makes the point through synthetic parallelism, the second line explaining the first.

The first line reads, most literally, 'He who finds a wife finds good.' Clearly, the implication is that she is a 'good' wife. But, she is not called a 'thing.' The word for 'good' is found often in Proverbs and, here, means something like 'fortune' or 'favor.'[33] A good wife and a good life are synonymous in God's plan most of the time (Gen. 2:18).

The second line explains how she becomes such a boon to the man – it is the Lord who has given her to him. She is an expression of God's favor resting upon him. A man cannot find a good wife and the favor that goes with her by his direct effort, but only as a divine gift. Surely he has a part in it, but not by directing his efforts at finding a wife, but by directing his energies in pleasing the Lord and walking in His ways. When a man is focused upon honoring God, He will, in His good time, care for the matter of granting a good wife. When God grants her to him, let him never stoop to believe he deserves her (or, heaven forbid, that he deserves better!). She is a gift.

The second line is identical to the second line of Proverbs 8:35. There, the favor comes from finding Lady Wisdom, here from finding a godly wife. The first and greatest attribute to look for in a wife is whether or not she possesses wisdom. Godly wisdom and a good wife are the two greatest evidences that a man's life is pleasing to the Lord, and how much better if the two are embodied as one! Indeed, as Kidner points out, both are said to be worth more than jewels (Prov. 8:11 and 31:10).[34]

Proverbs presents marriage as a great good (Prov. 12:4a; 19:14; 31:10-31), but also recognizes the hard realities of a bad marriage (Prov. 11:22; 12:4b; 19:13; 21:19; 25:24; 27:15). Let a man and woman walk with God and choose wisely!

18:23. The poor man utters supplications, But the rich man answers roughly.

This proverb states the ugly realities of life. The point is made by way of contrast. Does this contrast show the difference in how poor and rich answer others generally? Or, is it a contrast of the humble spirit of the poor as he approaches the rich and the rich man's attitude toward the poor man when he does? The answer is not clear, for it makes good sense either way. If the first, the point is that the rich are afforded some social buffer in their relationships that allows them to get away with being surly and unapproachable. If the second meaning is the point, the proverb simply exposes the humility that poverty invokes and the selfish pride riches can engender.

The word 'supplications' comes from a root meaning grace or favor. The root idea is usually that of finding favor in the eyes of another. It pictures weakness in the presence of power, poverty kneeling before wealth. Our particular word is most often used of making supplications to God, but can be used of human to human requests as well.[35] This contrasts with the way the rich answer those who speak to them. Because of presumption and social clout, the rich man 'answers roughly.' The word for 'roughly' figuratively describes that which is unbending, hard, or of haughty disposition.[36] Examples of such a response are plentiful (Gen. 42:30; Exod. 5:2; 1 Sam. 25:10; 1 Kings 12:13; 2 Chron. 10:13).

Proverbs has much to say about the plight of the poor. One's treatment of the poor reveals what he thinks of God (Prov. 14:31). Mocking the poor is mocking God (Prov. 17:5). The rich do well to remember that God made both them and the poor (Prov. 22:2). Likewise, Proverbs warns the rich of the intoxicating power of wealth. In such a state, a man may wrongly assess both his security (Prov. 10:15; 18:11) and his friends (Prov. 14:20).

Several proverbs in the next chapter add to the warning of this one. 'Better is a poor man who walks in his integrity Than he who is perverse in speech and is a fool' (Prov. 19:1). 'Wealth adds many friends, But a poor man is separated from his friend' (Prov. 19:4). 'Many will entreat the favor of a generous man, And every man is a friend to him to gives gifts' (Prov. 19:6). 'All the brothers of a poor man hate him; How much more do his friends go far from him! He pursues them with words, but they are gone' (Prov. 19:7). A careful reading of James 2:1-13 will shed much New Testament light on these verses as well.

18:24. A man of many friends comes to ruin, But there is a friend who sticks closer than a brother.

This antithetical proverb makes clear that one true friend is superior to having a multitude of casual friends. The first line describes the man who has focused on quantity of friends over the quality of their loyalty. He knows everyone. Everyone knows his name. When he enters the room, people slap him on the back and shake his hand. He wrongly assumes by such behavior that these are true friends. These relationships are built on social convenience. The word for 'friend' in the first line is a general one that can describe everything from a close friend to casual acquaintances. It is often descriptive of mere neighbors or associates.[37] Because his relationships lack depth, he eventually 'comes to ruin.' The verb is a play on words – r″eh ('friend') and r~'a' ('comes to ruin').[38] However, the kjv wrongly identifies the root as the same and thus translates as 'A man that hath friends must shew himself friendly.' The verb actually means to break in pieces and describes the ruin that awaits the one who assumes too much of casual acquaintances.[39]

The second line describes the wiser course for friendships: fewer friends (even just one) with whom one builds deeper ties. In times of adversity, such a friend 'sticks closer than a brother' (i.e. than one's own family). 'A friend loves at all times, And a brother is born for adversity' (Prov. 17:17). 'Better is a neighbor who is near than a brother who is far away' (Prov. 27:10b).

However trustworthy an earthly friend may prove, we must realize that relationships will disappoint. The fewer, deeper and more trustworthy the friendships, the more secure one's life. The word for 'friend' in this second line is different from that in the first. It, more literally, means 'one who loves.' It describes a deeper and more solid relationship than the first.[40] David and Jonathan provide an example of this kind of committed friendship (1 Sam. 18:1; 20:42; 2 Sam. 1:26).

Ultimately, however, even the closest of friends may back away when trouble comes. 'All the brothers of a poor man hate him; How much more do his friends go far from him! He pursues them with words, but they are gone' (Prov. 19:7). At such times, only Christ will refuse to abandon us (Matt. 28:18-20; Heb. 13:5-6). Thankfully, Jesus delights to call us not only servants, but His friends (John 15:13-15)! Abraham proved to be 'the friend of God' (2 Chron. 20:7; Isa. 41:8).

End Notes

1. Hess, Richard, 'פרד,' *New International Dictionary of Old Testament Theology and Exegesis* (Grand Rapids, Michigan: Zondervan Publishing House, 1997), 3:673-675.

2. Goldberg, Louis, '*yshh*,' *Theological Wordbook of the Old Testament* (Chicago: Moody Press, 1980), 1:413.

3. Bracke, John M., 'גלע,' *New International Dictionary of Old Testament Theology and Exegesis* (Grand Rapids, Michigan: Zondervan Publishing House, 1997), 1:870.

4. Ross, Allen P., 'Proverbs,' *The Expositor's Bible Commentary* (Grand Rapids, Michigan: Zondervan Publishing House, 1991), 5:1023.

5. Howard, David M., Jr., 'גלה,,' *New International Dictionary of Old Testament Theology and Exegesis* (Grand Rapids, Michigan: Zondervan Publishing House, 1997), 1:861-864.

6. Brown, Francis, S. R. Driver, Charles R. Briggs, *A Hebrew and English Lexicon of the Old Testament* (Oxford: Clarendon Press, n.d.), 162-163 and Kidner, Derek, *Proverbs* (Downers Grove, Illinois: InterVarsity Press, 1964), 127.

7. Murphy, Roland E., *Proverbs* (Nashville: Thomas Nelson Publishers, 1998), 135.

8. McComiskey, Thomas E., '*hārap*,' *Theological Wordbook of the Old Testament* (Chicago: Moody Press, 1980), 1:325-326.

9. Whybray, R. N., *Proverbs* (Grand Rapids, Michigan: William B. Eerdmans Publishing Company, 1994), 266.

10. Buzzell, Sid S., 'Proverbs,' *The Bible Knowledge Commentary* (Wheaton: Victor Books, 1985), 1:944.

11. Ross, 5:1024.

12. Ibid.

13. Murphy, 135.

14. Bowling, Andrew, '*hātat*,' *Theological Wordbook of the Old Testament* (Chicago: Moody Press, 1980), 1:336-337.

15. O'Connell, Robert H., 'להם,' *New International Dictionary of Old Testament Theology and Exegesis* (Grand Rapids, Michigan: Zondervan Publishing House, 1997), 2:766-767.

16. Wakely, Robin, 'רפה,' *New International Dictionary of Old Testament Theology and Exegesis* (Grand Rapids, Michigan: Zondervan Publishing House, 1997), 3:1181-1183.

17. Delitzsch, F., *Proverbs, Ecclesiastes, Song of Solomon* (three volumes in one) in C. F. Keil and F. Delitzsch, vol. 6, *Commentary on the Old Testament* (in ten volumes), (1872; rpt. Grand Rapids, Michigan: William B. Eerdmans Publishing Company, 1980), 2:7.

18. Adams, Jay E., *Proverbs* (Woodruff, South Carolina: Timeless Texts, 1997), 146.

19. Waltke, Bruce K., '*bā'al*,' *Theological Wordbook of the Old Testament* (Chicago: Moody Press, 1980), 1:119-120.

20. Hamilton, Victor P., '*shāhat*,' *Theological Wordbook of the Old Testament* (Chicago: Moody Press, 1980), 2:917-918.

21. Ross, 5:1025.

22. Oswalt, John N., '*kûl*,' *Theological Wordbook of the Old Testament* (Chicago: Moody Press, 1980), 1:432.

23. Whybray, 270.

24. Wolf, Herbert, '*hāqar*,' *Theological Wordbook of the Old Testament* (Chicago: Moody Press, 1980), 1:318.

25. Hamilton, Victor P., '*pārad*,' *Theological Wordbook of the Old Testament* (Chicago: Moody Press, 1980), 2:733.

26. Buzzell, 1:945.

27. Ross, 5:1028.

28. Bridges, Charles, *A Commentary on Proverbs* (Edinburgh: The Banner of Truth Trust, 1846, reprint 1998), 297.

29. Ibid.

30. Kidner, 130.

31. Whybray, 272-273.

32. Delitzsch, 2:14-15.

33. Ross, 5:1029.

34. Kidner, Derek, *Proverbs* (Downers Grove, Illinois: InterVarsity Press, 1964), 130.

35. Fretheim, Terence E., 'חנן,' *New International Dictionary of Old Testament Theology and Exegesis* (Grand Rapids, Michigan: Zondervan Publishing House, 1997), 2:203-204.

36. Delitzsch, 2:16.

37. Harris, R. Laird, 'rā'â,' *Theological Wordbook of the Old Testament* (Chicago: Moody Press, 1980), 2:853.

38. Buzzell, 1:945.

39. Brown, Driver and Briggs, 950.

40. Cohen, 123.

Proverbs 19

19:1. Better is a poor man who walks in his integrity Than he who is perverse in speech and is a fool.
This is another 'Better ... Than' proverb (Prov. 12:9; 15:16, 17; 16:8, 19, 32; 17:1; 19:22; 21:9, 19; 22:1; 25:7, 24; 27:5, 10; 28:6). The first line is repeated in Proverbs 28:6, but there the second line is 'Than he who is crooked though he be rich.' Many commentators and various ancient versions have sought to conform this proverb to that line, feeling it makes for better parallelism with the first line. The evidence is insufficient, however, to conclude that we know better than the ancient writer and the Holy Spirit. The point being made here is related to that in Proverbs 28:6, but is distinct.

The first line assumes that the man has had an opportunity to change his station in life, but because of 'integrity' he has chosen not to do so. The word translated 'integrity' (Prov. 2:7; 10:9, 29; 13:6; 20:7; 28:6; cf. 29:10) describes a whole and complete consecration of one's self to God which results in following God with one's whole heart and never failing to seek God's will in all areas of one's life.[1] It does not describe moral perfection, but the full-orbed and wholehearted submission of one's life to God. Because he has chosen to maintain his integrity in some given situation, it has meant continued or resultant poverty. The word for 'poverty' describes being destitute or hungry, but not poverty that has come about through laziness.[2]

Such a man, and even his condition, is 'Better ... Than' what is presented in the second line. Apparently, some opportunity had presented itself to him and, if only he had been willing to be 'perverse in speech,' he could have avoided poverty or risen above it. The word for 'perverse' describes that which has been twisted from its original or intended design (Prov. 2:15; 6:12; 8:8; 11:20; 22:5; 28:6). The original has not been obliterated, only 'tweaked,' 'twisted' or 'improved.' But, that slight twisting has destroyed its fundamental 'integrity' or 'wholeness,' thus it has become 'perverse' (NIV). A little white lie, an alternate version of the truth, or a half-truth may be easy to justify, but it distorts the truth and destroys integrity. It becomes ever so tempting, however, because of the promise of what can be gained or avoided by its use. In the end, however, they render one 'a fool.' The Hebrew word describes a thick-headed, stubborn fool.

But, he is not stupid. He has refused to listen to wise counsel, to God, and to his own conscience. His eyes saw potential material advantage, his ears closed, and his integrity paid the price.

19:2. Also it is not good for a person to be without knowledge, And he who makes haste with his feet errs.
The 'Also' is left untranslated by some versions (e.g. NIV), but is of significance. It may rather function much the same as the word does in Proverbs 17:26, introducing an argument from the lesser to the greater. If the matter stated in the first line is bad, how much worse that which is stated in the second line.[3] If it is a great tragedy for a person to stand uninformed about God and his circumstances, how much worse that, in zealous haste, he actually act upon such ignorance and end up with the consequences! It does not necessarily link what is said to be 'Better' (v. 1) with what is here 'not good.'[4]

The word translated 'a person' is *nephesh*, normally translated 'soul.' Here, the translators of the NASB have understood it as 'a person,' whereas the translators of the NIV have rendered it 'zeal.' The first is more woodenly literal, but the latter is probably more accurate. In certain contexts, the word can refer to one's 'desire,' 'hunger' or 'appetite' (Prov. 10:3; 13:2, 4, 25; 16:26; 23:2).[5] Here, the idea of eager desire or 'zeal' makes good sense.[6] Zeal without knowledge is not a virtue, rather a quick way toward ruin (Rom. 10:2).

The second line heightens everything that has been said in the first line. As bad as all that may be, how much worse to rush into action and unwittingly sin. The word for 'errs' means 'to miss the mark' and is often descriptive of sin (e.g. Exod. 20:20; Judg. 10:15; Ps. 51:6). Thus, the KJV translates 'he that hasteth with his feet sinneth.' Rather than moral failure, the idea may well be that of blundering past the path that would have led to success – 'may go the wrong way' (NLT), 'miss the way' (NIV), 'misses his way' (RSV).

This blunder may come because of 'haste.' The notion of 'haste' is particularly repugnant in Proverbs (Prov. 21:5; 28:20; 29:20). Overall, the proverb encourages a person to carefully study the facts before making a decision. It is better to restrain enthusiasm and risk delay, than it is to rush and make the wrong decision. In this case, our saying is true, 'Haste makes waste.'[7]

19:3. The foolishness of man subverts his way, And his heart rages against the Lord.
The word translated 'foolishness' is often rendered 'folly.' It is a reference to the outward manifestation of an inward disposition

of foolishness (e.g. Prov. 12:23; 13:16, 14:17, 24, 15:2).[8] It stands in contrast to the 'wisdom,' 'knowledge,' and 'understanding' of God. When one goes his own way rather than the way of submission and obedience to God, he 'subverts his way.' '... [I]n the greatness of his folly he will go astray' (Prov. 5:23). 'There is a way which seems right to a man, But its end is the way of death' (Prov. 14:12; 16:25). The word translated 'subverts' means to distort, twist, pervert or ruin something. Its root is found several times in Proverbs (Prov. 11:3; 13:6; 15:4; 21:12; 22:12). The fool shoots himself in the foot; he destroys his own life by his folly. 'Righteousness guards the one whose way is blameless, But wickedness subverts the sinner' (Prov. 13:6).

While the fool is his own undoing, he would never take personal responsibility for his condition. Rather 'his heart rages against the LORD.' The verb 'rages' means to be vexed, enraged or embittered against someone or something.[9] The noun form of the word is used in verse 12, where it describes anger which is like unto 'the roaring [raging] of a lion.' It is also used in Jonah 1:15 to describe the raging of a storm-tossed sea. Isaiah spoke of those who willfully sought guidance regarding the future from mediums and spirits instead of from God's word and said, 'And they will pass through the land hard-pressed and famished, and it will turn out that when they are hungry, they will be enraged and curse their king and their God as they face upward' (Isa. 8:21). Rather, we should take Jeremiah's counsel: 'Why should any living mortal, or any man, Offer complaint in view of his sins? Let us examine and probe our ways, And let us return to the LORD' (Lam. 3:39-40).

Frustration is found in the way of defensiveness, blame-shifting and finger pointing. The way of success, peace, joy and wholeness is in self-examination, personal responsibility, and repentance.

19:4. Wealth adds many friends, But a poor man is separated from his friend.

This adversative proverb makes a sad observation on the realities of human relationships. The first line describes the magnetic qualities of material wealth – suddenly everyone wants to be your friend! However, a true friend is hard to find. '... [T]hose who love the rich are many' (Prov. 14:20b). The thought of this first line is developed further two verses later: 'Many will entreat the favor of a generous man, And every man is a friend to him who gives gifts' (Prov. 19:6).[10]

If such friendship is based only on what one might gain, then it should come as little surprise that 'a poor man is separated from his friend.' Notice that the poor man has only one 'friend,' while the wealthy man has many 'friends.'[11] 'The poor is hated even by his neighbor' (Prov. 14:20a). The second line may be legitimately translated to understand the friend as separating himself from the poor man (NIV, RSV), or as simply a reporting of the fact that he is separated from his lone 'friend' by his calamity (NASB, KJV, NEB, JB).[12] This second line is developed further by verse 7: 'All the brothers of a poor man hate him; How much more do his friends go far from him! He pursues them with words, but they are gone.'

We would do well to count carefully who are our true friends and who are merely socially convenient acquaintances. Often, the hardships of life will help us sift through appearances to find those answers. We also do well to examine our commitments to those whom we call our 'friends.' Do we love them for who they are or for what they might do for us?

19:5. A false witness will not go unpunished, And he who tells lies will not escape.
Proverbs speaks often to the problem of false witnesses. This emphasis grew out of, and is backed up by, strong words in the law against lying (Exod. 23:1; Deut. 19:16-19). These two lines of synonymous parallelism once again make the point. The Lord hates a false witness; he is abomination to Him (Prov. 6:19). Such a one is deceitful (Prov. 12:17-18), speaking lies (Prov. 14:5). His speech is treacherous, putting innocent lives in jeopardy (Prov. 14:25). Such a one will perish (Prov. 21:28). A false witness might as well club his neighbor, run him through with a sword or shoot him with an arrow (Prov. 25:18).

This verse is almost perfectly repeated in verse 9, the only difference being that 'will not escape' is replaced by 'will perish.' The verb 'tells' in the second line is, more literally, 'breathes out.' A lie is to a liar like his own breath; it is what he is: his very nature. It is as easy for a liar to lie as it is to exhale; he does so without conscious thought. Seven of this word's ten appearances in the Old Testament are found here in Proverbs (Prov. 6:19; 12:17; 14:5, 25; 19:5, 9; 29:8). Most often, the word is associated with breathing out lies (Prov. 6:19; 14:5, 25; 19:9). Only in Proverbs 12:17 is one said to breathe forth truth.[13]

The fact that such a one 'will not go unpunished' and 'will not escape' must be taken as a reference to God's ultimate dealings with them. The false witnesses brought up against Naboth succeeded in the short term (1 Kings 23). But God made certain that Ahab and

Jezebel answered for their treachery (2 Kings 9:21-37). Likewise, the false witnesses brought against Jesus were also successful in the short term (Matt. 26:60). God will, however, find them out in the end. 'But for the cowardly and unbelieving and abominable and murderers and immoral persons and sorcerers and idolaters and all liars, their part will be in the lake that burns with fire and brimstone, which is the second death' (Rev. 21:8).

19:6. Many will entreat the favor of a generous man, And every man is a friend to him who gives gifts.
These two lines are synonymous in parallelism and expand upon the first line of verse 4 – 'Wealth adds many friends.'

The first line refers to 'a generous man.' The word describes one who is noble in character and generous with his things. He is magnanimous and free with that which he possesses.[14] 'Many will entreat the favor' of such a character. The verb means, most literally, 'to stroke the face of.'[15] It refers to insincere flattery and groveling. The niv well translates with 'Many curry favor with.' God encourages discerning and private generosity, but when a man is loose with his money he will accumulate a wealth of insincere 'friends.' Some take this as a reference to a man given to bribery (cf. Prov. 17:8; 18:16), but it appears to target undiscerning gift giving, perhaps subconsciously undertaken as an ego boost. Compare with Proverbs 29:26.

The second line echoes the principle of the first. Here, we should read 'friends' in quotation marks, for people attracted for such reasons seldom understand the depth of commitment involved in true friendship. We do well to remember Proverbs 18:24: 'A man of many friends comes to ruin, But there is a friend who sticks closer than a brother.'

19:7. All the brothers of a poor man hate him; How much more do his friends go far from him! He pursues them with words, but they are gone.
This proverb is unusual, in that it contains three lines. The first and second are roughly synonymous in parallelism. The third is notoriously difficult to translate. Many throw their hands up, declaring it helplessly corrupt. There is no good reason, however, to abandon it. Let's examine the first two lines and then take up the third.

The first line restates what Proverbs has already said – people, even one's own relatives, often stand aloof when poverty strikes you. It is an expansion of verse 4b as the previous proverb was an expansion of verse 4a. The verb 'hate' should not be read with the emotional charge with which the word is used today. It refers rather to a choice of one thing over another (Prov. 11:15; 14:20; 25:17). Given the option, most people would rather avoid the poor and needy.[16] This is tantamount to 'hate' in that, however it is arrived at, it is still a rejection of one who expects more of us.

The second line echoes the first. In the first, it was blood relatives who were in view. However, here, it is one's friends who back away during calamity. This point too has been stressed in Proverbs. 'The poor is hated even by his neighbor' (Prov. 14:20a). Solomon's father David knew the pain of such rejection (Ps. 38:11), as did Job (Job 19:19).

The third line, literally, reads 'He pursues words they are not.' This has yielded a wide variety of possible translations. We must make some insertions in order to yield readable English. The majority of the more literal translations view the friends/family as those who are pursued and yet 'are not,' though they are sought with words. 'Though he pursues them with pleading, they are nowhere to be found' (NIV). 'He may pursue them with words, yet they abandon him' (NKJV). 'When they call after them, they are not there' (NRSV). Some view the 'words' both as that which are pursued and as that which 'are not' (i.e. they can't find the words needed to successfully entreat their friends/family). 'He goes in search of words, but there are none to be had' (JB). Some follow the markedly different translation of the LXX: 'Practice in evil makes the perfect scoundrel; the man who talks too much meets his deserts' (NEB).

Overall, it seems best to allow the context to cast the determining vote. Proverbs 18:23 has already shed some light for us here: 'The poor man utters supplications, But the rich man answers roughly.' This finds the poor man taking words with him as he approaches those around him who might be of help to him in his plight. This should tip the scales in view of seeing the thing he pursues in verse 7c as his friends and family, and that they also are the ones who 'are not,' though he pleads his case with them.

19:8. He who gets wisdom loves his own soul; He who keeps understanding will find good.

These two lines are basically synonymous in their parallelism. 'He who gets wisdom' parallels 'He who keeps understanding' and 'loves his own soul' parallels 'will find good.' The point is that there is legitimate self-benefit that accrues to one who invests himself in wisdom.

The word 'wisdom' in the first line is the Hebrew word for 'heart.' Throughout Proverbs, the word 'heart' has been used metaphorically to refer to 'sense' (Prov. 6:32; 7:7; 11:12; 12:11; 15:21), 'wisdom' (Prov. 8:5), and 'understanding' (Prov. 9:4, 16; 10:13, 21; 15:32). Here, too, it describes not the physical organ of life, nor simply the normal sense of mind, emotions and will. It is, here, a picture of that which ideally fills the heart, controlling the thinking, feeling and choosing of a person.

When a person lays hold of that (or is laid hold of by it), then he 'loves his own soul.' This is a perfectly appropriate and healthy love. This is not sinful introspection or selfishness. This is simple self-preservation. '... [N]o one ever hated his own flesh, but nourishes and cherishes it ...' (Eph. 5:29). So too, here, there is a healthy self-interest that is evidenced not by self-focus, but by a fixed attention on wisdom and understanding. Personal health does not come by focusing on self, but by focusing on God and His wisdom. So true is this that wisdom personified can say, 'For he who finds me finds life, And obtains favor from the LORD. But he who sins against me injures himself; All those who hate me love death' (Prov. 8:35-36).

Similarly, the second line says that such a one 'will find good.' This echoes previous statements (Prov. 16:20; 17:20; 18:22), and points to the benefit derived from pursuing God's understanding.

19:9. A false witness will not go unpunished, And he who tells lies will perish.

This proverb is identical with that in verse 5, except for the final verb. Where verse 5 has 'will not escape,' this proverb has strengthened it to 'will perish.' Deuteronomy 19:18-19 provides justification from the Law: 'And the judges shall investigate thoroughly; and if the witness is a false witness and he has accused his brother falsely, then you shall do to him just as he had intended to do to his brother. Thus you shall purge the evil from among you.' Daniel 6:24a provides an illustration: 'The king then gave orders, and they brought those men who had maliciously accused Daniel, and they cast them, their children, and their wives into the lions' den.'

19:10. Luxury is not fitting for a fool; Much less for a slave to rule over princes.

Some things just ought not to be; this proverb points out two of them. The point of this proverb revolves around the words 'is not fitting' (cf. Prov. 17:7; 26:1). It speaks of the inappropriateness of something. In the first line, it is 'luxury' which 'is not fitting for a fool.' Sudden wealth does not lift a person devoid of wisdom to a level of competence in handling his affairs. Too many people have discovered that winning the lottery has not solved their problems, but only compounded them. Wealth works only to magnify the flaws already present. There is something learned through the hard work of acquisition which is necessary to retaining that wealth and to holding it with honor. Similarly, we discover that 'Excellent speech is not fitting for a fool' (Prov. 17:7a) and 'honor is not fitting for a fool' (Prov. 26:1b).

The second line escalates the sense of social shock through the words 'Much less' ('how much worse,' NIV). The more horrible thing in this second line is 'for a slave to rule over princes.' Suddenly being thrust into power leaves one unequipped to handle the unique pressures and responsibilities inherent in such a position. A 'slave' takes orders, has no need to think for himself, and may not be accustomed to the rigors of strategic planning. The power surge of sudden elevation may make the lowly slave in to an intolerable tyrant. Again, there is something to be learned in the ascent to leadership that is indispensable to faithfully carrying out its responsibilities.

'... [T]he earth quakes ... Under a slave when he becomes king ...' (Prov. 30:21-22a). 'There is an evil I have seen under the sun, like an error which goes forth from the ruler – folly is set in many exalted places while rich men sit in humble places. I have seen slaves riding on horses and princes walking like slaves on the land' (Eccles. 10:5-7; cf. Prov. 12:24; 17:2; 29:2; Isa. 3:4).

19:11. A man's discretion makes him slow to anger, And it is his glory to overlook a transgression.

Again, Proverbs praises the patient man. Here, it is a person's 'discretion' which enables him to have a long fuse. The word describes not only the ability to discern between things, but the insight to know why one is right and the other is wrong.[17] David prayed that his son Solomon might have this quality as he led Israel (1 Chron. 22:12). It is this quality which enables one, in the face of insult or injury, to restrain his anger. Solomon repeatedly underscores the value of putting off anger. 'A quick-tempered man acts foolishly, and a man of evil devices is hated' (Prov. 14:17). 'He who is slow to anger has great understanding, But he who is quick-tempered exalts folly' (Prov. 14:29). 'A hot-tempered man stirs up strife, But the slow to anger pacifies contention' (Prov. 15:18). 'He who is slow to anger is better than the mighty, And he who rules his spirit, than he who captures a city' (Prov. 16:32). 'Do not be eager in your heart to be angry, For anger resides in the bosom of fools' (Eccles. 7:9). The New Testament also underscores this: 'Let everyone be quick to hear, slow to speak and slow to anger; for the anger of man does not achieve the righteousness of God' (James 1:19-20). In contrast, the angry man is held up as a sorry soul (Prov. 19:19; 22:24; 29:22).

Of course, this does not necessarily mean that a man does not get angry. It means, rather, that he conceals that anger well (Prov. 12:16) and responds calmly (Prov. 15:1) until he can process the wrong that has been done to him. This ability to be slow to anger is so valuable because it is a reflection of God's own nature (Exod. 34:6; Num. 14:18; Neh. 9:17; Ps. 86:15; 103:8; 145:8; Joel 2:13; Jonah 4:2; Nahum 1:3).

The overlooking of a wrong is, according to the second line, a man's 'glory.' The word is used to describe the beauty or adornment of something. It can refer to a reputation, name, fame or renown.[18] Retaliation is not the badge to wear. Rather, let us be known for being adorned by the beauty of forbearance and a longsuffering spirit (Eph. 4:32; Col. 3:13). Love covers over another's sin (Prov. 10:12; 17:9), rather than laying it bare (Prov. 29:11).

19:12. The king's wrath is like the roaring of a lion, But his favor is like dew on the grass.

Twice this proverb uses the literary device of simile ('is like') to make a powerful comparison and contrast. The 'king's wrath' is likened unto 'the roaring of a lion.' A lion roars to paralyze its prey just before it strikes. So too, the king's anger may freeze all opposition, rebellion or treason in its tracks. This first line is nearly identical with Proverbs 20:2a, the only change being from 'wrath' to 'terror': 'The terror of a king is like the growling of a lion.' Compare also Proverbs 28:15: 'Like a roaring lion and a rushing bear Is a wicked ruler over a poor people.'

The second simile is the comparison of the king's 'favor' to 'dew on the grass.' The word translated 'favor' describes pleasure, delight, satisfaction or the disposition which shows kindness.[19] Clearly, the proverb is getting at the far extremes to which a monarch's disposition may swing. Unlike the deafening terror of a lion's roar, the dew quietly appears, does its work and, then, disappears, leaving its life-giving result. In the often arid climate of Palestine, the morning dew is essential to the life and growth of vegetation. The morning dews were often the metaphor of choice for describing God's blessings (Gen. 27:28; Deut. 33:28; Ps. 133:3; Hosea 14:5; Mic. 5:7).

An interesting comparison can be made between this proverb and Proverbs 16:14-15. The first line accords with 16:14: 'The wrath of a king is as messengers of death, But a wise man will appease it.' The second line matches up with 16:15: 'In the light of a king's face is life, And his favor is like a cloud with spring rain.'

We should also note this proverb's proximity to verse 11. Some make nothing of their like topics, believing that the proverbs are a jumbled collection of discordant wisdom sayings. Others believe that they are brought together here as a subtle message to the king to learn some forbearance.[20] At minimum, it tells us that, while it is desirable and prudent for any man to learn to control his temper, not just anyone can make such a suggestion to the king!

19:13. A foolish son is destruction to his father, And the contentions of a wife are a constant dripping.

The two lines of this proverb describe the surest way to ruin a home. This, of course, comes from the man's perspective and, no doubt, if things were viewed from the wife's side (or even the child's), other things could be listed as well. Yet, from a male perspective, there are two things that will make home life appear unlivable. The first is dealing with a 'foolish son.' Such a son is 'destruction' to the home, generally, and to the father, in particular. The word means calamity, wickedness or evil desire.[21] Proverbs often recounts the collateral damage a foolish son brings upon his family. There is 'grief' (Prov. 10:1), 'sorrow' and loss of joy (Prov. 17:21), and 'bitterness' (Prov. 17:25).

The second deathblow to a home is 'the contentions of a wife.' Such a woman is mentioned again in Proverbs 21:9, 19; 25:24; 27:15. By 'contentions' may be meant the nagging demands of an unhappy and discontent woman. There is always something wrong. The man feels he can never do anything right. Something is always not to her liking. Faced with constant failure, soon the man quits trying to please her at all. This only inflames her discontent and increases her complaints.

The result is like 'a constant dripping.' Here is pictured a roof full of holes. When rain comes, the home is awash with the incessant dripping of water. What begins as a problem to be fixed soon becomes maddening. There are not enough pots and pans in the house to catch all the dripping (i.e. he can never satisfy her demands)! This, all too soon, become overwhelming and, eventually, becomes a torturously unlivable situation for the man. She, no doubt, fails to understand the destruction she wreaks upon her home and marriage.

Yet, she ends up driving her husband away, at least emotionally, if not physically. This may have been the problem the king's advisor feared in Esther's day (Esther 1:16-18).

19:14. House and wealth are an inheritance from fathers, But a prudent wife is from the LORD.
The adversative at the head of the second line alerts us to an intended contrast between the two lines. That contrast seems to materialize as the first line declares that financial or material inheritance comes to one simply by birthright, while the second line demands that marital bliss can only come as a divine gift. So, the contrast is between what is expected as a matter of legal and social course (2 Cor. 12:14) and what comes surprisingly, as a matter of divine benefaction. The phrase 'from the LORD' is emphatic, being thrust forward in the layout of the second line.[22]

Is more intended by the contrast? Is there an implication here regarding how wives should be sought out? Does this encourage prayer early on for God's gracious gift of a good and godly wife, knowing only He is the source of such blessing? Is this a statement about the limitations of human fatherhood? In a culture where a father might well have found it in his power to bless his son materially, He was ultimately unable to assure marital blessing, even though he probably normally arranged marriage for his children. The father needed God's blessing in order to bless his son with a 'prudent wife'! A son was not simply to trust his father, but to trust God with his father.

The 'prudent wife' is a marked contrast to the wife pictured in verse 13 (cf. Prov. 12:4b). Here she is 'prudent,' a term that describes understanding, wisdom, insight or good sense.[23] She knows what a situation calls for and is able to respond accordingly. She is discerning and her judgment is trustworthy. Such a wife is more than a blessing; she is a gift from God Himself (Prov. 12:4a; 18:22)! For a fuller description of such a wife, read Proverbs 31:10-31.

19:15. Laziness casts into a deep sleep, And an idle man will suffer hunger.
Here, again, Solomon takes up the familiar theme of laziness (Prov. 6:9-11; 10:4; 12:11, 24, 27; 13:4; 14:23; 18:9; 24:30-34; 27:23-27; 28:19). The first line describes the cause, while the second line sets forth the result. 'Laziness' is self-perpetuating. This person doesn't do anything, because he is lazy. Then, that laziness brings on the feeling he 'can't' do anything, which, of course, he doesn't, because he

doesn't feel like it. This choice of laziness further feeds the emotions and he feels even more strongly that he 'can't' do anything. The vicious vortex of sloth gains power with each self-serving decision. The person ends up feeling trapped and powerless.

Such laziness 'casts into a deep sleep.' This verb points indisputably to the source of the problem: the benumbed stupor which begins with a personal decision not to work. What comes from this choice is 'a deep sleep.' The feminine noun occurs seven times in the Old Testament. The other six times all present this 'deep sleep' as something brought upon a person by the Lord. God brought it upon Adam (Gen. 2:21), Abram (Gen. 15:12), Saul and his army (1 Sam. 26:12), and the people of Judah (Isa. 29:10). It seems also, though not quite as clearly, that in Job 4:13 and 33:15 the Lord was at least indirectly the source of such 'deep sleep.'[24] It seems always to be a divinely induced insensitivity to surrounding conditions, so that a God-ordained purpose can be achieved. Only here does a source other than the Lord bring this deep stupor upon a person – the lazy man himself. The cognate noun is used in Proverbs 10:5 to describe the ill-timed sleep of the shameless son.[25] Here, as there, the only result is self-destructive. 'Do not love sleep, lest you become poor' (Prov. 20:13a).

The second line reinforces the first and presents the result of such sloth. Here, the person is called 'an idle man.' The word for 'idle' is used three other times in Proverbs (Prov. 10:4; 12:24, 27). It describes that which is slack, loose, deceitful or slothful.[26] It does not necessarily describe total inactivity, but rather one who does only half-hearted work. He has a poor work ethic. He does not care about the quality of his work. His heart is somewhere else. Such a man 'will suffer hunger.'

19:16. He who keeps the commandment keeps his soul, But he who is careless of his ways will die.

By means of antithetical parallelism, this proverb underscores the life and death proposition of obedience. The expression 'keeps the commandment' is in contrast to 'is careless of his ways' and 'keeps his soul' is the opposite of 'will die.'

The first line's 'the commandment' may point either to the ordinances of the Law or the instruction of Solomon (Prov. 13:13). To choose one over the other, however, is probably unnecessary. The wisdom teachings of Solomon are largely the practical outworkings of the divine Law.[27] Certainly, from our perspective, both are divinely inspired and in harmony.

The NASB has wisely translated 'keeps' twice in the first line, for the Hebrew has the same word in both places (contrast NIV). The root idea is 'to pay careful attention to' and, often, yields a translation of 'watch,' 'guard,' or 'keep.'[28] God's word and my welfare are intimately intertwined (Prov. 10:17; 19:8). To keep God's word is to keep one's own soul. To guard your life the best thing you can do is to guard your obedience to God's revealed will (Prov. 16:17).

In contrast is 'he who is careless of his ways.' The verb describes someone who seriously undervalues something, in this case the nature and consequences of 'his ways' (i.e. the way he conducts himself). The contrast here between 'careless' and 'keeps' reveals that such a person treats the matter of conforming his ways to God's word with contempt and irreverence.[29] Such a man unwittingly jeopardizes his own well-being, for he 'will die.' Certainly, short of the return of Christ, all die, but the idea here is that he will die prematurely or in a way, either directly or indirectly, related to his want of conformity to God's ways (Prov. 1:32; 6:32; 10:8, 10, 14, 29; 15:10).

19:17. He who is gracious to a poor man lends to the LORD, And He will repay him for his good deed.
Proverbs repeatedly encourages generosity toward the poor (Prov. 14:21, 31; 22:9; 28:27) and rails against insensitivity to their needs (Prov. 14:31a; 21:13; 22:16; 28:3, 27b). In this way, the wisdom of this book reflects the dictates of the Law (Deut. 15:7-8). The remarkable thing found in this proverb is the direct link made between the 'poor man' and 'the LORD.' Jesus made a similar connection, 'Truly I say to you, to the extent that you did it to one of these brothers of Mine, even the least of them, you did it to Me' (Matt. 25:40). The reverse is also true: that contempt for the poor is contempt for the Lord (Prov. 14:31a; 17:5).

This bit of wisdom seems to demand that what one does 'to a poor man' one is doing to 'the LORD.' But, closer examination reveals that the action is not exactly the same to one as the other. One is viewed as being 'gracious' to the poor (i.e. giving them a gift). The same action is viewed as 'lending' to the Lord. What is a gift to the one (knowing that they cannot repay and to demand such would be cruel), is a loan to the other (knowing He is the guardian of the poor and surety for all their needs).

The second line develops the notion of the Lord's reward to those who are thus generous with the poor. The promise is that 'He will repay him for his good deed.' The promise is not necessarily direct monetary or material benefit. The promise is that God rewards righteousness. Throughout Proverbs, generosity is viewed as an indispensable part of, and a nearly infallible evidence of, a righteous life. However, having noted this, Proverbs does often view the rewards of righteousness from a tangible, physical perspective (Prov. 11:24-26; 12:14). Again, Jesus spoke in such terms: 'Give, and it will be given to you; good measure, pressed down, shaken together, running over, they will pour into your lap. For by your standard of measure it will be measured to you in return' (Luke 6:38; cf. Matt. 19:27-30). The promise in both testaments is that God rewards the generous (Matt. 10:42; 2 Cor. 9:6-8; Heb. 6:10), therefore, the wise and righteous person gives freely as he becomes aware of needs.

19:18. Discipline your son while there is hope, And do not desire his death.
This proverb is a word of encouragement and exhortation to parents weary in their duties. The parallelism is synthetic. The first line encourages perseverance in discipline (Prov. 13:24; 22:6, 15; 23:13-14; 29:15, 17). The word translated 'Discipline' refers to correction of some kind that is aimed at educating the individual toward a better course. Its motive is always that of love and becomes one unfailing evidence of sonship (Prov. 3:11-12). It is never merely punitive, but instructional. The goal is not merely to mold ethical behavior, but to capture the heart for the Lord (Prov. 1:7). Proverbs does speak of corporal punishment (Prov. 22:15) as a legitimate form of discipline, but even more frequently of oral instruction.[30] Both must be wed together for effective discipline to take place.

The encouragement of the first line is to do this 'while there is hope.' Is this the correct translation, or is the NIV better ('for in that there is hope')? The former suggests that a child may arrive at a time and point beyond which parental discipline is no longer effective in reforming them for God, family and society. Certainly, no one is beyond the grace of God, but some seem to go beyond the normal means God has established for raising wise, mature adults. The later translation (NIV) suggests rather that a child never is beyond the hope of reformation, if parents will just everlastingly keep at discipline. Emotionally, we would prefer this translation.

The conjunction thus translated 'while' (NASB) or 'for in that' (NIV) has a broad range of possible translations including the causal (NIV) and the temporal (NASB).[31] Most translations and paraphrases seem to side with the NASB (KJV, NKJV, RSV, NRSV, Amplified, NEB, JB, NLT, Living, TEV). Interestingly enough, however, the ASV translates as the NIV does.

It is probably best to adopt the NASB translation with the understanding that a parent should never give up hope. No one is beyond God's reach. Parents may come to the end of their rope and the seeming end of their God-given resources in discipline, but God's ability to reach a child is never impaired. The encouragement is to keep disciplining their child, for, if they give up, what other hope do they have? Never write off a child as hopeless!

The second line, then, advances the thought of the first: 'do not desire his death.' This could mean either: (1) they should beware not to so severely discipline the child that he might die, (2) they should not throw up their hands and give up, leaving him to the 'death' so often spoken of as the end of the fool (Prov. 2:18; 5:5; 7:27; 8:36; 10:2; 11:4, 19; etc.), or (3) they should not wish for the capital punishment held out as a last resort by the Law for wicked sons (Deut. 21:18-21).

It is unlikely that this is an exhortation to avoid beating your child to death (option #1). Likewise, it is improbable that it looks to the extreme of capital punishment (option #3). The idea most parallel with line one is a warning against giving up on a child and abandoning him to folly and the inevitable death it will bring. This death may be viewed either as the calamitous outcome of dangerous living or of the slower outworking of the ultimate ends of foolishness that issues in death physically and spiritually. David refused to discipline Adonijah, and look what happened (1 Kings 1:5-6)!

The second line, literally, reads 'and on making him die do not set your soul.' To 'set your soul' is to 'direct one's desire toward' or 'long for' something.[32] Don't make it your ambition to free yourself of the draining and difficult work of parenthood by giving up on your child and abandoning him to his natural desires!

19:19. A man of great anger shall bear the penalty, For if you rescue him, you will only have to do it again.
This proverb is notorious for its translational difficulties, but the general sense is clear. The second line gives the reason for the stance taken in the first.

Proverbs warns often of the angry man. The angry man arrogantly blunders through life (Prov. 14:16-17, 29), stirring up trouble in his relationships (Prov. 15:18). Such a one is never far from sin (Prov. 29:22). For this reason, we are exhorted to stand away from a man of habitual anger (Prov. 22:24).

The point of line one is that a man given to such 'great anger' will have to stand alone when the consequence of his anger begin to blossom. He alone will pay the price. That is not to say that others will not experience difficult and often painful consequences as collateral damage. The point is explained in the second line. We are warned to count the cost before we bail out a man notorious for his anger, because 'you will only have to do it again.'

We only really help people when we assist them in dealing with the underlying source of their troubles.[33] Merely posting bail at the police station for an angry man does not truly help him. He must come to deal with his anger. If, over time, he resolutely refuses to do so, he should be left to his folly. Some people are quite skilled at manipulating such temporary 'help' from their friends, even while refusing their counsel regarding their fundamental problems. All such 'cosmetic' help only wastes our resources, enables the angry man to continue unchanged and opens us up to great pain. This is not a prohibition of all such practical help, but only a warning of the ultimate limited nature of its assistance.

19:20. Listen to counsel and accept discipline, That you may be wise the rest of your days.
In this proverb, we hear an echo of the first nine chapters and the father's instruction of his son. The two lines here work together as one, the latter giving the goal of the former.

The goal is wisdom. The means are 'counsel' and 'discipline.' The word for 'counsel' is found again in the next verse ('the counsel of the LORD'), tying the two together. The word can describe the rebellious plots of evil men against the Lord (Ps. 33:10). It can also describe good and wise counsel from other people, as here. Of course, as the next verse points out, only the counsel of the Lord will stand (Ps. 33:11). This proverb points out that one divinely granted way of coming to share His counsel is to listen with discernment to others. When we do not, we often do so to our own hurt (e.g. Absalom, 2 Sam. 17; Rehoboam, 1 Kings 12:8, 13).[34] We are to look and listen for the relative counsel of man that is in line with, and will steer us into, the unalterable counsel of God.

The other means toward wisdom is 'discipline.' The word describes learning through both exhortation and example. Such exhortations warn of the painful outcome of failing to heed the instruction: there will be a price to be paid for failure to listen and obey.[35]

The way we may enter into these means is to 'Listen to' and 'accept' them. The call to 'Hear, my son' echoed through the first nine chapters (e.g. Prov. 1:8; 4:10) and continues on in the second half of the book (Prov. 23:19, 22). We must be humble enough to not only hear good counsel when it comes, but to tune our ears to actively seek it out (cf. Prov. 12:15, where the same expression is used). The root idea of the word translated 'accept' means to receive something given.[36] There are two essential parts to a gift exchange. One is that the gift must be extended; the second is that the recipient must extend his arms and embrace it. Here, we are told that wisdom comes through the willingness to humbly extend our arms and embrace as a gift the correction that comes through discipline (Prov. 2:1-4; 4:10; 10:8).

What this stance toward life will gain you is that you will be 'wise the rest of your days.' Literally, the second line reads 'that you may be wise in your latter end.' Proverbs speaks in stark terms of the end of the fool (Prov. 5:4; 14:12; 16:25). Here, the expression likely does not mean simply the last moment of life or the culminating end of all one's life, but rather 'the rest of one's life' or 'one's future.'[37] The hope held forth is not that, at some fleeting moment at the end of life, you may be found wise, but that you may spend whatever days are ahead of you in wisdom.

19:21. Many are the plans in a man's heart, But the counsel of the Lord, it will stand.

This note of God's sovereignty rings in harmony with that sounded in Proverbs 19:1, 9. It connects with its immediate context by sharing the word 'counsel' with the previous verse. The two lines of the proverb are arranged in an antithetical parallelism. The contrast is between the diversity and instability of man's plots and the singularity and certainty of God's plan.

The first line casts emphasis on the multitude and variety of a man's plans – the word translated 'Many,' in Hebrew, as in English, is first in the word order. Proverbs 16:1, 9 reminded us that, being made in the image of God, we are able to think, reason and plot a course of action. Here the word translated 'plans' has, in its root, three strands of meaning: thought (Gen. 6:5), plan (Jer. 18:12) and invention (2 Chron. 2:14).[38] A man is driven by a sometimes unpredictable variety of thought processes, able to come up with a multitude of various plans and to creatively devise all manner of goals. This variety is in contrast to the singular 'counsel' of God.

The second line reminds us that, no matter how well thought out, how creatively devised or meticulously planned, unless a man's plans match with God's, they will not stand (Isa. 8:10). Like Isaiah, Solomon here sounds a reverberating tone for the absolute sovereignty of God (Isa. 14:24, 26-27; 31:2; 40:8; 46:10). 'The Lord nullifies the counsel of the nations; He frustrates the plans of the peoples. The counsel of the Lord stands forever, The plans of His heart from generation to generation' (Ps. 33:10-11; cf. Dan. 4:35). God 'works all things after the counsel of His will' (Eph. 1:11) and desired to show us 'the unchangeableness of His purpose' (Heb. 6:17).

Think of how Joseph's brothers considered his view of the future: 'And they said to one another, "Here comes this dreamer! Now then, come and let us kill him and throw him into one of the pits; and we will say, 'A wild beast devoured him.' Then let us see what will become of his dreams!"' (Gen. 37:19-20). In the end, however, Joseph said to them, 'And as for you, you meant evil against me, but God meant it for good in order to bring about this present result, to preserve many people alive' (Gen. 50:20).

The repetition of the word 'counsel' from the previous verse reveals that it can be used to describe the limited and relative 'counsel' of others and yet also the absolute 'counsel' (purpose) of God. It reminds us that we should seek out the wise counsel of others (v. 20), but, in so doing, we must recognize that it is only God's counsel that will stand in the end. We must, therefore, weigh and measure all earthly counsel according to the revealed purposes of God found in His written word.

19:22. What is desirable in a man is his kindness, And it is better to be a poor man than a liar.

This verse has been the subject of all manner of translational contortions in an attempt to make the two lines conform to one another. Rare meanings have been suggested for the words here translated 'desirable' ('lust,' 'greed') and 'kindness' ('shame'), but have proven themselves unnecessary.

The first line points to either what others desire in a man with whom they associate (nasb) or what that man desires for himself (niv). The nasb takes this as an objective genitive (the quality is what others desire in him). This seems a fair translation.

That which people long to find true in those they associate with is 'kindness.' This translates the rich Hebrew word *ḥesed*. The term is descriptive of covenant love and faithfulness. It is a mercy, kindness, love and compassion that flows from an unalterable commitment made to another. It is not hard to see why this is a quality desirable in those with whom one builds relationships. Ultimately, this is God's kind of love for those who trust Him.

This provides a suitable starting point from which to understand the second line, for here we meet 'a liar.' The term describes a person who perjures himself (e.g. Prov. 6:19; 14:5, 25; 19:9; 21:28).[39] In this instance, what it appears the man lies about it his inability to materially help those who are closest to him. He has the means to come to their aid, but deceitfully poses as unable to be of assistance. This not only provides a clear parallel to the first line, but such a contrast between covenant love and selfish lying is found in the New Testament: 'But whoever has the world's goods, and beholds his brother in need and closes his heart against him, how does the love of God abide in him?' (1 John 3:17).

For this reason, 'it is better to be a poor man' (i.e. to actually share the fate of the impoverished one before you) and be unable to help, than it is to be flush with money and bound by falsehood and selfish deceit. 'Better is a poor man who walks in his integrity Than he who is perverse in speech and is a fool' (Prov. 19:1). 'Many a man proclaims his own loyalty, But who can find a trustworthy man?' (Prov. 20:6).

19:23. The fear of the LORD leads to life, So that one may sleep satisfied, untouched by evil.
With the mention of the 'fear of the LORD,' the main theme of the book of Proverbs is reintroduced (Prov. 1:7; 9:10; 31:30). The first line lacks a verb; 'leads' has been supplied by the translators. This interpretation, however, is well founded, for what we have is very close to Proverbs 14:27a: 'The fear of the LORD is a fountain of life' (cf. Prov. 10:27; 22:4). But, perhaps there is an even better alternative to providing a verb. Walter C. Kaiser sees an emphatic emphasis and suggests the translation: 'The fear of the LORD is life indeed.'[40] The verb 'is' is still provided, but this may make better sense of the somewhat abrupt wording of the first line. This makes 'life' not so much a thing that is added to the fear of the Lord as a residual benefit, but that the fear of the Lord is the essence of what life itself is divinely designed to be.

By 'life' is meant all that God intended this life to be as well as the promise of life after death. It is a frequent promise in these proverbs (e.g. Prov. 10:11; 11:19; 12:28; 14:27; 22:4). The New Testament makes a similar promise to those who pursue godliness (1 Tim. 4:8).

The second line is in synthetic parallelism – taking the thought of the first line and explaining it more specifically. Two things are listed to expand upon the meaning of what 'life' means. The first is that 'one may sleep satisfied.' The word for 'sleep' is more literally 'lodge.' It refers to men finding lodging in some place for the night.[41] Thus, the word does, by extension, refer to sleep, but is somewhat broader in its meaning. The same word is found again in Psalm 25:13. The preceding verse begins, 'Who is the man who fears the Lord? ... His soul will abide [same word] in prosperity ...' (Ps. 25:12a, 13a). It is also found in the majestic promise of Psalm 91:1: 'He who dwells in the shelter of the Most High Will abide [same word] in the shadow of the Almighty.' 'When you lie down, you will not be afraid; When you lie down, your sleep will be sweet' (Prov. 3:24; cf. Ps. 3:3, 5; 4:8).

The second promise made to the man who fears the Lord is that he will be 'untouched by evil.' The man who fears the Lord will have the Lord for his constant guard and shield. Again, this promise is a familiar echo from other proverbs (Prov. 12:21; 14:26; 18:10). Even Psalm 91 is echoed again: 'No evil will befall you, Nor will any plague come near your tent' (v. 10). This safety comes because of the immediate intervention of the Lord, but also because the orientation to life that the fear of the Lord brings changes the way we make choices. Indeed, 'by the fear of the Lord one keeps away from evil' (Prov. 16:6). Thus, those who walk in the fear of the Lord do not put themselves in dangerous situations by poor choices.

19:24. The sluggard buries his hand in the dish, And will not even bring it back to his mouth.

This proverb makes its point by poking fun at the sloth of the lazy man. The 'sluggard' is a lazy slug who never seems to find the energy to overcome his inertia. He is spoken often of in these proverbs (Prov. 6:6, 9; 10:26; 13:4; 15:19; 20:4; 21:25; 22:13; 24:30; 26:13-16). The proverb we have here is virtually repeated in Proverbs 26:15.

The first line pictures the sluggard, motivated by his hunger, mustering all his strength to lift his hand and put it in the dish of food that has been prepared and placed before him. However, as the second line reveals, once he has exerted himself to get his hand into the food, he can't marshal enough strength to draw it back to his mouth!

Perhaps the choice of the word 'buries' is another intentional part of the fun.[42] The word, basically, means to hide something by burying it (Gen. 35:4; Exod. 2:12; Josh. 7:21; Jer. 13:4-7; 43:9).[43] Is this a comical picture of the lazy man's best efforts only serving to further bury himself in the mire of that which he just 'can't' do?

19:25. Strike a scoffer and the naïve may become shrewd, But reprove one who has understanding and he will gain knowledge.
This antithetical proverb encapsulates the Proverb's basic theory
of learning and discipline. Three classes of people are addressed.
The 'scoffer' despises being amended in his actions or thinking
(Prov. 9:7, 8; 13:1; 15:12). His independence makes movement
toward wisdom impossible (Prov. 14:6). The scoffer has long since
left his naïveté behind, but is confirmed in his reviling of all authority
(Prov. 21:24; 22:10; 29:8). The sad verdict awaiting the scoffer is that
the God whom he has scoffed will, in the end, stand and scoff over
his misfortune (Prov. 3:34).[44]

The second group are 'the naïve.' They are gullible and silly
(Prov. 14:15; 22:3). They love to exercise their willfulness and act
irresponsibly (Prov. 1:32). They tend to be thoughtless toward others.
Indeed, their folly is a source of pleasure to them (Prov. 15:21). They
waste their life chasing after what does not matter.

We all begin in this naïveté of the simple. Left undirected and
unrestrained, the power of folly's vortex begins the downward tug
of rebellion that will destroy our lives (Prov. 22:3). The 'naïve,' while
on dangerous ground, are still reachable and able to be rescued
from their folly.[45]

The third group is described as 'the one who has understanding.'
Such a person is able to look at circumstances with insight,
discerning the difference between competing statements, claims,
offers and actions. They have learned through training to see life
with different eyes than either the 'scoffer' or the 'naïve.' The 'one
who has understanding' possesses a clearer view of reality.

What does it take for each of these folk to learn? The 'scoffer' is
beyond learning (Prov. 9:8; 13:1; 15:12; 17:10; 21:11). Yet, he must be
disciplined anyway. The reason is found not in the hope that he will
respond, but that others around him will (Deut. 13:10-11; 1 Tim. 5:20).
When the 'naïve' see the 'Strike' (Prov. 14:3; 19:29) that a 'scoffer'
draws for his attitudes and actions, they 'may become shrewd.' The
'naïve' are capable of learning from someone else's mistakes.

There is, however, an even higher and more desirable level of
learning. The 'one who has understanding' learns wisdom by a
simple word of reproof. One word, the tone of voice, the expression
of another's face – all these are the hair trigger that sets in motion
his ability to 'gain knowledge.' 'Reprove a wise man, and he will
love you' (Prov. 9:8b). 'A rebuke goes deeper into one who has
understanding Than a hundred blows into a fool' (Prov. 17:10).

See Proverbs 21:11 for a virtual repeat of this proverb.

19:26. He who assaults his father and drives his mother away Is a shameful and disgraceful son.

Proverbs makes much of the proper relationship between children and parents (Prov. 10:1; 15:20; 17:21, 25; 23:22, 24, 25; 28:24). The Law set forth the necessity of proper honor by children to parents (Exod. 20:12; Deut. 5:16), holding forth the severest of penalties for violators (Exod. 21:15, 17). Here, a serious distortion of that ideal is considered.

The verbs in the first line give us the gist of the son's shameful actions. The word 'assaults,' in the form in which it is found, describes maltreatment, assault, or destruction. It is found again only in Proverbs 24:15.[46] The word 'drives ... away' is most often used to describe a frenzied flight from an enemy.[47] Thus, the proverb is pointing to a family relationship that has deteriorated to the place where the son is not above even physically assaulting or robbing his parents (Prov. 28:24; 30:11; Judg. 17:1-2). He is not above driving them, who once nurtured him, away from the home and land they worked years to acquire. In this litigatious society, we must not limit the application only to physical assault, for a legal assault in the courts amounts to the same thing. God would come to view the people of Israel as just such children to Him (Isa. 1:2).

Such a child is 'a shameful and disgraceful son.' The same word here translated 'disgraceful' is found again in Proverbs 13:5 where it describes 'a wicked man.' Oh, the heartbreak such a son brings to his parents (Prov. 10:5; 17:2; 19:13)! God promises that his life will be snuffed out in a painful and difficult way (Prov. 20:20).

19:27. Cease listening, my son, to discipline, And you will stray from the words of knowledge.

This proverb has presented a challenge to translators because of its form. The verse opens with an imperative: 'Cease listening.' Following such a form, one would expect something like 'Cease listening to folly.' But, instead, there is 'Cease listening ... to discipline.' The word for 'discipline' is always used in a positive sense in Proverbs.[48] Thus, the verse, taken at face value, seems contradictory to everything Solomon has said to this point. It would certainly be contradictory to the immediate context of the chapter (Prov. 19:20). The command to 'listen' or to 'hear' is found often in Proverbs (Prov. 1:8; 4:1, 10; 5:7; 7:24; 8:6, 32), always in a positive sense.

The vocative 'my son(s)' sounds like the instruction of chapters 1–9, where the expression is found some seventeen times (Prov. 1:8, 10, 15; 2:1; 3:1, 11, 21; 4:10, 20; 5:1, 7, 20; 6:1, 3, 20; 7:1, 24). It is found only here in Proverbs 10:1-22:16 and nowhere else between 7:1 and 23:15 (cf. Prov 23:15, 19, 26; 24:13, 21; 27:11; 31:2).[49]

Many find the key to understanding the proverb in reading it as a biting irony. In this sense the command is not to be taken seriously, but as tongue-in-cheek. The gist would then be: 'Go ahead, quit listening to what your father has to say! But, you'll end up straying from the words of knowledge, if you do.' The trouble is that no such irony is used anywhere else in Proverbs, and to expect a person to read it thus here is asking a great deal.[50]

The point is best understood, if we read the first line as a straightforward command: 'Cease listening, my son, to discipline.' As such it is a shock which makes one want to read on to discover how the father who has been so intent on selling his son on wisdom could say such a thing now. The second line then gives the answer – 'only to stray from the words of knowledge.' In other words, 'Stop sitting there, listening to godly instruction, only to turn around and do whatever it is you feel like doing!'[51]

Was this not the same point James sought to make (James 1:22-24; 4:17)? Luke and John both seemed intent on recording Jesus' mind on this (Luke 6:46-48; 10:12-15; 11:28; 12:47; John 13:17). Peter made the same point (2 Pet. 2:21), as did his disciple Mark (Mark 7:6-14).

Instead of being a command to discontinue listening to sound 'discipline,' the verse is an exhortation to stop hypocritically listening to it and then flaunting it, to go one's own way. The implication, of course, is that it is far better to listen to discipline and obey its instruction, as Proverbs has been so vigorous to prove (Prov. 22:17).

19:28. A rascally witness makes a mockery of justice, And the mouth of the wicked spreads iniquity.

This proverb again, like so many others, decries a false witness (Prov. 6:19; 12:17-18; 14:5, 25; 19:5, 9; 21:28; 24:28; 25:18). The phrase 'A rascally witness' is, literally, 'a witness of Belial.' The similar expression is found in Proverbs 6:12. The word 'rascally' is the Hebrew word belial, and describes a man who is actively wicked. The derivation of the word is not certain. But, it may come from a word meaning 'a place from which none arises,' a euphemism for Sheol. The word is used twenty-seven times in the Old Testament and describes a person who has become so wicked and perverse that he is a liability to the community. Such a person tries to turn people from God (Deut. 13:14), is sexually deviant (Judg. 19:22; 20:13; 1 Sam. 2:12), destructive in relationships (Deut. 15:19; 1 Sam. 30:22), rebellious toward authority (2 Sam. 20:1; 2 Chron. 13:7), and, as here, destructive with his lies (1 Kings 21:10).[52] Eventually, 'Belial' became a name for the embodiment of all wickedness, Satan himself (2 Cor. 6:15).

Such a person makes 'a mockery of justice.' The entire notion is illustrated in 1 Kings 21:10, where the same word is used to describe the two lying witnesses produced to destroy Naboth and give his vineyard to Ahab.

The second line is every bit as vivid as the first. The word 'spreads' is, literally, 'swallows.' The wicked man drinks down sin like a drunk after his drink. A deceitful witness gobbles down iniquity like a glutton devours the tidbits set before him (cf. Job 15:16; 20:12, 13; 34:7). Lying is a delicacy to the wicked. It is sport. It is pleasurable. In some twisted way, it satisfies, though momentarily, a sick hunger within. They 'swallow' their own lies, and, somehow, find satisfaction in doing so.

How sad, for '... [M]an does not live by bread alone, but man lives by everything that proceeds out of the mouth of the Lord' (Deut. 8:3; cf. Matt. 4:4).

19:29. Judgments are prepared for scoffers, And blows for the back of fools.

There is no escaping responsibility for the kind of person we become. The first line refers to the impending fate of 'scoffers.' Such folk are the hardened, arrogant mockers who revile God (Prov. 1:22; 3:34) and all authorities (Prov. 19:28, same root). 'Judgments are prepared' for them. The word 'Judgments' is always and only used of the punishments of God, even though they may at times be inflicted by human agents.[53] Such punishments are not for educational purposes, for the scoffer is beyond reform. Others may learn from the punishment of a scoffer, but not him (Prov. 19:25).

The second line considers 'fools.' They are not, in the wider teaching of Proverbs, as far gone as the scoffers, yet are far from being considered educable. It is 'blows' which await them (Deut. 25:2-3; Prov. 10:13; 14:3; 17:10; 18:6; 26:3). These are the physical disciplines inflicted by those charged with correcting and educating the wayward.

Thus, these two lines, while standing in synonymous parallelism, hold forth the certainty of divine judgments (Prov. 1:23-33), on the one hand, and the necessity of human discipline, on the other.[54] Folly is not only unwise, it is the path of pain and self-destruction. The confirmed fool will find no escape from discipline and punishment.

End Notes

1. Delitzsch, F., *Proverbs, Ecclesiastes, Song of Solomon* (three volumes in one) in C. F. Keil and F. Delitzsch, vol. 6, *Commentary on the Old Testament* (in ten volumes), (1872; rpt. Grand Rapids, Michigan: William B. Eerdmans Publishing Company, 1980), 2:78.

2. Buzzell, Sid S., 'Proverbs,' *The Bible Knowledge Commentary* (Wheaton: Victor Books, 1985), 1:945.

3. Cohen, A., *Proverbs* (London: The Soncino Press, 1946), 117, 124.

4. Kidner, Derek, *Proverbs* (Downers Grove, Illinois: InterVarsity Press, 1964), 131-132.

5. Fredericks, D. C., 'נֶפֶשׁ,' *New International Dictionary of Old Testament Theology and Exegesis* (Grand Rapids, Michigan: Zondervan Publishing House, 1997), 3:133.

6. Ross, Allen P., 'Proverbs' in *The Expositor's Bible Commentary* (Grand Rapids, Michigan: Zondervan Publishing House, 1991), 5:1030.

7. Buzzell, 1:945.

8. Goldberg, Louis, "*wl*,' *Theological Wordbook of the Old Testament* (Chicago: Moody Press, 1980), 1:19-20.

9. Butterworth, Mike, 'זֶעֶף,' *New International Dictionary of Old Testament Theology and Exegesis* (Grand Rapids, Michigan: Zondervan Publishing House, 1997), 1:1129-1130.

10. Buzzell, 1:946.

11. Cohen, 124.

12. Murphy, Roland E., *Proverbs* (Nashville: Thomas Nelson Publishers, 1998), 141.

13. Hamilton, Victor P., '*pûah*,' *Theological Wordbook of the Old Testament* (Chicago: Moody Press, 1980), 2:718-719.

14. Carpenter, Eugene and Michael A. Grisanti, 'נדב,' *New International Dictionary of Old Testament Theology and Exegesis* (Grand Rapids, Michigan: Zondervan Publishing House, 1997), 3:31-32.

15. Buzzell, 1:946.

16. Murphy, 143.

17. Goldberg, Louis, '*śākal*,' *Theological Wordbook of the Old Testament* (Chicago: Moody Press, 1980), 2:877.

18. Collins, C. John, 'כאר,' *New International Dictionary of Old Testament Theology and Exegesis* (Grand Rapids, Michigan: Zondervan Publishing House, 1997), 3:572-574.

19. Delitzsch, 2:27.

20. Whybray, 279.

21. Payne, J. Barton, '*hāwâ*,' *Theological Wordbook of the Old Testament* (Chicago: Moody Press, 1980), 1:209-210.

22. Kidner, 133.

23. Wolf, Herbert, '*śākal*,' *Theological Wordbook of the Old Testament* (Chicago: Moody Press, 1980), 2:877.

24. White, William, '*rādam*,' *Theological Wordbook of the Old Testament* (Chicago: Moody Press, 1980), 2:833-834.

25. Whybray, 281.

26. White, William, '*rāmâ*,' *Theological Wordbook of the Old Testament* (Chicago: Moody Press, 1980), 2:849.

27. MacArthur, John, *The MacArthur Study Bible* (Nashville: Word Publishing, 1997), 903.

28. Schoville, Keith N. 'שמר,' *New International Dictionary of Old Testament Theology and Exegesis* (Grand Rapids, Michigan: Zondervan Publishing House, 1997), 4:182-184.

29. Grisanti, Michael A., 'בזה,' *New International Dictionary of Old Testament Theology and Exegesis* (Grand Rapids, Michigan: Zondervan Publishing House, 1997), 1:628-630.

30. Gilchrist, Paul R., 'yāsar,' *Theological Wordbook of the Old Testament* (Chicago: Moody Press, 1980), 1:386-387.

31. Williams, Ronald J., *Hebrew Syntax: An Outline* (Toronto: University of Toronto Press, 1976), 72-73.

32. Hamilton, Victor, 'נשׂא,,' *New International Dictionary of Old Testament Theology and Exegesis* (Grand Rapids, Michigan: Zondervan Publishing House, 1997), 3:161.

33. Adams, Jay E., *Proverbs* (Woodruff, South Carolina: Timeless Texts, 1997), 154-155.

34. Gilchrist, Paul R., 'yāʿas,' *Theological Wordbook of the Old Testament* (Chicago: Moody Press, 1980), 1:390-391.

35. Merrill, E. H., 'יסר,' *New International Dictionary of Old Testament Theology and Exegesis* (Grand Rapids, Michigan: Zondervan Publishing House, 1997), 2:479-482.

36. Coppes, Leonard J., 'qābal,' *Theological Wordbook of the Old Testament* (Chicago: Moody Press, 1980), 2:783.

37. Cohen, 128.

38. Wood, Leon J., 'hāshab,' *Theological Wordbook of the Old Testament* (Chicago: Moody Press, 1980), 1:329-330.

39. Whybray, 284.

40. Kaiser, Walter C., 'lûn,' *Theological Wordbook of the Old Testament* (Chicago: Moody Press, 1980), 1:474-475.

41. Ibid.

42. Ross, 5:1037.

43. Hill, Andrew E., 'טמן,' *New International Dictionary of Old Testament Theology and Exegesis* (Grand Rapids, Michigan: Zondervan Publishing House, 1997), 2:376-378.

44. Kidner, 41-42.

45. Ibid., 39.

46. Van Dam, Cornelis, 'שׂרר,' *New International Dictionary of Old Testament Theology and Exegesis* (Grand Rapids, Michigan: Zondervan Publishing House, 1997), 4:48-49.

47. Kalland, Earl S., 'bārah,' *Theological Wordbook of the Old Testament* (Chicago: Moody Press, 1980), 1:131.

48. Kidner, 135.

49. Buzzell, 1:948.

50. Whybray, 286.

51. Delizsch, 2:37.

52. Wegner, Paul D., 'בלה,' *New International Dictionary of Old Testament Theology and Exegesis* (Grand Rapids, Michigan: Zondervan Publishing House, 1997), 1:662.

53. Delitzsch, 2:38.

54. Ibid.

Proverbs 20

20:1. Wine is a mocker, strong drink a brawler, And whoever is intoxicated by it is not wise.

With this proverb begins a recurrent theme of the dangers of alcoholic beverages (Prov. 23:20, 21, 29-35; 31:4-5). Two distinct alcoholic beverages are mentioned. 'Wine' was grape juice that had fermented; the amount of alcohol was probably between 7 to 10 percent. For common drinking purposes, it was normally mixed with generous portions of water.[1] The 'strong drink' ('beer,' NIV) was probably fermented drink from either grain or fruit. There is no evidence that distilled liquors were known this early in history. It is mentioned twenty-three times in the Old Testament, being coupled with 'wine' in all but two.[2] Both drinks were off-limits to priests while ministering (Lev. 10:9), and were, likewise, forbidden for Nazarites (Num. 6:3).

These two libations are personified as the actions they produce in those who imbibe in them. Wine is called 'a mocker,' coming from the same root as the word just found in Proverbs 19:25, 29. A 'mocker' is an arrogant reviler of God. Wine often gives expression to this inner, but, perhaps, as yet latent tendency in a person's heart. The other is 'a brawler.' The word describes an indiscreet, loud noise. It describes the chaotic whir of busy streets (Prov. 1:21), the voice of the adulteress (Prov. 7:11) and the Woman Folly (Prov. 9:13). It describes one bent on boorish self-expression, even at everyone else's expense. Anyone who has ever been around an inebriated person understands perfectly what both words describe. Anyone who has not should not seek the visual explanation.

In the second line, the word translated 'intoxicated' means, first, 'to stray' or 'to wander' from the right path. Then, it came to describe the staggering wobble of a drunkard's steps. 'And these also reel [our word] with wine and stagger from strong drink: The priest and the prophet reel [our word] with strong drink, They are confused by wine, they stagger from strong drink; They reel [our word] while having visions, They totter when rendering judgment' (Isa. 28:7).[3]

Anyone who lets himself be thus affected by a stimulant 'is not wise.' That is to say that either a wise person will not get drunk or a drunk person is not wise.[4]

It is true that wine was not categorically forbidden (Deut. 14:26). One should carefully consider, however, the vast difference between the wine, and even the strong drink, referred to in the Scriptures and the exceedingly more alcoholic and intoxicating drinks going by the same names today. Anything even approaching the alcohol content of today's liquors would have been strictly prohibited under Scriptural guidelines (Isa. 5:22; 56:12). Even so, wine led to Noah's sin (Gen. 9:21). It clouds one's ability to reason (Hosea 4:11). While the righteous man lives by faith, the one bent on intoxication gives expression to his worst urges (Hab. 2:4-5).

Alcohol makes you vulnerable to evil and all its dangers. It is associated with gluttony (Prov. 23:20), poverty (v. 21), personal pain, interpersonal strife (v. 29), distorted senses and thinking (v. 33), self-destruction (v. 34), personal abuse (v. 35), poor leadership (Prov. 31:4) and perverted justice (v. 5). Little wonder that Solomon concludes that 'he who is intoxicated by it is not wise'!

The 'fool,' Nabal (thus his name means), proved his character by his drinking party on the eve of his death (1 Sam. 25:36). Similarly, Ben-hadad was 'drinking himself drunk' with his cronies just before his overwhelming defeat (1 Kings 20:16).

20:2. The terror of a king is like the growling of a lion; He who provokes him to anger forfeits his own life.

This proverb echoes the note already sounded in Proverbs 16:14 and 19:12. One should walk humbly in the presence of an earthly ruler. Ultimate allegiances belong to God (Acts 5:29), but we owe earthly rulers honor and respect (1 Pet. 2:17). The 'king' is mentioned again in this chapter in verses 8, 26 and 28.

Here, it is the 'terror of a king' that is of concern. The word translated 'terror' describes an overwhelming dread or fear that engulfs a person. When a powerful horse stands over you, (Job 39:20) or when the teeth of the dreaded Leviathan begin to close around your body (Job 41:14), such dread takes hold of you. Anticipation of death brings such over-whelming terror (Ps. 55:4; 88:15). The presence of God is, thus, described as 'terror' (Gen. 15:12; Exod. 15:16; 23:27; Deut. 32:25; Josh. 2:9).[5] The displeasure of the king might be described as one's worst nightmare.

Such terror is likened to 'the growling of a lion.' A lion roars in order to paralyze its victim just prior to its strike. The lion's roar is used twice more in Proverbs (Prov. 19:12; 28:15). Interestingly, both times also refer to a king's anger.

Such authority should not deter us from righteous living, for, at least ideally, 'The king's favor is toward a servant who acts wisely,

But his anger is toward a servant who acts shamefully' (Prov. 14:35). Nevertheless, it is still true that 'The wrath of a king is as messengers of death, But a wise man will appease it' (Prov. 16:14). That is why the second line of this proverb warns: 'He who provokes him to anger forfeits his own life.' The word for 'forfeits' is, literally, 'sins.' The root means to 'miss' an appointed mark. The word almost always refers to moral sin against God, but not always (e.g. Prov. 8:36).[6] The sense of 'forfeit' best conforms to the context here. Scripture is filled with examples of such wrath from a king (1 Kings 2:23-24; Esther 7:7; Matt. 22:7; Luke 19:27).

20:3. Keeping away from strife is an honor for a man, But any fool will quarrel.

Once again, we encounter a proverb that condemns bickering and exalts harmony and all efforts to attain and maintain it. The first line contends that 'Keeping away' from conflict is a superior plan. The verb may come from either a root meaning to 'sit' or to 'remain' (and thus 'Keeping away from,' NASB; 'avoid,' NIV) or from a root meaning 'cease' ('stop,' NKJV).[7] The former speaks of doing what one can to never enter into an argument, the latter of giving up an argument that has already started. Either one, we may assume, would be the wise course of action, depending upon the circumstances. '... [A]bandon the quarrel before it breaks out' (Prov. 17:14b). '... [I]t is his glory to overlook a transgression' (Prov. 19:11b).

Such action is not just wise, but 'is an honor for a man.' When insulted, we are quick to defend ourselves: 'They can't get away with that!' 'What will people think, if I don't defend myself?' But, such attempts to defend one's honor only diminish it. Much more is gained in the eyes of others if we simply walk away from the fight.

In contrast to such honor is the way of the fool – 'But any fool will quarrel.' The verb is found also in Proverbs 17:14 and 18:1. The root idea is that of exposing or laying bare oneself.[8] It then extends to the idea of a snarling dog,[9] who has exposed his teeth in preparation for a fight.[10]

Such a person is not simply foolish, but 'A worthless person, a wicked man' (Prov. 6:12, 14). The reason for such a judgment, no doubt, is that he divides the covenant community by his actions. Unlike the wise man (Prov. 15:18), such a one has no restraint in his reactions (Prov. 12:16). Otherwise, he might be able to respond with grace (Prov. 15:1) or, at least, silence (Prov. 17:28). In fact, he loves a good fight (Prov. 17:19).

Note the example of that fool, Nabal (1 Sam. 25:11, 25). Also, contrast the responses of Jephthah (Judg. 12:1-6) and Gideon (Judg. 8:1-3) to the contentious Ephraimites.[11] Of course, not all conflict can be, or should, be avoided, but a general aversion to it is a sign of wisdom, righteousness and honor.

20:4. The sluggard does not plow after the autumn, So he begs during the harvest and has nothing.
As so often elsewhere in Proverbs, we meet up with the 'sluggard' (Prov. 6:6-11; 10:26; 13:4; 15:19; 19:24; 20:4; 21:25-26; 22:13; 24:30; 26:13-16). Proverbs generally condemns laziness (Prov. 10:4, 26; 12:24; 19:15). The indolent's problem here is that he 'does not plow after autumn.' The harvest was brought in by the end of autumn (Prov. 10:5). Then, as winter set in, the early rains came and the temperatures dropped. This was, however, the essential time for preparing the soil and planting the seed. The lazy man, contented by the abundance of the recent harvest and the warmth of his house, refuses to go out in the cold and mud to plow his field for next year's harvest. Immediate comforts speak more loudly than long-term needs. Laziness can abort the harvest on either end, here on the preparation end and, in Proverbs 10:5, on the gathering end. Regardless of the season, laziness impoverishes a man and those who depend upon him.

The second line sets forth the consequences of this man's sloth. 'So he begs during the harvest and has nothing.' It is not clear if he is begging his neighbors for grain, since he has not plowed or planted, or if perhaps he is viewed as begging his land for a harvest, since he may have gone ahead and planted without plowing and properly preparing the ground. In either case, he 'has nothing.' 'The soul of the sluggard craves and gets nothing' (Prov. 13:4a; cf. Prov. 21:25-26). He may end up destitute by never bringing in what he could have had, as here, or because he does not maintain what he does have (Eccles. 10:18).

20:5. A plan in the heart of a man is like deep water, But a man of understanding draws it out.
The word 'plan' is the same word translated 'counsel' in Proverbs 19:20, 21. As those two proverbs show, and our comments there bear out, the word may describe either the absolute, unalterable 'counsel' of God (Prov. 19:21b; cf. 21:30) or the tentative, moldable 'plans' of man (Prov. 19:20). Some have felt that the point of this proverb is that each man has a well of uncovered wisdom deep within him. All he needs is a good friend to draw it out of him. Or,

perhaps, what he needs is to become the 'man of understanding' the second line speaks of and, then, draw upon his own innate wisdom. Such a notion, however, flies in the face of all the Book of Proverbs has said about the natural bent of man's heart (Prov. 14:12; 16:25; 22:15). Rather, the translation 'plan' is a good one, for, here, the word seems to have the notion of 'intention,' 'motive' or 'assumption.'

Such 'motives' are 'like deep water' (cf. Prov. 18:4). That is to say, they are mysterious, unexamined and unexposed to the light of truth. 'The mind of man plans his way' (Prov. 16:9a). A person may operate off of those assumptions or motives without even understanding what they are. As such, he needs a good friend that 'draws it out.' The metaphor of 'deep water' continues with the imagery of 'draws out,' as the counselor/friend is pictured methodically reeling up a man's true motives from the murky depths below, where the light of truth and reality have never shone.

It takes 'a man of understanding' to do that kind of work. To become such a one, he must first admit his lack of 'understanding' and listen to God's wisdom (Prov. 2:2) and actively pray for God to give it (Prov. 2:3), for only the Lord can grant this insight (Prov. 2:6; 21:30). This is the timeless understanding of God, by which He created the universe (Prov. 3:19). One must listen to godly mentors – hopefully, parents, if one is ever to attain to it (Prov. 5:1). To a man who has tasted of such wisdom, finding more becomes his passion (Prov. 10:23). Such understanding is found in God's written word: 'For the word of God is living and active and sharper than any two-edged sword, and piercing as far as the division of soul and spirit, of both joints and marrow, and able to judge the thoughts and intentions of the heart' (Heb. 4:12).

We all desperately need to cultivate friendship with such 'a man of understanding,' for 'All the ways of a man are clean in his own sight, But the LORD weighs the motives' (Prov. 16:2).

20:6. Many a man proclaims his own loyalty, But who can find a trustworthy man?

This proverb is built around an antithetical parallelism, the contrast being between love professed in words and love proven in actions. The first line reminds us that 'Many a man proclaims his own loyalty.' The word 'loyalty' is the rich Hebrew word *ḥesed*, the word describing the divine covenant love and the love He enables and expects from those in covenant with him. A person may be quick to say 'I love you,' but the wise person only gives full trust to such a claim when a pattern of established behavior backs it up.

The second line rings with experience: 'who can find a trustworthy man?' The questioner appears to have been told how loyal his wife, children, friends or subjects are, only to be burnt when he trusted them (Ps. 12:1; Eccles. 7:28-29; Luke 18:8). Words are cheap (Prov. 25:14); actions are costly. For that reason, we ought to look for words backed up by sacrificial expressions of love. The question 'who can find ... ?' reminds one of the same question posed in the context of marriage in Proverbs 31:10. Thankfully, there is One who is ever faithful, 'a friend who sticks closer than a brother' (Prov. 18:24b)!

20:7. A righteous man who walks in his integrity – How blessed are his sons after him.

The previous proverb raised some doubt as to the actual existence of a 'trustworthy man.' This proverb immediately affirms that such men do exist. The first line asserts that there is a kind of man 'who walks in his integrity.' The word describes that which is complete or whole – all its parts are together and it is the same in all its parts.[12] That which proves consistent through all parts of such a man's life is his 'righteousness.' This marks the man out as a devout believer and follower of God, who has come to passionately integrate God into every avenue of his life.[13] Such a man is not sinless: 'Who can say, "I have cleansed my heart, I am pure from my sin"?' (v. 9). Rather, he has found a level of inner consistency. Even when he fails, he does the 'righteous' thing about it, confessing it to God and man in repentance (Prov. 11:3). This consistency is expressed through the word 'walks' (Prov. 10:9; 19:1). Thus, 'righteousness' and 'integrity' have become an established pattern of belief and behavior.

The second line extols the benefits others derive from knowing such a man – 'How blessed are his sons after him.' There is a solidarity among family members that our current culture has blinded us to (Exod. 20:5-6). Proverbs consistently affirms that an upright man's children will be richer for his righteousness (Prov. 13:22; 14:11, 26). Seeing their father's faithful consistency, the children have a model of what life is to be lived like. Such an inheritance is worth more than any amount of earthly wealth.

20:8. A king who sits on the throne of justice Disperses all evil with his eyes.

In ancient Israel the king held the position of chief judge and issued the final verdict in matters of dispute (Prov. 20:26) and was to be enabled by the Lord with the discernment necessary (Prov. 16:10; 1 Kings 3:16-28). No doubt, this is what drove Solomon to seek

God's wisdom when he began his reign (1 Kings 3:5-9). The ideal of this kind of judicial arrangement is expressed in Psalm 101 (cf. Ps. 72:1-4). To fulfill this role, the king needed to surround himself with wise counselors (Prov. 16:13; 20:28; 25:5). Soon enough, the emphasis would fall upon the Messianic King, who would fulfill this perfectly through the Spirit of the Lord (Isa. 11:1-4).

The word rendered 'justice' may well also be translated 'judgment' (kjv, cf. niv). However, here it seems best to see it as describing the qualitative nature of his rule (i.e. the throne upon which the king sits), rather than asserting the fact that, from such a throne, he renders judgment. The king's throne must be characterized by 'justice' (Isa. 11:5).

The second line sets forth the purpose of this 'throne of justice.' The word translated 'Disperses' is, more literally, 'sifts' or 'winnows.'[14] Grain was separated from the chaff by tossing it into the air and allowing the wind to blow away the chaff. As this was repeated, the result was, eventually, a 'pure' grain. The word is used in verse 26 to describe the king's separation of the wicked from the righteous. The king is said to accomplish this 'with his eyes.' Divinely given discernment was to be the heart desire and actual possession of every king (Prov. 16:10), but, sadly, few (then or now) sought this out. By looking with God-given discernment, the king was to be able to see through sham, cover-up and lies, and lay bare the truth about any given situation (1 Kings 3:16-28).

Every believer is to now desire and cultivate this kind of discernment (1 Cor. 2:15). Such discernment is required of anyone placed in any God-given position of leadership. Such leadership should covet this discernment and cry out to God for it. It is found through the discipline of repeatedly exposing one's self to God's revealed truth and applying it to the circumstances of life (Heb. 5:14).

20:9. Who can say, 'I have cleansed my heart, I am pure from my sin'?

Proverbs often neatly tucks all people into one of two categories: wise/foolish, righteous/unrighteous, godly/ungodly. This proverb reminds us that any such humanly devised division is never absolute.[15] No human is without sin. No human has ever freed himself from sin. The fact of universal human sin is widely taught in both the Old (Gen. 6:5; 1 Kings 8:46; 2 Chron. 6:36; Eccles. 7:20) and New Testaments (Rom. 3:9-12, 23; James 3:2). No one can stand before God in his own righteousness (Ps. 143:2). The Book of Job, with its struggle to understand the matter of suffering, especially expresses the common human problem of sin (Job 4:17; 9:30-31; 14:4; 15:14).

The question, as posed here, assumes a 'No' answer. Indeed, anyone who makes such a claim is deceived (1 John 1:8) and calls God a liar (1 John 1:10). 'Who can discern his errors? Acquit me of hidden faults.' (Ps. 19:12; cf. Jer. 17:9-10). That is why Proverbs asserts 'All the plans of a man are clean in his own sight, But the Lord weighs the motives' (Prov. 16:2; cf. 21:2; 1 Cor. 4:3-4). The proverb attacks not only the assertion of sinless actions, but of sinless motives as well.

The emphasis here is upon self-righteousness or self-purging. This, of course, does not negate the truth of the forgiveness of sins. Only God can make a man clean before Him (Ps. 32, 51). God has made this provision through Jesus Christ, Who alone is sinless (1 John 3:5) and has conquered sin for us (1 Pet. 2:22-24).

20:10. Differing weights and differing measures, Both of them are abominable to the LORD.

Ethics in business is a spiritual matter. Illegal and unjust business practices are detestable to the Lord. The first line, literally, reads 'A stone and a stone, an ephah and an ephah.' It describes someone with one set of weights (stones) and measures (ephah) for purchasing and another for selling. The weights for purchasing were heavier, so that he got more for his money, while the set for selling were lighter, so he gave up less for the agreed-upon price. A similar arrangement was made with the dry or liquid measure, perhaps by use of a false bottom to the container. Everyone, it seems, was trying to pull a fast one to better his deal (Prov. 20:14).

Such schemes were strictly condemned in the Law (Lev. 19:35; Deut. 25:13-16) and the Prophets (Ezek. 45:10; Amos 8:5; Mic. 6:10-11). Likewise, here in Proverbs, Solomon has no tolerance for such hucksters (Prov. 11:1; 16:11; 20:23). The emotional fervor behind such a denunciation is felt in that they are called 'abominable to the LORD.' An abomination is something that is repugnant to the Lord and which He cannot endure.[16] Because God loathes these things, they come under His judgment. Ultimately, it is not just the weights and measures that are abominable to the Lord, but the person who uses them: 'For the crooked man is an abomination to the LORD; But He is intimate with the upright' (Prov. 3:32).

Those tempted to 'adjust' their weights do well to remember that, ultimately, 'the Lord weighs the hearts' (Prov. 21:2; cf. 24:12).

Jesus said, 'Give, and it will be given to you; good measure, pressed down, shaken together, running over, they will pour into your lap. For by your standard of measure it will be measured to you in return' (Luke 6:38).

20:11. It is by his deeds that a lad distinguishes himself If his conduct is pure and right.

Through synthetic parallelism, this proverb tells us that lifelong tendencies can often be spotted early in life. The first line speaks of the 'deeds' of a young boy. The word translated 'deeds' describes habitual patterns of behavior or what has become one's practice.[17] So, it is not the occasional, but the established, actions that point to trends in a child's character. It is by these that a boy 'distinguishes himself.' The verb can have a shaded variety of meanings. Here, it seems to have the idea of recognizing someone or something. It can be used in the sense of distinguishing between two things (Ezra 3:13).[18] Here, the notion seems to be that a young boy 'distinguishes' (that is to say, makes recognizable his inner character) by what he does.

What is inwardly true of his character is outwardly made known by his 'conduct.' This word stresses the action of a man's work, again with an emphasis on the habitual nature of such action.[19] His regular way of behavior reveals whether his heart is 'pure' (v. 9; 21:8) and 'right' (v. 7). Though it is left unstated here, his conduct may also prove something less noble about his character.

This chapter has already stressed that we should not always believe what a person says of himself (Prov. 20:6). Before drawing any conclusions, we do well to use both our ears and our eyes (cf. v. 12) to examine what he says, as well as what he does. Jesus, too, stressed the revelatory nature of one's actions: 'For there is no good tree which produces bad fruit; nor, on the other hand, a bad tree which produces good fruit. For each tree is known by its own fruit. For men do not gather figs from thorns, nor do they pick grapes from a briar bush' (Luke 6:43-44).

This should be applied to adults as well as children. The NIV begins its translation of the verse with 'Even a child is known ...' (emphasis added), while NASB has, unfortunately, chosen to leave the Hebrew word (*gam*) untranslated. This word stresses that this is true 'even' in the case of a child and, therefore, is most certainly true in the case of an adult.

Proverbs teaches that every child begins with folly in his heart (Prov. 22:15a) and that, with proper discipline and instruction, a child may be brought to maturity as a wise adult (Prov. 22:6, 15b). So, this proverb does not speak of a child's unalterable destiny, but of the facts as they may be at the time the 'conduct' is observed. We should never give up on a child or label him as hopeless. Rather, we should accurately discern the truth of his inner character and employ the instruction of Proverbs to train and discipline him in the way of wisdom and righteousness.

20:12. The hearing ear and the seeing eye, The LORD has made both of them.

Taken at face value, this proverb is a simple affirmation of God's creative control of the human ear and eye and their physical functions (Exod. 4:11). The proverb, however, seems to point beyond this, to a meaning more in tune with the rest of Proverbs.

No doubt, there resides behind these lines the fact that God as the Creator of man's organs of sound and sight is the sole possessor of perfect knowledge (Ps. 94:9). While Proverbs speaks of God's unique ability to see the truth about all men (Prov. 5:21; 15:3; 21:2), and to hear what is going on inside a man's heart (Prov. 15:29), there seems to be another meaning that is primary here. The ear is often spoken of as a tool through which wisdom may be gained (Prov. 2:2; 4:20; 5:1; 15:31; 18:15; 22:17; 23:12; 25:12) or one which shuts out God-sent instruction (Prov. 5:13; 23:9; 28:9). In fact, the word for 'hearing' is the same one used to describe obedience. Thus, ideally, it describes 'hearing' with a predisposition to obey the truth. Similarly, Proverbs uses the eyes to speak of rightly focusing one's self on wisdom (Prov. 4:25; 7:2; 23:26) and rightly evaluating one's self (Prov. 3:7; 12:15; 21:2; 26:5, 12, 16; 28:11; 30:12, 13).

This very context has used the eyes to speak of discernment and insight (Prov. 20:8). People can say anything (Prov. 20:6), but it is one's actions which reveal the heart-reality (Prov. 20:11). For this reason, we need to employ both the ears and the eyes as we seek to discern the truth regarding any person or circumstance.

Hearing and sight are combined again in Proverbs 12:15.

20:13. Do not love sleep, lest you become poor; Open your eyes, and you will be satisfied with food.

Once again, we meet the lazy sluggard, though the name is not specifically used here (cf. v. 4). The two lines are arranged in an antithetical parallelism. The contrasts are between the one who loves sleep and the one who opens his eyes at the appropriate time and gets to work and, also, between the outcome of his actions: 'become poor' and 'will be satisfied with food.'

The first line commands us not to 'love sleep.' Sleep can be a great gift of God (Prov. 3:24; 19:23) and God promises to keep His obedient one even while he sleeps (Prov. 6:22). However, there are certain things that sleep should be sacrificed for, like getting out of surety (Prov. 6:4) and the harvest season (Prov. 10:5). To 'love sleep' is to crave it to the point that other more significant responsibilities are sacrificed to gain more of it, just for pleasure's sake. Be warned of the law of diminishing return – the more you sleep, the more you want (Prov. 19:15a; 24:33)! Rarely will you feel like you have had enough sleep (Prov. 26:14).

In contrast to this is the command to 'Open your eyes' (note the repetition of the noun from vv. 8, 12). This means not so much staying awake longer than one should. Nor is it an exhortation to spiritual alertness per se, though the Scriptures do command such vigilance (Rom. 13:11; 1 Cor. 15:34; Eph. 5:14). The point here is that, when it is time to get up, this person opens his eyes, gets up and takes up his responsibilities – whether or not he feels like it. Stewardship and responsibility before God and others drives this one to do what he may not feel like doing (i.e. getting out of bed and getting to work).

The tendency to sleep in means 'you become poor' (Prov. 10:4a; 19:15b; 24:33-34). The word, literally, means to be divested of that which one already possesses or which one is in line to possess by way of inheritance.[20] Love sleep and you will lose that which you have gained or even what your parents have labored their whole lives to accumulate and pass on to you.

On the other hand, the one who rises responsibly to engage in his assignments 'will be satisfied with food.' The promise is not outlandish wealth, but sufficiency for the needs of himself and his family (Prov. 10:4b; 12:24).

'How long will you lie down, O sluggard? When will you arise from your sleep? 'A little sleep, a little slumber, A little folding of the hands to rest' – And your poverty will come in like a vagabond, And your need like an armed man' (Prov. 6:9-11).

20:14. 'Bad, bad,' says the buyer; But when he goes his way, then he boasts.

This is more of a simple observation than a formal proverb. These two lines transport us to the ancient marketplace. The tricks of the seller have already been denounced (v. 10). Now, the huckstering ways of the buyer are laid bare.[21]

The seller has, no doubt, extolled the virtues of his product. So, now, the buyer proceeds to denounce it as worthless. He cries out

'Bad, bad'! Literally, the expression is 'Evil, evil,' but the words may be used, as here, in a non-moral sense. The claim is that the product is inferior. The goal is to drive the price down. The proverb proceeds upon the assumption that the seller, to some extent, believes the buyer's valuation of his product and, thus, drops the price.

The second line takes the reader down the road a bit after the transaction was made to reveal that the claim of 'Bad, bad' was a lie. The buyer had known all along that the product was good and that the price was remarkable. Only in the presence of his friends and family does he dare let out his true sentiments about the transaction.

What is the purpose of this proverb? It may have served to educate simple farmers about the slick business practices they might encounter as they sought to sell their products. Yet, though it is not openly stated, the mere presence of the observation tells us that the practice described is to be denounced as wrong. The buyer was lying. In his heart, he knew that both the product and the price were good. He, however, named it as something else. Our words should be plain and able to be taken at face value (Matt. 5:37). Better that we face the charge of naïveté than that of lying and falsehood.

20:15. There is gold, and an abundance of jewels; But the lips of knowledge are a more precious thing.

The Book of Proverbs often compares the relative value of gold, silver and jewels to the surpassing value of wisdom (Prov. 3:13-15; 8:10-11; 16:16). The first line of this proverb chimes in on the same note.

The second line stands in contrast to the glitter and gain of this world's treasures. Surpassing them all are 'the lips of knowledge.' This is not just an attempt to extol the value of wisdom. But, here, the point is that the lips communicate such wisdom to others.[22] The same phrase ('lips of knowledge') is found in Proverbs 14:7, where it also points to the articulation of wisdom in human words. This is not the first time the value of knowing what to say, when to say it, and how it ought to be said is compared with riches (Prov. 10:20; 25:11-12).

Such articulated knowledge is 'a more precious thing.' The word translated 'thing' most often points to some kind of 'vessel' or 'container.'[23] So, perhaps here, in context, a good translation would be 'a more precious vase.'[24]

20:16. Take his garment when he becomes surety for a stranger; And for foreigners, hold him in pledge.

Three people are in view in this proverb: the one making a loan, the one taking the loan and a third party who is guaranteeing repayment, if the one taking the loan defaults on payment. The object of the imperative 'Take' is the one making the loan. The person referred to by 'his' in the first line and 'him' in the second is the one guaranteeing repayment if the taker of the loan defaults.

Proverbs has warned of the foolishness of becoming 'surety' for another (Prov. 6:1-6; 11:15; 17:18). The man giving his promise to repay, should there be a default on the loan, is the one who should heed these warnings. However, if he is foolish enough to make such a promise, the one making the loan should take something in collateral, lest he never get repayment from either the one taking the loan or the one promising to make good on it if there is a default (cf. Prov. 22:26-27).

The law made provision for taking a man's coat as collateral. But, there were strict rules as to when it must be returned (Exod. 22:25-27; Deut. 24:10-13), as this could be abused by the unscrupulous (Amos 2:8).

The one taking out the loan is called 'a stranger' and 'foreigners.' The first refers to someone whose reliability is unknown. The second probably speaks of those who were not resident Israelites. For this latter term, the NIV has 'wayward woman,' but this has probably been influenced by the use of that term in Proverbs 1–9 and in the near repetition of this verse in Proverbs 27:13. The translation as a masculine plural ('foreigners') is probably the better one.[25]

20:17. Bread obtained by falsehood is sweet to a man, But afterward his mouth will be filled with gravel.

Here, we discover a connection of this and the surrounding verses. The word for 'sweet' has the same consonants as the word for 'becomes surety' in verse 16 and 'associate' in verse 19. While the words are distinct, it is clear that a connection is intended.[26] The exact nature of that connection is harder to determine. It may have simply been the similarity that caught the eye of the compiler of Proverbs and moved him to bring them together. It might also be that all have some application to business dealings.

The point of this proverb is made by antithesis. The first line describes the immediate pleasure of sin; the second contrasts it with the negative long-term consequences. The immediate lure of sin is that it looks 'sweet.' 'Stolen water is sweet; And bread eaten in secret is pleasant' (Prov. 9:17). Zophar made a similar description to Job (Job 20:12-18). This is 'Bread obtained by falsehood.' Not that it is literal bread, but it refers to the outcome of sin, that which is held forth with glitter and shine to the tempted mind. It promises to satisfy, to strengthen, to please. The application has to do with business practices (cf. vv. 10, 14).

The second line, however, holds forth the reality that lies behind the image. Instead of pleasure, 'his mouth will be filled with gravel.' Jeremiah confessed: 'He has broken my teeth with gravel' (Lam. 3:16a). 'Ill-gotten gains do not profit, But righteousness delivers from death' (Prov. 10:2).

We do well to look behind the immediate promise of temptation and study carefully the long-term consequences of our choices and actions. All that promises sweetness is not sweet and that which immediately denies the senses may, ultimately, prove to be most satisfying.

20:18. Prepare plans by consultation, And make war by wise guidance.

This proverb chimes in on the popular proverbial idea of making one's plans in consultation with others. Such a plan of action is often the difference between success and failure (Prov. 15:22). The difference between such failure and success can be vast when it comes to warfare (Prov. 24:6). The common people are, ultimately, the ones who will pay (often with their lives), so a wise ruler has surrounded himself with prudent men of understanding as his counselors (Prov. 11:14). 'And a man of understanding will acquire wise counsel' (Prov. 1:5b). It is sheer folly to hastily enter a war without first calculating the chances of winning. 'Or what king, when he sets out to meet another king in battle, will not first sit down and take counsel whether he is strong enough with ten thousand men to encounter the one coming against him with twenty thousand?' (Luke 14:31).

What is here applied to literal warfare is also applicable in the many decisions of life. Applicationally, we may take 'make war' in the metaphorical sense of dealing with the many obstacles of life.

20:19. He who goes about as a slanderer reveals secrets, Therefore do not associate with a gossip.

The first line of this proverb is nearly identical to the first line of Proverbs 11:13. The word for 'slanderer' is found only six times in the Old Testament (Lev. 19:16; Prov. 11:13; 20:19; Jer. 6:28; 9:4; Ezek. 22:9). Some translations render it as 'talebearer' or 'gossip,' but these are too weak.[27] Indeed, here, such a person 'reveals secrets.' He takes what has been shared in confidence and uses it to his own advantage and to your disadvantage. What was shared in an intimate, personal moment is now broadcast publicly.

For this reason, the second line warned against having anything to do with 'a gossip.' The word is, more literally, 'him who opens his lips.' The root has the idea of 'to be open,' 'to be spacious,' or 'to be wide.' It can, thus, in certain contexts, point to one who is naïve and immature. Indeed, it is related to the word so often rendered 'naïve' (e.g. Prov. 1:4, 22; 7:7; 8:5; 9:4; 14:15; 22:3). However, the real naïveté in view is not that of the one speaking (they simple-mindedly say more than they should), but of the one listening (they may not have the insight to discern the speaker's true motives for revealing information about another person). The word here came to mean 'entice,' 'deceive,' and 'persuade.'[28] The KJV wrongly took it as pointing to one who flatters with his lips.

We are told 'do not associate with' such a person. Literally, the word means 'do not mix' with such a person.[29] The less contact you have with a loose-lipped person, the better off you are. It is enticing to listen to their latest news (Prov. 18:8; 26:22; Rom. 16:18), but, even if their intent is not malicious, they cannot be trusted with confidential information. For this reason, Proverbs warns us of such characters (Prov. 11:13). Such a man can ruin even your most intimate friendships (Prov. 16:28). 'The one who guards his mouth preserves his life; The one who opens wide his lips comes to ruin' (Prov. 13:3). Who knows, it may be your unwillingness to listen to such a one that may save not only yourself, but others as well. 'For lack of wood the fire goes out, And where there is no whisperer, contention quiets down' (Prov. 26:20).

20:20. He who curses his father or his mother, His lamp will go out in time of darkness.
The act of cursing consists not simply in the use of foul language, but in treating with contempt someone to whom we owe respect. The root of the word means 'lightness' or 'slight.'[30] Thus, to curse someone is to treat them as less than they are in their God-given position. Respect is due to position, not just to persons. Our current culture has led us astray here.

In this proverb, it is the father and mother who receive such maltreatment. This is a violation of the fifth commandment (Exod. 20:12). The act of cursing one's parents put the person under a curse before God and the community (Deut. 27:16). That curse was punishable by death (Exod. 21:17; Lev. 20:9). If the community did not carry out the sentence (which was likely at the time of Solomon), God might (Prov 30:11, 17).

This capital punishment is reflected in the second line. The 'lamp' is a metaphor for the person's life (Prov. 20:27), and its being put out is figurative for his death (Prov. 13:9; 24:20; Job 18:5-6; 21:17). That happens 'in time of darkness.' The phrase is, literally, 'in the pupil of darkness.' The pupil being the center (and darkest part) of the eye means that this refers to the middle of the night or the darkest part of night (cf. Prov. 7:9). The notion may be that such a person will, in his darkest moment in this life, find himself without the help and support of his parents, the community or God. Or it may mean that he will die and be left in 'blackest darkness.' If this latter idea is the notion, this may be echoed in 2 Peter 2:17 and Jude 13 and point not just to the snuffing out of physical life, but of punishment in hell as well.

The New Testament confirms the Old Testament link between honor for parents and a long and successful life: 'Children, obey your parents in the Lord, for this is right. *Honor your father and mother* (which is the first commandment with a promise), *that it may be well with you, and that you may live long on the earth*' (Eph. 6:1-3; cf. Exod. 20:12).

So, what would make a child treat his parents this way? The reasons may be many, but perhaps the next proverb provides a clue: the request for an early bequeathing of the child's inheritance was denied. Perhaps the father of the prodigal son ran the risk of his son's profligate lifestyle rather than hold him up as one who cursed his parents (Luke 15:11-12).

20:21. An inheritance gained hurriedly at the beginning, Will not be blessed in the end.
Read this proverb with the one that precedes it. 'An inheritance' is land that comes to one by way of family inheritance (cf. Prov. 19:14).[31] Good parents strive to provide such an inheritance for their children (Prov. 13:22). But, the fact that it is 'gained hurriedly' implies that something about the passage from one generation to the next is either illegal or immoral (Prov. 19:26). Perhaps it is tantamount to a curse (v. 20). Haste in Proverbs generally points to a lack of wisdom or integrity (Prov. 1:16; 7:23; 19:2; 21:5, 6; 28:20, 22).

The contrast between the first and second lines is seen in the temporal designations of 'at the beginning' and 'in the end.' What looks successful, even if immoral or illegal, on the front end will be found out and recompensed on the back end. By 'Will not be blessed' is meant that it will be cursed. The curse of verse 20 will come back upon the head of the greedy, ungrateful and rebellious child. Get-rich-quick schemes rarely leave a person rich (Prov. 13:11). Let us not forget the destitute figure of the prodigal son (Luke 15:12-16).

20:22. Do not say, 'I will repay evil'; Wait for the Lord, and He will save you.
This verse matches well with the previous two, both of which expect divine justice to be meted out in the end. The first line issues a prohibition, the second a command. The prohibition 'Do not say' is found elsewhere in Proverbs (Prov. 3:28; 24:29). That which is forbidden is the self-indulgence of saying (whether audibly or only privately within one's heart) 'I will repay evil.' The warning of both testaments is that only God is in a position to exercise vengeance (Deut. 32:35; Ps. 94:1; Rom. 12:19; Heb. 10:30). For this reason, we are to avoid any such feelings, imaginations or actions of revenge ourselves (Prov. 24:29). Indeed, we are to return good for evil (Prov. 25:21; Matt. 5:38-42; Rom. 12:17-21; 1 Thess. 5:15; 1 Pet. 3:9). To take matters into our own hands is to invite God's judgment against ourselves (Prov. 17:13).

Interestingly, the promise of the second line is not that God will take revenge on our enemies, but that He will come to our aid. The picture is not of God as Judge, but as Savior. The command is to 'Wait for the Lord.' That probably means to wait for Him to do what is right in His eyes. 'Shall not the Judge of all the earth deal justly?' (Gen. 18:25b). This must be our attitude as we endure hostilities and injustices in Christ's name. His faithfulness is the issue, not our comfort.

20:23. Differing weights are an abomination to the Lord, And a false scale is not good.
Uprightness in business is of the utmost importance to God, as is seen from the three proverbs devoted to these matters in this chapter (vv. 10, 14, 23). This proverb makes the same point as verse 10. Here, too, 'Differing weights' is literally 'a stone and a stone.' Stones were used for weights in buying and selling. Here, one stone was used when purchasing (it was heavier in order to insure the acquisition of more product) and the other was used when selling, in order to give up as little of your product as possible. Such two-faced business dealings are 'an abomination to the Lord.' An 'abomination' is something so repugnant to the Lord that He cannot endure its

continuation. He must, thus, move in judgment against that thing or person. That such business practices are so labeled reminds us that such 'deals' prove in the end to be losing propositions.

Adding to the thought of verse 10 and the first line here, the second line states that 'a false scale' is also detestable to the Lord. See the comments on Proverbs 11:1 for this same expression. The result is the same as the dubious weights and measures, for deceit is the underlying motive. This 'is not good' (Prov. 16:29). This is simply a backward way of saying that such practices are evil. It 'is not good' in the sight of God and, thus, 'is not good' for the one working such a ploy.

20:24. Man's steps are ordained by the LORD, How then can man understand his way?

Ultimately, we are not directors, but followers. The first line of the proverb is a repeat from Psalm 37:23. There, Solomon's father used it in a context of blessing. Solomon repeats it here, as he contemplates the mystery of man's freewill and God's sovereignty. Here, as in the multiplied centuries of both Jewish and Christian theology, the two strains of truth are not reducible to the smallness of man's understanding. In the end, God's sovereignty must win out, though Scripture squarely puts responsibility upon us to choose the Lord's way. Solomon has probed this mystery before (Prov. 16:1, 3, 9; 19:21). The word translated 'Man's' is distinct from the word used for 'man' in line two. The first word is used in distinction from the second to describe man at his strongest and wisest.[32] The very highest of human insight, strength, wisdom and capability cannot ever search out completely the mystery of God's will and way with him.

The second line echoes this mystery in the form of a question: 'How then can man understand his way?' This is man, ordinary man – you and me, tangled in our frailties and faults. What hope do we have of ever tracing out God's way for us? Ultimately, we cannot. This can never become a cop-out, though, for it is the path of wisdom to understand one's way (Prov. 14:8). Yet, in the end we must confess: 'I know, O LORD, that a man's way is not in himself; Nor is it in a man who walks to direct his steps' (Jer. 10:23). Indeed, 'The mind of man plans his way, But the LORD directs his steps' (Prov. 16:9). Ultimately, our only hope lies in the fear of the Lord: 'Who is the man who fears the LORD? He will instruct him in the way he should choose' (Ps. 25:12; cf. Prov. 3:5-6).

This second line should not be read as expressing despair, but doxology. Though a sense of hopelessness can come to the one dependent upon his own resources, to the one shut up to the sovereign grace and providence of God, such surrender is the glad joy of worship. 'With Thy counsel Thou wilt guide me, And afterward receive me into glory' (Ps. 73:24). The so-called problem of God's sovereignty and man's free will always ends in either the folly of overemphasizing one over the other or in the doxology of holding both as absolute and non-competing truths of God's Word, whose interrelationship cannot be fully traced out by finite, human minds. Let us take the path of surrender, obedience and worship rather than self-reliance, arrogance and dogmatism.

20:25. It is a snare for a man to say rashly, 'It is holy!' And after the vows to make inquiry.
The two lines of this proverb form one continuous sentence. The thrust of the proverb is toward commitments made from mere sentimentalism or from peer pressure. It is easy, under the emotional or social pressure of the moment, to commit something to God. That is what is meant by saying 'It is holy!' It was tantamount to saying, 'This now belongs to God and I have no further rights over it. God may now do with it as He pleases and I will do with it as I have now committed.' Such commitments must be made with the utmost seriousness and forethought. The Mosaic Law demanded that a vow was unalterable and binding (Num. 30:2; Deut. 23:21-23), although it did make some very costly provisions for getting out of certain vows (Lev. 27:1-25; cf. Prov. 6:1-5). 'When you make a vow to God, do not be late in paying it, for He takes no delight in fools. Pay what you vow! It is better that you should not vow than that you should vow and not pay. Do not let your speech cause you to sin and do not say in the presence of the messenger of God that it was a mistake. Why should God be angry on account of your voice and destroy the work of your hands?' (Eccles. 5:4-6).

The second line provides some insight into the psychology of the situation: 'And after the vow to make inquiry.' Do not make a promise and, only afterward, think of what the price of actually keeping it might mean. That was Jephthah's problem (Judg. 11:30-35), but, in contrast, Hannah gave serious thought to the high cost of keeping her vow (1 Sam. 1:11). For other uses of the root word for 'rashly,' see Job 6:3 and Obadiah 16.

The problem is not that a vow is taken, but that it is undertaken 'rashly.' A vow was an act of worship. As such, it required a sacrifice to keep it. However, it was to be one that could be kept willingly, as a love expression to God. Hasty words are repeatedly identified as a major problem for man (Prov. 10:19; 18:13; Eccles. 5:2, 5). The word translated 'inquire' can mean either to check into something for ritual purity (Lev. 13:36; Lev. 27:33), or to give meditation and reflection to something personally (2 Kings 16:15; Ps. 27:4).[33] Such reflection should be entered into before the promise is made, not after.

God loves the sacrifices of worship His people make to Him. He, however, wants thoughtful worship, not mere emotionalism. Therefore, when a call for sacrifice or public commitment is made, carefully consider your response. To respond with love out of a fully informed heart is a beautiful thing. To respond shallowly and, then, wish you hadn't is a serious matter before God.

20:26. A wise king winnows the wicked, And drives the threshing wheel over them.

This chapter emphasizes the Divinely given responsibility and authority of the government ('king') to establish justice. Verse 8 spoke of the discernment needed to dispense justice. Verse 28 will describe the stability such justice brings to the ruler's government. Here, the issue is the means of dispensing that justice.

The first line returns to the imagery of winnowing first introduced in verse 8 (see the comments there). The second line introduces the metaphor of 'the threshing wheel' (lit., simply 'the wheel'). Do not read this as picturing some kind of torture inflicted upon the wicked. This, apparently, is a reference to the strong metal wheels of a cart driven back and forth ('drives' is, literally, 'causes to return') over the stalks of grain to separate the seeds from the stalk (Isa. 28:27-28).

In this way, the imagery of the two lines is complementary, though perhaps reversed from the order normally employed by the farmer. First, the farmer separated the grain from the stalk by means of threshing. Then, the grain was separated from the surrounding chaff through winnowing (tossing it in the air repeatedly to allow the breeze to blow away the lighter chaff). Just so, God has established the governing authorities to identify the evildoers in their jurisdiction, separate them from the law-abiding citizens and, then, punish them appropriately (Rom. 13:1-5; 1 Pet. 2:13-14).

No doubt, Solomon had seen his father's passion for justice, captured in Psalm 101:5-8: 'Whoever secretly slanders his neighbor, him I will destroy; No one who has a haughty look and an arrogant heart will I endure. My eyes shall be upon the faithful of the land, that they may dwell with me; He who walks in a blameless way is the one who will minister to me. He who practices deceit shall not dwell within my house; He who speaks falsehood shall not maintain his position before me. Every morning I will destroy all the wicked of the land, So as to cut off from the city of the LORD all those who do iniquity.'

Would to God that all earthly rulers shared such a passion for righteousness personally and justice socially! Of course, as John the Baptist reminded us, only the King of kings will bring such perfect justice: 'And His winnowing fork is in His hand, and He will thoroughly clear His threshing floor; and He will gather His wheat into the barn, but He will burn up the chaff with unquenchable fire' (Matt. 3:12).

20:27. The spirit of man is the lamp of the LORD, Searching all the innermost parts of his being.
The second line of this proverb explains the first. The first line contains an arresting metaphor. The 'spirit of man' is, literally, 'the breath of man.' This points back to Genesis 2:7, when God breathed into man the breath of life, thus setting him apart as the crown of creation and as distinct from the animal world. This is called 'the lamp of the LORD' (cf. v. 20). Interpretations have varied, but generally fall into two groups. Some see this as a reference to man's God-given conscience. In this sense, it is understood as man's built-in capacity for self-reflection (Job 32:8). The point is that man can think about and gain at least a measure of self-understanding that is beyond the rest of creation. The second line of interpretation understands this as God's way of searching out the truth about man's condition. The point is that God knows all about us and we can hide nothing from His all-knowing eyes (Prov. 5:21; 15:3, 11; 16:2; 21:2).

All things considered, even though the Bible has a clear doctrine of the conscience of man (Rom. 2:12; 2 Cor. 1:12; 1 Tim. 1:5, 19; 3:9; 4:2; etc.), the emphasis upon man's self-understanding through conscience seems to psychologize the text, by reading it through modern eyes. The emphasis in Proverbs on God's thorough knowledge of us tips the scales in favor of the second line of interpretation.

It is worthy of note that the spirit of man is called 'the lamp of the LORD,' not 'the light of the LORD.' It is through the impartation of God's own life to man that He is able to know, conclusively and completely, the truth of each man's deepest parts. A lamp is only an inanimate object until illuminated by fire. The 'light' in the lamp is God Himself investigating (all humans) and indwelling (all believers) His creature. The phrase 'all the innermost parts of his being' is, literally, 'all the chambers of the belly' (cf. the same phrase in v. 30). It describes the most inner and unreachable parts of the human creature. 'For who among men knows the thoughts of a man except the spirit of the man, which is in him? Even so the thoughts of God no one knows except the Spirit of God' (1 Cor. 2:11).

Of course, having established that it is God's knowledge of us that is in view, applicationally it is true that He delights then to let us know what He knows about the truth of our innermost being. He does this by the Spirit of God using the written word of God. 'For the word of God is living and active and sharper than any two-edged sword, and piercing as far as the division of soul and spirit, of both joints and marrow, and able to judge the thoughts and intentions of the heart. And there is no creature hidden from His sight, but all things are open and laid bare to the eyes of Him with whom we have to do' (Heb. 4:12, 13). A believer should welcome this ministry of God, though the unbeliever should be terrified by it.

20:28. Loyalty and truth preserve the king, And he upholds his throne by righteousness.

Now, again, for the third time in this chapter the stability of the king's rule is addressed (vv. 8, 26). Whereas those two proverbs recognize that the stability of the kingdom depends upon the righteousness of its subjects (and thus the king must act as judge), this proverb reminds us that the stability of the kingdom also rests upon the 'Loyalty and truth' of the king himself. What the king demands of the citizens (vv. 8, 26) he must demand of himself as well, for God certainly does.

The twin qualities of 'Loyalty and truth' are often found together in Scripture (e.g. Prov. 3:3). The word translated 'Loyalty' is the rich Hebrew term *ḥesed* which speaks of the commitment of covenant love (cf. v. 6). The same word is found in the second line, though it is translated 'righteousness.' It is both by strict adherence to the truth and by passionate and compassionate commitment to God and His people that the king wins their loyalty. In so seeking these qualities in his relations with his subjects, he imitates God's own rule (Ps. 89:14). God decreed that such qualities would be the foundation of the earthly kingdom of Israel (Isa. 16:5). It is God's own commitment to these qualities in His dealings with the king that solidify his throne (Ps. 40:11; 89:24).

The second line picks up again only on the first quality mentioned in line one. By such covenant love, a king 'upholds his throne.' This does not deny that the 'truth' mentioned in line one is less important, for Proverbs 29:14 says: 'If a king judges the poor with truth, His throne will be established forever' (cf. 16:12; 25:5). The promise of the permanence of his kingdom was God's word to David concerning his son Solomon (2 Sam. 7:12-17), so we should read great emotion into this proverb. Who can know what, or how much, this divine promise meant to him?

What is true for kings (and all rulers of nations) is also true for all who are called to exercise the authority of leadership in lesser roles. 'He who pursues righteousness and loyalty Finds life, righteousness and honor' (Prov. 21:21). Ultimately, however, these two qualities 'kiss' one another perfectly (i.e. come together in harmony) only in the rule of God Himself (Ps. 85:10). Thus, only Jesus' own rule will be indisputably established.

20:29. The glory of young men is their strength, And the honor of old men is their gray hair.

Each stage of life has its strong point (1 John 2:14). The particular adornment of a young person is their physical strength. While physical strength is nothing to rely upon absolutely, it is, nevertheless, a God-given quality that should be dedicated to the service of the Lord. The 'honor of old men is their gray hair.' When physical strength has passed, the wisdom, dignity and insight of a life lived righteously should become our badge of honor.

Of course, not all who are young are physically robust, nor are all who have gray hair wise. These are generalizations to make a point. Wisdom comes from having lived life righteously, to the glory of God (Prov. 16:31). If a young fool is a danger, how sad to encounter an elderly fool?

These two lines imply that the latter (wisdom of age) is superior to the former (strength of youth), yet they stop short of disparaging the former. Perhaps we should take note that each age has its contribution to make. Therefore, we should not give way to generational squabbles or competition. The old man should not try to be a young man any longer. The young man should begin now to learn from the old man (Lev. 19:32), for attaining wisdom is a lifelong pursuit.

Perhaps Jeremiah 9:23-24 helps us attain the needed balance: 'Thus says the Lord, 'Let not a wise man boast of his wisdom, and let not the mighty man boast of his might, let not a rich man boast of his riches; but let him who boasts boast of this, that he understands and knows Me, that I am the Lord who exercises lovingkindness, justice, and righteousness on earth; for I delight in these things,' declares the Lord.'

Let the young bring his strength into the service of the Lord, while sitting at the feet of those older and more righteous and experienced than he. Let the old make their years count for this one thing: growing intimacy with God.

20:30. Stripes that wound scour away evil, And strokes reach the innermost parts.

Corporal punishment is a recurrent theme of these proverbs (e.g. Prov. 22:15). Physical pain can bring spiritual and moral change. Discipline administered externally can have a redemptive effect on the internal life.

The expression 'Stripes that wound' describes, literally, a blow that leaves a striped bruise on the body.[34] It, thus, refers to severe discipline. We are told that God will resort to even this kind of discipline for His children (Ps. 89:32), but it is always an expression of His love (Prov. 3:11-12). Thus, we should embrace it, rather than flee it (Heb. 12:7-11).

It is said that such blows 'scour away evil.' The word means to rub[35] and, thus, the picture is of cleaning something with a scrubbing motion. Of course, this does not atone for sin, but is a deterrent to further 'evil.' Indeed, the second line demands that the physical discipline can 'reach' all the way down into 'the innermost parts' of a person's life and bring real change. The phrase 'innermost parts' is, literally, 'the chambers of the belly.' It is the same expression used in verse 27, and is descriptive of the most inaccessible and unreachable parts of a human being, those not being physical, but spiritual and moral.

We should find here not a command to spank until there is a bruise left, but an exhortation to continue with discipline (in all the forms prescribed in Proverbs, verbal and non-verbal), for without it there is no hope for our children (Prov. 19:18). The father who gives up on his child when he is incorrigible in no way reflects his heavenly Father. The father who, despite his frustrations, presses on in dealing with, and disciplining, his child follows in the path of obedience and hope.

This also applies more broadly than parent/child relationships. Proverbs has often spoken of how the fool invites blows upon his body (Prov. 10:13; 14:3; 27:22). We have, however, also been reminded that such means of discipline are not fool-proof (Prov. 17:10; 27:22). However, society at large would do well to, again, realize the connection between physical discomfort and inward reform.

Such times can become opportunities to proclaim the gospel of our Lord Jesus Christ, for 'He was pierced through for our transgressions, He was crushed for our iniquities; The chastening for our well-being fell upon Him, And by His scourging we are healed' (Isa. 53:5). 'He Himself bore our sins in His body on the cross, that we might die to sin and live to righteousness; for by His wounds you were healed' (1 Pet. 2:24). Does it not always seem odd, initially, that our cleansing comes by His wounds? Yet, this is the way of His grace. Thank God for it!

End Notes

1. Harris, R. Laird, '*yayin*,' *Theological Wordbook of the Old Testament* (Chicago: Moody Press, 1980), 1:375-376.

2. Hamilton, Victor P., '*shākar*,' *Theological Wordbook of the Old Testament* (Chicago: Moody Press, 1980), 2:926-927.

3. Hill, Andrew E., 'שָׁגָה,' *New International Dictionary of Old Testament Theology and Exegesis* (Grand Rapids, Michigan: Zondervan Publishing House, 1997), 4:43-44.

4. Whybray, R. N., *Proverbs* (Grand Rapids, Michigan: William B. Eerdmans Publishing Company, 1994), 288.

5. Van Pelt, M. V. and W. C. Kaiser, Jr., 'אֵימָה,' *New International Dictionary of Old Testament Theology and Exegesis* (Grand Rapids, Michigan: Zondervan Publishing House, 1997), 1:381-382.

6. Whybray, 289.

7. Murphy, Roland E., *Proverbs* (Nashville: Thomas Nelson Publishers, 1998), 149.

8. Kalland, Earl S., '*gāla'*,' *Theological Wordbook of the Old Testament* (Chicago: Moody Press, 1980), 1:165.

9. Ross, Allen P., 'Proverbs' in *The Expositor's Bible Commentary*, (Grand Rapids, Michigan: Zondervan Publishing House, 1991), 5:1040.

10. Whybray, 258.

11. Kidner, Derek, *Proverbs* (Downers Grove, Illinois: InterVarsity Press, 1964), 136.

12. Brown, Francis, S. R. Driver, Charles R. Briggs, *A Hebrew and English Lexicon of the Old Testament* (Oxford: Clarendon Press, n.d.), 1070.

13. Ross, 5:1042.

14. Whybray, 292.

15. Ibid.

16. Ibid., 73.

17. Carpenter, Eugene, 'עלל,' *New International Dictionary of Old Testament Theology and Exegesis* (Grand Rapids, Michigan: Zondervan Publishing House, 1997), 3:423.

18. Fretheim, Terence E., 'נכר,' *New International Dictionary of Old Testament Theology and Exegesis* (Grand Rapids, Michigan: Zondervan Publishing House, 1997), 3:108.

19. Delitzsch, F., *Proverbs, Ecclesiastes, Song of Solomon* (three volumes in one) in C. F. Keil and F. Delitzsch, vol. 6, *Commentary on the Old Testament* (in ten volumes), (1872; rpt. Grand Rapids, Michigan: William B. Eerdmans Publishing Company, 1980), 2:47.

20. Wright, Christopher J. H., 'ידשׁ,' *New International Dictionary of Old Testament Theology and Exegesis* (Grand Rapids, Michigan: Zondervan Publishing House, 1997), 2:547-549.

21. Bridges, Charles, *A Commentary on Proverbs* (Edinburgh: The Banner of Truth Trust, 1846, reprint 1998), 347.

22. Ross, 5:1044.

23. Hostetter, Edwin C., 'כְּלִי,' *New International Dictionary of Old Testament Theology and Exegesis* (Grand Rapids, Michigan: Zondervan Publishing House, 1997), 2:654-656.

24. Adams, Jay E., *Proverbs* (Woodruff, South Carolina: Timeless Texts, 1997), 160.

25. Whybray, 296.

26. Murphy, 152.

27. White, William, '*rākal,*' *Theological Wordbook of the Old Testament* (Chicago: Moody Press, 1980), 2:848.

28. Goldberg, Louis, '*pātâ,*' *Theological Wordbook of the Old Testament* (Chicago: Moody Press, 1980), 2:742-743.

29. Cohen, 135.

30. Coppes, Leonard J., '*qālal,*' *Theological Wordbook of the Old Testament* (Chicago: Moody Press, 1980), 2:800-801.

31. Whybray, 300.

32. Oswalt, John N., '*gābar,*' *Theological Wordbook of the Old Testament* (Chicago: Moody Press, 1980), 1:148-149.

33. Martens, Elmer A., '*bāqar,*' *Theological Wordbook of the Old Testament* (Chicago: Moody Press, 1980), 1:124-126.

34. Hamilton, Victor P., '*pāsa,*' *Theological Wordbook of the Old Testament* (Chicago: Moody Press, 1980), 2:730.

35. Whybray, 304.

Proverbs 21

21:1. The king's heart is like channels of water in the hand of the LORD; He turns it wherever He wishes.
This chapter is bracketed by an inclusio, focusing us upon the 'LORD' (vv. 1-3, 30, 31). Here, He is held forth as the only absolute Sovereign. Certainly, God controls the hearts of all men (Prov. 16:9; 19:21; 20:24). But, it may appear that kings, rulers and presidents hold absolute sway. They may even believe that they possess such power, yet they are 'in the hand of the LORD.' Their thinking, motives, inclinations and decisions are under the absolute control of God Himself.

By the king's 'heart' is meant all his powers of reasoning, feeling and choice. These are 'like channels of water.' The expression describes small irrigation ditches used to bring life-giving water to otherwise unusable land. The farmer directed the water by digging such ditches wherever he wanted and by, then, opening and closing the pathway for the water to flow (Deut. 11:10; Isa. 32:1-2). So, too, God 'turns it [the king's heart] wherever He wishes.' He is able to make even the evil intentions of a man's heart promote His glorious purposes (Ps. 76:10).

Scripture is filled with examples of such control by God over the hearts of rulers, particularly as they deal with His people and stand to influence His purposes: Abimelech (Gen. 20:6; Ps. 105:14-15), Pharaoh (Acts 7:10; Exod. 10:1-2), Artaxerxes (Ezra 7:21-23, 27), Tiglath-Pileser (Isa. 10:5-7), Cyrus (Ezra 6:22; Isa. 45:1-4), Nebuchadnezzar (Dan. 4:30-31, 34-37), Belshazzar (Dan. 5:22-28), and Pilate (John 19:11). This truth is affirmed throughout the Scriptures (Eccles. 9:1; Dan. 2:21; Ps.105:25; 106:46; Rev. 17:17).

Only God is absolute in His control. 'There is no wisdom and no understanding And no counsel against the LORD' (v. 30).

21:2. Every man's way is right in his own eyes, But the LORD weighs the hearts.
This antithetical proverb is a near repeat of Proverbs 16:2 (which see), with only an exchange of synonyms for some of the key words. Jeremiah lamented, 'The heart is more deceitful than all else And is desperately sick; Who can understand it?' (Jer. 17:9). The answer there (v. 10), and here (line b), is that only God knows us perfectly.

We think ourselves righteous or, at least, right (Prov. 12:15; 14:12; 16:25), but are in no position to make such judgments of ourselves. 'God sees not as man sees, for man looks at the outward appearance, but the Lord looks at the heart' (1 Sam. 16:7b).

Self-deception is a real danger to us all (Luke 16:15; 1 John 1:8). It is not only a terror, but a comfort, that 'the LORD weighs the hearts' (cf. Prov. 16:2b). 'The eyes of the LORD are in every place, Watching the evil and the good' (Prov. 15:3). 'Sheol and Abaddon lie open before the LORD, How much more the hearts of men!' (Prov. 15:11). He not only 'weighs' the hearts (as here), but He 'tests hearts' (Prov. 17:3). For this reason, we must ask with Solomon, 'Who can say, "I have cleansed my heart, I am pure from sin"?' (Prov. 20:9). God searches the depths of who we are, the places where no amount of self-reflection can probe (Prov. 20:27). Ignorance is no excuse (Prov. 24:12). Self-examination is necessary, but inevitably limited (1 Cor. 4:4-5). Yet, by His Spirit and through His written word, God delights to share with us what He finds as He examines our hearts (Heb. 4:12). Therefore, wise is the man who prays, 'Search me, O God, and know my heart; Try me and know my anxious thoughts; And see if there be any hurtful way in me, And lead me in the everlasting way' (Ps. 139:23-24).

21:3. To do righteousness and justice Is desired by the LORD rather than sacrifice.
Since God knows the heart (v. 2), mere religious ritual means nothing. In fact, it is worse than nothing; it is an abomination (Prov. 15:8; 21:27). To a large extent, it was confusion in this area that dethroned Saul, Israel's first king (1 Sam. 15:22) and made the way for David, Solomon's father, to be king. He appears to have understood God's priorities (Ps. 40:6-8). The Prophets repeatedly emphasize the proper relationship between right living and religious sacrifice (Isa. 1:11, 16, 17; Jer. 7:21-23; Hosea 6:6; Mic. 6:6-8). Jesus affirmed that sacrifice without righteous living is repugnant to God (Matt. 23:23; Mark 12:33).

Does this mean that God has no place for sacrifice? Solomon certainly did not understand it that way (1 Kings 3:4; 8:62-64). Clearly, since the sacrifice of Christ, the Jewish sacrificial system is defunct (Heb. 10:12). His sacrifice is once for all. This, however, does not rule out all sacrifice, for all worship is to be a sacrifice to God (Heb. 13:15-16; 1 Pet. 2:5). Such 'sacrifices' do not gain us merit before God, but evidence outwardly our inward delight over, and trust in, Jesus' once for all sacrifice for us.

What this proverb does warn us of is thinking that we can dis-connect true repentance and heart obedience from religious service of any kind. The moment our heart relationship with God is soiled by sin and is left unresolved, all religious or spiritual service or sac-rifice becomes worthless before God. In fact, it becomes worse than worthless. It becomes detestable in God's sight. The same act of sac-rifice can be either a pleasing aroma to God or an abomination, and it is the reality of repentance and obedience that makes the differ-ence.

21:4. Haughty eyes and a proud heart, The lamp of the wicked, is sin. One more time these Proverbs denounce pride (Prov. 3:34; 8:13; 16:5, 18; 21:24). The expression 'Haughty eyes' refers not so much to how one's eyes appear to others, but the way one looks at others.[1] In Proverbs 6:17, 'Haughty eyes' are listed as one of the seven things God finds most abominable (cf. also Prov. 30:13). The expression 'a proud heart' means, more literally, 'a broad heart.'[2] It too points to arrogance and pride (Ps. 101:5).

The difficult part of this verse comes in the second line. The expression 'The lamp of the wicked' is disputed. The Hebrew text has 'the plowing' or 'the tillage' rather than 'The lamp,' which the LXX and other versions supply. Most likely, the translation 'The lamp' is correct, following the use of this word several times in this context (Prov. 20:20, 27). The exact expression 'The lamp of the wicked' is found again in Proverbs 13:9; and 24:20. Most modern translations follow this understanding of the word (NASB, NIV, RSV, NRSV, JB).

The question then arises, Just what does 'The lamp of the wicked' refer to, and what does it mean? It appears that the expression is used in apposition to the first line. That is to say, it is a summary statement, gathering up the dual descriptions of pride. Pride is 'The lamp of the wicked.' It is almost a parenthetical phrase to explain what 'Haughty eyes and a proud heart' are – they are the very 'lamp of the wicked.' By 'lamp' is meant that, it is through the 'light' of pride and arrogance that the 'wicked' view all of life, just as the spirit of man is the 'lamp of the Lord' (Prov. 20:27) and is the way He investigates all of man's deepest parts. As such, it is more than a way of looking at life. It is the sum and substance of life, as he knows it (Prov. 13:9; 20:20). See also 2 Samuel 21:17; 22:29 and 1 Kings 11:36 for this expression. Jesus concluded the same about how one looks at life: 'The lamp of the body is your eye; when your eye is clear, your whole body also is full of light; but when it is bad, your body also is full of darkness' (Luke 11:34).

Such an outlook on life, Solomon concludes, 'is sin.' Note that the 'wicked' are a frequent subject in this chapter (vv. 7, 10, 12 [2x], 18, 27, 29).

21:5. The plans of the diligent lead surely to advantage, But everyone who is hasty comes surely to poverty.
Steady consistency brings gain, while haphazard hurriedness brings loss. This proverb makes its point by a stark contrast. The first line speaks, again, of the 'diligent.' Elsewhere, Proverbs has spoken of 'the soul of the diligent' (Prov. 13:4) and the 'the hand of the diligent' (Prov. 10:4; 12:24). Diligence is said to be a man's most prized possession (Prov. 12:27). Such enduring dedication is consistently praised throughout Proverbs (Prov. 6:6-8; 12:11; 14:23; 28:19).

We need, however, not simply diligence, but also 'plans.' The word for 'plans' can mean either to count, compute or calculate or, possibly, to plan, think out, devise, invent or scheme.[3] When we combine good thinking with consistent effort, they 'lead surely to advantage' (i.e. financial success). Think well, work hard – this is the key to success.

The second line spells out the formula for financial disaster. The key ingredient is haste. Haste can abide with neither the labor of good, clear thinking nor the toil of sustained hard work. The exact idea may point to being rash in actions (Prov. 19:2; 28:22), or to an attempt to by-pass the toil of good thinking and hard work, in order to get rich quick (Prov. 13:11; 20:21; 28:20).[4] The contrast is not only in process, but in outcome. In either case, the result will be 'poverty.' The contrast between 'advantage' and 'poverty' is made the more stark because the two Hebrew words have striking similarities in sound and form, but are polar opposites in meaning (cf. Prov. 14:23).[5]

This is the first of three proverbs pointing out unjust ways to attempt to make financial gain: hastily (here), deceitfully (v. 6), and violently (v. 7).[6]

21:6. The getting of treasures by a lying tongue Is a fleeting vapor, the pursuit of death.
As the previous verse condemns the hasty acquisition of wealth, this one attacks wealth attained through deceit. The problem is given in the first line: 'The getting of treasures by a lying tongue.' It is worthy of note that a 'lying tongue' is found also in Proverbs 6:17, where a list of seven abominations are outlined. There, it is immediately preceded by 'haughty eyes,' the very problem mentioned in the

preceding context here (v. 4). Of further note is that it is followed by 'hands that shed innocent blood' (Prov. 6:17c), as the next verse here (v. 7) speaks of 'violence.'[7] This underscores that these are not merely personal peccadilloes of Solomon, but are of a particularly despicable nature in the eyes of God. The particular problem of 'a lying tongue' (or 'lips') is often encountered in Proverbs (Prov. 6:17; 10:18; 12:19, 22; 17:7; 26:28). It is especially heinous when coupled with greed.

In the end, such tactics are like 'a fleeting vapor.' The word translated 'fleeting' means to be driven along. It describes the wind blowing smoke or chaff away. It is often used in the context of judgment.[8] The word for 'vapor' is found again in Prov. 13:11a: 'Wealth obtained by fraud [our word] dwindles' and Proverb 31:30a: 'Charm is deceitful and beauty is vain [our word].' Reaching for riches through deceit is like trying to grasp the wind (Prov. 23:4-5; 27:24; Eccles. 1:14; 2 Pet. 2:3). No one ever gets permanently rich through dishonesty. 'Ill-gotten gains do not profit' (Prov. 10:2a).

The most difficult part of this verse is in understanding the last phrase – 'the pursuit of death.' Several newer translations follow the LXX, Vulgate and several other ancient versions and emend the Hebrew text to read something like 'a deadly snare' (NIV; cf. RSV, NRSV). This is normally done with the rationalization that no good sense can be made of the sentence apart from such a reconstruction. If they are right, then the deceitful pursuit of riches is described through a double metaphor. It is like 'a fleeting vapor,' and it is also like 'a deadly snare.'

However, the reconstruction is probably unnecessary. The last phrase refers not to the practice of getting rich through lying, but is descriptive of what such a person is actually doing to himself. He thinks he is chasing down his fortune. But, in actual fact, he is fumbling headlong toward his own death. He grasps after wealth. But, in so doing, he unwittingly seeks his own undoing. Often, that which sparkles ultimately destroys. As he stumbles after the glittering prize, he is driving it along before himself (like a vapor one is never able to quite grasp, gather up and get one's arms around), all the while keeping it just out of reach. His pursuit is self-defeating ('a fleeting vapor') and self-destructive ('the pursuit of death').

21:7. The violence of the wicked will drag them away, Because they refuse to act with justice.

What goes around, comes around. When people practice violence, they invite violence. The first line of this proverb reminds us that we reap what we sow. This violence 'will drag them away.' The same Hebrew verb is used in Habakkuk 1:15 to describe a fisherman pulling fish up from the sea in a net. So, too, the one who resorts to violence will find himself ensnared in his ways and pulled into a vortex of reciprocal violence. Soon, the self-will that moved him to 'take matters into his own hands' will give way to involuntary submission to the violence of others. In this regard, we are reminded of the thuggery of the gangs spoken of in Proverbs 1:18-19 and of the retribution brought upon Abimelech by the men of Shechem (Judg. 9:23-24).[9]

The second line explains why the first is true: 'they refuse to act with justice.' What ends as involuntary destruction (line one) begins as sinful self-will ('refuse').[10] The pattern of sin always follows this pattern – self-will, leading to slavery. This 'justice' is the very thing that the Lord desires above all else (v. 3), and the thing that brings a rightly focused disciple the most joy (v. 15). Spurn what brings pleasure to the Lord in lieu of what brings pleasure to you and you will lose your joy.

21:8. The way of a guilty man is crooked, But as for the pure, his conduct is upright.

For the simple point that this proverb makes, it has created a lot of difficult discussion. Most of the commentaries have centered on identifying the meaning of the words translated 'guilty' and 'crooked,' since they occur nowhere else in the Old Testament.[11] Not so many disagree about the meaning of 'crooked.'[12] However, more ink has been spilt over the meaning of 'guilty.' The translators of the KJV believed it to be two words that had inadvertently been pushed together and the space between them removed: the Hebrew word for 'and' and a participle of the word meaning 'strange' (thus the KJV's 'The way of man is forward and strange').[13] It appears, however, that most experts see it as derived from two Arabic root words that, together, mean something like 'laden with guilt' (ASV).[14] In strong support of this understanding is the fact that the immediate context of the second line better supports such a translation, as it provides a better antithesis.

The simple point is that conduct points to character. When a man's way is 'crooked,' you can guess that he is 'guilty' of something. When his actions are 'upright,' you can bet his heart is relatively 'pure.' People are not something other than how they consistently behave. Examine a person's 'way' and 'work' (for thus is the literal meaning of the word translated 'conduct'[15]) and you will discover the fiber of his integrity.

Additionally, it reminds us that when a person carries around a burden of unresolved guilt, he resorts to all kinds of devious antics to keep his sin from being found out and his name sullied.[16] How complicated the life of sin becomes! On the other hand, when a man lives from a 'pure' heart, he can walk a straight line in this life, knowing that he has nothing to hide.

21:9. It is better to live in a corner of a roof, Than in a house shared with a contentious woman.
Again, we meet one of the numerous 'better ... than' proverbs (Prov. 12:9; 15:16, 17; 16:8, 19; 17:1; 19:1; 21:19; 25:7, 24; 27:5, 10; 28:6). The first line states that which is better – 'to live in a corner of a roof.' The roofs of homes in Israel were flat, providing a perfect place to erect a humble, but inhabitable, one room dwelling. That people actually did so is attested to in Scripture (1 Kings 17:19; 2 Kings 4:10). Such accommodations would be cramped and not nearly as comfortable as living in the house below. But, this would be far superior to living 'in a house shared with a contentious woman.'

The word translated 'contentious' means to quarrel, dispute, nag or enter into dissension. Many men, however, need no further explanation. The word is found almost exclusively in Proverbs. The plural, as here, points to multiplied instances of strife. Among those who create such disharmony, the contentious wife is the most frequently mentioned (Prov. 19:13; 21:9, 19; 25:24; 27:15).[17] Her incessant nagging is likened to the constant dripping of rain through a leaking roof (Prov. 19:13; 27:15). She makes even a luxurious home uninhabitable (Prov. 1:19; 25:24). This verse is nearly duplicated in Proverbs 25:24.

Though a man be married and conscious of his covenant commitment to his wife, his mind may wander to what might be 'better ... than' living with the woman his wife has become. He must guard himself, lest her nagging become the occasion for his failure to keep faith with her and God. She must hold her tongue and keep her peace.

21:10. The soul of the wicked desires evil; His neighbor finds no favor in his eyes.
The first line describes the problem. The word 'soul' stands for the person as a whole. We have seen how the word can describe the longings and passions of a person (Prov. 10:3; 16:26; 23:2), thus it is right in place with this talk of the one who 'desires evil.' Note that wrongdoing is not something done from weakness, nor because the

individual has been the victim of some wrong that now renders him incapable of better conduct.

This individual 'desires' evil (Prov. 12:12a). It is his longing. It is not an isolated failure or act or irrationality. For this person, 'evil' is fun (Prov. 2:14; 10:23a). 'He plans wickedness upon his bed; He sets himself on a path that is not good; He does not despise evil' (Ps. 36:4; cf. Prov. 4:16). 'You love evil more than good' (Ps. 52:3a). Much of Old Testament history is recorded to thwart such desires in us: 'Now these things happened as examples for us, that we should not crave evil things, as they also craved' (1 Cor. 10:6). When feelings, desires and appetites are allowed to be the determining factor in our thinking and conduct, no depths of depravity are unreachable.

The second line describes the outcome of such perverted desire – 'His neighbor finds no favor in his eyes.' Proverbs has strictly warned us of this: 'Do not devise harm against your neighbor, While he lives in security beside you' (Prov. 3:29). 'He who despises his neighbor sins' (Prov. 14:21a). It is this twisted, desire-driven philosophy of life that produces so much of our interpersonal strife (James 4:1-5).

21:11. When the scoffer is punished, the naïve becomes wise; But when the wise is instructed, he receives knowledge.
This verse is nearly identical to Proverbs 19:25 in meaning, if not in exact form. Three kinds of people are enumerated here. First, there is 'the scoffer.' Such a one rejects all attempts to curb his willfulness (Prov. 9:7, 8; 13:1; 15:12). Because he is confirmed in his rebellion, Proverbs considers him unreachable (Prov. 14:6). The 'scoffer' was once naïve, but has moved now into a confirmed state, where he rejects all authority (Prov. 21:24; 22:10; 29:8). As he now scoffs at God, so God will one day laugh over him in his destruction (Prov. 3:34).[18]

The second kind of person is 'the naïve.' Their basic traits are that they are gullible, silly and naïve (Prov. 14:15; 22:3). They delight in willful self-expression and, generally, fail to think or act responsibly (Prov. 1:32). They think little of others around them (Prov. 19:25). They find pleasure in their foolish lifestyle (Prov. 15:21). They throw their life away, chasing what, ultimately, does not matter (Prov. 15:21). We all start at this place of naïveté. Without someone to guide us into wisdom, we surely follow the downward pull of rebellion that will, ultimately, destroy us (Prov. 22:3). The 'naïve' are still reachable and able to be rescued from their folly.[19]

The third group is called 'the wise.' Those who make up this group have moved out of their initial naïveté and have started down the path of knowledge. They have sought God and His ways, walking obediently in them as they are revealed. Each nugget of knowledge has compounded into understanding and has now grown into wisdom. They are able to look at people and events around them with insight and discernment. They have learned through training (Heb. 5:14) to see the world through different eyes than the 'scoffer' or 'naïve.' The worldview of 'the wise' is a much more accurate representation of reality than that of either of the other two.

The point of this proverb, like that of its near twin (Prov. 19:25), is to outline the differences between how each of these folks learn. In the view of the Proverbs, the 'scoffer' is uneducable (Prov. 9:8; 13:1; 15:12; 17:10; 21:11). Perhaps this is why we are told 'Do not reprove a scoffer, lest he hate you' (Prov. 9:8a). Of course, no one is beyond the grace of God, yet apart from a supernatural intervention, the outcome of such a one is set. Yet, the 'scoffer' must be disciplined – 'Judgments are prepared for scoffers, And blows for the back of fools' (Prov. 19:29; cf. 14:3). The reason for his discipline is not his reformation, but that of the 'naïve' one who looks on (Deut. 13:11; 21:21; Prov. 19:25; 1 Tim. 5:20). When the 'naïve' watch the way a 'scoffer is punished,' it is possible that he 'becomes wise.' The 'naïve,' while silly and shallow, are capable of learning from the errors of another.

Yet, there exists a more desirable kind of learning. Here, 'the wise,' at a simple word of 'instruction' or reproof (Prov. 19:25), 'receives knowledge.' A simple 'word to the wise,' the way someone says something, even non-verbal cues like facial expression and body language, are often enough for 'the wise' to discover some new insight or take in 'knowledge' about the people and circumstances around them. 'A rebuke goes deeper into one who has understanding Than a hundred blows into a fool' (Prov. 17:10).

Some commentators debate over what the subject of the second line is.[20] Does 'he' refer to 'the naïve' of line one, or to 'the wise' of line two ? Does the word to 'the wise' in line two thus serve as a second way 'the naïve' can learn (in addition to the punishment of 'the scoffer'), or as a contrasting and superior way of learning altogether that only 'the wise' possess? It seems the second of these options is preferable. This not only is the most natural way of reading the proverb, but it also conforms to its near twin in Proverbs 19:25.

21:12. The righteous one considers the house of the wicked, Turning the wicked to ruin.

This proverb presents a couple of interpretational challenges. The first is the identity of 'The righteous one.' The NASB has taken it at face value and translated it as some individual (perhaps a judge, ruler or leader) that is just. This, however, makes the second line difficult to understand, for this one is said to overthrow the wicked man and bring him to ruin. This is a more active stance toward the wicked than the book of Proverbs usually seems to employ. On the other hand, the NIV ('the Just One'), the JB ('the Just One'), the NEB ('The Just God'), along with most modern commentators,[21] believe this to be a reference to God. Interestingly, the KJV has 'the righteous man,' while the NKJV has 'the righteous God' and, similarly, the RSV has 'the righteous,' while the NRSV has 'the Righteous One.' The trouble is that, not withstanding the fact that God is often called just or righteous, such a form is never anywhere used in the Old Testament as a title for God. Some point to Job 34:17 as a possible indicator, though it is not an exact match. This option is attractive, however, because it makes better sense out of the second line – God is the very One we would expect to be bringing such demonstrative judgment upon the wicked. All things considered, it is probably best to understand this as a reference to God.

The second challenge is that the same Hebrew word that was translated 'is instructed' in verse 11 is now used, but translated 'considers.' The word refers to knowledge, both held and passed on. In verse 11, such knowledge is being gained by one already 'wise.' Here, 'considers' describes an attempt to figure things out by the knowledge that has already been gained. The word can refer to the knowledge possessed only by God (Job 10:7; Ps. 139:6; Prov. 3:20).[22]

Thus, the first line of the proverb means that God, in His justice, knows perfectly the condition of 'the house of the wicked.' Then, add the thoughts of the second line: possessing such perfect knowledge, God, then, in His justice, overturns or subverts (the literal meaning of 'Turning,' Prov. 13:6; 19:3; 22:12) the wicked to their own ruin (Prov. 14:11). This understanding answers best to the whole of the Scripture's teachings about God and man and their response to the wicked.

21:13. He who shuts his ear to the cry of the poor Will also cry himself and not be answered.
'Blessed are the merciful, for they shall receive mercy' (Matt. 5:7). This proverb is the reverse image of Jesus' beatitude, revealing what happens to the unmerciful. Proverbs often demands ministry to the poor. We are to share our food (Prov. 22:9) and money (Prov. 28:8) when others are in need. We may be called upon to defend the rights of the oppressed (Prov. 31:9). Such a person recognizes that

God made both the poor man and himself (Prov. 22:2; 29:13). Such merciful generosity honors God (Prov. 14:31; cf. 17:5). All such acts of kindness are, ultimately, done to the Lord (Matt. 25:31-46) and, rather than giving away such resources, we are only lending to the Lord Himself (Prov. 19:17), who will ultimately repay the good deed. God Himself promises that such a person will never lack (Prov. 28:27) and will find happiness (Prov. 14:21).

The unrighteous man is self-centered and so caught up in his own desires that he either does not see his neighbor's need or does not care (Prov. 21:10, 26). Such a one has never truly tasted of God's love and mercy. 'But whoever has the world's goods, and beholds his brother in need and closes his heart against him, how does the love of God abide in him?' (1 John 3:17).

The second line of the proverb assumes that none of us is perfectly secure in our earthly wealth. One never knows what calamity may befall him. This second line also asserts the rigid and righteous impartiality with which the law of sowing and reaping operates. No mercy shown, no mercy received. 'For judgment will be merciless to one who has shown no mercy' (James 2:13a). God has already promised not to hear the ruthless, violent and unmerciful man when he calls (Prov. 1:28). For illustrations of this reciprocal law of recompense, see Jesus' account of the unmerciful servant (Matt. 18:30-34), the rich man and Lazarus (Luke 16:19-31) and the judgment of the last days (Matt. 25:31-46). We do well to remember, 'For in the way you judge, you will be judged; and by your standard of measure, it will be measured to you' (Matt 7:2).

21:14. A gift in secret subdues anger, And a bribe in the bosom, strong wrath.

This proverb, like Proverbs 17:8 and 18:16, speaks of bribery with no moral condemnation, a fact that seems odd, in view of the general denunciation of the practice throughout Proverbs and the rest of the Scriptures (Prov. 15:27; 17:23; Exod. 23:8; Deut. 16:19; 1 Sam. 12:3; Eccles. 7:7; Isa. 1:23; Amos 5:12). This proverb, however, simply states a fact of life that will help the wise one understand why certain situations work out as they do. It does not encourage the practice of bribery, but it lays bare the sad effectiveness of the ways of the world.

The first line names the practice as it is spoken of in the light, before the crowds: 'A gift.' The second line, however, confesses what it is in actual fact: 'a bribe.' That it does indeed arise from wrong motives and is employed with malicious intent is seen in that it is given 'in secret.' The expression is, literally, 'from the bosom.' The phrase points to covert actions and sinister intent (cf. also Prov. 6:27; 16:33; 17:23).

Just exactly the situation in which it is employed is not spelled out, but one illustration is given in Proverbs 6:32-35. Jacob and Esau provide another (Gen. 32:20). Whatever the specifics, a bribe can work to grease the wheels when relationships have been strained. Indeed, it 'subdues anger' and 'strong wrath.' It operates on the premise that 'Many will entreat the favor of a generous man, And every man is a friend to him who gives gifts' (Prov. 19:6).

Perhaps the moral note, left unstated here, is to be heard from the next proverb.[23]

21:15. The execution of justice is joy for the righteous, But is terror to the workers of iniquity.

This proverb of antithetical parallelism contrasts the response of 'the righteous' and 'the workers of iniquity' to the application of 'justice.' At first glance, it may appear that it is 'justice' in a general, and passive, sense that is being considered – others (rulers?) doing justice around them. However, it is the more active sense of the two contrasted groups actually doing the 'justice' themselves that is in view.[24]

To 'the righteous,' such an undertaking 'is joy.' The word describes being glad with the whole of one's person, as it is associated with the heart (Ps. 105:3), the soul (Ps. 86:4) and the eyes (Prov. 15:30). Many things can bring this 'joy' to a man, but it is God Himself, and His salvation, which is the most frequently cited reason. This 'joy of the Lord' is a person's very strength (Neh. 8:10).[25] This same word is found in verse 17, where it has become the sole objective of the person's life and, thus, has become his undoing. Such 'joy' or 'pleasure' is a wonderful, God-given byproduct of a rightly lived life, but it is an unworthy and self-destructive objective to pursue apart from God and His ways. Pursuing God's gifts rather than pursuing God is unholy and destructive.

In contrast, 'the workers of iniquity' find that this kind of justice 'is terror.' The word so translated describes both the emotion of terror and the event of destruction. It is found seven times in Proverbs (more than in any other book)[26] and describes the 'ruin' that results from foolish talk (Prov. 10:14; 13:3; 18:7), poverty (10:15; 14:28) and the path of evil (10:29; 21:15).[27]

This second line is a repeat of that found in Proverbs 10:29, where the thing spoken of is not 'The execution of justice,' but 'The way of the LORD.'

21:16. A man who wanders from the way of understanding Will rest in the assembly of the dead.

In this proverb, one can hear several echoes from the first nine chapters of Proverbs. We are familiar with 'the way' as a metaphor for the course of one's life, established through one's choices and acts (Prov. 1:15, 31; 2:8, 12, 20; 3:23, etc.). The word 'understanding' was introduced as early as Proverbs 1:3 and has reverberated often throughout these pages (Prov. 10:5, 19; 14:35; 15:24; 16:20, 23, etc.).

The phrase 'the dead' has been seen in Proverbs 2:18 and 9:18. Some translate the phrase 'the shades.' The Hebrew word here translated has Ugaritic origins. The Ugaritic word described 'the dead inhabitants of the netherworld.' The appearances of the Hebrew word are in poetic sections (Prov. 9:18; Job 26:5; Isa. 14:9; 26:14) and the word simply serves as a synonym for the other, more common, Hebrew words such as 'death' or 'Sheol.'[28] One should not read 'rest' with overtones of peaceful bliss, for it simply refers to the final state of their dwelling.[29]

Finally, the notion of a premature death for the fool is a frequent warning, especially for the man who would consort with the adulteress (Prov. 2:18-19; 5:23; 7:22-23, 26-27; 9:18). 'He who walks with wise men will be wise, But the companion of fools will suffer harm' (Prov. 13:20).

21:17. He who loves pleasure will become a poor man; He who loves wine and oil will not become rich.

Through synonymous parallelism, this proverb points out the self-defeating and self-destructive nature of an indulgent lifestyle. The word for 'pleasure' is the same one translated 'joy' in verse 15. The two verses help form a theology of pleasure. In verse 15, the 'joy' (or 'pleasure') is experienced as an outgrowth of having pursued righteousness. Here, the 'pleasure' is the thing targeted and sought out ('He who loves'). The focus makes all the difference. God is not a cosmic kill-joy who despises anyone's happiness and pleasure. True pleasure comes only from pursuing Him. Self-destruction comes from pursing 'pleasure' for pleasure's sake (Prov. 23:20, 21, 29-35; Eccles. 2:1, 2; 8:15).

The self-defeating nature of a hedonistic lifestyle is seen in the contrasting expressions 'will become a poor man' and 'will not become rich.' The 'wine and oil' are symbolic expressions that often represent 'the good life' of ease, leisure and wealth (Deut. 14:26; Judg. 9:9, 13; Neh. 8:12; Ps. 104:15; Amos 6:6; John 12:5). Such may be had within God's will, but it comes from pursuing righteousness and wisdom, not pleasure itself (vv. 20, 21).

21:18. The wicked is a ransom for the righteous, And the treacherous is in the place of the upright.

This proverb has puzzled commentators for some time. The thought appears to be much like that of Proverbs 11:8: 'The righteous is delivered from trouble, But the wicked takes his place.' If this is the case, then the point would seem to be that, when God's purposes are finally worked out, it is 'The wicked' who receive punishment, while the righteous are set free.

However, the proverb does not answer why 'the righteous' would be in need of 'a ransom.' The word translated as 'ransom' normally points to atonement and substitution. In what sense can the punishment of the 'wicked' be said to be atoning for the righteous? Or, how is their punishment a substitutionary act for 'the righteous'?

No doubt, 'ransom' must be understood somewhat metaphorically. Perhaps Isaiah 43:3 helps point the way, for there several nations are called a 'ransom' for Israel. They were conquered by Cyrus the Persian on his way to overthrow Babylon. In thus defeating Babylon, the Persians made way for the eventual release of the Israelites from exile. In this sense, the nations thus conquered were 'a ransom' given by God to free His people.

If this is the right understanding of the proverb, then its point is that, as God sovereignly rules the universe, He willingly uses the rebellious and unrighteous in order to bring about the eventual fulfillment of His plan, which ultimately means welfare for those who willingly follow Him in faith. For further reflection, consider Haman, who eventually stood in the place of Mordecai (Esther 7:9-10), and the tragic situation Jesus spoke of in Luke 13:1-5.

21:19. It is better to live in a desert land, Than with a contentious and vexing woman.

This proverb is a virtual repeat of the one found in verse 9 (cf. also Prov. 19:13; 25:24; 27:15). Two major differences are evident, however. The harried husband's preferable dwelling of verse 9 ('a corner of a roof') has now become 'a desert land.' The word largely signifies an uninhabited area, devoid of fruit, water supply or anything desirable and necessary.[30] Such a place is completely undesirable and normally considered nearly uninhabitable, yet, compared with 'a contentious ... woman,' the 'desert land' looks like a well-watered oasis to this frustrated man.

The second addition here is the word translated 'vexing.' It describes grief, anguish or sorrow.[31] The translation might be better: 'Than with the vexation of a contentious woman,' for 'contentious' and 'vexing' do not seem to be parallel comments on the kind of woman being considered. The 'vexing' is the overall result of living with a contentious woman, an additional editorial comment on the resulting home life.[32]

Some might read this proverb and its cousins and think they have found justification for an escape from a bad marriage. The word translated 'desert' is used in the memorable question, 'Can God prepare a table in the wilderness?' (Ps. 78:19b). This question, of course, was asked by the Israelites during their wilderness wanderings and they assumed the answer was 'No.' God, however, did set that table for them in the wilderness, providing manna, meat and water throughout their journeys. These proverbs do not provide an 'out' for frustrated husbands. Rather, it encourages them to embrace the hardships of their reality and call them what they are. These proverbs acknowledge such a man's pain, but the larger scope of Scripture promises God's sustaining grace, even as he remains faithful in the midst of it.

21:20. There is precious treasure and oil in the dwelling of the wise, But a foolish man swallows it up.
The Proverbs often view wisdom as having tangible rewards (Prov. 3:10, 16; 8:21; 15:6 22:4). Here, they are 'precious treasure and oil.' How this wealth happened to come into the possession of 'the wise' is not stated. We know it did not come because of ravenous pursuit on his part (cf. 'oil' in v. 17). It likely came by meticulous saving (Prov. 6:6-8) and careful self-discipline in consumption (Prov. 25:16). We know that, ultimately, 'It is the blessing of the LORD that makes rich, And He adds no sorrow to it' (Prov. 10:22). God delights to bless the homes ('dwelling') of those who walk in careful obedience to His precepts.

The second line presents a contrast, revealing the self-defeating ways of 'a foolish man.' He is, literally, 'a fool of a man' (cf. Prov. 15:20).[33] Instead of acquiring wealth, the fool 'swallows it up.' The verb in this form describes an engulfing, consuming and devouring action. The meaning is intensified into the idea of wiping out, or destroying, something.[34] In his rapaciousness, he gulps down any riches that come his way. There will be nothing left for coming days. He never discovers the cumulative blessings of self-discipline. Even his momentary pleasure is short-lived, for the riches he has devoured he 'will vomit them up' (Job 20:15, cf. v. 18).

The meaning, then, seems to be that the wise saves, or uses judiciously, his wealth when it comes and, as a result, will have more, while the fool squanders all he ever gains and, thus, rarely possesses anything. Some have suggested an alternative meaning. Perhaps it means that the wise may have wealth for a time, but, in the end, the fool will swallow up what he has saved. Therefore, the conclusion is that it is not wise to put your hope in the riches (Eccles. 2:18-19; Ps. 39:6; 49:10). This is a possibility, but, in the context of this chapter (v. 17), the former seems more likely.

20:21. He who pursues righteousness and loyalty Finds life, righteousness and honor.
The previous proverb held forth tangible rewards for the one who walks in wisdom. Here, the rewards are personal ('life'), spiritual ('righteousness') and social ('honor'). The first line sets out the conditions upon which such rewards are available. The individual must be one 'who pursues righteousness and loyalty.' These twin virtues summarize the requirements for one who would walk faithfully in covenant with God and man (Mic. 6:8). Righteousness is spiritual justification before God and social justice with one's fellow man. The word 'loyalty' is the rich Hebrew word *hesed*, which speaks of covenant love and faithfulness, again directed both vertically and horizontally. The faithful one 'pursues' this 'righteousness and loyalty.' The verb is nearly always negative in connotation, usually speaking of pursuing someone for purposes of war or revenge. While the meaning here is positive, the intensity of the word is profound.[35]

When a person stands rightly before God and man, dealing faithfully with Him and his neighbor, God promises there will be rewards. The second line delineates those rewards: 'life, righteousness and honor.' This trio of rewards are found often in Proverbs: 'life' (Prov. 2:19; 3:2, 18, 22; 4:10, 13, 22, 23; 5:6; 6:23; 8:35; 9:11; 10:11, 16, 17; 11:19, 30; 12:28; 13:12, 14; 14:27, 30; 15:4, 24, 31; 16:15, 22; 18:21; 19:23; 22:4; 27:27; 31:12); 'righteousness' (Prov. 8:18, 20; 10:2; 11:4-6, 18, 19; 12:28; 13:6; 14:34; 15:9; 16:8, 12, 31; 21:3); and 'honor' (Prov. 3:16, 35; 8:18; 11:16; 15:33; 18:12; 20:3; 22:4; 25:2, 27; 26:1, 8; 29:23).

Some have, unfortunately, considered the repetition of 'righteousness,' the middle of these three rewards, as 'suspicious,' seeing that it appears in the Hebrew text, but not in the LXX.[36] This unfounded suspicion is what led the translators of the RSV to drop the word all together and may have led to the unfortunate translation of 'prosperity' in the NIV. But, why should it be considered strange that God might bless the honest seeker with the very righteousness he has been seeking? Jesus later promised: 'Blessed are those who hunger and thirst for righteousness, for they shall be satisfied' (Matt. 5:6). Indeed, the promise is that God will bless such a one with not only what he has been seeking ('righteousness'), but with far more than he has been seeking ('life ... and honor'). Also, Jesus promised, 'But seek first His kingdom and His righteousness; *and all these things shall be added to you*' (Matt. 6:33, emphasis added). The wonder is that, when you seek God's righteousness, He guarantees that you will not only find it, but that you will also find much more than you ever sought!

21:22. A wise man scales the city of the mighty, And brings down the stronghold in which they trust.

These two synonymous lines remind us that wisdom is ultimately more powerful that a war machine. The imagery of armed military conflict is employed to give instructions more broadly about life in general. The 'wise man' is pictured as standing before a towering city of fortified battlements. The walls are lined with all the firepower that the city's resources can muster. Yet, everything 'mighty' has some point of weakness. The 'wise man,' spotting that place of vulnerability, 'scales' the walls unharmed and claims the victory.

Scripture is filled with examples of just such military exploits: Abram and the kings of the east (Gen. 14); Joshua over Jericho (Josh. 6) and Ai (Josh. 8); Gideon's band over Midian (Judg. 7).[37] Perhaps the most telling example, however, is that of David and his men taking the stronghold of Jerusalem (2 Sam. 5:6-9).

The second line echoes the first, but advances the imagery. The first line shows the 'wise man' merely scaling the walls of the city, in the second line he 'brings down' the trusted fortress of the mighty. Here, actual victory is attained. 'He who is slow to anger is better than the mighty, And he who rules his spirit, than he who captures a city' (Prov. 16:32). Wisdom strengthens a wise man more than ten rulers who are in a city' (Eccles. 7:19).

Notice over what the victory comes: 'the stronghold in which they trust.' Application demands that we now press beyond the imagery of military strategy, because there are many strongholds in which people trust and which they will defend with great passion and power. In the New Testament era, the battle is primarily seen to be on the spiritual level, 'For our struggle is not against flesh and blood, but against the rulers, against the powers, against the world forces of this darkness, against the spiritual forces of wickedness in the heavenly places' (Eph. 6:12).

The most formidable strongholds in our day are those in the mind, fortified with twisted logic and backed by immoral passions. Ideas are often more intimidating than infantrymen. Yet, 'though we walk in the flesh, we do not war according to the flesh, for the weapons of our warfare are not of the flesh, but divinely powerful for the destruction of fortresses. We are destroying speculations and every lofty thing raised up against the knowledge of God, and we are taking every thought captive to the obedience of Christ' (2 Cor. 10:3-5).

Ultimately, the power of wisdom outperforms the might of physical, military, social, spiritual or intellectual strength (Prov. 24:5). Eventually, we will all discover that 'Wisdom is better than strength' (Eccles. 9:16).

21:23. He who guards his mouth and his tongue, Guards his soul from troubles.

Again, we are reminded that less is more when it comes to speech. The two lines of this proverb function together to make one continuous sentence. The first line sets forth the prescribed action and the second the reward. In this regard, it is very near Proverbs 13:3a. Interestingly, the compactness of the Hebrew lines underscores the point made. Murphy tries to represent this terseness: 'One guarding mouth and tongue – one keeping self from troubles.'[38]

The same word is used twice (in both English and Hebrew): 'guards.' When one 'guards' what he says, he automatically guards himself from all kinds of troubles that would otherwise enter his life. The verb is used over four hundred times in the Old Testament. Its basic meaning is 'to exercise great care over' something.[39] Here, the thing carefully watched over is 'his mouth and his tongue,' a metaphorical reference to the words that proceed from the 'mouth' and the speech produced by the 'tongue.' Reminders to keep one's words few and judicious are plenteous in Proverbs (Prov. 10:19; 12:13; 14:3; 17:27, 28; 18:21).

When one keeps prudent track of one's words, he 'Guards his soul from troubles.' These 'troubles' may be in the spiritual, social, legal or physical realm. The word describes an intense inward agitation (Ps. 25:17). It is used to describe the pain of a woman's delivery of her first child (Jer. 4:31). It is the terror before a ravaging army (Jer. 6:24).[40]

We must each one take responsibility for our speech. There is 'A time to be silent, and a time to speak' (Eccles. 3:7b). Our highest motive should be the glory of God (Heb. 13:15) and the good of others (Eph. 4:29). Yet, there is worth even in the motive of sparing one's self 'troubles.' For these reasons, we must exercise great self-control in our speech. Yet, as the New Testament reminds us, no man can do this perfectly (James 3:2, 8). Therefore, it is wise to admit our inability and call out to God: 'Set a guard, O LORD, over my mouth; Keep watch over the door of my lips' (Ps. 141:3).

21:24. 'Proud,' 'Haughty,' 'Scoffer,' are his names, Who acts with insolent pride.

This proverb delineates the character and style of the 'Scoffer.' We have met him often in these proverbs (Prov. 1:22; 3:34; 9:7, 8, 12; 13:1; 14:6, 9; 15:12; 19:25, 28, 29; 20:1; 21:11; 22:10; 24:9). He represents the lowest possible descent into foolishness, pride taken to its extreme.

This first line is somewhat difficult to translate. Should the first three words all be translated as names for the 'Scoffer,' as here in the NASB? Or, does the NIV have it correct in making only the third ('Scoffer') a proper name, and translating the first two as descriptive terms ('The proud and arrogant man – "Mocker" is his name')? Seeing that the Hebrew word behind 'names' is singular, and the NASB has taken liberty to transform it to a plural, and seeing that the first two words ('Proud' and 'Haughty') do not appear to be in the class of a name, as does 'Scoffer,' it is probable that we should follow the NIV here.

Think, then, of the character of such a person. He is 'Proud.' The word describes one who is calloused and careless toward the rights and needs of others. Such a one assumes God's laws do not apply to him. He may even resort to violence against the godly (Ps. 86:14; Isa. 13:11). If unturned, he will reject God's grace (Jer. 43:2) and determine it is worthless to serve God (Mal. 3:13-14). A fiery judgment awaits such people (Mal. 4:1).[41]

He is also 'Haughty.' The word describes someone absorbed in self, who has, thus, lost all perspective and overestimates his worth.[42] This word is found elsewhere only in Habakkuk 2:5. There, we find a man who has distorted his thinking with too much alcohol and, in his drunken stupor, believes himself to deserve anything and everything: 'He enlarges his appetite like Sheol, And he is like death, never satisfied. He also gathers to himself all nations And collects to himself all peoples.'

With his character unveiled, his actions are then described: 'Who acts with insolent pride.' The word 'pride' is related to the first word in the proverb. The key to this word is its sense of presumption. Having too highly evaluated himself, the 'Scoffer' presumes that he has a right to things that are not his. In the end, however, he gets just what he deserves: 'dishonor' (Prov. 11:2).[43] The word 'insolent' describes that which is an overflow, excess or outburst. It can mean arrogance or fury as well. It describes the arrogant wrath of Moab against Israel (Isa. 16:6; Jer. 48:29). It can describe an overflowing fury which arises when others don't act in accord with one's presumptions about oneself.[44]

Such is the character and conduct of the 'Scoffer.' Little wonder, then, that Proverbs so soundly denounces him. God will scoff at him who has scoffed at His holiness and ways throughout his life (Prov. 3:34).

21:25. The desire of the sluggard puts him to death, For his hands refuse to work;

Here, again, we meet 'the sluggard.' Proverbs has often warned us of what such laziness produces: further laziness (Prov. 19:24), the lack of a harvest (Prov. 20:4), empty hands (Prov. 13:4), poverty (Prov. 6:11; 24:34), troubles (Prov. 15:19) and even forced labor (Prov. 12:24). Here, however, we come face to face with the stark reality of its end: 'death.'

Interestingly, it is his 'desire' which 'puts him to death.' Some take this to mean that 'desire' means hunger and, since he won't work, he actually starves himself to death.[45] However, it seems to point not so much at a legitimate hunger, but a lustful desire. The same word is used in Numbers 11:34-35 and 33:16-17 as part of the place named 'graves of craving.' When the people grumbled against God and Moses and demanded meat to eat, God sent an abundance of quail to fill their demand. Then He sent a plague in judgment. They got what they wanted and it killed them. They buried their dead and called the place 'graves of craving.'[46]

Here, too, the craving of the sluggard digs his grave, for, if he can muster any energy and take any initiative, it is spent on that which is frivolous ('desire') and not on what is essential ('work'). In the end, such a lifestyle destroys him. '... [I]f anyone will not work, neither let him eat' (2 Thess. 3:10).

21:26. All day long he is craving, While the righteous gives and does not hold back.

This verse and the previous one are linked. The obvious verbal link is found in the repeated Hebrew word translated 'desire' (v. 25) and 'craving' (here). Some believe that it was this commonality alone which led to these two proverbs being placed together. It seems more likely, however, that they were originally constructed together and form a larger thought unit. The first line here is, literally, 'All day long he is desiring a desire.' The subject is left general, with 'he.' The subject should be understood as the 'sluggard' of verse 25.

The shared Hebrew word is doubled to intensify the meaning. The NASB translators use 'craving' in an attempt to give this meaning, while the NIV has 'craves for more.' The 'sluggard' is not lazy for want of desire, but for want of initiative and drive. Indeed, he wants everything, but nothing moves him from his lethargy. He is full of dreams, ideas and grandiose plans. In the end, he wastes away in the wealth of his wishes.

How different for 'the righteous!' The very fact that the 'sluggard' is contrasted with 'the righteous' (rather than, say, 'the industrious') reveals that laziness is a spiritual matter. Where the lazy man only wants, constantly thinking of himself, the godly man thinks of others and thus 'gives and does not hold back' (Prov. 22:9; Ps. 37:26; 112:5, 9; Matt. 5:42). Laziness and righteousness are largely a matter of selfishness or servanthood. Selfishness is self-destructive (v. 25), while focusing on others leads to initiative, self-development, hard work, and spiritual progress (v. 26).

21:27. The sacrifice of the wicked is an abomination, How much more when he brings it with evil intent!
The first line of this proverb repeats that of Proverbs 15:8a, except that, there, the phrase 'to the LORD' is added.' The LXX has tried to conform this proverb to that one by adding the same phrase. Though the divine name is not found here, His presence is everywhere understood.

God is repulsed by the veneer of insincere acts of worship when the heart is not in it (Isa. 1:13-15; 66:3; Jer. 6:20; Amos 5:22). Ritualism is not only worthless before God, but it is profoundly repulsive. God refuses to endure hypocritical, insincere people who perform acts of worship. Even their prayer is an abomination to Him (Prov. 28:9).

Whereas the second line of Proverbs 15:8 presented a contrast ('But He loves him who pursues righteousness'), here the second line is in synthetic parallelism to the first – extending and developing the thought of the first. This takes the form of a 'How much more' statement. As unthinkable as blinded hypocrisy in worship is, there is something exceedingly worse. That something worse is 'when he [the worshiper] brings it [the sacrifice] with evil intent!' The Hebrew word translated 'evil intent' is used to describe actions that are particularly abhorrent to God, such as murder (Hosea 6:9), ruining another's life through false testimony (Isa. 32:7), gang rape (Judg. 20:6), parents using their daughter as a prostitute (Lev. 19:29), or a man sleeping with his daughter-in-law (Ezek. 22:11). It was such acts that caused God to spew out of the Promised Land its original residents (Lev. 18:24-30; 20:22-23).[47]

How incredible that God would consider these abominations on a par with what looks, at least from the outside, as an act of worship! In what sense has this person made his act of worship 'with evil intent?' While the first line may refer to the blinded person who is unaware of his hypocrisy and duplicity, this second line likely points to one who knowingly prostitutes the prescribed forms of worship in order to make personal gain. Perhaps he believes that such an act truly gains him merit with God, apart from genuine repentance and faith. Perhaps he uses the things of God to convince others of his piety, while he knowingly continues in his sin. Maybe he 'uses' church to gain community status and grow his business prospects. Whatever the specifics, God's judgment will fall swiftly upon such religious hucksters (1 Sam. 13:8-14; 15:21-23).

This reminds us that sincerity is not the test of true worship, nor is mere outward form. The true test is a repentant heart and a submissive, obedient will (Prov. 21:3; Mark 12:33).

21:28. A false witness will perish, But the man who listens to the truth will speak forever.
The first line sounds a now familiar denunciation of the 'false witness' (Exod. 20:16; Prov. 12:17-18; 14:5, 25; 25:18). Such lying is an abomination to God (Prov. 6:16, 19). For this reason, God promises that such a one 'will perish' (cf. Prov. 19:5, 9). In Old Testament days, this could mean that the death penalty would be exacted (Deut. 19:16-20). Or, it could mean, in a judicial setting, that the judge might cut short the witness's testimony. Or, in a more general application, it could mean that people simply may cease to listen to such a person.

The second line does not carry the thought in the expected direction. We might have anticipated a contrast something like, 'But he who tells the truth will be established.' But, rather than this, the writer has pointed us toward 'the man who listens.' This begs the question: listens to what or to whom? The NASB has supplied 'the truth' and the NKJV has inserted 'him' (i.e. the false witness). The meaning is likely more general, referring, in a courtroom scene, to all the evidence presented in a case, rather than selectively listening only to what one wants to hear (perhaps the case with the 'false witness').

If applied to more general circumstances, it may be a reference to listening with discernment, asking probing questions and a refusal to rush to judgment until the fuller context is understood. 'The first to plead his case seems just, Until another comes and examines him' (Prov. 18:17).

In whatever arena such a man is found, we are assured that he 'will speak forever.' That may mean that, in court, he speaks a complete testimony, which may not be refuted by a crafty defense attorney or cut short by an impatient judge. Such testimony will prove convincing to the judge or jury and, in this sense, will stand forever. 'Truthful lips will be established forever, But a lying tongue is only for a moment' (Prov. 12:19).

The NIV translates the second line as: 'and whoever listens to him will be destroyed forever.' This arises from the decision of the translators to solve the awkwardness of the relationship of lines one and two by following an alternative reading meaning 'perish,' rather than 'speak.'[48] The NIV marginal translation ('but the words of an obedient man will live on') is close to the NASB's translation, and should be preferred.

21:29. A wicked man shows a bold face, But as for the upright, he makes his way sure.

This proverb contrasts 'A wicked man' with 'the upright.' The characteristic in view for the 'wicked man' is that he 'shows a bold face.' The same expression in found in Proverbs 7:13, where it was used of the adulteress. The word means, more literally, to make something firm or strong (i.e. 'he hardens his face').[49] It speaks of a set disposition, a confirmed condition of the heart that reveals itself in one's countenance. His way is set; no amount of counsel, reproof or pleading will change his course (Isa. 48:4; Jer. 5:3; Ezek. 3:7).

The contrast in the second line describes 'the upright' as one who 'makes his way sure.' The NIV follows an alternative reading and translates as 'gives thought to his ways.' The commentaries are divided between the two readings. The basic notion, either way, is that, while the wicked man is hardened and confirmed in his sinful course, the wise man proceeds on the basis of wise counsel, proven principles, and discerning insight. He, thus, seeks to make 'his way sure' by giving 'thought to his ways.' In the end, such a disposition also affects this man's countenance: 'A man's wisdom illumines him and causes his stern face to beam' (Eccles. 8:1b).

No doubt, these two polarized attitudes affect the outward expression of one's face. But, the point has more to do with how

these individuals look at the world than what the world sees
when it looks at them. Here are two extreme approaches to life,
two worldviews, two attitudes toward God, others and self. Both
seek to establish themselves – one in independence and the other
in righteousness.[50] The difference is one not only of destiny, but of
process as well.

**21:30. There is no wisdom and no understanding And no counsel
against the Lord.**
As so many other times, this proverb sounds a note for God's
sovereignty. The lines form one continuous sentence. The proverb
begins with three negations. The terms 'wisdom' (Prov. 1:2, 7, 20; 2:2,
6, 10; 3:13, 19, etc.), 'understanding' (Prov. 2:2, 3, 6, 11; 3:13, 19, etc.)
and 'counsel' (Prov. 1:25, 30; 8:14; 12:15; 19:20, etc.) have been met
many times already and are standard wisdom-talk. Here, however,
they describe that which is generated, devised and employed apart
from God. As such, they do not qualify even to be called by these
names. There is a human, earthly, even Satanic, counterfeit to beware
of (James 3:13-18).

Kidner helpfully describes this trio of humanity's best as
synthesis ('wisdom'), analysis ('understanding') and policy
('counsel').[51] Only God possesses these things perfectly (Job 12:13).
Therefore, the fount of wisdom, understanding and counsel is the
fear of the Lord (Prov. 15:33; Jer. 9:23-24). Apart from Him, and
proper relation to Him, there is no clear analysis of the human
condition and predicament. There is neither any accurate synthesis
of his makeup, powers and purpose. And there cannot, then, be any
fruitful or lasting policy established for his advancement. Without
the Lord, all analysis fails due to a distorted view of the facts,
all attempts at synthesis are fractured and frayed, and all plans
and policies shut one up to his own woefully inadequate powers
(1 Cor. 3:19-20).

It comes as no surprise, then, that there can be none of these
'against the Lord.' The phrase means that no attempt to understand,
categorize and mobilize man 'against the Lord' and His truth will
prevail (Prov. 16:4, 9; 19:21; 21:1; 2 Chron. 13:12; Isa. 8:10; Acts 5:38-39).
To believe that it can is the height of arrogance (Isa. 40:13, 14). God
promises to confuse and frustrate all such humanistic attempts
at autonomy (Job 5:12, 13). We do well, then, to come to the same
conclusion as Job: 'I know that Thou canst do all things, And that no
purpose of Thine can be thwarted' (Job 42:2).

21:31. The horse is prepared for the day of battle, But victory belongs to the LORD.

Mention here of the Divine name rounds out an inclusio which brackets the chapter. As in verse 1, the head of state is seen to be in the Lord's hand. So too, here, the king's military might is seen to be subservient to God's plans. We have been reminded that man's wisdom is no match for the sovereign God (v. 30). So too, man's war machine is fruitless against God and His purposes (v. 31).

The first line parades before us man's greatest military weapon of the time: 'The horse.' With its superior speed came quick-strike capability. With the higher physical vantage point came increased leverage. The army that was dependent upon the foot soldier stood little chance, humanly speaking, of defeating the army with a cavalry. Yet, God consistently demanded that His people place their trust in Him, not the horse (physical, human or military might). 'Some boast in chariots, and some in horses; But we will boast in the name of the LORD, our God' (Ps. 20:7). 'A horse is a false hope for victory; Nor does it deliver anyone by its great strength' (Ps. 33:17). 'Woe to those who go down to Egypt for help, And rely on horses, And trust in chariots because they are many, And in horsemen because they are very strong, But they do not look to the Holy One of Israel, nor seek the LORD!' (Isa. 31:1; cf. Deut. 17:16; Ezra 8:22; Hosea 1:7).

The contrast of the second line provides the reason trust in man's power is fruitless: 'victory belongs to the LORD.' God wants all to 'know that the LORD does not deliver by sword or by spear; for the battle is the LORD's' (1 Sam. 17:47). The same note is sounded in the New Testament (Rom. 7:24-25; 1 Cor. 15:57). Let us beware of trust in human ingenuity (v. 30) and human might (v. 31), rather than in the Lord!

End Notes

1. Whybray, R. N., *Proverbs* (Grand Rapids, Michigan: William B. Eerdmans Publishing Company, 1994), 306.

2. Cohen, A., *Proverbs* (London: The Soncino Press, 1946), 138.

3. Hartley, John E., 'חשב,' *New International Dictionary of Old Testament Theology and Exegesis* (Grand Rapids, Michigan: Zondervan Publishing House, 1997), 2:303.

4. Barker, Kenneth, gen. ed., *The NIV Study Bible* (Grand Rapids, Michigan: Zondervan Publishing House, 1995), 967.

5. Whybray, 219.

6. MacArthur, John, *The MacArthur Study Bible* (Nashville: Word Publishing, 1997), 906.

7. Whybray, 308-309.

8. Coppes, Leonard J., '*nādap*,' *Theological Wordbook of the Old Testament* (Chicago: Moody Press, 1980), 2:557.

9. Kidner, Derek, *Proverbs* (Downers Grove, Illinois: InterVarsity Press, 1964), 142.

10. Ross, Allen P., 'Proverbs,' *The Expositor's Bible Commentary* (Grand Rapids, Michigan: Zondervan Publishing House, 1991), 5:1051.

11. Buzzell, Sid S., 'Proverbs,' *The Bible Knowledge Commentary* (Wheaton: Victor Books, 1985), 1:951.

12. Brown, Francis, S. R. Driver, Charles A. Briggs, *A Hebrew and English Lexicon of the Old Testament* (Oxford: Clarendon Press, n.d.), 246.

13. Weber, Carl Philip, '*wzr*,' *Theological Wordbook of the Old Testament* (Chicago: Moody Press, 1980), 1:230.

14. Ibid.; Brown, Francis, S. R. Driver, Charles A. Briggs, *A Hebrew and English Lexicon of the Old Testament* (Oxford: Clarendon Press, n.d.), 255; Carpenter, Eugene, Michael A. Grisanti, 'זָוַר,' *New International Dictionary of Old Testament Theology and Exegesis* (Grand Rapids, Michigan: Zondervan Publishing House, 1997), 1:1064-1065.

15. Brown, Francis, S. R. Driver, Charles A. Briggs, *A Hebrew and English Lexicon of the Old Testament* (Oxford: Clarendon Press, n.d.), 821.

16. Adams, Jay E., *Proverbs* (Woodruff, South Carolina: Timeless Texts, 1997), 165.

17. Schultz, Richard, 'דִּין,' *New International Dictionary of Old Testament Theology and Exegesis* (Grand Rapids, Michigan: Zondervan Publishing House, 1997), 1:938-942.

18. Kidner, 41-42.

19. Ibid., 39.

20. Murphy, Roland E., *Proverbs* (Nashville: Thomas Nelson Publishers, 1998), 157.

21. Delitzsch, F., *Proverbs, Ecclesiastes, Song of Solomon* (three volumes in one) in C. F. Keil and F. Delitzsch, vol. 6, *Commentary on the Old Testament* (in ten volumes), (1872; rpt. Grand Rapids, Michigan: William B. Eerdmans Publishing Company, 1980), 2:71; Kidner, 143; Murphy, 156-157; Ross, 5:1053.

22. Brown, Driver and Briggs, 395.

23. Murphy, 160.

24. Delitzsch, 2:73; Kidner, 143-144; Murphy, 160; Whybray, 312.

25. Waltke, Bruce K., '*śāmah*,' *Theological Wordbook of the Old Testament* (Chicago: Moody Press, 1980), 2:879.

26. Buzzell, 1:951.

27. Van Pelt, M. V. and W. C. Kaiser, Jr., 'חתת,' *New International Dictionary of Old Testament Theology and Exegesis* (Grand Rapids, Michigan: Zondervan Publishing House, 1997), 2:331-332.

28. White, William, '*rāphâ*,' *Theological Wordbook of the Old Testament* (Chicago: Moody Press, 1980), 2:858-859.

29. Cohen, 141.

30. Kalland, Earl S., '*dābar*,' *Theological Wordbook of the Old Testament* (Chicago: Moody Press, 1980), 1:178-181.

31. Creach, Jerome F. D., 'כעס,' *New International Dictionary of Old Testament Theology and Exegesis* (Grand Rapids, Michigan: Zondervan Publishing House, 1997), 2:684-686.

32. Delitzsch, 2:75.

33. Cohen, 142.

34. Els, P. J. J. S., 'בלע,' *New International Dictionary of Old Testament Theology and Exegesis* (Grand Rapids, Michigan: Zondervan Publishing House, 1997), 1:665-666.

35. White, William, '*rādap*,' *Theological Wordbook of the Old Testament* (Chicago: Moody Press, 1980), 2:834.

36. Murphy, 157.

37. Lane, Eric, *Proverbs* (Scotland: Christian Focus Publications, 2000), 235.

38. Murphy, 157, 161.

39. Hartley, John E., '*shāmar*,' *Theological Wordbook of the Old Testament* (Chicago: Moody Press, 1980), 2:939-940.

40. Hartley, John E., '*sārar*,' *Theological Wordbook of the Old Testament* (Chicago: Moody Press, 1980), 2:779.

41. Smith, Gary V., 'דיד,' *New International Dictionary of Old Testament Theology and Exegesis* (Grand Rapids, Michigan: Zondervan Publishing House, 1997), 1:1094-1096.

42. Gilchrist, Paul R., '*yhr*,' *Theological Wordbook of the Old Testament* (Chicago: Moody Press, 1980), 1:370.

43. Smith, Gary V., 'דיד,' *New International Dictionary of Old Testament Theology and Exegesis* (Grand Rapids, Michigan: Zondervan Publishing House, 1997), 1:1094-1096.

44. Brown, Driver and Briggs, 720.

45. Whybray, 314.

46. Alden, Robert L., ''*āwâ*,' *Theological Wordbook of the Old Testament* (Chicago: Moody Press, 1980), 1:18.

47. Hartley, John E., 'זמם,' *New International Dictionary of Old Testament Theology and Exegesis* (Grand Rapids, Michigan: Zondervan Publishing House, 1997), 1:1112-1114.

48. Ross, 5:1058.

49. Brown, Driver and Briggs, 738.

50. Adams, 169.

51. Kidner, 146.

Proverbs 22

22:1. A good name is to be more desired than great riches, Favor is better than silver and gold.
This proverb is constructed around a synonymous parallelism. This helps us in defining the terms, for the two lines work to explain one another. The first line exalts 'A good name.' Literally, it is simply 'A name,' but that it is 'good' is plain from the context and from other similar instructions (Prov. 3:4; 10:7; Eccles. 7:1). This 'good name' is paralleled with 'Favor' in the second line. This word appears sixty-nine times in the Old Testament, forty-three of which appear in the phrase 'to find favor in the eyes of' someone. It means favor, grace or charm.[1] Thus, reputation seems to be the point in sight here, though it is not simply being well thought of by others, but being well thought of by them for the right reasons (i.e. godly character and conduct). Ultimately, character is more important than reputation. You can control your character (by God's grace), but your reputation is not always within your power.

This 'name' is 'to be more desired than great riches.' Interestingly, the same valuation is made elsewhere in Proverbs, in comparison with wisdom and its synonyms (Prov. 2:4; 3:14; 8:10-11, 19; 16:16). Thus, again, we can see that the reputation or 'name' so cherished is that of being a person full of wisdom and righteousness (which is never far removed from 'wisdom' in Proverbs, cf. also Acts 6:3). The reputation in view is good, in a general sense (1 Tim. 3:7), though because of the context it might be appropriate to understand this as particularly true in the way one relates and responds to money, wealth and possessions (1 Tim. 3:3). One will get further in business, ministry and relationships on the wealth of a good name than on the size of one's investment portfolio.

22:2. The rich and the poor have a common bond, The LORD is the maker of them all.
Here, again, as in the first verse, we encounter the rich, something that becomes a theme of this chapter (vv. 1, 2, 4, 7, 9, 16, 22-23). The point here is made through a synthetic parallelism – the second line explaining more specifically the first.

The first line tells us that both those with and those without material goods 'have a common bond.' The word means, basically,

491

'to meet together,' whether in an affable, neutral or unfriendly encounter.[2] The lives of the poor and rich seem to be lived on two completely separate planes. Seldom, if ever, do they meet. The circumstances of their daily activities simply do not make for social interchange. However, there is one inescapable point where their paths do meet. The second line of the proverb tells us that this place is their point of origin – 'The LORD is the maker of them all' (cf. 1 Sam. 2:7; Job 31:15; 34:19).

It is true that the rich and poor shall both meet the same end (James 1:9-11). Yet, Proverbs stresses their common point of origin. 'The poor man and the oppressor have this in common: The LORD gives light to the eyes of both' (Prov. 29:13). 'He who oppresses the poor reproaches his Maker, But he who is gracious to the needy honors Him' (Prov. 14:31). 'He who mocks the poor reproaches his Maker' (Prov. 17:5a).

Is the point that God has simply made both and, now, they have made themselves either rich or poor? Or, is it that God has actually not only created them as individuals, but that He has created them as 'poor' or 'rich' individuals? Has He not only created them, but also appointed their circumstances? Proverbs has told us: 'The LORD has made everything for its own purpose, Even the wicked for the day of evil' (Prov. 16:4). Proverbs tells us that riches are dispensed by God, but not apart from our cooperation with wisdom and righteousness (Prov. 22:4, 9). Likewise, poverty comes from God's hand, sometimes as a chastening for wrong attitudes or actions (Prov. 22:13, 16). What is clear is that we are all blessed beyond what we deserve. We all share in the outpouring of God's general grace: 'He causes His sun to rise on the evil and the good, and sends rain on the righteous and the unrighteous' (Matt. 5:45; cf. Acts 14:17).

22:3. The prudent sees the evil and hides himself, But the naïve go on, and are punished for it.
An adversative makes the point here by contrasting two opposing views of one's circumstances (Prov. 27:12 is a virtual repeat, with only slight variations). The 'prudent' stands over against the 'naïve.' The 'naïve' are open-minded to a fault. They believe anything, and everything, they hear. The wind of popular opinion blows them wherever it will. Assuming the best in another can be a virtue (love 'believes all things,' 1 Cor. 13:7), but it can also be a fault. Here, it represents a willful disregard for the danger inherent in a chosen course. The 'naïve' have no sound judgment (Prov. 1:4, 22, 32; 7:7; 8:5; 9:4, 6, 16). The 'prudent,' on the other hand, is shrewd in the

best sense of the word. While the word can be used with sinister connotations (Gen. 3:1; Job 5:12; 15:5), here it describes one possessing the caution of wisdom (Prov. 12:16, 23; 13:16; 14:15, 18). 'The wisdom of the prudent is to understand his way' (Prov. 14:8a).

It is worthy of note that the Hebrew word for 'prudent' is singular, while the word for the 'naïve' is plural. Does this indicate that, in terms of sheer numbers, one is far more likely to encounter a 'naïve' individual than a 'prudent' one?[3]

The one's prudence is evident, in that he 'sees the evil' before it arrives. Because he has been trained by wisdom, knowledge, and instruction, he can spot problems before they arise and thus avoid them. Perhaps the 'naïve' also 'see the evil' (because they 'go on,' in spite of what they see?), but it is more in keeping with the meaning of the word to see them as so caught up in their pleasures that all the red flags and warning lights are left unobserved. But, what is this 'evil' that they see? The word can refer to either moral evil or a calamitous event. Since wisdom and righteousness are never far from one another in Proverbs, perhaps it is best to see this as some moral choice that will yield potentially dangerous ramifications.

The action each takes further differentiates between them. The 'prudent ... hides himself.' Verse five describes this further: 'Thorns and snares are in the way of the perverse; He who guards himself will be far from them.' 'A wise man is cautious and turns away from evil' (Prov. 14:16a). If the 'evil' is seen as moral temptation to wrong, then the thought here is not far from Paul's admonition to the Romans: 'But put on the Lord Jesus Christ, and make no provision for the flesh' (Rom. 13:14). If the emphasis falls on the side of calamity, then the seeking of refuge has to do more generally with avoiding foreseen troubles.

The 'naïve' plunge blindly ahead and 'are punished for it.' The Hebrew word normally means to punish by imposing a monetary fine (Prov. 17:26; 19:19), but it can also refer to punishment more generally (Prov. 21:11).[4] Perhaps the translation 'pays the price' would be best here.[5] There is a penalty for walking in the folly of sin, and that price will be paid eventually (Rom. 6:23).

22:4. The reward of humility and the fear of the LORD Are riches, honor and life.

This proverb forms one continuous sentence, containing two foundational qualities of life (in the first line) and, then, three consequences that flow from possessing them (in the second line). The twin qualities we are to make ours are 'humility and the fear of the Lord.' Just what these mean, and how they relate to one another, have been the focal point of much debate by scholars. The primary problem seems to be that the proverb provides no verbs and the conjunction 'and,' found between 'humility' and 'the fear of the Lord,' has been supplied, not existing in the Hebrew text. The text would, literally, read: 'The consequence of humility the fear of the Lord riches and honor and life.' This makes it difficult to understand the relationships between the words and is, obviously, difficult to render in English.

We appear to have a grammatical construction known as asyndeton, i.e. the absence of connective conjunctions in a sentence.[6] What is meant by humility is more fully explained by the familiar term 'the fear of the Lord' (Prov. 1:7; 9:10; 31:30). In fact, these two terms are found together again in Proverbs 15:33. By humility is meant that which arises naturally from properly reverencing the Lord. When you see Him for who He is, you see yourself for who you really are (Isa. 6:1-5).

When such a worldview has gripped the heart of a man, three consequences will be found to be his. The translation 'reward' is permissible, but the word means that which follows upon the heels of something else.[7] It is a natural progression, a consequence of a given set of facts.

These consequences are designated 'riches, honor and life.' When a man rightly reverences God and rightly views himself, he will be blessed materially ('riches'), socially ('honor') and personally ('life'). In Proverbs 3:16, this trio of blessings are seen as the reward bestowed by Lady Wisdom. In Proverbs 21:21, the same three qualities are seen as the possession of 'He who pursues righteousness.' Once again, wisdom, righteousness and the fear of the Lord are never far removed from one another. The New Testament equivalent of this verse is found on the lips of Jesus in Matthew 6:33.

22:5. Thorns and snares are in the way of the perverse; He who guards himself will be far from them.

This proverb is an echo, and further development, of the thought already set forth in verse 3. Through a basic contrast, these two lines mark out the kind of path the 'perverse' and the righteous find themselves on in this life. The 'perverse' is one who has twisted or distorted reality (Prov. 2:15; 6:12; 11:20; 17:20; 19:1; 28:6). Thus, he makes what appears to him to be wise choices, but they are based upon a distorted view of reality. His opposite is not named here, but, because he 'guards himself,' we may intimate that he is upright and wise. He sees life straight, understands its issues as they confront him and is, thus, able to chart a safe course through them.

The path of 'the perverse' is said to be filled with 'Thorns and snares.' The Hebrew word for 'Thorns' is rare.[8] Thus, some demand an emendation, suggesting that 'Thorns' do not make a suitable companion to 'snares.'[9] The LXX, however, has the same wording and, to be circumspect, a commentator's discomfort with the parallelism of the biblical writer is not sufficient grounds to alter the text. Indeed, Scripture affirms that 'The way of the sluggard is as a hedge of thorns, but the path of the upright is a highway' (Prov. 15:19). Also, 'the way of the treacherous is hard' (Prov. 13:15b). The imagery of thorns describes that which makes one's way nearly impassible and, certainly, painful. If one does emerge on the other side, he is bleeding and wounded. Such a one's way is also filled with 'snares' (Prov. 7:23). Not only does the 'perverse' face the obvious difficulty of snarled, sharp obstacles that bind his feet and rip at his flesh, but he also discovers that hidden traps have been set to prevent him from escaping the twisted path he has chosen.

How different for 'He who guards himself.' God promises that, as we walk in the way of faith and wisdom, He will make our paths straight (Prov. 3:5-6). In contrast are the twisted paths of wasted effort and needless pain which the 'perverse' choose. Indeed, God speaks of 'The highway of the upright' (Prov. 16:17; cf. 15:19b) and a 'path of life' (Prov. 10:17). This guarding takes place as an individual keeps watch for wisdom, listens carefully to God's word, and is quick to learn and obey. When one takes this stance toward life, he 'will be far from' the twisted way of hardship and danger.

22:6. Train up a child in the way he should go, Even when he is old he will not depart from it.
This is among the best-known, as well as most quoted and controversial, of all the proverbs. The first line sets forth, via an imperative, the proper conduct of parents; the second line then presents the consequence that follows upon that conduct.

The verbal command 'Train up a child' comes from a Hebrew word that most frequently refers to beginning, initiating or inaugurating something.[10] The Temple was dedicated (1 Kings 8:63), as could be a person's house (Deut. 20:5). Such a dedication of a structure referred to its initial use for its intended purpose. This may have included a formal dedication ceremony. Some scholars see in this a cognate to an Egyptian word which means to consecrate something to divine service or to give something to the gods.[11] If this is the case, then the point would be that parents are to absolutely consecrate their children (and, thus, their parenting) to God and begin early to channel all their efforts and resources into training that child for the service of God. It is never too early to begin to teach and train our children in the truths and ways of God.

The particular direction of this training is 'in the way he should go.' This phrase has been the center of the most speculation and controversy in recent years. The phrase in Hebrew is literally 'on the mouth of his way.' Does this refer to the way the child ought to go (i.e. the way of righteousness and wisdom) or does it refer to the child's natural bent and personality (i.e. his natural inclinations, gifts and talents)? The cryptic expression 'on the mouth of' is a Hebrew idiom meaning 'according to the measure of' or 'in accordance with.'[12] The key, then, remains to determine just what is meant by 'his way.'

The Hebrew word for 'way' is used nearly seventy times in the book of Proverbs. It describes the choices and direction one takes in life. It forms one of the key themes of the book, particularly the first nine chapters. That theme develops clearly and without ambiguity – we are to choose the way of God, wisdom and righteousness and we are to shun the way of evil, folly and sin. The 'way' here in verse 6, also, then, describes the way one ought to go, the right way, the divine way, the wise and righteous way. That this is 'his' (the child's) way may mean no more than that this is the way God has laid out before him as His appointed way for his life. To find here warrant for the contemporary notion of non-directive parenting, dictated by the whims and wants of the child, is to rip the verse from its context and to read it for what we want it to say, rather than what it, in fact, does say.

That having been said, there is wisdom in understanding the individuality and personality of each child and, thus, adapting discipline and training (within the Scriptural instruction, Prov. 13:24; 19:18; 22:15; 23:13-14; 29:17) to best reach the divinely appointed goal. Every child is different and learns differently. This is true, but it is not the major point being made in this proverb.

So, one dedicates his child to God and begins early to teach, train and guide him on the path God would have him to walk. What can one expect will happen, if this course is consistently taken? The second line tells us, 'Even when he [the child] is old he [the child] will not depart from it [the way that has been set before him].' Here it is not the grammatical, syntactical and lexical matters that complicate our understanding. What makes this second line hard is the question as to whether this is a promise and guarantee. Does this dogmatically demand that, if proper parenting is employed, all children in the household will walk with God obediently? Personal examples abound that seem to contradict such a view.

This takes us back to the nature of an ancient proverb. The ancient proverb was never designed to be an absolute guarantee of what will always be true, in every case, without exception, but rather as an accurate observation of the basic laws of life. More often than not, children who have been reared by loving parents, who have patiently and consistently taught them God's truth and ways through instruction, discipline, and modeling, will grow up to walk obediently with God. This is the general case. Yet, because of the mysterious interplay of human will and divine sovereignty, this is never absolutely assured to us. We are not computers to be programmed, but living beings to be trained, loved, wooed, and won. Such a process is as heartbreaking in some lives as it is rewarding in others. Every parent who truly loves God and his child will give himself to the service of God in so raising his child, with the prayerful hope that, when he is called to take his hands off and release his child into the world as an adult, the child will indeed 'not depart from' his God and His ways (Eph. 6:4).

22:7. The rich rules over the poor, And the borrower becomes the lender's slave.
This proverb states one of life's hardest facts. Solomon has just said that 'The rich and the poor have a common bond, The Lord is the maker of them all' (v. 2). Yet, while this is true, they have harsh realities to face in this life. Too often 'The poor man utters supplications, But the rich man answers roughly' (Prov. 18:23; cf. James 2:6). Those with material advantage too often come to that position on the backs of those less privileged. Once in the position of wealth, clout and leverage, the pressure is great to lord it over those they deem to be beneath them.

The second line makes the matter more specific, taking it out of the general realm of 'rich' and 'poor' and applying it to 'the borrower' and 'the lender.' The former becomes the latter's 'slave.' This, often, became the literal fact in Hebrew society (Neh. 5:4-5; 2 Kings 4:1). God had promised that His people would become the lender, not the borrower, if they would obediently follow Him (Deut. 28:12). Solomon has made clear the folly of being security for another's loan (e.g. v. 26). Here he implores every person about to take on personal debt to stop and think carefully before doing so.

The same warning of slavery is made a matter of foolishness and wisdom in Proverbs 11:29. For this reason, every person about to take on a loan must weigh the wisdom of doing so. If a loan is necessary for life's necessities, it may be considered, but we should never take a loan to fund our luxury.

22:8. He who sows iniquity will reap vanity, And the rod of his fury will perish.

The law of the harvest is as inescapable in the field of the heart as in the field of grain. Sow righteousness, reap a reward (Prov. 11:18; Hosea 10:12; Gal. 6:8b). Sow wickedness, reap judgment (Job 4:8; Hosea 10:13; Gal. 6:7-8a). We reap what we sow (Gal. 6:7-8) and, sometimes, more than we sow (Hosea 8:7). Here it is 'iniquity' that is sown. The harvest is 'vanity.' The word means trouble or sorrow (cf. Prov. 12:21, 'trouble').

The second line makes more specific the harvest that is brought in. The expression 'the rod' is often representative of power.[13] The word translated 'fury' can describe an overflowing rage[14] or arrogant pride.[15] This power to discharge his anger and advance his self-centered agenda at the expense of the unsuspecting and undefended 'will perish' (Ps. 125:3). God will make such arrogance serve His purposes (Ps. 76:10), but, in the end, he will still bear responsibility for his sinful choices (cf. Assyria, Isa. 10:5; 14:5-6). The ego-driven manipulator may seem to reign for the moment, but his moment in the sun will be short-lived.

22:9. He who is generous will be blessed, For he gives some of his food to the poor.

The law of sowing and reaping (v. 8) applies especially to one's benevolent giving (2 Cor. 9:6). The expression 'He who is generous' is, literally, 'The good of eye.' The opposite is seen in the Hebrew expression 'the evil of eye' (Prov. 23:6; 28:22, 'stingy'; cf. Matt. 20:15). How one looks upon others is evidence of the condition of one's heart. The Law raised high the standard of generosity to the poor (Deut. 14:29; 15:7-11). This emphasis continued consistently through the Wisdom Literature (Job 31:16-20; Prov. 11:25; 19:17; 28:27; Eccles. 11:1-2) and the Prophets (Isa. 58:7-12; Ezek. 18:7, 16; Dan. 4:27).

God promises that He has built a reciprocal effect into giving to the poor (Prov. 11:25). In fact, giving to the poor is but lending to the Lord Himself, who promises to repay (Prov. 19:17). But, stinginess also has its own repercussions (Prov. 21:13). Jesus said, 'It is more blessed to give than to receive' (Acts 20:35). The New Testament consistently reinforces the notion of rewards for those who give to help the poor in their need (Luke 6:35-38; 1 Tim. 6:18-19; Heb. 13:16). Generosity is the pathway to personal happiness (Prov. 14:21). How contrary to our twenty-first century, Western way of looking at things! But Jesus said that our attitude and giving toward the poor will have effects reaching all the way into eternity (Matt. 25:34-40), for few things more accurately reveal the true condition of our hearts even now.

22:10. Drive out the scoffer, and contention will go out, Even strife and dishonor will cease.
We meet again 'the scoffer,' the fool that is now hardened in his folly to the point of reviling all that is sound, wise, godly and good (e.g. Prov. 3:34; 13:1; 15:12). The only thing to do when a 'scoffer' resides among the group is to 'Drive out' the person and, with him, his influence. The word implies that such a person should be banished from the people of God.[16] This same verb is used to describe what God did with Adam and Eve (Gen. 3:24) and Cain (Gen. 4:14). It is also used to describe what Abimelech did to David (Ps. 34:1) and what God did, through the Israelites, with the nations (Ps. 78:55; 80:9). Though this may seem harsh, it is but joining God in what He is doing, for He scoffs at the scoffer (Prov. 3:34). Correcting such a one only brings trouble (Prov. 9:7, 8). It will not help him, but it will help others who look on (Prov. 19:25; 21:11; 1 Tim. 5:20). It is, ultimately, what Abraham had to do with Ishmael (Gen. 21:9, 10).

A trio of problems are promised to disappear, if we will but remove 'the scoffer.' The first is 'contention.' It refers to the discord, division and strife that is inevitable around the 'scoffer.' The second problem to flee is 'strife.' This word most often means 'rights' or a legal decision (Prov. 20:8; 29:7; 31:5, 8). It often indicates a legal dispute.[17] Perhaps here it points to the removal of the scoffer's judgmental and arrogant attitude. The third problem to leave is 'dishonor.' The word is used eight times in Proverbs (e.g. 6:33; 13:18) and describes shame or disgrace.[18] A 'scoffer' is a disgrace to those who seek to live for righteousness and his removal lifts a reproach from God's people.

Both testaments recognize that, sometimes, this difficult work is a necessity if the people of God are to survive and remain unified (Matt. 18:17). 'Reject a factious man after a first and second warning, knowing that such a man is perverted and is sinning, being self-condemned' (Titus 3:10, 11). In the absence of the troublemaker, it is amazing how many problems simply disappear (Prov. 26:20). David's commitment must be that of God's collective people as well:

'Whoever secretly slanders his neighbor, him I will destroy; No one who has a haughty look and an arrogant heart will I endure' (Ps. 101:5).

22:11. He who loves purity of heart And whose speech is gracious, the king is his friend.

The literal rendering of this verse is difficult: 'He who loves purity of heart, grace his lips, his friend the king.' The struggle is both the decision of where to divide the lines and the determination of what verbs to understand in order to make sense of it.

What is clear is that this proverb stands in stark contrast to the previous one. In contrast to the brazen mockery of the 'scoffer' (v. 10), we meet one 'who loves purity of heart' and 'whose speech is gracious.' Such purity of heart marks one as welcomed into God's presence and granted intimacy with Him (Ps. 24:4; Matt. 5:8). Ultimately, of course, such purity is not gained by effort, but given by grace. By 'one whose speech is gracious' is meant one who is able to frame his words in such a way as to both express accurately his thoughts and gain an appreciation for them. This is more than slick talk, for it arises from a heart of sincere and genuine motives. Such speech is the product of wisdom (Eccles. 10:12).

The reward for such a one is that 'the king is his friend.' He becomes a delight (Prov. 14:35) and pleasure (Prov. 16:13) to the ruler. This is the path to high places – genuine holiness and a guarded tongue.

22:12. The eyes of the Lord preserve knowledge, But He overthrows the words of the treacherous man.

This proverb makes its point by an antithesis, the second line contrasting the first. The opening line is difficult, at first glance, for we are not used to seeing 'The eyes of the Lord' set upon an abstract such as 'knowledge' rather than upon something concrete. Many commentators take 'knowledge' as representative of those who possess it. The 'eyes of the Lord' speak of God's omniscience (2 Chron. 16:9; Ps. 11:4; Prov. 5:21; 15:3, 11; Heb. 4:13). The verb 'preserve' has the notion of watching over, keeping or guarding something. The point is that, wherever truth is found, God is setting guard over it. This is seen in that the contrast is His overthrow of 'The words of the treacherous man.' The verb 'overthrows' has the connotation of twisting or perverting something (Prov. 15:4), but it also means to subvert someone's plans (Prov. 11:3; 13:6; 19:3; 21:12). Here, the Lord 'overthrows' the lies of the wicked by twisting them away from their intended target.[19] God foils the plots and intents of the deceitful. In so doing, He stands guard over the truth and makes certain that it prevails. Those who stand with God in the truth should find comfort in His absolute, sovereign control of all things (Prov. 16:4, 9; 19:21; 21:1, 30). What encouragement to stand fast in what we know to be true and the right course of action!

22:13. The sluggard says, 'There is a lion outside; I shall be slain in the streets!'
Here, again, we meet the 'sluggard' (e.g. Prov. 6:6, 9; 13:4; 15:19; 19:24; 20:4; 21:25). And, once again, we discover God using abrasive humor to shame the lazy man into action (Prov. 19:24; 26:13-16). This proverb is nearly repeated in Proverbs 26:13.

When we do not want to do something, we can invent a multitude of reasons why it makes no sense. Laziness is fertile soil for paranoia and excuses. Here, the 'sluggard' is afraid that, if he goes outside, a lion will devour him. While there were lions known in the area (1 Sam. 17:34), it was a highly improbable excuse for not going to work.

The lazy one also cried out: 'I shall be slain in the streets!' The NASB has rendered this quite literally, and makes it sound like an outgrowth of his fear of a lion. The NIV, however, makes this to be a second and separate excuse: 'I will be murdered in the streets.' This is probably because elsewhere the Hebrew word rendered 'slain' (NIV, 'murdered') is used only of humans.[20] It points to a murderous robber.[21] That such persons did roam the countryside is clear (Prov. 1:10-19; Luke 10:30), but, again, it was a lame excuse for not leaving one's home.

Eric Lane reminds us, 'This applies in the Christian life: God calls to obedience and service, and we reply, "It's too difficult, and I am inadequate."'[22] So, soon, we forget the promises of God, when we find something that frightens us or that we don't wish to do because of its difficulty. 'For He will give His angels charge concerning you, To guard you in all your ways. They will bear you up in their hands, Lest you strike your foot against a stone. You will tread upon the lion and cobra, The young lion and the serpent you will trample down' (Ps. 91:11-13).

22:14. The mouth of an adulteress is a deep pit; He who is cursed of the Lord will fall into it.
Now the 'adulteress,' so prominent in the prologue (Prov. 2:16-19; 5:3-6; 6:24-29; 7:5-27), is mentioned for the first time in the collection

of Proverbs 10:1-22:16.[23] Review those passages to better understand
the perspective of Proverbs on sexual sin. The word, literally, means
'stranger.' It can refer to a non-Israelite (Ruth 2:10), but here it means
one who is outside the bounds of proper relationship for a given
man (Prov. 5:3, 20; 23:27).[24] The word is in the plural form, being,
more literally, 'adulteresses.'

Here, it is her 'mouth' that is so dangerous. We have been warned
often of the alluring nature of her words (Prov. 2:16; 5:3; 6:24; 7:5,
14-21). When she begins to speak, do not stand and argue or even
try to resist. Run until out of the sound of her words! Silence her
by your distance, for her words are called 'a deep pit.' It represents
the hunter's snare that, once fallen into, is inescapable and renders
one nearly irretrievable. Here, it is her seductive words, but, in
Proverbs 23:27, it is the harlot herself who is called 'a deep pit.'

The word for 'cursed' is also found in Prov. 24:24 and 25:23. It
describes extreme indignation and anger ('he who is under the
Lord's wrath,' NIV).[25] Free sex is never free. There is always a horrible,
incalculable price to be exacted. Solomon himself later confessed,
'And I discovered more bitter than death the woman whose heart
is snares and nets, whose hands are chains. One who is pleasing to
God will escape from her, but the sinner will be captured by her'
(Eccles. 7:26).

**22:15. Foolishness is bound up in the heart of a child; The rod of
discipline will remove it far from him.**
The need for discipline arises not just from the individual offenses
committed, but from the condition of heart which gives them birth.
What is in that pastel-colored bundle that we carry home from the
hospital so tenderly? One made in God's image (Gen. 1:26), to be
sure. But, one in whom, through Adam (Rom. 5:12), that image has
been marred. The problem is here called 'Foolishness.' It describes a
hardened case of moral stubbornness and stupidity.[26] The same word
is used in Proverbs 27:22 to remind us that, if left undisciplined, this
condition is nearly impossible to remove later in life. We begin with
it 'bound up in' our hearts. The Hebrew word describes tying two
things together. In contrast, it is used of tying the commandments and
instructions of one's parents about one's neck (Prov. 3:3; 6:21).[27] The
metaphor is one of inextricable intimacy, likened to writing something
upon the very fabric of one's heart (Prov. 3:3). That which is thus bound
to the heart becomes nearly inseparable from the heart itself.

The child left to himself does not tend toward improvement, but
toward degeneration, morally and spiritually. Only the intervention

of loving parents to discipline, instruct and guide that child offers hope for his life and those around him (Prov. 19:18).

Such intervention is here called 'the rod of discipline' (Prov. 13:24; 19:18; 23:13-14; 29:15). This may serve as a metaphorical way of referring to all forms of discipline held forth in Proverbs (such as verbal instruction, reproof and correction, Prov. 15:5), but it most often describes corporal punishment. To ears trained by the culture around us rather than by God's word, this may sound frightening and dangerous. Withdrawing corporal punishment (and all forms of discipline) is not a sign of superior love, but of lack of love (Prov. 13:24). God loves His children enough to discipline us (Deut. 8:5; Prov. 3:11-12; Heb. 12:5-11). Our discipline must arise out of a similar love (Prov. 13:24).

While the condition of the heart is serious, and, if left unattended, may harden beyond repair (Prov. 27:22), there is every hope that, if confronted early with loving discipline, we can 'remove it far from' the child (cf. Prov. 22:6). The parent's joy (Prov. 10:1; 15:20; 17:21; 23:15, 16, 24, 25; 29:17) and hope (Prov. 19:18), as well as the child's safety and maturity (Prov. 23:13-14), rest upon the surety of this word from God.

22:16. He who oppresses the poor to make much for himself Or who gives to the rich, will only come to poverty.

We come now to the end of the main section of Solomon's proverbs (Prov. 10:1–22:16). This section contains 375 individual proverbs. The numerical value of the Hebrew name 'Solomon' found in Proverbs 10:1 is exactly 375. It is highly improbable that this happened by chance.[28] The start of the next section is clearly marked by the statement 'the words of the wise' and is also clearly marked off at its end (Prov. 24:34) by the introduction of a new section in Proverbs 25:1.

This proverb is comprised of a compacted Hebrew text that has challenged commentators mightily. It reads, literally, 'One oppressing the poor to multiply to him; One giving to the rich only to poverty.' The proverb is constructed around a formal parallelism. The first line has 'One oppressing the poor' and is answered in the second line by 'One giving to the rich.' The result in the first line is 'to multiply to him' and is matched in the second by 'only to poverty.'

Two questions surface immediately. Who is the 'him' at the end of line one, and who is the one who gets only poverty at the end of the second line? It seems unlikely that the first line would be asserting that, when a person oppresses the poor, it actually ends

up being the poor who gain. It, therefore, must be a stark statement
of fact: when a person unscrupulously takes advantage of the poor,
he does gain a measure of wealth. We would wish for some kind of
qualification (e.g. that such wealth will not last) or judgment (e.g. he
will be condemned), but that is not the point of the proverb. That is
dealt with elsewhere (Prov. 14:31; 22:22-23; 28:3). Who, then, is the
one who comes to poverty in the second line? It seems unlikely that
the point of the proverb would be to say that, by giving to those
who already have wealth, we will bring them down to poverty. It
is more likely that the point is that we waste our gifts ('bribes?' cf.
Prov. 17:8, 23; 18:16; 19:6) when we give them to the rich, for they
take them and, then, fail to grant us what we hoped to gain by
them.

Between the two lines, the NASB supplies 'or' and the NIV provides
'and,' attempting to make the final comment ('to poverty') apply to
both lines. Yet, there is no corresponding particle in the Hebrew
text. It would appear that the first line states a simple fact: when one
oppresses the poor, he gains some measure of wealth (albeit limited,
temporary, and unrighteous). The second line, similarly, simply
presents reality: give to the one who already has and you will not
only fail to get what you hoped the bribe would manipulate them
into providing, but you will lose the thing you gave as well.

The proverb points out the folly of giving bribes to the rich. This
is more stupid even than oppressing the poor (which has already
been denounced in the Proverbs). Jesus, similarly, warned that we
must examine our motives in how we relate to those of higher station
in life (Luke 6:32-35; 14:12-14).

22:17. Incline your ear and hear the words of the wise, And apply your mind to my knowledge;

This verse begins a new section of Proverbs, which extends through
24:22. The title 'the words of the wise' clearly marks this out as a new
beginning and is matched by the title 'These also are the sayings
of the wise' in Proverbs 24:23-34. Commentators have long noted
the similarity between this section and that of the ancient Egyptian
work The Wisdom of Amenemope. That ancient pagan work
was comprised of thirty chapters. Some, who accept an emended
Hebrew text, say this section purports to be divided into thirty
sayings (cf. 'Have I not written thirty sayings for you,' NIV, v. 20).
This emendation is not accepted by all, however, as the NASB text
indicates.[29] Though there is no universal agreement about how the
thirty sayings should be identified, the NIV has arranged its text to

represent how it believes these thirty saying fall out. The supposed parallelisms between the two writings follow no particular order and appear to be selected at random.

Neither is there any agreement as to whether the Hebrew borrowed from the Egyptian, the Egyptian from the Hebrew, or both from some other more ancient (Hebrew?) source. What does appear undeniable is that there are some remarkable, though not exact, parallels between this section of Proverbs and The Wisdom of Amenemope.

Does this suggest that there can be something learned from non-Christian (in this case non-Hebrew) writings? Scripture does say, 'How blessed is the man who does not walk in the counsel of the wicked' (Ps. 1:1a). Yet does that require that nothing can be learned from those who possess no vital relationship with God? Paul read pagan poetry and the Holy Spirit even incorporated some of it into the inspired Scriptures (Acts 17:28; Titus 1:12). This does not in any way call into question the uniqueness and inspiration of Scripture. Nor does it elevate any pagan writing to the status of holy revelation. It simply raises the question as to whether God's general grace might enlighten an unredeemed mind to the point it can recognize and record measured portions of reality, a reality which was then built upon by those with the insight of the indwelling Holy Spirit and, at His direction, recorded in the sacred text of Scripture. Even if Solomon, or some other Hebrew editor, borrowed from the Egyptian writing (which has not been definitively proved), they nevertheless were moved by the Holy Spirit to bring it in line with the truth and transform it into God's inerrant, infallible written revelation for man.

Verses 17-21 serve as a kind of prologue to the remainder of the section (Prov. 22:17-24:22), just as Proverbs 1:1-7 served as a prologue to chapters 1–9. There is a clear contrast in style. The collection of Proverbs 10:1–22:16 is made up of single, two line proverbs. Here the proverbs run on into paragraphs and more closely resemble the discourses of chapters 1–9, though in a more condensed form.

Who was the author/editor of this section? Who is speaking when he says 'apply your mind to *my* knowledge' (emphasis added)? The noun 'the wise' is in the plural, indicating that this may be a collection of sayings made by others. This editorial work may have been done by Solomon himself, though we cannot be certain.

As for this verse, the call to 'incline your ear' reminds us of Proverbs 2:2; 4:20 and 5:1. The verb is one of broad meaning, from 'to extend' or 'to stretch out,' presumably in an exertion of effort, all the way to 'bow down.'[30] It reminds us that both personal effort and humility are required on the path of wisdom. Those of unyielding pride or slothful laziness will never know the sweet fruits of wisdom (vv. 18-21). The command to 'hear' is similar to Proverbs 1:8 and 4:1, 10. And the demand to 'apply your mind to my knowledge' is not far from the call to 'Incline your heart to understanding' in Proverbs 2:2.[31] The imperatives of this verse are followed by three compelling reasons why they should be heeded (one each in vv. 18, 19, 20-21).

22:18. For it will be pleasant if you keep them within you, That they may be ready on your lips.
The first reason to listen to the wisdom of Proverbs, in general, and this section (Prov. 22:17–24:22), in particular, is that it will be a personally positive thing to learn and obey them. We are promised 'it will be pleasant' to make these wise sayings a part of one's life. The word for 'pleasant' describes that which is agreeable, lovely and pleasing. It speaks of the five senses finding delight in something, including the eyes (Song of Sol. 1:16), the tongue (Ps. 141:4), and the ears (Ps. 141:6; Prov. 15:26; 16:24).[32] Learning and integrating the wisdom of Proverbs into one's experience leads to a happy life. This requires, however, that you 'keep them within you.' The phrase is, literally, 'within your belly.' It is equivalent to our saying 'in the depths of your heart' (Prov. 18:8; 20:27, 30). This must be descriptive of memorizing these proverbs. But, it extends beyond the ability to merely rattle off the words from memory. It means that, as food is ingested and becomes inseparable from one's own body as it becomes strength and life, so too these proverbs must become the very fabric of one's approach to, and response to, life.

That this kind of thoroughgoing integration is in view is obvious from the second line. To 'be ready on your lips' is, more literally, 'They shall be fixed together on your lips.' Here to 'be ready' (or 'be fixed') means to be so established as to be prepared for what is necessary. Such a one has so thoroughly incorporated the truths of this book into his life that his life may be said to be established upon this wisdom. In such a state of established wisdom, these sayings reside upon 'the tip of the tongue' at all times, ready to be applied personally and shared interpersonally at any moment.

22:19. So that your trust may be in the LORD, I have taught you today, even you.
Here is the second reason for the instructions that follow: that our trust may be squarely established on the Lord. This goal of 'trust'

sounds like an echo of Proverbs 3:5 – 'Trust in the LORD with all your heart.' Instruction/revelation builds faith – this sounds much like an Old Testament version of Romans 10:17.

Notice that the instruction is timely, for 'I have taught you *today*' (emphasis added). The Hebrew stresses the particularity of this specific day out of all days.[33] The instruction is also personal, 'I have taught *you* today, *even you*' (emphasis added). The addition of the 'even you' at the end of the sentence has left many commentators scratching their heads. Some suggest following the LXX, which reassigns its connections within the sentence. It is intended, however, to stress the deliverance of instruction to a particular person and his personal responsibility to heed it. The phrase could be translated 'to you personally.'[34] It stresses the intimacy of relationship between the teacher and pupil,[35] which now, of course, means God's instruction to each of us. Do we approach these proverbs that personally? Do we approach the Author of these proverbs that intimately?

The high purpose of these instructions – 'that your trust may be in the LORD' – marks this work out as unique from The Wisdom of Amenemope.[36] The goal is not individual, independent competence. The Proverbs are not given to make us autonomous. The goal is to put us in a place where we are actively dependent upon God at each instant and with each endeavor. The point is not simply to believe what these instructions teach, but to actively trust the One who speaks them by acting upon them personally ('even you') and immediately ('today').[37]

22:20. Have I not written to you excellent things Of counsels and knowledge,

This verse is famous for the controversial debate over how to render the Hebrew word here translated 'excellent things.' This translation is favored by the NASB, KJV and NKJV, while the translation 'thirty sayings' is supported by the NIV, RSV, NEB and JB.

The consonantal Hebrew text has been traditionally translated with the idea of 'heretofore' or 'previously.' When the Hebrew word is vocalized, it yields a word referring to military officers. It reminds one of the three-fold team of crack military elites that surrounded David (2 Sam. 23:8-12). This is, then, metaphorically translated 'excellent [princely? or chief?] things.'[38] Compare this with the idea expressed in Proverbs 8:6 ('I will speak noble things'). Some offer an emendation to the reading that is then rendered as the number 'thirty.' Here, then, some find a point of comparison with The

Wisdom of Amenemope which is also divided into thirty sections, albeit thirty chapters.[39]

Obviously, the older translations favor 'excellent things,' while most newer translations render with something like 'thirty sayings.' However, rather than choosing between the vocalized Hebrew text ('excellent things') and the emended Hebrew text ('thirty sayings'), it is better to stay with the consonantal Hebrew text ('heretofore' or 'previously').[40] This is not without its problems, though, for the expression in Hebrew normally is a combination of two words, and, here, the first would be missing.[41] If, however, this is accepted, the point would be that what is about to be taught by way of written instruction has previously been passed on to them via verbal instruction. Verbal instruction often became written, enduring revelation (Rom. 15:15; 2 Thess. 2:5).[42] We need to learn and re-learn the same truths again and again, taking them in through a variety of means, until they become the very fabric of our thinking and the lens through which we view the world.

This which was previously spoken and is now underscored in writing is called 'counsels' and 'knowledge.' The former term refers to advice, plans and input. Unlike the temporal and shifting counsel of man, the counsels of the Lord stand forever (Isa. 46:9-11). Jesus is the 'Wonderful Counselor,' who can, and will, guide the willing disciple into the paths of God's will (Isa. 9:6).[43] The latter term is a now familiar one in Proverbs (Prov. 1:4, 7, 22, 29; 2:5, 6, 10; 3:20; 5:2, etc.).

22:21. To make you know the certainty of the words of truth That you may correctly answer to him who sent you?
Here, then, is the third purpose of these 'sayings of the wise' (v. 17) – the ability to become a faithful conveyor of truth. The word 'certainty' comes from what appears to be an Aramaic word used nowhere else in the Hebrew Old Testament, but showing up in the Aramaic sections of Daniel (Dan. 2:47; 4:34).[44] Delitzsch says that the noun describes not only right behavior and correct measure, but balance. From that, it extends to describe that which is the rule or norm.[45]

It may be that the Hebrew editor then added the Hebrew words translated 'the words of truth' to explain more precisely what was meant by the less familiar Aramaic word. The NIV makes the Aramaic and Hebrew words parallel with one another – 'true and reliable words' – instead of the NASB's 'the certainty of the words of truth.' The Hebrew word for 'truth' carries a sense of that which is reliable and certain. For this reason, the NIV's translation of 'reliable' may be preferable. The word is used to describe God's nature (e.g. Exod. 34:6; Ps. 25:5; Jer. 4:2; 10:10, etc.). It is, thus, true of God's words (Ps. 119:142, 151, 160).[46]

Line one, therefore, describes the nature of the instruction, while the second line now gives the point of it all: 'That you may correctly answer to him who sent you.' The word translated 'correctly' is the same Hebrew term translated 'truth' in the first line. The point is that what one is taught, one is expected to pass on – words that conform to reality in a God-ruled universe and that prove reliable and trustworthy as one seeks to live out life under this sovereign God.

Proverbs has spoken of the trust placed upon messengers (Prov. 10:26; 13:17; 25:13; 26:6). But, just who it is that sends this student is not entirely certain here. The disciple's parents may have sent the youth to learn wisdom from the instructor. The goal is not simply that they return to answer the parents well, but that they are then able to return and respond with wisdom to all whom they may encounter in life.[47] The student is to learn well from his teacher that he might, in turn, become the teacher and others might gain what he has gotten. In God's school of wisdom, every lesson is an investment not only in the one taught, but in every person that student may ever encounter. Every lesson is a stewardship!

As it relates to those within the family of God, it is He 'who comforts us in all our affliction so that we may be able to comfort those who are in any affliction with the comfort with which we ourselves are comforted by God' (2 Cor. 1:4). In terms of relating to those outside the family of God, the sense may not be far from the New Testament exhortation: '[A]lways being ready to make a defense to everyone who asks you to give an account for the hope that is in you' (1 Pet. 3:15).

22:22. Do not rob the poor because he is poor, Or crush the afflicted at the gate;

The prologue behind us (vv. 17-21), the actual 'words of the wise' now begin. And, they begin where the first collection left off (Prov. 10:1–22:16). This verse is completed by the next, where we find the reason that stands behind these commands.

The first line warns against plundering the poor. Such sin is warned of in the Law (Exod. 23:6; Lev. 25:17), and elsewhere, in the Wisdom Literature (Job 31:16; Prov. 22:16; 14:31). The point here, however, gets at the motive as well as the action – don't do it 'because he is poor.' That is to say, just because we are able to do something does not mean that we should.

The second line clarifies just what is in view in the first. It is not so much violent thievery that is in view (though that certainly is condemned as well), but ruthless legal action. It was in 'the gate' where the ancients transacted their business and legal matters were settled (Prov. 1:21; 31:23). Thus, the niv's 'in court,' while more interpretation than translation, gets at the point. All that is within legal bounds is not necessarily also within the moral bounds of God's will. Money and power are not the bottom line for those whose hearts would be conformed to the heart of God.

22:23. For the Lord will plead their case, And take the life of those who rob them.

The justification for the prohibitions of verse 22 is now presented. The reason to avoid treating the poor and needy unjustly is because the Lord Himself is their defender (Prov. 23:10, 11). He 'will plead their case.' The words 'will plead' and 'their case' translate two words from the same Hebrew root. In both cases, the words describe division, quarreling, or strife between people. It can, then, describe the conducting of a lawsuit.[48] God Himself, with all His infinite wisdom and power, will serve as the legal counsel of those who are out-manned by worldly adversaries (1 Sam. 25:39; Ps. 12:5; 35:10; 140:12; Isa. 3:13-15). This is metaphorical, of course. So it therefore does not prohibit one taken to earthly courts of law from securing good legal counsel. The assurance is that God will be working through all means to protect His own.

The second line makes more specific what kind of action God is willing to take. The line is difficult to translate because the word translated 'take the life of' is of uncertain meaning. It appears again only in Malachi 3:8, 9. It seems to mean something along the lines of 'robbing' or 'plundering.'[49] Literally, it reads 'and will plunder those plundering them in soul.' Thus, the niv translates 'will plunder those who plunder them.' The point seems to be that, whatever it is the oppressors do to God's vulnerable people, He is willing to return upon their heads, even to the point of taking their life ('soul'), if need be.

22:24. Do not associate with a man given to anger; Or go with a hot-tempered man,

Here again, we are reminded that 'bad company corrupts good morals' (1 Cor. 15:33). The concern relates specifically to relationships with those who lack self-control over their feelings. Two expressions are used to describe such people. The first is called 'a man given to anger.' It means, literally, 'an owner of nostril.' That makes little sense to twenty-first century ears. The first word is the one from which the false god Baal gets its name. It means more generally 'lord' or, if followed by a genitive, 'owner' of that thing.[50] The second word can describe the facial feature of the nose, but as anger is often seen on the face (through a snort, or redness of pigment) it came to express a state of anger. It describes especially the emotional element of wrath.[51]

The second expression is 'a hot-tempered man.' It means, literally, 'a man of heats.' The word 'heats,' by extension, describes anger, wrath and indignation.[52] The expression is a superlative descriptive of one who is the poster boy for hot-heads.[53] The warning is against the one who is given to being 'hot under the collar.'

We are warned 'Do not associate with' 'Or go with' such individuals. The first expression comes from the word that means 'to feed' and, then, became descriptive of a shepherd pasturing his sheep. Further, it came to mean a friend or companion, whether it be an intimate or casual relationship.[54] The second expression ('go with') has the idea of walking down the path of life with another.[55] Don't 'fall in' with one given to outbursts of anger!

This same warning is outlined in more detail in Proverbs 1:10-19. We may mean to influence them away from their wrath, but the tug is often stronger the other way (Prov. 12:26). The angry man is seen as a fool (Prov. 14:17, 29), who stirs up trouble in all his relationships (Prov. 15:18) by his sinful lack of self-control (Prov. 29:22). Such a man dies lonely, for those without wisdom cannot endure his contentions and those with wisdom avoid him at God's command.

22:25. Lest you learn his ways, And find a snare for yourself.
Here, now, we have the reason that stands behind the prohibitions of verse 24. The concern is an accommodation to the ways of the angry man, rather than a drawing of him into your more peace-loving way of life.

The word 'ways' harkens back to the repeated theme of chapters 1–9 (e.g. Prov. 1:19, 31; 2:8, 13, 15, 20; 3:6, etc.). In Proverbs, life is a path to be walked. If we start walking in the way with the angry, we will soon find ourselves down their path (behaving like them), and be unable to escape. In that path, there is 'a snare.' Like the unsuspecting animal suddenly, and irreversibly, caught by the hunter, so is the sudden revelation to the one who chums with the wrathful (Prov. 5:22; 12:13; 13:14; 29:6).

The undertow of fellowship with the sinful was a point of failure for the Israelites (Ps. 106:35) and can continue to be for the New Testament believer (1 Cor. 15:33).

22:26. Do not be among those who give pledges, Among those who become sureties for debts.
This verse and the next raise a cry now familiar throughout Proverbs. The fullest treatment is given in Proverbs 6:1-5 (which see for comments), though it is dealt with elsewhere as well (Prov. 11:15; 17:18; 20:16; 27:13).

The warning is against giving 'pledges.' The expression is, literally, 'strike hands' and was a way of sealing a legal transaction. It is akin to, but certainly more binding than, our modern handshake. The commitment here pointed to is further explained by the expression 'become sureties for debts.' It means to become responsible for the debt of another, should they default on the loan.

We should not bank our financial security (and that of those who depend upon us) on the faithfulness of another. The Old Testament encourages generosity in giving and even in making interest-free loans. It warns in the strictest terms, however, against guaranteeing the repayment of another's loan. The next verse gives a vivid and compelling reason for this.

22:27. If you have nothing with which to pay, Why should he take your bed from under you?
Here, now, is the answer to the warnings of verse 26. A hypothetical situation is set up: What 'If you have nothing with which to pay'? You have made yourself responsible for someone else's debt, assuming that it will be no great risk to you. 'It's just a signature! They'll never come after me!' Foolish thinking!

The second line raises the question: 'Why should he take your bed from under you?' The 'he' is, presumably, the creditor who demands to be satisfied and is willing to follow the legal trail to obtain it (Prov. 20:16; 27:13). The ancients often used their outer cloak for their 'bed.' As such, the law required that any cloak taken in pledge must be returned by sundown (Exod. 22:26-27; Deut. 24:10-13). Apparently, the creditor in this situation does not feel the constraint of the law. Here the 'bed'/cloak represents the very last, and most inviolable, of a man's possessions. Nothing shall be untouchable, if you put yourself up for someone else's debts (Prov. 11:15).

22:28. Do not move the ancient boundary Which your fathers have set.

In Israel, land was a holy thing, given by God Himself (Deut. 19:14). A family, then, presumably parceled out among its members the individual plots. Thus the descriptive phrase: 'Which your fathers have set.' This meant that any tampering with the boundary markers was not only treachery against one's neighbor (Job 24:2) and disrespect toward one's ancestors, but also sacrilege against God. A divine curse rested upon any who dared try to enlarge their land holdings (Isa. 5:8) by subtle movements of the boundary markers (Deut. 27:17; Prov. 15:25). No amount of social status could protect one from such a curse (1 Kings 21:16-19; Hosea 5:10).

This proverb is nearly repeated in Proverbs 23:10, the first lines being identical. There a justification clause is added (Prov. 23:11), where one is lacking here. The underlying motive appears to be greed and thirst for larger land holdings. The ultimate issue is contentment with what God has granted to you.

22:29. Do you see a man skilled in his work? He will stand before kings; He will not stand before obscure men.

We meet here an unusual three line proverb. Its central figure is 'a man skilled in his work.' The Hebrew word for 'skilled' combines the ideas of skill and speed. It is used of Ezra the scribe (Ezra 7:6), a singer whose tongue is like 'the pen of a ready writer' (Ps. 45:1), and of a future Davidic king who will 'be prompt [skilled] in justice' (Isa. 16:5).[56] Skilled craftsmanship was considered a form of wisdom (Exod. 31:3; 35:30-35; Prov. 8:30).

Promotion should come as a reward of diligent acquisition of skill, not from ladder climbing and unholy ambition. Proverbs has already extolled the rewards of diligence (Prov. 10:4; 12:24). Now, it specifically addresses the outcome of focusing on work ethic before advancement. One who sets himself to be 'skilled' in his job will not fail to 'stand before kings.' The Scriptures are filled with examples of just such rewards: Joseph rose to serve, first, Potiphar (Gen. 39:4) and, then, Pharaoh himself (Gen. 41:46); David stood before Saul (1 Sam. 16:21-23); and Hiram stood before Solomon (1 Kings 7:14). The promise is then reversed: 'He will not stand before obscure men.' The word translated 'obscure' refers to that which is dark and, thus, hidden or obscured.[57]

In the Hebrew mind, to 'stand before' meant to 'serve' or to 'stand ready to serve.' Thus, the promise here is not advancement to a place where one no longer must work, but to further, albeit recognized, service. 'He who loves purity of heart And whose speech is gracious, the king is his friend' (Prov. 22:11; cf. 27:18).

End Notes

1. Yamauchi, Edwin, '*ḥānan*,' *Theological Wordbook of the Old Testament* (Chicago: Moody Press, 1980), 1:302-303.

2. Grisanti, Michael A., 'פּגשׁ,' *New International Dictionary of Old Testament Theology and Exegesis* (Grand Rapids, Michigan: Zondervan Publishing House, 1997), 3:577-578.

3. Delitzsch, F., *Proverbs, Ecclesiastes, Song of Solomon* (three volumes in one) in C. F. Keil and F. Delitzsch, vol. 6, *Commentary on the Old Testament* (in ten volumes), (1872; rpt. Grand Rapids, Michigan: William B. Eerdmans Publishing Company, 1980), 2:84.

4. Allen, Ronald B., ''*ānash*,' *Theological Wordbook of the Old Testament* (Chicago: Moody Press, 1980), 2:685-686.

5. Cohen, A., *Proverbs* (London: The Soncino Press, 1946), 145.

6. Murphy, Roland E., *Proverbs* (Nashville: Thomas Nelson Publishers, 1998), 164.

7. Delitzsch, 2:85-86.

8. Feinberg, Charles L., '*snn*,' *Theological Wordbook of the Old Testament* (Chicago: Moody Press, 1980), 2:771.

9. Ross, Allen P., 'Proverbs,' *The Expositor's Bible Commentary* (Grand Rapids, Michigan: Zondervan Publishing House, 1991), 5:1060-1061.

10. Naude, Jackie A., 'חנך,' *New International Dictionary of Old Testament Theology and Exegesis* (Grand Rapids, Michigan: Zondervan Publishing House, 1997), 2:200-201.

11. Archer, Gleason L., *Encyclopedia of Bible Difficulties* (Grand Rapids, Michigan: Zondervan Publishing House, 1982), 252.

12. Brown, Francis, S. R. Driver, Charles A. Briggs, *A Hebrew and English Lexicon of the Old Testament* (Oxford: Clarendon Press, n.d.), 805.

13. Cohen, 147.

14. Buzzell, Sid S., 'Proverbs,' *The Bible Knowledge Commentary* (Wheaton: Victor Books, 1985), 1:953.

15. Murphy, 164.

16. Cohen, 147.

17. Whybray, 320.

18. Buzzell, 1:953.

19. Cohen, 148.

20. Ross, 5:1064.

21. Delitzsch, 2:92.

22. Lane, Eric, *Proverbs* (Scotland: Christian Focus Publications, 2000), 250.

23. Ibid.

24. Buzzell, 5:910.

25. Wood, Leon J., '*zāʻam*,' *Theological Wordbook of the Old Testament* (Chicago: Moody Press, 1980), 1:247.

26. Kidner, Derek, *Proverbs* (Downers Grove, Illinois: InterVarsity Press, 1964), 41.

27. Coppes, Leonard J., '*qāshar*,' *Theological Wordbook of the Old Testament* (Chicago: Moody Press, 1980), 2:818-819.

28. Murphy, 164.

29. Whybray, 324, 327-328.

30. Wilson, Marvin R., '*nāṭâ*,' *Theological Wordbook of the Old Testament* (Chicago: Moody Press, 1980), 2:573-575.

31. Buzzell, 1:955.

32. Meier, Samuel A., 'נעם,' *New International Dictionary of Old Testament Theology and Exegesis* (Grand Rapids, Michigan: Zondervan Publishing House, 1997), 3:121-123.

33. Delitzsch, 2:94.
34. Whybray, 327.
35. Cohen, 149.
36. Murphy, 170.
37. Lane, 252.
38. Delitzsch, 2:97-98.
39. Konkel, A. H. 'אָמֵשׁ,' *New International Dictionary of Old Testament Theology and Exegesis* (Grand Rapids, Michigan: Zondervan Publishing House, 1997), 1:449-450.
40. Brown, Driver and Briggs, 1026.
41. Kidner, 149.
42. Lane, 252-253.
43. Gilchrist, Paul R., 'yā'as,' *Theological Wordbook of the Old Testament* (Chicago: Moody Press, 1980), 1:390-391.
44. Murphy, 169.
45. Delitzsch, 2:98.
46. Scott, Jack B., ''āman,' *Theological Wordbook of the Old Testament* (Chicago: Moody Press, 1980), 1:51-53.
47. Delitzsch, 2:99.
48. Bracke, John M., 'דּיב,' *New International Dictionary of Old Testament Theology and Exegesis* (Grand Rapids, Michigan: Zondervan Publishing House, 1997), 3:1105-1106.
49. Brown, Driver, and Briggs, 867.
50. Waltke, Bruce K., 'bā'al,' *Theological Wordbook of the Old Testament* (Chicago: Moody Press, 1980), 1:119-120.
51. Van Groningen, Gerard, ''ānēp,' *Theological Wordbook of the Old Testament* (Chicago: Moody Press, 1980), 1:58.
52. Van Groningen, Gerard, 'yāham,' *Theological Wordbook of the Old Testament* (Chicago: Moody Press, 1980), 1:374-375.
53. Delitzsch, 2:101.
54. White, William, 'rā'â,' *Theological Wordbook of the Old Testament* (Chicago: Moody Press, 1980), 2:852-853.
55. Brown, Francis, Driver and Briggs, 98.
56. Tomasino, Andy 'מהר,' *New International Dictionary of Old Testament Theology and Exegesis* (Grand Rapids, Michigan: Zondervan Publishing House, 1997), 2:857-859.
57. Murphy, 169.

Proverbs 23

23:1. When you sit down to dine with a ruler, Consider carefully what is before you;
The first three verses of this chapter form a thematic whole. The picture is that of a dinner party ('When you sit down to dine') in the setting of high society ('with a ruler'). Should you find yourself elevated to the invitation list, be careful how you think about your good fortune and how you conduct yourself. The point seems to be that there is often more going on at such functions than immediately meets the eye. We are tipped off to this by the fact that the delicacies are called 'deceptive food' (v. 3).

The second line warns us to 'Consider carefully what is before you.' The marginal readings of both the NASB and NIV suggest that this may be translated 'Consider carefully *who* is before you' (emphasis added). The Hebrew text appears to favor the translation 'what'[1] and is supported by the LXX.[2] In the end, the difference is probably small. The point is that one must not be lured by the draw of riches and its luxuries, for, in its spell, he may be blinded to more important realities that are at play.

Daniel is a classic example of one who carefully discerned the eternal as he was invited to 'dine with a ruler' (Dan. 1:8ff). Jesus also warned of the undisclosed motives of those who flaunt their wealth and resources at dinner parties (Luke 14:7-14).

23:2. And put a knife to your throat, If you are a man of great appetite.
Here is the answer to the deceptive charm of luxuries dangled before one – 'put a knife to your throat.' The shocking expression points to a ruthless self-control. The call is not to suicide, but to moderation. Undiscerning feeding of simple appetites can lead to an unseen snare of untold miseries. Is it intentional irony that the call is to put the knife to 'your throat' rather than to your meal?[3]

Jesus called His followers to just such a fierce temperance (Matt. 18:8, 9) and Paul reiterated that command (1 Cor. 9:24-27).

This is all predicated upon a condition – 'If you are a man of great appetite.' The Hebrew text is, literally, 'an owner of soul.' Elsewhere in Proverbs, we have already seen that the Hebrew word 'soul' can

517

describe the immaterial and intangible cravings and needs of the physical body (e.g. Prov. 10:3; 16:26). The one whose appetites are routinely unrestrained makes himself vulnerable to the intrigues of unscrupulous persons who possess the means to draw him in. Gluttony is routinely condemned in Proverbs, sometimes because of its encouragement toward laziness (Prov. 23:20, 21), and other times because of its effect upon relationships (Prov. 28:7).

23:3. Do not desire his delicacies, For it is deceptive food.

A third exhortation is added to those of verses 1-2, and then they are justified. The first line exhorts one to 'not desire his [the ruler's] delicacies.' Such people possess the resources to awaken our previously untapped appetites. We may not perceive our vulnerabilities here, because such temptations are so rare. How often does one dine with a person of such means? It is easy to reason, 'When will I ever get an opportunity like this again?' The same exhortation is found in a different context in verse 6. Note the prayer of David in Psalm 141:4!

The second line provides the reason for all these extreme exhortations – 'it is deceptive food.' The expression is, literally, 'bread of lies.' This could, of course, simply mean that, while such food tastes good, it cannot ultimately satisfy. This may be because you'll never be able to afford such delicacies again or that such frivolous pleasures are empty in the end. Or, it could mean that the ruler himself is using the food for some ulterior motive in dealing with you. This latter option seems the most likely.

Again, Daniel provides the best example of one who saw past the sumptuously spread table before him and chose God's better way (Dan. 1:5, 8, 13-16).

23:4. Do not weary yourself to gain wealth, Cease from your consideration of it.

This warning against pursuing wealth is somewhat new in Proverbs. Proverbs promises wealth as a reward for wisdom (Prov. 8:21; 14:24), righteousness (Prov. 15:6), generosity (Prov. 11:25) and diligence (Prov. 10:4; 12:27). It roundly condemns ill-gotten gains (Prov. 10:2; 15:27). True, Proverbs tells us that God promises to redistribute the wealth of those who are greedy after gain (Prov. 21:6; 28:8), that clamoring after riches is a trap whose jaws are seldom seen in time to do anything about it (Prov. 11:4; 28:22), and that it is better to be poor and possess integrity than it is to possess things but lack honesty (Prov. 16:8). But, Proverbs does not, generally, cast a negative light upon wealth itself.

Here, the warning is against exhausting oneself and all one's resources in an effort to gain a life of luxury. This does not denounce hard work to provide well for one's family, to meet one's obligations and to keep from being a burden to others. Here, the concern is the person who sacrifices everything (family, health, time, God, etc.) in an effort to gain a life of untouchable wealth.

The second line adds the warning 'Cease from your consideration of it.' The NIV renders it 'have the wisdom to show restraint.' Both translations are an effort to translate the more literal Hebrew: 'from your understanding cease.' This could mean either that, because you possess understanding, give up this senseless pursuit of wealth. Or, it could mean that you are to stop trying to understand just what you have to do to get rich.

The next verse will provide the justification for such warnings. This is a theme, however, that is sounded throughout the Scriptures (Prov. 28:20, 22; Matt. 6:19; 1 Tim. 6:9-11, 17; Heb. 13:5). Note especially Ecclesiastes 5:10-16.

23:5. When you set your eyes on it, it is gone. For wealth certainly makes itself wings, Like an eagle that flies toward the heavens.

This verse follows upon the previous one, providing here the justification for the warnings sounded there. The first line is literally, 'Will your eyes fly on it?' The question is translated here as a temporal expression ('When'). The idea is that of letting your eyes fly away from what they should be fixed upon and, in a fancied flight of imagination, letting them become transfixed upon the luxuries of wealth. The trouble with such a make-believe world is that, soon, the bubble pops and 'it is gone.'

Indeed, 'wealth certainly makes itself wings, Like an eagle that flies toward the heavens.' Ironically, when you have let 'your eyes fly' to the covetous world of wealth, that wealth 'makes itself wings' and 'flies toward the heavens' (cf. Isa. 11:14). The same root verb is used in both instances.

Pursuing riches is like grasping wind, nearly impossible and certainly frustrating. When given as a gift from God, wealth can be a great blessing (Prov. 15:6). But, when pursued for its own sake, it is unattainable or, at least, unretainable (Prov. 27:24). Eric Lane describes it well: 'The nest-egg you have laid with such trouble hatches out, sprouts wings and disappears *into the sky like an eagle*, never to be seen again, gone where you can't recover it' (emphasis his).[4]

23:6. Do not eat the bread of a selfish man, Or desire his delicacies;
In this and the following two verses, we meet a social situation not
dissimilar to that of verses 1-3. The major difference is the nature and
character of the host of the dinner party. There, it was a ruler; here it
is 'a selfish man.' The phrase is, literally, 'an evil eye.' The phrase is
found again in Proverbs 28:22, where it describes one who rushes after
riches. The expression 'a good eye,' found in Proverbs 22:9, appears to
be its opposite and clearly points to generosity of heart. The contrast
and comparison point toward a meaning of 'selfish' (NASB) or 'stingy'
(NIV), rather than 'malicious,' as some scholars suggest.

We are warned not to share a meal with such a one. The reasons
will be provided in verses 7, 8. For now, the second line expands
upon the warning of the first. The second line is, in fact, a repeat
of verse 3a. The word 'delicacies' refers to food that is especially
tasty.[5] It describes something that might be saved for special guests,
but, here, it is offered begrudgingly, for 'his heart is not with you'
(v. 7b). The Mosaic Law warned about performing outward forms of
generosity without an inward heart of sincerity (Deut. 15:9).

**23:7. For as he thinks within himself, so he is. He says to you, 'Eat
and drink!' But his heart is not with you.**
We are now given justification for the commands in verse 6. The
greatest challenge of this verse comes in its first line. At first glance,
the NIV ('for he is the kind of man who is always thinking of the cost')
differs significantly from the NASB. The Hebrew is, most literally, 'as
he calculates within his soul, so [is] he.' This means simply that it
is not what he says or how he behaves outwardly that determines
who he truly is. Rather, it is what he is thinking within himself as
you eat of his food and partake of his drink that defines the reality
of his character.

The word translated 'he thinks' means to calculate or measure.[6]
This form is found only here in the Old Testament. For this reason,
no doubt, the LXX has read it as the word for 'hair' and translates
as 'Eating and drinking [with him] is as if one should swallow a
hair.'[7] This provides some reason for the regurgitation mentioned in
verse 8, but is, ultimately, an unnecessary stretch. It is the disgusting
selfishness of the calculating host that makes one sick, not the ill-
prepared food.

One must note the context of verses 6 and 8 to come to an accurate
understanding. Some have abandoned the context, plucked this
from its setting and developed an entire doctrine of the mind from
these words. Let the text say what it says – no more and no less.

Outwardly, this host is the picture of generosity, saying to you, 'Eat and drink!' But, this is not reality. Don't be fooled, for 'his heart is not with you.' 'He who hates disguises it with his lips, But he lays up deceit in his heart. When he speaks graciously, do not believe him, For there are seven abominations in his heart' (Prov. 26:24, 25).

23:8. You will vomit up the morsel you have eaten, And waste your compliments.

The character of the host has been discovered ('a selfish man,' v. 6). His attitude toward you, and what he has offered you, has been laid bare ('his heart is not with you,' v. 7). Suddenly, his sweet 'delicacies' (v. 6) turn sour in your stomach. As the realization of the situation's reality washes over you, it makes you sick ('will vomit up'). The vomiting is, no doubt, intended metaphorically, pointing to the social embarrassment you feel. You may not have eaten much in volume ('the little you have eaten,' NIV), but it is unsettling nevertheless.

Suddenly, you replay every moment since the invitation was given. You process all the hypocritical words of invitation extended to you. You realize now how untrue all your kind 'compliments' have been and wish they had never left your mouth.

Note the irony of the vile, sour vomit that proceeds from the mouth in the end (line one), in contrast to the 'compliments' (lit., 'pleasant words') that first passed over the lips (line two).[8]

23:9. Do not speak in the hearing of a fool, For he will despise the wisdom of your words.

This proverb is unusual in this section (Prov. 22:17–24:34), in that it stands by itself. The command limits the counsel of the wise man. There are some we should not continue to counsel, for they prove that they will not listen to wisdom. This verse is Proverbs' equivalent to Jesus' more graphic warning of Matthew 7:6. The warning is against directing your counsel to 'a fool' personally. Literally, the line reads 'In the ears of a fool do not speak.' The expression 'in the ears of' indicates an urgency of speech to a particular person.[9] The picture is that of directly challenging a fool in a personal, one-on-one confrontation. Such people have already determined not to learn from another; you are wasting your breath.

The second line underscores this resolute attitude: 'For he will despise the wisdom of your words.' The Hebrew word here translated 'wisdom' is normally translated 'prudence,' 'insight' or 'understanding' (e.g. Prov. 12:8; 13:15; 16:22; 19:11). It describes a practical ability to think straight. It pictures one who is able to deliberate clearly in all his encounters.[10] The folly of the 'fool' is seen in that 'he will despise' any such clear-headedness. He treats the wisdom of God, which is more valuable than gold, silver or riches (Prov. 2:4; 3:14, 16), as an insignificant thing.[11] For this reason, Proverbs often warns against engaging such folk (Prov. 1:7b, 22; 9:7, 8; 12:1).

23:10. Do not move the ancient boundary, Or go into the fields of the fatherless;
The first line here is a repeat of the first line in Proverbs 22:28. Possession of land in Israel was a sacred right, a gift handed down by God through the fathers (Prov. 22:28b). Some would attempt to increase their land holdings by moving another's 'boundary' markers by stealth. Subtle movements over time of such official markers would likely not be detected and would rob the individual or family of precious property. Such behavior was nothing less than theft (Deut. 19:14; 27:17; Job 24:2; Prov. 22:22-23, 28; Hosea 5:10).

Whereas the second line in Proverbs 22:28 emphasizes the ancient character of such boundary lines, here the second line makes more specific the kinds of people particularly vulnerable to such schemes. The 'fatherless' were considered especially prone to the deceitful plots of opportunists (Deut. 10:18; Ps. 10:14, 17-18; 68:5; 82:3; 146:9). If the 'fatherless' were to be protected, then, obviously, widows were also a group to be guarded (Prov. 15:25; Isa. 10:2; Jer. 22:3; Zech. 7:10). The warning here is against even going into the fields of such folk – to move their boundary stones, to lay claim to their land, or simply to take of their crops.

23:11. For their Redeemer is strong; He will plead their case against you.
This verse provides the justification that stands behind the commands of verse 10. Do not take liberties with the defenseless, because 'their Redeemer is strong.' The word translated 'Redeemer' is used elsewhere to describe the next of kin who is responsible to buy back lost family holdings (Lev. 25:25-28; Ruth 4:1-12), or to avenge the blood of a family member (Num. 35:12, 19). The most famous example of the work of a human kinsman-redeemer is that of Boaz with Ruth (Ruth 2:20; 3:9, 12, 13; 4:1-14). The expression is also used of God, particularly as it relates to His care for His otherwise defenseless people (Gen. 48:14-16; Exod. 6:6; Job 19:25-27; Isa. 41:14; 43:14; 44:24; Jer. 31:11; 50:34). The warning is that, while what is seen (the condition of the individual as weak and defenseless) appears

vulnerable, what is unseen (God as their omnipotent protector) is formidable.

The second line explains God's actions: 'He will plead their case against you.' God appoints Himself 'A father of the fatherless and a judge for the widows' (Ps. 68:5a; cf. Exod. 22:22-24). God has pledged to personally 'establish the boundary of the widow' (Prov. 15:25). The phrase 'plead their case' has already been used in Proverbs 22:23 in a similar warning. It is a translation of two Hebrew words from the same root, both describing division, quarreling and strife between people. The expression, then, came to describe the bringing of a lawsuit.[12] God will stand beside His people when they are unjustly taken advantage of and out-manned, out-gunned and out-numbered.

The Wisdom of Amenemope has a similar warning and justification. However, after this verse, the similarities between that bit of ancient pagan wisdom literature and this holy, inspired book of wisdom diminish.[13]

23:12. Apply your heart to discipline, And your ears to words of knowledge.

This verse stands by itself, but serves as an introduction designed to prepare the reader to receive the instructions that follow. It has much in common with similar calls to pursue and embrace wisdom. Proverbs is thoroughly salted with such exhortations (e.g. Prov. 1:8; 2:1-4; 3:1; 4:1, 10; 5:1; 6:20; 7:1; 19:20; 22:17). Nearly every word in this verse is used frequently in Proverbs 1–9.

Literally, the first line commands us to 'Bring your heart in for discipline.' Our attention wanders and our hearts become preoccupied. We must be ever diligent to rein them in and focus them upon 'discipline.' We need to be regularly reminded of this necessity, as the testimony of these frequent exhortations bears witness.

The word translated 'discipline' is also found in the next verse as it applies to corporal punishment of a child. This reminds us that a complete understanding of Biblical discipline involves not simply physical actions, but, first and always, 'words of knowledge' as well. It also reminds us that we never outgrow the need of 'discipline.' Instructor and student, parent and child alike all continue in the need to embrace discipline. Hopefully, the form in which it comes and the attitude with which it is embraced changes as we grow older. But, we never outgrow the need to conform our lives to 'discipline.' He who would discipline rightly and effectively must himself be the student of discipline.

23:13. Do not hold back discipline from the child, Although you beat him with the rod, he will not die.

Whereas the previous verse was the address of the teacher/parent to the student/child, here the call is made to the teacher/parent. There, it was a call to apply the heart to discipline, here it is a call to apply discipline to the student/child ('the board of education to the seat of learning'!). The repeating of the Hebrew word for 'discipline' from the previous verse helps develop the full picture of Biblical discipline – it involves both 'words' (v. 12) and physical discipline (v. 13).

We have encountered previously 'the rod' as a means of disciplining a child (Prov. 13:24; 22:15), and shall again (Prov. 29:15). It is also referred to more generally in Proverbs 10:13; 14:3; 22:8; 26:3. The 'rod' may, more metaphorically, refer to all Biblical forms of discipline, but it especially points to corporal punishment. Such discipline is not cruel, but an expression of a parent's love (Prov. 13:24). As God disciplines His children because of His love (Deut. 8:5; Prov. 3:11-12; Heb. 12:5-11), so too earthly parents must at times express their love for their children in this way.

There are many reasons parents withhold both verbal and physical discipline from their children – fear of rejection, selfishness, laziness, social pressure. Here, the second line points out one particular reason – 'Although you beat him with the rod, he will not die.' The concern here could be that the child would die from the spanking itself, but, more likely, it is a reassurance that the use of 'the rod' will, far from harming the child, deliver such a one from the paths that may, eventually, lead to an untimely death. We are exhorted 'Discipline your son while there is hope, And do not desire his death' (Prov. 19:18). This implies that, should discipline be withheld, there may come a point at which an undisciplined child will move beyond the hope and help of parental discipline. To withhold discipline is to fail to hold the child back from that which may be death to him both spiritually and physically. This is true, because 'Foolishness is bound up in the heart of a child' (Prov. 22:15a). The hope is 'The rod of discipline will remove it far from him' (Prov. 22:15b).

23:14. You shall beat him with the rod, And deliver his soul from Sheol.

This verse answers to and clarifies the previous one. Far from 'the rod' being the means of the child's death (v. 13), it is the means of his deliverance from death.

The first line is more accurately cast as a command (NASB, NIV), not a condition (RSV). Discipline is a divine commission laid upon parents. The Hebrew pronoun translated 'You' is thrust forward in the sentence and has great stress laid upon it.[14] Discipline is the parent's role. It is not all he or she does, but a major part of his or her ministry as a parent. Parents cannot farm out the responsibility of discipline and instruction to another – whether grandparents, schools, churches or daycare providers.

The result of parents carefully and Biblically disciplining their child is that they will 'deliver his soul from Sheol.' The Hebrew word sheol refers to the grave and, thus, to the death that places one there. The translation 'hell' (KJV) is unfortunate and leads the mind away from the point being made. Here, it is probably intended to point to a premature and untimely death that may come due to living an undisciplined and ungodly life.[15] That could legally come at the hands of the community (Deut. 21:18-21), but is more likely a picture of the consequences of sin as its own worst judgment in this life. The 'soul' may represent the whole of one's life, not simply the immaterial part of one's being (Ps. 63:1; Isa. 10:18).[16]

23:15. My son, if your heart is wise, My own heart also will be glad;
We continue on the parent/child theme. The personal appeal 'My son' has been heard many times in chapters 1–9 (e.g. Prov. 1:8, 10). That it is found elsewhere in this section (vv. 19, 26) reminds us of the unity of the book as a whole.

The great desire of all parents is that wisdom might come to roost in their child's heart. We long for our children to have good health, to enjoy good friends, to excel at their studies. In the end, however, the thing we covet most is wisdom of heart. Note that 'heart' is found twice in these two lines. The parent's heart condition is wrapped up in the condition of their child's heart. As the child's heart rises to meet wisdom (v. 19), knowledge, discipline (v. 12), instruction and understanding (v. 23) the parent's heart swells with a delight no words can express (Prov. 10:1; 15:20; 23:24, 25; 27:11; 29:3). Conversely, nothing can crush the heart of a parent more than his child's pursuit of folly (Prov. 17:21; 28:7).

Those who would conclude that the discipline of verses 13-14 proceeds from a cruel, unloving heart need only to read on to these verses to discover the tenderness of heart that calls for, and governs, such discipline.

23:16. And my inmost being will rejoice, When your lips speak what is right.
This verse connects with the prior one to form a chiastic construction.[17] That is to say that verse 15a ('My son, if your heart is wise') corresponds with verse 16b ('When your lips speak what is right') and verse 15b ('My own heart also will be glad') matches up with verse 16a ('And my inmost being will rejoice'). Recognizing this helps the proverb to interpret itself and draws us to its main point.

The words 'inmost being' translate the Hebrew word for kidneys. They were considered to be the seat of one's deepest emotions. We might similarly describe something as touching 'the core of my being,' or that I feel it 'in my bones,' or that something is felt 'in my heart of hearts.'[18] Few things reach so deep into a person's emotions, but children have a unique and privileged access to the deep chambers of a parent's heart.

The cause of rejoicing is that the child's 'lips speak what is right.' This answers to 'if your heart is wise' (v. 15a). The point, then, is that the heart that has been captured by wisdom is, now, revealed through the lips. Jesus pointedly reminded us that, what is in the heart shows up on the lips, whether for good or ill (Luke 6:45). Proverbs makes the same point (Prov. 15:28; 16:23; 22:17, 18).[19] Wisdom herself promises such words from her lips (Prov. 8:6); all who love her will likewise speak with wisdom. This child does not merely rattle off memorized rules handed down by his parents, but has come to embrace their God and to pursue their wisdom. What could delight a parent more (vv. 24, 25)?

23:17. Do not let your heart envy sinners, But live in the fear of the Lord always.
At times, the present lot of the unrighteous appears preferable to the disciplined way of righteousness. The Psalms attest to this inner struggle (Ps. 37:1; 73:3) and the Proverbs recognize it as well (Prov. 3:31; 24:1, 19). But, theirs is a temporary condition. Thus, we are warned: 'Do not let your heart envy sinners.'

The word translated 'envy' is one that describes a fervent, animated sort of thinking that propels one forward into action.[20] In fact, this yields what can appear to be two decidedly different shades of meaning – a sinful envy or a righteous zeal. This helps us here, because the second line of the proverb does not have a verb. It reads, most literally, 'but only in the fear of the Lord all the day.' Some simply insert a verb they believe to be understood here, like the verb for 'be': 'but be in the fear of the Lord always' ('live,' NASB). However, it is likely that the verb from the first line is to be understood as governing the second line as well. The meaning would then be 'Do not sinfully envy the temporal and momentary benefits the sinful seem to enjoy, but rather set your heart upon zealously possessing the fear of the Lord.' The NIV captures this idea well: 'Do not let your heart envy sinners, but always *be zealous* for the fear of the LORD' (emphasis added).

'The fear of the LORD' brings us back to the theme around which the book is structured (Prov. 1:7; 9:10; 31:30) and with which it is peppered throughout (e.g. Prov. 3:7; 19:24; 28:14). The expression 'always' (both NASB and NIV) translates the literal expression 'all the day.' The point is that, at every waking moment, we must set our passion and drive upon fearing the Lord. We must be incessantly clinging to His promises, applying ourselves to His commands, governing our lives by His purposes, pursuing His objectives and fulfilling His desires. In everything and at every moment, we must think His thoughts, feel His affections and choose His will. Even as we sleep, we should do so in the knowledge of His constant lordship (Prov. 19:23; cf. Ps. 3:5; 4:8). As we do, we will discover that the present perceived advantage of the wicked is nothing compared to the actual hope that belongs to the righteous (v. 18).

23:18. Surely there is a future, And your hope will not be cut off.
This verse provides motive for obedience to the commands of the previous verse. 'Surely' translates two Hebrew words that are also found in the previous verse and are there translated with 'but.' The exact meaning is difficult to ascertain, but clearly cannot be translated identically in both cases. The NASB translation probably captures it well.

We are reminded here that what looks like a present advantage for the sinful (v. 17a) is nothing compared to the future advantage the righteous will enjoy (v. 18). 'Surely there is a future' for the one who walks in the fear of the Lord. The same expression is repeated in Proverbs 24:14. There it is wisdom, rather than the fear of the Lord, which ushers in this hope. This, once again, underscores that wisdom and righteousness are never far apart in Proverbs.

The word translated 'a future' describes that which comes after something else, that which is last or behind.[21] It is found often in Proverbs (Prov. 5:4, 11; 14:12, 13; 16:25; 19:20; 20:21; 24:14, 20; 25:8; 29:21) and is worthy of reflective meditation. Its combination with the word translated 'hope' calls to mind the promise of Jeremiah 29:11, where the two words are again found together: 'For I know the plans that I have for you,' declares the Lord, 'plans for welfare and not for calamity to give you a future and a hope.'

The promise that the hope of those who fear the Lord 'will not be cut off' also implies that the fleeting, temporal advantage of the unrighteous will suffer that fate. 'For there will be no future for the evil man; The lamp of the wicked will be put out' (Prov. 24:20).

How different the future of the godly! 'For the needy will not always be forgotten, Nor the hope of the afflicted perish forever' (Ps. 9:18). When David struggled with the apparent blessing of the wicked (Ps. 37:1), he counseled himself to 'Trust in the Lord, and do good; Dwell in the land and cultivate faithfulness. Delight yourself in the Lord; And He will give you the desires of your heart' (vv. 3-4). Later, he declared, 'Mark the blameless man, and behold the upright; For the man of peace will have a posterity' (v. 37).

Be faithful and, one day, 'men will say, 'Surely there is a reward for the righteous; Surely there is a God who judges on earth!' (Ps. 58:11). The answer to envy of the wicked, as Kidner so well states it, is to look up (v. 17) and look ahead (v. 18).[22]

23:19. Listen, my son, and be wise, And direct your heart in the way.

This verse serves to prepare the way for the commands of verse 20, which, in turn, gives way to the justification of those commands in verse 21. This verse sounds like an echo from chapters 1–9. Five distinct themes from those chapters are sounded again here: the command to 'Listen' (e.g. Prov. 1:8; 4:10); the call 'my son' (e.g. Prov. 1:8, 10, 15; 2:1; 3:1, 11, 21); the command to 'be wise' (e.g. Prov. 6:6); the emphasis on 'the way' (e.g. Prov. 1:15; 2:20; 4:11, 14; 9:6); and the focus upon the 'heart' (e.g. Prov. 2:2, 10; 3:1, 3, 5; 4:4, 23).

The call 'my son' does have a unique feature, however. Here, it is combined with the emphatic pronoun 'you,' which is left untranslated in the nasb and niv. [23] It is, most literally, 'Listen you, my son!' This underscores the dramatic nature of the call and the urgency of its plea. Gluttony, drunkenness and sloth (vv. 20-21) are no trifles!

The 'way' must be the way of wisdom (Prov. 4:11), understanding (Prov. 9:6), righteousness (Prov. 16:31), and of good men (Prov. 2:20).

There are especially great affinities between this verse and the fourth chapter of Proverbs. The command to 'Listen' is matched by Proverbs 4:10. The 'way of wisdom' is the designated course (Prov. 4:11). The command there is keep your feet on the path and your eyes straight ahead (Prov. 4:25-27).

23:20. Do not be with heavy drinkers of wine, Or with gluttonous eaters of meat;
The introduction of 'wine' returns us to the theme of Proverbs 20:1, and prepares us for the more extended discourse of verses 29-35. Such carousing and drinking parties are roundly condemned in Scripture (Isa. 5:11, 22; 56:12; Hab. 2:15; Matt. 24:49; Luke 21:34; Rom. 13:13; Eph. 5:18). Note that, here, the warning is not even specifically about avoiding drunkenness, but against even being with 'heavy drinkers of wine,' for 'bad company corrupts good morals' (1 Cor. 15:33). Despite our best intentions, we tend to be influenced more than we influence in such situations.

Notably, such drunkards are coupled with 'gluttonous eaters of meat.' Both reveal a lack of self-control and inner discipline. Both are descriptive of the rebellious son, who is brought before the community for their judgment (Deut. 21:20). While in our society alcohol abuse has more of a stigma than overeating, such was not the case in Biblical times. The Scriptures roundly denounce gluttony (Prov. 23:2; 28:7; Matt. 11:19; Phil. 3:19; Titus 1:12).

The verb form of the word translated 'gluttonous' describes someone who is reckless and extravagant. In this case, it is an extravagance in catering to his own appetites.[24] The Hebrew text ends with a word that, literally rendered, means 'for themselves' (untranslated in NASB). This points to the essentially selfish nature of both alcohol abuse and overeating.[25]

23:21. For the heavy drinker and the glutton will come to poverty, And drowsiness will clothe a man with rags.
Here, then, is the motive clause. The end of such overindulgence is 'poverty' and being clothed 'with rags.' Industry gives way to indulgence and, soon, indolence and indigence follow. The urge to 'sleep it off' is too overwhelming and, soon, business ventures suffer. If the pattern persists, poverty is inevitable. 'He who loves pleasure will become a poor man; He who loves wine and oil will not become rich' (Prov. 21:17).

How odd that the enemies of Jesus charged Him with these two excesses (Matt. 11:19). He was the epitome of self-control (John 8:29). Yet, it reveals the ancient attitude toward these two sins.

23:22. Listen to your father who begot you, And do not despise your mother when she is old.
This appears to begin a related set of proverbs running through verse 25. The theme is the relation of children to their ageing parents.

Some would include verses 26-27, because of the word 'son' in verses 26, but this seems unlikely to be a part of the grouping. The present set is marked off by a dual reference to the parent's begetting of the child: 'your father who begot you' (v. 22a) and 'let her rejoice who gave you birth' (v. 25b).[26]

The call to 'Listen to your father' harkens back to chapters 1–9 (e.g. Prov. 1:8; 2:1; 3:1; 4:1; 5:1). But, the foundation goes all the way back to the Mosaic Law and its fifth commandment (Exod. 20:12). This law is still the path of God under the New Covenant (Eph. 6:1). The present command to 'Listen' makes specific in one avenue of life what it means to honor one's father and mother.

The second line makes clear that the relationship in view is that of an adult child relating to his ageing mother. The concern is how he treats her 'when she is old.' The relationship between parents and children certainly changes when the child arrives at adulthood and departs to establish his own family. But, the relationship continues to change as both parents and child age further. Advancing age, with all of its challenges to the physical body, changes in one's social role, and digressing mental acuteness, demands that the child now consciously continue to work at honoring his parents. One of the best ways is to make a concerted effort to 'Listen' to them. To fail to do so is not a practical necessity due to the demands of life, but is to 'despise your mother' (cf. Prov. 15:20; 30:17; Lev. 19:32). The Hebrew verb means to hold something as insignificant.[27] An ageing adult may seem to rattle on incessantly, complain profusely or have advice about everything. But, the wise and godly child neither takes the words personally nor treats them as unimportant. Rather, he takes the time to listen, weeding out the unimportant and discerning the blossom of wisdom.

23:23. Buy truth, and do not sell it, Get wisdom and instruction and understanding.

What pleases parents more than anything else (vv. 22, 24, 25)? It is to see their child(ren) walking in the truth (3 John 4). This realization steers us away from concluding, with so many commentators, that this verse is dislocated or a fabrication to be discarded. The verse does not exist in the LXX. But, it matches the familial context here perfectly.

The command is to 'Buy truth.' This echoes David's call to Solomon, rehearsed in Proverbs 4:5, 7. The verb is used in most contexts to describe the financial acquisition of land or slaves (e.g. Gen. 39:1). This developed, over time, into the picture of God's

redemption of His people (Exod. 15:16; Ps. 74:2). This helps us
understand the repeated command to acquire wisdom (Prov. 1:5;
4:5, 7; 15:32; 17:16; 18:15; 19:8), though clearly the word has no
literal commercial sense here in Proverbs.[28] Clearly, no one can
literally purchase wisdom (Job 28:15-19). The point of the command
is that we should consider no price too high to pay in order to lay
hold of truth (Matt. 13:44-46). Every drop of energy, every penny
of provision, every resource of our lives should be devoted to the
priority of gaining truth.

Conversely, the first line then reverses course and demands that,
having once obtained truth, 'do not sell it.' So, treasure the possession
of truth that no enticement can seduce you into surrendering it.
Clearly, there is a price to be paid for attaining wisdom, but there is
also a price to be paid for retaining wisdom.

The second line, then, adds three more words to the goal to
be pursued: 'wisdom,' 'instruction' and 'understanding.' These
three terms further identify just what is meant by 'truth' in
line one.[29] This 'wisdom' can describe the skills of a craftsman,
but here points to the skillful application of moral and ethical
principles. Likewise, 'instruction' is the same word translated
'discipline' in verses 12, 13. It describes moral correction. And,
'understanding' describes the discernment necessary to see
between two issues.[30]

Let a child lay hold of these treasures and his parents' hearts will
be contented whatever else may come.

23:24. The father of the righteous will greatly rejoice, And he who begets a wise son will be glad in him.

A parent's pride in a wise child swells beyond description! Here,
the father is featured; in the next verse, the mother is in view. This
verse forms a chiastic construction with the next verse, in that 'will
greatly rejoice' is the same Hebrew verb as 'rejoice' in verse 25, and
'will be glad' is the same word as 'be glad' in verse 25.[31] The verses
work together to underscore the delight of parents in their children's
social and spiritual maturity.

The echo of verses 15 and 16 can be heard here. Proverbs speaks
often of the delight of parents in their children's progress in wisdom
(Prov. 10:1; 15:20; 27:11; 29:3). Proverbs also presents the contrasting
gloom for a parent of a fool (Prov. 17:21). Note the parallelism of
'righteous' and 'wise.' Once again, we note that to be wise is to be
righteous, and to be righteous is to be wise.

23:25. Let your father and your mother be glad, And let her rejoice who gave birth to you.

The previous verse reverberates again here, only, this time, 'your mother' is primarily in view, rather than just one's 'father.' Here, the chiastic pattern begun in verse 24 is completed as well. The pages of Proverbs reverberate with this note of parental gladness over a wise child (see on v. 24).

Interestingly, the father is said to 'beget' the child (vv. 22, 24) and the mother is said to give him 'birth' (v. 25).[32] No great distinction may be intended, but it underscores what common sense should have told us long ago: God designed a mother and a father to be a part of, not only bringing children into this world, but also in raising them to maturity and wisdom.

23:26. Give me your heart, my son, And let your eyes delight in my ways.

A new passionate appeal (vv. 26-28) opens with an appropriately tender and compelling call. The father/teacher is making his appeal by the familiar address 'my son' (cf. vv. 15, 19). The request is 'Give me your heart.' Since the 'heart' is the seat of the mind and volition, this is not a request for affectionate love, but thoughtful allegiance of will. The father is asking the son to imitate his conduct. A wise father not only tells his son the correct path to walk, but goes before him, demonstrating by his consistent conduct what such instruction looks like in the daily path of life.

The second line connects the 'heart' (vv. 15, 17, 19) with the 'eyes.' The more common combination is that of the heart and the ears (Prov. 2:2; 22:17; 23:12, 19), but what one watches is often as enchanting as what one hears (Prov. 4:25-27), particularly in regard to a young man's sexual desires (vv. 27-28). We have been warned of this before (Prov. 6:25).

23:27. For a harlot is a deep pit, And an adulterous woman is a narrow well.

Two women are spoken of. The first is called 'a harlot' and the second 'an adulteress.' The 'harlot' is a prostitute who sells sex to willing men (cf. Prov 2:26; 7:10; 29:3). The term 'adulterous woman' means, literally, 'foreigner' or 'alien' (Prov. 2:16; 5:20; 6:24; 7:5),[33] but it is because she resides outside a marriage covenant with you that she is 'foreign' to you.

Consorting with a woman who is not given to you by God in marriage is like falling into 'a deep pit' (Prov. 22:14) or 'a narrow well.' Some want to see sexual references to a woman's anatomy here,[34] but the point is more likely to be that he who enters into such a relationship will become unable to save himself, just as a man who has become helplessly wedged in a narrow hole. This may be meant as a metaphor for death and the grave, generally (Prov. 2:18; 5:5; 7:27), or, more specifically, as a 'black hole' into which one may sink all his wealth and possessions, in order to satisfy the woman's demands for payment or blackmail (Prov. 5:10; 6:35).

23:28. Surely she lurks as a robber, And increases the faithless among men.

Some women are not passively seduced, but actively play the seductress. They actively seek out men as 'a robber' seeks an unsuspecting target. They 'lurk' for their targets, lying in wait to rob them of that which is reserved for their wives alone. Proverbs 7:7-23 provides powerful imagery to supplement this picture of thievery (cf. Prov. 6:26; Eccles. 7:26).

Such a woman 'increases the faithless among men.' There is debate about whether this means she multiplies the number of unfaithful men or whether she repeatedly is unfaithful herself. It appears more likely that the reference is to the multiplying of the number of men who prove unfaithful to God, their wives, and the others in their lives who have come to expect their faithfulness to God, marriage and family.[35]

This triplet of verses then warns us that sexual promiscuity is a danger to oneself (v. 27), to one's possessions (v. 28a), and to one's relations, specifically, and to the larger society, more generally (v. 28b). Mess around, and you will be trapped and unable to save yourself (v. 27), robbed and unable to vindicate yourself (v. 28a), and defamed and unable to clear your name (v. 28b).

23:29. Who has woe? Who has sorrow? Who has contentions? Who has complaining? Who has wounds without cause? Who has redness of eyes?

This begins a remarkable, and unique, discourse on the evil effects of alcohol (vv. 29-35). We have already been warned of this danger (Prov. 20:1; 23:20-21), and will be again (Prov. 31:4-5). But, this presentation is distinctive among them all, both for its length and its style. The six-fold riddle of this verse gives way to the answer in the next. Exhortations follow (v. 31), along with motivation based upon alcohol's allurements (v. 31), its effects (vv. 32-34) and the drunkard's own witness (v. 35).

Here, the riddle consists of six questions designed to unveil the emotional ('woe,' 'sorrow'), relational ('contentions,' 'complaining') and physiological ('wounds,' 'redness of eyes') effects of alcohol abuse.[36] Each question lacks the verb and begins most literally with 'To whom ...?' The verb 'is' ('has' in NASB) should be understood.

The onomatopoetic interjection 'woe' is the cry of one's emotions caught speechless. The English expression 'Oy!' may be a direct transliteration of the Hebrew word.[37] The woes of drink are recounted throughout Scripture (e.g. Isa. 5:11, 22). A drunkard ends in 'sorrow.' The Hebrew word is found only here in the Old Testament, and may be translated simply as 'Oh!'[38] It, like the word translated 'woe,' is an interjection of sorrowful lament.[39]

The relational havoc is described with the words 'contentions' and 'complaining.' The former is found most often in Proverbs and describes quarreling, disputing and nagging. The plural form lays bare the multiplied incidents provoked by the inebriated fool.[40] The latter is a word whose root means to rehearse, repeat or go over something repeatedly in one's mind. It is often translated 'meditation,' which can eventually move into outward 'babbling.' So, what we have here is a tormented mind that, in its solitary misery, begins to pour out to others (who would rather not hear!) its assessment of its miserable lot in life.

The physiological results are 'wounds without cause' and 'redness of eyes.' The 'wounds' are, more literally, 'bruises.'[41] These presumably will have come either from the stumbling fool careening into objects in his stupor, a fight he has provoked by his ranting, or a public beating resulting from his rancor (Prov. 19:29). The word translated 'redness' probably means something more like 'dull' (Gen. 49:12).[42] It would point, then, not to the color of the eyes after a long drink, but to the impaired vision during the intoxication.

23:30. Those who linger long over wine, Those who go to taste mixed wine.

Who suffers the effects described in the previous verse? The answer is given here. It is 'Those who linger long over wine.' The word is used in Isaiah 5:11 of those who stay up late to drink.[43] The self-discipline of sleep would have guarded their lives, but their 'freedom' for more ends up enslaving them. As with Nabal, the result is disastrous (1 Sam. 25:36). Both the Old (Prov. 20:1; 21:17; 23:20-21; Isa. 28:7) and New Testament warn of becoming addicted to alcohol (Eph. 5:18; 1 Tim. 3:3; Titus 1:7).

The parallel problem is 'Those who go to taste mixed wine.' The wine was probably mixed with spices in order to enhance both its taste and potency (Ps. 75:8; Prov. 9:2; Isa. 5:22; Song of Sol. 8:2). They are being led by their senses, rather than by their minds and wills.

23:31. Do not look on the wine when it is red, When it sparkles in the cup, When it goes down smoothly;

As with sexual appetites (v. 26), so also with appetites of taste – the organs of sight must be brought under control ('Do not look on the wine'). Both visual attraction ('when it is red,' 'When it sparkles in the cup') and the seduction of the pallet ('When it goes down smoothly') must be guarded against.

The more literal rendering of the second line is 'when it gives in the cup its eye.' This would almost make the wine more than an attractive inanimate object, but an active seducer.[44] As with the human seductress (Prov. 6:25), one must not allow one's eyes to be caught by the mistress alcohol ('Do not look ... it gives in the cup its eye'). The third line is matched by a similar third line in Song of Solomon 7:9.

These phrases describe those smitten by and addicted to, not merely the physiological grip of alcohol, but also the aesthetic experience of drinking. They have become champions of drinking. They are not merely those who can 'hold their drink,' but are connoisseurs of alcohol and its consumption. This is about more than thirst and drunkenness; this has become an art to them.

23:32. At the last it bites like a serpent, And stings like a viper.

What begins so delightfully (v. 31), now ends with displeasure and destruction. The word translated 'At the last' means that which comes after something else. Here, it reflects the logical outcome of excessive drinking. Just as wanton sensuality has a bitter price to pay in the end (Prov. 5:4, 11), so too indiscretion with drink demands a painful payoff.[45] Wisdom is found by measuring one's present actions by future outcomes (Prov. 5:4; 14:12; 16:25; 19:20; 25:8; 28:23; 29:21).[46]

That price is found, in that alcohol 'bites like a serpent' and 'stings like a viper.' The latter refers to a poisonous snake, though the exact identity and method of dispersing its venom is unknown (Jer. 8:17). The bite of snakes was often viewed as an expression of God's judgment (Jer. 8:17; Amos 5:19; 9:3; Acts 28:3-4). Here that judgment may come more by natural consequences than by the direct hand of God. Nevertheless, the price is both painful and deadly.

23:33. Your eyes will see strange things, And your mind will utter perverse things.

Drunkenness produces distortions of reality. The 'eyes ... see strange things,' things that are not there or misperceptions of what is there. A few have favored a word that means 'strange women' rather than 'strange things.' This, however, disrupts a coherent parallelism with the second line.

Here, 'mind' is the Hebrew word referring to the heart. The heart is said to speak ('utter'). While, technically, the vocal chords, tongue and mouth form and articulate the words, their substance arises from the heart (Luke 6:45). In this sense, it is perfectly natural to refer to the heart speaking. What comes from the heart and, thus, the mouth of a drunken person is said to be 'perverse things.' The same Hebrew word appears eight other times in Proverbs (Prov. 2:12, 14; 6:14; 8:13; 10:31-32; 16:28, 30) and only elsewhere in Deuteronomy 32:20.[47] It means to turn or to turn upside down. Both what is perceived (line one) and what is produced (line two) are twisted, backward and at odds with reality. Such an individual is destined to live a miserable life, demanding that his dreamworld is true reality.

The general description (vv. 29-32) is now cast as personal experience ('your'), and continues in this vein through verse 35.

23:34. And you will be like one who lies down in the middle of the sea, Or like one who lies down on the top of a mast.

Not only are one's perceptions and proclamations distorted (v. 33), but one's physical equilibrium is askew. By 'the middle of the sea' may be meant either the bottom of the sea (Exod. 15:8) or the surface of the water (Prov. 30:19).[48] By the 'one who lies down' there may be meant either that the drinker eventually dies from his drink (as a man might die of drowning if he tried to sleep on or in the ocean), or that, as the drunkard tries to sleep, it is as though he were trying to sleep in a boat bobbing and swaying on the waves. The latter is probably the point, for this renders the better parallelism with the second line.

The meaning of the word rendered 'mast' is debated and the translation is uncertain, though it most likely has a meaning something like this. The point is that the one who has succumbed to the effects of alcohol is dizzy, sick to his stomach and left reeling – like a person might be if he tried to sleep at the top of the mast, where the pitching of the vessel is most violent.

Psalm 107:27 employs a reverse image – a sailor being like a drunken man, rather than the other way around, as here.[49]

23:35. 'They struck me, but I did not become ill; They beat me, but I did not know it. When shall I awake? I will seek another drink.'

As the drunkard struggles toward consciousness, he recognizes from the marks upon his body that, in his revelry, he has gotten into a fight (v. 29), though, at the time, he did not feel a thing. The word for 'become ill' may have the sense of 'feel pain' (Jer. 10:19). He does not even remember the bout that has brought about his bruises ('I did not know it'). As with the fool, the drunkard learns no lessons from a beating (Prov. 27:22).

As the pain of reality begins to dawn upon him, all he can think of is finding more alcohol, so as to disappear once again into his drunken stupor. He asks, 'When shall I awake?' He wants to know, because he is calculating how soon he can get his hands on 'another drink' (Prov. 26:11; Isa. 56:12). Simple indulgence gives way to drunkenness, which soon becomes full-blown addiction.

End Notes

1. Cohen, A., *Proverbs* (London: The Soncino Press, 1946), 152.

2. Murphy, Roland E., *Proverbs* (Nashville: Thomas Nelson Publishers, 1998), 174.

3. Buzzell, Sid S., 'Proverbs,' *The Bible Knowledge Commentary* (Wheaton: Victor Books, 1985), 1:956.

4. Lane, Eric, *Proverbs* (Scotland: Christian Focus Publications, 2000), 257.

5. Alexander, Ralph H., 'ta'am,' *Theological Wordbook of the Old Testament* (Chicago: Moody Press, 1980), 1:351-352.

6. Fuller, Russell, 'שׁער,' *New International Dictionary of Old Testament Theology and Exegesis* (Grand Rapids, Michigan: Zondervan Publishing House, 1997), 4:208.

7. Buzzell, 5:1069.

8. Murphy, 175.

9. Whybray, R. N., *Proverbs* (Grand Rapids, Michigan: William B. Eerdmans Publishing Company, 1994), 334.

10. Cohen, 74.

11. Martens, Elmer A., 'bûz,' *Theological Wordbook of the Old Testament* (Chicago: Moody Press, 1980), 1:95-96.

12. Brake, John M., 'דיב,' *New International Dictionary of Old Testament Theology and Exegesis* (Grand Rapids, Michigan: Zondervan Publishing House, 1997), 3:1105-1106.

13. Murphy, 174, 175.

14. Whybray, 336.

15. Delitzsch, F., *Proverbs, Ecclesiastes, Song of Solomon* (three volumes in one) in C. F. Keil and F. Delitzsch, vol. 6, *Commentary on the Old Testament* (in ten volumes), (1872; rpt. Grand Rapids, Michigan: William B. Eerdmans Publishing Company, 1980), 2:112.

16. Waltke, Bruce K., 'nāpash,' *Theological Wordbook of the Old Testament* (Chicago: Moody Press, 1980), 2:587-591.

17. Ross, Allen P., 'Proverbs,' *The Expositor's Bible Commentary* (Grand Rapids, Michigan: Zondervan Publishing House, 1991), 5:1070.

18. Kidner, Derek, *Proverbs* (Downers Grove, Illinois: InterVarsity Press, 1964), 152.

19. Lane, 260.

20. Peels, H.G.L., 'קנא,' *New International Dictionary of Old Testament Theology and Exegesis* (Grand Rapids, Michigan: Zondervan Publishing House, 1997), 3:937-940.

21. Harris, R. Laird, "*āhar*,' *Theological Wordbook of the Old Testament* (Chicago: Moody Press, 1980), 1:33-34.

22. Kidner, 152.

23. Whybray, 337.

24. Ibid, 338.

25. Ibid.

26. Lane, 260.

27. Martens, Elmer A., '*bûz*,' *Theological Wordbook of the Old Testament* (Chicago: Moody Press, 1980), 1:95.

28. Cornelius, Izak and Raymond C. Van Leeuwen, 'קנה,' *New International Dictionary of Old Testament Theology and Exegesis* (Grand Rapids, Michigan: Zondervan Publishing House, 1997), 3:940-941.

29. Murphy, 176.

30. Buzzell, 1:907.

31. Ibid., 1:957.

32. Ibid.

33. Konkel, A. H., 'נכד,' *New International Dictionary of Old Testament Theology and Exegesis* (Grand Rapids, Michigan: Zondervan Publishing House, 1997), 3:108.

34. Murphy, 177 and Adams, Jay E., *Proverbs* (Woodruff, South Carolina: Timeless Texts, 1997), 183.

35. Delitzsch, 2:119-120.

36. Buzzell, 1:957.

37. Goldberg, Louis, "*ôy*,' *Theological Wordbook of the Old Testament* (Chicago: Moody Press, 1980), 1:19.

38. Coppes, Leonard J., "*ābâ*,' *Theological Wordbook of the Old Testament* (Chicago: Moody Press, 1980), 1:4-5.

39. Delitzsch, 2:120.

40. Schultz, Richard, 'דין,' *New International Dictionary of Old Testament Theology and Exegesis* (Grand Rapids, Michigan: Zondervan Publishing House, 1997), 1:938-942.

41. Hamilton, Victor P., '*pāsâ*,' *Theological Wordbook of the Old Testament* (Chicago: Moody Press, 1980), 2:730.

42. Delitzsch, 2:121.

43. Whybray, 340.

44. Murphy, 171.

45. Hill, Andrew E., 'אחרית,' *New International Dictionary of Old Testament Theology and Exegesis* (Grand Rapids, Michigan: Zondervan Publishing House, 1997), 1:361-362.

46. Buzzell, 1:957.

47. Ibid., 1:910.

48. Cohen, 158.

49. Murphy, 177.

Proverbs 24

24:1. Do not be envious of evil men, Nor desire to be with them;
This chapter opens by addressing envy, a theme common to the Wisdom Literature (e.g. Ps. 37:1; 73:3; Prov. 1:11, 14, 15; 3:31). Yet, it is its three-fold repetition within this subsection (Prov. 22:17-24:22) which is most remarkable (Prov. 23:17; 24:19).

The command is to not look longingly at 'evil men.' The Hebrew is, more literally, 'men of evil.' These are not individuals who, at a given time, may go the way of sin, but those who have habitually chosen that path. They have become consumed with evil. They are tainted through and through by its darkness. No part of their lives is untouched by evil's influence. Rightly does Scripture counsel us away from fellowship with such men (Ps. 1:1).

The opposite of such 'envy' and 'desire' is the fear of the Lord (Prov. 23:17). The particular bent of this temptation appears to be not the longing for the wickedness itself, but for the apparent success and material prosperity it affords (Ps. 37:7; 73:3; Prov. 1:10-15; 24:19). Elsewhere, we are counseled to look at their latter end (Ps. 37:2). Here, the motivation, while not contradictory, is slightly different. This motivation is presented in the next verse.

24:2. For their minds devise violence, And their lips talk of trouble.
The reason for the admonitions of verse 1 are now provided. Study the kind of people your heart has begun to envy. In both their thinking and their speaking, they show they are consumed with violence and hatred. The root of the Hebrew word translated 'devise' describes a low, muttering sound. It refers to talking to one's self under one's breath. It came to refer to meditation or planning, plotting and devising something.[1] What they mumble under their breath, what their minds meditate upon, what they devise, scheme and work out in their thoughts is only 'violence' (cf. v. 8; Prov. 1:10-11; 6:14). The envy may blind us to the self-judgment such violence is (Prov. 21:7).

As so often, what is conceived in the heart ('minds') is then given birth upon the lips through our words. So, too, with 'violence' – 'Their lips talk of trouble' (cf. Ps. 10:7). Again, the 'mouth speaks from that which fills his heart' (Luke 6:45).

What once looked so desirable, upon closer examination is nothing to envy. It destroys others and even oneself.

24:3. By wisdom a house is built, And by understanding it is established;

This verse and the next form a couplet about how to establish a godly home. The word translated 'house' may, in Proverbs, refer either to the physical structure (e.g. Prov. 1:13; 14:1; 19:14) or the family which inhabits it (e.g. Prov. 11:29; 15:27; 31:15, 21, 27). One is reminded of the metaphorical enterprise of Woman Wisdom in Proverbs 9:1, and of the literal undertaking of the woman in Proverbs 14:1. When one remembers that, in Proverbs, wisdom and righteousness are never far apart, it is helpful to compare this statement with Psalm 127:1.

The verbs 'built' and 'established' work together to remind us that this is about more than simply laying good footings for the physical structure. It is just as much about the hard work that makes a family flourish in God's ways.

There is a trio of virtues which form this foundation: wisdom, understanding (v. 3) and knowledge (v. 4). These have become stock elements within the book. Interestingly, these same three are found previously in Proverbs 3:19-20, where they are the key elements upon which God founded the entire created order.[2] Creation has foundation and order. This arises from, and is an extension of, God's own nature. Both our houses and our households must be set upon and secured by God's own presence and precepts. As they are, we will begin to experience the result described in the next verse.

24:4. And by knowledge the rooms are filled With all precious and pleasant riches.

The household founded upon this trinity of wisdom ('wisdom,' 'understanding,' and 'knowledge') will experience not only stability (v. 3), but also substance (v. 4). Proverbs does not blush from associating material reward with wise and righteous living (e.g. Prov. 3:9, 10; 8:21; 15:6; 22:4).

An interesting parallel exists between this verse and Proverbs 1:13. There, the gang members call to the unwary youth promising to fill their dwellings with 'all kinds of precious wealth.' This is the same expression as 'precious ... riches' here.[3] Of course, the rebels do not recognize that they fight against God when they scheme so (Prov. 1:15-19). Their plan is doomed from the start. How different for the one who applies himself to wisdom! Here, the very riches the rebels sought on their own terms are given by God as a reward to the wise. When we seek riches without wisdom, we likely end up with neither. When we search for wisdom before riches, we end up with both. God Himself assures us of this equation.

24:5. A wise man is strong, And a man of knowledge increases power.
More often than not, victory goes to the wise, not the strong. Proverbs has reiterated this repeatedly. The one willing to humble himself and listen to counsel will win (Prov. 11:14; 20:18). The stiff-necked and independent find frustration and failure (Prov. 15:22). Few obstacles are insurmountable to the one armed with wisdom and insight (Prov. 21:22). 'So I said, "Wisdom is better than strength." ' ... The words of the wise heard in quietness are better than the shouting of a ruler among fools. Wisdom is better than weapons of war ...' (Eccles. 9:16-18).

The LXX makes this a comparative and the NRSV follows: 'Wise warriors are mightier than strong ones, and those who have knowledge than those who have strength.'[4] However, the Hebrew text is, more literally, 'A wise warrior [is] in strength; and a man of knowledge firms up might.'

He is not fully armed who does not possess wisdom.

24:6. For by wise guidance you will wage war, And in abundance of counselors there is victory.
What is stated generally (v. 5) is now made specific and given motivation. The first line is close to the second line of Proverbs 20:18 (cf. also Prov. 21:22). Only a fool (and a loser!) enters battle without a plan. Jesus, likewise, made this simple observation (Luke 14:31). Wise and victorious is the one who seeks 'wise guidance' before the fracas breaks out. The word translated 'wise guidance' is used elsewhere only in Proverbs 1:5; 11:14; 12:5; 20:18 and Job 37:12, and is related to the word for rope or cord. A metaphor for what is intended comes from the world of sea navigation. Ropes were used to steer a ship; thus, the sailor pulled on the ropes to steer a true course.[5] So the wise person will seek the guidance of many counselors as he fights the battles of life.

The second line is nearly identical with Proverbs 11:14b. 'Without consultation, plans are frustrated, But with many counselors they succeed' (Prov. 15:22). 'He who walks with wise men will be wise' (Prov. 13:20a). Isolation usually means defeat, while vibrant, discerning interaction with the community of believers speeds one down the path toward victory.

24:7. Wisdom is too high for a fool, He does not open his mouth in the gate.
Wisdom lies beyond the reach of the fool. The word for 'Wisdom' is here in the plural, as in Proverbs 1:20; 9:1. By this form, the fullness, depths, intensity and profundity of wisdom is emphasized.[6] The subject is a hardened, obstinate fool. Such a one may never obtain wisdom. The word translated 'too high' is hard to identify. It is the exact form of the rare Hebrew word for corals (cf. Job 28:18). Corals were considered rare, valuable and highly desirable treasures by the Israelites. They were imported from distant places and were, thus, quite expensive. They became a metaphor for that which is unattainable and unpurchasable. Others have read this to be a rare form of the word for 'high' or have adopted an emendation of the text to arrive at this word. The NIV and NASB have both followed this path.

The point is not entirely lost by either translation. It is that no amount of money (Prov. 17:16) or effort (Prov. 14:6; 17:24) can enable a fool to attain to wisdom. Wisdom is had through a change of heart, not a pocket full of money. Because the fool's heart is set, wisdom is beyond him.

The second line pictures the public revelation of the fool's shallowness. The 'gate' served the ancient Hebrews as the place of major public debate and as their legal courts (Prov. 1:21; 22:22). In the normal course of life, the fool is never at a loss for words (Prov. 10:14; 12:23; 14:3; 15:2; 18:6, 7). But, when the conversation turns serious, he has nothing of substance to contribute. While silence may be mistaken for wisdom (Prov. 17:28), here we discover it can also be a shameful verdict on one's superficiality.

24:8. He who plans to do evil, Men will call him a schemer.
When wisdom is refused and folly embraced, sin moves from being a singular event to an obsession. The fool 'plans to do evil.' To 'plan' sin is to invent new expression of wickedness. The word so translated emphasizes the creating of new ideas.[7] Sin is subject to the law of diminishing return. The pleasure a particular expression of sin brought in the past now fails to arouse the same excitement. Therefore, deeper, more dangerous and blatant forms must be invented so that the pleasure pulse of sin may be maintained. Those addicted to sin are consumed with thoughts of how to gain their next 'fix' of illicit pleasure.

This chapter has already condemned one who makes such plans (v. 2), as does the Proverbs (Prov. 1:10-16; 6:14; 9:13-18; 14:22) and the Scriptures as a whole (Job 15:35; Ps. 38:12; Rom. 1:30).

Such a person soon gains a reputation. 'Men will call him a schemer.' Here 'schemer' is, more literally, 'master of evil plans.' This one becomes known as the 'Lord of Intrigue,' because everyone knows his mind is always whirling, driven by a lust for the fleeting thrill of iniquity. Such a one soon is despised by the community (v. 9; Prov. 14:17). God has pronounced his condemnation (Prov. 12:2) and rejects his overtures of worship (Prov. 21:27).

24:9. The devising of folly is sin, And the scoffer is an abomination to men.
What we suspected in verse 8 now becomes clear – the scheming of the fool is directed toward sin. The word for 'devising' is often used of lewd and morally outrageous actions, such as incest (Lev. 18:17; 19:29; 20:14; Judg. 20:6).

Along with his designation as a 'schemer' (v. 8), he is also labeled 'the scoffer.' This translates the word representing the lowest level of foolishness in Proverbs. This is the confirmed, rancourous fool who is beyond reproof (Prov. 9:7, 8; 15:12). He is arrogant (Prov. 21:24) and divisive (Prov. 22:10). Such folk are 'an abomination to men.' The term 'abomination' is most often reserved for the revulsion of God to sin, but here it describes the community's utter distaste for the scheming fool.

24:10. If you are slack in the day of distress, Your strength is limited.
There is some debate as to whether this should be stated as a conditional statement (as here), or whether it should be set forth as an interrogative ('Are you slack in the day of distress? Then your strength is limited.'). The point is much the same either way. The major concern is the 'day of distress.' The word translated 'distress' comes from a root that describes that which is constricted, narrow or confining. This particular form is used of intense inner struggle (Ps. 25:17), a woman in labor (Jer. 4:31), and the horror felt in the face of a foreign military (Jer. 6:24). It is used of Judah's darkest days of discipline (Jer. 30:7).[8] Clearly, the concern here is no mere inconvenience! These are days of darkness, discipline, and difficulty.

The concern is that such days may make one 'slack.' The word has a broad range of meaning, covering ideas like sink, slacken, relax, decline, or drop. The idea here appears to be that of a heart which grows faint and drops its guard in the face of adversity.[9]

The same root word as in 'distress' is found again in the word translated 'limited.' In the Hebrew text, the two words appear side

by side and form a play on words. This particular form describes
something narrow, like a passageway that permits only traffic in one
direction (Num. 22:26), or the narrowing of a river that causes the
water to rush at high speed (Isa. 59:19).

Some people flee when the pressures mount (Deut. 20:8;
Heb. 12:3). But, it is the day of compression and constriction that
reveals your strength. Confident words uttered in the day of blessing
mean little. It is the ability to stand up under the pressures of dark
days that lays bare the reality of one's backbone and substance. The
wisdom that gives strength (v. 5) is only actually visible under the
microscope of testing.

One does well to study this proverb (along with the next two
verses) in comparison with Psalm 82, where judges and leaders are
tested under difficulty. See, particularly, verses 3-6. Such trials are
necessary, for they not only reveal strength, but they produce it in
the wise. The New Testament insists that tribulations bring about
perseverance, perseverance produces proven character, and proven
character develops hope (Rom. 8:3-5).

**24:11. Deliver those who are being taken away to death, And those
who are staggering to slaughter, O hold them back.**
This verse and the next form a powerful exhortation. There are a
couple of interpretational challenges here. The first is to determine
under what conditions these folk are 'being taken away to death' and
'staggering to slaughter.' Are they unjustly condemned or are they
rightly convicted? Proverbs speaks specifically against standing in
the way of justice for the guilty (Prov. 28:17). The whole of Scripture
echoes this sentiment. It should be clear, therefore, that the people
under consideration here are those who have been wrongly accused
and perhaps convicted. They are about to be unjustly disciplined
for a crime they did not commit. The discipline here is of the most
extreme kind, capital punishment, but this should not stop us from
applying it in cases of less severe injustice.

The second major decision regards a short Hebrew particle
in the second line that normally means 'if.' Understanding it as
a conditional clause makes no sense here. The word may also be
understood as part of an expressed longing, as part of an oath. In
such cases, it might be translated 'O that ...!' This appears to be the
use here – 'O hold them back.'[10]

As with the previous verse, this and the next should be compared
to Psalm 82:3-6. Repeatedly, the Scriptures exhort God's people to
stand with the oppressed (Isa. 58:6, 7).

24:12. If you say, 'See, we did not know this,' Does He not consider it who weighs the hearts? And does He not know it who keeps your soul? And will He not render to man according to his work?
God now removes all excuses for failing to stand up for the abused and downtrodden. The lame excuse 'I didn't know!' is summarily set aside as weak and pointless. Notice that while 'If you say' is in the singular, the excuse ('we did not know this') is in the plural. Some claim a defective text and side with the LXX, which has 'repaired' the discrepancy.[11] But, is this not evidence that we are forever trying to spread the blame, broaden the responsibility and blend into the crowd? The destroyer of such justifications is the omniscience of God. He 'weighs the hearts' (Prov. 21:2) of all. He Who is the keeper of your soul (Ps. 121:3-8) is also the great knower of your motives (1 Sam. 2:3; 16:7; Ps. 94:9-11; 139:2; Prov. 16:2).

Out of God's omniscience grows His ability to judge and recompense justly. He will 'render to man according to his work' (Job 34:11; Ps. 62:12; Prov. 12:14; Matt. 16:27; Rom. 2:6). This is clearly the territory of deity, not humanity (v. 29), for only His knowledge is perfect and His heart pure.

24:13. My son, eat honey, for it is good, Yes, the honey from the comb is sweet to your taste;
The introductory call 'My son' reminds one of the frequent usage of the phrase in chapters 1–9, and also in these later chapters (23:15, 19, 26; 24:21). The bold command to 'eat honey' seems abrupt and out of place, if the verse is read alone. It should, however, be taken with the next verse. This clarifies that the command is not concerned with food intake or with commending tasty treats, but rather that 'honey' is used as an analogy for wisdom. God's word and wisdom are elsewhere linked with honey (Ps. 19:10; 119:103; Prov. 16:24). Honey is mentioned elsewhere in Proverbs as dangerous in excess (Prov. 25:16; 27:7), but the analogy should not be carried over to this comparison with wisdom.

The point is that we naturally seek out, and consume, what is both beneficial and pleasant. If that holds true for the foods we consume, it should certainly hold true as well for what we feed our hearts and minds upon.

The word for 'comb' is a word that, more literally, means 'the drippings' and refers to the purity of honey that flows directly from the comb (cf. RSV).[12] The expression 'your taste' is, more accurately, 'your palate.'[13]

24:14. Know that wisdom is thus for your soul; If you find it, then there will be a future, And your hope will not be cut off.

The first line here is regarded by nearly all translators as difficult. Some believe an emendation of 'Know' to 'Seek' would be preferable.[14] However, the Hebrew text, despite their pleas to the contrary, appears to make good sense and is followed by most modern translations (e.g. NASB, NIV). The pleasant 'taste' of wisdom to the soul is by now well established in Proverbs (e.g. Prov. 2:10). This first line makes clear that the previous verse was not an independent thought, but meant as an analogy not to be divorced from these lines.

The remainder of the second and third lines (except for 'If you find it, then') are an exact duplication of Proverbs 23:18. There, it is the fear of the Lord, rather than wisdom, which is the foundation of this hope. We are reminded again that wisdom and righteousness are never far apart in Proverbs.

The word translated 'a future' is a frequent feature in Proverbs (Prov. 5:4, 11; 14:12, 13; 16:25; 19:20; 20:21; 23:18; 24:20; 25:8; 29:21), and describes that which comes after something else, that which is last or behind.[15] In tandem with the word translated 'hope,' it reminds us of Jeremiah 29:11, where the two words are also found together: '"For I know the plans that I have for you," declares the Lord, "plans for welfare and not for calamity to give you a future and a hope."'

The longer one pursues wisdom, the better and more pleasant it tastes to the soul, for the rewards keep getting better and the future keeps getting brighter!

24:15. Do not lie in wait, O wicked man, against the dwelling of the righteous; Do not destroy his resting place;

The concern is for those who 'lie in wait' for the righteous. Previously, the exhortation has been directed against the gang of young thugs who would wish to inflict bodily injury upon the innocent (Prov. 1:11; cf. 12:6) and the immoral woman who, likewise, wished to ruin the unsuspecting, though obviously in a different way (Prov. 7:12; 23:28). Here, however, the violence is directed not so much against the person physically as against his 'dwelling' and 'resting place.' This includes violent thievery, but also the plotting and intrigue of the one who would bring down the righteous to gain their property and possessions in a more underhanded way. Note that God protects both the person of righteousness and his possessions. Though the latter are clearly not valued as the former, they are, nonetheless, drawn under the umbrella of God's protection. Did not Abraham recover not only his family, but all their possessions as well (Gen. 14:16)? The home of the righteous is a sacred place, guarded and protected by God. That does not mean harm cannot come there, only that God sovereignly allows, and tenaciously avenges, it when it does.

The vocative expression 'O wicked man' (NASB, NKJV) is unusual and unexpected. It is the only place in Proverbs where the wicked are addressed directly.[16] This would seem to contradict the frequent admonition not to reprove a fool (Prov. 9:7, 8; 13:1; 17:10; 23:9). For this reason, though the Hebrew text is clear and there is no textual warrant for it, some commentators simply omit it.[17] Others render it as an apposition, which describes the class of people being discussed (thus 'like an outlaw,' NIV, NRSV, NLT).[18] However, Proverbs does not completely prohibit reproof for the wicked (Prov. 24:25). In fact, we are taught that there is a time to rebuke the foolish, not because they will learn from it, but because the righteous will (Prov. 19:25). Perhaps then, the translation as a vocative ('O wicked man') is correct and this is the appropriate identification of the motives and methods of the sinner. The appeal is then made with the hope that someone else, if not the man himself, will learn from it. Could it be we have here modeled the lesson of Proverbs 19:25?

24:16. For a righteous man falls seven times, and rises again, But the wicked stumble in time of calamity.
Now, we encounter the motivation for the exhortations of verse 15 – the ultimate invincibility of the one guarded by God Himself and the inevitable stumbling of the schemer. The 'righteous man' is described as falling 'seven times.' This should not be taken as limited to the literal number, but as a proverbial expression meaning something like 'many times,' 'over and over' or 'numerous times' (Job 5:19). Proverbs realistically recognizes the hardships that may come upon the righteous (Prov. 10:25; 11:8, 9; 12:7; 18:5; 28:1). Yet, though these hardships will come, and perhaps come often, each time the righteous man 'rises again.' Though not explicit in the text, the assumption is that it is through Divine aid that he stands again. 'When he falls, he shall not be hurled headlong; Because the LORD is the One who holds his hand' (Ps. 37:24). The prophet Micah echoes the declaration of the one who walks with God, 'Do not rejoice over me, O my enemy, Though I fall I will rise' (Mic. 7:8a). The vindication of the righteous is not always as swift as we might like, but it is certain.

On the other hand, 'the wicked' will be undone by a lone 'calamity.' Note that, in contrast to the repeated hardships of the righteous, who yet recover, here the wicked's undoing is spoken of in the singular ('calamity'). The wicked bring their judgment upon themselves as the consequences of their sin rebounds upon them (Prov. 11:5; 14:32). Such disaster will seem to spring upon them in an instant, leaving no time to regroup and recover (Prov. 6:15; 24:22; 29:1). For all of their supposed stealth, the wicked fumble about in the darkness, not even seeing what it is that eventually undoes them (Prov. 4:19). Consider the examples of Haman (Esther 7:10) and those who plotted against Daniel (Dan. 6:23-24).

24:17. Do not rejoice when your enemy falls, And do not let your heart be glad when he stumbles;
The admonitions here are built off of those in the preceding two verses. The verb here translated as 'falls' is the same as that in verse 16a, and the verb translated as 'stumbles' here is the same as the one translated 'stumble' in verse 16b. The motivation for obedience to these demands is to be found in the next verse.

The Scriptures soundly denounce gloating over the misfortune or judgment that falls upon one's enemy (Job 31:29; Prov. 17:5; Mic. 7:8). The Edomites, in their relationship to Israel, seemed to exemplify failure in this area (Lam. 4:21, 22; Ezek. 35:12-15; Obad. 12). This does not censure simply outward expressions of delight, but goes to the very 'heart' and gets at our inward thoughts.

David describes his mourning over the calamity of his enemies in Psalm 35:13, 14, but laments that they did not return the favor (Ps. 35:15). Note also David's response to Abner's death (2 Sam. 3:32). Rather than gloating, we should respond with kindness to our enemy's calamity (Prov. 25:21-22), a demand that Jesus invoked as the rule of His kingdom (Matt. 5:44; Luke 6:28).

24:18. Lest the LORD see it and be displeased, And He turn away His anger from him.
Here, then, is the motive for the admonitions of verse 17. The reason for not rejoicing over the downfall of one's enemy is, first, that the Lord perceives what is going on in one's 'heart' (v. 17). 'And there is no creature hidden from His sight, but all things are open and laid bare to the eyes of Him with whom we have to do' (Heb. 4:13). Having established that all our thoughts and inward responses are known by God, we are then confronted with the problem that He may be 'displeased' with what He finds there! Our word 'displeased' is in Hebrew, more literally, 'evil in His eyes.' We now have the problem of compounded evil. The evil began with the wrongdoing of one's enemy. God has judged this evil, whether directly or indirectly, by

the consequences of that enemy's sin. If, however, you take pleasure in his downfall, there is a new evil introduced to the equation.

Presumably, the Lord will now have to deal with this new evil as He has the first. The fact of God's knowledge of, and displeasure with, one's delight (line one) then leads to the fact that God must act upon this knowledge and displeasure (line two). Just what this divine response is said to be is a matter of some debate. Does the second line here simply imply that God will withdraw His judgment upon your enemy if you delight over it? If this is the case, then the second line would seem to encourage the very spirit condemned in verse 17 and the first line of verse 18.[19] More likely is the implied meaning that, not only will God 'turn away His anger from him [one's enemy],' but that He will then direct it toward you! This understanding finds support among both Jewish and Christian interpreters.[20]

The Edomites illustrated this as they took pleasure in Israel's discipline. 'Rejoice and be glad, O daughter of Edom, Who dwells in the land of Uz; But the cup will come around to you as well, You will become drunk and make yourself naked. The punishment of your iniquity has been completed, O daughter of Zion; He will exile you no longer. But He will punish your iniquity, O daughter of Edom; He will expose your sins!' (Lam. 4:21-22; cf. Ezek. 35:12-15). Similarly, it is illustrated by the warning of Christians regarding their attitude toward unbelieving Jews in Romans 11:18-21.[21]

24:19. Do not fret because of evildoers, Or be envious of the wicked;

This verse and the next have much in common with Psalm 37. Was the author familiar with David's writings? The word translated 'fret' means to burn or to glow with heat. It, then, became expressive of anger. The same word is found three times in Psalm 37 (vv. 1, 7, 8), where, similarly, David warned against anger and envy toward the wicked. This has become a theme of this section (Prov. 23:17; 24:1), though it is found elsewhere as well (Prov. 3:31).

Note how fine the line is between anger ('fret') and envy ('envious'). What seem to be polar opposites exist on two sides of a razor's edge. What may manifest itself as indignation at the apparent prosperity of the sinful can quickly become envy of the goods they seem to have achieved. The envy may not be directed at their sin, but at the apparent products of it. The attitude which says 'I serve God faithfully and get nothing, but look at those who give no care to God's ways!' is a toxic combination of anger (at God?) and envy (of the wicked's apparent blessing).

24:20. For there will be no future for the evil man; The lamp of the wicked will be put out.

Here is the motive for the exhortations of verse 19. The connections with Psalm 37 continue, as in the previous verse. There, it was the fretful envy of the righteous over the wicked that found a parallel. Here, it is the assurance that 'there will be no future' for the wicked (Ps. 37:2, 28, 38; cf. Ps. 73). The word translated 'future' means something like 'that which comes after' or 'end.'[22] The idea might be: there will be no 'tomorrow' or no 'next time' for the evil man. This stands in marked contrast to the future of the righteous, now twice referred to as 'a future and a hope' (Prov. 23:17-18; 24:14).

The second line reaffirms the first, though with different imagery. Hebrew poetry seems to have favored the picture of 'the lamp' being 'put out' (Job 18:5, 6; 21:17; Prov. 13:9; 20:20). The 'lamp' is a metaphor for life (Job 3:20), and its being 'snuffed out' (NIV) refers to the inevitable, hopeless death of the evil person.

Interestingly, while the parallels with Proverbs 23:17-18 are close, the reasoning is reversed. There, the reason not to fret over sinners is stated positively – the future and the hope of the righteous. Here, the same exhortation is backed up with the negative – the lack of a future and hope for those who have become the object of envy.

24:21. My son, fear the LORD and the king; Do not associate with those who are given to change;

This verse co-mingles the familiar and the new. The call 'My son' is echoed here again, reminiscent of chapters 1–9, but also in the collections of proverbs (e.g. Prov. 23:15, 19, 26; 24:13). Also, the familiar theme of the fear of the Lord is echoed again (e.g. Prov. 1:7; 9:10; 31:30).

What is not so familiar is the almost shocking combination of fearing the Lord 'and the king.' Certainly, under the Old Covenant, God was intimately invested in His 'king' of the nation Israel. David, himself anointed by God as king (1 Sam. 16:13), refused to touch God's anointed, even though King Saul was already condemned (1 Sam. 24:10; 26:9). Yet, even under the New Covenant, God commands both fear of God and honor to those whom He has set in the place of delegated authority (Rom. 13:1-7). In fact, this proverb is echoed in 1 Peter 2:17, where Peter applies the same principle to the Christian's relationship to the ungodly, pagan emperor.

God has invested a measure of His authority in the civil leader. He is to be a wise steward of this authority by using it to reward the righteous and judge the ungodly (Prov. 20:8, 26; Rom. 13:3-4). What if he fails in this stewardship? Not even the vile Nero invalidated this command for the apostles and those to whom they had been sent (Rom. 13:1-7; Titus 3:1-7).

The second line adds the exhortation: 'Do not associate with those who are given to change.' This, presumably, refers to those who would like to throw off the fetters of authority – whether that be God's or the established civil order. There may be a time for civil disobedience (e.g. Exod. 1:15-22; Dan. 3), but it comes only when compelled to do that which violates the express will of God and is always undertaken with a spirit of submission, even if the act of obedience must be withheld.

The word 'associate' has already been met at Proverbs 20:19, and has the idea of 'mix with' or 'mingle with.' Recreating with subversives is dangerous. What begins as a curiosity over their ways may, in time, become a conviction of our hearts.

'I say, "Keep the command of the king because of the oath before God. Do not be in a hurry to leave him. Do not join in an evil matter, for he will do whatever he pleases." Since the word of the king is authoritative, who will say to him, "What are you doing?" He who keeps a royal command experiences no trouble, for a wise heart knows the proper time and procedure' (Eccles. 8:2-5).

24:22. For their calamity will rise suddenly, And who knows the ruin that comes from both of them?

Now, we encounter the incentive which adds punch to the exhortations of verse 21. The relation of the 'calamity' to what precedes has been cause for much discussion. Does 'their' refer to the calamity that comes upon 'those who are given to change' (objective genitive), or is it a reference to the cause of such judgment, meaning God and the king (subjective genitive)? It would seem wisest to understand 'both of them' (line two) to refer to God and the king (v. 21) and, therefore, read this understanding forward and understand 'their calamity' to refer to that judgment which flows from their hands upon those who would rebel against them.

Such judgment is called a 'calamity.' The Hebrew word combines the ideas of destruction, ruin, disaster, distress, vengeance, trouble, misfortune, doom, terror, downfall and peril. Approximately one third of its usages appear in the expression 'day of calamity.' It is used almost exclusively (except for 2 Sam. 22:19; Job 30:12; 31:23; Ps. 18:18) in reference to those deserving of this judgment.[23] This judgment is also called 'ruin.' This is the translation of a rarely used Hebrew word (Job 30:24; 31:29).[24]

Such judgment 'will rise suddenly' (Ps. 73:19; Prov. 29:1). The question 'who knows...?' reminds us that this is a matter of both suddenness and surprise. Such disaster will also be permanent (Prov. 24:16).

That this warning is still in effect is witnessed by Paul's possible allusion to it in Romans 13:4.

24:23. These also are sayings of the wise. To show partiality in judgment is not good.

A new subsection begins here, running through verse 34. This is not a typical two-line proverb. Rather, we have a heading (v. 23a) that introduces verses 23b-34 and a one-line proverb (v. 23b) which introduces one thematic treatment of that subsection (vv. 23b-26). The first line echoes Proverbs 22:17, where another more extended subsection is introduced with similar words (see discussion there). That the present section is related to that one is clearly seen by the addition of 'also' here. Solomon prepared us for these kinds of proverbs: 'The words of the wise and their riddles' (Prov. 1:6). This subsection is devoted to themes of impartiality (vv. 23b-26), diligence (v. 27), neighborly relations (vv. 28-29), and a moral story (vv. 30-34).

The second line introduces a theme spanning several verses (vv. 23b-26). Impartiality was demanded in the Law, both of judges (Deut. 1:17; 16:19) and ordinary citizens of Israel (Lev. 19:15). Jesus demanded no less of His followers (John 7:24), nor did the apostles (James 2:1-13).

The more literal Hebrew behind 'show partiality' is 'know faces.' The point is not to render a verdict based upon your relationship (past, present or potential) to one of the parties involved. This is becoming a familiar theme (Prov. 18:5; 28:21).

24:24. He who says to the wicked, 'You are righteous,' Peoples will curse him, nations will abhor him;

The theme of impartiality continues and is made more specific. The concern here appears to be a judge or official who renders an unjust verdict, rather than simply an improper personal judgment (which, however, would also be condemned by implication). This is seen in that the 'Peoples' and 'nations' both are disgusted with him. This assumes someone of a public enough nature to observe the injustice. Perhaps this is why the NIV interprets with 'the guilty' and 'innocent,' rather than 'the wicked' and 'righteous,' trying to conform the image to a legal setting. Something is lost, however, in such interpretive translation.

The particular problem here is the inversion of justice – saying to 'the wicked, 'You are righteous.' Such practices were condemned in the Law (Exod. 23:6, 7). The Prophets backed them up as well: 'Woe to those who call evil good, and good evil; Who substitute darkness for light and light for darkness; Who substitute bitter for sweet, and sweet for bitter!' (Isa. 5:20).

Such injustice brings a 'curse' upon the judge; indeed, even the 'nations will abhor him'! Note that this presumes an agreed-upon standard of right and wrong. How far we have wandered when the judicial system cannot agree upon what is darkness and light, let alone the larger national culture and the very nations of the world! God is repulsed by such backward 'justice' (Prov. 17:15); we should be as well.

24:25. But to those who rebuke the wicked will be delight, And a good blessing will come upon them.

Now we gain the reverse image of that presented in the previous verse. While the one who inverts justice receives the contempt of others (v. 24), here we find the blessings that abound to him who judges justly. The words 'the wicked' are an addition, but are appropriate, because the subject is inferred from the previous verse. The word translated 'delight' refers to that which is found to be pleasant, sweet, delightful and beautiful.[25] This 'delight' appears to be the inward experience of the individual who confronts wrong, rather than the experience of those who watch on and see his unwavering commitment to right, although that may also be true (Prov. 25:12).

The word translated 'rebuke' can have the sense of a legal verdict of guilty (cf. 'those who convict the guilty,' NIV). Yet, this seems to limit the application to only those in official judicial roles, when it should also be applied more widely. This is what God does to the child He loves (Prov. 3:12).

The 'delight' and 'good blessing' may not be immediate, as with John the Baptist when he reproved Herod (Matt. 14:4). On the other hand, the results may follow more quickly, as with Elijah when he rebuked Ahab (1 Kings 21:19-29). The 'delight' and 'good blessing' will likely not come from the one rebuked (Prov. 9:7; 15:12), though, if he is a wise man, he will respect you (Prov. 9:8; 25:12). It may just be found in a bystander who observes your just actions and takes them to heart (Prov. 19:25). Whatever the immediate response of people, we will eventually find that 'He who rebukes a man will afterward find more favor Than he who flatters with the tongue' (Prov. 28:23).

The 'good blessing' is, more literally, 'a blessing good.' The word 'good' describes the contents of the blessing rather than the subjective experience it produces on the one who receives it. The word 'delight' appears to point to the inward, subjective experience of the one who rebukes wrong, while the 'good blessing' points to their outward, objective experience. God will make certain that 'good' things come the way of the one who judges impartially. Eli forfeited both of these when he refused to rebuke his ungodly sons (1 Sam. 3:13).

While rebuking wrong is often hard to do, God promises good rewards upon those who stand with Him. The command to impartially confront wrong continues to be a requirement of the servant of God in the New Testament (1 Tim. 5:20; 2 Tim. 4:2; Titus 1:13; 2:15).

24:26. He kisses the lips Who gives a right answer.

The connection of this proverb to the previous verses is of some debate. It may be understood as a separate saying. But, despite its more general nature, it was probably placed here in order to round off the instructions of verses 23b-25.

This is the only place the Bible makes reference to kissing on the lips.[26] The more general brotherly kiss was on the cheek and was an expression of brotherhood and friendship (Rom. 16:16; 1 Cor. 16:20; 2 Cor. 13:12; 1 Thess. 5:26; 1 Pet. 5:14). Usually, this reference to a kiss on the lips is understood as a heightened expression of affection and loyal friendship. We should not read into it the sensual connotations our culture associates with kissing on the lips (but cf. Prov. 7:13).

This metaphor describes 'a right answer.' The word translated 'right' means straight. The root of the word described that which is straight, as opposed to that which is crooked. It describes that which is rightful, true, correct or appropriate, as opposed to that which is bad, false and inappropriate.[27] The kind of speech under consideration appears, then, to be that which is straightforward, true, honest and unambiguous. A friend is honest. A friend tells you the truth. A friend does not mince words, shade meanings, hint, wink, or beat around the bush. Words from a plainspoken friend may be taken at face value and have no hidden agendas. This kind of speech is the greatest expression of love, friendship and affection. 'Better is open rebuke Than love that is concealed. Faithful are the wounds of a friend, But deceitful are the kisses of an enemy' (Prov. 27:5, 6; cf. also 16:13; 25:11, 12; 28:23).

On the other hand, such an outward expression of friendship may be used to deceive. 'Faithful are the wounds of a friend, But deceitful are the kisses of an enemy' (Prov. 27:6). Was this not the strategy of Judah Iscariot (Matt. 26:48, 49; Luke 22:47, 48)?

Better a friend who cuts with honest words than an enemy who cajoles with pleasant words that carry a hidden motive. Not every smiling face is that of a friend, and not every hard word comes from an enemy.

24:27. Prepare your work outside, And make it ready for yourself in the field; Afterwards, then, build your house.
This proverb is a call to well-ordered priorities. The phrase 'build your house,' as in verse 3, may refer either to the construction of a physical dwelling (Prov. 1:13; 14:1; 19:14) or to the establishing of a marriage and family (Prov. 11:29; 15:27; 31:15, 21, 27; cf. Ruth 4:11).

The concern here is that 'your work outside' and work 'in the field' be done before this takes place. This presupposes an agrarian lifestyle. The point is that one must undertake marriage and family, or even significant financial obligations (like building a house), with careful thought and preparation. A single man may live less comfortably and make the sacrifices necessary to lay a base of financial security. He would not want to make his wife and children make those same sacrifices. Indeed, having the responsibility of a wife and children may hinder or delay his ability to firm up that base. Or, if a man undertakes to build a house first and uses the growing season to tend to his own comforts, winter will soon come upon him and he will have no food with which to feed his family. The bottom line here is: First things first (Luke 14:28-30). Contrast the lazy man who never thinks ahead (cf. vv. 30-31).

This is a wise word in a culture where toys and creature comforts seem to be all-important and responsibilities appear boring and insignificant. On the other hand, we should not use this as affirmation of those who hesitate to marry or have children, because they have greedy financial goals that may never be met, if they take on the 'burden' of investing their time and attention in others.

24:28. Do not be a witness against your neighbor without cause, And do not deceive with your lips.
Verses 23-26 used courtroom imagery to make their point. We now return to that venue. The problem is one who is willing to 'be a witness against [a] neighbor without cause.' Note that the problem is not specifically a false witness. That the Law (Exod. 20:16; Lev. 6:2-4;

Deut. 19:18-21) and Proverbs often condemns such a false witness (Prov. 6:19; 12:17; 14:5, 25; 19:5, 9; 21:28; 25:18) and that the LXX of this verse makes an interpretive translation to that effect may point to this as the best way of understanding the more general wording here. At least, the point is that one should not be willing to bear witness against a neighbor (taken broadly as anyone with whom one is acquainted) without substantial cause. Does this condemn the practice of being an 'expert witness for hire' as our litigious society has made popular?

The second line may be best translated as an interrogative: '[A]nd have you deceived ... with your lips?' The verb lacks the object and seems incomplete.[28] Perhaps the void serves much in the same way a fill-in-the-blank would today, leaving the issue generic and allowing the individual mind to supply the name of the person whom he is tempted to bring witness against. When is it ever right to deceive someone with your lips? Never! The reference to 'your lips' hearkens back to verse 26. The New Testament standard is no different, and, indeed, broadens the application to all speech (Eph. 4:25).

24:29. Do not say, 'Thus I shall do to him as he has done to me; I will render to the man according to his work.'
Commentators are divided as to whether or not this verse connects logically with the preceding one. It seems wise to follow the trend of this subsection and see the proverbs grouping together, instead of standing in isolation. The context would then be a powerful aid in understanding, making personal retaliation the motive of the 'false witness' in verse 28. A wrong has been done ('as he has done to me'), now the spirit of revenge wants its due ('I shall do to him'). Proverbs has already warned of this toxic spirit (Prov. 20:22), as do the rest of the Scriptures (Matt. 5:38-41; Rom. 12:17). God alone possesses the right to avenge wrong (Deut. 32:35; Ps. 94:1; Heb. 10:30). The wise man finds the opposite response is best on a personal level (Prov. 25:21, 22). Samson (Judg. 15:11) and Absalom (2 Sam. 13:22-28) both illustrate the gall of a vengeful heart.

The second line ('according to his work') sounds very much like an echo of the divine assurance given at the end of verse 12. 'Do not say, 'I will repay evil'; Wait for the Lord, and He will save you' (Prov. 20:22).

24:30. I passed by the field of the sluggard, And by the vineyard of the man lacking sense;
Here begins a short story (vv. 30-34) in which the teacher reflects upon a personal experience for didactic purposes. It is, as such,

not dissimilar to Proverbs 7:6-23, though it addresses a different issue. The 'sluggard' is met fourteen times in Proverbs (Prov. 6:6, 9; 10:26; 13:4; 15:19; 19:24; 20:4; 21:25; 22:13; 24:30; 26:13-16). The best commentary on this account is Proverbs 6:6-11.

Whether or not this reflects an actual event or is a moral story manufactured for purposes of instruction is beside the point. What should not be lost, however, is how much can be learned if one simply keeps his eyes open. We would be surprised how many moral and spiritual lessons unfold about us if we only observed life more carefully as we 'passed by.'

The 'field' or 'vineyard' apparently was obtained at some expense (even if by relatives from whom they were handed down). No doubt an investment of labor and seed had been made at some point. This investment was not nurtured by consistent labor, however. This is obvious from the state of the field/vineyard in verse 31. This reveals that the man was not only lazy ('the sluggard'), but was 'lacking sense.' The expression is, literally, 'lacking heart' and is found also in Proverbs 6:32; 7:7; 9:4; 10:13; 12:11; 17:18; 24:30. It is equivalent to saying that such a person is a fool.

Investments require nurture in order to return a good yield. To make the initial investment without following through with that required to make the venture fruitful is folly fed by laziness.

24:31. And behold, it was completely overgrown with thistles, Its surface was covered with nettles, And its stone wall was broken down.

This unusual three-line verse adds fine detail to the picture already begun in broad strokes in the previous verse. This 'field' in which a 'vineyard' (v. 30) was once planted has become overrun with brush due to the owner's neglect. Indeed, instead of a bountiful crop, 'thistles' (Isa. 34:13; Hosea 9:6) and 'nettles' (Zeph. 2:9) abound. God's curse upon the ground assured that, apart from 'the sweat of your face,' the ground would produce nothing but 'thorns and thistles' (Gen. 3:18-19). The sluggard is giving way before the curse upon sin. 'The way of the sluggard is as a hedge of thorns, But the path of the upright is a highway' (Prov. 15:19). Even the protective rock wall built around the vineyard, to protect it from both human and animal intruders, has been allowed to crumble (Isa. 5:5). His inverted values are becoming evident to all (Prov. 24:27).

For a contrast, read both Isaiah 5:1-7 and 28:24-29 for a picture of the measures taken by the wise farmer to assure a bountiful crop.

24:32. When I saw, I reflected upon it; I looked, and received instruction.

Open eyes can lead to an informed heart. The speaker has taken visual notice of the condition of the sluggard's field, but the eyes of his heart (Eph. 1:18) have also been opened. The Hebrew word translated 'saw' speaks not only of the literal sight of the physical organs (Prov. 22:29; 29:20), but is often used of studying, gazing at or scrutinizing something. It describes the prophetic insight and vision of the prophets as well. So, this is more than a mere passing glance; this is insightful study.[29] Similarly, the word translated 'I looked' is the one used more than any other word to describe what happens when the prophet receives a vision from God. Thus, it too can describe more than the mere act of light rays being collected by the physical organs of sight.[30] It is not merely sight that we meet here, but insight.

That which is seen with the eyes soon engages the heart. Beware what you set before your eyes (Ps. 101:3)! The expression 'I reflected upon it' is, more literally, 'I set my heart.' The expression 'to set the heart' is used ten times in Scripture. It can have a negative connotation, as when Pharaoh ignored, dismissed and refused to take notice of what God was doing in the first plague (Exod. 7:23). It can also be used positively, as here, to describe considering something (Prov. 22:17; 27:23).[31] The use of the word 'heart' echoes verse 30, where it was the sluggard's lack of heart that started his troubles.

The result of open eyes and a reflective heart is that we may receive 'instruction.' The word refers to education through correction. It often describes discipline and even chastening.[32] The wise man is the one who chastens himself through reflective study and insight. Such a one, often, is able to bypass the discipline inflicted by the consequences of foolish choices.

24:33. 'A little sleep, a little slumber, A little folding of the hands to rest,'

This verse and the next are a virtual repetition of Proverbs 6:10-11. In both Proverbs 6:10 and here, the words appear to be a derisive quotation of the sluggard, as he attempts to justify his laziness. Note the nasb's use of quotation marks. Sufficient rest is a carrot the lazy never seem to actually acquire (Prov. 26:14). The pursuit lengthens legitimate leisure into consuming laziness. Delay and procrastination set him up for only increased want (v. 34) and more excuses.

For the phrase 'folding of the hands,' see Ecclesiastes 4:4-8, where the polarized dangers of workaholism and laziness are set in contrast to responsible labor.

24:34. Then your poverty will come as a robber, And your want like an armed man.
This continues the near perfect repetition of Proverbs 6:10-11. We meet now the logical outgrowth of the faulty reasoning espoused in verse 33. This outcome is set forth in two similes set off in synonymous parallelism.

The sluggard's demise is called both 'poverty' and 'want.' The problem of 'poverty' is met often in Proverbs (e.g. Prov. 10:15; 13:18; 24:34; 30:8; 31:7). It describes one who is utterly destitute.[33] The Hebrew word translated 'want' describes a simple lack of that which is needed.[34] Here, unlike in Proverbs 6:11, it is in the plural and denotes the multiplied 'wants' of the lazy man.

This condition is fleshed out for us in the metaphors of 'a robber' and 'an armed man.' Such stalkers were a common occurrence along ancient roadways. The expression 'an armed man' literally means 'a man of a shield.' It refers to a light infantryman.[35] The emphasis is on the fact that the man is well armed, but moves with swiftness and stealth.

The point is that the lazy man, one day, awakens from his stupor to discover that he has become poverty-stricken. The poverty did not spring up overnight, but the realization of it has suddenly dawned upon him. With arms folded, eyes closing in slumber and mouth muttering rationalizations (v. 33), sudden economic destruction overtakes the sluggard unawares. 'Poor is he who works with a negligent hand, But the hand of the diligent makes rich' (Prov. 10:4; cf. Prov. 13:4; Eccles. 10:18).

End Notes

1. Wolf, Herbert, 'haga,' *Theological Wordbook of the Old Testament* (Chicago: Moody Press, 1980), 1:205.

2. Whybray, R. N., *Proverbs* (Grand Rapids, Michigan: Zondervan Publishing House, 1994), 344.

3. Ibid., 334.

4. Murphy, Roland E., *Proverbs* (Nashville: Thomas Nelson Publishers, 1998), 179.

5. Ross, Allen P., 5:906.

6. Cohen, A., *Proverbs* (London: The Soncino Press, 1946), 5.

7. Wood, Leon J., 'hāshab,' *Theological Wordbook of the Old Testament* (Chicago: Moody Press, 1980), 1:329-330.

8. Hartley, John E., 'sārar,' *Theological Wordbook of the Old Testament* (Chicago: Moody Press, 1980), 2:778-779.

9. Wakely, Robin, 'דפה,' *New International Dictionary of Old Testament Theology and Exegesis* (Grand Rapids, Michigan: Zondervan Publishing House, 1997), 3:1181-1182.

10. Brown, Francis, S. R. Driver, Charles A. Briggs, *A Hebrew and English Lexicon of the Old Testament* (Oxford: Clarendon Press, n.d.), 50.

11. Whybray, 348.

12. Lane, Eric, *Proverbs* (Scotland: Christian Focus Publications, 2000), 270.

13. Whybray, 349.

14. Kidner, Derek, *Proverbs* (Downers Grove, Illinois: InterVarsity Press, 1964), 155.

15. Harris, R. Laird, ''āhar,' *Theological Wordbook of the Old Testament* (Chicago: Moody Press, 1980), 1:33-34.

16. Murphy. 181.

17. Ibid, 180.

18. Whybray, 349.

19. Kidner, 155.

20. Cohen, 162.

21. Kidner, 155.

22. Whybray, 337.

23. Alden, Robert L., ''wd,' *Theological Wordbook of the Old Testament* (Chicago: Moody Press, 1980), 1:17.

24. Harris, R. Laird, 'pyd,' *Theological Wordbook of the Old Testament* (Chicago: Moody Press, 1980), 2:722.

25. Wilson, Marvin R., 'nā'ēm,' *Theological Wordbook of the Old Testament* (Chicago: Moody Press, 1980), 2:585.

26. Ross, Allen P., 5:1077.

27. Jonker, Louis, 'נכח,' *New International Dictionary of Old Testament Theology and Exegesis* (Grand Rapids, Michigan: Zondervan Publishing House, 1997), 3:105-106.

28. Whybray, 355.

29. Naude, Jackie N., 'חזה,' *New International Dictionary of Old Testament Theology and Exegesis* (Grand Rapids, Michigan: Zondervan Publishing House, 1997), 2:56-61.

30. White, William, 'rā'â,' *Theological Wordbook of the Old Testament* (Chicago: Moody Press, 1980), 2:823-825.

31. Hamilton, Victor P., 'shît,' *Theological Wordbook of the Old Testament* (Chicago: Moody Press, 1980), 2:920-921.

32. Gilchrist, Paul R., 'yāsar,' *Theological Wordbook of the Old Testament* (Chicago: Moody Press, 1980), 1:386-387.

33. White, William, 'rûsh,' *Theological Wordbook of the Old Testament* (Chicago: Moody Press, 1980), 2:840.

34. Scott, Jack B., 'hāsēr,' *Theological Wordbook of the Old Testament* (Chicago: Moody Press, 1980), 1:309.

35. Smith, James E., 'gānan,' *Theological Wordbook of the Old Testament* (Chicago: Moody Press, 1980), 1:168-169.

Proverbs 25

25:1. These also are proverbs of Solomon which the men of Hezekiah, king of Judah, transcribed.
Here begins another major section of Proverbs (Prov. 25:1–29:27). The present verse and Proverbs 30:1 clearly mark out this section. The proverbs we encounter here were authored by Solomon, but were compiled into the present arrangement by 'the men of Hezekiah.' Hezekiah reigned approximately 250–275 years after the time of Solomon. No doubt, it was during the spiritual revival under his reign (2 Kings 18:1-8; 2 Chron. 29:1–31:21) that King Hezekiah saw with fresh eyes the value of the wisdom God entrusted to Solomon and had his works reissued in the present form. Solomon wrote 3,000 proverbs (1 Kings 4:32), so these 138 were, no doubt, selected from among the best of them. This process was superintended by the Holy Spirit, so that what we have in our present form of the book of Proverbs is breathed out by Him (2 Tim. 3:16). Perhaps Shebna, the scribe (2 Kings 18:18, 37; 19:2), led the group who carried out this sacred work.[1]

Many scholars have noted that the first three chapters (25–27) show an affinity with one another, while the last two (28–29) reveal a character all their own. The first three chapters use little antithetical parallelism, and are filled with more similes, metaphors and admonitions. The latter two chapters return to a more frequent usage of the contrasting lines within the proverbs.[2]

The exact meaning of the verb translated 'transcribed' is of some debate among scholars, but it appears to mean something like move, snatch away or transfer from one place to another.[3] In this context, then, it would describe the copying out of an existing collection of proverbs into a new one. It points clearly to Solomonic authorship and a Holy Spirit-guided compilation by Hezekiah's men.

25:2. It is the glory of God to conceal a matter, But the glory of kings is to search out a matter.
Hezekiah's men begin by selecting proverbs that concern 'kings' and arranging them into a thematic section (vv. 2-7).

This proverb contrasts that which 'is the glory' of God and kings. The word 'glory' refers to that which brings honor to an individual.[4] God's glory, in this case, is found in that He conceals a good deal about Himself and His ways. What we know of God is by His condescending revelation. This, by no means, implies that He has revealed all of Himself. On the contrary, God has left much about Himself and His ways veiled (Exod. 33:20; Job 11:7-8; 15:8; 26:14; Isa. 45:15; John 1:18). Solomon himself admitted, 'The LORD has said that He would dwell in the thick cloud' (1 Kings 8:12). He knows all (Heb. 4:13), but not all about Him is known (Isa. 55:8-9). This brings God great honor – for He is unsearchable. McKane was correct: 'When it is supposed that everything is known about God, it is no longer possible to worship him.'[5] 'The secret things belong to the LORD our God, but the things revealed belong to us and to our sons forever, that we may observe all the words of this law' (Deut. 29:29). What God has revealed, we must fully and fervently search out. What God has left veiled in mystery must serve to remind us of our rightful place before the infinite God of the universe. We are called to be worshipers as well as wise men (Rom. 11:33).

The glory of God is found in the fact that, while He is omniscient, He remains personally unsearchable. The glory of the earthly ruler, on the other hand, is found in that, while he is limited in knowledge, he never rests in searching out the state of his kingdom and its subjects. When it is found that not all is known about God, we gladly become worshipers. When it is discovered that the king is hiding something, we quickly become disgruntled. People desire a king who can say, 'I have seen and applied my mind to every deed that has been done under the sun wherein a man has exercised authority over another man ...' (Eccles. 8:9). His search will, ultimately, end against the broad wall of God's inscrutability – 'I concluded that man cannot discover the work which has been done under the sun. Even though a man should seek laboriously, he will not discover; and though the wise man should say, 'I know,' he cannot discover' (Eccles. 8:17).

God is always worthy of our worship. The mortal men who rule over us on earth, however, are often a disappointment. Our calling is to find the balance in Peter's counsel: 'fear God and honor the king' (1 Pet. 2:17). Only the unsearchable, inscrutable God is worthy to be reverenced and worshiped. But, we should grant honor to the earthly ruler to whom God has delegated a measure of His authority and whom He has set over us for our good.

25:3. As the heavens for height and the earth for depth, So the heart of kings is unsearchable.

This verse introduces the first of twelve comparisons in this chapter ('like' or 'as,' vv. 11-14; 18-20; 23; 25-26; 28) and thirteen in the next

(Prov. 26:1, 2, 7-11, 14, 17-18, 21-23).[6] That this verse is connected with the preceding is also clear, in that the word 'kings' is repeated, as is the root word found in both 'search out' (v. 2) and 'unsearchable' (v. 3).

Verse two looked at the king in comparison to God; this verse views him in relationship to his subjects. While it is true that, ultimately, only God is inscrutable (v. 2), every earthly ruler has motives and missions that remain concealed from public view (v. 3). This may be for reasons both personal and political. At such times, one might as well attempt to measure off the 'height' of the heavens or run a tape to the center of the earth to find its depth as discover the royal 'secret.'

At times, Proverbs seems drawn to the mysteries of that which cannot be understood (Prov. 30:18-19).

25:4. Take away the dross from the silver, And there comes out a vessel for the smith;
This verse provides the analogy, while the next provides the point. Silver, in its natural state, is always found alloyed with impurities. Heat must be applied in order to separate the lead, copper and other contaminants from the silver. This smelting process stands behind the imagery of these two lines. The 'dross' is the scum of pollutants that rises to the top of the molten metal and must be skimmed off. When the process is completed, there remains the pure, precious metal, which is then fit for fashioning 'a vessel.'

There is some debate over the second line of this proverb. Technically, simply removing 'the dross from the silver' does not create 'a vessel for the smith.' The refining process will provide the material for 'the smith' to produce such an article, but the process itself will not do so.[7] This hair-splitting has led to proposed emendations and alternate meanings for words.[8] The NIV has translated with 'material' instead of 'a vessel.' The LXX has apparently added that this process makes the silver pure. The problem, however, is probably not as large as it may appear. The picture is painted with broad, but clear, strokes by the Hebrew text and the meaning is not obscured.

This 'dross' is often used in Scripture as an emblem of moral filthiness (Ps. 119:119). The process of separating, and removing, these impurities is picturesque of God's judgment (Isa. 1:22-25; Ezek. 22:18-19; Mal. 3:2-3). It can also describe a more general process of refinement in a man's life (Prov. 27:21). This imagery, then, becomes the artistic fabric upon which the moral point of verse 5 will be made.

25:5. Take away the wicked from before the king, And his throne will be established in righteousness.

Analogous to the dross being removed from silver (v. 4) is the removal of unrighteous advisors from a leader (v. 5). When 'the wicked' are taken from the place where they can exert an influence upon the leading decision-maker, then that head's leadership is 'established in righteousness.'

God promised to David, through the prophet Nathan, that He would thus establish his son Solomon's reign (2 Sam. 7:13). David had previously made such a personal commitment concerning his rule (Ps. 101:4-8). How much of this was in Solomon's mind as he wrote these proverbs?

Note, however, the horrors that came upon Rehoboam and his subjects, because of his refusal to listen to the right kind of advisors (1 Kings 12:6-15). Unfortunately, this devastating failure was compounded by later rulers of Israel, like Joash (2 Chron. 24:17-24). But, righteousness reigned where leaders like Asa refused to allow even his own family to manipulate him in unrighteousness (1 Kings 15:13; 2 Chron. 14:1-7).

If 'Righteousness exalts a nation' (Prov. 14:34), then the leader of that nation must stand and swiftly disperse the unrighteousness that threatens his subjects (Prov. 20:8, 26). Then will 'Loyalty and truth preserve the king' as he 'upholds his throne by righteousness' (Prov. 20:28). 'If a king judges the poor with truth, His throne will be established forever' (Prov. 29:14). 'It is an abomination for kings to commit wickedness, For a throne is established on righteousness' (Prov. 16:12, note the near repetition of the last line here).

25:6. Do not claim honor in the presence of the king, And do not stand in the place of great men;

We continue in the vein of royal proverbs (vv. 1-7). This verse and the next appear to have been in the mind of Jesus when He told His parable in Luke 14:7-11. His adaptation from the courts 'of the king' to the setting of a wedding feast reveals that the principle set forth here applies more broadly than simply in the political world. The admonitions of this verse are supported by the 'it is better' statement of the next.

The problem addressed is that of self-promotion. The expression 'Do not claim honor' is, more literally, 'Do not honor yourself.' The self-promoting are, often, the self-defeating. The king has no time for those with personal agendas; he needs people who will carry out his program for the kingdom. To rush for position and power is to set yourself up for the embarrassment of public demotion.

The good scribe Baruch was warned by the prophet Jeremiah: '[A]re you seeking great things for yourself? Do not seek them ...' (Jer. 45:5). The disciples repeatedly struggled with thoughts of self-promotion (Matt. 18:1-4; Mark 9:33-37; Luke 9:46-48; 22:24-27). Diotrephes exemplifies the problem ('who loves to be first among them') and the product ('if I come, I will call attention to his deeds'; 3 John 9, 10).[9]

Proverbs assures us that true greatness will not go unrecognized (Prov. 22:29).

25:7. For it is better that it be said to you, 'Come up here,' Than that you should be put lower in the presence of the prince, Whom your eyes have seen.

This is the motivation for the exhortations of verse 6. There is a much greater glory in being promoted by another in the presence of others (Luke 14:10) than in trying to advance yourself and being humiliated by being demoted (Luke 14:8-9). The honor of being advanced by another is illustrated in David (2 Sam. 7:8), while the disgrace of unveiled self-promotion is illustrated by Shebna in Isaiah 22:15-19. Better to pray with David, 'O Lord, my heart is not proud, nor my eyes haughty; Nor do I involve myself in great matters, Or in things too difficult for me' (Ps. 131:1). 'It is better to be of a humble spirit with the lowly, Than to divide the spoil with the proud' (Prov. 16:19). 'Let another praise you, and not your own mouth; A stranger, and not your own lips' (Prov. 27:2).

Jesus' summary statement of His parable reveals that the principle espoused here applies more widely than to just the king's court: 'For everyone who exalts himself shall be humbled, and he who humbles himself shall be exalted' (Luke 14:11).

The final phrase ('Whom your eyes have seen') has been the source of much discussion. Though the Hebrew text affixes it to this verse, it seems somewhat unnecessary and awkward here. The LXX, Syriac and Vulgate all connect it with the beginning of verse 8.[10] Many modern translations follow this lead and change 'Whom' to 'what' (NIV, RSV, NRSV, JB).

25:8. Do not go out hastily to argue your case; Otherwise, what will you do in the end, When your neighbor puts you to shame?

The final phrase of verse 7 may be best coupled with these lines. Note the discussion there.

The warning 'Do not go out hastily to argue your case' seems to be a warning about rushing to judgment about what you have seen (v. 7c). Specifically, it appears to be a warning against rushing to court to press charges or to bring witness against a neighbor. However, the application may fall within a wider circle than just the courtroom.

The motivation seems to be that what you have taken as fact, in a rush to judgment, may not actually hold up in the courts (either of law or common opinion). Thus, 'in the end' there will be 'shame' upon you.

The Hebrew word translated 'Otherwise' is somewhat awkward grammatically and has led commentators to suggest an emendation. However, it is probably best understood along the lines of 'Lest ... what will you do in the end?'[11]

What seems obvious may not be accurate and, thus, it is best to hold one's tongue till the facts are in (Prov. 18:17). The rush may cause a world of hurt (Prov. 17:14). Your neighbor's welfare is your divine responsibility. Be careful, then, how you treat him (Prov. 24:28). Jesus spoke along similar lines, though with a twist (Matt. 5:25).

25:9. Argue your case with your neighbor, And do not reveal the secret of another,

Rather than hasty legal action, the wise man takes his 'case' (now personal, but potentially legal) not to the courts, but to the offending party. Go straight to 'your neighbor' and try to resolve your concerns privately. Jesus counseled this as the first, and necessary, step to all personal disputes (Matt. 18:15). Only after this has taken place and been left unresolved, can we find justification for going to a third party (Matt. 18:16-18).

The second line warns against dredging up privileged information ('the secret of another'), which you may have access to in order to win your dispute with your neighbor. Presumably, this is information from, or about, someone outside the two people currently in conflict. Such information was gained through the confidence of the third party and divulging it for personal advantage would be a disgrace (Prov. 11:13). If you handle your personal associations in this way, you may find it difficult to make and retain friends in the future (Prov. 20:19).

25:10. Lest he who hears it reproach you, And the evil report about you not pass away.

A warning ('Lest') is now added to the admonitions of verse 9 and serves as motivation. The fear is that 'he who hears it (your revelation of privileged information, v. 9) reproach you.' The expression 'he who hears it' refers to the party with whom you are in a dispute. It can, however, have legal overtones and refer to a judicial figure.[12] If the legal imagery continues from v. 8, then this may help with the identification of the one who will 'reproach you.' Whether it be the one you are in a dispute with, or the judge hearing your case in court, you will be branded as a gossip. Your reputation will be sullied and people will no longer consider you worthy of their trust.

The second line underscores the seriousness of such a reputation. Most literally, it reads, 'and your evil report not returns.' Does this mean the evil report about another that you spread will be unretrievable and you'll never be able to take your words back (cf. NEB)? Or, does it refer to a bad reputation about you as a gossip? It is probably the latter, a view supported by most major modern translations (NASB, NIV, RSV, NRSV, JB). 'The evil report about you [will] not pass away.' Proverbs consistently affirms the value of a good name (Prov. 3:4; 10:7; 22:1). We should take great care what we say in the heat of an argument. We should avoid unloading all we know just to win an argument. We may discover that, in so doing, we have won a battle, but lost the war.

25:11. Like apples of gold in settings of silver Is a word spoken in right circumstances.

This introduces a series of proverbs on speech (vv. 11-15). While the imagery of this proverb is beautiful, the actual translation is complex. Several words are disputed as to their meaning. The word translated 'apples' is an obvious reference to some kind of fruit, but which one? Suggestions have included apples, apricots, oranges, pomegranates, citrons and quinces. Since many believe the apple was not yet introduced to Palestine,[13] it possibly refers to one of the other fruits. Some have taken 'gold' to speak of the color of the fruit rather than the substance of which it is made.[14] If this is true, then perhaps the orange or apricot lead the way. The precise identification of the fruit meant is, however, not absolutely essential to understanding the proverb. The reference to 'gold' should likely be taken literally, as it is in the next verse. These are actual fruit-shaped decorations made of gold and placed in 'settings of silver.' The word translated 'settings' is difficult. It may, generally, describe an image, sculpture or relief of some kind.[15] It can be used to describe the physical structure of an idol (Lev. 26:1; Num. 33:52; Ezek. 8:12). It is also used to describe the imaginary constructions of the heart (Ps. 3:7; Prov. 18:11).[16] Here, it appears to simply describe some ornate craftsmanship of an artisan skilled in metalworking. The imagery of 'apples of gold in settings of silver,' while not entirely clear, is obviously meant to describe that which is beautiful, valuable and carefully crafted.

That which is likened to this is 'a word spoken in right circumstances.' The exact derivation of the Hebrew word translated 'in right circumstances' is difficult to ascertain. It is found only here. Some have traditionally linked it to the word for wheel.[17] Thus, they suggest the literal reading is 'on its two wheels.'[18] Many claim that a link with this root word is unlikely.[19] So, what is beautiful about these words? Is it their timing (NASB, NIV)? Or, is it their substance? The former translations may build off of the idea of timeliness in Proverbs 15:23. The second may be supported by the idea of a well-turned phrase (a proverb) being likened to a cart with two wheels being well-balanced.[20] Probably both the fitness of time and substance are in view.[21] A good word at the wrong time can fail to produce its intention. There may be a time for speaking, but not just any word will do. Indeed, 'He kisses the lips Who gives a right answer' (Prov. 24:26)!

The Suffering Servant would be granted 'the tongue of disciples' so that he would 'know how to sustain the weary one with a word' (Isa. 50:4). Jesus still operates thus through those who yield their lives to Him and walk sensitively with those about them. The New Testament calls us to this kind of speech as well (Eph. 4:29). It is to be a balance of well-chosen ('only such a word as is good for edification') and well-timed words ('according to the need of the moment').

25:12. Like an earring of gold and an ornament of fine gold Is a wise reprover to a listening ear.
The golden imagery of the previous verse pours over into this one. Here, the metaphors are of 'an earring of gold' and 'an ornament of fine gold.' Both articles were emblematic of wealth, blessing, and beauty. The Hebrew word translated 'fine gold' appears to heighten the imagery yet again. The first word translated 'gold' is the most basic reference to this precious metal.[22] The second apparently refers to a more precious form of gold,[23] perhaps because of the location from which it was mined, the advanced process of refinement it has been through, or the quality of its workmanship.

The presence of wisdom has been compared to such personal adornment (Prov. 1:9; 3:22; 4:9). Yet, here, it is not a personal character quality that is considered beautiful and worthy of display. Rather, it is a personal acquaintance that is valued in this way. The person is called 'a wise reprover.' They may be so esteemed and, thus, labeled because they are adept at bringing 'a word spoken in right circumstances' (v. 11). Their words are well-thought-out, well-timed and well-delivered. The beauty of such reproof is not obvious to all (Prov. 1:25, 30; 5:12; 10:17; 12:1; 15:10). It takes a person with 'a listening ear' to detect their beauty and to rightly estimate their worth. The expression 'a listening ear' is, more literally, 'a hearing ear.' This 'listening' or 'hearing' requires more than simply good auditory equipment. It requires the humility of heart and hunger after wisdom that puts one in a place to gladly receive a reproof if it will advance one in the school of insight and understanding. To 'hear' or to 'listen' is to hear with a view toward conformity and obedience (Prov. 15:31).

The 'wise reprover' holds his insight until he discovers one with 'a listening ear.' The 'listening ear' seeks diligently for one who might serve him as a 'wise reprover.' When the one meets the other, he wears that relationship like his most valuable possession.

25:13. Like the cold of snow in the time of harvest Is a faithful messenger to those who send him, For he refreshes the soul of his masters.
The three-line format of this proverb stands out in a chapter dominated by two-line proverbs. However, this is no reason to side with the commentators who consider this a gloss.

The simile ('Like') sets up the point about faithfulness. It is the simile that has created the most discussion. It seems that 'snow in the time of harvest' [i.e. the hot summer months] would not only be highly unlikely (Prov. 26:1), but disastrous for the crops. The heat of the harvest season could be intense. Compare the fate of one young man in the fields under the sweltering heat of harvest time (2 Kings 4:18-20).[24]

If snowfall in Palestine would be unlikely at this time of year, what would be the explanation? Suggestions are plenteous: snow brought from the mountains and kept in an ice hole, a cool mountain breeze blowing down over the snow, a drink from a stream cooled by melting snow in the mountains, a drink iced by snow, cold compresses to the forehead, or even simply the imagined pleasure of such an occurrence at the hottest time of the year.[25] Note the similar comparison in verse 25.

Whatever the exact meaning is, the point is clear – faithfulness 'refreshes.' Literally, 'refreshes the soul of his masters' is 'his master's soul he makes return.' A 'messenger' was used to convey important information for business transactions, social dealings and personal communications. As such, the character and performance of one's messenger could radically affect one's station in life. When one sent a messenger on his behalf, he was entrusting to him his very 'soul' or life (Prov. 10:26; 26:6). The faithful messenger carried away not just a message, but his master's reputation and well-being. Thus, when he returned, having faithfully completed his task, there was great relief for the one who sent him (Prov. 13:17).

It is worthy of note that the same words used here ('refreshes the soul') are employed in Psalm 23:3 ('He restores my soul') to describe the effect of God's ministry to the one who trusts Him.[26] To do your job well is holy work. To be faithful to those over you is to join God in His ministry to another human heart.

25:14. Like clouds and wind without rain Is a man who boasts of his gifts falsely.

The previous verse spoke of the refreshment of a faithful messenger. Here, we find his opposite and the inverse effect.

The imagery here is both simple and picturesque. Drought covers the land and all, together, pray for rain and watch the horizon. In time, a cloud materializes, then another and yet another. Hopes soar! The inhabitants watch with anticipation as the clouds draw near. They can feel their soothing coolness. They can hear the glad sound of the drops on parched earth. They can smell the fresh scent of the earth washed clean. They can taste the food it will produce. Yet, sadly, the clouds come, casting their shadow of promise, but depart having left nothing behind but the scorching sun, searing temperatures, parched earth, and hungry bellies.

'Like' this is 'a man who boasts of his gifts falsely.' This does not mean his personal talents, but promises he makes of work done, presents given, goods donated, money contributed, etc.[27] The line, literally, reads 'a man boasting himself in a gift of falsehood.' The 'gift' is a 'falsehood' in that he promised it, but does not deliver. His promises are bigger than what he produces (Prov. 20:6). Such a one leaves those around him utterly disappointed.

The metaphor of rainless clouds and vacuous winds is used of false prophets (2 Pet. 2:19; Jude 12; cf. Jer. 5:13). This reminds us that the false promiser par excellence was Satan himself, who deceived Adam and Eve with the promise 'you will be like God' (Gen. 3:5). What they received was death, not life. Jesus was not deceived by his tactics, however (Matt. 4:1-11). But, still today, 'such men are false apostles, deceitful workers, disguising themselves as apostles of Christ. And no wonder, for even Satan disguises himself as an angel of light. Therefore it is not surprising if his servants also disguise themselves as servants of righteousness' (2 Cor. 11:13-15).[28]

Any promises you have not kept? If so, you are keeping bad company!

25:15. By forbearance a ruler may be persuaded, And a soft tongue breaks the bone.

Self-controlled persistence will, generally, yield far better results than hot-headed force. The first line presents the hardest of cases: 'a ruler' whom we may assume is set on a particular course of action that is contrary to the counsel of one of his advisors. The ruler wins; end of discussion. That will be the case, if the advisor takes the course of letting his emotions boil over to the surface (Prov. 14:29; 15:18). But, if he chooses 'forbearance' instead, he might find that his boss 'may be persuaded.'

The second line presents a roughly synonymous idea, though the picture is very different. What seems impossible may not actually be so. The 'soft tongue' may indeed break the hard 'bone.' The 'soft tongue' pictures the gentle, careful speech (Prov. 15:1) of one who has come up against firm resistence ('the bone'). How can the weaker win out over the stronger? By its gentle response to the firm resolve of the other. The one in a position of authority, despite appearances, may yet be won over. Stay calm, stay the course, remain in his circle of influence. Bide your time. Serve him well, despite your setback (Eccles. 10:4). The day may just come when your idea will have a hearing and win the day. 'The wrath of a king is as messengers of death, But a wise man will appease it' (Prov. 16:14). 'He who is slow to anger is better than the mighty, And he who rules his spirit, than he who captures a city' (Prov. 16:32).

25:16. Have you found honey? Eat only what you need, Lest you have it in excess and vomit it.

All things in moderation! The proverb opens with the assumption that one has either stumbled upon or discovered through diligent search some wild honey. Both Sampson and the armies of Saul fill in the details of our sketchy backdrop (Judg. 14:8; 1 Sam. 14:25). Solomon is not against the pleasures of food, for he has counseled us to enjoy the sweetness of honey (Prov. 24:13). Here, however, he demands 'Eat only what you need.' 'It is not good to eat *much* honey' (v. 27, emphasis added).

Why this restraint? Is it for purely dietetic reasons? Is health his concern? Is it because of weight gain? Those may be remotely related as negative side effects of overindulgence in sweets. But, the point made has more to do with a general theology of pleasure than it does with health issues. This is about more than simply 'honey.'

The world believes that pleasure is found through 'more.' If a little is pleasurable, then 'more' will increase that pleasure. Solomon tested this theory and found it to be false (Eccles. 2:1-11). He testified '... all that my eyes desired I did not refuse them. I did not withhold my heart from any pleasure ...' (Eccles. 2:10). In the end he found such a philosophy to be '... vanity and striving after wind ...' (Eccles. 2:11). What overindulgence gets you is not more pleasure, but less. '... [Y]ou have it in excess and vomit it.' 'A sated man loathes honey, But to a famished man any bitter thing is sweet' (Prov. 27:7).

Ultimate pleasure can be found only on the other side of self-restraint. Kidner well says: 'Since Eden, man has wanted the last ounce out of life, as though beyond God's 'enough' lay ecstasy, not nausea.'[29]

Could it be, then, that God's boundaries are not designed to restrict our freedom and dull our enjoyment, but to expand our boundaries and heighten our pleasure?

25:17. Let your foot rarely be in your neighbor's house, Lest he become weary of you and hate you.
The principle of moderation, which was stated generally (v. 16), is now applied specifically. The first line, most literally, reads 'Make your foot rare from your neighbor's house.' The word translated 'rarely' means precious or valuable.[30] Negatively, that would speak to the frequency of your visits ('Seldom set your foot in your neighbor's house,' NIV). Positively, it would speak to the value of your calls. Make your visits something that bring blessing to the home and its residents, rather than simply something designed for your benefit. Leave more than you take.

The most obvious clue that this proverb is an extension and application of the previous one is that 'Lest he become weary' is the identical verb translated 'Lest you have it in excess' (v. 16). In that case, the concern was becoming sated personally with honey; here, the fear is that your neighbor begin to feel that way about you! The first made a person want to physically 'vomit' (v. 16), the second brings a similarly violent interpersonal reaction – 'hate.'

25:18. Like a club and a sword and a sharp arrow Is a man who bears false witness against his neighbor.

A 'false witness' is condemned in the ninth commandment (Exod. 20:16; Deut. 20:5) and frequently in Proverbs (Prov. 12:17; 14:5, 25; 19:5, 9; 21:28; 24:28). This is one sin God particularly hates (Prov. 6:19).

Why this particular revulsion for one who bears false testimony against his neighbor? Because such words are 'Like a club and a sword and a sharp arrow.' The Hebrew text has, more literally, 'Like one who scatters' rather than 'a club.' Most translations appear to follow the LXX and emend the word (to 'a club') in order to preserve a tight parallelism of the three terms. All three refer to weapons of death. The 'club' crushes. The 'sword' divides (Ps. 57:4; Prov. 12:18). The 'sharp arrow' pierces (Jer. 9:8).[31] The words of a false witness crush the reputation, livelihood and social standing of the object of the lies. Those lies divide them from trusted friends. They pierce to the depths of their souls and put hope to death. All it takes for any of us is one rumor – life as we know it can be over that quickly.

25:19. Like a bad tooth and an unsteady foot Is confidence in a faithless man in time of trouble.

Here again the metaphor opens the proverb, but here there are two, rather than three emblems (cf. v. 18). The 'bad tooth' seems to point to a tooth that shatters, crumbles or gives way under the pressure of chewing.[32] Just what is meant by the foot being 'unsteady' is hard to pinpoint. It has been translated as 'lame' (NIV, NRSV), 'out of joint' (NKJV), 'limping' (NEB), and a foot 'that slips' (RSV). The root of the word points toward the action of slipping, sliding or shaking.[33] This action may come about from a lack of structural integrity or strength within the leg itself or because of the poor choice of footing upon which a strong leg is placed. The feet of those with integrity will not suffer from this instability (Ps. 26:1; 37:31), while those of the unfaithful will never fail to shake and slip (Job 12:5).

That which is 'Like' these two ineffective and insecure members of the body is 'confidence in a faithless man in time of trouble.' The form of the text can mean either trust in one who is unfaithful or, with a few modifications of the text, that which the unfaithful have placed the weight of their trust in.[34] The former seems the more likely meaning here, given the close proximity to the problem of a person of falsehood (v. 18).

Trust in those of low integrity is both deeply painful and disastrously ineffective. David knew this (Ps. 55:12-14), as did Israel as a whole (Isa. 36:6; Ezek. 29:6-7), Jesus (Matt. 26:56) and Paul (2 Tim. 1:15; 4:16).[35]

25:20. Like one who takes off a garment on a cold day, or like vinegar on soda, Is he who sings songs to a troubled heart.
Commentators tend to make much over supposed corruptions in the text of this proverb, but they have seldom offered any convincing emendations. The first line is said to be a dittogram, with the Hebrew consonants being closely related to those in verse 19.[36] The LXX has a radically different proverb altogether ('As vinegar is bad for a wound. So a pain which afflicts the body afflicts the heart. As moth in a garment and a worm in wood, the pain of a man wounds the heart').[37] Nothing should dissuade us from simply taking the Hebrew text at face value.

The proverb consists of two metaphors that, then, set up the moral point made in the last line. To take a person's 'garment on a cold day' would be cruel, inhumane and provoke an altercation. It was forbidden in the Law (Deut. 24:12-17) and frowned upon generally in society (Job 24:7-10; Isa. 58:7).

The addition of 'vinegar on soda' produces a violent reaction. The LXX has 'wound' where the Hebrew has 'soda.' There is no good reason to abandon the Hebrew text. This appears to refer to sodium carbonate (i.e. baking soda),[38] which, when combined with vinegar, provides an illustration of two elements not comfortable with one another.

These two vivid similes are 'Like ... Is he who sings songs to a troubled heart.' Literally, it is 'evil heart.' This is not a reference to the moral depravity of the heart, but to its emotional state. Light, happy songs do not meet the need of such a heart, and may provoke an undesired reaction. The exiles of Israel found it difficult to sing their songs in captivity (Ps. 137:3-4). Darius removed music from his presence when he worried over Daniel (Dan. 6:18). While David played for Saul when he was in a foul mood (1 Sam. 19:9), it proved only a fleeting success and did not forestall the reaction this proverb warns of (1 Sam. 19:10).

Truly, there is 'A time to weep, and a time to laugh; A time to mourn, and a time to dance' (Eccles. 3:4). This proverb warns us against applying frivolous balms to deep hurts. We must listen well to the condition of people's hearts. We must take seriously their troubles. We must 'Rejoice with those who rejoice, and weep with those who weep' (Rom. 12:15).

25:21. If your enemy is hungry, give him food to eat; And if he is thirsty, give him water to drink;

This verse and the next form a noble proverb made the more famous by its quotation by the Apostle Paul in Romans 12:20. The Law taught that one must give back his enemy's possessions when stumbled upon (Exod. 23:4-5). Proverbs prohibited revenge (Prov. 17:13; 20:22; 24:17-18, 29). This appears, however, to go beyond either of these prescriptions. Far from simply returning what rightly belongs to another, we must give what belongs to us. This is more than simply refraining from revenge. Here, we meet the positive action of giving 'him food to eat' and 'water to drink.' Jesus took such instruction to yet another level: 'I say to you, love your enemies' (Matt. 5:44).

Elisha's counsel to the King of Israel about the appropriate treatment of captured Aramean soldiers is illustrative of this teaching (2 Kings 6:22). Consider also the prophet Oded's advice to King Ahaz regarding treatment of captured soldiers of Judah (2 Chron. 28:15). Compare the good Samaritan in the New Testament (Luke 10:33-36).

Here 'your enemy' is, more accurately, 'your hater' or, perhaps, 'the one who hates you.' This removes the application from the vague world of case studies and plants it in the concrete world of our relationships.[39] The next verse describes the results of taking such a radical and selfless approach to conflicted relationships.

25:22. For you will heap burning coals on his head, And the LORD will reward you.

The outcome of returning love for hate is here stated in an enigmatic metaphor: 'you will heap burning coals on his head.' Just what this refers to, and what its effect is, upon the 'enemy' (v. 21) is not stated explicitly. Interpretations have ranged from a helpful act of kindness to one whose fire at home has gone out to the railing judgment of God (Ps. 140:10). Most see it as some kind of resulting shame or contrition on the part of the enemy. Experiencing such kindness in the face of one's hatred is humbling. Just how the 'burning coals on the head' picture this shame is not plainly stated. Some point to an Egyptian ritual wherein the penitent carried hot coals on this head as an outward expression of remorse for a wrong committed. There is, however, no clear connection linking that ritual to Israel.

Certainly, whatever the final conclusion, it must be balanced with the overall teaching of Scripture, in general, and Proverbs, in particular. We have been instructed that we are never to repay evil for evil (Prov. 20:22; 24:29) and not to rejoice when an enemy falls (Prov. 24:17). Certainly, a brother offended is difficult to win over (Prov. 18:19), but, if it is to happen, it will come about through gentleness and kindness (Prov. 25:15), rather than triumphalism. The Holy Spirit guided the Apostle Paul to use it in the context of teaching about revenge (Rom. 12:17-21). This seems to rule out the idea of some kind of backhanded judgment. It certainly affects the motives with which the act of kindness is undertaken. There is no seething bitterness behind this smiling face! This seems to describe a result of the kindness described in the previous verse, rather than a motive for it. Paul summarizes his whole point by saying, 'Do not be overcome by evil, but overcome evil with good' (Rom. 12:21).

An additional result will be 'And the Lord will reward you' (something Paul drops from his quotation). God is the great equalizer. He is the only rewarder. David's response concerning the Benjamite's cursing is instructive here (2 Sam. 16:12), as is Saul's response to David's kindness (1 Sam. 24:18-20). God always makes sure there is a reward for righteousness (Prov. 11:18; 19:17).

25:23. The north wind brings forth rain, And a backbiting tongue, an angry countenance.

We have here what appears to be a simple comparison made in two lines. The trouble is that the 'north wind' typically does not bring rain to Palestine. Rather, rain comes normally from the west (1 Kings 18:41-44; Luke 12:54). Numerous attempts have been made to explain, or explain away, the 'north wind' reading. Some think it must mean 'northwest,' a direction from which rain might sometimes come to Israel. This, however, reads something into the language that is not there. Others conclude that this proverb was imported from Egypt where the weather patterns do bring rain from the north. But, what good would this proverb be in a land where the comparison did not hold true to the facts? Still others see a connection between the Hebrew words 'north' and 'backbiting' (lit., 'hidden') and, thus, translate as 'The hidden wind brings forth rain, and a hidden tongue, an angry countenance.' This stretches the language in ways that seem unnatural to its normal usage. Still others change the word 'brings forth' to mean 'repels' and, thus, understand the second line to mean that, if a person gives a would-be gossip an angry glance, it will stop the spread of slander. The Jewish commentators tend to understand it in this latter sense. This, however, requires emendations that seem gratuitous.

In the end, the mystery of just how the words 'north wind' should be understood remains unclear. However, the meaning of the proverb as a whole remains obvious. The cause and effect relationship of gossip and strife is clear. Proverbs roundly condemns gossip (Prov. 10:18; 11:13; 20:19), even while recognizing its alluring nature (Prov. 18:8; 26:22). It remains unclear also whether the 'angry countenance' is found on the face of the one spoken about or the one spoken to. It seems more likely that it refers to the one about whom the gossip has spoken.

25:24. It is better to live in a corner of the roof Than in a house shared with a contentious woman.
This proverb is repeated nearly verbatim from Proverbs 21:9. See the comments there. The question of why this would be repeated is natural. Some suggest that it indicates two collections of proverbs made independent of one another, but using similar sources.[40] Whatever took place at the human level, God the Holy Spirit superintended to make certain the point was driven home. The repetition serves to underline, circle and highlight the point being made.

In this context, the close proximity to the 'backbiting tongue' is not to be overlooked.[41] The betrayal of a neighbor hurts (v. 23), but nothing seems quite as unlivable as life in the same home with 'a contentious woman' (v. 24). The damage done by treachery cloaked in hushed tones (v. 23) is bad enough, but it is nothing compared to the raucous brawling of a henpecking wife (v. 24). How much harder when 'your enemy' (v. 21) seems to live within your home! How much more we need to return good for evil to those we live with (v. 21).

25:25. Like cold water to a weary soul, So is good news from a distant land.
In verse 13, the metaphor was 'the cold of snow;' here, it is 'cold water.' There, it was the cool refreshing at an unexpected time ('in the time of harvest'); here, it is to 'a weary soul.' There, it was the messenger himself that was the refreshment ('a faithful messenger'); here, it is the message the courier bears ('good news').

A little 'good news' may only fall on the ear, but it brings life to the whole of the body (Prov. 15:30) and 'soul.' Proverbs occasionally uses 'soul' to speak of the appetite (e.g. Prov. 10:3; 16:26; 23:2). Nevertheless, the translation 'throat' is probably not as good,[42] for certainly the point goes beyond mere physical refreshment.[43]

Solomon, who, through commerce, sent men far and wide, knew well the refreshing of 'good news from a distant land'

(1 Kings 9:26-28). Jacob was revived in his old age at the news of Joseph's good fortune in Egypt (Gen. 45:25-28). Think of how wonderful the sight of Jesus was to Simeon (Luke 2:25-35) and Anna (Luke 2:36-38). Paul's spirit leapt at the news of the strength of the Thessalonians' faith (1 Thess. 3:5-8) and the Corinthians' zeal (2 Cor. 7:5-7). And, so it is to every soul that hears, understands, and embraces the good news of God's salvation (Isa. 52:7-8)!

25:26. Like a trampled spring and a polluted well Is a righteous man who gives way before the wicked.
Two emblems are used in this comparison. The first is 'a trampled spring.' In an arid land, where fresh water supplies were few and far between, to have walked through a clear pool of water and, thus, stirred up the silt was unthinkable and calamitous in its effect. It could mean the difference between life and death for a traveler dependent upon the water's purity. The second metaphor is 'a polluted well.' The word 'polluted' primarily describes destruction. But, such destruction may not come simply by overwhelming force, but through inward corruption.[44] Thus, the picture is of a well that has not been filled in (and thus destroyed), but of one which still appears functional, but whose water has been fouled through contaminants of some kind. A well came at a high cost and was guarded like life itself (Gen. 21:25-30; 26:15-33). Such a loss was of great magnitude. See Ezekiel 32:2 and 34:18-19 for another use of these metaphors.

That which is compared to these two pictures is 'a righteous man who gives way before the wicked.' The verb 'gives way' may simply mean 'moved,' but speaks, generally, of great instability and insecurity.[45] Does this describe a good man who succumbs to the moral pressure of wickedness and willingly enters into sin, thus destroying his testimony and harming those who have looked to him as a model? Or, does it refer to the 'righteous man,' who is run over and destroyed by the wicked in some calamity and there is no apparent response from the 'righteous' God he serves? Both decry the loss of God's glory in the eyes of those who look on – the first, through the loss of a good man's witness; the second, through God's apparent inaction to protect His own. The first sees the 'spring' that is 'trampled' and the 'well' that is 'polluted' as the reputation of the 'righteous man.' The second views them as the moral order of the universe. The first implicitly admits the power of one man's testimony for good or ill; the second the fact that, sometimes, God allows the wicked to triumph temporarily, for reasons known only to Him. The first laments the failure of a man to his God; the second the apparent failure of God to uphold His commitment to His people. The first highlights the darkness of our own hearts; the second the darkness of the times in which we live.

Proverbs has used the same verb to describe the Divinely assured immovability of the righteous. 'The righteous will never be shaken, But the wicked will not dwell in the land' (Prov. 10:30). 'A man will not be established by wickedness, But the root of the righteous will not be moved' (Prov. 12:3). But, Proverbs also uses the same word for 'well' to describe the moral influence of the godly. Thus, we read that 'the righteous is a fountain of life' (Prov. 10:11).

Ultimately, the decision is arbitrary. We must determine to learn both lessons.

25:27. It is not good to eat much honey, Nor is it glory to search out one's own glory.

Any difficulty in understanding this proverb lies not at the fault of the first line, but the second. The opening line accords with verse 16 and affirms that moderation in good things is honorable and wise (cf. Prov. 27:7). The trouble is with the parallel found in the second line. It reads, literally: 'and to search out their glory [is] glory.' Just how this relates to the first line is not clear. Some words were spared in attempting to capture the punch that comes with brevity. But, what words are we to understand as we read this line? Many suggestions have been made to 'correct' the text, ranging from emendations, changing vowel points, word divisions and attributing unusual meanings to words.[46]

The best answer would appear to be found by staying in the immediate context. Given the clear point of line one, what would we logically understand to be the point of line two which presumably parallels it in some way? This would include supplying a negative to match the 'not' in line one. This the KJV, NASB and NIV have done. All present a translation whose point is that, as it is not good to pursue and overindulge in eating sweets ('honey'), so it is not a good thing to seek out and overindulge oneself in affirmations, awards, recognition and building of reputation. This point has already been made in this context (vv. 6-7), and seems to accord well with the first line. 'Let another praise you, and not your own mouth; A stranger and not your own lips' (Prov. 27:2). An illustration of this problem may be found in the servant Shebna (Isa. 22:15-19) and in Jesus' parable (Luke 14:7-11).

25:28. Like a city that is broken into and without walls Is a man who has no control over his spirit.
A city without strong walls around it is easy pickings for any, and every, foe that sets his sights upon its possessions and people. Failure to have fortified walls around one's city was a disgrace and disaster (Neh. 1:3). This same vulnerability is true of 'a man who has no control over his spirit.' The word 'spirit' describes the immaterial part of man, the place where passions of all types operate (Prov. 16:32; 17:27). A man's passions (ranging from anger to lust and beyond) do not define the man; rather, he must define them. One of the great lies of our age is that self-control is neither desirable nor do-able.

While, here, the city without walls pictures the vulnerabilities of a man without self-control, the reverse image is found in Proverbs 16:32: 'He who is slow to anger is better than the mighty, And he who rules his spirit, than he who captures a city.'

End Notes

1. Cohen, A., *Proverbs* (London: The Soncino Press, 1946), 166.

2. Murphy, Roland E., Proverbs (Nashville: Thomas Nelson Publishers, 1998), 189; and Whybray, R. N., *Proverbs* (Grand Rapids, Michigan: William B. Eerdmans Publishing Company, 1994, 356-357.

3. Delitzsch, F., *Proverbs, Ecclesiastes, Song of Solomon* (three volumes in one) in C. F. Keil and F. Delitzsch, vol. 6, *Commentary on the Old Testament* (in ten volumes), (1872; rpt. Grand Rapids, Michigan: William B. Eerdmans Publishing Company, 1980), 2:149.

4. Whybray, 360.

5. McKane, William, *Proverbs: A New Approach*, Old Testament Library (Philadelphia: Westminster, 1970), 579; quoted in Ross, Allen P., 'Proverbs,' *The Expositor's Bible Commentary* (Grand Rapids, Michigan: Zondervan Publishing Company, 1991), 5:1079.

6. Buzzell, Sid S., 'Proverbs,' *The Bible Knowledge Commentary* (Wheaton: Victor Books, 1985), 1:960.

7. Ross, 5:1079-1080.

8. Whybray, 361.

9. Bridges, Charles, *A Commentary on Proverbs* (Edinburgh: The Banner of Truth Trust, 1846, reprint 1998), 465.

10. Ross, 5:1080.

11. Murphy, 188.

12. Ibid., 192.

13. Whybray, 364.

14. Cohen, 168.

15. Hadley, Judith M., 'מַשְׂכִּית,' New International Dictionary of Old Testament Theology and Exegesis (Grand Rapids, Michigan: Zondervan Publishing House, 1997), 2:1116.

16. Cohen, Gary G., 'śkh,' Theological Wordbook of the Old Testament (Chicago: Moody Press, 1980), 2:876.

17. Feinberg, Charles L., ''pn,' Theological Wordbook of the Old Testament (Chicago: Moody Press, 1980), 1:65.

18. Murphy, 189.

19. Tomasino, Anthony, 'אָכֵן,' *New International Dictionary of Old Testament Theology and Exegesis* (Grand Rapids, Michigan: Zondervan Publishing House, 1997), 1:481.

20. Ross, 5:1081.

21. Lane, Eric, *Proverbs* (Scotland: Christian Focus Publications, 2000), 277-278.

22. Wolf, Herbert, 'zhb,' *Theological Wordbook of the Old Testament* (Chicago: Moody Press, 1980), 1:236.

23. Whybray, 364.

24. Cohen, 169.

25. Ross, 5:1082.

26. Cohen, 169.

27. Kidner, Derek, *Proverbs* (Downers Grove, Illinois: InterVarsity Press, 1964), 158.

28. Bridges, 469-470; and Lane, 279.

29. Kidner, 159.

30. Hartley, John E., 'yāqar,' *Theological Wordbook of the Old Testament* (Chicago: Moody Press, 1980), 1:398-399.

31. Buzzell, 1:961.

32. Livingston, G. Herbert, 'ra'a,'' *Theological Wordbook of the Old Testament* (Chicago: Moody Press, 1980), 2:856-857.

33. Van Pelt, M. V. and W. C. Kaiser, Jr., 'מעד,' *New International Dictionary of Old Testament Theology and Exegesis* (Grand Rapids, Michigan: Zondervan Publishing House, 1997), 2:1011; Victor P. Hamilton, 'mā'ad,' *Theological Wordbook of the Old Testament* (Chicago: Moody Press, 1980), 1:518; Francis Brown, S. R. Driver, Charles A. Briggs, *A Hebrew and English Lexicon of the Old Testament* (Oxford: Clarendon Press, n.d.), 588.

34. Kidner, 159.

35. Lane, 281.

36. Ross, 5:1084.

37. McKane, 588.

38. Harris, R. Laird, 'neter,' *Theological Wordbook of the Old Testament* (Chicago: Moody Press, 1980), 2:610-611.

39. Murphy, 194.

40. Whybray, 369.

41. Lane, 283.

42. McKane, 589-590.

43. Ibid., 590.

44. VanDam, Cornelis, 'שׁחת,' *New International Dictionary of Old Testament Theology and Exegesis* (Grand Rapids, Michigan: Zondervan Publishing House, 1997), 4:92-93.

45. Kaiser, Walter C., 'môt,' *Theological Wordbook of the Old Testament* (Chicago: Moody Press, 1980), 1:493-494.

46. Whybray, 370.

Proverbs 26

26:1. Like snow in summer and like rain in harvest, So honor is not fitting for a fool.

This chapter bears the marks of careful arrangement by Hezekiah's editors (cf. Prov. 25:1). It breaks neatly into three thematic sections. Verses 1-12 speak of the 'fool,' the term *kᵉsîl* occurring in every verse except verse 2. The second section takes up the topic of the 'sluggard' (vv. 13-16). The chapter closes with an extended section, which, in a variety of ways, makes reference to the man who maliciously uses his tongue to wound and divide. Of the twenty-eight verses of the chapter, thirteen employ simile ('like,' 'as') to make their point.[1] Yahweh is never mentioned in this chapter.[2]

In Palestine, 'snow in summer' and 'rain in harvest' is unheard of. It simply doesn't happen in the normal course of events. Samuel, in rebuking the nation for demanding a king like other nations, said he would call upon God to send rain during the wheat harvest (1 Sam. 12:17). Such an event would be so unusual as to be considered a sign of God's judgment. If such mistimed rain or snow should occur, it would have been more than unusual and inconvenient; it would have been disastrous to the crops and those who depended upon them.

'Like' this is the exaltation of a 'fool.' The term used here describes the stubborn, thick-headed individual who has resolutely set his face against social order and God's revelation. His problem is not mental deficiency, but a negative spiritual resoluteness. He brings disaster upon himself, but also his parents (Prov. 10:1; 17:21, 25; 19:13). He even despises them (Prov. 15:20).[3]

The term 'honor' can describe both the innate, inner worth of a person as well as some external means of recognizing and rewarding that inner substance.[4] But, the 'fool' is devoid of moral and spiritual substance. There is nothing within him that is worthy of 'honor' outwardly. Thus, it is completely incongruous ('is not fitting,' cf. Prov. 17:7; 19:10) to exalt such a one to an honored position. What such a one deserves is 'a rod for the back' (v. 3). Such misplaced honor is not just against the social order. It destroys society. Such a move only invites trouble: 'Like one who binds a stone in a sling, So is he who gives honor to a fool' (Prov. 26:8).

26:2. Like a sparrow in its flitting, like a swallow in its flying, So a curse without cause does not alight.
This is the only verse in the subset (vv. 1-12) which does not specifically mention the 'fool.' Although unnamed, his presence is clearly detected, for only a 'fool' would utter 'a curse without cause.'

Such a baseless invective is treated, metaphorically, as some objective reality which 'Like a sparrow in its flitting, like a swallow in its flying ... does not alight.' This may mean simply that, when someone curses you without reason, you should consider the source and shrug it off.[5] It may also take a more serious view of cursing, one which was generally adhered to by the ancients. It was generally held that a curse possessed some objective reality and was something to be greatly feared.[6] Here, the implicit promise is that God watches over His people and does not allow a baseless curse to 'alight.' He kept Baalam's curse from having power over Israel (Num. 23:8; Deut. 23:5; Neh. 13:2). He kept Saul's curse from affecting Jonathan (1 Sam. 14:28-29), Goliath's curse from affecting David (1 Sam. 17:43), and Shimei's curse from alighting on David (2 Sam. 16:12).

Yet, for purposes known only to Him, God may sovereignly allow Satan access to one of His children 'without cause' (Job 2:3). This will be for the outworking of His plan and, ultimately, to work out to the good of His child (Job 42:10; cf. Rom. 8:28).

The effect of this verse is to counter the superstition rampant then and now. We should consider the source of a baseless curse, examine our own lives for any grounds for such an imprecation and, then, set our eyes upon our Father who keeps His own.

26:3. A whip is for the horse, a bridle for the donkey, And a rod for the back of fools.
The fool refuses to listen to counsel. The only option left is physical discipline or restraint. Just as the 'whip' and 'bridle' were necessary to rein in a dumb beast, so 'a rod' is required to restrain a fool. Do not make much out of the seeming reversal of 'a whip ... for the horse' and 'a bridle for a donkey.' The point is simply that physical force is the only means available to direct his actions.

This proverb should be read in close relationship to Psalm 32:8-9. God promises 'I will instruct you and teach you in the way which you should go; I will counsel you with My eye upon you' (Ps. 32:8). Yet, the fool is beyond counsel. He is resolute in his direction. Therefore, God warns 'Do not be as the horse or as the mule which have no understanding, Whose trappings include bit and bridle to hold them in check, Otherwise they will not come near to you' (Ps. 32:9).

Honor 'is not fitting for a fool' (v. 1b). The only thing that is fitting is a physical deterrent (v. 3b). The power of position ('honor,' v. 1b) is not what a fool needs, but the power of physical discipline (v. 3b).[7] Proverbs elsewhere speaks of physical force being the only means of restraint and constraint for the fool (Prov. 10:13; 14:3; 19:29). For this reason, we should withhold counsel from the fool, but let us discern carefully before ever applying that label to anyone (cf. discussion on vv. 4-5)!

26:4. Do not answer a fool according to his folly, Lest you also be like him.

This verse and the next seem to give contradictory counsel. The first line of each is identical in the Hebrew, except for the negation 'not.' The key to resolving the apparent contradiction is found in understanding the second line of each. It should also be noted that these proverbs were carefully collected and compiled into their present form (Prov. 25:1). Thus, the compilers must have, knowingly and wisely, placed these two proverbs in juxtaposition to make a point.

Here, the command is to resolutely refuse to 'answer a fool according to his folly.' Proverbs offers ample warning about avoiding conversation with the fool (Prov. 17:12; 23:9; 29:9). Hezekiah gave his men this order as they listened to the taunts of Sennacherib's army (Isa. 36:21). Jesus, 'while being reviled ... did not revile in return; while suffering, He uttered no threats' (1 Pet. 2:23). We are to do the same (1 Pet. 3:9). Jeremiah seemed to do the same in the face of the false prophet, Hananiah (Jer. 28:11). David nearly failed in this regard with Nabal, whose name, remember, means 'fool' (1 Sam. 25:21-22).

The reason we are told to take this course is 'Lest you also be like him.' This second line seems to help us understand what is meant by 'according to his folly' in the first line. The point seems to be not to lower oneself to the fool's methods and manner of argumentation. It is easy to be drawn into a tit-for-tat exchange. What begins as a simple attempt to silence the folly can soon become an argument, which leaves you looking as foolish as the 'fool.'

Jesus warned: 'Do not give what is holy to dogs, and do not throw your pearls before swine' (Matt. 7:6).

26:5. Answer a fool as his folly deserves, Lest he be wise in his own eyes.

This verse must be read with the previous one and the comments there. Here, 'Answer' must have some different nuance of meaning than in verse 4. Again, the key to understanding is found in the second line. The command rests upon the concern 'Lest he be wise in his own eyes.' Is this genuine concern for rescuing the fool from his folly? More likely, it is a concern that he view himself as having outwitted you, silencing you by his 'wisdom.' Thus, others, observing his assumed victory, may conclude, by your silence, that he is correct and his folly will spread.

Being wise in one's own eyes is the opposite of the fear of the Lord, the most basic need of man according to Proverbs (Prov. 3:7). Indeed, verse 12 seems to conclude that the one who is 'wise in his own eyes' is all but unredeemable. Not even multiplied attempts by many persons will deliver him from his folly (v. 16). The snare of self-congratulated wisdom is open to all, the fool (Prov. 26:12) and the rich (Prov. 28:11) alike. When the condition sets in, the fool can see nothing else (Prov. 12:15). The New Testament also warns against it (Rom. 12:16).

Thus, the concern here seems to be for those who observe the fool who believes, because of a lack of response from the wise man, that he has overcome him. As he struts about in his arrogance, others will be prone to follow him without discernment. For this reason, in some cases, it is right to 'Answer a fool as his folly deserves.'

Jesus exemplified both the silence that is enjoined by verse 4 (Matt. 26:63; Mark 14:61; 1 Pet. 2:23) and the answer that is commanded here (Matt. 16:1-4; 21:24-27; Luke 13:10-17). He proved the reality of this proverb's effectiveness by His ability to silence His critics (Mark 3:1-4; Luke 14:1-6; 20:21-26). Also, the Apostle Paul was, when in extremity over wandering disciples, willing to 'speak like a fool' (2 Cor. 11:16-17; 12:11).

There is indeed 'A time to be silent, and a time to speak' (Eccles. 3:7). May God enable us to know what time it is in every encounter!

26:6. He cuts off his own feet, and drinks violence Who sends a message by the hand of a fool.

The chronicle of the fool continues. Here the problem is trusting significant business to him. Messengers were a staple of commerce and social transactions in that culture. The incidence of their use is reflected in the frequency with which they appear in Proverbs

(Prov. 10:26; 13:17; 25:13). Here, 'sends a message' is, literally, 'sends words.'[8] Thus, the picture is of an individual who has a timely and important message that must reach another party. He hires a man to take that oral message, who then turns out to be 'a fool.'

The effect of this poor choice of couriers is set forth in two metaphors. The first is 'He cuts off his own feet.' The hiring of a messenger was to provide, in effect, a second set of feet for the master. But, instead of doubling his capacity, he incapacitated himself. He has cut his own legs out from under himself. Evidently, the message never arrives or, at best, arrives in corrupted form.

The second image is so powerful that many have suggested that the text must be corrupt.[9] The word 'violence' is a strong one, describing sinful violence (as opposed to natural calamity) and extreme wickedness.[10] The failure to deliver a message upon which great matters rest, or to deliver a distorted message, can bring great damage to many people. Those who are heavily invested in the venture may be incited thereby to extreme, sinful reactions. Thus, one 'drinks' such reactions – that is, they take them into themselves, to the depths of their persons (cf. Prov. 4:17; Job 34:7). Though some suggest it, there appears no good reason to emend the Hebrew text.

Elsewhere, the 'lazy one' (Prov. 10:26) and a 'wicked messenger' (Prov. 13:17) are types of unfaithful couriers. Proverbs 25:13 presents the reverse image – the refreshing nature of 'a faithful messenger' who carries out his duties faithfully. Choose carefully whom you send to represent you! Give only measured tasks to those of whom you are unsure.

26:7. Like the legs which hang down from the lame, So is a proverb in the mouth of fools.

The second line is identical with that in verse 9. Both seek to make the point of the uselessness and damage of a wisdom saying employed by a fool. Here, the simile is 'the legs which hang down from the lame.' The verb, 'which hang down,' is obscure, as it appears in the Hebrew text. This has led to a variety of suggested emendations. Most commentators and translators appear to agree that the verb is related to one describing drawing water from a well (Prov. 20:5).[11] The picture, then, is the dangling bucket at the end of a rope.[12] This action (or lack of it!) is, then, applied to the feeble legs of the lame man. The unreliability of a lame foot has been used already (Prov. 25:19). Note also that 'legs' and 'feet' (v. 6) link this proverb with the previous one.

A proverb is designed to communicate wisdom. The 'fool' is full of folly and devoid of wisdom. So, for him to rattle off from rote memory the words of a wise saying is worthless to him and to those who hear him. A proverb in the head and on the lips of a fool will no more make him wise than the dead limbs of a lame man can make him walk.

26:8. Like one who binds a stone in a sling, So is he who gives honor to a fool.

The metaphor in this simile is somewhat difficult to understand. The translation is complicated by the fact that the Hebrew word behind 'a sling' appears only here in the Old Testament. Some have suggested a translation something like this: 'Like one who places a precious gem stone among a heap of stones.' This, however, requires understanding 'a stone' as a precious stone of some kind, a meaning it does not normally have.[13] Others have suggested following the Latin, which speaks of placing a stone in a pile of stones set up in memorial to the Roman god Mercury. This, however, would require either an intolerably late date for the book of Proverbs or an impossibly early existence for the Greek/Roman culture.[14] It is best to understand, with the LXX, that the Hebrew does indeed refer to 'a sling,' and that it is the binding of a stone into that sling which is in view.

Why would one tie a stone into the pouch of a sling? The very reason for the sling's existence is that it might hurl the stone, not hold on to it. Such action is nonsensical; it contradicts the very reason for the sling's existence. So, too, is 'he who gives honor to a fool.' Honor is designed for people of wisdom (Prov. 3:16, 35; 4:8; 8:18), grace (Prov. 11:16), humility (Prov. 15:33; 18:12; 29:23), peace making (Prov. 20:3), righteousness, faithfulness (Prov. 21:21), and the fear of the Lord (Prov. 22:4). How incongruous, then, to place honor upon one who possesses none of these qualities! Indeed, 'honor is not fitting for a fool' (v. 1).

26:9. Like a thorn which falls into the hand of a drunkard, So is a proverb in the mouth of fools.

The second line of this proverb is identical to that in verse 7. More difficult to understand is the first line here. Most literally, it reads: 'A thorn goes up into the drunkard's hand.' The word translated 'thorn' can describe a thorn bush, a branch from such a bush or the single torn itself.[15] Similarly, just what is meant by 'falls into the hand' is difficult to pinpoint. The verb means simply 'go up,' with a diversity of nuances possible.[16] Does this mean a thorn goes up into the hand of the drunkard (i.e. pierces it)? Or, does it mean he takes up a thorn bush or branch by grabbing it intentionally?

The ambiguity of the first line yields a number of possible understandings. It could describe an inebriated person stumbling along and, inadvertently, piercing his hand with a thorn. The point, in such a case, might be that he can't control his own actions and protect himself or that, being drunk, he has rendered himself insensitive to pain and, thus, does not even know that he has injured himself. If the first is the intention of the proverb, then the comparison would be that a fool is liable to harm himself by quoting a proverb. If the second is in view, then it likely means that a fool quoting a proverb is insensitive to the pain he inflicts upon himself by quoting, but failing to live out, the wisdom of which he speaks.

The point might also be that the drunkard has picked up a thorn bush or one of its branches and is wielding it as a weapon in his drunken rage. In such a case, the point of the comparison might be either that, just as a drunk with a sharp stick in his hand might harm those around him, so a fool who employs a proverb might harm those around him. Or, it could point to the comic figure of a stumbling drunk waving a thorn stick about, shouting out threats and invectives. In this case, the comparison would be to the obvious folly of a fool quoting a proverb.

Perhaps this latter view is to be favored, for it matches the imagery of a useless weapon already encountered in the previous verse.

26:10. Like an archer who wounds everyone, So is he who hires a fool or who hires those who pass by.

The text of this proverb is obscure and exceedingly difficult to translate. The confusion of translators is apparent immediately: 'The great God that formed all things both rewardeth the fool, and rewardeth transgressors' (KJV), 'The great God who formed everything Gives the fool his hire and the transgressor his wages' (NKJV), 'Like an archer who wounds everybody is he who hires a passing fool or drunkard' (RSV), 'Like an archer who shoots at any passer-by is one who hires a stupid man or a drunkard' (NEB). The LXX is not much help, for it is even more different: 'All the flesh of fools endures much hardship; for their fury is brought to nought' (LXX).

The first line is the most disputed. Two of the words have a wide range of meanings. The Hebrew word translated 'an archer' can also mean either 'great' or 'chief.'[17] The word rendered 'wounds' can also mean 'bring forth.'[18]

Most modern translations (NASB, NIV, RSV, NRSV, NLT) take the first word, not in its more common meaning of 'much' or 'more,' but as a rarer word meaning 'archer' (cf. Job 16:13; Jer. 50:29).[19] This might have in its favor the presence of similar imagery in the general context (v. 18).

Whatever the exact translation, it seems clear that the point of the proverb has to do with imprudent hiring practices. Putting a fool on your payroll is a roll of the dice, not unlike hiring a total stranger who just happens to be passing you by at the time. You never know what you will get. Chances are that they will hurt you and your clients ('Like an archer who wounds everyone') more often than not. Abimelech's hiring of worthless no-goods to help murder his half-brothers did indeed set up a short-lived rule, but, ultimately, it backfired (Judg. 9:4-6, 53-57).

26:11. Like a dog that returns to its vomit Is a fool who repeats his folly.

A more disgusting picture is hard to imagine! We shudder under the very thought of the dog frantically returning again to lap up that which it has regurgitated. So is the 'fool who repeats his folly.' He will never learn. No one can teach him, not even experience. So, we see here the power of sin's gravitational pull. Having once drawn near enough to come within its pull, it is exceedingly difficult and rare for a person to break free.

Behold the addictive nature of sin! The drunkard feels powerless before his drink (Prov. 23:35). So it is with drug addiction, pornography, promiscuity, gambling and a host of other destructive and dominating vices. Family and friends beg and plead with their loved one to leave their sin behind, but to no avail. The first line is quoted in 2 Peter 2:22, to describe the 'folly' of the one who turns away from God in favor of sin. In this regard, consider also Hebrews 6:4-8 and 1 John 2:19.

Pharaoh (Exod. 8:8, 15; 9:27, 34-35), Ahab (1 Kings 21:27-29; 22:8) and Herod (Mark 6:20-27) all contribute varying examples of this proverb's point.[20]

26:12. Do you see a man wise in his own eyes? There is more hope for a fool than for him.

We come now to the end of this subsection on the 'fool' (vv. 1-12). However, the section does not end by focusing upon the fool. He is only brought in as a contrasting figure to the truly hopeless one. The proverb, then, serves to temper and balance the disparaging view of the 'fool' given in the preceding verses and to guard against the arrogant assumption that it does not apply to oneself.

Being wise in one's own eyes is a special concern of this section (vv. 5, 16). The warning was sounded early in Proverbs and set in contrast to the fear of the Lord (Prov. 3:7). It is, then, possible to immerse oneself in the proverbs and yet fail in their most basic instruction: the fear of the Lord. Indeed, that seems to be the height of folly! It is a trap into which both the lazy (Prov. 26:16) and the rich (Prov. 28:11) may equally fall. Both Pharisees (Luke 18:11-12) and Christians (1 Cor. 3:18; 8:2; Rev. 3:17) may stumble over pride.

The second line is repeated verbatim in Proverbs 29:20. It gives the impression that there may be degrees of folly. The worst form of folly, however, is the impression that you stand above it! Only here is there any hint of danger in wisdom.[21] The peril is grave, leaving you nearly beyond rescue, drowning in a sea of the only thing that can save you, yet without eyes to see and ears to hear.

26:13. The sluggard says, 'There is a lion in the road! A lion is in the open square!'

We here begin a new subsection, and this time the 'sluggard' is the subject (vv. 13-16). The collection contains some near repeats – this verse answers to Proverbs 22:13 and verse 15 to Proverbs 19:24. The entire subject of laziness is quite fully developed in Proverbs 6:6-11 and 24:30-34.

Paranoia and excuse-making are always evidence enough to convince the 'sluggard' that this is not a good day to work. Generally speaking, lions prowl at night and sleep during the day, when men are at work (Ps. 104:21-23). This is pure fancy, but the lazy man has convinced himself. The veneer of his excuses may not persuade others, but they are not the target of his logic. He is convinced, so what else matters?

It is the places of commerce, business and exertion that he avoids: 'the road' and 'the open square.' How unlikely is that which turns him back: 'a lion in the road!' or 'A lion ... in the open square!' It is all-consuming self-centeredness which provides the soil for the paranoia to grow so quickly and convincingly. The mind will never lack for reasons not to do something it does not want to do (Eccles. 11:4). Every shadow is a monster. Every possibility is a probability.

The 'sluggard' soon forgets God's enabling and protecting presence: 'For He will give His angels charge concerning you, To guard you in all your ways. They will bear you up in their hands, Lest you strike your foot against a stone. You will tread upon the lion and cobra, The young lion and the serpent you will trample down' (Ps. 91:11-13).

26:14. As the door turns on its hinges, So does the sluggard on his bed.

Humor can, at times, achieve what direct address cannot. The humor of this proverb has a biting edge to it and is meant to provoke 'the sluggard' to meaningful action.

The lazybones is here likened to a door that 'turns on its hinges.' The door moves, but goes nowhere. It is motion without march, movement without mobility. Just so, 'the sluggard' flips and flops from side to side, but never makes any progress toward getting out of bed and making his life useful. His excuse is, 'A little sleep, a little slumber, A little folding of the hands to rest' (Prov. 6:10; 24:33). But, his family and friends wonder, 'How long will you lie down, O sluggard? When will you arise from your sleep?' (Prov. 6:9).

26:15. The sluggard buries his hand in the dish; He is weary of bringing it to his mouth again.

We have here a near repeat of Proverbs 19:24 (which see). The main variation is that, instead of 'And will not even bring it back to his mouth' (Prov. 19:24b), we have 'He is weary of bringing it to his mouth again.' What was 'I won't' (Prov. 19:24) has now become 'I can't.' How quickly that transition is made in the rationalizations of one's mind! The unwilling often convince themselves that they are the unable.

One should note that the King James Version has 'A slothful man hideth his hand in his bosom,' rather than 'in the dish.' The LXX and Syriac have 'bosom' and the Vulgate and Targums have 'armpit,' rather than 'in the dish,' as the Hebrew text has it. There appears no good reason to abandon the Hebrew. Even the New King James Version has made that transition.

The proverb pictures one so lazy that it affects his physical well-being. He'd rather starve than move! If a person is not willing to muster the small amount of energy to feed himself physically, how much less likely is he to undertake the discipline to feed himself on 'the bread of life' (John 6:35-40)?

26:16. The sluggard is wiser in his own eyes Than seven men who can give a discreet answer.

The lazy man's sloth makes perfect sense to him. Generally, we do what we do for reasons that sound convincing to ourselves. The 'sluggard' has marshaled a self-convincing array of reasons for his lifestyle. In that sad world of illusion, he is beyond counsel, for not even 'seven men who can give a discreet answer' are able to dislodge his misplaced thinking. He has added folly to his laziness (v. 5). Being convinced of the soundness of his thinking, he has placed himself beyond counsel and is, therefore, beyond hope (v. 12).

He is, first and foremost, unwilling to do the hard work of good, clear thinking. This, then, blocks him from seeing the wisdom in a disciplined life of wisdom. Insightfully, Greenstone says, 'Much anti-intellectualism may be traced to such rationalization for laziness.'[22]

The portrait of the 'sluggard' now comes full circle (vv. 12-16). Fearful and paranoid of what might happen if he applied himself and left the safe confines of his comfortable, self-controlled world (v. 13), the sluggard cloisters himself in his self-made safe haven (v. 14) and, there, slowly degenerates into an obsessively self-consumed lifestyle that, eventually, destroys him (v. 15). There, he is unreachable, for he has shut out all reason and counsel by the self-convincing arguments of folly dressed in the robes of wisdom (v. 16).

26:17. Like one who takes a dog by the ears Is he who passes by and meddles with strife not belonging to him.
This closing section (vv. 17-28) primarily focuses on how the tongue stirs up trouble in a variety of ways. There are four subsections, each consisting of three verses:[23] troubles arising from senseless actions (vv. 17-19), troubles arising from a slanderous tongue (vv. 20-22), troubles arising from a sinful heart (vv. 23-25), and troubles arising from scheming deception (vv. 26-28). Note the following repetition of words: 'strife' (vv. 17, 21); 'fire' (vv. 20, 21) and 'Firebrands' (v. 18); 'contention' (v. 20) and 'contentious' (v. 21); 'whisperer' (vv. 20, 22); and 'hates' (vv. 24, 28), 'hatred' (v. 26).[24]

Several issues must be settled to understand this particular proverb. Does 'passes by' refer to the person who happens to wander by a dispute? Or, does it refer to the dog who happens to wander by the individual who provokes it (cf. RSV)? The accenting of the Hebrew text would make it refer to the man. But, some have emended the text to make it refer to the dog. The latter feel this is a better option, for a stray dog would be more likely to be provoked. However, the concern appears to be getting involved in matters that are not one's own business, so we should side with the former.

Also, what exactly does 'meddles' mean? The Hebrew text is, more literally, 'makes himself angry' or 'makes himself excited' over some quarrel that is not one's own. The Vulgate and Syriac, however, point to the meaning 'meddles.'[25] It is probably better to stay with the Hebrew text, understanding that such heated passion is aroused over business that is not one's own (thus, the sense of 'meddles' is retained as well).[26]

'Mind your own business!' seems to be the moral of this story (Prov. 3:30). It is senseless to stick your nose in where you are not invited (Prov. 20:3). Refuse to be needlessly drawn into another man's quarrels. Note Jesus' example (Luke 12:13-14). To fail in this regard is likened to grabbing a junkyard dog (dogs were seldom domesticated) by the ears, thus bringing needless trouble upon one's self.

26:18. Like a madman who throws Firebrands, arrows and death,
This begins a four line proverb that encompasses both this verse and the next. The simile is begun with 'Like' here and is answered by 'So' in verse 19.

That which begins the comparison is 'a madman.' The word occurs only here in the Old Testament. In its verb form, it seems to describe being amazed or startled. In its substantive form, it points to one, as here, who has gone mad.[27] But, this maniac has taken up arms (cf. v. 10)!

The 'Firebrands' were flaming arrows (cf. Isa. 50:11),[28] while the 'arrows' were the non-ignited variety of the same weapon. The third word in the trio, which seems mismatched, is 'death.' While the translation is literal and accurate, the word may well be meant to flavor the previous two, rendering a meaning of 'deadly flaming arrows and deadly arrows' (cf. NIV).[29] On the other hand, it may stand as a separate, climactic expression: 'flaming arrows, arrows, yes even death!'[30]

26:19. So is the man who deceives his neighbor, And says, 'Was I not joking?'
The 'Like' of verse 18 is now answered by the 'So' of this verse. The simile comes full circle. The comparison was the lunatic with a weapon. The reality is 'the man who deceives his neighbor.' Nothing more is said about the nature or specifics of the deception. Was it a practical joke? Was it a malicious ruse that is quickly passed off as jesting when exposed to the light? But, deceit in any variety is condemned in the Proverbs (e.g. Prov. 24:28).

Excuses in any form seldom gain a hearing in heaven or on earth (Prov. 24:12a). Thus, whether malicious or not, the excuse 'It was only a joke!' does not pass muster. Only a fool finds pleasure in another's misfortune. 'Folly is joy to him who lacks sense' (Prov. 15:21a). 'Doing wickedness is like sport to a fool' (Prov. 10:23a).

Humor is a good gift of God (Eccles. 3:4), but never when it is enjoyed at the expense of another (Eph. 5:4).

26:20. For lack of wood the fire goes out, And where there is no whisperer, contention quiets down.

This subsection (vv. 20-22) addresses the problem of a slanderous tongue. The problem person is called a 'whisperer,' a character we meet four times in Proverbs. Such a person's gossiping ways are tantalizingly fun to enter into (Prov. 18:8; 26:22), but, when the fun is over, a string of broken relationships is left (Prov. 16:28). In Proverbs, the problem of gossip is dealt with more generally as well (Prov. 11:13; 20:19; 25:9). Ultimately, the gossip is no better than the mocker, in that both wreak the same havoc upon relationships (Prov. 22:10). Such an individual is the fuel that fires 'contention' (Prov. 6:14; 15:18; 16:28; 17:14; 18:19; 21:19; 22:10; 23:29; 25:24; 26:20, 21; 27:15; 28:25; 29:22).

Once the 'whisperer' is removed, the strife 'quiets down.' That is because 'For lack of wood the fire goes out.' But, oh, how difficult it is to collectively shut down such a talker! You may change the arena in which they do their talking, but will likely never quiet them completely. 'And the tongue is a fire, the very world of iniquity; the tongue is set among our members as that which defiles the entire body, and sets on fire the course of our life, and is set on fire by hell' (James 3:6).

26:21. Like charcoal to hot embers and wood to fire, So is a contentious man to kindle strife.

The repetition of the words 'wood' and 'fire' links this verse with the one that precedes it. The point is nearly the same as well. What is stated negatively there ('For lack of wood a fire goes out') is now cast in the positive ('Like charcoal to hot embers and wood to fire'). When one piles fuel on an existing fire (or even a smoldering ember), one produces a greater conflagration.

The effect of 'a contentious man' is much the same. He is fuel to all the smoldering embers of bitterness in the lives of those he comes in contact with (Prov. 15:18; 29:22). He is, ultimately, deemed a fool, for 'a fool's lips bring strife' (Prov. 18:6). 'Keeping away from strife is an honor for a man, But any fool will quarrel' (Prov. 20:3). The remedy is the same as that stated in verse 20: the 'contentious man' must be removed. 'Drive out the scoffer, and contention will go out, Even strife and dishonor will cease' (Prov. 22:10).

Whereas, in verse 20 the problem was a 'whisperer' (i.e. a gossip), here the problem is 'a contentious man.' While they present themselves differently socially, the two are conjoined twins, sharing a corrupt heart. The gossip moves with stealth, while the 'contentious man' is loud and brash. Yet their impulses are not far apart and their results are much the same. Each 'with perversity in his heart devises evil ... [and] spreads strife' (Prov. 6:14).

26:22. The words of a whisperer are like dainty morsels, And they go down into the innermost parts of the body.
This proverb is an exact repetition of Proverbs 18:8. The 'whisperer' of verse 20 is reintroduced, binding this triplet of verses together.

The problem is this individual's words. Indeed, he is one who murmurs and whispers about others behind their backs. He is a gossip, and what he has to say is 'like dainty morsels.' This expression is found only here and in Proverbs 18:8. It is derived from a root that means to devour, swallow or gobble up.[31] Listening to gossip is as easy as downing a delightful dessert. Putting a stop to gossip is as difficult as refusing that tantalizing confection when everyone else is indulging. Such words are 'dainty morsels,' in that they are something rare, special, and something you believe not everyone has the privilege of enjoying. How could you pass them up?

The danger is found in that, once indulged, the gossip goes 'down into the innermost parts of the body.' The expression 'innermost parts of the body' is found again only in Proverbs 18:8; 20:27, 30. Most literally, it means 'inner chambers [rooms] of the belly' (the farthest depths of a man). Gossip does not merely fall upon your ears; it settles deep within you. You cannot help but be influenced by it. You will never look at the person of whom the gossip spoke in the same way again. Gossip irrepressibly shapes our view of people, no matter how hard we try to discount it as probably untrue.

Oddly, a wise man's words also are pleasant (Prov. 16:21, 24), but their consumption yields a much different outcome. They are life and health to the whole body (Prov. 4:22), while the gossip warps a man's mind, distorts his perceptions and destroys his relationships.

26:23. Like an earthen vessel overlaid with silver dross Are burning lips and a wicked heart.
Simile is again employed to make the point, a point that is expanded and expounded further in verses 24-26. The conversation on this

proverb usually revolves around two proposed emendations. The first is to read 'glaze' (NIV, RSV, NRSV), rather than 'silver dross.' The second is to change 'burning' to 'smooth.' As for the former, some feel 'silver dross' makes for an unnatural reading. They, then, propose understanding this as an example of an otherwise unknown Hebrew word that is related to a Ugaritic word meaning 'glaze.'[32] This is creative, but probably unnecessary. The substance skimmed off of molten silver in the refining process (cf. Prov. 25:4) was at times used as a kind of veneer over common pottery, to make it appear like true silver.[33] As for the latter proposed emendation, this too is unnecessary. The proposal is made because 'burning lips' seems to some an obscure metaphor and the proposed word 'smooth' is used elsewhere of deceitful speech (Prov. 6:24) and seems to be the choice of the LXX. Yet, the point of 'burning lips' is not hard to see. They are 'burning,' in that they are warm and full of affectionate praise and affirmations of friendship. Yet, they are insincere, covering 'a wicked heart.'

The point of the proverb is the condemnation of hypocrisy and the threat of being drawn in by excessive praise. Beware of the words of the harlot (Prov. 2:16; 5:3-4). Jesus condemned the Pharisees as 'whitewashed tombs which on the outside appear beautiful, but inside they are full of dead men's bones and all uncleanness' (Matt. 23:27). 'Even so,' He said, 'you too outwardly appear righteous to men, but inwardly you are full of hypocrisy and lawlessness' (Matt. 23:28). He also charged them, saying, 'Now you Pharisees clean the outside of the cup and of the platter; but inside of you, you are full of robbery and wickedness' (Luke 11:39).

Further examples of this problem include the insincere comfort of Jacob's sons, after they had sold Joseph into slavery and concocted a lie about his death (Gen. 37:35), and the kiss of Judas upon the cheek of our Lord (Matt. 26:25, 49-50; Luke 22:47-48).[34]

26:24. He who hates disguises it with his lips, But he lays up deceit in his heart.

Verses 24-26 now enlarge upon the simile of verse 23. The Hebrew words translated 'lips' (vv. 23, 24) 'heart' (vv. 23, 25) and 'hates'/'hatred' (vv. 24, 26) help link these verses. The problem is hatred concealed. This one 'disguises' it. The same word was employed when Joseph disguised his true identity from his brothers (Gen. 42:7) and when Jeroboam's wife used a covering to veil her true identity from the prophet (1 Kings 14:5-6).[35] The cloak this time is not makeup, hairstyle or clothing, but the 'lips.' The words rolling

over his tongue carry no resemblance to the reality of his heart. The
heart reality is that he 'lays up (literally, 'puts') deceit in his heart.'
The 'deceit' reconnects us with verse 19 and many other proverbs
(Prov. 11:1; 12:5, 17, 20; 14:8, 25; 20:23). 'Deceit is in the heart of those
who devise evil' (Prov. 12:20a).

The word translated 'heart' is different from the normal Hebrew
word translated this way (cf. vv. 23, 25), though it is, at times, parallel
to it. It refers to that which is inward, thus often representing the
inward parts of both humans and animals. It can also refer to the
internal workings of a gathering of people, like a community.
Though inward, and thus subject to disguise, God knows what is
within a man (Gen. 18:12-13; Ps. 64:6).[36] *God not only hears what comes
off the lips, but He knows what festers within the heart!*

**26:25. When he speaks graciously, do not believe him, For there
are seven abominations in his heart.**
This continues the thought from verse 24. The idea of 'gracious'
speech is not that it is full of good fruits, but that it is what one wants
to hear. It is smooth (cf. the glaze of v. 23). The warning is 'do not
believe him.' That is to say, do not take him at face value and place
any weight upon his words. There is something terrible beneath the
surface. There 'are seven abominations in his heart.' The number
seven is not to be taken literally (cf. v. 16), but points to any large
number. One should carefully read the 'six things which the LORD
hates, Yes, seven which are an abomination to Him' (Prov. 6:16-19).

Beware the smiling face! We must guard against a suspicious
nature, but we must not be taken in by the flattery of every smooth
talker. David warned of those 'Who speak peace with their neighbors,
While evil is in their hearts' (Ps. 28:3), and Jeremiah took note of
the one who 'speaks peace to his neighbor, But inwardly he sets an
ambush for him' (Jer. 9:8). *May God grant us the discernment to see the
heart and not just hear the words!*

**26:26. Though his hatred covers itself with guile, His wickedness
will be revealed before the assembly.**
This proverb both continues the preceding theme and introduces
the next. In this way, it serves as something of a Janus – looking both
backward and forward. It continues the theme of deceitful speech
(vv. 23-25), but it also introduces the last triplet of verses which
focus on the consequences of one's actions (vv. 26-28).

The pronoun 'his' has no equivalent in the Hebrew text. The
'hatred' echoes the verb 'hates' in verse 24. The verb 'covers' is used

both positively (Prov. 10:12; 11:13; 12:16, 23; 17:9) and negatively (Prov. 10:6, 11, 18; 28:13) to describe the concealment of something. In this case, the animosity lay beneath a covering of 'guile' (a Hebrew form found only here). The root describes leading astray, seduction, misleading and deception.[37]

Though this social veneer is carefully crafted, the truth will, eventually, be known. The 'wickedness' of such a one's heart 'will be revealed before the assembly.' The word translated 'assembly' is a general one, describing a collection of people for any of a broad range of purposes.[38] Some commentators assume this is a judicial body,[39] but there is no good reason to be so specific. The point is likely that, what has been withheld from society (the wickedness of heart) will sooner or later become evident to all.[40] Like the man of lust, the man of guile will cry out 'I was almost in utter ruin In the midst of the assembly and congregation' (Prov. 5:14). Truly, '[N]othing is hidden that shall not become evident, nor anything secret that shall not be known and come to light' (Luke 8:17).

26:27. He who digs a pit will fall into it, And he who rolls a stone, it will come back on him.

The public exposure of verse 26 now becomes the ironic retribution of verse 27. The poetic sections of the Old Testament often speak of this kind of wry justice (Ps. 7:15-16; 9:15; 35:8; 57:6; Prov. 1:18; 28:10; 29:6; Eccles. 10:8-9). The narrative sections even furnish examples in Haman's hanging on the gallows of his own invention (Esther 7:10) and Daniel's enemies' demise by the lions they designated for him (Dan. 6:24-28).

The first line pictures a man who digs a large hole and, then, covers it up in an attempt to waylay someone. In the outworking of his carefully laid plan, however, he forgets where he dug the hole and, rushing along, becomes victim of his own plot. The second line is more difficult to picture. The idea is, likely, that of rolling a stone in an attempt to hit someone with it. But, the fact that gravity only makes a stone roll downward makes it difficult to picture how one could get around on the other side of the stone fast enough to have it fall on them. Perhaps the picture is best understood as a person rolling a stone up a hill from which he plans to send it cascading down upon an unsuspecting enemy. Part way up the hill, however, the stone gets away and comes tumbling back on the mischief-maker.

We all recognize that the whiplash of justice is not always so immediate in its recoil. While perfect justice awaits the return of the perfect Judge, there are still enough examples of this kind of irony to warn us of what will surely come someday. In context, this is a warning against the kind of syrupy insincerity described in verses 23-26, for the deceiver can easily become the deceived.

26:28. A lying tongue hates those it crushes, And a flattering mouth works ruin.

The emphasis on deceit and hatred resurfaces (vv. 23-26). The two lines are not perfectly synonymous, but, generally, reflect the same thought. The first line speaks of a 'lying tongue' (Prov. 10:18), while the second looks at 'a flattering mouth' (cf. vv. 23-26). The manifestation is different, but the essence is the same. The overly flattering one is as dangerous as the bald-faced liar. 'A man who flatters his neighbor Is spreading a net for his steps' (Prov. 29:5).

The results of these seemingly divergent actions are quite similar as well. The first 'crushes' its victims with premeditated hatred and the second 'works ruin.' There is some debate as to whether 'works ruin' is a reference to the result in the object of the hatred or if it is a reciprocating self-judgment that comes back on the hateful, as in verse 27. While the larger context may point to the latter, the parallelism seems to tip the scales in favor of the former.

In the end, we must admit, 'Faithful are the wounds of a friend, But deceitful are the kisses of an enemy' (Prov. 27:6). And, we must pray 'May the LORD cut off all flattering lips' (Ps. 12:3a).

End Notes

1. Buzzell, Sid S., 'Proverbs,' *The Bible Knowledge Commentary* (Wheaton: Victor Books, 1985), 1:961.

2. Whybray, R. N., *Proverbs* (Grand Rapids, Michigan: William B. Eerdmans Publishing Company, 1994), 371.

3. Kidner, Derek, *Proverbs* (Downers Grove, Illinois: Inter Varsity Press, 1964), 40-41.

4. McKane, William, *Proverbs: A New Approach* (Philadelphia: The Westminster Press, 1970), 595.

5. Adams, Jay E., *Proverbs* (Woodruff, South Carolina: Timeless Texts), 197.

6. Ross, Allen P., 'Proverbs,' *The Expositor's Bible Commentary* (Grand Rapids, Michigan: Zondervan Publishing House, 1991), 5:1087.

7. Lane, Eric, *Proverbs* (Scotland: Christian Focus Publications, 2000), 286.

8. Cohen, A., *Proverbs* (London: The Soncino Press, 1946), 174.

9. Whybray, 373.

10. Harris, R. Laird, '*hāmās*,' *Theological Wordbook of the Old Testament* (Chicago: Moody Press, 1980), 1:297.

11. Kidner, 162.

12. Delitzsch, F., *Proverbs, Ecclesiastes, Song of Solomon* (three volumes in one) in C. F. Keil and F. Delitzsch, vol. 6, *Commentary on the Old Testament* (in ten volumes), (1872; rpt. Grand Rapids, Michigan: William B. Eerdmans Publishing Company, 1980), 2:179-180 and McKane, 597-598.

13. Whybray, 374.

14. Delitzsch, 2:181.

15. Murphy, Roland E., *Proverbs* (Nashville: Thomas Nelson Publishers, 1998), 197.

16. Schultz, Carl, "*ālâ*,' *Theological Wordbook of the Old Testament* (Chicago: Moody Press, 1980), 2:666-670.

17. Johnston, Gordon H., 'רַב,' *New International Dictionary of Old Testament Theology and Exegesis* (Grand Rapids, Michigan: Zondervan Publishing House, 1997), 3:1028-1034.

18. Kidner, 163.

19. Whybray, 374-375.

20. Bridges, Charles, *A Commentary on Proverbs* (Edinburgh: The Banner of Truth Trust, 1846, reprint 1998), 490-491.

21. Murphy, 201.

22. Greenstone, Julius H., *Proverbs With Commentary* (Philadelphia: The Jewish Publication Society of America, 1950), 269; quoted in Ross, 5:1091.

23. Murphy, 198, 201.

24. Whybray, 376.

25. Kidner, 163.

26. Cohen, 176.

27. Brown, Francis, S. R. Driver, Charles A. Briggs, *A Hebrew and English Lexicon of the Old Testament* (Oxford: Clarendon Press, n.d.), 529.

28. Younger, K. Lawson, Jr., 'זִיקוֹת,' *New International Dictionary of Old Testament Theology and Exegesis* (Grand Rapids, Michigan: Zondervan Publishing House, 1997), 1:1096-1097.

29. Whybray, 377.

30. Delitzsch, 2:191.

31. O'Connell, Robert H., 'להם,' *New International Dictionary of Old Testament Theology and Exegesis* (Grand Rapids, Michigan: Zondervan Publishing House, 1997), 2:766-767.

32. Ross, 5:1092-1093.

33. Cohen, 177.

34. Bridges, 497.

35. Wilson, Marvin R., '*nākar*,' *Theological Wordbook of the Old Testament* (Chicago: Moody Press, 1980), 2:579-580.

36. Coppes, Leonard J., '*qereb*,' *Theological Wordbook of the Old Testament* (Chicago: Moody Press, 1980), 2:813.

37. Fisher, Milton C., '*nāshā*',' *Theological Wordbook of the Old Testament* (Chicago: Moody Press, 1980), 2:603-604.

38. Carpenter, Eugene, 'קהל,' *New International Dictionary of Old Testament Theology and Exegesis* (Grand Rapids, Michigan: Zondervan Publishing House, 1997), 3:888-892.

39. Cohen, 178.

40. McKane, 604-605.

Proverbs 27

27:1. Do not boast about tomorrow, For you do not know what a day may bring forth.

The Hezekiah collection of Solomon's proverbs continues (Prov. 25:1–29:27). As in the previous chapter, Yahweh's name does not appear here. Some proverbs form pairs (vv. 1-2, 3-4, 5-6, 9-10, 15-16). Verses 23-27 form an extended collection, building upon the metaphor of shepherding.

The chapter opens by warning of the folly of presuming upon one's future. The demand is: 'Do not boast about tomorrow.' By 'tomorrow' is meant plans for any future date. The word 'boast' means 'praise' and is repeated in verse 2, and its near relative is found in verse 21.[1] The picture is of one praising himself for deeds envisioned, but, as yet, undone.

The reason this is folly is that 'you do not know what a day may bring forth.' Jesus warned of the presumptuous folly of kingdom building (Luke 12:19-20) and Isaiah of a party mentality (Isa. 56:12). The future lies solely in God's hands (Prov. 16:1, 9). Wise is the man who lives one day at a time, maximizing each moment for God's glory. This does not preclude careful planning, however (cf. vv. 23-27). Rather, it is an understanding of one's inability to sustain, or advance, his own life and existence. Such an outlook not only saves one from arrogance, but also from worry (Matt. 6:34).

Read James 4:13-16 with this proverb to gain a fuller understanding of the mindset God seeks to instill in us.

27:2. Let another praise you, and not your own mouth; A stranger, and not your own lips.

This proverb makes its point through synonymous parallelism. It is linked with the previous verse through the repetition of the root word found, there, in 'boast' and, here, in 'praise.' That verse warned against boasting about that which is ahead, this one against what one believes to be past and present.

The Hebrew word translated 'another,' more specifically, describes one with whom you are not acquainted or related.[2] It is often translated as 'stranger' in Proverbs (e.g. Prov. 5:10, 17; 6:1; 11:15; 14:10; 20:16) or as 'adulteress' ('strange woman,' a woman foreign to your commitments to God and family; e.g. Prov. 2:16; 5:3, 20; 7:5; 22:14). Similarly, the word 'stranger' is used of a 'foreigner' in general (Prov. 5:10; 20:16) or of an adulterous woman, more specifically (Prov. 2:16; 5:20; 6:24; 7:5; 23:27; 27:13).[3]

Mere 'praise' is not the problem, though it is a test of any man (v. 21). The issue, here, is tooting one's own horn. '... Nor is it glory to search out one's own glory' (Prov. 25:27b). Because of our self-absorption, any self-evaluation is inherently skewed (Prov. 16:2; 21:2). Those who 'measure themselves by themselves, and compare themselves with themselves ... are without understanding. ... For not he who commends himself is approved, but whom the Lord commends' (2 Cor. 10:12, 18). Even Jesus announced, 'I do not seek My glory; there is One who seeks and judges' (John 8:50).

Reputation is something that is formed in the mind of another, not one's own. If it becomes obvious you are bent on building your own reputation, you will have just defeated the very thing you seek. We are better off seeking to simply obey in every way, moment by moment, and allowing God to take care of any recognition that may come our way.

27:3. A stone is heavy and the sand weighty, But the provocation of a fool is heavier than both of them.

The form of this proverb and the next are similar. Using two negative illustrations, the proverb produces an even worse scenario. Here, the negative illustrations are of the weight of carrying around a cumbersome stone, or of lugging about a large sandbag. Either one would exhaust the physical resources of any man, given enough time.

In contrast ('But') to these is an even greater weight to bear: 'the provocation of a fool.' The word translated 'provocation' is used elsewhere to describe a sinful man who provokes, agitates and prods God into a response (1 Kings 15:30; Ezek. 20:28).[4] It is also used of the effect of a foolish son upon his parents (Prov. 17:25) and of the discontented man's search for meaning (Eccles. 1:18; 2:23; 5:17; 11:10).[5]

A fool's nonsense is a constant jab in the side of the wise man, an irritation that, like a grain of sand in the shoe, may seem hardly noticeable at first, but soon wears thin one's reserves of patience and tact. To live with such an individual is to bear a burden greater than any physical load that could be laid upon you.

Rare is the one married to a fool and yet able to hold the tongue and stay the course! Consider Abigail's plight in marriage to Nabal ('fool'): 'now the man's name was Nabal, and his wife's name was Abigail. And the woman was intelligent and beautiful in appearance, but the man was harsh and evil in his dealings, and he was a Calebite' (1 Sam. 25:3).

27:4. Wrath is fierce and anger is a flood, But who can stand before jealousy?

As in the previous verse, here, the point is made by using two negative illustrations, and, then, producing an even worse case. The first line sets up the second by describing the overwhelming nature of 'Wrath' and 'anger.' It is both 'fierce' and 'a flood.' The former word has the connotation of cruelty.[6] Unrestrained anger can become almost unhuman, forgetting the basic decency that comes with being stamped in the image of God. Similarly, the latter word pictures a raging torrent, swollen by melting snows in the mountains or a heavy downpour in the plains. Moving along in a wall of water, it takes with it everything in its path: trees, homes, wildlife, man. As with the flood, anger may appear irresistible and overwhelming.

'But,' worse than this is the power of 'jealousy.' The word can describe both a healthy and righteous zeal and an unrighteous, all-consuming jealousy. Here the latter is in view. It eats one away from the inside ('rottenness to the bones,' Prov. 14:30), as well as consuming one's relationships like a cancer (Prov. 6:32-35). It is what led Cain to murder Abel (1 John 3:12). So prevalent is it that it required a special provision in the Mosaic Law (Num. 5:14). It led to our Lord's death (Matt. 27:18). So powerful is the grip of jealousy that it can only be likened to the strength of death itself (Song of Sol. 8:6).

The jealousy here is not from lack of possessions (wishing you had what someone else has), but from an over-possessiveness (unhealthy dominance of what one does have).[7] It consumes the emotions, blinds the mind to reason, seizes the will and dominates the soul. The power of jealousy is here highlighted by the rare use of a rhetorical question.

27:5. Better is open rebuke Than love that is concealed.

This is another example of a 'Better ... Than' proverb (Prov. 12:9; 15:16-17; 16:8, 16, 19, 32; 17:1; 19:1, 22; 21:9, 19; 22:1; 25:7, 24; 27:10; 28:6).[8] This verse and the next form another of the pairs that open this chapter, being bound both by theme and the related words translated 'love'/'friend.'

That which is 'Better' is 'open rebuke.' Proverbs has had much to say about 'rebuke,' a great deal of it to make us open to it. Indeed, rebuke is the path of life (Prov. 6:23; 15:31), honor (Prov. 13:18), understanding (Prov. 15:32) and wisdom (Prov. 29:15). He who rejects a needed rebuke is stupid (Prov. 12:1), a fool (Prov. 15:5) and despises himself (Prov. 15:32). Little wonder that 'open rebuke' is considered a good thing, even though painful. The word 'open' means uncovered.[9] When it is needed, blessed is the one who has a friend willing to throw the wraps off of the rebuke he so desperately needs!

The contrast is 'love that is concealed.' What good does 'love' do in theory? How can 'love' be known unless it is released from the closet of self-protection and made known? Just why the love is concealed is not stated, but perhaps it is out of fear of hurting the one loved or out of concern that the relationship will suffer damage beyond repair. In either case, there would seem to be more self-love involved than selfless love. We need to learn that 'He who rebukes a man will afterward find more favor Than he who flatters with the tongue' (Prov. 28:23). With David, we need to pray, 'Let the righteous smite me in kindness and reprove me' (Ps. 141:5a). Such love is like unto that of our Master (Rev. 3:19). Thus, Paul rebuked Peter, not as a sign of discord, but of ultimate love (Gal. 2:14). It is the sign of true brotherliness and commitment to another's welfare more than one's own comfort (Matt. 18:15).

27:6. Faithful are the wounds of a friend, But deceitful are the kisses of an enemy.

Like the preceding proverb, this one prefers the pains of true friendship to the professions of false love. When a 'friend' (lit., 'one who loves') confronts, it may feel like 'wounds' (or 'bruises').[10] Love sometimes hurts in order to heal. But, such 'wounds' are 'faithful.' That is to say, they arise from a heart that is true and pure in its commitment to our welfare. Such were the words of Nathan to David (2 Sam. 12:7) and such are God's to us (Job 5:17-18). Such words go to the depths of or our 'innermost parts' (Prov. 20:30) and work change for the better. We should wear such marks of friendship like a prize (Prov. 25:12). Such friendship risks the relationship on the hope that 'He who rebukes a man will afterward find more favor Than he who flatters with the tongue' (Prov. 28:23).

In contrast ('But') are the supposed marks of commitment from 'an enemy' (lit., 'one who hates'). Like Judas to Jesus (Matt. 26:49), the false friend feigns friendship to achieve a personal goal. Such a one prostitutes (Prov. 5:3-4) the friendship. Despite what is on his lips, 'he lays up deceit in his heart' (Prov. 26:23-24).

The greatest challenge of this proverb is the translation of the word standing behind our 'deceitful.' The word is obscure, and many translations have resulted ('multiplies' NIV, 'profuse' RSV and NRSV, 'deceitful' KJV and NKJV, 'perfidious' NEB, 'ominous' JB). Generally, either translators have looked for an emendation to the Hebrew text or link it to an Arabic word, from which they seek to derive a suitable contrast to 'faithful' in the first line. Though suggested translations have been abundant, generally, modern translators have sided either with a meaning something like 'profuse' or 'deceitful.' The former follows the suggestion that the Hebrew form is identical to the more common Hebrew word meaning 'to pray. But, that it is a totally unique word carrying this new meaning. The actual existence of such a word is somewhat doubtful, since this would be the only occurrence we have of it.[11] The latter translation requires an emendation of the Hebrew text to recreate a word that makes a suitable parallel to the 'faithful' found in the first line. This has yielded a variety of guesses.[12] In the end, a translation something like 'profuse' may be preferable, because it does the least violence to the Hebrew text as we have it, though it should be considered tentative at best.

27:7. A sated man loathes honey, But to a famished man any bitter thing is sweet.

This proverb is built around an antithetical parallelism. In both lines, the word 'man' is, more literally, 'soul.' As we have seen in Proverbs, the 'soul' can also describe the cravings, hungers and desires of a person's life (e.g. Prov. 6:30; 10:3; 13:2, 4, 25). In the first line, that 'hunger' has been muted by the sheer abundance enjoyed. So 'sated' is this soul that it 'loathes' what is normally a sweet find (Prov. 25:16). The expression is even stronger than appears here, for 'loathes' is more literally 'tramples.' This is the most extreme expression of derisive spite[13] (cf. Heb. 10:29).

The second line holds forth a soul that has been deprived of any luxury and, indeed, probably many necessities – it is 'famished.' When the taste buds have been so long deprived, 'any bitter thing' tastes 'sweet.'

The proverb probably applies more widely than just to food and physical appetites. Proverbs has used 'honey' as a vehicle to get at issues like 'wisdom' (Prov. 24:13-14), 'glory' (Prov. 25:27), and sexual desire (Prov. 5:3). What is said here of physical appetite may be applied more broadly to possessions, money, experiences, etc. These lines may be taken both as a condemnation of over-indulgence as well as a plea for moderation. Indeed, moderation is ultimately not a denial of pleasure, but a heightening of pleasure!

Verse 20 reminds us that some things are never really 'satisfied' (same root word as 'sated' here). One satisfaction of an illegitimate desire only feeds the monster of lust, leading to more extreme measures to satisfy the desire again. But, with the all-out pursuit to indulge the desire, one embraces the law of diminishing returns. What once thrilled, thrills no longer. More extreme pleasures are needed to gain the same high. Soon, one is destroyed by the pleasures one pursues.

How much better the man who practices moderation, knowing that the temporary restraint of desire means, ultimately, more intense delight and a more targeted pursuit of that which ultimately satisfies.

27:8. Like a bird that wanders from her nest, So is a man who wanders from his home.

The simile upon which this proverb is founded ('Like ... So') works from the picture of a fowl that 'wanders' far from the nest she has called home. The exact nature of the wandering has been highly disputed, however. Some feel that this represents an irresponsible itch to search for excitement.[14] Others feel it points to a forced evacuation because of threat.[15] The fact is that the proverb does not tell us which reason is in view. The former may be supported by the apparently mindless flutter of the sparrow in Proverbs 26:2, the latter by the picture painted in Isaiah 16:2 (cf. Ps. 11:1).

We note that this is a mother bird, for it is 'her' nest that is left.[16] If driven off, was she forced to abandon her young and, thus, her posterity? If through neglect, is she so selfish that no mother-love stirs the strings of her heart?

What is clear is that the second line focuses upon 'a man,' who, in some sense, also 'wanders from his home.' The word 'home' is, more literally, 'place.' We all have somewhere that, in the arrangement of God, is our appointed assignment. Flight from it, for whatever reason, should not be undertaken lightly. Certainly, the urge to excitement and change is an unworthy motive and leads to destructive consequences (Luke 15:11-32). Our God-appointed assignment is to this 'place' and to the people whom God has placed there. Our faithfulness must be worked out in this 'place.' Our mark for God is to be made in this 'place.' *Do not allow either fear or fancy to rob you of the destiny God has marked out for you!*

27:9. Oil and perfume make the heart glad, So a man's counsel is sweet to his friend.
This verse and the next are linked by the theme of friendship (cf. v. 6). The first line is clear enough. The use of 'Oil and perfume' was widespread. In a day when bathing was difficult and the conditions often sweltering, the use of scented lotions and incense was a welcome luxury to those who could afford them. To greet a friend by anointing his head with 'Oil' was a sign of welcome and respect (Ps. 23:5; 141:5). Such action made one's 'heart glad' over the bond of friendship.

The second line, then, builds off of this emblem in the first ('So'). Just exactly the point of this second line, however, has been a matter of considerable debate. The second line, literally, reads, 'and sweet one's friend from the counsel of soul.' Some, concluding that the Hebrew is hopelessly corrupt, have followed the entirely different text of the LXX: 'but the soul is torn by trouble' (RSV), 'but trouble shatters your peace of mind' (TEV), 'but cares torment a man's very soul' (JB). Others have attempted all manner of emendations – ending up with either a comparison with trees ('one's friend is sweeter than fragrant trees,' Driver) or one's self ('is better than one's own counsel').[17]

Despite the interpretational gymnastics, it seems best to simply read it as a comparison with the first line – as simple luxuries like perfume and oil makes life more sweet, so does a friend who gives counsel out of the deep well of his life's experience and wisdom ('the counsel of the soul'). As one might indulge in the simple luxuries of life, so indulge yourself in deeper levels of friendship with those God's has sovereignly placed about you. Don't fail to find this sweetness in life because of a refusal to hear a reproof (v. 6). Rebuke need not be a sour experience, but can actually sweeten the way life unfolds.

27:10. Do not forsake your own friend or your father's friend, And do not go to your brother's house in the day of your calamity; Better is a neighbor who is near than a brother far away.
This unusual three line proverb continues the theme of friendship from verse 9. Many complain of the lack of continuity between the three lines, concluding that these are three fragments thrown together without much thought as to their relationship.

The first line is a plea for the preservation of friendships, particularly longstanding family friendships ('your father's friend'). Solomon's son, if he heard or read this bit of wisdom from his

father, did not heed it, for he rejected his father's faithful advisors
(1 Kings 12:6-8; 2 Chron. 10:6-8).

The second line seems to discourage seeking family support
in difficult times. It appears to stand in direct opposition to
Proverbs 17:17: 'A friend loves at all times, And a brother is born for
adversity.' The prohibition here, however, is not to be considered
absolute. It must be read with the first and third lines.

The third line affirms that, when life is cruel, we are better served
by a near friend ('a neighbor') than a distant relative ('a brother
far away'). It is not that we shun family at such times, but that we
realize the depth of our need and the obstacle of distance and the
time needed to cover it. The brother who 'is born for adversity,' if far
away, could do little (in a day of limited communication and travel)
to help in time of need. But, there is a 'friend who sticks closer than
a brother' (Prov. 18:24b). Rely upon, and accept, the help of such a
brother.

What we have, then, is an encouragement to cultivate friendships
(line one), not to the exclusion of family relationships (line two),
but so that in days of need (line two) you may find the immediate
support you need (line three). A friend who is willing to confront
us when needed (v. 6), share out of the depths of his soul (v. 9),
and reciprocate mutual edification (v. 17) is an asset not to be
taken lightly. The comparison of 'friend', 'brother,' and 'neighbor'
do not depreciate the value of family, but celebrate the worth of
friendship.[18]

**27:11. Be wise, my son, and make my heart glad, That I may reply
to him who reproaches me.**

As so often in chapters 1–9, this proverb employs the direct address
'my son' (Prov. 1:8, 10, 15; 2:1; 3:1; etc.), though it is the only such
usage in chapters 25-29.[19] The now familiar call is to 'Be wise,' and
the first of two reasons given for the action is also familiar: 'make
my heart glad' (Prov. 10:1; 15:20; 23:15-16, 24-25; 29:3). There is no
limit to the joy a wise son or daughter can bring to a parent's heart!
Of course, Proverbs makes profoundly clear the depths of sorrow
and grief that the foolish child can plunge a parent into (Prov. 17:25;
19:13). These kinds of effects are not confined only to familial
relationships, but also spiritual ones (1 Thess. 2:19-20; 3:8; 2 John 4;
3 John 4).

What is new in this verse is the second reason given: 'That I
may reply to him who reproaches me.' The more normal ending
would be to give some reason why such a course is good for the

'son.'[20] Here, however, the benefit espoused is for the parent. The word translated 'reproaches' carries the idea of taunting, mocking, insulting or defying someone.[21] Presumably, the derision is directed at what some might perceive to be irresponsible, inept or ineffective parenting practices and skills. Among all the unselfish things a child is to learn to embrace is the reputation of his parent.

The proverb also reminds us that the greatest apologetic we can ever give to the world is the wise children we send into it.

27:12. A prudent man sees evil and hides himself, The naïve proceed and pay the penalty.

This proverb is a near perfect repetition of Proverbs 22:3. In this, it is not alone, for two other proverbs in this chapter come close to repeating previous ones: verse 13 (cf. Prov. 20:16) and verse 15 (cf. Prov. 19:13).[22]

Here, the 'prudent' stands over against the 'naïve.' The 'naïve' are open-minded to a fault. They believe anything and everything they hear. The wind of popular opinion blows them wherever it will. Assuming the best in another can be a virtue (e.g. love 'believes all things,' 1 Cor. 13:7), but it can also be a fault. Here, the problem is a willful disregard for the danger inherent in a chosen course. The 'naïve' have no sound judgment (Prov. 1:4, 22, 32; 7:7; 8:5; 9:4, 6, 16). The 'prudent' man, on the other hand, is shrewd in the best sense of the word. While the word can be used with sinister connotations (e.g. Gen. 3:1; Job 5:12; 15:5), here, it describes one possessing the caution of wisdom (e.g. Prov. 12:16, 23; 13:16; 14:15, 18). 'The wisdom of the prudent is to understand his way' (Prov. 14:8a).

It is worthy of note that the Hebrew word for the 'prudent' is singular, while the word for the 'naïve' is plural. Does this indicate that, in terms of sheer numbers, one is far more likely to encounter a 'naïve' individual than a 'prudent' person?[23]

The one's prudence is evident in that he 'sees evil' before it arrives. Because he has been trained by wisdom, knowledge and instruction, he can spot problems before they arise and, thus, avoid them. Perhaps the 'naïve' also 'sees [the] evil,' (because they 'proceed;' in spite of what they see?), but it is more in keeping with the meaning of the word to picture them as so caught up in their pleasures that all the red flags and warning lights are left unobserved. But, what is this 'evil' that they see? The word can refer to either moral evil or a calamitous event. Since wisdom and righteousness are never far from one another in Proverbs, perhaps it is best to see this as some moral choice that will yield potentially dangerous ramifications.

The action each takes further differentiates between them. The 'prudent ... hides himself.' 'Thorns and snares are in the way of the perverse; He who guards himself will be far from them' (Prov. 22:5). 'A wise man is cautious and turns away from evil' (Prov. 14:16a). If the 'evil' is seen as moral temptation to wrong, then the thought here is not far from Paul's admonition to the Romans: 'But put on the Lord Jesus Christ, and make no provision for the flesh' (Rom. 13:14). If the emphasis falls on the side of calamity, then the seeking of refuge has to do, more generally, with avoiding foreseen troubles.

The 'naïve' plunge blindly ahead and 'pay the penalty' for it. The Hebrew word normally means to punish by imposing a monetary fine (Prov. 17:26), but it can also refer to punishment more generally (Prov. 19:19; 21:11).[24] A translation something like 'pays the price' is best here.[25] There is a penalty for walking in the folly of sin, which price will be paid eventually (Rom. 6:23). Consider the example of the naïve youth who does not avoid the snares of illegitimate sexual experimentation (Prov. 7:22-23; 9:16-18).

27:13. Take his garment when he becomes surety for a stranger; And for an adulterous woman hold him in pledge.

This proverb serves as a negative example of what a lack of prudence can do (v. 12).[26] The connection with verse 12 is both thematic and linguistic, there appears to be a play on words between 'prudent' ('ārûm, v. 12) and 'becomes surety' ('ārab, v. 13).[27] This proverb is also a virtual repeat of Proverbs 20:16.

Three people are in view in this proverb: the one who makes a loan, the one who takes the loan and a third party who guarantees repayment of the loan if there is a default in payment. The one addressed by the imperative 'Take' is the one who makes the loan. The person referred to by 'his' in the first line and 'him' in the second is the one who guarantees repayment of the loan, if the one taking it defaults.

Proverbs has already warned repeatedly of becoming 'surety' for another (Prov. 6:1-6; 11:15; 17:18; 20:16; 22:26-27). The man giving his promise to repay, should there be a default on the loan, is the one to whom these many warnings are directed. However, if he is foolish enough to make such a promise, the one making the loan should take something in collateral, lest he never get repayment from either the one taking the loan or the one promising to make good on it, if there is a default (cf. Prov. 22:26-27).

The Law made provision for taking a man's coat as collateral. But, there were strict rules as to when it must be returned (Exod. 22:25-27;

Deut. 24:10-13), as this could be abused by the unscrupulous (Amos 2:8).

The one taking out the loan could be either 'a stranger' or 'an adulterous woman.' The first refers to someone whose reliability is unknown. Where the second line has the singular feminine ('an adulterous woman'), Proverbs 20:16 had a textual question between whether it was a masculine plural ('foreigners,' so NASB) or, like here, a feminine singular ('a wayward woman,' so NIV). The term in the masculine referred to those who were of another land or nation other than Israel. They were strangers to the covenant. In the feminine form, it could also refer to a 'foreign woman,' that is, a woman who is a stranger to your covenant of marriage. Here, the feminine singular form points to this latter meaning.

In either case, the point is their unreliability. If anyone is stupid enough to become surety for such characters, you had better protect the investment of your loan by taking some security. This, of course, does not eliminate kindness. It merely emphasizes that virtue must move arm in arm with prudence.

27:14. He who blesses his friend with a loud voice early in the morning, It will be reckoned a curse to him.
Do not believe every smiling face. This proverb seems, at first, to be overly critical of the greeter. Is it not a good thing to bless your friends and neighbors (vv. 9, 10)? The proverb leaves a good deal to interpretation. However, it is the timing ('early in the morning') and manner ('with a loud voice') of the blessing that gives away its insincerity.

Why the rush? Has some recent good fortune come your way and he wants to be the first at your side to share in it? Why so loud? Do his cartoonish, overdone blessings hint at some duplicity? Is this man on a par with the hypocrite of Proverbs 26:23-26? The wise man will carefully consider these questions before being taken in by the overdrawn display of friendship.

The second line lays bare the ultimate end of such insincerity – 'It will be reckoned a curse to him.' To whom exactly does the 'him' refer? Is it the one being greeted? Does he see through the act and discern the true motives behind it? Or, does it mean that, if taken in by the display of friendship, he will eventually discover what a curse this all was? Or, does the 'him' point to the one making the blessing (i.e. this plot will backfire on him as either God or the one being blessed lays bare his intentions)? It probably points to the former, but either option is a possibility.

We are duly instructed to observe socially appropriate ways of address. Timing, manner, and motive all should combine, if our desire is to pass on a true blessing.

27:15. A constant dripping on a day of steady rain And a contentious woman are alike;

This verse and the next form yet another couplet. The 'contentious woman' is not new to the Proverbs (Prov. 21:9, 19; 25:24). Better a life of physical deprivation on the corner of a roof (Prov. 21:9; 25:24) or in a desert land (Prov. 21:19) than life in a spacious house with her! The picture of 'constant dripping' has also been encountered already in Proverbs 19:13. What is new here is that it is on a 'day of steady rain.' The word describes a downpour, not just a light drizzle (not a 'winter day,' as per the LXX).[28]

Outside, the storm is nearly unbearable; inside, the dripping is insufferable. Charles Bridges aptly observes, 'The storm within is however much the most pitiless. Shelter may be found from the other. None from this. The other wets only to the skin; this even to the bones.'[29]

It was the stemming of this kind of storm which must have been in the mind of King Ahasuerus's advisor in Esther 1:18.

27:16. He who would restrain her restrains the wind, And grasps oil with his right hand.

This verse continues the discussion of life with a 'contentious woman' from verse 15. Not only is there the maddening effect of her constant bickering, but there is wider social embarrassment. What will the neighbors think? The henpecked husband tries desperately to still his loquacious wife, but to no avail.

Attempting to keep her bombastic ways a private matter is like trying to hold the wind in check. The first line, more literally, reads: 'Those who would hide her, hide the wind.' The sense of 'hide' is 'treasure' or 'cover up.' The poor husband cannot cover the fact that his marriage is miserable and that his wife dominates him.

The second line is more difficult to translate and has led to various translations. The most literal rendering is simply: 'and oil his right hand calls.' One problem is that 'right hand' is a feminine form with a masculine suffix. Another is the word 'grasps' ('calls'). Many simply see this as another metaphor to describe that which is unrestrainable (i.e. trying to grab a handful of oil). In this sense, it would be on a par with trying to nail jelly to the wall. It simply can't be done. The trouble is that this must assume a meaning for 'calls' that is unnatural for it.

Perhaps a better understanding is that the 'oil' be understood as the perfumed ointments so common among the Jews of the time. The right hand would have been the most natural hand with which to apply this lotion-like substance. When once the hand has been filled with the fragrant oil, it is impossible to hide the fact, for the fragrance betrays the oil's presence. In this sense, then, the wife is like the perfume upon the hand – you can't keep her a secret.[30] The fragrance (stench?) of her turgid ways is effusive.

Wise is the young person who enters the covenant of marriage with caution and discerning wisdom! The marriage covenant is for a lifetime, so make certain the result is something you can live with.

27:17. Iron sharpens iron, So one man sharpens another.

This proverb makes its point by comparative parallelism. The first line sets the image clearly. A blade is fashioned, honed to an edge and polished to a fine finish by the use of other metal – the one working over against the other. The process, though for a different purpose, is described in Isaiah 44:12: 'The man shapes iron into a cutting tool, and does his work over the coals, fashioning it with hammers, and working it with his strong arm.'

In a similar fashion, 'one man sharpens another.' The verb translated 'sharpens' in both lines describes making something sharp or keen. This may refer to the edge of a literal cutting tool (Ezek. 21:14-16) or, metaphorically, to the adeptness of an animal (Hab. 1:8) or the tongue (Ps. 57:4; Isa. 49:2).[31] The literal meaning is clear in line one, but the second line must mean something more metaphorical. The second line is, more woodenly translated, 'a man sharpens his friend's face.' Just why 'face' is employed is not clear, and it makes the second line more awkward (thus, many translations fail to translate it; but, see NKJV). The word translated 'face' has a broad range of meaning, including describing the person as a whole and his personality. No doubt, here, it has a sense something like that.

We are better for our social interactions, even the ones we least appreciate. We are a debtor to every man whose path we have crossed, for no social contact need be a waste if we will but learn from it. How much more valuable, then, those friendships in which our companion has our highest good in mind! 'Two are better than one' (Eccles. 4:9a). 'He who walks with wise men will be wise' (Prov. 13:20a). Indeed, as we have just discovered, 'a man's counsel is sweet to his friend' (v. 9b). Think of Jonathan's benefit to David, for he 'arose and went to David at Horesh, and encouraged him in

God' (1 Sam. 23:16). Little wonder we are exhorted, 'let us consider how to stimulate one another to love and good deeds, not forsaking our own assembling together' (Heb. 10:24-25a).

No man can be his best or reach the heights God intends for him without those blessed friends who comfort, provoke, challenge, rebuke, chide, affirm, stimulate and encourage until his thinking is clear, his wisdom mature, his purpose refined, and his faculties sharp.

27:18. He who tends the fig tree will eat its fruit; And he who cares for his master will be honored.

This proverb is simple, making its point through synonymous parallelism. The figure in the first line is that of a farmer who carefully tends his fig tree. The fig was a fixture in Palestine. It required careful attention and took several years of such doting commitment before it would yield its fruit. Scripture often employs the agricultural picture of a farmer's faithful labor to make a point (1 Cor. 3:8; 9:7; 2 Tim. 2:6). Such faithfulness is rewarded: 'He who tills his land will have plenty of bread' (Prov. 12:11a; cf. 28:19).

The point made in the second line has to do with faithfulness, not to crops, but to those to whom we are accountable. The verb here ('cares for') is different from that in line one ('who tends'), but they function as near synonyms. The notion here in the second line is that of exercising great care over something.[32] The parallel to the 'fruit' of line one is, here, the experience of being 'honored.' If careful attention to our God-given leaders and places of service is rendered, God will take care of our reward.

Joseph found it to be so in Potiphar's house (Gen. 39:4), though his betrayal by Potiphar's wife reveals that God may suspend momentarily this pattern of faithfulness-reward to achieve His higher purposes. In the end, however, the promise holds true, as even Joseph discovered (Gen. 41:39-45). 'Do you see a man skilled in his work? He will stand before kings; He will not stand before obscure men' (Prov. 22:29). Jesus took pains to reveal that the same principle proves true on the heavenly plane (Matt. 25:21, 23; Luke 12:42-44; 19:17; John 12:26).

The need, then, in every situation is to find our God-given assignment and perform it well to the glory of God. If we attend to His honor, He will care for ours. Our first charge is to find the person or people under whom God has placed us and, then, to serve Him by serving them. He will care for notice, honor, recognition, and reward. P. T. Forsyth was correct: 'The first duty of every soul is to find not its freedom but its Master.'

27:19. As in water face reflects face, So the heart of man reflects man.
The Hebrew text is terse and concise, making the exact understanding of this proverb a challenge. The absence of verbs adds to the difficulty. The verse, literally, reads, 'As water the face to face, so the heart of man to man.' Presumably, we should understand some verb, such as 'reflects,' in both lines (as most translations do).

The thought of the first line is simple enough. When one looks into a pool of still, clear water, he sees a near perfect representation of his face looking back at him. Mirrors were not as refined as they are today. So, perhaps the smooth surface of water gave the most accurate reflection possible of one's true appearance.

The second line presents more challenges. How many men are referred to? Does it mean that, when you see another's true character ('heart'), you are seeing a reflection of the same human condition in which you share? Or, does it mean that, when you look within your own heart, you see the real you?

The former tells us that the truth about ourselves is discovered in deeper fellowship with others. It is a warning against being judgmental of others, since what we quickly identify in others is likely a problem for us as well.

The latter demands that the discovery of our true selves is to be found in introspection. It is a warning against denial, since we easily excuse what we find in ourselves.

The former has, to its advantage, that it seems to echo something in verse 17. The latter, however, seems to hold more closely to the parallelism of the first line.

In the end, it is impossible to decide absolutely which is meant. Both represent the facts. Perhaps we must settle with something like 'we need the other to know ourselves; we know the other by (knowing) ourselves.'[33]

27:20. Sheol and Abaddon are never satisfied, Nor are the eyes of man ever satisfied.
The word 'Sheol' describes the realm of the dead, generally. The word 'Abaddon' is used six times in the Old Testament, all in the Wisdom Literature (Job 26:6; 28:22; 31:12; Ps. 88:11; Prov. 15:11; 27:20). It seems to refer to the condition of punishment and ruin, coming from a word meaning 'to perish' or 'to destroy,'[34] or it may refer to the deepest, darkest recesses of the realm of the dead.[35] Interestingly, later in Scripture the word is transliterated and becomes a name for one of the highest-ranking demons in Satan's forces (Rev. 9:11). While in Proverbs 15:11 the two refer to that which is farthest from

God (yet known thoroughly by Him; cf. Job 26:6), here, the point is their insatiable appetite. They 'are never satisfied' (cf. Prov. 30:15-16; Isa. 5:14; Hab. 2:5). 'Sheol and Abaddon' are viewed like a yawning, mythical monster unable to assuage its appetite, regardless of the countless victims it devours.[36]

For all the power of the imagery, death and destruction are not the point of the proverb. Behind this emblem (and strengthened by it) stands the issue: 'Nor are the eyes of man ever satisfied.' The eye is the body's primary point of contact with the world around it. It can, therefore, represent the avarice and greed of the human heart as it wants to take in, consume and dominate the world around (Eccles. 1:8; 4:8).

The 'lust of the eyes' is not from our Father, but from the world system (1 John 2:16). 'And the world is passing away, and also its lusts' (1 John 2:17a). There is no end to the possessions, experiences, curiosities and pleasures the human heart can consume. Like drinking salt water to assuage one's thirst, we find that which satisfies only deepens the thirst it momentarily quenched. Soon, the act of getting transitions from pleasure to pain. In the end, the consumer is consumed by his consuming. The shopper becomes the shopped. The owner becomes owned.

Thankfully, Jesus offers water that permanently satisfies (John 4:13-14) and His grace frees from the grip of covetousness (Phil. 4:11-13).

27:21. The crucible is for silver and the furnace for gold, And a man is tested by the praise accorded him.
The first line of this proverb is identical to that in Proverbs 17:3. The image of metal testing is often used in Scripture (e.g. Ps. 66:10; Isa. 1:25; 48:10; Jer. 6:29; Ezek. 22:17-22; Mal. 3:3). Precious, but impure, metals were fired until they became liquid. The impurities rose to the top as dross and were skimmed away. Such testing both proved the value of the metal and improved it, as the impurities were taken away (Prov. 25:4).

The second line, here, varies significantly from that in Proverbs 17:3. There, it was the Lord who was testing the man's heart; here, it is 'praise.' The second line contains no verb and, literally, reads, 'and a man by the mouth of his praise.' But, what exactly is intended by 'his praise'? Does it refer to how he responds to the praise that comes to him from others? Does it mean that a man's real worth is proven by the reputation he comes to have over time? Or, does it mean that a man's inner self is revealed by what he praises? All are possible and commentators are divided over the options.

Most modern translations have followed the first option (NIV, NASB, NLT, NRSV, NEB). This is probably to be preferred. Proverbs 12:8a puts the words in the mouth of others: 'A man will be praised according to his insight.' The word for 'praise' we find here is related to the one found in verses 1-2. There, we are warned about speaking too confidently about what we think we know (v. 1), and letting words of praise come from others, not from our own mouths (v. 2). Jesus warned, 'Woe to you when all men speak well of you, for in the same way their fathers used to treat the false prophets' (Luke 6:26). The words of others, often, prove the reality of one's discipleship (John 12:42-43).

When praised, do we swell? Do we gush with feigned humility? Both lay bare a destructive pride. Humble is the man who can receive such praise and still maintain an accurate estimation of himself, while passing on the credit to God. 'I say to every man among you not to think more highly of himself than he ought to think; but to think so as to have sound judgment, as God has allotted to each a measure of faith' (Rom. 12:3).

Not only is our heart revealed by our response to others' praise of us, but perhaps even more so by people's praise of others instead of us. Saul's great failure came in his inability to handle the public recognition of David (1 Sam. 18:7-8, 15-16, 30; 19:1). How exceedingly difficult it is when others receive the praise we desire or believe we deserve! It is humility indeed that can rejoice at the recognition of another.

27:22. Though you pound a fool in a mortar with a pestle along with crushed grain, Yet his folly will not depart from him.
Like the preceding proverb, this one discusses separating the unwanted from the valuable. The imagery, however, is different. Instead of a smelter's pot (v. 21), we have before us, here, the 'mortar' and 'pestle' of the flour-maker. The 'mortar' was the bowl in which rough grain was placed and the 'pestle' was the stone hammer with which it was then pulverized to remove the worthless husk from the valuable grain. The word translated 'mortar' is the noun form of the verb translated 'pound.' It was a 'pounding-bowl.'[37] The imagery is of violent, crushing blows that separate the inferior from the invaluable.

The powerful imagery is transferred to the problem of a 'fool' and his 'folly.' No amount of physical discipline can remove the 'folly' from a 'fool.' It is such an innate part of who he is that it cannot be separated from his substance. Folly is not material, but spiritual. For this reason, it cannot be separated physically from a person.

True, Proverbs does occasionally call for physical discipline for the fool (Prov. 10:13; 14:3; 19:29; 20:30). But, we are also told that this is more for the benefit of those looking on than for the fool himself (Prov. 19:25; 21:11). Indeed, 'A rebuke goes deeper into one who has understanding Than a hundred blows into a fool' (Prov. 17:10).

In the end, we discover that folly must be 'graced' out of a fool, not beaten out of him. This is Divine work, and only God can accomplish it.

27:23. Know well the condition of your flocks, And pay attention to your herds;

The closing five verses are unified into a poetic description of pastoral life (vv. 23-27). Just what is the point? Is this to be taken strictly as a recounting of the life of a farmer? Or, is there a more metaphorical meaning? The imagery of the shepherd in the Old Testament is almost always used in metaphorical terms. God is seen as the Shepherd of Israel (Gen. 49:24; Ps. 80:1; Isa. 40:11; Jer. 31:10; Ezek. 34:12) and of individual believers (Gen. 48:15; Ps. 23:1). The human leader of Israel is set forth as a shepherd, whether that be the judges (1 Chron. 17:6), Joshua (Num. 27:17) or David (2 Sam. 5:2; 1 Chron. 11:2; Ps. 78:71). Even Cyrus the Persian would be used of God as a sort of shepherd for His people (Isa. 44:28). The Old Testament describes the coming Messiah as a Shepherd (Ezek. 34:23; 37:24). Of course, in the New Testament Jesus is set forth as the Good Shepherd (John 10:3, 11). Then, the elders of a local church are called to the task of shepherding the people under their charge (1 Pet. 5:2).

Of course, the word 'shepherd' does not occur in verses 23-27. Yet, its image is everywhere understood behind these descriptions. With this figurative predominance in the use of the imagery of the shepherd and his flock, it seems likely that this is both a description that makes perfect sense when applied to the farmer and a metaphorical message for broader application.

The command of verse 23 is given justification in verse 24. Verse 24 introduces a hint of the royal courts with the mention of 'a crown,' which may direct us to a wider application. After Solomon's death, the kingdom was split because of his son Rehoboam's insensitivity to the needs of the people (1 Kings 12:1-17). He did not 'Know well the condition of [his] flocks, And pay attention to [his] herds.' As a result, he lost the kingdom, except the tribe of Judah (1 Kings 12:16-17). Could it be that the later collectors of these Solomonic proverbs (Prov. 25:1) had this in mind as a broader application of these truths?

Any who might serve in a shepherding role should pay careful attention to these admonitions and assurances.

The opening exhortation ('Know') is quite emphatic in form.[38] The expression 'the condition' is, more literally, 'the face,' which meant the appearance, which, of course, pointed to the actual condition of the flock. Thus, the translation is appropriate. The second line parallels the first and reaffirms its point.

No one is so secure that he need not bother himself with his responsibilities. No one is so important that he need not consider those to whom, and over whom, he is responsible.

27:24. For riches are not forever, Nor does a crown endure to all generations.

Verse 23 provided the exhortation, this verse the motivation. The reason to carefully watch over all who are put under your leadership is that those things to which you might be tempted to divert your attention and care are, at times, fleeting and elusive. One may be tempted to trust in either wealth ('riches') or position ('a crown') and, thus, become lax in his responsibilities. Yet, wealth is 'not forever.' Indeed, 'When you set your eyes on it, it is gone. For wealth certainly makes itself wings, Like an eagle that flies toward the heavens' (Prov. 23:5).

Also, there is no guarantee that even royal position and power ('a crown') will 'endure to all generations' (lit., 'to generation, generation'). The term translated 'a crown' describes the princely dignity of the royal family.[39] But, Proverbs has cast the royal family's security in less than absolute terms (Prov. 14:28), and other Scriptures confirm this to be the case in actual experience (Job. 19:9; Ps. 89:39; Jer. 13:18; Lam. 5:16; Ezek. 21:26). As noted in verse 23, Rehoboam found this to be true.

The call here is to fix one's hope rightly (not in possession or position) and to focus oneself rightly (on that which or those whom God intends). 'Instruct those who are rich in this present world not to be conceited or to fix their hope on the uncertainty of riches, but on God, who richly supplies us with all things to enjoy. Instruct them to do good, to be rich in good works, to be generous and ready to share, storing up for themselves the treasure of a good foundation for the future, so that they may take hold of that which is life indeed' (1 Tim. 6:17-19).

27:25. When the grass disappears, the new growth is seen, And the herbs of the mountains are gathered in,
Those who live responsibly with their God-given assignments (vv. 23-24) will discover the rhythms of nature and the interventions of providence harmonizing in the fulfillment of their needs.

What happens to 'the grass' of the first line? Is it that it 'disappears' ('is gone,' RSV) or that it is 'removed' (NIV, KJV)? Is this from man's hand (i.e. it is mowed or harvested)? Or, is this from a seasonal change or climactic calamity ('disappears' or 'is gone')? The Hebrew word in the present form means 'to depart' or 'to go into exile.'[40] It would appear, then, that the idea is not that it is harvested ('removed'), but that, through natural grazing patterns, seasonal change or, perhaps even adverse weather conditions, it 'disappears.' Understood in this way, it sets this up a natural illustration of the financial or social calamity of verse 4. The idea here, then, is that, even if that upon which you depend for the sustenance of your flocks ('the grass') vanishes, God, through the patterns of nature He has established, will provide – 'the new growth is seen, And the herbs of the mountains are gathered in.' This is all from God's hand, for 'He causes the grass to grow for the cattle, And vegetation for the labor of man, So that he may bring forth food from the earth' (Ps. 104:14).

When we responsibly care for our charge, we find ourselves cooperating with the God-ordained rhythms of nature and the interventions of His providence. How much better to be responsibly moving in concert with God (v. 25) than to be blindly trusting in our own power, position or possessions (v. 24)!

27:26. The lambs will be for your clothing, And the goats will bring the price of a field,
The final two verses of this closing poem (vv. 23-27) confirm that living responsibly pays. Whereas the security of wealth (v. 24a) or social position (v. 24b) can quickly disappear, a life spent faithfully caring for one's responsibilities will yield up the provision for one's needs. 'The lambs' will provide wool 'for your clothing' (Prov. 31:13, 19, 21-25). And 'the goats' can be sold for a price to purchase more land (Prov. 31:16), which may, in turn, allow for larger herds to be grazed.

27:27. And there will be goats' milk enough for your food, For the food of your household, And sustenance for your maidens.
In addition to clothing and additional lands (v. 26), responsible living provides daily food for one's household. This verse is unusual, in

that it contains three lines. The LXX omits the middle line and it is conjectured that it is an addition, due to the fact that the other two lines do not mention male members of the household.[41] This is speculative, however, and there appears to be no good reason to abandon the Hebrew text as we have it.

The first line speaks of 'goats' milk' as a staple of one's diet (Deut. 32:13-14; Isa. 7:21-22). Oddly 'food,' both in the first and second lines, is, more literally, 'bread.' To our modern ears, the notion of 'milk' as 'bread' sounds like nonsense. The Hebrews, however, used the most staple part of the diet ('bread') to represent the whole and it can be translated more generically 'food,' when the context dictates.[42] The third line makes mention of one's 'maidens.' They were likely female servants who perhaps, among other chores, took care of the milking (Prov. 31:15).[43] The 'sustenance' is, more literally, 'life.'

End Notes

1. Buzzell, Sid S., 'Proverbs,' *The Bible Knowledge Commentary* (Wheaton: Victor Books, 1985), 1:963.

2. Wood, Leon J., '*zûr*,' *Theological Wordbook of the Old Testament* (Chicago: Moody Press, 1980), 1:238.

3. Wilson, Marvin R., '*nākar*,' *Theological Wordbook of the Old Testament* (Chicago: Moody Press, 1980), 2:579-580.

4. Van Groningen, Gerard, '*kā'as*,' *Theological Wordbook of the Old Testament* (Chicago: Moody Press, 1980), 1:451.

5. Creach, Jerome F. D., 'כעס,' *New International Dictionary of Old Testament Theology and Exegesis* (Grand Rapids, Michigan: Zondervan Publishing House, 1997), 2:684-686.

6. Brown, Francis, S. R. Driver, Charles A. Briggs, *A Hebrew and English Lexicon of the Old Testament* (Oxford: Clarendon Press, n.d.), 470.

7. Kidner, Derek, *Proverbs* (Downers Grove, Illinois: InterVarsity Press, 1964), 165.

8. Buzzell, 1:931.

9. Waltke, Bruce K., '*gld*,' *Theological Wordbook of the Old Testament* (Chicago: Moody Press, 1980), 1:160-161.

10. Hamilton, Victor P., '*pāsa'*,' *Theological Wordbook of the Old Testament* (Chicago: Moody Press, 1980), 2:730.

11. Whybray, R. N., *Proverbs* (Grand Rapids, Michigan: Zondervan Publishing House, 1994), 380-381.

12. Ibid.

13. Delitzsch, F., *Proverbs, Ecclesiastes, Song of Solomon* (three volumes in one) in C. F. Keil and F. Delitzsch, vol. 6, *Commentary on the Old Testament* (in ten volumes), (1872; rpt. Grand Rapids, Michigan: William B. Eerdmans Publishing Company, 1980), 2:202.

14. Bridges, Charles, *A Commentary on Proverbs* (Edinburgh: The Banner of Truth Trust, 1846, reprint 1998), 507-509.

15. Lane, Eric, *Proverbs* (Scotland: Christian Focus Publications, 2000), 296.

16. Kidner, 165.

17. Ibid., 166.

18. Buzzell, 1:964.

19. Ibid.

20. McKane, William, *Proverbs: A New Approach* (Philadelphia: The Westminster Press, 1970), 616.

21. Hartley, John E., 'חרף,' *New International Dictionary of Old Testament Theology and Exegesis* (Grand Rapids, Michigan: Zondervan Publishing Company, 1997), 2:280-282.

22. Murphy, Roland E., *Proverbs* (Nashville: Thomas Nelson Publishers, 1998), 206.

23. Delitzsch, 2:84.

24. Allen, Ronald B., *''anash,' Theological Wordbook of the Old Testament* (Chicago: Moody Press, 1980), 2:685-686.

25. Cohen, A., *Proverbs* (London: The Soncino Press, 1946), 145.

26. Bridges, 514.

27. Whybray, 383.

28. Patterson, R. D., 'sgr,' *Theological Wordbook of the Old Testament* (Chicago: Moody Press, 1980), 2:618, Whybray, 383 and McKane, 616.

29. Bridges, 515.

30. Cohen, 182.

31. Southwell, P. J. M., 'חדד,' *New International Dictionary of Old Testament Theology and Exegesis* (Grand Rapids, Michigan: Zondervan Publishing House, 1997), 2:24.

32. Hartley, John E., 'shāmar,' *Theological Wordbook of the Old Testament* (Chicago: Moody Press, 1980), 2:939-940.

33. Schökel, Alonso, quoted in Murphy, 209.

34. Harris, R. Laird, *''ābad,' Theological Wordbook of the Old Testament* (Chicago: Moody Press, 1980), 1:3.

35. Delitzsch, 2:322.

36. McKane, 617; and Whybray, 385.

37. Kidner, 168.

38. Whybray, 387.

39. Delitzsch, 2:219.

40. Waltke, Bruce W., 'gālâ,' *Theological Wordbook of the Old Testament* (Chicago: Moody Press, 1980), 1:160-161.

41. Whybray, 388.

42. Brown, Francis, S. R. Driver, Charles A. Briggs, *A Hebrew and English Lexicon of the Old Testament* (Oxford: Clarendon Press, n.d.), 537.

43. Delitzsch, 2:220-221.

Proverbs 28

28:1. The wicked flee when no one is pursuing, But the righteous are bold as a lion.

We continue in Hezekiah's collection of Solomon's proverbs (Prov. 25:1–29:27). The closing portion of chapter 27 (vv. 23-28) seemed to signal the close of a subsection (25:1–27:28). Indeed, there are cues in chapters 28 and 29 that they constitute another subsection. Antithetical parallelism predominates here (Prov. 28:1, 2, 4, 5, 7, 10-14, 16, 18-20, 25-28; 29:2-4, 6, 8, 10, 11, 15, 16, 18, 23, 25, 26), whereas, in chapters 25-27, only six proverbs employ such contrasts (25:2; 26:24; 27:3, 4, 6, 7). The contrast of the wicked (Prov. 28:1, 4, 12, 15, 28; 29:2, 7, 12, 16, 27) and the righteous (28:1, 12, 28; 29:2, 6-7, 16, 27) is frequent here. Indeed, it forms an inclusio that wraps the section in this theme (Prov. 28:1; 29:27). The poor are also frequently mentioned (28:3, 6, 8, 11, 19, 22, 27; 29:7, 13-14). Four times, the Law is referred to here (Prov. 28:4, 7, 9; 29:18).[1]

This antithetical proverb demonstrates the power of conscience. The first line pictures a man with a defiled conscience ('The wicked'). His imagination runs wild with paranoia. His sin hounds him (Num. 32:23) and he ever wonders when, and how, it will catch up with him. Like the Arameans in Elisha's day, he flees when there is no tangible threat (2 Kings 7:5-7). Indeed, this very experience was promised by God to be reality for the disobedient (Lev. 26:17, 36). 'A man who is laden with the guilt of human blood Will be a fugitive until death; let no one support him' (v. 17). Every sound in the night becomes his undoing. Every look is interpreted as having sinister motives. Every potentiality becomes a probability.

The second line, in contrast, pictures a man with a clean conscience ('the righteous'). His mind is freed up to focus upon the future, rather than worrying about how the past is going to catch up with him. This man faces opportunities and obstacles with confidence ('bold'). Like young David before Goliath, he knows only that God's honor is at stake and he trusts Him wholly (1 Sam. 17:46; cf. Ps. 18:33-38; 138:3).

Thank God for the privilege of 'having our hearts sprinkled clean from an evil conscience' through Christ (Heb. 10:22)! In so doing, He frees us 'from dead works to serve the living God' without fear

(Heb. 9:14), so that we may, most assuredly, say 'I serve with a clear conscience' (2 Tim. 1:3). What liberty! What confidence!

28:2. By the transgression of a land many are its princes, But by a man of understanding and knowledge, so it endures.

The compounded sinfulness of a nation's people make it tend toward fracture and instability (Prov. 14:34). Never was this illustrated more than in the nation of Israel. During the days of the judges, 'every man did what was right in his own eyes' (Judg. 17:6b) and the result was lawlessness and a succession of deliverers who rescued the nation just long enough to allow it to return to its selfishness. Solomon's words proved accurate in the experience of the nation after his death. The ten northern tribes rebelled and the result was two centuries in which it had nine dynasties with twenty different kings (e.g. 1 Kings 16:8-28; 2 Kings 15:8-15).[2] The Prophets identified this as a part of God's judgment (Isa. 3:1-7; Hosea 7:16; 8:4; 13:11).

In contrast ('But'), a nation is blessed when it has an 'understanding' leader who possesses 'knowledge.' Such a man is blessed by God and the people (Prov. 11:11). He brings stability and a lasting tenure to the throne. Here, note the lasting nature of David's dynasty in Judah. 'He who hates unjust gain will prolong his days' (Prov. 28:16b).

The principle which is here exemplified by a nation and its ruler(s) applies more broadly to include churches and their pastors, organizations and their leaders, and homes and their parents.[3]

28:3. A poor man who oppresses the lowly Is like a driving rain which leaves no food.

Because a 'poor man' acting as an oppressor upon other poor men ('the lowly') seems unlikely to some, they push for an emendation here. The NIV, as do many commentators, changes 'A poor man' into 'A ruler.' But, there is no textual support for such an emendation. The picture, as the Hebrew text has it, is not so unheard of, and, in fact, matches the entire proverb better.

Verse 2 has already led us to anticipate a succession of rulers who are not likely or desirable candidates for office. Here, then, is an example: a poor man who has risen suddenly to a position of power. The oppressed and underprivileged of the nation rejoice, thinking: 'Finally, someone who understands us!' They are overly optimistic, however. When the power surge hits, the once oppressed becomes the worst oppressor. Did not Jesus even use such an illustration (Matt. 18:28)? Proverbs also pictures such a scene elsewhere (Prov. 30:21-22).

This plain understanding of the Hebrew text prepares us perfectly for the simile of line two. When a dirt farmer sees a rain cloud, he rejoices in hope. But, sometimes, that rain cloud turns into a downpour that wipes him out. So, the surprise ruler that is greeted with high expectations disappoints all the more sorely because of the high hopes his coronation engendered. The King of Assyria is thus pictured (Isa. 28:2). Solomon himself uses the picture of a gentle, nourishing rain as the ideal for an upright ruler (Ps. 72:6-7).

Let us remember that it is character that counts in leadership, not simply background and pedigree.

28:4. Those who forsake the law praise the wicked, But those who keep the law strive with them.

This antithetical proverb shows that one's response to the revelation of God's will determines the moral lines for the rest of life (cf. v. 5). Commentators are divided over whether the 'law' should be understood as the Mosaic Law or, more generally, as the teaching of the wise, as found throughout Proverbs (e.g. Prov. 1:8; 3:1). The context here seems to point to the Mosaic Law, in view of the fact that the Law is again mentioned in verses 7 and 9, and God's own name is introduced in verse 5. In the end, the point is not affected, for either is an expression of God's authoritative standard.

Once we 'forsake' God's authority over us, we make morality a sliding scale, determined by personal preference. Once relativism is embraced, we are free to also embrace whatever the moment makes expedient. Without the external standard of God's truth, the moment will rarely provide enough to make a stand against evil convenient.

Note that doing violence to God's word often brings peace with man, while keeping peace with the God of truth frequently brings conflict with men. The way of earthly peace brings the wrath of God, while the way of heavenly peace brings the wrath of man.

The righteous will never be completely at rest in this life (Ps. 119:53), while those who exchange slaps on the back will soon enough find their party has been marching toward destruction (Rom. 1:32). Those who resist the urge to make instant peace (Prov. 18:5; 24:25) will find some strife inevitable in this present life (Eph. 5:11), but are laying up a good reward for the next. 'Where there is no vision [i.e. divine revelation], the people are unrestrained, But happy is he who keeps the law' (Prov. 29:18). This was true of Elijah with Ahab (1 Kings 18:18), Nehemiah with the officials of his day (Neh. 13:11, 15), and John the Baptist with the Pharisees and Sadducees (Matt. 3:7) and Herod the tetrarch (Matt. 14:4).

28:5. Evil men do not understand justice, But those who seek the LORD understand all things.
This verse and the preceding one must be read together, for they develop similar ideas along slightly different lines of thought. Again, the form is antithetical, contrasting 'Evil men' and 'those who seek the LORD,' as well as their outcome: 'do not understand' and 'understand all things.'

The placement of 'Evil men' is emphatic. It describes those who are committed to corruption.[4] Because of their prior commitment to a way of thinking and living, they 'do not understand justice.' It should be carefully noted that 'justice' is something which lies outside of a man. It is objective, rather than subjective and situational. It is something a man conforms his life to, rather than something moldable to the human circumstance. To 'understand' this is impossible for one thus committed. The word 'understand' might also be translated 'discern.' It points to the ability to look at two things and see what God sees. It is the ability to see through the fog of situational details and personal agendas and see what God knows to be primary and foundational.[5] '... [T]hey did not honor Him as God, or give thanks; but they became futile in their speculations, and their foolish heart was darkened.... And just as they did not see fit to acknowledge God any longer, God gave them over to a depraved mind ...' (Rom. 1:21, 28; cf. Isa. 6:9; 44:18).

The second line, in contrast, describes 'those who seek the LORD.' This was an expression often on the lips of Solomon's father (Ps. 14:2; 22:26; 27:4; 34:10; 40:16). It describes one who passionately thirsts for God and the understanding of His thoughts and will. Such a person 'understands all things.' This is a quite literal translation. But, is this intended to broaden the scope of understanding beyond 'justice' to 'all things,' or is it a way of saying that such a one will understand justice thoroughly (NIV)? In context, it probably points, most specifically, to the latter, yet not losing the broader connotation altogether. 'Then you will discern righteousness and justice And equity and *every good course*' (Prov. 2:9, emphasis added). 'I have more insight than all my teachers, For Thy testimonies are my meditation. I understand more than the aged, Because I have observed Thy precepts' (Ps. 119:99-100). 'But he who is spiritual appraises all things' (1 Cor. 2:15a; cf. 1 John 2:20, 27).

Note that there is a moral condition that must be met if one is to apprehend justice. Jesus also insisted on this: 'If any man is willing to do His will, he shall know of the teaching, whether it is of God, or whether I speak from Myself' (John 7:17). What does all this tell us about our legal system?

28:6. Better is the poor who walks in his integrity, Than he who is crooked though he be rich.

This is the last example of a 'Better … Than' saying (e.g. Prov. 12:9; 15:16, 17; 16:8).[6] The first line is identical to that in Proverbs 19:1. The second line differs only in that the individual finds himself 'rich' rather than 'a fool,' and that the problem is his 'ways' (NIV), rather than his 'speech.'

As in Proverbs 19:1, the first line assumes that the man has had an opportunity to change his station in life, but, because of 'integrity,' he has chosen not to do so. The word translated 'integrity' (Prov. 2:7; 10:9, 29; 13:6; 20:7) describes a complete consecration of one's self to God, which results in a person who follows God with his whole heart and who, without fail, seeks God's will in all areas of his life.[7] It does not describe moral perfection, but the full-orbed and wholehearted submission of one's life to God. Because he has chosen to maintain his integrity in some given situation, it has meant continued or resultant poverty. The word for 'poverty' describes being destitute or hungry, but not poverty that has come about through laziness.[8]

Such a man, and even his condition, is 'Better … Than' what is presented in the second line. Apparently, some opportunity had presented itself to him and, if only he had been willing to be 'crooked,' he could have avoided poverty or risen above it. The word for 'crooked' describes that which has been twisted from its original or intended design (Prov. 2:15; 8:8; 10:9; 11:20; 17:20; 19:1; 22:5; 28:18). The original has not been obliterated, only 'tweaked,' 'twisted' or 'improved.' But, that slight twisting has destroyed its fundamental 'integrity' or 'wholeness.' Thus, is has become 'perverse' (NIV).

What has become 'crooked' is not made manifestly clear in the NASB's translation, but the NIV makes it more obvious when it calls it 'his ways.' The word is the one used so often in Proverbs to describe our path in life as a 'way' in which we walk. Especially in Proverbs 1–9, the theme of a good way and an evil way is developed (e.g. Prov. 2:8, 12-13, 20). Here, the word is in the plural form, indicating that this man's crookedness has led him to have multiple 'ways' in which he works with people. He is a double-dealer. He is shifty, tricky and deceitful. He is double-minded, making his moral decisions based on the expediency of the moment. He does it because of the promise of getting 'rich.'

A little white lie, an alternative version of the truth, or a half-truth may be easy to justify, but they distort the truth and destroy integrity. They become ever so tempting, however, because of the promise of what can be gained or avoided by their use.

The theme of the 'poor' (vv. 3, 8, 11, 19, 22, 27) and the 'rich' (vv. 8, 11, 20, 22, 25) continues throughout this chapter.

28:7. He who keeps the law is a discerning son, But he who is a companion of gluttons humiliates his father.

The form is antithetical parallelism. The point is the effect of children's behavior and choices upon their parents. The first line presents the 'discerning' child. The word is found often in Proverbs, generally, and in this chapter, specifically (vv. 2, 5, 11). It can describe both the knowledge of something and the faculty that allows you to come to that knowledge.[9]

To keep something is to guard, watch over or preserve it from danger. The word came to mean something like 'obey,' with the nuance of carefully watching over the truth by preserving it in one's life. We met the 'law' in verse 4 and will again in verses 9 and 18. The debate about whether this is the Mosaic Law or simply the instruction of the father is moot, for, in Proverbs, the instruction of the father is always in the Law of God. It should be understood as the teaching of God as it comes through the father. When the next generation embraces the truth and faith that has anchored the previous generation, there is much to rejoice over. 'The father of the righteous will greatly rejoice, And he who begets a wise son will be glad in him. Let your father and your mother be glad, And let her rejoice who gave birth to you' (Prov. 23:24-25).

The contrast is found in the second line. Rather than the son who carefully keeps the truth instilled by his father, we meet one 'who is a companion of gluttons.' The word for 'companion' is, more literally, 'feed,' 'shepherd' or 'pastor,' but can also mean 'to associate with' or 'be a friend.'[10] So, instead of guarding, watching over and protecting the law through his obedience, this son gives harbor to, and enables, the lifestyle of those who are 'gluttons.' The word describes one who despises or regards something lightly. Presumably, that which these folk despise and treat with contempt is the 'Law' that the father has tried to instill in the son. They are given to gluttony and drunkenness (Deut. 21:20; Prov. 23:20-21). Such a lifestyle is self-destructive, and leads to poverty (Prov. 23:21).[11]

When a son thus flaunts his disregard for the truth of God and the faith of his father, it 'humiliates his father.' The idea is that of public disgrace.[12] A father's plea is 'Be wise, my son, and make my heart glad, That I may reply to him who reproaches me' (Prov. 27:11). Sadly, however, 'a foolish son is a grief to his mother' (Prov. 10:1b).

The goal of the Book of Proverbs is to bring the son into the experience of this discernment (Prov. 1:1-4) through his father's instruction (v. 8). The opening plea was to guard against the wrong kind of companions (vv. 10-19).[13]

28:8. He who increases his wealth by interest and usury, Gathers it for him who is gracious to the poor.

The Mosaic Law forbade taking interest from fellow Israelites (e.g. Exod. 22:25; Lev. 25:36; Deut. 23:19-20) and the Prophets similarly condemned the practice (e.g. Ezek. 18:8; 22:12). But, it appears to have been practiced at various times and in various forms (Ps. 15:5; Neh. 5:7, 11). It appears there was no such ban on taking interest from foreigners (Deut. 23:20a). The first line, apparently, then, views the unscrupulous business dealings of brother-Jews.

The condemnation is of both 'interest and usury.' The former is condemned in Exodus 22:25 and Deuteronomy 23:20-21, while both are banned in Leviticus 25:36-37.[14] Some say the rabbis understood 'interest' to be the repayment of more than was loaned (e.g. borrow $100 and repay $120) and 'usury' to be the advantage gained by buying low and then holding back the needed goods from those who depended upon them, until the market could bear selling them at an excessively high increase (e.g. purchasing apples at .50 apiece and selling them for $1 to the starving).[15] Others say that 'interest' meant that an amount was deducted from the loan amount and held back as the 'interest' (e.g. the loan amount is $100, but the borrower only gets $90, while being required to repay the entire $100) and that 'usury' described the levying of an additional charge upon repayment of the principle of the loan (e.g. loan amount was $100, repayment was $100, but was also met by a surcharge of $20).[16]

Whatever the exact financial arrangements, the problem is that of motive. The loaner is using the needy for his own advancement. Such a one will find that, in the end, he 'Gathers it for him who is gracious to the poor' (cf. Job 27:17). The wheels of providence may appear to turn slowly, but they will come around to justice in each and every case. Perhaps, if the desired justice is not meted out in this life, it will mean that the son to whom he leaves his wealth will have a more benevolent heart toward the poor and give his father's wealth away (Prov. 13:22).[17] Only God knows His means, but He has made clear the end of such selfishness.

How different the legacy of the generous! 'He has given freely to the poor; His righteousness endures forever; His horn will be exalted in honor' (Ps. 112:9). The one who is 'gracious to the poor' may show it through giving some of his food to the needy (Prov. 22:9), defending their rights (Prov. 31:9) or lending to them without interest. In such a case, he is actually lending to the Lord (Prov. 19:17). As he does so he honors God (Prov. 14:31; 17:5) and has the divine assurance that he will not lack (Prov. 28:27).

28:9. He who turns away his ear from listening to the law, Even his prayer is an abomination.
The first line presents the character to be considered, the second the divine evaluation of his action. The one in view wishes to pray, but, at the same time, 'turns away his ear from listening to the law.' As noted at verse 4, the 'law' normally refers to the wisdom instruction of a father or teacher, but here, given its intimate connection with God it probably has reference to God's Law given through Moses (cf. v. 7 also). This individual 'turns away his ear' from what God has said. The expression implies a willful decision to refuse God's voice.[18] The Hebrew word translated 'listening' means not simply to hear, but to hear and obey.

In the case of such a person, 'Even his prayer is an abomination' to God. If you won't listen to God, He won't listen to you. God is speaking to us through His written revelation (at that time, the Mosaic Law). When we refuse to listen to Him in His word, our prayers are worse than of no effect. They are an absolute 'abomination.' This powerful word has been reserved for the worst of offenses (cf. Prov. 3:32; 6:16-19; 8:7; 11:1, 20; 12:22; 15:8, 9, 26; 16:5, 12; 17:15; 20:23; 21:27). It describes an unendurable emotional revulsion to something. This is what God experiences toward some praying people! They fool themselves, but they do not fool God. Others may think them spiritual, but not Him who weighs all hearts. No amount of sacrifice will win God's favor when our hearts are not with Him (Prov. 15:8; 21:27). It is not just broken relationships (1 Pet. 3:7) or unrepentant sin (Ps. 66:18; 109:7; Isa. 1:15; 59:1-2) that keeps God from hearing and answering our prayers, but a stout heart of pride that refuses to hear what God says. 'The Lord is far from the wicked, But He hears the prayer of the righteous' (Prov. 15:29).

This proverb links Bible study and prayer as indivisible spiritual disciplines.[19] Prayer is not simply speaking, but also listening. We must pray with our Bibles open! We must seek not only to speak, but to listen; Not just to be heard, but to hear; not simply to inform, but to learn (James 1:19, 23).

28:10. He who leads the upright astray in an evil way Will himself fall into his own pit, But the blameless will inherit good.
This is one of the rare three-line proverbs. Whereas the previous proverb set forward one who 'turns away his ear' from God's truth, here, he has gone the next step and seeks to turn 'the upright astray in an evil way.' Wanting company in his rebellion, he proselytizes for wickedness. Jesus reserved some of His strongest words of condemnation for such folk (Matt. 5:19; 18:6; 23:15).[20]

In the end (and God controls the timetable), he 'Will himself fall into his own pit.' He has set a trap for 'the upright' and, in the end, he will stumble headlong into it himself. This is a picture repeated often in the Wisdom Writings (Ps. 7:15; 57:6; Prov. 26:27; Eccles. 10:8). The same truth is also presented in an agricultural metaphor (Job 4:8; Gal. 6:7). Compare this warning with the outcome of the ruthless gang members of Proverbs 1:11, 18.

While the unscrupulous fall into the consequences of their own schemes, 'the blameless will inherit good.' The 'blameless' are not morally perfect, but those whose lives are given over to God in wholehearted devotion (cf. Prov. 2:21).[21] No time sequence is given, only the ultimate outcome. Perseverance in God's path will bring His 'good' reward (Prov. 3:35; Matt. 6:33; Heb. 6:12; 10:36; 1 Pet. 3:9). Ultimately, if not always quickly, the wicked come into their own trap, while the righteous are lifted up into the bounty of the Lord. 'He who walks blamelessly will be delivered, But he who is crooked will fall all at once' (v. 18).

28:11. The rich man is wise in his own eyes, But the poor who has understanding sees through him.
We return again to the 'rich man' and 'the poor,' which is a prominent feature of this chapter (vv. 3, 6, 8, 11, 19, 20, 22, 25, 27).[22] Here, it is assumed that the 'rich man' is 'crooked' (v. 6), unscrupulous (v. 8), and selfish (v. 27) in his rush (vv. 20, 22) to make his fortune. Such a man may become 'wise in his own eyes' because of his apparent success. In so doing, however, he has rejected the fear of the Lord (Prov. 3:7) and moved into the domain of the fool (Prov. 26:5, 12) and sluggard (Prov. 26:16). He believes himself secure in his riches (Prov. 10:15; 18:11), which should be one of the first clues that wisdom is eluding him.

By contrast ('But'), in this case, 'the poor' possess 'understanding.' The same Hebrew word is found in verses 2, 5 and 7. Such discernment belongs to 'those who seek the Lord' (v. 5), so apparently, that is what this poor man has done. It is this sort of man who is, ultimately, secure (v. 2), not the man who trusts in his riches. From the security of the fear of the Lord and the stability He brings, the poor man 'sees through' the deceitfulness of the wealthy man's riches. The word always denotes an energetic and arduous investigation.[23] With applied wisdom, 'the poor' is able to see the truth about what the 'rich man' says, does, is, and has.

It is certainly not always the case that wisdom comes with poverty and deception with riches. But, often, it is true. The socially superior are not always truly superior. Success, all too often, blinds its victims.

28:12. When the righteous triumph, there is great glory, But when the wicked rise, men hide themselves.
The rulers of a nation, in large measure, determine the quality of life its people enjoy. The first line pictures 'the righteous' in 'triumph.' The word translated 'triumph' means, more literally, 'rejoices.' This, in the opinion of some, does not provide a suitable parallel to 'rise' in the second line. For this reason, they postulate an emendation that will yield a meaning like 'triumph.'[24] The emendation is unnecessary, however. Why would 'the righteous' rejoice? Because they have come to have a place of influence upon the larger society and are able to spread such righteousness as a blanket over their people. In such a case, 'there is great glory.' The idea is that of boasting or glorying in one's lot. It is used of a son's boasting over his father (Prov. 17:6) and of boasting of the ability to overlook an offense (Prov. 19:11).[25] Such righteous revelry is magnified when a nation's ruler seeks after what is right. 'When it goes well with the righteous, the city rejoices, and when the wicked perish, there is glad shouting' (Prov. 11:10). 'When the righteous increase, the people rejoice' (Prov. 29:2a).

However ('But') 'when the wicked rise, men hide themselves.' This second line is nearly identical to the first line of verse 28, except for the main verb. Just what is meant by 'hide themselves'? It is, more literally, 'will be sought,' which, of course, would mean that they are not to be easily found (i.e. they hide themselves). Some, however, take this as 'will be searched' (for their possessions). They understand the point to be that the righteous are being plundered (cf. Obad. 6).[26] Yet, the translation 'hide' is confirmed by the clear meaning of the verb used in verse 28a.[27]

As an example of such hiding, consider how Obadiah hid 100 prophets during the tenure of Ahab (1 Kings 18:13), and how Joash was hidden in the temple for six years, while Athaliah ruled (2 Kings 11:2-3). As an illustration of line one, observe the response of the people when Athaliah was put to death and Joash crowned (2 Kings 11:20). '... [W]hen a wicked man rules, people groan' (Prov. 29:2b). Note verses 15 and 16, as you study verses 12 and 28 of this chapter.

28:13. He who conceals his transgressions will not prosper, But he who confesses and forsakes them will find compassion.

Here Proverbs comes closer to the gospel than in perhaps any other place. Through Jesus' fulfillment of the law and the sacrifice of Himself as the Lamb of God, this proverb is more obviously powerful today than even in ages past.

The first line describes one who 'conceals' his sins. Proverbs counsels us to cover over the sins of others (Prov. 10:12; 17:9), but never our own. 'Love covers a multitude of sins' (1 Pet. 4:8), but only as you extend that to another, not as you seek to hide your own. The pressure of social embarrassment coupled with contemptuous pride often controls us. Job boasted, asking, 'Have I covered my transgressions like Adam, By hiding my iniquity in my bosom, Because I feared the multitude, and the contempt of families terrified me, And kept silent and did not go out of doors?' (Job 31:33-34). The effect is disastrous: 'He ... will not prosper.' The root of the word means to achieve adequately what is planned.[28] In this case, it refers first to the total inability to succeed at keeping one's sin hidden (Num. 32:23).[29] Then, it also means, secondarily, that no success envisioned possible by the concealment of the sins will be attainable.

Indeed, far from prospering, such a man suffers unsearchable spiritual, psychological, emotional, and physical torture. 'When I kept silent about my sin, my body wasted away Through my groaning all day long. For day and night Thy hand was heavy upon me; My vitality was drained away as with the fever heat of summer' (Ps. 32:3-4).

How we thank God for the contrast ('But') of line two! We are able to find God's 'compassion.' The word describes a deep love that normally extends from one raised above the object of the love.[30] The verbal form here intensifies the meaning even further. Oh, how God loves us and longs to have mercy upon us!

We move into God's favor and blessing through two acts. We must confess our sin. The word is used of confessing not only our sins, but also God's attributes and accomplishments (Ps. 89:5; Ps. 105; 106; 145). In this latter sense, it becomes a key term for praise.[31] Here, however, the admission is to 'transgressions.' Of the numerous Hebrew words for sin, this one stresses the rebellious nature of revolt against God's will (e.g. Isa. 43:27). To experience God's mercy, we must name ourselves as rebels against a holy God. Broad, sweeping, general confessions will not do (i.e. 'I'm as big a sinner as the next guy' or 'I'm sorry'). We must be specific and we must be ruthless with ourselves, our sin, and our tender egos.

Having suffered for his sinful silence, David finally broke down. He later wrote, 'I acknowledged my sin to Thee, And my iniquity I did not hide; I said, "I will confess my transgressions to the LORD"; And Thou didst forgive the guilt of my sin' (Ps. 32:5; cf. 2 Sam. 12:13). The Apostle John also wrote, 'If we say that we have no sin, we are deceiving ourselves, and the truth is not in us. If we confess our sins, He is faithful and righteous to forgive us our sins and to cleanse us from all unrighteousness' (1 John 1:8-9).

But, not even this, alone, is enough. We must also forsake our sin. In its more literal sense, the word describes leaving, abandoning or losing something.[32] Here, then, it demands not only admitting the sinfulness of our rebellion, but a willful determination, by the grace of God, to walk away from, and have no further involvement with, our particular sin. This essential component of true biblical repentance is often missing in today's presentation of the gospel. The Mosaic Law required this of the Jews (Lev. 5:5; 26:40-42). Daniel required it of Nebuchadnezzar (Dan. 4:27). John the Baptist would later demand that those coming to him for a baptism of repentance 'bring forth fruit in keeping with repentance' (Matt. 3:8). The church later continued to preach this same requirement. As Paul summarized his message for King Agrippa, he told all people 'that they should repent and turn to God, performing deeds appropriate to repentance' (Acts 26:20).

When we both confess and forsake our sins, God promises we will experience His 'compassion.' 'How blessed is he whose transgression is forgiven, Whose sin is covered! How blessed is the man to whom the LORD does not impute iniquity, And in whose spirit there is no deceit! ... Many are the sorrows of the wicked; But he who trusts in the LORD, lovingkindness shall surround him. Be glad in the LORD and rejoice you righteous ones, And shout for joy all you who are upright in heart' (Ps. 32:1-2, 10-11; cf. also Ps. 51).

28:14. How blessed is the man who fears always, But he who hardens his heart will fall into calamity.
This proverb follows logically on the heels of the previous one. Verse 13 initiates the process, but verse 14 is the life that issues from

that event. There must be the event of confessing and forsaking sin. But, if that is genuine, there will come a lifestyle that is characterized by new direction.

The first line views 'the man who fears always.' There is no object of his fear stated. Some translations have added 'the Lord' (NIV, RSV, NRSV). But, the word translated 'fears' is not used of the fear of the Lord (cf. Prov. 1:7, 9:10; 23:17). That word speaks of holy reverence and awe, whereas our word here is a strong one that described a quaking dread (Prov. 1:26, 27, 33; 3:24, 25). It is in an intensive verbal form and the accompanying 'always' stresses the continuous nature of the fear. The only other occasion of this verb in this form is found in Isaiah 51:13, and there it also has our same word for 'always.'[33] The implied object should be considered sin, or its consequences. Of course, in view of what has taken place in verse 13, the necessary and appropriate fear of the Lord stands everywhere behind this fear of sin and its consequences.

'A wise man is cautious and turns away from evil, But a fool is arrogant and careless' (Prov. 14:16). The result of living such a lifestyle is to be 'blessed' (cf. Ps. 1:1).

The adversative form of this proverb then sets forth the contrast ('But') of the first line – both in attitude and outcome. Instead of one who 'fears always,' we have here 'he who hardens his heart.' Presumably, the hardening is toward God, His word, the truth about the man's sin, and anyone who might represent any of the above. The example of Pharaoh immediately comes to mind (Exod. 7:13, 22; 8:15, 19, 32; 9:7, 12, 34, 35; 10:1, 20, 27). Also, we should not forget that a similar hardness of heart set in on the people of Israel not long afterward (Exod. 17:7; Ps. 95:8). We are reminded that incomplete repentance renders a person no better off than the entirely unrepentant person (cf. Rom. 2:5).

The result is that such a person 'will fall into calamity.' The word translated 'calamity' is, more literally, 'evil.' It has here, however, the sense of sudden downfall. Such a man 'falls into' it as into a trap. 'A man who hardens his neck after much reproof Will suddenly be broken beyond remedy' (Prov. 29:1).

28:15. Like a roaring lion and a rushing bear Is a wicked ruler over a poor people.
This verse and the next take up the matter of tyrannical rulers. The simile ('Like ... Is') is provided by the translators to smooth over the abruptness of the Hebrew (literally, 'A roaring lion and a bear charging; a wicked ruler over a weak people'), which may be actually more of a metaphor.[34]

The evil ruler behaves like a ravenous beast, which stops at nothing to satisfy its impulses. 'The king's wrath is like the roaring of a lion' (Prov. 19:12). 'The terror of a king is like the growling of a lion; He who provokes him to anger forfeits his own life' (Prov. 20:2). Satan himself is thus represented (1 Pet. 5:8). The word translated 'roaring' appears to point to the sound emitted by a beast driven by hunger (Isa. 5:29-30).[35]

Such a potentate is compared also to 'a rushing bear.' Elsewhere, a fool in his folly is likened unto a bear (Prov. 17:12). Solomon's father was thus characterized by an enemy, because of his expertise at making war (2 Sam. 17:8). God compares Himself to both the lion and the bear in His judgment (Hosea 13:7-8). The Hebrew participle translated 'rushing' describes the rapacious maneuvers of a bear 'lingering about, running hither and thither, impelled by extreme hunger.'[36]

In Daniel's vision of the future, he saw the kingdoms of man represented as brute beasts, the first two of which were like a lion (Dan. 7:4, Babylon) and a bear (Dan. 7:5, Medo-Persia).

What is 'Like' this is 'a wicked ruler over a poor people.' The word 'poor' has been met already in verses 3, 8, and 11. It refers not to the destitute, but those who find themselves among the lower classes of society. The primary emphasis is on material want, but it can also describe lack of social clout (Amos 2:7) and, more rarely, spiritual poverty (Jer. 5:4).[37] Is it any wonder that, when evil people find political power, such folks 'hide themselves' (Prov. 28:12b)? When the king 'roars,' the people 'groan' (Prov. 29:2b)!

28:16. A leader who is a great oppressor lacks understanding, But he who hates unjust gain will prolong his days.
The Hebrew of this verse is difficult to translate and has led to a long list of suggested emendations. The first line has, literally, 'A ruler lacking understanding and adds oppressions.' Perhaps this should be understood as an exclamation[38]: 'A ruler lacking understanding and adding oppressions!' In this case, it would be tantamount to saying, 'Look! Look at the folly of such a ruler!' However it is translated, the first line does not provide a neat parallelism for the second line. When read together, the implication in the first line is that such a 'leader' is not wise, because those he rules will not long put up with his selfish ('unjust gain') oppressions. They will, eventually, rise up against him and remove him from power. In contrast is the one 'who hates unjust gain' (cf. Prov. 1:19; 10:2) and, thus, does not use the people and their resources to his selfish ends. Such a leader 'will

prolong his days' (lit., 'extends days'). Throughout Proverbs, long life is seen as a reward of the wise (e.g. Prov. 3:2, 16, 18, 22; 4:10, 13, 22, 23; 15:27).

Taken with the preceding verse, we observe that God sees tyrannical rulers as animal-like (v. 15), ruthless, foolish and greedy (v. 16).

28:17. A man who is laden with the guilt of human blood Will be a fugitive until death; let no one support him.

Behold, the iron grip of a guilty conscience!

The first portion reads, literally, 'A man oppressed by the blood of a soul.' The word translated 'laden' normally carries the idea of the ruthless oppression of the unfortunate and socially helpless.[39] Here, it is uniquely used to picture the man as residing under the oppressive weight of a guilty conscience. Such oppression makes the individual 'a fugitive until death.' The Hebrew reads, literally, 'to a pit shall flee.' As in Proverbs 1:12, 'pit' is a metaphorical reference to Sheol, the grave or, more pointedly, death itself.

One remembers Cain, who for the shedding of his innocent brother's blood, was cursed to 'be a vagrant and a wanderer on the earth.' He mourned, realizing that 'whoever finds me will kill me' (Gen. 4:11-14).

The command 'let no one support him' should be carefully weighed with the injunction of Proverbs 24:11-12 to help deliver the innocent. As Kidner reminds us, the one 'forbids indifference to suffering,' while the other 'forbids interference with justice.'[40]

Such a stance toward a murderer is founded upon the pre-Mosaic ordinance that whoever destroyed the image of God in another human through murder should have his life taken (Gen. 9:6). The Mosaic Law later upheld this law (Exod. 21:14; Num. 35:19-31). But, in this proverb, the point is not that society will catch up to him, but that God has already begun his punishments through the insufferable weight of his guilty conscience. Such a burden is not escapable by physical exertion or by spatial distance, but must continue pressing pressed down upon the mind and heart and will be lugged about wherever the fugitive wanders.

28:18. He who walks blamelessly will be delivered, But he who is crooked will fall all at once.

Here again, as in v. 6 (cf. Prov. 19:1), we find contrasted 'He who walks blamelessly' with 'he who is crooked.' The former describes not moral perfection, but the integrity of a whole and complete consecration of one's self to God. Such a consecration results in a person who follows God with his whole heart, and who consistently seeks God's will in all areas of his life.[41] The latter describes that which has been twisted from its original or intended design (e.g. Prov. 2:15; 8:8; 11:20; 17:20; 22:5; 28:6). The original has not been obliterated, only 'tweaked,' 'twisted' or 'improved.' But, that slight twisting has destroyed its fundamental 'integrity' or 'wholeness.' Thus, it has become 'perverse' (NIV).

Literally, it is 'the crooked in his ways' (cf. NIV). The 'ways' are dual, as was the case in verse 6. In Proverbs 1–9, the theme of a good way and an evil way was developed (e.g. Prov. 2:8, 12-13, 20). Here, the plural form indicates that this man's crookedness has led him to have multiple 'ways' in which he works with people. He is a double-dealer. He is shifty, tricky, and deceitful. He is double-minded, making his moral decisions based on upon the expediency of the moment.

The individual who walks in integrity 'will be delivered.' The welfare and divine protection of the upright is often testified to in Proverbs (e.g. Prov. 1:33; 3:23; 18:10; 28:26). In contrast, the 'crooked will fall all at once.' The last phrase is difficult, being, more literally, 'will fall in one.' Some see no hope of making sense of it, and emend to read 'will fall into a pit' (RSV). Others see 'in one' referring to one of the two ways. The point, then, would be that, if you try to lead a double life, one or the other will eventually catch up with you. More likely is that 'in one' means something like 'suddenly' (NIV) or 'all at once' (NASB).[42] His judgment will come like a whirlwind (Prov. 10:25), in which he is found out and exposed (Prov. 10:9) and, thus, his days will be cut short (Prov. 10:27). Such a man destroys himself (Prov. 11:3, 5-6), as his devices become a trap set for himself (Prov. 28:10). He 'Will suddenly be broken beyond remedy' (Prov. 29:1b). Wicked Haman provides the best Biblical example of such a man and his end (Esther 7).

28:19. He who tills his land will have plenty of food, But he who follows empty pursuits will have poverty in plenty.
This antithetical proverb contrasts the fruitfulness of hard work with the foolishness of get-rich-quick schemes (cf. v. 20). The first line promises that the one who works diligently, applying consistent effort to his fields, will find he always has enough. The second line speaks of the one who seeks an easier way. The noun 'vain things' has the idea of 'delusions' or 'fantasies.'[43] These appear to be schemes bent on quick, easy money. It is not that such a man does not work

hard, for the participle 'who follows' is in a verbal form, pointing to an intensified action (i.e. 'who pursues diligently'). It is simply that he believes his yield will be higher, if he pursues his racket.

These proverbs resolutely deny any such notion. Proverbs 12:18 is nearly identical: 'He who tills his land will have plenty of bread, But he who pursues vain things lacks sense.' Yet, here, we have 'will have poverty' instead of 'lacks sense.' The parallelism is more powerful here. The contrast of 'plenty of food' and 'poverty in plenty' is stark.

This begins a series of proverbs that develop the themes of poverty and wealth (vv. 19-22). We should carefully read Proverbs 27:18, 23-27 with this verse also. 'In all labor there is profit, But mere talk leads only to poverty' (Prov. 14:23; cf. 6:6-11; 20:4; 24:30-34). The proverb should not be read to elevate either farming, in particular, or manual labor, in general, above other less strenuous forms of employment today. Rather, it is pointing to one's motivation: attempting to get something for nearly nothing. 'Do not love sleep, lest you become poor; Open your eyes and you will be satisfied with food' (Prov. 20:13). 'In all labor there is profit, But mere talk leads only to poverty' (Prov. 14:23).

28:20. A faithful man will abound with blessings, But he who makes haste to be rich will not go unpunished.
Here, again (cf. v. 19), God contrasts the fruitfulness of hard work with the folly of trying to get rich quick. The first line pictures the 'faithful man.' The Hebrew word translated 'faithful' has the notion of steadiness, reliability, honesty, and duty.[44] The word is often used to describe the faithfulness of God (e.g. Deut. 32:4; Ps. 33:4; 143:1). It is used of God in that great passage recounting His faithfulness (Lam. 3:21-23). Thus, God calls us to display the faithfulness that He Himself possesses.[45] Here such a man is contrasted with 'he who makes haste.' Perhaps, then, the particular nuance in mind is that of faithfulness through perseverance.[46]

When a man is found to be 'faithful,' he 'will abound with blessings.' These 'blessings,' contrasted with the lust after material gain in the second line, no doubt should be viewed as also material in some sense. Yet, ultimately, it is God's smile that is intended (Prov. 10:22). With it come a host of spiritual, physical, and social rewards (Prov. 3:13-18; 10:6).

The second line is concerned with the fellow 'who makes haste to be rich.' Such schemes consistently end in want, not wealth (Prov. 12:11; 13:11; 23:4-5; 28:19). The point is that he 'makes haste' after a lifestyle without willingness to endure the process of gaining it legally, ethically, and uprightly (Prov. 20:21; 28:22). 'But those who want to get rich fall into temptation and a snare and many foolish and harmful desires which plunge men into ruin and destruction. For the love of money is the root of all sorts of evil, and some by longing for it have wandered away from the faith, and pierced themselves with many a pang' (1 Tim. 6:9-10).

Proverbs tells us that adultery (Prov. 6:29), evildoing (Prov. 11:21), pride (Prov. 16:5), delighting in another's misfortune (Prov. 17:5), and false testimony (Prov. 19:5, 9) 'will not go unpunished.'[47] We are to add to this list the one who cares more for finances than faithfulness.

28:21. To show partiality is not good, Because for a piece of bread a man will transgress.

In the context of making haste after riches (vv. 20, 22), we have here exemplified one means of doing so: bribery. The expression 'show partiality' is, more literally, 'know faces.' It points to a less-than-just decision rendered because of a relationship (past, present or future) with one of the parties involved. The law explicitly condemned such a practice (Deut. 1:17; 16:19). It is not wise (Prov. 24:23a), 'is not good' (Prov. 24:23b) and is immoral (Exod. 23:3; Lev. 19:15). Jesus condemned it (John 7:24), as did the apostles (e.g. James 2:1-13).

The expression 'is not good' is used repeatedly in Proverbs (Prov. 17:26; 18:5; 19:2; 24:23; 25:27; cf. 16:29). The expression may be an understatement, implying something criminal or self-destructive.[48] Sadly, bribes seem to continue to find willing takers (Prov. 17:8). This first line is nearly identical to Proverbs 24:23b.

The second line demonstrates just how low this practice can take a person. He can be bought 'for a piece of bread' (cf. Ezek. 13:19). One who accepts a bribe brings trouble, not only upon himself, but also upon those he loves (Prov. 15:27). He will become the target of deserving public outrage (Prov. 24:24).

28:22. A man with an evil eye hastens after wealth, And does not know that want will come upon him.

The first line presents 'A man with an evil eye.' The only other Old Testament usage of the expression is in Proverbs 23:6, where we are warned 'Do not eat the bread of a selfish man [literally, an evil eye].' The opposite expression is found in Proverbs 22:9, where it is translated 'He who is generous,' but it is, literally, 'the good of eye.' The point seems to be, as the translations demonstrate, that of a stingy, selfish, covetous attitude toward things. Jesus may have approached this expression when He asked, 'Or is your eye envious because I am generous?' (Matt. 20:15).

The problem, as in verses 19-20, continues to be that the man 'hastens after wealth.' His rush toward riches betrays his avaricious attitudes.

The warning is that such a man 'does not know that want will come upon him.' Because he fails to calculate God into his economic agenda, he does not realize that his strategies are self-defeating. '... [E]veryone who is hasty comes surely to poverty' (Prov. 21:5). Generosity is divinely rewarded (Prov. 11:24a), and miserliness is divinely chastened (Prov. 11:24b; cf. 20:21). 'The generous man will prosper, And he who waters will himself be watered' (Prov. 11:25). 'Do not weary yourself to gain wealth, Cease from your consideration of it' (Prov. 23:4).

28:23. He who rebukes a man will afterward find more favor Than he who flatters with the tongue.
Proverbs has consistently spoken of reproof or rebuke as a means of growth, health and life (Prov. 1:23; 9:8; 15:5, 12, 31; 19:25; 25:12; 27:5-6). Little wonder that 'He who rebukes' is so highly spoken of here. The Hebrew word translated 'afterward' is problematic. As it stands in the Hebrew text, the word normally means something like 'following my instructions,' which makes little sense here.[49] All manner of emendation and correction have ensued. In the end, no answer seems completely satisfactory. The context seems to point to a meaning like 'afterward,' and most of the modern translations follow this (NASB, NIV, RSV, NRSV, NKJV, NLT).

The contrast is between 'He who rebukes' and 'he who flatters with the tongue.' The latter is the same expression used of the immoral woman in Proverbs 2:16 and 7:5. Flattery is never looked upon favorably in the Proverbs, for 'a flattering mouth works ruin' (Prov. 26:28b). Wisdom reveals that 'A man who flatters his neighbor Is spreading a net for his steps' (Prov. 29:5).

If you are wise, 'He who rebukes' you 'will afterward find ... favor' with you more than the smooth-talking flatterer. The word translated 'favor' means acceptance, goodwill or approval. It comes from a root meaning 'to be pleased with.'[50] The combination 'afterward ... favor' implies that the first response to rebuke is not pleasant, but that, in time, one learns to rightly value the honest person as a friend and to see through the flattery of the other.

As nice as it is to have someone say only favorable things to us, wisdom teaches us to provide an even greater welcome for the one who speaks the truth for our own good. 'Do not reprove a scoffer, lest he hate you, Reprove a wise man, and he will love you' (Prov. 9:8, cf. 15:12). Listening to an honest, truthful rebuke ushers in greater measures of God's Spirit and God's word (Prov. 1:23). For this reason, we should delight in and love such a friend (Prov. 16:13). This welcome proves you are wise (Prov. 9:8; 15:31), prudent (Prov. 15:5), and knowledgeable (Prov. 19:25). The wise man will regard such a friend as a precious possession (Prov. 25:12). 'Better is open rebuke Than love that is concealed. Faithful are the wounds of a friend, But deceitful are the kisses of an enemy' (Prov. 27:5-6).

Peter exemplifies the kind of wisdom described here. Paul openly rebuked him for his hypocrisy regarding eating with Gentile believers (Gal. 2:11-14), but later Peter was able to call him 'our beloved brother Paul,' ascribe to him 'wisdom' and set his writings on a par with 'the rest of the Scriptures' (2 Pet. 3:15-16).[51]

28:24. He who robs his father or his mother, And says, 'It is not a transgression,' Is the companion of a man who destroys.
Proverbs speaks often of the responsibility of children to parents and the effect of one's living upon one's parents (Prov. 10:1; 15:20; 17:21, 25; 20:20; 30:11, 17). Here, the effect is, again, negative. The problem is that the child 'robs his father or his mother.' This may come in the form of literal theft, helping oneself to the family resources, and reasoning that it is yours by virtue of your family standing, running up debts that are left to the parents or – and perhaps this is most likely here – attempting to obtain one's inheritance before its time (Prov. 20:21). This was the particular sin of the prodigal son (Luke 15:12). It is the responsibility of children to care for ageing parents (1 Tim. 5:4, 8), not to use them to one's own personal gain.

The horror here, however, exceeds simply the theft. Making matters worse is the brazenness with which it is undertaken. The child says, 'It is not a transgression.' The Law set down strict guidelines for those who dishonor their parents (Exod. 20:12; 21:15, 17), but this specific problem is not addressed there. The child might audaciously challenge, 'Show me in God's Law where this is wrong! Give me the chapter and verse! I'll do whatever God's word tells me to do, but you can't prove to me that this is wrong!'

Jesus encountered just such people in the Pharisees and scribes (Matt. 15:4-6; Mark 7:10-12). He reminded them that such was implied in the commandment 'Honor your father and mother' (Exod. 20:12).

In actual fact, this robbery is no better than assault (Prov. 19:26). We are also reminded that such schemes do not secure anything, but only destroy (Prov. 18:9). Such a child destroys the security he thinks he gains himself, along with his family relationships, the latter-year comforts of his ageing parents, and the entire social order.

28:25. An arrogant man stirs up strife, But he who trusts in the LORD will prosper.
This verse and the next are tied together by the common word 'trusts.' It leads the way in the next verse, while, here, it closes the contrast.

Here, 'An arrogant man' is, more literally, 'the wide of soul.' Most interpret this along the lines of greed or covetousness (NIV, RSV, NRSV, JB) rather than pride, as here in the NASB (cf. KJV, NKJV). This seems to follow the notion found elsewhere in Proverbs, where 'soul' describes the appetites or cravings of a man (Prov. 10:3; 13:25; 27:7).[52]

When one is committed to complete satisfaction of personal appetites, he inevitably 'stirs up strife' in the process. Other things leading to such conflict are deceit (Prov. 6:14), hatred (Prov. 10:12), presumptuous pride (Prov. 13:10), a quick temper (15:18), perversity (Prov. 16:28), scoffing (Prov. 22:10), alcohol (Prov. 23:29), and anger (Prov. 29:22).

A commitment to gratify one's desires and urges will, of necessity, destroy relationships in the process. 'What is the source of quarrels and conflicts among you? Is not the source your pleasures that wage war in your members? You lust and do not have; so you commit murder. And you are envious and cannot obtain; so you fight and quarrel' (James 4:1-2a). In his greed, this person not only alienates others by his covetousness, but he enlists them as agents to oppose his selfish pursuits.[53] Grasping greedily after things is ultimately self-defeating (Prov. 28:20, 22).

In contrast ('But') is 'he who trusts in the LORD.' Blessing (Prov. 16:20) and exaltation (Prov. 29:25) are elsewhere assured the one who so rests himself and his desires on the Lord. Here the promise is that such a one 'will prosper' ('will be made fat'). Elsewhere, this is assured to the generous (Prov. 11:25) and diligent (Prov. 13:4) one. Truly, 'godliness ... is a means of great gain, when accompanied by contentment' (1 Tim. 6:6).

28:26. He who trusts in his own heart is a fool, But he who walks wisely will be delivered.
In the previous verse, trust in the Lord was commended. Here, 'He who trusts in his own heart' is condemned. What could be more

foolhardy than reliance upon one's own sinful, subjective, self-absorbed thoughts? We have been warned 'do not lean on your own understanding' (Prov. 3:5), and told 'There is a way which seems right to a man, But its end is the way of death' (Prov. 14:12; 16:25). Such a one earns the title 'fool.'

In contrast ('But') to such an approach to life is 'he who walks wisely.' Clearly, in Proverbs, to walk wisely is to trust in the Lord (cf. v. 25). 'Trust in the Lord with all your heart, And do not lean on your own understanding' (Prov. 3:5). Indeed, Proverbs 29:25 virtually replaces this line with 'he who trusts in the Lord will be exalted.'

The promise is that reliance upon God, rather than upon self, will bring the needed deliverance in the day of trouble. 'He who walks blamelessly will be delivered' (Prov. 28:18). 'In all your ways acknowledge Him, And He will make your paths straight' (Prov. 3:6).

Self-reliance is the pathway to trouble, while reliance upon God is a divinely guarded course. What is needed is the humility to admit that we do not possess within ourselves the wisdom needed to both honor God and successfully navigate life in His world. 'Thus says the Lord, "Let not a wise man boast of his wisdom, and let not the mighty man boast of his might, let not a rich man boast of his riches; but let him who boasts boast of this, that he understands and knows Me, that I am the Lord who exercises lovingkindness, justice, and righteousness on earth; for I delight in these things," declares the Lord' (Jer. 9:23-24). 'Let no man deceive himself. If any man among you thinks that he is wise in this age, let him become foolish that he may become wise' (1 Cor. 3:18).

28:27. He who gives to the poor will never want, But he who shuts his eyes will have many curses.
Proverbs has much to say about the poor. Here, the concern is to give to them in their need. This may include lending them money (Prov. 28:8), giving food (Prov. 22:9), and even standing up for their rights (Prov. 31:9). The Law commanded such generosity (Deut. 15:7; 24:19), and God is honored by those who display such generosity (Prov. 14:31; cf. 17:5). Such a stance is only logical, since God made both the poor and the rich (Prov. 22:2; 29:13), and those with means are only in that position by His grace. God calls these folks 'righteous' (Prov. 29:7), for he who overlooks the needy sins (Prov. 14:21a).

The assurance here is that, when we do share with the poor, we 'will never want.' When we give to the poor, we are actually making a loan to God (Prov. 19:17), who promises to reward us. As our

Shepherd, He promises we 'shall not want' (Ps. 23:1). He assures us that happiness will follow in the wake of generosity (Prov. 14:21b). God's promise is that giving will not lessen one's assets, but increase them (Prov. 11:24-25; 19:17; 22:9).

In contrast ('But') is the one 'who shuts his eyes' toward those less fortunate. He 'will have many curses.' It is not immediately clear who will issue these curses. It could be God (Prov. 3:33) or those he has snubbed (Prov. 11:26). We must understand this warning in context for the ancient world. A curse was not just mean words and a blessing was not just kind thoughts. It was believed that a curse or a blessing possessed power to effect change in one's life. To be cursed was most serious indeed. Here we are assured that God, either directly or indirectly, will make certain the stingy one misses out on the abundant blessings that come to those who are generous with their worldly wealth (Prov. 11:26b; 28:20). The day is coming when the stingy man will be in need, will cry out and no one will answer him (Prov. 21:13).

28:28. When the wicked rise, men hide themselves; But when they perish, the righteous increase.
This verse is very much like verse 12. Whereas that proverb began with the triumph of the righteous, this begins with the ascendancy of the wicked. The result is that 'men hide themselves.' Tyranny drives righteousness underground. 'Like a roaring lion and a rushing bear Is a wicked ruler over a poor people.' (Prov. 28:15). However, 'A leader who is a great oppressor lacks understanding ...' (Prov. 28:16a) because history has taught us that, in such conditions, the righteous are not destroyed, but strengthened. That is why 'when they [the wicked] perish [and perish they will, Prov. 11:10b; 29:16b], the righteous increase.' The word 'increase' can mean either multiply in number or advance in influence.[54] Commentators are divided over which is intended here.[55]

'When it goes well with the righteous, the city rejoices, And when the wicked perish, there is glad shouting' (Prov. 11:10). 'When the righteous increase, the people rejoice, But when a wicked man rules, people groan' (Prov. 29:2). 'When the wicked increase, transgression increases; But the righteous will see their fall' (Prov. 29:16).

End Notes

1. Buzzell, Sid S., 'Proverbs,' *The Bible Knowledge Commentary* (Wheaton: Victor Books, 1985), 1:965.

2. Ibid.

3. Adams, Jay E., *Proverbs* (Woodruff, South Carolina: Timeless Texts, 1997), 209.

4. Whybray, R. N., *Proverbs* (Grand Rapids, Michigan: William B. Eerdmans Publishing Company, 1994), 390.

5. Goldberg, Louis, 'bîn,' *Theological Wordbook of the Old Testament* (Chicago: Moody Press, 1980), 1:103-4.

6. Buzzell, 1:965.

7. Delitzsch, F., *Proverbs, Ecclesiastes, Song of Solomon* (three volumes in one) in C. F. Keil and F. Delitzsch, vol. 6, *Commentary on the Old Testament* (in ten volumes), (1872; rpt. Grand Rapids, Michigan: William B. Eerdmans Publishing Company, 1980), 1:78.

8. Buzzell, 1:945.

9. Brown, Francis, S. R. Driver, Charles A. Briggs, *A Hebrew and English Lexicon of the Old Testament* (Oxford: Clarendon Press, n.d.), 108.

10. White, William, 'rā'â,' *Theological Wordbook of the Old Testament* (Chicago: Moody Press, 1980), 2:852-853 and R. Laird Harris, 'rā'â,' *Theological Wordbook of the Old Testament* (Chicago: Moody Press, 1980), 2:853.

11. Grisanti, Michael A., 'זלל,' *New International Dictionary of Old Testament Theology and Exegesis* (Grand Rapids, Michigan: Zondervan Publishing House, 1997), 1:1109-1110.

12. Oswalt, John O., 'kāllam,' *Theological Wordbook of the Old Testament* (Chicago: Moody Press, 1980), 1:442-443.

13. Lane, Eric, *Proverbs* (Scotland: Christian Focus Publications, 2000), 306.

14. McKane, William, *Proverbs* (Philadelphia: The Westminster Press, 1970), 626.

15. Cohen, A., *Proverbs* (London: The Soncino Press, 1946), 187.

16. Whybray, 391.

17. Lane, 304.

18. Cohen, 187.

19. Adams, 211.

20. Kidner, Derek, *Proverbs* (Downers Grove, Illinois: InterVarsity Press, 1964), 170.

21. Cohen, 187.

22. McKane, 621.

23. Wolf, Herbert, 'hāqar,' *Theological Wordbook of the Old Testament* (Chicago: Moody Press, 1980), 1:318.

24. Whybray, 392.

25. Collins, C. John, 'פאר,' *New International Dictionary of Old Testament Theology and Exegesis* (Grand Rapids, Michigan: Zondervan Publishing House, 1997), 3:572-574.

26. Cohen, 188.

27. Whybray, 392.

28. Hartley, John E., 'sālēah,' *Theological Wordbook of the Old Testament* (Chicago: Moody Press, 1980), 2:766.

29. Cohen, 188.

30. Coppes, Leonard J., 'rāham,' *Theological Wordbook of the Old Testament* (Chicago: Moody Press, 1980), 2:841-843.

31. Alexander, Ralph H., 'yādâ,' *Theological Wordbook of the Old Testament* (Chicago: Moody Press, 1980), 1:364-366.

32. Schultz, Carl, "āzab,' *Theological Wordbook of the Old Testament* (Chicago: Moody Press, 1980), 2:658-659.

33. VanPelt, M. V., and W. C. Kaiser, Jr., 'פחד,' *New International Dictionary of Old Testament Theology and Exegesis* (Grand Rapids, Michigan: Zondervan Publishing House, 1997), 3:597-598.

34. Whybray, 393.

35. Ibid., 88.

36. Delitzsch, 2:231.

37. Coppes, Leonard J., '*dālal*,' *Theological Wordbook of the Old Testament* (Chicago: Moody Press, 1980), 1:190.

38. Murphy, 213 and Delitzsch, 2:231-232.

39. Swart, I., 'עשק,' *New International Dictionary of Old Testament Theology and Exegesis* (Grand Rapids, Michigan: Zondervan Publishing House, 1997), 3:557-558.

40. Kidner, 171.

41. Delitzsch, 1:78.

42. Ross, Allen P., 'Proverbs,' *The Expositor's Bible Commentary*, (Grand Rapids, Michigan: Zondervan Publishing House, 1997), 5:1108; Delitzsch, 2:234; Murphy, 212-213.

43. Shepherd, Jerry, 'ריק,' *New International Dictionary of Old Testament Theology and Exegesis* (Grand Rapids, Michigan: Zondervan Publishing House, 1997), 3:1106-1109.

44. Moberly, R. W. L., 'אמן,' *New International Dictionary of Old Testament Theology and Exegesis* (Grand Rapids, Michigan: Zondervan Publishing Company, 1997), 1:427.

45. Ibid., 1:429-430.

46. Cohen, 190.

47. Buzzell, 1:966.

48. Whybray, 251.

49. Ross, 5:1109.

50. Buzzell, 1:923.

51. Lane, 309.

52. Cohen, 57.

53. McKane, 627.

54. Whybray, 397.

55. Compare, for example, Delitzsch, 2:240; McKane, 624-625; and Whybray, 397.

Proverbs 29

29:1. A man who hardens his neck after much reproof Will suddenly be broken beyond remedy.

As to form, this chapter is dominated by antithetical proverbs (vv. 2, 3, 4, 6, 8, 10, 11, 15, 16, 18, 23, 25, 26). There are notable examples of continuous sentence proverbs as well (vv. 1, 5, 9, 12, 14, 21).

Proverbs has spoken often of the beneficial effects of reproof (e.g. Prov. 1:23, 6:23; 13:18; 15:31-32) and of the danger of spurning such (e.g. Prov. 3:11; 10:17; 12:1; 15:10). Now, that theme reaches an apex. Our character is, literally, 'a man of reproofs.' The plural points to the multiplied attempts to reason with the individual and is represented in the English translation by 'after much.'

The problem is that such a one 'hardens his neck.' This is a stock phrase describing an ineducable spirit, a willful self-sufficiency, and a resolute rebellion. The phrase is often translated as 'obstinate' (Exod. 32:9; 33:3, 5; 34:9) or 'stubborn' (Deut. 9:6, 13). Such was Pharaoh's condition (Exod. 7:13). The Israelites chose this course at Massah and Meribah (Exod. 17:7). The sons of Eli exemplified this implacable stubbornness (1 Sam. 2:25). And Zedekiah and his subjects evidenced it (2 Chron. 36:12-16). The best expansion on this condition is Proverbs 1:24-31.

The second line is identical to Proverbs 6:15b. Judgment comes 'suddenly' to the one who listens to no one. The word has the sense of splitting, opening, breaking out, and breaking forth.[1] Unawares, out of nowhere, the judgment befalls him (cf. Prov. 4:22; 28:18). Compare the example of Judah in Jeremiah's day (Jer. 19:10-11, 15).

The calamity of the wicked is spoken of in final terms, for he will be 'beyond remedy.' Again, his calamity is further described as being 'broken.' Like a shattered earthenware jar (Ps. 2:9; Isa. 30:14), whose pieces cannot be restored, the rebel will be swiftly broken in the midst of his plot.[2] No explanation can restore him or clear his name. The one who hates reproof will come to poverty and shame (Prov. 13:18), fall into calamity (Prov. 28:14), disappear (Prov. 10:25), and die (Prov. 15:10).

29:2. When the righteous increase, the people rejoice, But when a wicked man rules, people groan.
This same note has been sounded before (Prov. 11:10; 28:12, 28). There is glad celebration when 'the righteous increase.' The same word for 'increase' is used in Proverbs 28:28. The word can describe either multiplication of numbers or advancement in influence.[3] Here, the contrast is with 'rules,' which indicates that the notion is that of influence. 'When the righteous triumph, there is great glory' (Prov. 28:12a). Consider, as an example, the celebration over Mordecai in Esther's day (Esther 8:15).

The contrasting ('But') response is pictured in line two. Here, it is 'a wicked man' that is the concern. The Hebrew text is singular, though it can have a collective meaning.[4] We should not, however, rush past the contrast between the collective influence of the righteous in line one and the singular will of 'a wicked' individual in line two.[5]

The trouble is that such a one now 'rules.' 'Like a roaring lion and a rushing bear Is a wicked ruler over a poor people' (Prov. 28:15; cf. 29:16). Under such leadership, 'people groan' and 'hide themselves' (Prov. 28:12b, 28a). Little wonder 'there is glad shouting' (Prov. 11:10b) when such a leader is removed from power. As an example, consider the experience of the Hebrews under the thumb of Egypt (Exod. 2:23-24; 3:9; 6:5) and, later, in the days of the judges (Judg. 2:18).

Considering that this section of Proverbs (Prov. 25:1–29:27) was assembled by servants of Hezekiah, it seems likely that the concentration of this theme here (Prov. 28:12, 28; 29:2) is some statement about his times. After sixteen years of wickedness under the rule of Ahaz (2 Kings 16), the people, no doubt, celebrated the revival of righteousness under Hezekiah (2 Kings 18-19).

29:3. A man who loves wisdom makes his father glad, But he who keeps company with harlots wastes his wealth.
This verse harkens back to themes repeated often in Proverbs 1–9. What is unusual is the reference to 'A man' rather than 'A son' (e.g. Prov. 10:1). Perhaps this means that the son has moved into adulthood and the father is now aged.[6] In such a situation, the father may well have turned over the inheritance to his son and is now dependent upon him for his daily sustenance and security.

What could make an aged father happier ('glad') than to see in his son one who 'loves wisdom'? 'A wise son makes a father glad' (Prov. 10:1a; 15:20a). 'My son, if your heart is wise, My own heart also will be glad; And my inmost being will rejoice, When your lips speak what is right' (Prov. 23:15-16). 'The father of the righteous will greatly rejoice, And he who begets a wise son will be glad in him' (Prov. 23:24). 'Be wise, my son, and make my heart glad' (Prov. 27:11a).

In contrast ('But'), what could make a father more heartsick than to see his son wantonly wasting all the family wealth on riotous living? '... [H]e who is a companion of gluttons humiliates his father' (Prov. 28:7b). This aged father, now destitute and living hand-to-mouth, has watched his son lustfully consume all he spent a lifetime building, in order that he might pass it on to his child. Here, the problem is that the son 'keeps company with harlots.' Repeatedly, Proverbs has warned of the devastation such illicit sexual activity inevitably brings, often singling out the financial ramifications of such action (Prov. 5:9-10; 6:31). 'For on account of a harlot one is reduced to a loaf of bread' (Prov. 6:26). This was the problem of the prodigal son (Luke 15:30). Proverbs has often reminded us that wisdom turns one back from adultery (Prov. 2:16-19; 5:1-14; 7:1-27).

29:4. The king gives stability to the land by justice, But a man who takes bribes overthrows it.

Here is the pathway to the longevity of a nation. The word translated 'stability' means to stand, remain or endure.[7] In the present verbal form, it means 'to cause to stand.' What is required for such a state is a leader who rules 'by justice.' 'For a throne is established on righteousness' (Prov. 16:12b). 'And he upholds his throne by righteousness' (Prov. 20:28). 'Take away the wicked from before the king, And his throne will be established in righteousness' (Prov. 25:5). 'If a king judges the poor with truth, His throne will be established forever' (Prov. 29:14). Consider what the Queen of Sheba noted about the source of Solomon's successful reign (2 Chron. 9:8). Behind the righteousness and justice stands wisdom (Prov. 8:15-16).

In contrast ('But') to this wise, just, and righteous ruler stands 'a man who takes bribes.' The phrase is, more precisely, 'a man of exactions.'[8] The term normally describes offerings made according to the rituals outlined in the Mosaic Law. Here, however, it may describe either bribery or taxation, more likely the latter.[9] While bribes are repeatedly condemned in Proverbs (Prov. 15:27; 17:23; 28:16; cf. Prov. 17:8; 18:16; 21:14) and elsewhere (Deut. 16:19; 1 Sam. 12:3; Eccles. 7:7; Isa. 1:23; Amos 5:12), the point here seems to be excessive taxation for selfish purposes. This was the end Samuel predicted when the nation asked for a king (1 Sam. 8:11-18) and just what they got by the time of Rehoboam, Solomon's son (1 Kings 12:1-19).

29:5. A man who flatters his neighbor Is spreading a net for his steps.

The two lines make one continuous sentence. The problem is the one 'who flatters.' More literally, it means 'A man who makes smooth.' This is in the style, if not the content, of the 'smooth' flattery of the seductress (Prov. 2:16; 5:3; 7:5). Proverbs looks down sternly upon any form of flattery, viewing it as a mortal danger (Prov. 26:28b). It is nothing less than lying (Prov. 26:28a). Today, we might name the offender 'a smooth-talker.' He identifies a point of pride or ego weakness in his intended victim and then begins to lay it on thick, smoothing it over with suave finesse. Job detested it (Job. 32:21), as did Solomon's father (Ps. 5:9).

The second line can be a bit ambiguous. It could mean either that the flattery of the first line is malicious (the net is spread for the one being flattered) or self-destructive (the flattery backfires, and the net is being unwittingly spread for the flatterer). In favor of the latter view is the fact that the next verse reminds us that 'By transgression an evil man is ensnared' (v. 6a). Proverbs often warns of the self-destructive nature of sin (Prov. 1:18; 26:27; 28:10). In the end, honest speech gets you much farther than smooth-talking manipulation (Prov. 28:23).

29:6. By transgression an evil man is ensnared, But the righteous sings and rejoices.

The first line has no verb: 'In the transgression of an evil man [is] a snare.' The NASB has rightly supplied one. Is the snare for the evil man himself? Or, is it for another against whom he plots? The NIV has taken some liberties, but has probably captured the intent: 'An evil man is snared by his own sin.' The poetic literature often speaks of the irony of an evil person being caught in the trap he has set for another (Job 5:13; Ps. 7:15-16; 35:7-8; Prov. 1:18; 12:13; 22:5; 26:27; 28:10; Eccles. 9:12).

In contrast ('But') to this ironic self-destruction is 'the righteous' one. Instead of falling in judgment, he 'sings and rejoices.' This speaks of the carefree peace that can be had by those who deal rightly with others. They can live unafraid that their schemes might backfire.

Some want to emend the text and change 'sings' to 'runs.' They do so for primarily two reasons. The first is that they believe that the active idea of the first line must be met with a more mobile picture in the second. The second reason is that Proverbs seldom employs two verbal ideas like this ('sings and rejoices').[10] The emendation is unnecessary, for the contrast is sufficient and the uniqueness of the combination does not prohibit its usage here.

29:7. The righteous is concerned for the rights of the poor, The wicked does not understand such concern.

A man's standing before God affects how he views those who stand before him. The contrast is between 'The righteous' and 'The wicked.' What separates the two, in this case, is that the former are 'concerned for the rights of the poor,' while the latter do 'not understand such concern.'

The Scriptures speak often of concern for the poor (Job 29:16; Ps. 41:1; Prov. 31:5, 8-9). Here, the verb 'is concerned' is, more literally, 'knows.' It appears to be used in the same sense as in Proverbs 12:10a: 'A righteous man has regard for his beast.'[11]

The word used here for 'poor' means those who are defenseless through economic or physical misfortune.[12] It is easy to take advantage of the poor simply because they are so disadvantaged that they seldom have anyone both leveraged and concerned enough to defend them (Prov. 22:22). It often appears to be of little economic or social value to side with such folk. Yet, God promises that, when we do so, we are only lending to Him who repays in full and more (Prov. 19:17). God assures lasting stability to those who take up the cause of the poor (Prov. 29:14).

Such logic escapes 'The wicked.' While the word translated 'concern' in the second line is different from the word so translated in the first line, the parallelism carries over and gives the same sense here. The phrase 'understand such concern' is, literally, 'do not discern knowledge.' On the landscape of their thinking, there is no recognition that the poor exist or that, if they do, they are of any concern to such an individual. They are pawns to be used and sacrificed as they may serve the 'wicked' man's personal agenda. 'Evil men do not understand justice, But those who seek the LORD understand all things' (Prov. 28:5).

29:8. Scorners set a city aflame, But wise men turn away anger.

The problem here are the 'Scorners.' Such persons have become so independent as to render themselves incapable of learning wisdom (Prov. 14:6). Unwilling to receive reproof or teaching (Prov. 9:7, 8; 13:1; 15:12), they are confirmed in their rejection of authority (Prov. 21:24; 22:10). They are, more literally, 'men of mocking.' The exact phrase is found elsewhere only in Isaiah 28:14, where it is used of unrighteous political leaders. It may have the same sense here, though it can apply more broadly. The entire first line, literally, reads: 'Men of mocking blow against a city.' Here, 'blow' is interpreted as 'set ... aflame,' picturing one blowing upon smoldering embers to fan them again into flame (Prov. 26:21). The word is used often in Proverbs in connection with speaking lies (Prov. 6:19; 14:15, 25; 19:5, 9), but can also be used of speaking truth (Prov. 12:17). Such folks often perceive themselves as social reformers. But, they are, in fact, anarchists for whom God has the sternest of warnings (Prov. 6:12, 14-15; 11:10-11). 'Like charcoal to hot embers and wood to fire, So is a contentious man to kindle strife' (Prov. 26:21).

Fortunately, there are, at times, 'wise men' in leadership. Through wisdom, they 'turn away anger.' Such a one is able to sooth contentions, win the loyalties and trust of divergent splinter groups, and find common ground where the scoffer only further divides (cf. Prov. 16:14). True wisdom is peaceable (James 3:17-18), but, at times, such peace can be had only through the radical step of removing the mocker (Prov. 22:10). For an example of this very wisdom, see 2 Samuel 22:14-22.

29:9. When a wise man has a controversy with a foolish man, The foolish man either rages or laughs, and there is no rest.
There is no dealing with a fool. The first line pictures 'a wise man' and a 'foolish man' with 'a controversy.' Just what is meant by 'a controversy' is not immediately clear. Does it refer to a lawsuit (NIV, NEB) or a personal controversy of a more general nature (NASB, KJV, NKJV, RSV, JB)? The word is broad in describing actions that seek to bring order to a community of people, guaranteeing that justice is done.[13] It is largely used as expressive of the exercise of government.[14] The reference likely describes a personal dispute that has remained unresolved and has been pushed to the level of public litigation. No resolution had come as the wise man and the foolish man sought to work out their differences, just between the two of them. Now, because of the nature of the fool, there is little expectation that any such resolution will be had, even with the intervention of outside parties.

The second line is ambiguous, without a subject specified. The NASB has understood it to refer to the fool (thus the translators' addition of 'The foolish man'), which is the most likely referent. Some contend, however, that it may refer to the wise man (e.g. KJV, following the Vulgate). In this sense, it would mean that, no matter what tactics the wise man uses (either anger ['rages'] or scorn ['laughter']), he cannot move the fool to a resolution. It has even been suggested that the first ('rages') refers to the wise man, who takes the matter seriously, and the second ('laughter') refers to the fool, who mocks the whole process.[15] In the end, it is probably best to see 'the fool' as the one parading this wide-ranging display of emotion across all efforts to bring harmony. The wise man never knows for sure what he will get when he tries for a resolution. The fool's feelings are in constant flux and every option across the continuum of emotion will be used to deflect from the real issues.

In the end, as at the beginning, 'there is no rest.' The word describes a heart and mind at peace, in stillness, restful (Eccles. 9:17; Isa. 30:15).[16] When working with a fool, no technique and no amount of effort can make such a state yours. 'Do not answer a fool according to his folly, Lest you also be like him' (Prov. 26:4).

29:10. Men of bloodshed hate the blameless, But the upright are concerned for his life.

Intolerance lies not with the righteous, but with the wicked. The subject of line one is 'Men of bloodshed,' or, literally, 'men of bloods' (cf. this type in Prov. 1:11-16). They 'hate' those who possess integrity. The word describes a strong emotional reaction to that which is, or those who are, detested or abhorred. This emotional response moves toward action designed to distance oneself from the person or thing hated.[17] In this case, the hatred moves the bloodthirsty to try to do away with 'the blameless.' These folks are not morally perfect, but rather people of integrity, persons whose inner and outer life are one (Prov. 10:9, 29; 13:6; 19:1; 20:7; 28:6, 10).

The best illustration of such integrity, and such violent hatred of it, is the response of the Jewish leadership to Jesus (Matt. 17:23; 26:4; Mark 14:1; John 5:18; 7:1; 11:53). Jesus promised His followers would face the same kind of enmity from the world (Matt. 10:22; John 15:18-21). Consider also the response of Cain to Abel's acceptance before God (Gen. 4:5-8; 1 John 3:12).

The exact referent of the second line is somewhat difficult to identify. The line reads literally, 'but the upright seek his soul.' The problem here is that 'seek his soul [i.e. life]' normally means to seek to kill someone. This seems an impossible thing to assign to 'the upright.' The RSV, without justification, simply changes 'the upright' to 'the wicked.' The NRSV has changed it to a generic 'they,' but still sees it as referring to the bloodthirsty of line one. The NIV is similar: 'and seek to kill the upright.' The change of subject is gratuitous and without warrant. The best option seems to be to see this as a unique usage of the verb and to read it as expressive of the concern of the upright for the welfare of the blameless.[18] Proverbs 24:11-12 expresses the attitude well: 'Deliver those who are being taken away to death, And those who are staggering to slaughter, O hold them back. If you say, 'See, we did not know this,' Does He not consider it who weighs the hearts? And does He not know it who keeps your soul? And will He not render to man according to his work?'

29:11. A fool always loses his temper, But a wise man holds it back.

Here, as in verses 8-9 and 22, the problem is that of anger. Throughout Proverbs, the 'fool' is pictured as unable to control his emotions, even for a moment (Prov. 12:16). His arrogance makes him careless and quick-tempered (Prov. 14:16-17). His lack of control leaves himself vulnerable (Prov. 25:28). The verbal form points out that he causes all his emotion to be spilled out through his lack of self-control.[19] The word translated 'his temper' is, literally, 'his spirit.' Elsewhere, however, it is similarly used of one's anger (Prov. 16:32; 25:28).[20] Such a person is subject to every whim of passion and makes everyone in his life ride the roller coaster to the peaks and through valleys of his emotions.

There is a better way, however. It is the way of the 'wise man.' Such a one 'holds it [the anger] back.' The construction of this second line is somewhat challenging, but, upon some reflection, yields helpful insight. A more literal reading would be, 'but the wise man holding back, quiets it.' The verb ('quiets') means to soothe or to still.[21] It is used also in Psalms 65:7 and 89:9 to describe the stilling of a storm at sea.[22] The metaphor is picturesque of an inwardly raging anger. The One who stills the storms (Matt. 8:23-27; Mark 4:36-41; Luke 8:22-25) can surely help quell the surges of a person's anger. The 'holding back' represents a word whose verbal root means to continue somewhere for a longer period of time than was anticipated.[23] In our form, it can mean 'back' or 'after' and can refer either to a spatial distancing or a temporal delay.[24] The sense is that the wise man retains his anger as an invisible inner struggle until such time or place as he may appropriately work it through with God. Such a person 'has great understanding' (Prov. 14:29), 'is better than the mighty' (Prov. 16:32) and full of 'discretion' (Prov. 19:11).

This denies the demand that anger is uncontrollable and must always be vented. This reminds us that self-control is possible by God's Spirit (Gal. 5:22-23). It also tells us that, while anger may be controlled, it should always be thoroughly processed before God. Denial is unhealthy emotionally, psychologically, spiritually, and even physically. We must measure all our communication with others according to the principle of ministry to them (Eph. 4:26-27, 29). God is, ultimately, the only one with whom we may be utterly forthcoming and still be safe.

29:12. If a ruler pays attention to falsehood, All his ministers become wicked.

Like prince, like people. A leader sets the standard of integrity for those around him. Here, the problem is a ruler who 'pays attention to falsehood.' The Hebrew word translated 'pays attention' means to listen, but it represents more than just hearing. It describes listening with a view to embracing or obeying what is said.[25]

The word 'falsehood' is, more literally, 'a lying word.' It only takes a single incident like this to signal an invitation for more of the same. Soon, 'All his ministers become wicked.'

When a leader countenances a false report, an intentional misrepresentation to advance a cause, or a bending of the truth, he sends clear signals that will draw every unscrupulous character within his realm of leadership. David had, obviously, taught his son well regarding the importance of surrounding himself with upright advisors (Ps. 101). Would that Solomon's son, Rehoboam, had learned the same lesson (1 Kings 12:13-14)! Ahab allowed his wife, Jezebel, to convince him of this course against Naboth (1 Kings 21:1-13).

'If a king judges the poor with truth, His throne will be established forever' (Prov. 29:14). 'Take away the wicked from before the king, And his throne will be established in righteousness' (Prov. 25:5). A wise leader makes certain he is getting the straight scoop from his advisors (Prov. 25:2). 'Loyalty and truth preserve the king, And he upholds his throne by righteousness' (Prov. 20:28). Knowing this a leader is wise to quickly disperse evildoers from his presence (Prov. 20:8). 'It is an abomination for kings to commit wickedness, For a throne is established on righteousness' (Prov. 16:12).

29:13. The poor man and the oppressor have this in common: The Lord gives light to the eyes of both.

The point is made through a synthetic parallelism – the second line explaining more specifically the first. This verse is a near repeat of Proverbs 22:2. Here, the first line contrasts 'The poor man' with 'the oppressor,' while in Proverbs 22:2 the contrast is between the poor and the rich. Surely, this is assumed here, but is taken further in noting that the man with goods either got them through oppression, keeps them through oppression, or both. The LXX has the contrast of debtor and lender. This may mean that the rich 'oppressor' came to his wealth by either high taxation or charging unscrupulously high interest rates for his loans.[26]

The first line tells us that both those with, and those without, material goods have something 'in common.' The word means basically 'to meet together,' whether in an affable, neutral or unfriendly encounter.[27] Most of the time, the lives of the poor and rich are lived on two completely separate social planes. Seldom do their lives intersect. The course of their daily affairs simply does not make for social interchange. There is, however, one inescapable point where their paths do cross. The second line of the proverb tells us what this place is: 'The LORD gives light to the eyes of both.' To give light is expressive of giving life (Job 33:30; Ps. 13:3; 49:19). The point is that they share a common origin from a common Maker (Prov. 22:2b; 1 Sam. 2:7; Job 31:15; 34:19).

Both the oppressor and the ones oppressed have a common origin. 'He who oppresses the poor reproaches his Maker, But he who is gracious to the needy honors Him' (Prov. 14:31). 'He who mocks the poor reproaches his Maker' (Prov. 17:5a). They both shall meet the same end (Job 3:19; James 1:9-11). And, both are sustained by the same Creator along the path between (Matt. 5:45; Acts 14:17).

Is the point that God has simply made both and now they have made themselves (either rich or poor)? Or, is it that God has actually not only created them as individuals, but has created them as 'poor' or 'rich' individuals? Has He not only created them, but also appointed their circumstances (though without approving the oppression that may have brought them about)?

Proverbs has told us that 'The Lord has made everything for its own purpose, Even the wicked for the day of evil' (Prov. 16:4). Proverbs tells us that riches are dispensed by God, but not apart from our cooperation with wisdom and righteousness (Prov. 22:4, 9). Likewise, poverty comes from God's hand, sometimes as a chastening for wrong attitudes or actions (Prov. 22:13, 16).

What is clear is that we are all blessed beyond what we deserve. We all share in the outpouring of God's prevenient grace: 'He causes His sun to rise on the evil and the good, and sends rain on the righteous and the unrighteous' (Matt. 5:45; cf. Acts 14:17).

29:14. If a king judges the poor with truth, His throne will be established forever.
The path to longevity is through uprightness. The first line is concerned with 'a king' and the appropriate manner of his judgments. The way commended is 'truth,' meaning dedication to

his charge and a commitment to fully discharge his duties through the exercise of justice.[28] Such a ruler perceives reality and holds it accurately against the standard of law, making all decisions on the basis of this valuation. This should never be more true of a leader than in the case of those least likely to gain his attention, pad his pockets or jeopardize his agenda ('the poor,' cf. vv. 7, 13). In a psalm penned by Solomon, he prays for the ability to judge with God's righteousness and compassion (Ps. 72:1-4, 12-15). As a royal psalm, it not only applies to Solomon, but also, prophetically, to the ultimate King, Jesus Christ. Elsewhere, the Messiah is pictured as ruling with just this kind of 'truth' (Isa. 11:4; 9:7; Luke 1:32-33; Heb. 1:8-9).

Where God finds a leader willing to take up the cause of the powerless, He promises security – 'His throne will be established forever.' The word translated 'established' is used twenty-five times of the establishment of a dynasty.[29] The same promise is made elsewhere when the king detests wickedness (Prov. 16:12), loves loyalty and truth (Prov. 20:28), and removes the wicked counselors from before himself (Prov. 25:5). Similarly, the ruler who hates oppression and making wealth unjustly will 'prolong his days' (Prov. 28:16). Not only is his throne thus secured, but the entire land finds 'stability' (Prov. 29:4). God has pledged Himself as the Protector of the poor (Prov. 22:22-23; 23:10-11) and, thus, the Guardian of all who take up their cause as well.

29:15. The rod and reproof give wisdom, But a child who gets his own way brings shame to his mother.
The path of good for a child and of joy for his parents inevitably passes through the hour of discipline. Such discipline is always dual: words ('reproof') and actions ('rod'). The NIV follows some commentators in understanding this dual reference as an example of the literary form hendiadys ('The rod of correction'). This, however, masks the point of the dual nature of discipline (cf. Eph. 6:4, 'the discipline and instruction of the Lord'). The 'rod' represented physical, corporal discipline (Prov. 13:24; 22:15; 23:13-14). Such discipline is a sign of love, not hate (Prov. 13:24), and is a Divinely given corrective for the folly of inborn sin (Prov. 22:15). But, discipline is never merely physical. It must, first and always, be verbal as well ('reproof'). Repeatedly, in Proverbs, 'reproof' is seen as the pathway to life, not only for children, but any caught in the clutches of folly (e.g. Prov. 1:23, 25, 30; 3:11, 12; 5:12; 6:23, 33). Significantly, God's discipline is mentioned in Proverbs before He requires it of parents (Prov. 3:11-12).[30] His discipline is always motivated by love, as ours

should be. Anger, embarrassment or frustration should never launch one into the use of either the 'rod' or 'reproof.'

In contrast to this loving discipline of word and act is the parent who allows the child to get 'his own way.' The verb here is a broad one, meaning 'to send,' 'to send away,' 'to let loose,' and 'to spread.'[31] Closer to the imagery of our context, Delitzsch notes that the root is used of animals allowed to wander at will in order to find refuge (Job 39:5; Isa. 16:2).[32] The picture here, then, is of a child allowed to do his own thing. Boundaries are never imposed. Actions are never restrained. Attitudes are never checked.

Such a child inevitably 'brings shame to his mother [and father].' The mention here of only the mother may indicate either that it is the child's earliest training that is in view[33] or that it is a mere stylistic variation and includes the father as well (cf. mention of only the father in v. 3).[34] Proverbs often warns of the heartache that awaits the parents who do not deal early, consistently, and decisively with the folly born into the heart of their child (Prov. 10:1; 17:21, 25; 19:13a, 26; 28:7). On the other hand, 'The father of the righteous will greatly rejoice, And he who begets a wise son will be glad in him' (Prov. 23:24). 'Correct your son, and he will give you comfort; He will also delight your soul' (Prov. 29:17). Nothing guarantees the extremes of emotion like parenthood!

29:16. When the wicked increase, transgression increases; But the righteous will see their fall.

This antithetical proverb, as so many others do, contrasts 'the wicked' and 'the righteous.' Here, the view is of a time 'When the wicked increase.' The same word for 'increase' is used in verse 2 and in Proverbs 28:28. The word can describe either multiplication of numbers or advancement in influence.[35] In Proverbs 28:28, the contrast was with 'rules,' which indicates that the notion there is one of influence. Here, however, the word occurs twice, describing both the 'increase' of the wicked and, when that happens, the commensurate 'increases' in acts of sin. There is a momentum to sin. Inhibitions are demolished when the popular culture embraces sin. The picture is of a day when long-standing, commonly agreed-upon moral boundaries are removed and both society and those who make it up find themselves in a place they never dreamed they would be. In such a day, men 'hide themselves' (Prov. 28:12b, 28a). It is the exact opposite of the picture in verse 2a and in Proverbs 28:12a.

The second line contrasts ('But') this seeming triumph of 'the wicked' and their 'transgression.' The Proverbs often promise the downfall of the wicked (e.g. Prov. 10:25; 14:11; 21:12). Here, however, the promise is taken even farther and 'the righteous' are assured of a day when they 'will see their fall.' The notion is that they will look with triumph over the fall of those who have reviled God.[36] The Psalms often speak of the righteous looking upon the wicked in their judgment (Ps. 37:34; 54:7; 58:10; 91:8; 92:11). This proverb does not specify when this will happen, but assures that it will indeed take place. This assurance has been a major stabilizing factor in the lives of God's people for thousands of years.

29:17. Correct your son, and he will give you comfort; He will also delight your soul.

The joys of parenthood are, generally, a matter of delayed gratification. One must 'Correct' his 'son, and [then] he will give you comfort.' The root of 'Correct' describes correction that results in learning. It is substantially verbal in nature (cf. v. 15 and the dual nature of discipline). It is, first, God's work with His people (Prov. 3:11-12) and, then, also that of the parent with his child. Hence, the love of God (Prov. 3:12), the fear of the Lord (Prov. 1:7), and the instruction of His Word (Prov. 1:8) are closely tied to all such parental correction.[37]

When the child responds to such correction and walks in a path of wisdom, 'he will give [his parents] comfort.' The word translated 'comfort' describes lack of movement and a sense of security.[38] No more frantic activity. The adult child has come to an established pattern of wise living and the parent can settle in his joy. The worrisome shame of verse 15 is the opposite of this.

Using synthetic parallelism, the second line extends further the blessing of the first. The 'comfort' of line one is expanded here by noting that the adult son 'will also delight your soul.' The word for 'delight' is one that normally refers to culinary delicacies. Interestingly, 'soul' is sometimes used as descriptive of one's appetite (Prov. 10:3; 16:26; 23:2; 27:7). Here, the meaning appears to be metaphorical and speaks of the utter joy of seeing your child walk in wisdom.

Heartache is not far from the parents who do not deal early, consistently, and decisively with the foolishness in the heart of their child (Prov. 10:1; 17:21, 25; 19:13a, 26; 28:7). We are also, gladly, promised the joys that come to the parent whose children embrace wisdom. 'A wise son makes a father glad' (Prov. 10:1). 'The father of the righteous will greatly rejoice, And he who begets a wise son will be glad in him' (Prov. 23:24). The key is to not loose heart and to 'Discipline your son while there is hope' (Prov. 19:18a). We count on the hope that if we 'Train up a child in the way he should go, Even when he is old he will not depart from it' (Prov. 22:6; cf. 13:24; 23:13).

29:18. Where there is no vision, the people are unrestrained, But happy is he who keeps the law.

This antithetical proverb contrasts the state of those who possess the word of God and obey it (line two) with those who have no revelation of God's will (line one). The word 'vision' is descriptive of the revelation given by God to one of His prophets (1 Sam. 3:1). The word is used in the titles of some books of the prophets (Isa. 1:1; Amos 1:1; Mic. 1:1; Nahum 1:1).[39] Note that in the second line the reference is to 'the law.' The Hebrew word here is *torah*, one often referring to the Law of God given through Moses. We have seen that, in Proverbs, the word often refers in a more limited sense to the instruction of one's father (Prov. 1:8; 3:1; 4:2; 6:20; 7:2) or the wisdom teacher (Prov. 13:14). Given its parallel with prophetic 'vision' in line one, it here seems (as in Proverbs 28:4, 7, 9) to refer to the Divine Law through Moses. Walls astutely observes: 'The law, the prophets and the wisdom literature meet in this verse.'[40]

While noting the unique referent of each word, we should probably not try to make too fine a distinction between prophetic 'vision' and divine 'law' here. Some picture the scene as one in which the prophets have been silenced, but the written Law of God is still available. The counsel would then be something like 'Where God does not speak in contemporary terms, return to the objective written word.'[41] While that may be wise counsel, it is probably making too much of the wording here.

The first line warns of the time and place when such a revelation of God's will is absent. Oded told Asa that '[F]or many days Israel was ... without a teaching priest and without law' (2 Chron. 15:3). God warned the people of Amos's day: 'Behold, days are coming ... When I will send a famine on the land, Not a famine for bread or a thirst for water, But rather for hearing the words of the Lord ... They will go to and fro to seek the word of the Lord, But they will not find it' (Amos 8:11, 12b). Ezekiel promised a day would come when '... [T]hey will seek a vision from a prophet, but the law will be lost from the priest and counsel from the elders' (Ezek. 7:26). Micah warned of a time when '[I]t will be night for you – without vision, And darkness for you – without divination. The sun will go down on the prophets, And the day will become dark over them. The seers will be ashamed And the diviners will be embarrassed. Indeed, they will all cover their mouths Because there is no answer from God' (Mic. 3:6-7). In exile, the people lamented that 'There is no longer any prophet' (Ps. 74:9).

Where God's word is absent, 'the people are unrestrained.' The Hebrew verb means 'to let loose.' It can refer to the cutting (Lev. 10:6; 13:45; 21:10) or unbraiding (Num. 5:18) of one's hair.[42] Still today, we speak of 'letting one's hair down' as a metaphor of living a wild, undisciplined life.[43] In Proverbs, it is used of neglecting (in the sense of letting slip through one's fingers) God's word and discipline (Prov. 1:25; 8:33; 13:18; 15:32). When one 'lets go' of God's revealed will (through either willful neglect or rebellion), he also lets go of the reins of his conduct and character. Believing in nothing, he comes to believe anything. He is at the whim of circumstances, hormones, and emotions.

Perhaps most notably, the word is used twice in Exodus 32:25 to describe the riotous orgy of the Hebrews under Aaron's watch, as Moses was on Mount Sinai receiving God's Law. This may well form a historical backdrop for the proverb, or, at least, serve as a dramatic illustration of its truth. Without God's revealed will, every opinion is equally valid and no truth is had to guide the way (Prov. 28:4a; Judg. 17:6; 21:25). Not only does such a one not hear from God, but God refuses to hear him (Prov. 28:9).

On the other hand, where God's word is preached, embraced, and obeyed, we find 'happy' individuals (Ps. 1:1, 2; 19:11; 106:3; 119:2; Prov. 8:32). Hezekiah, whose men compiled these proverbs at his direction (Prov. 25:1), 'kept His commandments, which the LORD had commanded Moses' and as a result 'the LORD was with him, wherever he went he prospered' (2 Kings 18:6-7). When in distress over the impending attack of Assyria, Hezekiah listened to the prophetic word through Isaiah (2 Kings 19:2-7, 20-34) and the nation was miraculously delivered (vv. 35-37). Later, Isaiah sent a word about Hezekiah's impending death (2 Kings 20:1), but Hezekiah begged God not to honor this word (vv. 2-3) and God sent Isaiah back with word of His change of heart (vv. 4-11). Hezekiah later received another rebuke from Isaiah and, again, accepted it (vv. 12-21).

How powerful is the faithful preaching of God's word! Through it, God can tame an entire society. Where it is missing, every form of evil is eventually embraced.

29:19. A slave will not be instructed by words alone; For though he understands, there will be no response.
This verse arose from a day where the work arrangements were very different than in our own. Often, a 'slave' was a part of the household life and industry. For that reason, that 'slave' was often treated more as one of the family (cf. vv. 15, 17 and the discipline of children) than as a modern day employee. Thankfully, today, in the western world, slavery has been obliterated. For this reason, our application of such passages must not be wooden, but in principle.

The first line makes a blanket statement that, at first blush, would seem to be true of all who held the station of 'slave.' Certainly, we know from Scripture that not every slave was of the poor moral quality of the one pictured here (e.g. Joseph in Egypt, Daniel in Babylon; cf. Prov. 17:2).[44] Generally, however, slaves were considered to be of low character.[45]

The problem envisioned is of a slave who 'will not be instructed by words alone.' As we have discovered in the case of children, words are a very important part of the overall discipline of a family (cf. Prov. 1:8). However, in the case of this slave, the words are useless. Mental inability is not this slave's problem 'For ... he understands.' The words are clear. The master has communicated well. The slave understands the master's wishes. There simply is 'no response.' The word translated 'response' means to answer. Here, it is not simply that there is no verbal response from the slave, but that there is no obedient response to the instructions given by the master.[46]

The particular 'slave' in view here is obstinate and willful. What should be done with such a one when verbal instruction lays bare his resolute defiance (cf. v. 21)? The implication of the proverb is that it will take corporal discipline to move this defiant servant. This was recognized as permissible, perhaps even advisable here (cf. Papyrus Insinger, 14:11: 'If the stick is far from the master, the servant does not listen to him.'),[47] but there were divine regulations to keep it from being extreme (Exod. 21:20, 26-27). Certainly, today, this measure would be out of the question. When an employer finds an employee surly and unresponsive to direction, he must be willing to up the ante to get that employee's attention. That may take the form of withholding pay increases or incentives, passing over the employee during promotions, and even dismissal. Some employees will respond to no other type of motivation.

Certainly, Christians in the workplace should exhibit a better attitude toward those in authority over them (1 Tim. 6:1-2; Eph. 6:5-9; Col. 3:22-4:1; Titus 2:9-10). As with the individual and God, so the employee may find that, through conscientious commitment to the success of his employer, he becomes less of a 'slave' and more a part of the larger 'family' the business place can sometimes offer (John 15:14-15; Gal. 4:7).

29:20. Do you see a man who is hasty in his words? There is more hope for a fool than for him.
The previous verse dealt with defiant silence, this with unrestrained babble.[48] This saying has already appeared in Proverbs 26:12, with but one change. Instead of 'a man who is hasty in his words,' there it is 'a man wise in his own eyes.'

Proverbs views haste, in general, as a pathway to trouble. It can lead to rash actions (Prov. 19:2), loss of advantage in social interchange (Prov. 21:5), and punishment (Prov. 28:20). When one is hasty to get rich (Prov. 13:11; 28:20), he ends up only in poverty (Prov. 21:5).

Here the problem is 'hasty ... words.' While 'There is more hope for a fool than for him,' it is precisely the fool who is quick to speak (Prov. 12:16, 23). Such a one speaks without first listening (Prov. 18:13). He gushes forth whatever comes to mind (Prov. 15:2, 28). 'Where there are many words, transgression is unavoidable' (Prov. 10:19a).

The contrast, of course, is that wisdom is found in holding one's tongue. '... [H]e who restrains his lips is wise' (Prov. 10:19b). 'He who restrains his words has knowledge, And he who has a cool spirit is a man of understanding. Even a fool, when he keeps silent, is considered wise; When he closes his lips, he is counted prudent.' (Prov. 17:27-28). 'Let everyone be quick to hear, slow to speak and slow to anger' (James 1:19). 'Do not be hasty in word or impulsive in thought' (Eccles. 5:2).

The second line demands that 'There is more hope for a fool than for him.' As noted above, the proper label for one who is hasty in speech is 'fool,' but the point here is that even a fool has some hope (however slim) of coming to wisdom. But, the one who is 'hasty in his words' has little or no opportunity. Having blurted out his ill-conceived and poorly thought-through ideas, he finds his thoughts on public record. His pride demands that he defend those ideas to the end. His resolute will refuses to budge even when the weight of evidence rests with the other side. He dies defending his rightness. Here, the word for 'fool' describes one who is dull, but not necessarily defiant.[49] At least, the 'fool' might learn something.

29:21. He who pampers his slave from childhood Will in the end find him to be a son.

The great struggle in understanding this verse lies in the fact that the Hebrew words translated 'pampers' and 'a son' both appear only here in the Old Testament. The former seems surely to have some such meaning as is represented here, for it is later attested to in other Hebrew writings.[50] The first line, then, pictures a slave that has probably been born into a family of slaves, all of whom serve a particular master. That master, then, determines under what conditions that child is raised. He apparently sees that he is raised in a soft manner, perhaps out of tender sentiments. The trouble is that he raises him to enter a life that can never be his. He is left completely unprepared for the hash realities of the toilsome experience that will be his for a lifetime as a slave (cf. v. 19). This appears to be a major argument for the 'nurture' rather than 'nature' debate. You will get what you raise.

The second line is more difficult to understand. That it presents some negative consequence which flows from the actions of the first line seems clear. But, commentators and translators have been baffled as to the meaning of 'a son.' Along with the NASB, the RSV, KJV and NKJV understand it as coming from a Hebrew word meaning offspring, progeny or heir. The NIV follows the LXX and translates as 'he will bring grief in the end.' The NRSV seems to follow suit: 'will come to a bad end.' The NEB and JB take it as a reference to his lack of gratitude ('ungrateful'). While certainty will elude us, probably some notion of 'son' or 'heir' is best, for Proverbs has often compared the slave and the 'son' or 'heir' (Prov. 17:2; 19:10; 30:22).[51]

While the meaning of one word may be obscure, the point of the proverb is not. We must train people to succeed in the life they will lead. Slavery is rightly abhorrent to us and we should seek, like our best forefathers, to end it wherever it may still be practiced. Beyond that, we can learn here, however, that we best serve an individual by helping him succeed in the realities he will have to live in, rather than those which we would wish he might live in. This is particularly applicable to those who serve to fulfill the Great Commission in cross-cultural contexts. The goal is not to raise up Christians after the model of our culture of origin, but to raise up disciples of Christ who will live out His commands in the midst of their own culture. We fail both them and our Master unless we train them to live in this way.

29:22. An angry man stirs up strife, And a hot-tempered man abounds in transgression.
The first line of this proverb is nearly identical to Proverbs 15:18. There, it is used in an adversative parallelism, here in a synonymous one.[52] The word used there of anger points to heat, this word is, more literally, 'nose.' The word came to be used for anger because the nostrils might flare in anger or the angry man might let forth a snort through the nose, indicating his ire. This word points particularly to the emotional aspects of anger.[53]

A man with a bent toward this uncontrollable emotion 'stirs up strife.' The precise phrase is found in Proverbs 15:18. The word 'stirs up' is most often used in Scripture in contexts of warfare.[54] If there is any ember of contention still smoldering beneath the surface of formal social conventions, then this man can find it and fan it to flame once again (Prov. 6:14; 14:17, 29; 19:19; 22:24; 30:33). He joins with the 'perverse man' (Prov. 16:28), the 'contentious man' (Prov. 26:21) and the 'arrogant man' (Prov. 28:25) in their ability to agitate any social setting.

The parallel expression in the second line is 'a hot-tempered man.' He is, more literally, 'an owner of wrath.' The word translated 'hot-tempered' comes from the verb to 'be hot' and is the word used in Proverbs 15:18 in the first line. It describes heat, hot displeasure, indignation, anger or wrath.[55]

A man in such a condition is not just occasionally angry, but is given to anger. Anger colors most of what he sees, thinks, feels, and does. The result is that his relationships horizontally ('stirs up strife') and vertically ('abounds in transgressions') are broken. Note, he 'abounds' in transgression. He not only owns wrath, but is a champion at sin. Where there is anger, sin is seldom far behind. 'A quick-tempered man acts foolishly' (Prov. 14:17a). '... [H]e who is quick-tempered exalts folly' (Prov. 14:29b). Indeed, 'A man of great anger shall bear the penalty' (Prov. 19:19a).

It is self-control this man needs: 'A fool always loses his temper, But a wise man holds it back' (Prov. 29:11a). 'He who is slow to anger has great understanding' (Prov. 14:29a). '... [T]he slow to anger pacifies contention' (Prov. 15:18b). 'He who is slow to anger is better than the mighty, And he who rules his spirit, than he who captures a city' (Prov. 16:32). We should not even 'associate with a man given to anger; Or go with a hot-tempered man' because we might 'learn his ways, And find a snare' for ourselves (Prov. 22:24-25).

29:23. A man's pride will bring him low, But a humble spirit will obtain honor.
Here, again, is the oft-repeated theme of 'pride' and 'a humble spirit.' Proverbs repeatedly tells us that God is opposed to the proud. It stands directly opposed to the fear of the Lord, the major theme of this book (Prov. 8:13; 15:33; 22:4). Indeed, the proud man is an abomination to the Lord (Prov. 16:5). Little wonder that God guarantees to 'bring him low.' Pride pulls 'dishonor' (Prov. 11:2), 'destruction' (Prov. 16:18; 18:12), and 'stumbling' (Prov. 16:18) in its train. Nebuchadnezzar boasted of his sovereignty, but was brought down by the true Sovereign (Dan. 4:30-31). Jesus added His voice to this assurance: '[W]hoever exalts himself shall be humbled' (Matt. 23:12a), as did his half-brother James: 'God is opposed to the proud' (James 4:6).

On the other hand ('But'), one who possesses humility 'will obtain honor.' Humility not only pulls 'honor' (Prov. 15:33; 18:12b) in its train, but also 'riches' and 'life' (Prov. 22:4). Humility is paralleled with the fear of the Lord (Prov. 15:33; 22:4). 'But to this one I will look, To him who is humble and contrite of spirit, and who trembles at My word' (Isa. 66:2b). Jesus promises, '[H]e who humbles himself shall be exalted' (Luke 14:11; 18:14b). 'Humble yourselves in the presence of the Lord, and He will exalt you' (Prov. 4:10). 'Humble yourselves, therefore, under the mighty hand of God, that He may exalt you at the proper time' (1 Pet. 5:6).

The irony of God's justice is inescapable: By lifting yourself up, you bring yourself low, and by recognizing your lowliness, you incite God to lift you up.

29:24. He who is a partner with a thief hates his own life; He hears the oath but tells nothing.
This proverb employs synthetic parallelism – the second line explains and expands upon the first. The first line pictures one 'who is partner with a thief.' He is a partner in the sense that for whatever service rendered in the plot he receives a divided portion of the goods taken.[56] Was he enticed (Prov. 1:11-19)? Did he see and enter in on his own initiative (Ps. 50:18)? We aren't told the circumstances, but we are called to discern that such a one 'hates his own life.' Proverbs speaks often of actions that are ultimately self-destructive (Prov. 6:32; 8:36; 15:32; 20:2). Playing any knowing part in a crime is just such an act.

In just what way his involvement proves to be self-destructive is now explained in the second line. The accomplice 'hears the oath.' The Hebrew word for 'oath' refers to a curse which clings to an individual who breaks a contract.[57] For example, in Judges 17:2, the one from whom something has been stolen pronounces a curse upon the thief.

Here, the problem is that 'He hears the oath' (a call for all who have any knowledge of the crime to come forward with testimony), yet he 'tells nothing.' Leviticus 5:1 called upon all who had knowledge of a theft to come forward with information, on punishment of a curse. Thus, in addition to his guilt over participating in a theft, he now adds the crime of perjury. The emphasis may not be so much upon the addition of another legal charge, but the fear of the curse that now pursues him wherever he goes. Whatever his primary concern (and probably it was both), the answer is full and open disclosure and confession.

29:25. The fear of man brings a snare, But he who trusts in the LORD will be exalted.
As we near the conclusion of the Hezekiah collection (Prov. 25:1–29:27), the scribes bring us back to the primary theme of the entire book: the fear of the Lord (e.g. Prov. 1:7; 9:10; 31:10). It is not arrived at directly, but by contrast. Here, the concern is the 'fear of man.' The Hebrew word for 'fear' is not the same as that found in the references to the fear of the Lord. Rather than pointing to reverence, this word describes the quaking terror elicited by an unexpected happening.[58]

The 'fear of man' is 'a snare' that tripped up some of God's greatest servants. Abraham feared Abimelech and twice lied about his wife Sarah (Gen. 12:11-13; 20:2, 11). His son Isaac followed his father's example (Gen. 26:7). While Moses beheld the glory of God on the mountain, Aaron was succumbing to the fear of man in the valley (Exod. 32:22-24). Israel's first king stumbled here (1 Sam. 15:24), as did the prophet Elijah (1 Kings 19:3). The 'fear of man' incited Peter to deny Christ (Matt. 26:69-74). Even after his restoration and the coming of the Holy Spirit, he was beset by it (Gal. 2:11-13). Many of the rulers believed in Jesus, but for fear of the Pharisees did not go public with their faith (John 12:42). Nicodemus came under cover of night to Jesus (John 3:1-72; 19:39).

The 'fear of man' is that which entices us to change our character, conviction or conduct because of the intimidation of standing alone for God. Jesus warned against it in the strongest terms: 'Do not fear those who kill the body, but are unable to kill the soul; but rather fear Him who is able to destroy both soul and body in hell' (Matt. 10:28). You cannot fear both God and man: 'Of whom were you worried and fearful, When you lied, and did not remember Me, Nor give Me a thought? Was I not silent even for a long time So you do not fear Me?' (Isa. 57:11; cf. 51:12).

This 'brings a snare' in that it promises one thing and delivers another. It appears expedient to curb our convictions to the opinions of those around us. It appears the better part of wisdom to alter our God-directed course. There will be time to return and take up God's agenda. We will live for another day and can then do His bidding. This is always a deception. This 'snare' is a trap set by oneself when he chooses to fear man more than honor God. 'He who trusts in his own heart is a fool' (Prov. 28:26a).

The alternative to the 'fear of man' is to trust in the Lord. Elsewhere in Proverbs, we are exhorted to trust in the character (or name, Prov. 18:10) and word of God (Prov. 16:20; cf. 30:5) with all our hearts (Prov. 3:5-6). Such a man 'will prosper' (Prov. 28:25b). To trust God rather than to fear man is to obey God's clear directives, regardless of popular opinion, apparent wisdom or the prospects for success. Consider Daniel (Dan. 6:1-23), his three friends (Dan. 3:1-28), and the apostles (Acts 5:29) as examples.

The one who demonstrates his trust through obedience 'will be exalted.' The word is a military term which means, literally, 'set on high' (i.e. they are kept above the threats of the enemy).[59] For similar expressions by Solomon's father, David, see Psalm 27:4-5; 69:29 and 91:14. Solomon apparently had learned well from his father (Prov. 14:26). Indeed, 'It is better to take refuge in the Lord Than to trust in man' (Ps. 118:8).

29:26. Many seek the ruler's favor, But justice for man comes from the Lord.

Whereas the previous proverb spoke of the trap of the fear of man, this proverb addresses the folly of ultimate reliance upon man.

Once again, as often in this chapter, the center of attention is upon the ruler of the nation (vv. 2, 4, 12, 14). It is the normal course for humans ('Many') to look to those persons about them whom they believe possess the power or position to grant what they think is due them. The 'ruler's favor' is, more literally, 'the face of the ruler.' The face often reveals the mood and feelings of a person. It, thus, was used as an expression for one's emotions, attitudes, and biases.[60] A similar expression is found in Proverbs 19:6, where people are seeking the face of the generous man.

Solomon knew whereof he wrote, being the goal and hope of many a person's pursuit. The Queen of Sheba came looking for an audience with the king (1 Kings 10:1-4). Indeed, it was said that the entire world wanted to court his favor (1 Kings 10:24)!

Of particular concern here is the king's perceived ability to bring 'justice.' That is why he enjoys the position he does (Prov. 8:15; 16:10; Rom. 13:1-5).[61] Yet, ultimately, one's 'justice ... comes from the LORD' and not a person He has set in place to administer His authority on earth. 'The king's heart is like channels of water in the hand of the LORD; He turns it wherever He wishes' (Prov. 21:1). Only God 'gives justice to the afflicted' (Job 36:6b). God controls even the outcome of what appears a random roll of the dice (Prov. 16:33). '... [S]urely the justice due to Me is with the LORD' (Isa. 49:4). 'Therefore, let those also who suffer ... entrust their souls to a faithful Creator in doing what is right' (1 Pet. 4:19).

'Do not trust in princes, In mortal man, in whom there is no salvation. His spirit departs, he returns to the earth; In that very day his thoughts perish. How blessed is he whose help is the God of Jacob, Whose hope is in the LORD his God; Who made heaven and earth, The sea and all that is in them; Who keeps faith forever; Who executes justice for the oppressed; Who gives food to the hungry. The LORD sets the prisoners free' (Ps. 146:3-7).

29:27. An unjust man is abominable to the righteous, And he who is upright in the way is abominable to the wicked.
Justice and injustice, righteousness and wickedness share a mutual dislike for one another. The word behind both occurrences of 'abominable' is a strong one, normally translated 'abomination.' An abomination is an attitude or action that is found to be so repugnant as to be unendurable.[62] Proverbs speaks often of that which is an abomination to the Lord (e.g. 6:16; 11:20; 15:9). Because God loathes these things, they come under His judgment. Things elsewhere listed as an abomination to the Lord include idolatry (Deut. 7:25), homosexuality and other sexual perversions (Lev. 18:22-30; 20:13), human sacrifice (Deut. 12:31), occult activity (Deut. 18:9-14), ritual prostitution (1 Kings 14:23f.), dishonest business practices (Deut. 25:13-16), and sacrificing unclean, or defective, animals (Deut. 14:3-8; 17:1).[63]

Here, 'he who is upright' feels this way toward 'the wicked' (cf. Ps. 139:21-22), and, in so doing, he sides with the Lord (Prov. 11:20). There is no surprise here, except to the sinner. What is astonishing is that the 'unjust man' feels this revulsion toward 'the righteous' (cf. v. 10). There is an air of righteous superiority in his disgust. Having chosen a path of unholiness, he, nevertheless, is so deluded as to defend with 'holy' zeal his ungodly ways from the 'infidels' who would dare censure his conduct and threaten his rights! In his sin, he has embraced an inverted ethic and morality. God still says to such folk: 'Woe to those who call evil good, and good evil; Who substitute darkness for light and light for darkness; Who substitute bitter for sweet, and sweet for bitter!' (Isa. 5:20).

This mutual enmity is a product of the fall of man and God's curse (Gen. 3:15). Jesus reminded His followers often that they would feel the sulfurous breath of such hatred (Matt. 10:22; 24:9; John 15:18; 17:14; 1 John 3:13). The Apostle Paul made clear the definite divide between righteousness and unrighteousness (2 Cor. 6:14-18).

With this proverb, the Solomonic collection comes to an end (Prov. 1:1–22:16; 25:1-29:27), as well as the subsection of Hezekiah's editors (Prov. 25:1-29:27). Solomon's proverbs began by introducing the 'king' (Prov. 1:1) and, fittingly, have ended on the same note (v. 26). Proverbs has rigorously detailed the divide between the righteous and the wicked. It is fitting that the whole should be concluded by the starkest statement of that contrast here.

There remain before us only the three appendices (The words of Agur: Prov. 30:1-33; The words of Lemuel: Prov. 31:1-9; and the poem about the virtuous woman: Prov. 31:10-31).

End Notes

1. Delitzsch, F., *Proverbs, Ecclesiastes, Song of Solomon* (three volumes in one) in C. F. Keil and F. Delitzsch, vol. 6, *Commentary on the Old Testament* (in ten volumes), (1872; rpt. Grand Rapids, Michigan: William B. Eerdmans Publishing Company, 1980), 1:145.

2. Ibid., 146.

3. Whybray, R. N., *Proverbs* (Grand Rapids, Michigan: William B. Eerdmans Publishing Company, 1994), 397.

4. Cohen, A., *Proverbs* (London: The Soncino Press, 1946), 193.

5. Murphy, Roland E., *Proverbs* (Nashville: Thomas Nelson Publishers, 1998), 221.

6. Cohen, 193.

7. Allen, Ronald B., "*āmad*,' *Theological Wordbook of the Old Testament* (Chicago: Moody Press, 1980), 2:673.

8. Cohen, 194.

9. Ross, Allen P., 'Proverbs,' *The Expositor's Bible Commentary* (Grand Rapids, Michigan: Zondervan Publishing House, 1991), 5:1112; Delitzsch, 2:242-243.

10. Ross, 5:1112.

11. Whybray, 399.

12. Cohen, 150.

13. Schultz, Richard, 'שׁפט,' *New International Dictionary of Old Testament Theology and Exegesis* (Grand Rapids, Michigan: Zondervan Publishing House, 1997), 4:213-220.

14. Culver, Robert D., '*shāpat*' *Theological Wordbook of the Old Testament* (Chicago: Moody Press, 1980), 2:947-949.

15. Cohen, 195.

16. Brown, Francis, S. R. Driver, Charles A. Briggs, *A Hebrew and English Lexicon of the Old Testament* (Oxford: Clarendon Press, n.d.), 629.

17. Van Groningen, Gerhard, 'ŝāmah,' *Theological Wordbook of the Old Testament* (Chicago: Moody Press, 1980), 2:879-880.

18. Ross, 5:1113; Cohen, 195; Murphy, 220; Delitzsch, 2:246-248.

19. Gilchrist, Paul R., 'yāsā',' *Theological Wordbook of the Old Testament* (Chicago: Moody Press, 1980), 1:393.

20. Cohen, 195.

21. Cohen, Gary G., 'shābah,' *Theological Wordbook of the Old Testament* (Chicago: Moody Press, 1980), 2:896.

22. Buzzell, Sid S., 'Proverbs,' *The Bible Knowledge Commentary* (Wheaton: Victor Books, 1985), 1:968.

23. Arnold, Bill T., 'אחר,' *New International Dictionary of Old Testament Theology and Exegesis* (Grand Rapids, Michigan: Zondervan Publishing House, 1997), 1:360-361.

24. Murphy, 220 and Whybray, 401.

25. Coppes, Leonard J., 'qāshab,' *Theological Wordbook of the Old Testament* (Chicago: Moody Press, 1980), 2:817.

26. Delitzsch, 2:249.

27. Grisanti, Michael A., 'פגשׁ,' *New International Dictionary of Old Testament Theology and Exegesis* (Grand Rapids, Michigan: Zondervan Publishing House, 1997), 3:577-578.

28. Delitzsch, 2:250.

29. Oswalt, John N., 'kûn,' *Theological Wordbook of the Old Testament* (Chicago: Moody Press, 1980), 1:433-434.

30. Lane, Eric, *Proverbs* (Scotland: Christian Focus Publications, 2000), 123.

31. Austel, Hermann J., 'shālah,' *Theological Wordbook of the Old Testament* (Chicago: Moody Press, 1980), 2:927-928.

32. Delitzsch, 2:250.

33. Whybray, 402.

34. Allen, 5:1115.

35. Whybray, 397.

36. Ibid., 402.

37. Gilchrist, Paul R., 'yāsar,' *Theological Wordbook of the Old Testament* (Chicago: Moody Press, 1980), 1:386-387.

38. Coppes, Leonard J., 'nûah,' *Theological Wordbook of the Old Testament* (Chicago: Moody Press, 1980), 2:562-563.

39. Naudé, Jackie A., 'חזה,' *New International Dictionary of Old Testament Theology and Exegesis* (Grand Rapids, Michigan: Zondervan Publishing House, 1997), 2:58-59.

40. Walls, A. F., 'Proverbs' in *The New Bible Commentary: Revised* (Grand Rapids, Michigan: William B. Eerdmans Publishing Company, 1970), 568.

41. McKane, William, *Proverbs: A New Approach* (Philadelphia: The Westminster Press, 1970), 640-641.

42. Hamilton, Victor P., 'par'ōh,' *Theological Wordbook of the Old Testament* (Chicago: Moody Press, 1980), 2:736-737.

43. Kidner, 176.

44. Ross, 5:1116.

45. Cohen, 197.

46. Delitzsch, 2:253.

47. Murphy, 223.

48. Bridges, Charles, *A Commentary on Proverbs* (Edinburgh: The Banner of Truth Trust, 1846, reprint 1998), 579.

49. Goldberg, Louis, 'kāsal,' *Theological Wordbook of the Old Testament* (Chicago: Moody Press, 1980), 1:449-450.

50. Whybray, 404.

51. Lane, 320.

52. Whybray, 404.

53. Van Groningen, Gerard, ''ānēp,' *Theological Wordbook of the Old Testament* (Chicago: Moody Press, 1980), 1:58.

54. Waltke, Bruce K., '*gara*,' *Theological Wordbook of the Old Testament* (Chicago: Moody Press, 1980), 1:171.

55. Van Groningen, Gerard, '*yaham*,' *Theological Wordbook of the Old Testament* (Chicago: Moody Press, 1980), 1:374-375.

56. Wiseman, Donald J., '*hālaq*,' *Theological Wordbook of the Old Testament* (Chicago: Moody Press, 1980), 1:292-293.

57. Gordon, Robert P., 'אלה,' *New International Dictionary of Old Testament Theology and Exegesis* (Grand Rapids, Michigan: Zondervan Publishing House, 1997), 1:403-405.

58. Van Pelt, M. V. and W. C. Kaiser, Jr., 'חרד,' *New International Dictionary of Old Testament Theology and Exegesis* (Grand Rapids, Michigan: Zondervan Publishing Company, 1997), 2:263-265.

59. Ross, 5:1025.

60. Hamilton, Victor P., '*pānâ*,' *Theological Wordbook of the Old Testament* (Chicago: Moody Press, 1980), 2:727-728.

61. Lane, 314.

62. Whybray, 73.

63. Youngblood, Ronald F., '*to'eba*,' *Theological Wordbook of the Old Testament* (Chicago: Moody Press, 1980), 2:977.

Proverbs 30

30:1. The words of Agur the son of Jakeh, the oracle. The man declares to Ithiel, to Ithiel and Ucal:

With Solomon's proverbs now behind us, chapter 30 begins a series of three appendices: (Prov. 30:1-33; 31:1-9; 31:10-31). That this opening verse serves as a title for the first appendix is apparent. Beyond this, virtually every word of this verse has been disputed and debated by commentators.

'Agur' was taken by older Jewish commentators as a veiled reference to Solomon. This view, however, holds little in its favor. What would be gained by such a riddled reference to the one who has been so obviously touted as the author of the earlier parts of the book? The name 'Agur' appears to be non-Hebrew, and is probably of non-Israelite origin.[1] It is a name not otherwise known to us. The only textual help we have in identifying 'Agur' is in the designation 'the son of Jakeh.' But, this actually helps us little, for this too appears to be a non-Hebrew name that is not otherwise found in the Scriptures.

What follows are called 'The words ... the oracle.' The Hebrew word for 'oracle' normally describes a prophetic message given by God and poured through a messenger (prophet), who personally feels the weight of this message (e.g. Zech. 9:1; Mal. 1:1). It may be translated 'burden' because of its weighty subject matter and import. This would seem to add great gravity to the words that follow in the rest of the chapter. However, because the term is normally reserved for prophetic utterances and not Wisdom Literature, some (cf. RSV and the NIV margin) have seen in it a reference to a personal name (Massa, a son of Ishmael and his clan, Gen. 25:14-16; 1 Chron. 1:30) or a place-name (Massa, the region in northern Arabia where he lived).[2] The same word occurs in Proverbs 31:1, and if it is a reference to a place, then Lemuel would have been Agur's ruler.[3] The matter is not easy to settle, but there seems no compelling reason to read this as other than 'oracle.'

Beyond this, we may assume that he was likely one of the other recognized sages that ministered in Solomon's day (1 Kings 4:30-31).

677

If the Hebrew is read as 'the oracle the man spoke,' then it is a phrase also used of Balaam (Num. 24:3) and David (2 Sam. 23:1).

The second line is even more disputed than the first. 'Ithiel' and 'Ucal' are names otherwise unknown to us, except for a reference to one 'Ithiel' in Nehemiah 11:7. They may have been disciples or pupils of Agur, but we are not certain.

Because of this obscurity, many have concluded that, instead of reading them as personal names, the Hebrew consonantal text should be divided and vocalized differently, yielding a meaning that does not designate the recipients of these words, but rather serves as the beginning of the 'oracle' itself. The LXX lends some support to this hypothesis, but the problem is that no consistent translation of the text results. The suggestions range from 'I am weary, O God, and am consumed' to 'O that God would be with me that I might understand' to (viewing it as Aramaic instead of Hebrew) 'I am not a god that I should have power.'[4] Given the difficulty in deciding just what the text should be if it is thus re-divided and vocalized, it is probably best to retain the understanding that these are obscure personal names.

The style of this chapter is markedly different from that which has preceded, confirming the introduction of a different author. We find here a style that does not quite conform to either the discourses of Proverbs 1–9 or the sentence literature of Proverbs 10–29. Verses 1-4 tend toward the discourse style, but are cut short of the normal length. Numeric proverbs collect in most of the rest of the chapter (vv. 7-9, 15-17, 18-20, 21-23, 24-28, 29-31), though there are notable exceptions to this as well (vv. 5-6, 10, 11-14, 32-33).

All this debate about the exact identity of 'Agur' and the recipients of this portion does serve to remind us that wisdom is not the exclusive domain of only one man, no matter how great, but is available to anyone who will humble himself (as this author so obviously does, vv. 2-4) and seek God. What an honor it must have been for 'Agur' to have his writings recognized as Holy Spirit-inspired and placed alongside those of Solomon!

30:2. Surely I am more stupid than any man, And I do not have the understanding of a man.

To our twenty-first-century ears, these opening words of Agur seem overstated almost to the point of being phony. Yet, understood in context, they make a profound and needed point.

The word translated 'stupid' is cognate with the word for 'cattle.'[5] The translation 'brutish' has been suggested.[6] Agur sees himself as moving forward only in animal-like instincts (Ps. 49:10; 73:22). The point is that Agur sees himself as having risen barely above the animal level in his ability to search out and know God (v. 4ff). The second line affirms and reinforces the first, in that he has failed to attain to even the insight that his being made in the image of God should afford him.

These broad-ranging statements must be understood in context. The particular want of knowledge and insight is not all-inclusive, but related to 'the knowledge of the Holy One' (v. 3b). When it comes to searching out and knowing God, Agur sees his utter bankruptcy. The rhetorical questions of verse 4 provide the contemplative soil out of which Agur's despair in this verse has grown.

The book opened by asserting that 'The fear of the Lord is the beginning of knowledge' (Prov. 1:7a). What, then, we find here is, in actual fact, not total despair of wisdom, but the beginning of its discovery. Agur has seen something of God (v. 4) and, now, in His light, he has seen himself (vv. 2-3). Paul's view of himself changed when he saw the glorious Christ and he could never escape it (1 Tim. 1:15). He came to insist that, 'If anyone supposes that he knows anything, he has not yet known as he ought to know' (1 Cor. 8:2). He demanded that God's wisdom was not to be found along the plane of human reasoning, but by divine revelation to the human soul (1 Cor. 2:6-16). Agur would agree heartily with Paul.

30:3. Neither have I learned wisdom, Nor do I have the knowledge of the Holy One.

Agur's lament over his lack of wisdom continues from verse 2. All this sounds like Solomon's complaint in Ecclesiastes 7:23-24: 'I tested all this with wisdom, and I said, "I will be wise," but it was far from me. What has been is remote and exceedingly mysterious. Who can discover it?'

Note the parallelism of 'wisdom' and 'the knowledge of the Holy One.' True wisdom is not anthropocentric, but theocentric. We will never truly discover wisdom by looking inward, but only by looking upward. To know God is to begin to discover His world. To study His world without knowing Him is to consign one's self to futility.

Without expressly stating it, Agur has brought us back again to the theme of the book of Proverbs: The fear of the Lord. 'The fear of the LORD is the beginning of wisdom, And the knowledge of the Holy One is understanding' (Prov. 9:10; cf. Prov. 1:7; 2:5; 15:33). The title 'Holy One' is found in Proverbs only here and in 9:10 (cf. Hosea 11:12). Both times it is in the plural form, serving as a plural of majesty.

30:4. Who has ascended into heaven and descended? Who has gathered the wind in His fists? Who has wrapped the waters in His garment? Who has established all the ends of the earth? What is His name or His son's name? Surely you know!

The crisis of spiritual and intellectual darkness described in verses 2-3 now reach its climax. Employing a series of five rhetorical questions reminiscent of Job 38–41 and Isaiah 40:12-25, Agur now calls all within the sound of his voice to join him in confessing such human inability. Commentators debate whether Agur is still speaking or whether another human, or even God, has taken center stage and is now putting these questions to Agur. While God asks the questions in Job 38 and Isaiah 40, there is no compelling reason to see a shift in speakers here.

The first four questions should be answered simply with the response: 'God!' The first question inquires about who is able to make the descent and ascent necessary to be intimately, and actively, involved in the affairs of both heaven and earth (Gen. 11:7; 28:12; Exod. 19:18; Deut. 30:12; Ps. 68:18; John 3:13; Eph. 4:8-9). Answer: God alone!

The second question employs anthropomorphism to inquire as to who might gather up the winds in his hands (Exod. 15:10; Ps. 104:3; 135:7; Isa. 40:12; Amos 4:13). Answer: God alone!

The third question uses the metaphor of a 'garment' to describe the clouds in the sky as they hold 'the waters' in them (Job 26:8; 38:8, 9). Who is capable of creating and sustaining such a process? Answer: God alone!

The fourth question examines the ability to set the boundaries ('has fixed the boundaries of the earth,' NEB; 'has set all the ends of the earth,' JB) of the created world (Job 38:4; Ps. 24:1-2; Prov. 8:27-29; Isa. 45:18). Who is capable of this? Answer: God alone!

The fifth question, which is actually a double inquiry, is of a different nature from the first four. Whereas the first four questions inquired about a 'Who,' this question asks 'What?' The 'Who' of each of the first four questions is obviously God alone. Now, Agur wants to know 'What' is His name and that of His son. In the Hebrew mind, to know a person's name is to know his nature and character. Agur longs not just to examine the works of God (first four questions), but to know God Himself (fifth question). How can this be? As impossible as it is for man to search out all the wonders of God's creation, it is infinitely more difficult for him to discover God Himself. 'What is His name'? It is 'the Holy One' (v. 3), 'God (vv. 5, 9), and Yahweh ('LORD,' v. 9).

The second part of the question is even more arresting: 'What is... His son's name?' It is interesting that Agur saw God as possessing both an essential unity, as well as a plurality that allowed for such a question. Jewish interpreters understood this to be a reference to Jacob, others to a personification of wisdom (as in chapters 1–9), and still others to a demiurge.[7] The Jewish answer of Jacob (Israel) is probably closest to the point. God commanded Moses: 'Then you shall say to Pharaoh, 'Thus says the LORD, "Israel is My son, My first-born"' (Exod. 4:22; cf. Jer. 31:9; Hosea 11:1). Luke traced the genealogy of Jesus through Joseph, back through Jacob and, ultimately, to 'Adam, the son of God' (Luke 3:23-38). We who enjoy the full scope of Scriptural revelation under the illuminating influence of the Holy Spirit know that the answer to Agur's final question is Jesus Christ! We have the privilege, not of understanding every detail of how God designed and sustains His creation, but of knowing Him deeply in an intimate, personal, eternal relationship (John 17:3).

The verse ends with the challenge: 'Surely you know!' This sounds very much like God's demand of Job: 'Tell Me, if you have understanding ... Tell Me, if you know all this' (Job 38:4, 18). Is this sarcasm or a deep spiritual hunger? Having concluded that these are Agur's words and not God's, it appears that here we have Agur's pleading before anyone, and everyone, who might give his hungry heart direction toward the true knowledge of God.

30:5. Every word of God is tested; He is a shield to those who take refuge in Him.

Into Agur's dark despair of ever finding and knowing God (vv. 2-4) now breaks the brilliant rays of divine revelation. There is no finding and knowing God on man's terms (vv. 2-4), but God has revealed Himself to man. No knowledge of God is possible apart from His condescension to reveal Himself. Gladly, God has done this through the 'word of God.' Whoever Agur was, he was apparently acquainted with the Scriptures, for this is a virtual quotation of David's words in Psalm 18:30 and 2 Samuel 22:31. We have transitioned from 'The words of Agur' (v. 1) to the 'word of God.'[8]

The word for 'God' is 'ĕlōah, a name of disputed origin. It is found in Job forty-one times. It is found only here in Proverbs. It appears to be a very ancient term, being found in some of the oldest Scriptural poetry (Deut. 32:15, 17; Job). It is used sparingly in the rest of the Old Testament (e.g. Isa. 44:8; Hab. 3:3) and is then picked up later in post-exilic books like 2 Chronicles (32:15), Nehemiah (9:17) and Daniel (11:37-39).[9]

The emphasis of the first line is upon 'every word of God' (cf. 2 Tim. 3:16).[10] Each and every word in each and every line is 'tested' and found true. The Hebrew word describes the process of testing and purifying metal through the smelting process. Being found thus purified and proven, God's word is trustworthy in its revelation of Himself and His truth.[11] 'The words of the Lord are pure words; As silver tried in a furnace on the earth, refined seven times' (Ps. 12:6). 'Thy word is very pure, Therefore Thy servant loves it' (Ps. 119:140). 'The commandment of the Lord is pure, enlightening the eyes ... They are more desirable than gold, yes, than much fine gold' (Ps. 19:8b, 10a). To one desperate to know God, how precious His word is!

God's word is marvelous, not simply for the knowledge it imparts, but for the One it reveals! This God-who-speaks 'is a shield to those who take refuge in Him.' Our trust must be seen in active obedience ('takes refuge,' cf. Prov. 16:20). When God is thus trusted and obeyed, He is a 'refuge' that not even death can overcome (Prov. 14:32). 'But Thou, O Lord, art a shield about me' (Ps. 3:3a). 'For the Lord God is a sun and a shield' (Ps. 84:11a). 'He is a shield to those who walk in integrity' (Prov. 2:7b).

30:6. Do not add to His words Lest He reprove you, and you be proved a liar.

God's word is not only without error (v. 5), it is sufficient in its revelation of God and His ways (v. 6). In view of this sufficiency, Agur warns 'Do not add to His words.' This is an echo of Moses' warning in Deuteronomy 4:2 and 12:32, except that Moses added the warning of not taking away from what God has said. A similar warning serves to seal the canon of Scripture in Revelation 22:18: 'I testify to everyone who hears the words of the prophecy of this book: if anyone adds to them, God shall add to him the plagues which are written in this book.'

People have added to God's word in many ways. The false prophets added their own interpretations and passed them off as of divine authority (Jer. 28:15-17; 29:21-22, 31-32; Ezek. 13:7-9). The Jews added their meticulous rules and regulations (Matt. 15:9). The pre-Gnostics of Paul's day added their observations (Col. 2:21-22). Some, even after the apostles, have laid their tradition alongside the Scriptures. Cults lay their leader's books alongside the Scriptures and hold them to be of similar authority. Many today continue the trend in less formal ways, building their lives on a series of hunches, speculations and feelings, rather than upon the clear commands, prohibitions, and principles of Scripture.

The warning here is that God will 'reprove you' for supplementing His words. To be laid bare before the Lord is enough, but His reproof will also expose you as 'a liar' to all creation. Here, too, there are echoes of Job: 'Will you speak what is unjust for God, And speak what is deceitful for Him? Will you show partiality for Him? Will you contend for God? Will it be well when He examines you? Or will you deceive Him as one deceives a man?' (Job 13:7-9).

The Bible does not tell us everything there is to know. 'The secret things belong to the LORD our God, but the things revealed belong to us and to our sons forever, that we may observe all the words of this law' (Deut. 29:29). Scripture does give us more than we deserve to know and sufficient light to be brought to a saving relationship with God and enabled to walk with God in joyful and fruitful obedience. The Scriptures 'are able to give you the wisdom that leads to salvation through faith which is in Christ Jesus' (2 Tim. 3:15b). They are sufficient to render us 'equipped for every good work' (2 Tim. 3:17b). 'His divine power has granted to us everything pertaining to life and godliness ... He has granted to us His precious and magnificent promises, in order that by them you might become partakers of the divine nature' (2 Pet. 1:3a, 4a).

30:7. Two things I asked of Thee, Do not refuse me before I die:
This verse introduces the first of six numeric proverbs (vv. 15-17; 18-20; 21-23; 24-28; 29-31). Proverbs 6:16-19 provides the only other such numeric proverbs in this book.

The form is that of prayer, even though there is no mention of the divine name.[12] The plea is found in this verse, the content of the request in verse 8 and the motive for the petition in verse 9. Agur says that he has only two requests that he would like to be proved true in the rest of his earthly experience. Some commentators insist that there are actually three requests given (kept from lying, kept in neither wealth nor poverty, and kept with daily provision).[13] In actual fact, the last two probably form one petition, seen from two sides. To be kept from the extremes of wealth and poverty is to be given just what one needs each day.

The expression 'Do not refuse me before I die' does not necessarily mean that Agur felt his end was near. These are not the pleas of a dying man. He asks that these two things be true of his experience for the rest of his life, however long that may be.[14]

Agur's requests reflect a good deal of humility (for he knew his areas of greatest weakness) and self-control (for he could have asked for many things).

30:8. Keep deception and lies far from me, Give me neither poverty nor riches; Feed me with the food that is my portion,
Following the introduction to his prayer (v. 7), Agur now lays out the specifics of his requests. As mentioned under the previous verse, some have concluded that there are three, not two requests, as advertised (v. 7). There are three lines to this verse, yet the final two form one request.

Agur begins his petitions: 'Keep deception and lies far from me.' The word behind 'deception' is the one used in the third commandment: 'You shall not take the name of the Lord your God in vain' (Exod. 20:7; Deut. 5:11). The word basically describes that which is empty, hollow, unreal, unsubstantial and, therefore, worthless. In this connection it is, then, used often to describe idols. Thus, idols are considered to be a deception.[15] Perhaps the point is that Agur wishes to be saved from spiritual deception, whether that means his being deceived or his deceiving others.[16] After all, being deceived and becoming a deceiver are never far removed from one another (1 John 1:6-8). The second word is a more standard word for lying, deception and falsehood.

The second request consists of two lines. Agur first asks that God keep him from the extremes of financial life: 'poverty or riches.' God is the One who makes both the rich and the poor (1 Sam. 2:7). The request is somewhat surprising, given that Proverbs generally speaks of riches as a reward for wise living (e.g. Prov. 3:16; 8:18; 10:22). At the same time, the lack of riches is at times preferred (Prov. 15:16-17; 16:8; 17:1).

The second part of this request is that God would 'Feed me with the food that is my portion.' By 'portion' is not meant simply what I need to sustain life for that day, but the allotment which God, in His wise sovereignty, deems to be correct for me.[17] The Apostle Paul found this restful place of contentment: 'I have learned to be content in whatever circumstances I am. I know how to get along with humble means, and I also know how to live in prosperity; in any and every circumstance I have learned the secret of being filled and going hungry, both of having abundance and suffering need' (Phil. 4:11b-12). He knew where His portion came from: 'And my God shall supply all your needs according to His riches in glory in Christ Jesus' (Phil. 4:19).

Were these two requests in some way behind Jesus' model prayer ('Give us this day our daily bread ... do not lead us into temptation,' Matt. 6:11-13)?[18] The motive behind these petitions awaits us in the next verse.

30:9. Lest I be full and deny Thee and say, 'Who is the Lord?' Or lest I be in want and steal, And profane the name of my God.
The motivation behind Agur's passionate pleas (vv. 7-8) is now revealed. Standing behind his petitions are the twin temptations of the spiritual sloth that ease can bring and the moral decay that want can lead to.

That one might 'be full' and, thus, 'deny' God seems an odd thing. How can the multiplication of divine blessings compound our independence from Him? Yet, that is precisely the human condition. Too soon, we forget the source of the provisions that flood our lives. Abundance tends toward arrogance and independence. Moses warned of such (Deut. 8:12-17; 31:20), the Prophets saw it as reality (Isa. 1:4; 59:13; Hosea 13:6), and the postexilic community confessed it was true (Neh. 9:25-26). The question 'Who is the Lord?' implies the height of hubris and self-reliance (Deut. 6:12; 32:15; Josh. 24:27; Job 21:14-16; 31:28). How can this be? Should not the mercies of God lead to denial of self and submission to God (Rom. 12:1-2)? Yet, like the rich man who built bigger barns, we are blinded to the Giver by the very gifts He gives (Luke 12:16-21).

Dangerous as prosperity is, the opposite pole proves no safer. A severe lack ('poverty,' v. 8 and 'be in want,' v. 9) may not guide one into reliance upon God, but rather impetuous self-preservation ('steal'). While some might try to understand (Prov. 6:30), the overall result could be that I would 'profane the name of my God.' The word translated 'profane' means to grasp, seize or lay hold of. It can describe both a literal, physical action as well as a mental one. In this case, it pictures the name of God being handled roughly, treated commonly or, as it is translated here, 'profaned.'[19]

Because of the dangers of living at the economic extremes, Agur wisely prayed 'Give me neither poverty nor riches; Feed me with the food that is my portion' (v. 8b).

30:10. Do not slander a slave to his master, Lest he curse you and you be found guilty.
Mind your own business and stay out of the affairs of others! This practical word from Agur, along with verse 17, appear to be the only two of his which stand alone as singular verses, unconnected to the verses that surround them.

The warning is to 'not slander a slave to his master.' The verb for 'slander' means, literally, to use the tongue and can refer to speech with either a neutral or evil intent. Here, the motive appears to be vicious – thus the translation 'slander.' A slave, as the lowest of the social classes, would be powerless to defend himself against the accusation of an upstanding citizen. The slave's only recourse would be to 'curse' the one making the false accusation and trust that God would bring the justice that society would surely withhold. In this case, the accusation is false, for the accuser will 'be found guilty' and, thus, God will allow the 'curse' to have its effect (Prov. 26:2). It is the master's business to deal with his own slave (Rom. 14:4). So, keep yourself focused on your own affairs.

30:11. There is a kind of man who curses his father, And does not bless his mother.
Verses 11-14 hang together as a unit, introducing four distinct classes of people. This is signaled by the fact that each verse begins simply with the Hebrew word for 'generation' (here translated as 'There is a kind of man who.' The word apparently arose from a more ancient word meaning 'lap in a race, cycle of time, [or] lifetime.'[20] It, then. came to describe the span of a man's life. Then, also, as here, it designated a class, group, breed or circle of people characterized by particular moral or spiritual issues.[21] Individual cases of the attitudes and actions described here (vv. 11-14) are bad enough, but woe to the land whose people as a whole take them on! Taken together, the problems are rebellion (11), self-righteousness (12), pride (13), and lack of mercy (14).

Here, the problem is that of rebellion against one's parents (cf. Prov. 19:26; 28:24). The one who cursed his parents could have been subject to the death penalty (Exod. 21:17; Lev. 20:9). While no such condemnation is here prescribed, Proverbs 20:20 makes plain that it had not been forgotten entirely, and 30:17 paints a graphic scene of such a man's dead corpse being picked clean by the birds of the air.

The parallelism reveals that the failure to 'bless' is tantamount to the action of cursing one's parents. The sin of omission is as condemnatory as the sin of commission. According to the Apostle Paul, failure to adequately care for one's ageing parents was enough to call into question one's salvation (1 Tim. 5:4, 8).

30:12. There is a kind who is pure in his own eyes, Yet is not washed from his filthiness.
Here, again, is another 'generation' (class, breed, group) of people. This people is characterized by their self-righteousness. Whereas the previous group (v. 11) let it all hang out, withholding nothing of their defiance, this group conceals reality behind a thin veneer of

sanctity.[22] Such a one is 'pure in his own eyes.' What he has forgotten is that 'All the ways of a man are clean in his own sight' (Prov. 16:2a). What he fails to remember, to his own peril, is that 'the Lord weighs the motives' (Prov. 16:2b). Isaiah denounced those who said to others 'Keep to yourself, do not come near me, For I am holier than you!' (Isa. 65:5).

'Who can say, "I have cleansed my heart, I am pure from sin"?' (Prov. 20:9). 'If we say that we have no sin, we are deceiving ourselves, and the truth is not in us' (1 John 1:8). Such self-deception was the problem of Jeremiah's day (Jer. 2:23, 35). Jesus pointed out a Pharisee that exemplified this sort of spiritual pride: 'God, I thank Thee that I am not like other people: swindlers, unjust, adulterers, or even like this tax-gatherer' (Luke 18:11). He denounced them as a class of people, warning 'Woe to you, scribes and Pharisees, hypocrites! For you are like whitewashed tombs which on the outside appear beautiful, but inside they are full of dead men's bones and all uncleanness' (Matt. 23:27). But, given time, the same attitude can creep into the church: 'you say, "I am rich, and have become wealthy, and have need of nothing," and you do not know that you are wretched and miserable and poor and blind and naked' (Rev. 3:17).

Despite the fact that such a one is 'pure in his own eyes' he 'is not washed from his filthiness.' The word translated 'filthiness' is a powerful and descriptive word, revealing just what God thinks of the self-righteous. It can describe human excrement. Isaiah used it to describe vomit-covered tables after a drunken party (28:8).[23] In God's eyes, spiritual pride is the most revolting sin to which we can yield.

30:13. There is a kind – oh how lofty are his eyes! And his eyelids are raised in arrogance.

This third 'generation' (cf. vv. 11, 12) is characterized by 'arrogance.' There is a whole class of people who have succumbed to such pride. Their hubris is most profoundly expressed through their 'eyes.' They are 'lofty' (or, more literally, 'high') and their 'eyelids are raised.' This is expressive of the viewpoint from which they perceive life and the others around them. When a conscious act, they look over them in supposed superiority. When an unconscious act, they overlook those around them in arrogant 'disdain' (NIV).

They forget that 'There are six things which the Lord hates, Yes, seven which are an abomination to Him' and that the first item on the list is 'Haughty eyes' (Prov. 6:16-17a). Such a stance is sin (Prov. 21:4) and God has no patience with such folk (Ps. 101:5). 'The proud look of man will be abased, And the loftiness of man will be humbled, And the LORD alone will be exalted in that day' (Isa. 2:11).

This attitude stands in direct contrast to the humility of Agur (vv. 2-4). Better to be able to pray authentically, 'O LORD, my heart is not proud, nor my eyes haughty; Nor do I involve myself in great matters, Or in things too difficult for me' (Ps. 131:1).

30:14. There is a kind of man whose teeth are like swords, And his jaw teeth like knives, To devour the afflicted from the earth, And the needy from among men.
We meet now a fourth 'generation' of folk who view others as expendable commodities, existing only for the consumption and strengthening of the more powerful. They are oppressive, ruthless, rapacious, covetous, greedy, and cruel.

The first two lines picture the 'teeth' and 'jaws' of the oppressive as 'swords' and 'knives' (cf. 'spears and arrows' in Ps. 57:4). David said of ruthless Doeg, 'Your tongue devises destruction, Like a sharp razor, O worker of deceit' (Ps. 52:2).

The third and fourth lines picture such a one as a wild, ravenous beast bent on consumption. David referred to 'the workers of wickedness ... Who eat up my people as they eat bread' (Ps. 14:4). Micah spoke of those who 'tear off their skin from them And their flesh from their bones, And who eat the flesh of my people, strip off their skin from them, Break their bones, And chop them up as for the pot And as meat in a kettle' (Mic. 3:2-3). All of this is toward 'the afflicted' and 'the needy.' Such a stance toward the poor is a reproach to their Creator (Prov. 14:31), who will make certain that all such efforts to get rich will fail (Prov. 22:16). The same word for 'needy' is found in Proverbs 31:9, where we are told to 'Open your mouth' (vv. 8, 9) for the afflicted, not to devour them, but to speak for the justice that is due them (cf. also Prov. 31:20).

It is a part of our nature to flock with those of like heart, even of like sin. Thus, we have met here whole generations given over to a particular sin (vv. 11-14). We are more a product of our culture than we would wish to think. When a sin predominates among an entire people, it can become an almost irresistible drawing power that pulls even the righteous into its vortex. Thus, we must ask ourselves whether we also have become a people of disrespect and rebellion (v. 11), self-righteousness (v. 12), arrogance (v. 13) and selfish manipulation (v. 14)?

30:15. The leech has two daughters, 'Give,' 'Give.' There are three things that will not be satisfied, Four that will not say, 'Enough':
We meet here the second of six numeric proverbs, a form especially enjoyed by Agur (vv. 7-9; 18-20, 21-23, 24-28, 29-31). The Hebrew word for 'leech' does not occur elsewhere in the Old Testament, but this meaning is attested by the Arabic and Syriac languages.[24] It has been identified, more specifically, as the horse leech of the Middle East.[25] 'The leech' is presented here as having 'two daughters.' Just what is referenced by this expression is not certain, though most point to the dual suckers at either end of the leech and through which it draws the blood of the host.[26] Then, follows two imperative verbs – 'Give,' 'Give.' The NIV interprets these to be the cry of the two daughters, and adds the words 'it cries' to make this point, though they do not exist in the Hebrew text. A better solution is to see '"Give," "Give"' as the names of these metaphorical daughters, names which express the characteristic nature of the individuals being depicted.[27] The picture is that of insatiable greed.

The connection of the second half of the verse to the first has been debated. Some conclude that verse 15a is a fragment of an otherwise unrecoverable proverb and has no formal connection to what follows in verses 15b-16.[28] Though the transition is not smooth, based upon content, it seems clear that the two verses were intended to be joined in one continuous thought.

The expression 'Three things ... Four' introduces a formula used elsewhere (Job 5:19; Prov. 6:16; Amos 1:3, 6, 9, 13; 2:1, 4, 6; cf. Eccles. 11:2; Mic. 5:5). It reveals that the list that follows is selective and representative, not exhaustive. The characteristic common of all that follows in verse 16 is that they 'will not be satisfied' and 'will not say "Enough".' The former describes being satisfied by nourishment,[29] the latter means, literally, 'wealth' or 'riches.' Here, the context demands something like our 'Enough' or 'Satisfied.'[30] The greedy never arrive at the place where they say 'I've got more than I can use or enjoy. Stop!' (contrast Exod. 36:5-6). 'All a man's labor is for his mouth and yet the appetite is not satisfied' (Eccles. 6:7).

30:16. Sheol, and the barren womb, Earth that is never satisfied with water, And fire that never says, 'Enough.'
Here are four examples of the insatiable greed introduced in verse 15. The first is 'Sheol.' It refers to the place of the dead. The NIV has well translated it as 'the grave.' 'Sheol and Abaddon are never satisfied' (Prov. 27:20a). 'Sheol has enlarged its throat and opened its mouth without measure' (Isa. 5:14a). 'He enlarges his appetite like

Sheol, And he is like death, never satisfied' (Hab. 2:5b). The grave has never turned back a corpse saying it is satisfied!

The second is 'the barren womb' or, more literally, 'the closing of the womb.' A woman who longs for children and cannot bear them cries out like Rachel 'Give me children, or else I die' (Gen. 30:1; cf. 16:1-2). Consider, also, Hannah's torment as long as she could not bear children (1 Sam. 1:6-11).

The third picture of insatiability is that of the 'Earth that is never satisfied with water.' In arid regions like Israel, it was rare to have enough consistently supplied rain for the crops. It would seem that, no matter how often it rained, it was never quite enough. The earth would continue to swallow up the water.

The fourth metaphor is that of 'fire.' Fire continues to burn as long as it is fed fuel. It never ceases to flame as long as tinder is supplied. It 'never says, 'Enough.'' The last word is the same as the one that closed the previous verse.

Each of these figures is employed as merely reflective of the human condition of avarice. How difficult it is for us to learn, as Paul did, 'I know how to get along with humble means, and I also know how to live in prosperity; in any and every circumstance I have learned the secret of being filled and going hungry, both of having abundance and suffering need ... I have received everything in full, and have an abundance; I am amply supplied,' (Phil. 4:12, 18a).

30:17. The eye that mocks a father, And scorns a mother, The ravens of the valley will pick it out, And the young eagles will eat it.
Verses 10 and 17 stand alone as the only two of Agur's proverbs (30:1-33) which are unconnected to their surrounding context. However, the topic of unfilial relations to one's parents is also taken up in verse 11, and the 'eye' is also seen in verse 12 and 13.

Here, the problem is the 'eye' which 'mocks ... And scorns.' The 'eye' is often employed in Scripture to be descriptive of the nature of one's heart (Matt. 5:29; 6:22-23; Luke 11:34-36). The issue, then, is that of a heart that despises the authority and teaching of parents. How often such arrogance is seen first through the expression of the eyes (vv. 12-13)!

The NASB has left a Hebrew word untranslated in the second line. The Hebrew text reads, more literally 'and despises to obey a mother' (cf. NIV). The Hebrew word for 'obey' is found elsewhere only in Genesis 49:10. Some find this troublesome and look to reconstruct the clause. The Syriac, Targums and LXX have all translated along the lines of 'old age' ('scorns a mother's old age,' NEB).[31] However, an Arabic cognate carries the meaning of obedience as well. This, coupled with the reference in Genesis 49:10, leads us to conclude that it is obedience to both father and mother that is found so distasteful here.[32]

Such defiance will be met with the most severe discipline. The Hebrew Law called for the penalty of capital punishment for rebellious children (Deut. 21:18-21). Though the death of the child is not explicitly stated here, it is probably in view, whether from the community's judgment or from the sovereign strike of God (Prov. 20:20). Whatever the means, the end is that the corpse of the rebel is apparently thrown aside, exposed to the elements, and made food for the birds of the air. Such a death was a sign of judgment (Deut. 28:26; 1 Sam. 17:44; 2 Sam. 21:10; 1 Kings 14:11; Jer. 16:4; Ezek. 29:5; 39:17).

We should recalculate the seriousness of disrespect of and rebellion toward parents, computing, this time, not from culture, but from Scripture. When a child's defiance is tolerated in the home, it will become his pattern in the community. Such an attitude mitigates against everything that makes for success and advancement in this life or the next.

30:18. There are three things which are too wonderful for me, Four which I do not understand:
This is another numeric proverb. The formula of 'three things ... four' was met in verse 15 and is found again in verses 21 and 29. 'Four things' also are enumerated in verses 24-28, but with a slightly different introduction. We, surprisingly, discover here that a fifth element has been added (v. 20). It is of a jarring nature, does not appear to match the first four elements and upsets the numeric development. Yet, verse 20 should be read with verses 18 and 19, for it is attached through the common word 'way.'

The exact relation of each of the four items has been greatly debated. What we are told is that all four are 'too wonderful' for Agur, and that he could not 'understand' them. The former word points to something beyond what is conventional, customary or expected. It is often used of God's actions in salvation.[33] Perhaps, here, a word like 'incomprehensible' conveys the meaning. The latter word is the rich Hebrew word for knowledge. It refers to more than mere cognition of facts, but to a deep experiential knowledge. Agur here laments that the wonders enumerated in verse 19 still remain somewhere beyond him. He has not entered into them, been able to dissect and classify them, or disassemble them and discover the secret of their 'way.'

Thus, we discover that Agur's humility is not confined to the theological (vv. 2-4), but also includes the natural, physical and interpersonal.[34] Here, then, in a book that extols the virtues of wisdom, is a confession of the limitations of human wisdom. Ironically, it is just such humility that paves the way for wisdom. What a wondrous thing we lose, when we lose our sense of wonder!

30:19. The way of an eagle in the sky, The way of a serpent on a rock, The way of a ship in the middle of the sea, And the way of a man with a maid.

That which verse 18 declared 'too wonderful' and difficult to 'understand' is here enumerated. Each of the four items listed begins with the word 'way.' This is the word so often used in Proverbs, especially chapters 1–9, to describe the course of an individual's life. Here, it probably has the idea of manner or behavior.[35]

Just how each of these four items is 'too wonderful' to 'understand' is not specified. This has given rise to many speculations and interpretations. Here are some of the more common: (1) All four describe something obscured from sustained scrutiny, for they are majestic in their expression, but then gone quickly, without leaving a trace; (2) All four have a mysterious and unexplainable means of movement; (3) All four describe the motion of one thing within the arena or realm of another; (4) The first three serve as illustrations of the final, most mysterious marvel;[36] (5) All four seem to master something that is apparently unmanageable; (6) Each travel where there are no previous pathways;[37] and (7) All four leave no recoverable trail, making it impossible to tell how they got from point A to point B.[38]

Several things do appear to be clear. Neither the 'eagle,' 'serpent,' 'ship' or 'man' are strictly the point of comparison. Rather, it is the 'way' of each that is in view. It also seems clear that the first three items build toward, and serve as illustrations of, the fourth. This is seen, in that there is a transition from the animal world to the human world, and because verse 20 seems to take up the last and make an additional, shocking point from it.

Perhaps our demand to scrutinize and dissect each of these illustrations in order to isolate just exactly what it is that is so 'wonderful' and beyond 'understanding' misses the point, precisely because they are mysterious and beyond our understanding. Even with our advanced scientific knowledge, who does not marvel at an eagle soaring in the sky? Has our learning rendered us beyond wonder at the sight of a snake moving along the surface of a rock? Have we become too smart to still marvel at the wonder of taming the seas through nautical travel? All are still a spectacle that captures the human imagination and incites wonder in the human heart. Do they not still make us stop and stare?

The final item is the true wonder of the four. The Hebrew word translated 'with' can also be translated 'in.'[39] Ross observes, 'This mystery ... focuses on the most intimate part of human relationships. So the most intimate moments of love are at the heart of what the sage considers to be wonderful. All of it is part of God's marvelous plan for his creation and therefore can be fully enjoyed and appreciated without fully comprehending it.'[40] The sexual act is more than a culture plate of throbbing hormones to be studied under a microscope. It is a mystery – a holy, spiritual act. How shocking, then, that it could be so callously engaged in (v. 20)!

30:20. This is the way of an adulterous woman: She eats and wipes her mouth, And says, 'I have done no wrong.'

That this verse is related to the previous two is clear in the continuation of the theme of 'the way.' Verse 18 led us to anticipate only four elements, all of which were presented in verse 19. Here a jarring fifth is introduced, an intruder, not only to the rhythmic expectation of the poetry, but also to the beauty of the scene. Gone are the natural wonders of 'an eagle in the sky,' 'a serpent on a rock,' 'a ship in the middle of the sea' and 'a man with a maid.' Suddenly, 'an adulterous woman' crashes into the serene, reflective scene. She is brazen, brash and insensible to the wonders just contemplated. We have met the likes of her before (Prov. 2:16-19; 5:1-14, 20-23; 7:1-27; 22:14; 23:27-28).

The second line euphemistically pictures her illicit sexual encounters as the eating of a meal. The metaphor has also been met before (Prov. 7:18; 9:17; Song of Sol. 4:16-5:1). Here is her 'way': Sex is just another appetite to be satisfied. She finds no spiritual dimension to her sexuality. She discerns no moral implications. She does not imbibe the mysteries and meanings of the sexual act. 'She eats and wipes her mouth.' Ho, hum.

Should anyone raise an objection, or call her to deeper reflection upon her 'way,' she simply replies, 'I have done nothing wrong.' She is immoral precisely because she is amoral.[41] She has 'seared [her] own conscience as with a branding iron' (1 Tim. 4:2; cf. Prov. 5:6; 28:24). The greatest wonder of all, and that which is most beyond understanding (v. 18), may just be her utter insensibility to the creation and gifts of God. How can a creature so quickly and thoroughly forget her Creator?

30:21. Under three things the earth quakes, And under four, it cannot bear up:

Here, again, we meet the formula 'three things ... four' (vv. 15-16, 18-20, 29-31, cf. vv. 24-25). This time, however, it does not introduce three things that lead to a climatic fourth, as in verses 18-19. The four items enumerated in verses 22-23 are held in a relative parallelism.

These four items are said to represent things 'Under' which 'the earth quakes' and 'cannot bear up.' The word translated 'Under,' employed twice here, is repeated at the head of each of the next two verses. It tells us that each of the scenarios is pictured as something with wider social implications. Others must try to 'bear up' under them. This, they find, is almost impossible.

The verb 'quakes' can describe the literal, physical shaking of the earth (1 Sam. 14:15). But, more often, it is used metaphorically, as here, of an irresistible disturbance.[42] The verb 'bear up' is a common one that describes lifting something up, carrying it and bearing it away.[43] Here, it is negated and pictures a situation that is so oppressive that it cannot be managed in the normal way.

Does this describe a rigid social order that, rightly understood, exists still today and must not be upset, lest chaos reign? Or, is this a more humorous look at some things that simply are overwhelmingly irritating? We should first identify the figures of speech employed here. That the 'earth quakes' and that it 'cannot bear up' under these situations is hyperbole – an intentional overstatement to make a point. Additionally, 'the earth' serves as a metonymy – a way of referring to the people who live upon it.[44] Of the four situations named, only the first approaches any true sense of cataclysmic anarchy. The succeeding three seem to point to unfortunate, and irritating, people in circumstances inappropriate to them.

Rather than making a dogmatic designation of social stations in life, this appears to describe certain social situations in which people may become insufferably obnoxious to others. These are not insignificant, for we should each seek to live to the benefit of others, but neither are they necessarily cataclysmic to society as a whole.

30:22. Under a slave when he becomes king, And a fool when he is satisfied with food,

Following the introduction in verse 21, we are now introduced to the four unbearable situations. Two examples from each sex are presented. The first intolerable circumstance is 'a slave when he becomes king.' This is incongruent: 'I have seen slaves riding on horses and princes walking like slaves on the land' (Eccles. 10:7). 'Like snow in summer and like rain in harvest, So honor is not fitting for a fool' (Prov. 26:1). A leader does not appear suddenly without preparation, but is made fit for the office through years of preparation. Without such preparation, the power rush may go to his head and he, who was once oppressed, may now become the oppressor. 'A poor man who oppresses the lowly Is like a driving rain which leaves no food' (Prov. 28:3). Consider the historical example of Adolph Hitler. Born a peasant and raised in poverty, he became the archetype of the ruthless dictator. Such an arrangement is a curse from God (Isa. 3:4). Consider the chaos that reigned after the servant Zimri took Asa from the throne and then took Asa's throne to himself (1 Kings 16:9-20).

The second individual is markedly less far-reaching in his folly, but nevertheless still insufferable for those who come into proximity with him. He is 'a fool' who has become 'satisfied with food.' The word for 'fool' is *nābāl*, referring not to a dimwit, but to the obstinate, irreligious, unbelieving, and defiant rebel (Ps. 14:1; Prov. 17:7, 21). Here, being 'satisfied with food' does not point to gluttony per se, but to prosperity in general.[45] This defiant one has 'made it' in this world and flaunts his goods as evidence that he does not need God. Throughout Proverbs, provision of food, specifically, and prosperity, generally, is viewed as the fruit and reward of hard work and diligence (Prov. 12:11; 20:13; 28:19). Such a man, however, does not see his 'food' as a sign of God's blessing, but of the success of his autonomy. He flaunts his wealth obnoxiously before the faithful, defying the God they worship and seek for their daily bread. He cares little of thinking 'lightly of the riches of His kindness and forbearance and patience' and does not allow the 'kindness of God' to lead him 'to repentance' (Rom. 2:4). Interestingly, Agur has already confessed his fear of rejecting God because of entering into prosperity (Prov. 30:8-9).

Wicked Nabal is an example of just such a man. His name is fitting. When David's men sought him for support, he asked, 'Shall I take my bread and my water and my meat that I have slaughtered for my shearers, and give it to men whose origin I do not know?'

(1 Sam. 25:11). When Nabal's wife returned from making peace with David, did she not find him 'holding a feast in his house, like the feast of a king' and was not his 'heart ... merry within him, for he was very drunk' (1 Sam. 25:36)? She had rightly confessed that he was 'a worthless man, Nabal, for as his name is, so is he. Nabal is his name and folly is with him' (1 Sam. 25:25).

Interestingly, the two concerns of this verse also make up Proverbs 19:10, but in reverse order: 'Luxury is not fitting for a fool; Much less for a slave to rule over princes.'

30:23. Under an unloved woman when she gets a husband, And a maidservant when she supplants her mistress.

Two more examples of that which is insufferable are now added. And, this time, both illustrations involve females. The first concerns 'an unloved woman.' She is, more literally, a 'hated' woman. That may mean that she is positively odious or that, on a relative scale, compared to others, she is not chosen (and thus hated). Is this an old maid who has, time and again, hoped for a husband, but repeatedly had those hopes dashed? Has she been the butt of ridicule and mocking by her peers who have married? Another possibility is that she is one of several wives in a polygamous marriage and has fallen into disfavor with her husband for some reason. The law recognized this possibility (Deut. 21:15). If this is the case, then Leah serves as an example (Gen. 29:31-33). The former of these two possibilities seems the more likely meaning here. In either case, once she finds a favorable status, she holds her head high and never lets her former mockers fail to recognize her present good fortune.

The final example is of 'a maidservant when she supplants her mistress.' The Hebrew word translated 'supplants' can refer to inheritance, but, here, probably has a meaning of take or gain possession of.[46] The same word is used in verse 9 to speak of being 'in want.' The picture here, then, appears to be that of a maidservant who has become the object of her master's affections and, thus, displaces (and impoverishes) 'her mistress' by becoming his bride. It is not difficult to imagine the vexing circumstance that would create for the former 'mistress!' This is the situation that Sarah feared with Hagar (Gen. 16:1-6; 21:10). This may seem a circumstance unrepeatable in modern Western society. But a wife's friend, a family acquaintance or an employee of a family business could all take her place should the husband not walk with discretion. In such a case, the insufferable circumstances would not be markedly different from the case presented here.

30:24. Four things are small on the earth, But they are exceedingly wise:

Here we encounter yet another of Agur's numerical proverbs. This opening is distinctive, however, in that it is missing the now familiar 'three things ... four' formula (vv. 15, 18, 21, 29), and proceeds simply with the fullest number ('Four things'). What is common among the examples that stretch out over the next four verses is that they are 'small.' The Hebrew word carries the idea of not only 'small' in size, but also weak in strength or insignificant in comparative contribution.[47] This relative evaluation is made against other things 'on the earth.' The two animals and two insects used for illustration and instruction are not creatures that immediately demand your attention. Yet, 'they are exceedingly wise.' The expression is, more literally, 'they [are] the wise ones of those made wise.' The point seems to be that, while they do come bigger and stronger, they don't come any wiser than the four creatures set forth here. Though not intimidating, they are instructive.

Another lesson that should not escape us here is that, through sanctified, Spirit-led reflection on the created order, we can learn wisdom. The governing principle in such reflection must be that deductions made serve as illustrations of already revealed truth found in Scripture, rather than as revelation independent and outside of God's word.

Let us hear Agur clearly: size does not always win the prize! Girth does not equal greatness! Through industrious preplanning (v. 25), cautious defense (v. 26), organized cooperation (v. 27), and courageous boldness (v. 28), victory may be gained by those lacking the might and fight of the world. 'A wise man scales the city of the mighty, And brings down the stronghold in which they trust' (Prov. 21:22). 'A wise man is strong, And a man of knowledge increases power' (Prov. 24:5).

30:25. The ants are not a strong folk, But they prepare their food in the summer;

The first of the four wise creatures presented are 'The ants.' They are tiny to be sure, and 'not a strong folk.' The word 'folk' is the normal word for 'a people.' The word often points to the unity of the people designated.[48] What they lack in strength, the ants make up for in unity and industrious preplanning. For a reason that escapes empirical observation, they have the foresight to 'prepare their food in the summer.' Solomon longed that the lazy man would show as much wisdom: 'Go to the ant, O sluggard, Observe her ways and be wise, Which, having no chief, Officer or ruler, Prepares her food in the summer, And gathers her provision in the harvest' (Prov. 6:6-8; cf. 13:4; 20:4).

30:26. The badgers are not mighty folk, Yet they make their houses in the rocks;

The second group is 'The badgers.' The specific identification of this animal is somewhat tenuous, but probably points to the rock-badger, a small animal about the size of a rabbit. It was considered unclean for eating (Lev. 11:5). They 'are not mighty folk' ('folk' is the same word as in v. 25). That is to say, they are vulnerable to the many predators who would like to make a meal of them. Their wisdom is found in that 'they make their houses in the rocks.' Elsewhere, they are said to dwell among the cliffs (Ps. 104:18).

By living out their lives away from the presence of their natural enemies, they prove that wisdom is found in avoiding the places and people where trouble might crop up. It is better to avoid a confrontation than to win one.

30:27. The locusts have no king, Yet all of them go out in ranks;

Here is our third seemingly insignificant group: 'The locusts.' Whereas ants and badgers lack strength (vv. 25-26), the locusts are missing authoritative leadership ('have no king'). In this, they are like the ant (Prov. 6:7). Despite lacking a central head, 'all of them go out in ranks.' The verb for 'go out' is a common one used to describe the advance of an army's ranks of soldiers.[49] The expression 'in ranks' is a translation of a Hebrew word whose root means to 'cut' or 'divide.' By this is meant that, as they go out, they instinctively (without central leadership) divide themselves into organized ranks and move distinctly, but as one (Joel 2:7-8).[50]

Teeming locusts are, in this way, transformed from a mob of individuals into a fierce war machine, capable of wreaking vast destruction and inciting awesome fear (Joel 1:4-7; 2:3-9; Amos 7:1-2). Just ask Egypt (Exod. 10:4-15)!

How much we could learn from these loathsome insects, if only we would! How much could we do for the glory of God, if we as God's people moved as one (John 17:22)? How many could be rescued from an eternity of torment, if we would but focus the vast resources God has put at our disposal on His great purpose (Matt. 28:18-20)? What could we accomplish, if we would learn to recognize both our God-given diversity and unity and truly move as Christ's body (1 Cor. 12)?

30:28. The lizard you may grasp with the hands, Yet it is in kings' palaces.
Here is the fourth of our small, but wise creatures (vv. 24-28). The subject this time is 'The lizard.' The Hebrew word is rendered 'spider' by the King James Version (and NKJV), but the choice of more modern translators is 'lizard.' The exact kind of lizard is unknown.[51]

The point is that such a creature 'you may grasp with the hands.' They are defenseless, having no poison, barbs or means of attack with which to fend you off. You can gather up their whole existence in the palm of your hand and end that existence, if you so wish. 'Yet it is in kings' palaces.' Despite their lack of superior protective qualities, they consistently put themselves in the very places of power that we could try with all our might to enter and be turned back. Yet, in the inner chambers of the most powerful men on earth, this helpless creature can gain access! It is unabashed boldness that gets him there.

30:29. There are three things which are stately in their march, Even four which are stately when they walk:
Here, again, as in verses 15-16; 18-19; 21-23, we meet the 'three things ... four' formula. As in verses 18-19, the first three build toward and serve as illustrations of the fourth climactic element.

What links these four is that they 'are stately in their march' and 'stately when they walk.' The translation 'stately' is probably the best translation in this context of participles that mean simply to do well. What these four creatures do well is move along their path. Is this a big deal? Oh, it is! Just look at them! They are impressive in their carriage, gait, stride, step or march. Who cannot help but be impressed? In this, they stand in direct contrast to the four small, but wise, creatures of verses 24-28.

No clear moral is stated. No obvious conclusion is drawn. Is this to be a positive lesson – they are each leaders in their own realm (lion – among the beasts; cock – in the barnyard; male goat – among the herd; the king before his people or his enemy)?[52] Or, is this to be a negative lesson – the king struts when with his army, but what is he without them? Or, is this a subtle warning against offending the king?

Most likely, these four characters are not held up in order than we might emulate them, but rather as a negative example of how not to carry ourselves (note the negative examples of vv. 15-16). This chapter has focused on the theme of humility throughout. The closing exhortations (vv. 32-33) seem to warn us against such high-

minded pride. In this context, it seems wisest to read verses 29-31
as an indirect warning, rather than as some kind of subtle nudge
toward stately bearing.

30:30. The lion which is mighty among beasts And does not retreat before any,

The first of the 'stately' animals is now led before us. 'The lion'
receives a more extended presentation than the other three, which
are bunched together in verse 31.

What makes the lion special is that he 'is mighty among the
beasts.' The lion has no natural predators in the animal world. He is
never the hunted, but always the hunter. For this reason, he 'does not
retreat before any.' He walks with 'stately' dignity as an expression
of his power, confidence and fearlessness.

Elsewhere in Proverbs, the king (v. 31) and the 'lion' are brought
together: a king's wrath is like a roaring lion (Prov. 19:12), and his
terror like a growling lion (Prov. 20:2). A wicked king ruling over
a poor people is likened to a roaring lion (Prov. 28:15). In a more
positive illustration, the righteous are said to be bold as a lion
(Prov. 28:1). King Saul and his son, Jonathan, are both also likened
to a lion (2 Sam. 1:23).

30:31. The strutting cock, the male goat also, And a king when his army is with him.

The final three of the four beings which are 'stately in their march
... stately when they walk' (v. 29) are now enumerated. To the
'lion' (v. 30) is now added 'The strutting cock.' This translation is
highly uncertain. Other possibilities offered include the war-horse,
greyhound, starling, zebra, raven, and cockerel.[53] The Hebrew text
has simply 'girded of loins.' This served as some kind of nickname or
catchword that signaled a particular animal to the ancient readers,
but which connection eludes us. The translation 'cock' wisely follows
the LXX and ancient versions.[54]

The third animal is 'the male goat.' He was often used to lead out
the rest of the flock (Jer. 50:8; Dan. 8:5). He walks with what would
appear to be a proud prance. His intimidating glare is renowned.
He is a picture of dignity and bearing.[55]

The 'lion' (v. 30), the 'cock' and 'male goat,' for all of their
arrogant pomp, serve only to set the stage for the final, climactic
creature: 'a king when his army is with him.' The translation 'king'
is quite certain, but that which follows has been of some debate.
Other possible translations include 'a king against whom there is no

uprising,' 'a king standing over his people' or, as the LXX has it, 'a king haranguing his people.'[56] Whatever the exact translation, it is clear that the text points to an unrivaled king.

The exact point of these three verses remains unstated. It is possible that they serve as a warning similar to several previous proverbs. 'The wrath of a king is as messengers of death, But a wise man will appease it' (Prov. 16:14). 'The terror of a king is like the growling of a lion; He who provokes him to anger forfeits his own life' (Prov. 20:2). Probably more to the point is that they stand as a warning against pride, for it must be carefully considered how the theme of humility has been developed throughout the chapter, as well as in the warnings that follow (vv. 32-33).

30:32. If you have been foolish in exalting yourself Or if you have plotted evil, put your hand on your mouth.

The non-specific illustrations of verses 29-31 are now set in a context of warning against pride. The theme of humility that runs throughout the chapter is now appropriately concluded through this call to desist from 'exalting yourself.' The word translated 'you have been foolish' is a strong one, deriving from the same root as the noun that forms the name Nabal ('fool,' 1 Sam. 25:25). The noun form is found in verse 22 and refers not to a simpleton, but to a forward, godless, cynical and insolent rebel (cf. Ps. 14:1; Prov. 17:7, 21). Such a person exalts himself above all need of God and others.

The second part of the warning is concerned with whether 'you have plotted evil' (Prov. 6:14; 16:27). The verb is here translated in order to signal an evil bent to these plans, but is a neutral word that can be used in either a positive or negative sense (cf. Prov. 31:16). Perhaps, here, it is not to be seen as a second, separate warning from 'exalting yourself,' but as the mental plans and plots to make a name for yourself.[57]

If such a heart is within you, 'put your hand on your mouth'! This action appears to signal stunned respectful awe (Job 29:9), astonished amazement (Job 21:5) or repentant conviction (Job 40:4; Mic. 7:16). It is this latter sense which is intended here. The next verse gives the motive which stands behind these exhortations.

30:33. For the churning of milk produces butter, And pressing the nose brings forth blood; So the churning of anger produces strife.

Why desist from self-exaltation (v. 32)? You should do so because there are inevitable, and disastrous, consequences which lie down that path. Here, two similes lead the way to the point in the final line. This connection is clearly seen in the Hebrew text, where the same word is used in each line (in English 'churning,' 'pressing,' 'churning'). This verb is found only here in the Old Testament, and seems to have the sense of squeezing, pressing or wringing something.[58]

When one churns milk, he initiates a process that, if persisted in, produces butter. If one, in anger, punches his neighbor in the nose, he will, as a result, bring forth blood. Just so, persisting in, giving in to, or dwelling upon anger 'produces strife.' The logic is made even more obvious when we note that the words 'nose' and 'anger' are two forms (the singular and plural) of the same root. The term 'anger' is, literally, 'nostrils,' a Hebrew expression used to describe anger. It picks up on the reddening of the nose, the flare of the nostrils or a snort that betrays an inner rage.

If you continue to think only of self, promote self and exalt self, you will inevitably rouse the anger of those over whom you exalt yourself. In so doing, you will destroy relationships and defeat your very purpose. 'An angry man stirs up dissension ... A man's pride brings him low' (Prov. 29:22a, 23a). How much better to walk humbly and remember that 'A gentle answer turns away wrath, but a harsh word stirs up anger' (Prov. 15:1)!

End Notes

1. Whybray, R. N., *Proverbs* (Grand Rapids, Michigan: William B. Eerdmans Publishing Company, 1994), 407.

2. Kidner, Derek, *Proverbs* (Downers Grove, Illinois: InterVarsity Press, 1964), 178.

3. Lane, Eric, *Proverbs* (Scotland: Christian Focus Publications, 2000), 323.

4. Whybray, 407-408.

5. Ibid., 190.

6. Cohen, A., *Proverbs* (London: The Soncino Press, 1946), 200-201.

7. Ross, Allen P., 'Proverbs,' *The Expositor's Bible Commentary* (Grand Rapids, Michigan: Zondervan Publishing House, 1991), 5:1119.

8. Murphy, Roland E., *Proverbs* (Nashville: Thomas Nelson Publishers, 1998), 229.

9. Scott, Jack B., ''ĕlōah,' *Theological Wordbook of the Old Testament* (Chicago: Moody Press, 1980), 1:43-44.

10. Murphy, 229.

11. Wakely, Robin, 'צרך,,' *New International Dictionary of Old Testament Theology and Exegesis* (Grand Rapids, Michigan: Zondervan Publishing Company, 1997), 3:847-853.

12. Whybray, 411.

13. Ibid.; and Murphy, 229.

14. McKane, William, *Proverbs: A New Approach* (Philadelphia: The Westminster Press, 1970), 649, and Cohen, 202.

15. Hamilton, Victor P., 'שוא,' *Theological Wordbook of the Old Testament* (Chicago: Moody Press, 1980), 2:908.

16. Delitzsch, F., *Proverbs, Ecclesiastes, Song of Solomon* (three volumes in one) in C.

F. Keil and F. Delitzsch, vol. 6, *Commentary on the Old Testament* (in ten volumes), (1872; rpt. Grand Rapids, Michigan: William B. Eerdmans Publishing Company, 1980), 2:282.

17. Ibid., 283.

18. Whybray, 411; and Lane, 325.

19. Konkel, A. H., 'תפל,' *New International Dictionary of Old Testament Theology and Exegesis* (Grand Rapids, Michigan: Zondervan Publishing House, 1997), 4:326-327.

20. Hamilton, Victor P., 'דור,' *New International Dictionary of Old Testament Theology and Exegesis* (Grand Rapids, Michigan: Zondervan Publishing House, 1997), 1:930-931.

21. Culver, Robert D., '*dûr*,' *Theological Wordbook of the Old Testament* (Chicago: Moody Press, 1980), 1:186-187.

22. Lane, 326.

23. Hayden, Roy E., 'צאה,' *New International Dictionary of Old Testament Theology and Exegesis* (Grand Rapids, Michigan: Zondervan Publishing House, 1997), 3:726.

24. Whybray, 414.

25. Cohen, 204.

26. Murphy, 234.

27. Kidner, 180; and Cohen, 204.

28. McKane, 652-653.

29. Waltke, Bruce K., '*śāḇēa*',' *Theological Wordbook of the Old Testament* (Chicago: Moody Press, 1980), 2:869.

30. Weber, Carl Philip, '*hûn*,' *Theological Wordbook of the Old Testament* (Chicago: Moody Press, 1980), 1:213.

31. Whybray, 415,

32. Gilchrist, Paul R., '*yqh*,' *Theological Wordbook of the Old Testament* (Chicago: Moody Press, 1980), 1:397.

33. Kruger, Paul A., 'פלא,' *New International Dictionary of Old Testament Theology and Exegesis* (Grand Rapids, Michigan: Zondervan Publishing House, 1997), 3:615-617.

34. Lane, 328.

35. Merrill, Eugene H., 'דרך,' *New International Dictionary of Old Testament Theology and Exegesis* (Grand Rapids, Michigan: Zondervan Publishing House, 1997), 1:989.

36. Ross, 5:1123.

37. Buzzell, Sid S., 'Proverbs,' *The Bible Knowledge Commentary* (Wheaton: Victor Books, 1985), 1:970.

38. Murphy, 235.

39. Delitzsch, 2:296.

40. Ross, 5:1124.

41. McKane, 658-659.

42. Bowling, Andrew, '*rāgaz*,' *Theological Wordbook of the Old Testament* (Chicago: Moody Press, 1980), 2:830-831.

43. Kaiser, Walter C., '*nāśā*',' *Theological Wordbook of the Old Testament* (Chicago: Moody Press, 1980), 2:600.

44. Buzzell, 1:971.

45. Walls, A. F., 'Proverbs' in *The New Bible Commentary: Revised* (Grand Rapids, Michigan: Zondervan Publishing House, 1970), 569.

46. Wright, Christopher J. H., 'ירש,' *New International Dictionary of Old Testament Theology and Exegesis* (Grand Rapids, Michigan: Zondervan Publishing House, 1997), 2:547-549.

47. Coppes, Leonard J., '*qāṭōn*,' *Theological Wordbook of the Old Testament* (Chicago: Moody Press, 1980), 2:795.

48. Van Groningen, Gerard, '*mm*,' *Theological Wordbook of the Old Testament* (Chicago: Moody Press, 1980), 2:675-677.

49. Whybray, 419.

50. Murphy, 233.

51. Ibid.

52. Lane, 331.

53. McKane, 663-664; Cohen, 208; and Whybray, 420.

54. Walls, 569.

55. Cohen, 208.

56. Ross, 5:1126.

57. Cohen, 208.

58. Kaiser, Walter C., '*mys*,' *Theological Wordbook of the Old Testament* (Chicago: Moody Press, 1980), 1:504.

Proverbs 31

31:1. The words of King Lemuel, the oracle which his mother taught him.

A second appendix to the whole of Proverbs now appears. It is signaled by 'The words of King Lemuel,' just as the first appendix was signaled by 'The words of Agur' (Prov. 30:1; cf. 22:17). This 'King Lemuel' is otherwise unknown to us and appears to be, like Agur, of non-Hebrew origin. The words 'the oracle' face the same interpretational and translational challenges as they did in Proverbs 30:1. Do they refer to a prophetic oracle (e.g. Zech. 9:1) or to a region in northern Arabia? As in Proverbs 30:1, there appears to be no compelling reason not to accept this in the traditional sense of prophetic oracle. This is the only such direct address to a king in the Book of Proverbs. Such addresses to a king were not uncommon in Egyptian and Mesopotamian literature.[1] That this comes from 'his mother' is unusual. While Proverbs 1:8 and 6:20 speak of a mother's instruction, and while the influence of a king's mother was sometimes substantial (1 Kings 1:11-13; 15:13), this is the only example of a royal oracle coming from the queen mother, rather than the king's father.

31:2. What, O my son? And what, O son of my womb? And what, O son of my vows?

Hear now the anguished cry of the queen mother's heart for her son, the king! Three times the word 'what' is repeated, indicating the passion and urgency with which she sets forth these three searching questions. This mother, seeing the direction of her royal son's choices (vv. 3ff), is nearly beside herself with concern. The lack of verbs in each line serves to heighten the intensity of their examination. She might be asking 'What are you, a king, doing?' or 'What are you thinking?' or 'What is required of one who holds the privilege of your office?'

Each successive question serves to strengthen her clout, as she exhorts her son to listen. He is, first, her 'son.' All the influence the filial relationship should afford is now called upon. But he is more: he is the son of her 'womb' – out of her very body, flesh of her flesh, birthed in agonizing pain! Yet, he is still more: he is the son of her 'vows.' Perhaps as Samuel came to Hannah (1 Sam. 1:11, 27-28), this son was granted to her on the basis of vows made to God. Or, perhaps she simply dedicated him to God upon his birth.

As she warns him against the vices of women (v. 3) and wine (vv. 4-7), she reminds him that he does not live and die just to himself. He has responsibilities to her as his mother, to his subjects, and to God as his Sovereign. Before he was a king, he was a son. And before he was her son, he was dedicated to God. Not only had he been vowed to God, but his very name (v. 1) means 'belonging to God.'[2] Though those in positions of authority and influence may have the power to do as they please, they do not have the right.

Interestingly, the thrice-repeated 'son' is not the Hebrew form, but the Aramaic.

31:3. Do not give your strength to women, Or your ways to that which destroys kings.

The gasping urgency of the queen mother (v. 2) now gives way to specific warnings. Her first concern is her son's vulnerability to sensual enticements. The 'strength' she exhorts him to vigilantly guard is a Hebrew word that can refer to male virility and sexual power.[3] Like so many other calls within Proverbs (Prov. 2:16-19; 5:1-14; 7:6-27; 22:14; 23:27-28), the warning here is to bring one's amorous desires under the control of God's higher purposes. Immorality, like the wine that will be warned of next (vv. 4ff), has an intoxicating and addictive nature (Hosea 4:11). The warning is not against marriage, for, in fact, that is the appropriate arena for the healthy expression of these God-given desires (Prov. 5:15-23).

The second breath speaks, now, of his 'ways.' The word can imply sexual intimacy, as it appears to do in Proverbs 30:19, or it may speak, more generally, of the concentration and desires of one's heart.[4] The translation 'that which destroys kings' should probably be rendered as 'those who destroy kings' (cf. NIV).[5] The word 'destroys' means to 'wipe out,' and is used of the destruction of the flood (Gen. 7:22-23). Moses used the word when he prayed to be blotted out of God's book, if He would not forgive Israel of their sins (Exod. 32:32-33). When God did judge Israel, he wiped Jerusalem out as one would clean out a dish by turning it upside down and wiping it (2 Kings 21:13). Interestingly, the word is also used in Proverbs 30:20 of the adulteress, who is likened to one who eats, wipes her mouth and, then, contends she has done no wrong.[6]

That such a thoroughgoing judgment falls upon those who abuse their authority by indulging in sexual gratification was predicted by God (Deut. 17:17) and illustrated by Samson (Judg. 16), David (2 Sam. 5:13; 12:1-12) and Solomon (1 Kings 11:1-8; Neh. 13:26).

Notably, like 'son' in verse 2, 'kings' is an Aramaic word.

31:4. It is not for kings, O Lemuel, It is not for kings to drink wine, Or for rulers to desire strong drink,

Now, the queen mother's counsel sounds a second warning. She reminds us that those who carry the responsibility of leadership surrender certain freedoms that those in lesser circumstances may be able to enjoy (vv. 6-7). 'It is not for kings ... It is not for kings.' Authority brings responsibility. Our lives are not our own. Great matters weigh in the balance and the king's verdict will make the difference. He needs a clear head and a keen mind (v. 5) to render just and wise decisions. Alcohol stands alongside immorality in impairing judgment (v. 3; cf. Hosea 4:11).

The repetition (v. 1) of the name 'Lemuel' may be to sound a contrast between his high calling (Lemuel means 'belonging to God') and the low living that alcohol, inevitably, seems to bring.[7]

The word 'wine' is the common one throughout the Old Testament. The 'strong drink' ('beer,' NIV; cf. Prov. 20:1) was probably fermented drink from either grain or fruit. There is no evidence that distilled liquors were known this early in history. It is mentioned twenty-three times in the Old Testament, in all but two being coupled with 'wine.'[8] Both drinks were off-limits to priests, while ministering (Lev. 10:9), and were, likewise, forbidden for Nazarites (Num. 6:3).

Little wonder that Solomon would later declare 'Blessed are you, O land, whose king is of nobility and whose princes eat at the appropriate time – for strength, and not for drunkenness' (Eccles. 10:17). Note his similar, but more general, warnings in Proverbs 20:1 and 23:29-35.

Think of the damage done by rulers like Ben-hadad (1 Kings 20:12-20), Ahasuerus and Haman (Esther 3:15), Belshazzar (Dan. 5:2-4), and Herod (Mark 6:21-28) while they were inebriated!

31:5. Lest they drink and forget what is decreed, And pervert the rights of all the afflicted.

Behold, now, the horrors of the drunken ruler! In his abuse of alcohol, he may 'forget what is decreed.' That is to say, his clouded mind may forget the laws and constitution that govern him. He may become a law unto himself and, in his drunken state, twist the laws to his satisfaction or of those who have gained his ear.

If not this, he may 'pervert the rights of all the afflicted.' God places the ruler on his throne (Rom. 13:1), so that he may make certain that justice is maintained in his realm. From Moses (Exod. 23:6; Deut. 16:19) to the Prophets (Isa. 5:23; 10:2), the Old Testament writers were concerned that rulers might fail in justice. It is 'all the afflicted' (literally, 'the sons of affliction') that are the very ones the king is to be most concerned with protecting (v. 8). Little wonder that his failure in justice is an abomination to the Lord (Prov. 17:15). The drunken ruler should be, and probably will be, replaced (e.g. Elah of Israel, 1 Kings 16:9).

31:6. Give strong drink to him who is perishing, And wine to him whose life is bitter.
If taken out of context, this verse and the next would form a surprising, even shocking, requirement of those who lead a nation. Is it really the responsibility of a ruler to provide the 'lower levels of society' with an opiate to dull their minds, numb their sensitivities, and quiet their complaints? Does God really intend to tell the leader of a nation to drug the people to keep them comfortable and quiet? Certainly, 'wine ... makes man's heart glad' (Ps. 104:15). Assuredly, in days before the medical advances we enjoy, it had some medicinal value (Luke 10:34; 1 Tim. 5:23). Apparently, it was used to numb the pain of those in the throes of death (Matt. 27:34; Mark 15:23).

Yet, we need to read these lines in their immediate context. This section warns against royal excesses (vv. 2-9). The reason given is that the king must have a clear mind, so that he may provide justice for the people (v. 5). This responsibility is not required of others. The point is that, with authority comes responsibility. Those in positions of leadership do not have the liberties of those with lesser responsibilities. They may end up drinking themselves silly, but he cannot! These two verses should not be read as authorization for drunkenness to avoid responsibilities and problems, but as a backhanded way of underscoring the responsibility of one placed in a position of leadership and authority.

31:7. Let him drink and forget his poverty, And remember his trouble no more.
That verses 6 and 7 are not to be taken as authorization for inebriation, but as a reminder of the disciplines required of those who would lead (see on v. 6) is clear when we compare this verse with verse 5. The responsibilities of those in authority (v. 5) are paralleled directly with the supposed liberties of the down and out (v. 7). In the former case, they should not imbibe 'Lest they drink and forget' (v. 5a). And, in the latter case, they should drink in order to 'forget his poverty, And remember his trouble no more' (v. 7).

The point is not to drug the lowly, but to make responsible the privileged and powerful. With rank comes responsibility.

31:8. Open your mouth for the dumb, For the rights of all the unfortunate.

The queen mother, having discoursed on what is not the rightful exercise of royal authority (vv. 3-7), now states positively what it is the king should do with his position – namely, defend the cause of the less fortunate. The repetition of the word 'rights' from verse 5 reminds us that this has been the point all along. Verses 8 and 9 both begin identically, with the command 'Open your mouth,' revealing that they stand together in making the final point of this subsection.

Appropriately the king is exhorted to 'Open [his] mouth for the dumb.' The word translated 'dumb' is probably not intended to refer literally to those who have lost the physical ability to speak. Rather it is likely intended metaphorically of those who do not, because of the hard realities of life, have a voice in the arena of the decision-makers and are, thus, likely to be treated less than fairly.

The expression 'all the unfortunate' is difficult to translate, because this is its only occurrence in the Old Testament. The word describes that which is passing away or vanishing.[9] In this view, it may refer to those unjustly under the death penalty. The word can also have the idea of substitution, however.[10] In this case, it would refer to those who, because of their low social estate, need an advocate to stand in their place in the court and plead their case.[11]

It is the divinely delegated duty of the ruler of the nation to make sure that justice is done, even for those who could easily be discarded, cast aside or unthought of (Prov. 16:10). In so doing, he not only secures the rights of the defenseless, but he secures his own throne (Prov. 20:28), because God rewards those who take up the cause of the poor (Prov. 19:17). When he fails to defend the needy, he is making a theological statement about his view of their Creator (Prov. 14:31; 17:5). When he takes up their cause, he has chosen to see himself alongside the less fortunate, both of them being creatures of the one great Creator (Prov. 22:2; 29:13). David viewed his rule in this light (2 Sam. 14:4-11), as did Solomon (1 Kings 3:16-28; Ps. 72:4), at least initially. Job also exemplified this commitment to justice (Job 29:12-17). Jesus Christ, the Messiah, will rule the nations and dispense perfect justice to the needy (Isa. 9:6-7; 11:4).

31:9. Open your mouth, judge righteously, And defend the rights of the afflicted and needy.
Now again, as in verse 8, the command is issued to King Lemuel: 'Open your mouth.' The theme of his speech is to be along the same lines as the previous verse. He is to 'judge righteously,' taking up 'the rights of the afflicted and needy.' This is a concern that echoes throughout God's revelation, from the Law (Lev. 19:15; Deut. 1:16; 16:18-20), through the poetic books (Job 29:12-17; Ps. 72:1-4; Prov. 16:10; 20:8; 24:23; 29:7), and finding special emphasis in the Prophets (Isa. 1:17, 23; 11:4; 32:1-2; Jer. 5:28; 22:3, 15-16; 23:5; Dan. 4:27; Amos 5:11-12; Zech. 7:9; 9:9).

Do not forget the lesson of Lemuel's mother! Our personal responsibility as agents of righteousness (vv. 8-9) supersedes any perceived rights we may feel we possess to indulge ourselves (vv. 3-7).

31:10. An excellent wife, who can find? For her worth is far above jewels.
We now come to the climactic, and concluding, section of the entire book: the well-known treatise on the 'excellent wife.' This section serves not only as an outline of the individual qualities and cumulative worth of a fine wife, but also as a fitting literary conclusion to the whole of Proverbs. The authorship of this section is uncertain. We could conclude that Lemuel continues (with his mother's words as in vv. 1-9?) as author here. It may be that Solomon penned these words, though one would expect that the one so obviously recognized (Prov. 1:1; 10:1; 25:1) as the primary author of the book would be reintroduced here as well. It is probably best to determine that we simply do not know with certainty who penned these words, but that the Holy Spirit was indeed the ultimate author, as with the rest of Scripture (2 Tim. 3:16).

What is more manifestly clear is that this description of the 'excellent wife' stands as an appropriate literary conclusion to the whole of the book. In the opening section (chs. 1–9), wisdom was personified as a woman (Prov. 1:20-33; 8:4-36; 9:1-6). Here, again, as the book concludes, wisdom appears, this time in the picture of the wise domestic partner. This serves as a fitting inclusio to wrap the whole in the picture of wisdom's beauty and virtues. That such an inclusio is intended by the author is clear from the emphasis on the fear of the Lord both at the beginning (Prov. 1:7) and, here, at the end (Prov. 31:30). The ideals of wisdom presented throughout the Book of Proverbs are now gathered up and presented in a beautiful, breath-taking, but practical, presentation of wisdom embodied and in motion. This portrait of womanly virtue stands in stark contrast to the adulteress of the earlier chapters (Prov. 2:16-19; 5:3-14, 20; 6:24-35; 7:5-27; 8:13-18).[12]

This poetic description of the ideal woman is presented as an acrostic poem. Each of the twenty-two verses begins with the succeeding letter of the Hebrew alphabet. This is not the only place in Scripture that this is found (e.g. Ps. 119; Lam. 1, 2, 3, 4), and signals that the poem was to be committed to memory. This arrangement in composition was to provide a helpful aid to one's memory.

Notable is her title as an 'excellent wife.' The term translated 'excellent' is the same one used to describe the heroic 'mighty man of valor' (e.g. Judg. 6:12; 11:1; 1 Sam. 16:18). Here, however, it appears to speak of her capability, efficiency, and character.[13] Interestingly, the term is used of Ruth as 'a woman of excellence' and of her soon-to-be husband Boaz as 'a man of great wealth' (same term). The same word is used to close this description of the 'excellent wife' (v. 29, 'nobly'). Earlier, we learned that 'An excellent wife is the crown of her husband' (Prov. 12:4a).

The question 'who can find?' (cf. Prov. 20:6) can imply impossibility.[14] But, would a book so intent on holding wisdom up as the ideal of life, and to setting it forth in such practical portals, in the end, tell us to throw up our hands and give up pursuing it? Rarity, rather than impossibility, is the point here. Truly, such a wife is a gift from the Lord (Prov. 19:14) and a sign of His favor (Prov. 18:22).

To underscore the point, we are told 'her worth is far above jewels.' The word translated 'worth' is a commercial term that normally refers to the price of something.[15] The point may be that, even if such a woman were for sale (a crass idea perhaps used to make a point by contrasting her character with such a motive), the price would be beyond us. Probably, the point is that no dowry, no matter how large, can balance the worth of such a gift from the Lord.

The term 'jewels' has been used before to refer to the value of wisdom (Prov. 3:15; 8:11; 20:15; cf. Job 28:18), another key bit of evidence to suggest this is an intentional picturing of the ideals of Lady Wisdom once again. While the picture is metaphorical and, thus, in contrast to the personification of wisdom found in chapters 1–9, 'Wise daughters aspire to be like her, wise men seek to marry her (v. 10), and all wise people aim to incarnate the wisdom she embodies, each in his own sphere of activity.'[16]

31:11. The heart of her husband trusts in her, And he will have no lack of gain.

This woman is completely trustworthy. It is, particularly, 'her husband' who finds her faithful. He 'trusts her' with the home, his wealth, his reputation, their children, and the whole of their domestic life. This is a remarkable statement, for this verb is almost exclusively used for trust in the Lord. Only twice in the Old Testament is it used of trust in another human being: here and in Judges 20:36.[17] The husband is seldom seen in this ode to the woman of valor, except as a man free from domestic worries, so that he can give himself to civic leadership (v. 23), or as turning from his preoccupations to praise his wife (v. 28). His conspicuous absence in the poem is not a signal of an estranged relationship, but underscores his trust in her.[18] 'An excellent wife is the crown of her husband' (Prov. 12:4a).

The second line tells us that his trust is not misplaced, for 'he will have no lack of gain.' Rather than consuming the family resources, this woman multiplies them! The word translated 'gain' is the normal word used to describe the spoils of war – a seemingly odd application here. Perhaps the word was chosen because it refers to 'an increase in wealth which does not result from one's personal labors.'[19] The husband finds his household's net worth has increased because of his wife's industrious ways.

31:12. She does him good and not evil All the days of her life.

The trust her husband has placed in her (v. 11) is, at first, a gift and, then, a reward, because, time and again, she provides 'good' for him. This 'good' is not only psychological and relational, but tangible, as the following verses show. Note that, despite her far-flung entrepreneurial ways, her focus is upon the home and her husband. She is, first, a 'keeper of the home' (Titus 2:5) and only secondarily a career woman. Her focus is fixed and helps to secure the marriage and home ('All the days of her life').

31:13. She looks for wool and flax, And works with her hands in delight.

The flurry of activity the 'excellent wife' gives herself to now begins to come into view. That she looks for 'wool and flax' is a signal that she has the clothing of her family in mind. Obviously, 'wool' was spun into material for warm clothing. She also sought out 'flax,' that linen might be made from it (Isa. 19:9). She herself will do some of the spinning (v. 19). Much of the material will be used to clothe her family (v. 21), but some of the articles will adorn herself (v. 22), and still others will be sold for a profit (v. 24). She is industrious, conscientious, and unselfish in her labors.

The second line reveals that such labor is a 'delight' to her. The expression is, literally, 'she makes according to the pleasure of her hands.'[20] Of course, her hands represent the whole of herself. She finds pleasure in such labors; she finds meaning and purpose in the tasks that fill her days. Both Testaments recognize such a person as blessed, whether they be male or female (1 Thess. 4:11-12).

31:14. She is like merchant ships; She brings her food from afar.
The shocking comparison of the 'excellent wife' to 'merchant ships' is not a reflection of her stature, but of her far-ranging business dealings. She treats her family to a wide variety of 'food from afar.' She likely funds her exotic menu from the garments she makes (vv. 13, 19, 24) and trades with businessmen from afar (v. 18, NIV) with the proceeds from her land dealings (v. 16).

At the height of Israel's prosperity under Solomon, foreign trade via ships was highly developed (1 Kings 9:26; 10:11, 22; 2 Chron. 8:18; 9:20-21). The Jews, however, were never great sailors of the high seas. This fell to their neighboring Phoenicians, who dwelt on the coast of the Mediterranean (Isa. 23:1, 14).

31:15. She rises also while it is still night, And gives food to her household, And portions to her maidens.
Not only does this remarkable woman carefully, and broadly, shop for her household (v. 14), but she takes charge personally of the meal preparation. Sleep has generally been regarded by Proverbs as an impoverishing indulgence (Prov. 19:15; 20:13). The sluggard thereby casts himself into poverty (Prov. 6:9-11; 24:33-34). In contrast, before the light of dawn begins to brighten the landscape, this woman is up and diligently preparing the food for the day. She thinks of her family's needs before her own need for rest.

The word for 'food' in the second line normally refers to the 'prey' of an animal. In later Hebrew writings (e.g. Mal. 3:10), it did come to have the more general meaning of simple 'food,' as here.[21]

This is the only verse in the poem that contains three lines. For this reason, some are suspicious that this may be a carry-over from the very similar wording in Proverbs 27:27.[22] There is, however, no good reason to reject it as genuine here. The word for 'portions' can refer to either provisions of food or assigned work tasks. Its meaning is, most simply, 'what is appointed.'[23] The ASV, RSV, and NRSV all take this to be a reference to assigning the appointed labors to the household servants. It is probably better here, given the context referring to food, to see it as a reference to the food needed for the servant girls. Its use in Proverbs 30:8 lends support to this translation.

It seems odd to some that a woman wealthy enough to afford household servants is up early, preparing food. However, she views her resources not as license for personal ease, but as a gift demanding personal responsibility. We all would do well to learn from her!

31:16. She considers a field and buys it; From her earnings she plants a vineyard.
Now, we discover that the 'excellent wife' knows not only how to spend money, but how to invest it wisely as well. 'She considers a field.' The verb is one that can be used negatively of plotting evil (Prov. 30:32), but, here, it has the positive meaning of bringing together a discerning plan or strategy for action.[24] She weighs out not only the wisdom of investing in land, generally, but she also evaluates the worth of the particular field which she is considering. In the end, she is convinced of this financial venture 'and buys it.' That this kind of liberty was not the norm for women of the ancient Near East only underscores that 'The heart of her husband trusts in her' (v. 11a). That confidence in these kinds of financial ventures was intended is clear, because it is stated that 'he will have no lack of gain' (v. 11b).

She is not contented with simply becoming a land baroness. She wants her property to become a money-making venture yearly, not simply when it is resold. For this reason, 'she plants a vineyard.' The money, not only to purchase the land, but to cultivate the vineyard, comes 'From her earnings.' She has been purchasing the best of materials (v. 13a), and works joyfully (v. 13b) and diligently (vv. 18b, 19), making garments not only for her family (vv. 21-22), but also for resale (v. 24). This diligence has paid off in a second-level business venture, as she takes those earnings and reinvests them in land and agriculture.

31:17. She girds herself with strength, And makes her arms strong.
She is not only a shrewd business woman, but a diligent and hard worker. She is not afraid of physical labor. The first line reads, literally, 'She has girded her loins with strength.' The physical act of girding involved gathering up the loose, flowing robes of one's tunic and tucking them into one's belt. This was done to grant freedom of movement for physical labor or armed battle. This is an expression typically used of men and warriors (1 Kings 18:46; 2 Kings 4:29).

It came to have a metaphorical meaning as well (Job 38:3; Ps. 93:1; Eph. 6:14; 1 Pet. 1:13). It may mean here either that she, literally and physically, 'rolls up her sleeves' and gets 'dirt under her fingernails' by helping to plant the vineyard (v. 16), or that, more generally, 'She sets about her work vigorously' (NIV). Though she had servant girls at her bidding (v. 15), she is not above working alongside of them. Sarah (Gen. 18:6-8), Rebekah (24:18-20) and Rachel (Gen. 29:9, 10) reveal that women of means could be found putting their hands to difficult tasks (Exod. 2:16; 2 Sam. 13:5-9).[25]

The second line says she 'makes her arms strong.' The same word for strength is used to describe the military power of the soldier to stand his ground (Nahum 2:1) and of the political might to secure the kingdom under Rehoboam (2 Chron. 11:17).[26] Here, it means not that she is a body builder, but that she applies herself to her work and is thereby fit and capable for it.

31:18. She senses that her gain is good; Her lamp does not go out at night.
Here we gain an understanding of that which motivates such an entrepreneurial woman. The verb translated 'She senses' means, basically, to taste or sample food or beverage. It is used often in a literal sense, though also metaphorically, as here, to speak of testing, discerning or sensing something (cf. 'O taste and see that the Lord is good,' Ps. 34:8a).[27] She has begun to eat of the fruit of her labors in buying, selling, producing, and trading ('her gain') and it whets her appetite for more ('is good'). The word 'gain' is from a root that is a commercial term, referring to the increase made through business ventures.[28] Line one informs us, quite simply, that she knows how to discern when business is good. While she can enjoy the fruits of her labor, she is doing more than simply consuming them. She is, in a good sense, consumed by them and motivated to multiply them.

Motivated by the 'good' business, 'Her lamp does not go out at night.' This could simply mean that she doesn't retire at sunset, but continues to work by artificial light to make sure she doesn't miss the wave of good business fortune that has come to her. Paul spoke of working 'night and day' in order to supply his needs and those of his ministry companions, that they might not be a burden to those to whom they ministered (1 Thess. 2:9; 2 Thess 3:7-9). That this woman was, in some sense, 'driven,' is beyond question. We should beware, however, of taking the wording here too woodenly. She has already risen before dawn to prepare food for her family and servants (v. 15), worked hard throughout the day in manual labor (v. 17), agricultural pursuits (v. 16b), commercial transactions (vv. 13a, 16a), and the production of goods (v. 13b). To insist that she, literally, forgoes sleep is both unrealistic and to miss the point. Wisdom realizes that 'It is vain for you to rise up early, To retire late, To eat the bread of painful labors; For He gives to His beloved even in his sleep' (Ps. 127:2).

The expression 'lamp ... go out' can speak metaphorically of calamity (Job 18:6; Prov. 13:9; 20:20; 24:20; Jer. 25:10), rather than sleeplessness. Here, that the 'lamp does not go out' would then be a symbol of the safety, security, and prosperity of her household.

31:19. She stretches out her hands to the distaff, And her hands grasp the spindle.

Among her nocturnal activities (v. 18) is the spinning of wool and flax (v. 13) into useable form for the garments she makes for her family (v. 21), herself (v. 22), and for resale (v. 24).

The words for 'distaff' and 'spindle' are used only here in the Old Testament and, for this reason, it is impossible to picture exactly what they looked like or how they functioned. What is clear is that she is spinning out the material for purposes of making cloth.[79]

This verse must be read with the next, if its meaning is to be clear. That they are connected is seen from the chiastic arrangement of their words. We encounter the word 'hands' twice in this verse, but they are two different Hebrew words. The first means 'hands' and the second 'palms.' These are presented in the reverse order in the next verse so that we have an A-B-B-A arrangement. Also, the verb 'stretches' appears at the head of this verse and at the close of the next. All of this simply points out to us that she 'stretches out her hands' to labor and work late into the night, so that she will be in a position to make the same motion toward those who are in need (v. 20). Having worked hard all day, she employs her hours of rest for labor that she might be able to bless those who cannot pay her for her goods. She is a tireless, thoughtful, and unselfish woman!

31:20. She extends her hand to the poor; And she stretches out her hands to the needy.

The hands (note the chiasm with verse 19) that have labored into the night hours (v. 19) are now opened and generous to those less fortunate. In fact, she seems to have given herself, at least in part, to her labors for the express intent of being in a position to help those in need. 'Let him who steals steal no longer; but rather let him labor, performing with his own hands what is good, in order that he may have something to share with him who has need' (Eph. 4:28, emphasis added).

The Law required generosity to the poor (Deut. 15:11) and the Gospels did no less (Matt. 6:2, 3; Mark 14:7; Luke 6:38; see also Heb. 13:16). Proverbs has said much concerning 'the poor.' As the embodiment of wisdom, this woman understands the central place of benevolence. One's response to 'the poor' is expressive of one's attitude toward God (Prov. 14:21, 31; 17:5). The wise see that giving to 'the poor' is simply lending to the Lord, who repays such faithfulness (Prov. 19:17). The one who withholds from the needy invites his own poverty (Prov. 21:13), and the one who gives, ends up getting more in return (Prov. 11:25; 22:9). 'He who gives to the poor will never want, But he who shuts his eyes will have many curses' (Prov. 28:17). In fact, the one who labors only for self ends up leaving it all to someone who will be more generous than he (Prov. 28:8).

Her open palm and extended hands hold not only a gift, but are a signal that she gives more than her goods. She gives her time and attention – indeed, her very self.[30] This woman is as godly and generous as she is diligent and productive.

31:21. She is not afraid of the snow for her household, For all her household are clothed with scarlet.
Among her many qualities is foresight – 'She is not afraid of the snow.' She knows what the future brings, regarding weather. Because of her pre-planning and industry, 'she smiles at the future' (v. 25b). She has prepared her family well, for they 'are clothed with scarlet.' The word for 'scarlet' may refer to expensive, high quality fabric or clothing (2 Sam. 1:24; Jer. 4:30; Rev. 18:16). Obviously, it is not the color that keeps them warm, but the quality that the color signals. The form of the word, however, is odd, having a plural ending. Some have suggested an emendation meaning 'double' (i.e. she has purchased them layers of clothing or doubly thick cloth). This requires no change of the Hebrew consonants and the re-pointing of the vowels is supported by the LXX and Vulgate.[31] This having been said, however, there appears to be no good reason for the change from 'scarlet,' if we understand it as a signal of the quality of the garment, rather than simply to its color.

31:22. She makes coverings for herself; Her clothing is fine linen and purple.
This woman knows how to work hard, providing food (vv. 14-15) and clothing (vv. 13, 19-21) for her household. Yet, she also knows

how to take care of herself and present herself appropriately for her station in life. She is the wife of a city elder (v. 23) and she appropriately presents herself as a leading lady of the community.

The first line says, 'She makes coverings for herself.' The various translations are uncertain as to just what these 'coverings' are for: 'her bed' (NIV), her floor (ASV), her walls (NKJV) or simply 'herself' (NASB, RSV, NRSV). The Hebrew simply has 'for herself' and the NASB, RSV and NRSV are probably wise in stating it generally.[32] The word for 'coverings,' however, is used in Proverbs 7:16 to refer to coverings the adulteress used for her couch or bed (thus the NIV's rendering here). On the other hand, viewing them as coverings for her own body would maintain the imagery of the second line.

The second line clearly refers to her own personal apparel. The 'fine linen' was probably made from flax, and may well have been imported (or she may have made them herself, verses 13, 24). Such garments were given by Pharaoh to Joseph upon his appointment as prime minister (Gen. 41:42), will be given to the church at the marriage supper of the Lamb (Rev. 19:8), and the armies of heaven when they return with Jesus in His glory (Rev. 19:14). Her garments of 'purple' were rich and expensive. Such garments were probably made of wool and imported from Phoenicia, where they extracted the dye from Mediterranean shellfish.[33] The color is the same as the robes of the kings of Midian (Judg. 8:26) and the upholstery of Solomon (Song of Sol. 3:10). The clothing of the rich man Jesus referred to was fine linen and purple (Luke 16:19).

Has this woman, in presenting herself in this way, violated the principles of modesty and appropriateness later found in 1 Timothy 2:9-10 and 1 Peter 3:3-6? Not at all. The New Testament passages call women to not neglect the development of their inner life, something this woman clearly has not failed in (v. 30). The warning there is not simply against outward adornment, but outward adornment without inner substance. Here, she wears clothing appropriate to her God-given station in life and wears it with dignity and humility.

31:23. Her husband is known in the gates, When he sits among the elders of the land.

Not much has been heard of the 'husband,' except that he trusts his wife and is duly rewarded through her (vv. 10-12). But, he is not indolent. The freedom from domestic concerns that his wife has afforded him has allowed him to develop a wider ministry to the community. In the Hebrew culture, 'the gates' of the city were where

legal and social decisions and transactions took place. The elders sat
at 'the gates' to render rulings for the people of the city (Ruth 4:1, 11;
Job 29:7). There, among the elders, he is 'known' – that is, he is
respected as a wise and contributing member of their group. It is
just here that wisdom wishes to make itself known (Prov. 1:21; 24:7),
and is able to do so, not just because the man is wise, but because
his wife is as well. This reveals that a woman's contribution to the
world can be multiplied as she wisely, energetically, and gladly
serves the interests of her home. In fact, the influence she wields in
this way reaches beyond the city 'gates' and moves out to 'the elders
of the land.' This probably refers to a wider territory, perhaps an
administrative region of some kind.[34]

31:24. She makes linen garments and sells them, And supplies belts to the tradesmen.

This woman is prolific in her production of goods! She selected the
raw goods (v. 13), transformed it into cloth (v. 19), made clothing
for her family (v. 21) and for herself (v. 22), and, now, she produces
enough to sell to the foreign traders who pass through! The word
for 'linen garments' is not the same as the one found in verse 22.
This word is of foreign origin, possibly Egyptian.[35] It is found again
in Judges 14:12-13 and Isaiah 3:23.

The 'belts' were sashes used to gird all the other garments
together. The word 'tradesmen' is literally 'Canaanites,' though here
it is not so much an ethnic or nationalistic reference as it is to the
lingering peoples of the land who did business with the Israelites.
She has labored into the night to make certain that she can make
good on this business opportunity (v. 18).

31:25. Strength and dignity are her clothing, And she smiles at the future.

Her adornment is not merely outward (v. 22), but also the inner
beauty of substance and character (1 Tim. 2:9-10). Here, she is
pictured as wearing 'Strength and dignity' as 'clothing.' That is to
say, these are essential character qualities of her inner person that
cannot help but be seen by those about her. 'Strength,' though used
of humans, is a word that essentially speaks of the power of God.
As an attribute of God, it is something God gives to His people,
not as a 'thing,' but by His own personal presence with them.[36]
This woman walks with God and He dwells with her. The word
translated 'dignity' points to being raised up above that which is
low, common, or little. It speaks of a just pride or true dignity.[37] She

is not arrogant, but because of her relationship to God (v. 30) and her industrious ways (vv. 13ff), she is recognized as a woman who is a cut above those around her.

The future is not a fearful prospect to her. Indeed, she 'smiles at' it! The word for 'smiles' means to laugh.[38] The future for the mocker is a frightful thing, a time when God will laugh at him in his calamity (Prov. 1:26). But, this woman has chosen her fears well. She does not fear the future (v. 21), but has appropriately set her fear upon the living God (v. 30)! Thus, she is at peace with uncertainties.

31:26. She opens her mouth in wisdom, And the teaching of kindness is on her tongue.

For the first time, we learn something of the speech of this 'excellent wife.' Until now, we have observed her behavior and studied her character, but her speech has been unexamined. Not surprisingly, when 'She opens her mouth,' we discover 'wisdom' flowing from it. Who she speaks to is not designated, but it likely includes her household servants (v. 15), her children (vv. 21, 28), and her husband (vv. 11-12, 25). A mother is to give instruction to her children (Prov. 1:8; 6:20), and this she faithfully carried out. 'The mouth of the righteous flows with wisdom' (Prov. 10:31).

Not only does she speak wisdom, but 'the teaching of kindness is on her tongue.' This brings together two of the richest Hebrew words in the Old Testament: *torah* ('teaching' or law) and *hesed* ('kindness' or covenant love).[39] These two words might be said to embody Old Testament religion. The Law and the covenant love of God were the pillars upon which the Israelite's relationship to God rested. Here, she has so thoroughly integrated them into her life that her very words are salted with their flavor.

31:27. She looks well to the ways of her household, And does not eat the bread of idleness.

This woman is a amazing blend of hands-on worker and efficient manager of her staff and family. As a faithful administrator, 'She looks well to the ways of her household.' The form is participial, the only one in the poem, and unusual. Some have tried to make this a veiled word play on the Greek word *sophia* (wisdom), but this would require an unacceptably late date for the poem.[40] What should be obvious is that, despite her far-flung enterprises and broad-sweeping investments, this woman is absorbed in her home and family (Titus 2:4-5). She knows well the condition of her flock (Prov. 27:23).

The second line is an understatement of her industrious ways. The 'bread of idleness' would be a reference to eating food for which one did not labor. Or, understood more generally, it would refer to entering into the benefits of something for which one did not work. She is a woman who understands well both Paul's example ('nor did we eat anyone's bread without paying for it, but with labor and hardship we kept working night and day so that we might not be a burden to any of you,' 2 Thess. 3:8) and his principle ('if anyone will not work, neither let him eat,' 2 Thess. 3:10b).

31:28. Her children rise up and bless her; Her husband also, and he praises her, saying:

As the poem comes to a close, those near her cannot contain their praise. It begins with her children (v. 28a), and moves on to her husband (v. 28b-29), God (v. 30), and the broader community (v. 31). They see her for what she is: an 'excellent wife' and mother (v. 10).

The action indicated by the verb 'rise up' was one necessary before an important declaration was about to be made (Mic. 6:1; Jer. 1:17; 1 Chron. 28:2; 2 Chron. 30:27).[41] Today, it might picture one calling for the attention of assembled guests and clearing his throat to make a toast, or of a crowd leaping to its feet in a thunderous standing ovation.[42] What her children do when they arise is 'bless her.' More literally, they 'call her blessed.' The word means to pronounce one blessed or happy. It is a word never used of God's praise for another, but only of man's praise.[43] She has come to enjoy the benefits of having reared wise children (Prov. 23:25; 29:17).

Paul praised Timothy's grandmother Lois and mother Eunice for their faith and for passing it on to Timothy (2 Tim. 1:5). Later, Paul reminded Timothy, 'You, however, continue in the things you have learned and become convinced of, knowing from whom you have learned them; and that from childhood you have known the sacred writings which are able to give you the wisdom that leads to salvation through faith which is in Christ Jesus' (2 Tim. 3:14-15). How Timothy must have thanked God for his godly mother and grandmother!

In the second line, the husband chimes in as well. He 'praises her.' The form of the root word is used both of the light emitted by celestial bodies ('shine') and of the praise that is given off by man concerning someone or something else ('praise,' or 'boast').[44] Obviously, here it is the latter that is intended. The exact content of such praise is quoted in the next verse.

31:29. 'Many daughters have done nobly, But you excel them all.'
The husband's praise (v. 28b) is now quoted. The word 'nobly' is
the same Hebrew word translated 'excellent' in verse 10, forming an
inclusio to frame this subsection. At the start, the author wondered
aloud: 'An excellent wife, who can find?' This man has raised his
voice to claim that he had! If 'her worth if far above jewels' (v. 10b),
then this man is claiming to be a rich man indeed.

The word 'daughters' is a poetic reference to the broad view of
all the women available for consideration.[45] We are reminded that,
while such a woman is rare, she is not singular, for 'Many daughters
have done nobly.' Yet, in her husband's view, she surpasses even the
best of the best.

The wise husband is reminded that it is not sufficient to simply
estimate his wife's worth (vv. 10-28a), but he must also voice it
(v. 28b-29).

**31:30. Charm is deceitful and beauty is vain, But a woman who
fears the Lord, she shall be praised.**
Having skillfully instilled a gnawing hunger to know what makes
this woman tick, the poet now reveals the source of her excellence.
The first line instructs us concerning what makes an insufficient
grounds for life and relationships: personal 'Charm' and physical
'beauty.' The former is 'deceitful.' The word normally refers to words
or actions that are untrue and without foundation in fact or reality.[46]
By her charms, a woman is able to set forth an impression of herself
which will not hold up over time and under the pressures of real life
(Prov. 5:3; 11:22). The latter is said to be 'vain.' The word, literally,
means 'breath' or 'vapor.' It is here today and gone tomorrow. We
should not read these as a denouncement of physical beauty, for
Proverbs has counseled a man to find delight in his wife's body
(Prov. 5:15-19). Rather, the point is that there must be much more
than physical attraction and general enchantment if the marriage is
to last and reflect God's ways.

Above all else, that which makes her an 'excellent wife' is her fear
of the Lord. It is her spiritual life which gives strength and beauty
to the rest of her being. This reference to the fear of the Lord serves
as an inclusio with Proverbs 1:7, the key verse of the book. We do
well to remember that the book began here and that the first major
section of the book ended here as well (Prov. 9:10). So, now, the book
as a whole also ends upon this theme. 'The fear of the Lord is the
beginning [and ending] of wisdom' (Prov. 1:7, parenthesis added).
The first word in wisdom is also the last: rightly reverencing the Lord.

The wise man was introduced to the Woman Wisdom in chapters 1–9, and, now, he has wedded her (Prov. 31:10-31). He has rejected the adulteress and harlot (e.g. Prov. 2:16-19; 5:1-6; 7:1-23), and has found delight in a woman of true integrity and substance (1 Tim. 2:9-10; 1 Pet. 3:1-6). For this decision, he is blessed forevermore.

31:31. Give her the product of her hands, And let her works praise her in the gates.
In the end, this virtuous woman receives back for all her unselfishness. The poet demands that we 'Give her the product of her hands.' The expression is, more literally, 'the fruit of her hands,' an expression resembling the one in verse 16. This may include the literal fruit of her new vineyard (v. 16), the food for which she has bartered (v. 14), and her clothing (v. 22). However, the expression seems to be a broader, sweeping description of the many good things that her godly, disciplined life yields. 'A man will be satisfied with good by the fruit of his words, And the deeds of a man's hands will return to him' (Prov. 12:14). The God she has feared (v. 30) has rewarded her in tangible ways.

The book closes with the poet's last call: that we 'let her works praise her in the gates.' We are reminded of her husband's influence there (v. 23). Perhaps he starts the chorus of cheers. Perhaps her glory is found in his respect there, and 'her works praise her' in some reflective or residual manner. It would have been unusual in Jewish culture for a woman to be directly praised at the city gates. But, this is no ordinary woman. 'A gracious woman attains honor' (Prov. 11:16a). She has joyfully learned the truth of Proverbs 22:4: 'The reward of humility and the fear of the LORD Are riches, honor and life.'

We are reminded that this book opened with Woman Wisdom raising her voice 'At the head of the noisy streets ... At the entrance of the gates in the city ...' (Prov. 1:21). Appropriately, as the book closes, she has found a hearing, has been embraced, and is now being praised there.

Boaz's words to Ruth seem to reflect both his familiarity with this passage and her likeness to this virtuous woman: 'And now, my daughter, do not fear. I will do for you whatever you ask, for all my people in the city know that you are a woman of excellence' (Ruth 3:11).

Thus ends this remarkable book of wisdom. Wisdom has spoken. Life (Prov. 3:2, 16, 18, 22; 4:10, 13, 22-23; 6:23; 8:35; 9:11) and death (Prov. 1:19; 2:18-19; 5:5; 7:23, 27; 8:36) have been set before us. Let us choose life (Deut.30:19)!

End Notes

1. Bullock, C. Hassell, *An Introduction to the Old Testament Poetic Books* (Chicago: Moody Press, 1988), 176.

2. Kidner, Derek, *Proverbs* (Downers Grove, Illinois: InterVarsity Press, 1964), 182.

3. Wakely, Robin, 'חַיִל,' *New International Dictionary of Old Testament Theology and Exegesis* (Grand Rapids, Michigan: Zondervan Publishing House, 1997), 2:117.

4. Ross, Allen P., 'Proverbs,' *The Expositor's Bible Commentary* (Grand Rapids, Michigan: Zondervan Publishing House, 1991) 5:1127.

5. Kidner, 183; Murphy, Roland E., *Proverbs* (Nashville: Thomas Nelson Publishers, 1998), 240; Whybray, R. N., *Proverbs* (Grand Rapids, Michigan: William B. Eerdmans Publishing Company, 1994), 423.

6. Kaiser, Walter C., '*māhâ*,' *Theological Wordbook of the Old Testament* (Chicago: Moody Press, 1980), 1:498-499.

7. Cohen, A., *Proverbs* (London: The Soncino Press, 1946), 209.

8. Hamilton, Victor P., '*shakar*,' *Theological Wordbook of the Old Testament* (Chicago: Moody Press, 1980), 2:926-927.

9. Brown, Francis, S. R. Driver, Charles A. Briggs, *A Hebrew and English Lexicon of the Old Testament* (Oxford: Clarendon Press, n.d.), 322.

10. Cohen, 210; Delitzsch, F., *Proverbs, Ecclesiastes, Song of Solomon* (three volumes in one) in C. F. Keil and F. Delitzsch, vol. 6, *Commentary on the Old Testament* (in ten volumes), (1872; rpt. Grand Rapids, Michigan: William B. Eerdmans Publishing Company, 1980), 2:324.

11. Cohen, 210.

12. Ross, 5:1128-1129.

13. Wakely, Robin, 'חַיִל,' *New International Dictionary of Old Testament Theology and Exegesis* (Grand Rapids, Michigan: Zondervan Publishing House, 1997), 2:116-126.

14. Murphy, 246 and Whybray, 426.

15. Cornelius, Izak, 'מכר,' *New International Dictionary of Old Testament Theology and Exegesis* (Grand Rapids, Michigan: Zondervan Publishing House, 1997), 2:937-939.

16. Waltke, Bruce K., 'The Role of the "Valiant Wife" in the Marketplace,' *Crux* (Vancouver, British Columbia: Regent College, September 1999), 31.

17. Ibid., 26.

18. Murphy, 246.

19. Cohen, 211.

20. Ibid.

21. Whybray, 427.

22. Murphy, 244, 247.

23. Kidner, 184.

24. Hartley, John E., 'זמם,' *New International Dictionary of Old Testament Theology and Exegesis* (Grand Rapids, Michigan: Zondervan Publishing House, 1997), 1:1112.

25. Waltke, 28.

26. Feinberg, Charles L., ''*āmēs*,' *Theological Wordbook of the Old Testament* (Chicago: Moody Press, 1980), 1:53-54.

27. O'Connell Robert H., 'טעם,' *New International Dictionary of Old Testament Theology and Exegesis* (Grand Rapids, Michigan: Zondervan Publishing House, 1997), 2:378-380.

28. Cornelius, I., 'סחר,' *New International Dictionary of Old Testament Theology and Exegesis* (Grand Rapids, Michigan: Zondervan Publishing House, 1997), 3:242-243.

29. Murphy, 247.

30. Delitzsch, 2:333-334.

31. McKane, 668-669.

32. Lane, 339.

33. Whybray, 429.

34. Ibid.

35. Murphy, 244.

36. Shultz, Carl, "*āzaz*,' *Theological Wordbook of the Old Testament* (Chicago: Moody Press, 1980), 2:659-660.

37. Delitzsch, 2:337.

38. Payne, J. Barton, 's*āhaq*,' *Theological Wordbook of the Old Testament* (Chicago: Moody Press, 1980), 2:763-764.

39.Lane, 341.

40. Murphy, 244.

41. Whybray, 430.

42. Lane, 341.

43. Hamilton, Victor P., "*āshar*,' *Theological Wordbook of the Old Testament* (Chicago: Moody Press, 1980), 1:80.

44. Coppes, Leonard J., '*hālal*,' *Theological Wordbook of the Old Testament* (Chicago: Moody Press, 1980), 1:217-218.

45. Cohen, 215.

46. Austel, Hermann J., '*shāqar*,' *Theological Wordbook of the Old Testament* (Chicago: Moody Press, 1980), 2:955-956.

Appendix A

Wisdom and Folly

To understand Proverbs in its individual parts, it helps to stand above its astounding detail and scan the panorama of its movements and emphases. Never is this more valuable than in regard to its teaching on both wisdom and folly. Turn randomly in Proverbs and you will be confronted by either or both. Yet, when immersed in an individual text, it is sometimes difficult to fully appreciate its richness without the perspective of the book's whole teaching on wisdom and folly. To that end, we dare ask, 'What does the Book of Proverbs teach about wisdom and folly?' We seek an answer with enough breadth to be comprehensive and, yet, with enough brevity to be comprehensible.

Wisdom

Proverbs employs a rich vocabulary to set wisdom before us in all her beauty. These varied terms are often used interchangeably, the synonyms standing in parallel not as distinct objects on the artist's canvas, but in shaded transitions from one hue of truth to another. Admittedly, any attempt to dissect and individualize the meaning of the terms is somewhat artificial, yet such 'science' need not destroy the beauty of the flower it studies. Such detailed study may in fact bring a greater appreciation for not only its function, but its loveliness.

The most frequently used, and overarching, term for wisdom is *hokmâ*. If *hokmâ* is at the heart of the flower, the other complementary terms make up the graded transition of colors stretching to the tip of its petals. To employ a different metaphor, *hokmâ* is the diamond *par excellence* and the other complementing terms are her facets, which catch the light of truth and spray it forth in a rainbow of colors.

Hokmâ, succinctly stated, is skillful living. Beyond the Book of Proverbs, such skill can include physical aptitude and excellence in endeavors such as sewing (Exod. 28:3), metalwork (Exod. 35:31, 32), working with gemstones, woodworking (v. 33), weaving and embroidery, and other skills of craftsmen (Exod. 35:35). It can describe skill in leadership generally (Deut.34:9; 2 Sam. 14:20; Isa. 29:14), as well as political (1 Kings 2:6), military (Isa. 10:13), and nautical (Ps. 107:27) skill more specifically.

In Proverbs, such skillful living relates primarily to the world of relationship with both God and man. Here the intellectual, spiritual, and moral aspects are primary. Yet *hokmâ* is more than mere theory. It is practical know-how in the hard realities of living with others before God in the world He has created. As such, *hokmâ* enables us to make our way through life with eyes to see what really is, ears to hear what God is saying, and a will to walk in His way with Him.

Hokmâ guides us aright in matters religious, ethical, moral, relational, and financial. With *hokmâ*, we discover that we see clearly, hear accurately, discern distinctly, speak circumspectly, and choose wisely. *Hokmâ* steers us from many a pitfall and guides us into success. Strikingly, the best of all *hokmâ's* emphases are summarized and embodied in the Messiah (Isa. 11:2).

Such *hokmâ*, along with all its attendant emphases, fundamentally arises from, and rests upon, the foundation of an appropriate fear of the Lord (Prov. 1:7; 9:10). The pivotal problem of folly is its failure to discern God's glory, His sovereign administration of the world, and His rightful place in each individual's life (Prov. 19:3).

The facets of the 'diamond' that is *hokmâ* send forth a rainbow spectrum of light.[1] Let us examine the beauty in the spectrum of this truth's colors. Note how each succeeding step takes us into a life of wisdom that is less dependent upon external restraint and instruction and ever more dependent upon the intimacy of personal relationship with God Himself.

1. Discipline. Two words in the wisdom-complex make the point here. The first, *mûsār*, describes correction, discipline, or chastisement which results in learning. It arises out of love (Prov. 3:11-12; 23:13). The most fundamental form of *mûsār* is verbal (Prov. 3:11) and visual (Prov. 24:32), but, if unheeded, it can become physical (Prov. 22:15).

Often found in parallel with, and complementing, the emphasis of *mûsār* is *tôkaḥat*. In formal legal contexts, it could refer to an attorney's arguments in the presentation of his case (Job. 13:6). In Proverbs, it refers more generally to reproof, rebuke, or correction that yields a disciplined change in course. Clearly, the verbal aspect is primary here.

2. Discernment. The key term here is *bînâ*. *Bînâ* is often translated as understanding, but its root idea is most clearly expressed in the way its related preposition, *bên*, is rendered: 'between.' Such understanding is a result of studied observation (Job 13:1; Ps. 119:104) where the data gathered through one's senses is then clarified by the reproofs and corrections that have already come. Such insightful observations begin to highlight in the individual's mind distinctions between right and wrong, wisdom and folly, truth and falsehood, God's way and the way of the tempter. The possessor of *bînâ* begins to understand the lessons that external discipline has taught and now begins, internally, to render wise judgment in the affairs of life.

Nearly synonymous with *bînâ* is *t^ebûnâ*. The intelligence, aptitude and skill of *t^ebûnâ* similarly arise from eyes that increasingly see with the clarity of wisdom. While functionally synonymous with *bînâ*, the two terms only appear in synonymous parallelism in Proverbs 2:3.

3. Understanding. The noun *śēkel* and its verb, like *bînâ*, describe discernment and yet take it a step further. *Śēkel* emphasizes not only the ability to discern between two options and identify God's choice, but it also implies the ability to understand why one option is His preference.[2] The word might well be communicated today as simply 'common sense.' It describes the ability to wade through data, sort and reason it into logical arrangement and then project a course of action that will arrive at success.[3] Insight, comprehension, and discernment all help round out the essence of this practical common sense.

Similarly, the term *tûšiyyâ* describes sound, efficient wisdom which advances one toward success. It describes the Spirit-guided human mind moving upward toward God's mind, rather than simply God imparting information through a heaven-sent revelation. It describes a God-given ability to use God's revealed truth to deduce the wisest and most efficient course in achieving His will in a given situation.[4] These two terms extend the experience of wisdom yet one more step.

4. Prudence. The term *'ormâ* can be used negatively to describe guile and craftiness (Exod. 21:14). In this regard, it is descriptive of the serpent's wiles in the Garden (Gen. 3:1). Yet, in Proverbs, it describes the positive sense of prudence and shrewdness. This Spirit-born cleverness understands the trend of events (Prov. 14:8) and inherent dangers (Prov. 22:3; 27:12), and turns one's steps (Prov. 14:15) to a path that avoids pitfalls and finds a passage through the challenges of doing God's will.[5]

Similarly, *m^ezimmâ* describes a studied, resourceful discretion (Prov. 1:4). It keeps its possessor from falling prey to the strong enticements of evil tempters (Prov. 2:11, 12). The word *tahbûlōṯ* vividly describes such direction. Many scholars believe it is derived from a word for rope and was used in the nautical world to describe the pulling of ropes to manipulate a ship's rudder and, thus, steer it in its course.[6] The one who possesses *tahbûlôt* steers a clear course along God's path. Or, in other words, he 'knows the ropes' of life.[7]

5. Knowledge. The noun *da'at* and its kindred verb describe knowledge that is not merely intellectual, but deeply personal and experiential. The irreplaceable foundation of all wisdom is the fear of the Lord (Prov. 1:7; 9:10), but such fear is not the end of wisdom. '… [F]ear of God is reverential awe, finding expression in uprightness and devotion; knowledge of God means a fullness of relationship with God and walking in his ways.'[8] This brings wisdom to its fullest expression – not merely rightly reverencing God, but also deeply knowing Him (Prov. 2:5; 3:6) in a walk of active faith that enables us to successfully fulfill His purposes in the world He has created. The God we rightly tremble before is also the God who draws us near and reveals Himself to us in personal relationship (Prov. 9:10).

Leqaḥ describes learning. Its root means to take or seize, and, thus, the learning it depicts is that in which the mind reaches out to perceive the truth. Four of the word's nine appearances in Proverbs are as the object of *yāsap*, meaning to add or increase (Prov. 1:5; 9:9; 16:21, 23).[9] Wisdom is, thus, seen not as a plateau to achieve, but a

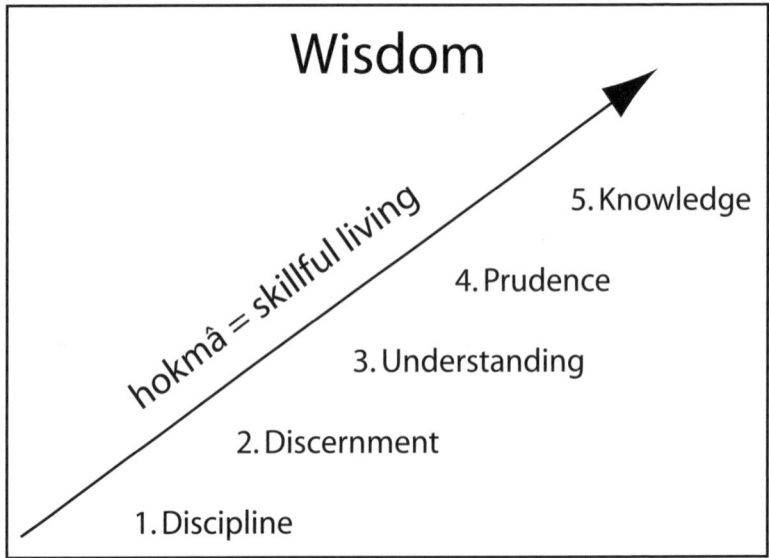

journey to continue in – ever learning, always coming to know God more deeply.

Folly

If wisdom is a diamond set forth in multifaceted splendor, folly is a descending staircase, leading to ever deeper levels of grim futility, frustration, and finality (Prov. 5:5).[10] No one left to himself ever arrives at wisdom. We begin our journey in foolishness and folly (Prov. 22:15). Apart from the loving discipline and guidance of wise parents and counselors, we are caught helplessly in the downward vortex of our own sinful nature.

Again, as with wisdom, Proverbs employs a rich vocabulary to describe the complexities of folly. As with wisdom, these terms often serve as synonyms for one another. The distinctions are not drawn in fine lines, but with gradual, yet clear, transitions in emphasis.

The fool's fundamental problem is that he stands alone. He needs no other resources and recognizes no other authority. His failure began where wisdom's ascent launched – the fear of the Lord (Prov. 1:7; 9:10). The rock that becomes the foundation of a life of wisdom for some is the stumbling stone over which many others trip. He has chosen to live in God's world without God. His worldview is skewed. He is disconnected from reality. He is fighting against the gravitational pull of God's nature, the laws He has fixed in the nature of His creation, and His sovereign purposes for man.

Having chosen to go his own way and depend upon his own resources, the fool sets in motion a process that must end in disaster. What looks like the autonomy of selfhood moves downward from plain simpleness (*petî*) to foolishness and folly (*kᵉsîl*). From here, the fool, left to himself, falls even deeper into more serious foolishness (*'ewîl*), and from there he descends to an even denser state of folly (*nābāl*). The vortex's power eventually pulls the foolish down to the level of what the Proverbs call a scoffer (*lēs*).[11]

Ponder this descent into futility, depravity, and death:

1. The naïve. The *petî* is a gullible, silly simpleton (Prov. 14:15; 22:3). He loves to exercise his willfulness and act irresponsibly (Prov. 1:32). He tends to be thoughtless toward others (Prov. 19:25). Indeed, his folly is a source of pleasure to him (Prov. 15:21). He wastes his life chasing after what does not matter (Prov. 15:21). He lacks wisdom (Prov. 21:11, *hokmâ*), discernment (Prov. 9:6, *bînâ*), and prudence (Prov. 1:4; 8:5; 19:25, *'ormâ*).

The naïve has no experience to warn him of the dangers that lie in his path (Prov. 27:12). All people begin with the naïveté of inexperience and youth. Left undirected and unrestrained, the power of the vortex begins the downward tug of rebellion that will destroy our lives (Prov. 22:3). Vulnerable though the naïve are, there is hope. At this stage the naïve one is still reachable and able to be rescued from the current of his foolishness (Prov. 19:25; 21:11).[12]

2. The fool[1]. The *kᵉsîl* is the next downward step for the simpleton who refuses to learn. This is the most common term referring to the fool in Proverbs. It indicates one who is thick-headed and stubborn. He is not stupid, but has, by his refusal to listen to the wisdom of his parents and wise counselors, chosen a recalcitrant outlook on life. He is impenitent and falls into the same errors repeatedly (Prov. 13:19). He likes to hear himself talk (Prov. 12:23; 15:2), but has nothing of substance to say. He is unreliable (Prov. 26:6, 10) and squanders what money he does have (Prov. 21:20).

The source of his problem is a spiritual, not a mental, deficiency. He is invited to learn wisdom (Prov. 1:22; 8:5), but has no place for truth in his life and no time for the fear of the Lord (Prov. 1:29). He enjoys his folly too much (Prov. 15:14; 18:2). The *kᵉsîl* brings agony, bitterness and catastrophe to his parents (Prov. 10:1; 17:21; 17:25; 19:13). Not only does he bring his parents to ruin, he despises them (Prov. 15:20).[13]

3. The fool[2]. Without restraint and serious intervention, the *kᵉsîl* moves downward further, to the level of the *'ewîl*. The *'ewîl* shares many of the same characteristics of the *kᵉsîl*, but his moral insolence is taken even further.[14] He refuses counsel (Prov. 1:7; 10:8; 12:15; 15:15) and mocks at sin (Prov. 14:9). Unless this kind of attitude and behavior is corrected early in life, the downward pull of the vortex can become nearly irreversible (Prov. 22:15; 27:22).[15]

4. The nabal. There is, however, yet another step down for the fool. From the derision of the *'ewîl*, he falls to the level of the *nābāl*. The term is used just a handful of times in Proverbs (Prov. 17:7, 17; 30:22, 32), but, influenced by its wider use in the Old Testament, we find him to be a dark figure.[16] He shares many of the same character traits of the *kᵉsîl* and *'ewîl*. Yet, the *nābāl* goes even further by closing his mind completely to God, even denying His existence altogether (Ps. 14:1). The godless *nābāl* is illustrated for us by the husband of Abigail (1 Sam. 25:25), whose own name, ironically, was Nabal. Of him, his own wife confessed 'one cannot speak to

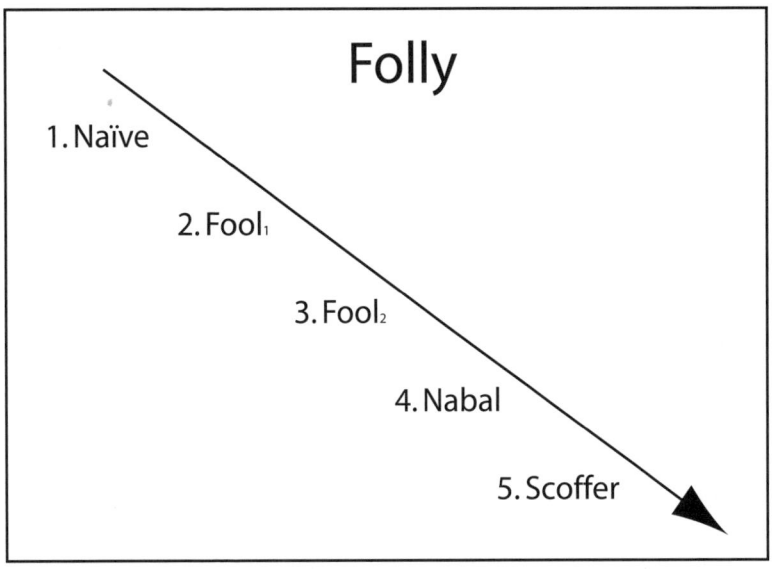

him' (1 Sam. 25:17).[17] How telling that his wife was noted for her discerning wisdom (1 Sam. 25:3; N~kal, see above) while, in a very real sense, he became the poster-child for folly!

5. The scoffer. The deepest level of descent described in Proverbs is that of the scoffer (*lēs*). The *lēs* despises being amended in his actions or thinking (Prov. 9:7, 8; 13:1; 15:12). His arrogant independence makes movement toward wisdom impossible (Prov. 14:6). He has long since rendered himself insensitive to any positive benefit from discipline (Prov. 9:7), rebuke (Prov. 9:8; 15:12), or instruction (Prov. 13:1).[18] The scoffer is no longer a simpleton who curiously investigates folly here and there, but is one who has become confirmed in his reviling of all authority (Prov. 21:24; 22:10; 29:8). The sad verdict awaiting the scoffer is that the God toward whom he has scoffed will, in the end, return the favor (Prov. 3:34).[19]

Two Ways

Proverbs repeatedly sets before us a choice of two paths we may walk in this life. There are two calls given by two women who have two houses. Each calls us to walk one of two paths, which lead inevitably to one of two destinies (Prov. 7:27; 8:35, 36). Over seventy times in Proverbs, we are brought to this fork in the road and told to choose which path we will travel. One path is variously labeled as the way of the evil, wicked, angry, perverse, treacherous, sluggard, devious, and violent. Ultimately, it ends in death (Prov. 1:19; 7:27; 14:12; 16:25).

The other is the way of righteousness, justice, understanding, and blamelessness. Ultimately, it issues in life (Prov. 6:23; 8:35; 12:28; 16:17). This is the way of the Lord (Prov. 10:29).

Though they bear many names, these are the only two ways. By any other name, they remain the paths of wisdom and folly in the final analysis.

Proverbs is the call of a father to his 'son.' We hear the voice of godly wisdom and experience calling to the naïveté of youth, begging him, at his most vulnerable time of life, to choose the way of life. Heightening the drama and the eternal nature of the choice, Bruce Waltke tells us that the son is '… probably about twenty years of age, standing on the threshold of full adulthood. The time is at hand when the line must be crossed to move into maturity. Two conflicting worldviews make their appeal.'[20]

As we discovered above, these two paths lead us through five progressions on the way to our final destination. The way of wisdom leads us higher into fellowship with God Himself; the way of folly draws us away from God and toward destruction. The one way appears logical and right to the uninformed human mind (Prov. 14:12; 16:25). The other, at first, appears fraught with hardships and discipline (Prov. 6:23; 15:10). Our selection of a path

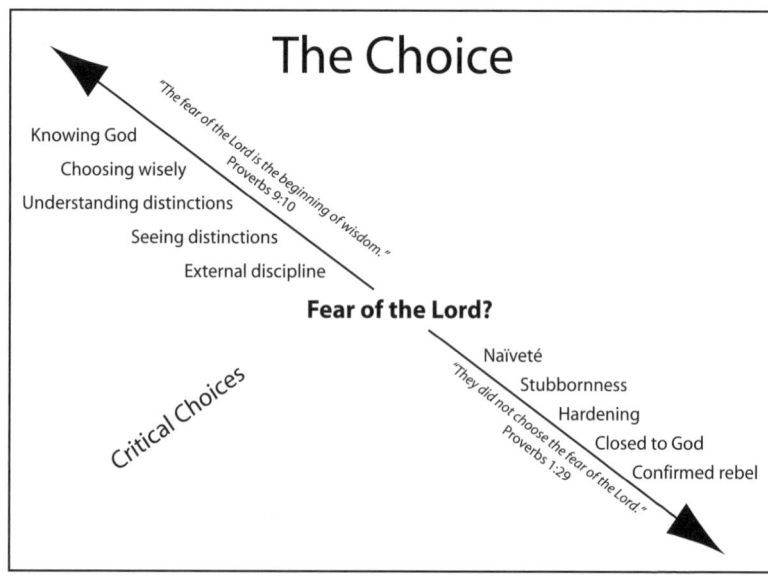

may come quickly and without much thought, and the descent or ascent it initiates may be gradual. But, once the path is chosen, the destiny is determined.

We must not miss this fundamental fact: The choice of a path is also the choice of a destiny. If we choose poorly, repentance is possible, but it grows more difficult and unlikely the further down the path we travel. With great urgency, the competing calls of Lady Wisdom and Madame Folly set before us life's most fundamental choice. Our choice in this matter will not only affect our quality of life now, but will reverberate through eternity as well.

End Notes

1. I was first alerted to the basic differences in the terms by, and am thus indebted to, Derek Kidner, *Proverbs* (Downers Grove: InterVarsity Press, 1964), 36, 37, 39-42.

2. Goldberg, Louis, 'śākal,' *Theological Wordbook of the Old Testament* (Chicago: Moody Press, 1980), 1:877.

3. Ibid.

4. Archer, Jr., Gleason L., *A Survey of Old Testament Introduction: Revised and Expanded* (Chicago: Moody Press, 1964, 1974, 1994), 517.

5. Luc, Alex, 'ערם,' *New International Dictionary of Old Testament Theology and Exegesis* (Grand Rapids, Michigan, 1997), 3:540.

6. Brown, Francis, S. R. Driver, Charles A. Briggs, *A Hebrew and English Lexicon of the Old Testament* (Oxford: Clarendon Press, n.d.), 287.

7. Kidner, 37.

8. Fretheim, Terence E., 'ידע,' *New International Dictionary of Old Testament Theology and Exegesis,* (Grand Rapids, Michigan: Zondervan Publishing House, 1997), 2:411.

9. Kaiser, Walter C., 'lāqah,' *Theological Wordbook of the Old Testament* (Chicago: Moody Press, 1980), 1:482.

10. This discussion of the fool and his folly is adapted from the author's work: John A. Kitchen, *Embracing Authority* (Scotland: Christian Focus Publications, 2002), 128-130.

11. Kidner, 39-42. Also, see Louis Goldberg, ''ĕwîl', *Theological Wordbook of the Old Testament,* (Chicago: Moody Press, 1980), 1:19-20.

12. Kidner, 39 and Chou-Wee Pan, 'פתה,' *New International Dictionary of Old Testament Theology and Exegesis* (Grand Rapids, Michigan: Zondervan Publishing House, 1997), 3:714-716.

13. Kidner, 40-41 and Chou-Wee Pan, 'כסל,' *New International Dictionary of Old Testament Theology and Exegesis* (Grand Rapids, Michigan: Zondervan Publishing House, 1997), 2:678-680.

14. Goldberg, ''ĕwîl,' *Theological Wordbook of the Old Testament* (Chicago: Moody Press, 1980), 1:19-20.

15. Kidner, 41.

16. Pan, Chou-Wee, 'נבל,' *New International Dictionary of Old Testament Theology and Exegesis* (Grand Rapids, Michigan: Zondervan Publishing House, 1997), 3:11-13.

17. Kidner, 41.

18. Powell, Tim, 'ליץ,' *New International Dictionary of Old Testament Theology and Exegesis* (Grand Rapids, Michigan: Zondervan Publishing House, 1997), 2:798-800.

19. Kidner, 41-42.

20. Waltke, Bruce K., 'Proverbs: Theology of,' *New International Dictionary of Old Testament Theology and Exegesis*, (Grand Rapids, Michigan: Zondervan Publishing House, 1997), 4:1085.

Appendix B

Thematic Index of Proverbs

This index has been prepared using the New American Standard Bible to aid the student in discovering, then digging more deeply into, some of the rich themes of Proverbs. The index spans both the extended discourses of chapters 1–9 and the individual proverbs that predominate in chapters 10–31.

A quick perusal of the list reveals the amazing breadth of human experience which Proverbs addresses. Just as startling, however, may be some of the words that Proverbs does not use.

In a few cases, the treatment of a word or theme is so expansive that I have directed the student to a concordance rather than list every usage here. Most importantly, use this index as a doorway, not a wall. Its intent is not to contain all that could be said about the themes of Proverbs (how arrogant to assume any list could!), but to open a door of discovery into the wonderful world of God's truth.

Bibliography

Adams, Jay E. *Proverbs*. The Christian Counselor's Commentary. Woodruff, South Carolina: Timeless Texts, 1997.

Aitken, Kenneth T. *Proverbs*. The Daily Study Bible Series. Philadelphia: The Westminster Press, 1986.

_____. 'Proverbs, Sayings and Themes,' *New International Dictionary of Old Testament Theology and Exegesis*, Volume 4. Grand Rapids: Zondervan Publishing House, 1997.

Archer, Gleason, Jr. *A Survey of Old Testament Introduction*. Chicago: Moody Press, 1964, 1974, 1994.

Baxter, J. Sidlow. *Explore the Book*. Grand Rapids: Zondervan Publishing House, 1960.

Bradshaw, Robert I. 'Wisdom,' www.biblicalstudies.org.uk/article_wisdom2.html.

Bridges, Charles. *A Commentary on Proverbs* (Edinburgh: The Banner of Truth Trust, 1846, reprint 1998).

Bullock, C. Hassell. *An Introduction to the Old Testament Poetic Books: Revised and Expanded*. Chicago: Moody Press, 1979, 1988.

Buzzell, Sid S. 'Proverbs,' *The Bible Knowledge Commentary: Old Testament* (Wheaton: Victor Books, 1985).

Cohen, A. *Proverbs: Hebrew Text and English Translation with Introduction and Commentary*. Soncino Books of the Bible. London: Soncino, 1946.

Delitzsch, Franz. *Proverbs, Ecclesiastes, Song of Solomon*. Commentary on the Old Testament. Translation by James Martin. 3 volumes in 1. Reprint. Grand Rapids: William B. Eerdmans Publishing Company, 1980.

Estes, Daniel J. *Hear, My Son: Teaching and Learning in Proverbs*. New Studies in Biblical Theology. Grand Rapids: William B. Eerdmans Publishing Company, 1997.

Fox, Michael V. *Proverbs 1–9*. The Anchor Bible, Volume 18a. New York: Doubleday, 2000.

Gaebelein, F. E. 'Proverb,' *The Zondervan Pictorial Encyclopedia of the Bible*, Volume 4. Grand Rapids: Zondervan Publishing House, 1975, 1976.

Garrett, Duane A. *Proverbs, Ecclesiastes, Song of Songs*. The New American Commentary, Volume 14. Nashville: Broadman Press, 1993.

Genung, John Franklin. 'Proverb,' *The International Standard Bible Encyclopaedia*, Volume 4. James Orr, gen. ed. Grand Rapids: William B. Eerdmans Publishing Company, 1939, 1956.

_____. 'Proverbs, Book of,' *The International Standard Bible Encyclopaedia*. Volume 4. James Orr, gen. ed. Grand Rapids: William B. Eerdmans Publishing Company, 1939, 1956.

Gesenius, William. *A Hebrew and English Lexicon of the Old Testament with an Appendix Containing Biblical Aramaic*. Translated by Edward Robinson. Oxford: Clarendon Press, n.d.

Harris, R. Laird, editor. *Theological Wordbook of the Old Testament*. 2 volumes. Chicago: Moody Press, 1980.

Helmbold, A. K. 'Proverbs, Book of,' *The Zondervan Pictorial Encyclopedia of the Bible*. Volume 4. Grand Rapids: Zondervan Publishing House, 1975, 1976.

Henry, Matthew. *Matthew Henry's Commentary on the Whole Bible*. Complete and unabridged in one volume. Peabody, Massachusetts: Hendrikson Publishers, 1991, 2001.

Hildebrant, Ted. 'Proverbs 22:6a: Train up a Child?,' *Grace Theological Journal* 9:1 (1988).

Hubbard, D. A. 'Proverb,' *New Bible Dictionary*, 2nd edition. Wheaton: Tyndale House Publishers, Inc., 1962.

_____. 'Proverbs, Book of,' *New Bible Dictionary*, 2nd edition. Wheaton: Tyndale House Publishers, Inc., 1962.

Kaiser, Walter C., Jr. *Toward an Old Testament Theology*. Grand Rapids: Zondervan Publishing House, 1978.

Kidner, Derek. *The Proverbs: An Introduction and Commentary*. Tyndale Old Testament Commentary. Downers Grove: InterVarsity, 1964.

_____. *The Wisdom of Proverbs, Job & Ecclesiastes*. Downers Grove: InterVarsity Press, 1985.

Lane, Eric. *Proverbs*. Focus on the Bible. Scotland: Christian Focus Publications, 2000.

McKane, William. *Proverbs: A New Approach*. Old Testament Library. Philadelphia: Westminster, 1970.

Murphy, Roland E. *Proverbs*. Word Biblical Commentary. Nashville: Thomas Nelson Publishers, 1998.

Parsons, Greg W. 'Guidelines for Understanding and Proclaiming the Book of Proverbs,' *Bibliotheca Sacra* 150 (1993): 151-170.

Ross, Allen P. 'Proverbs.' *The Expositor's Bible Commentary*, Volume 5. Grand Rapids: Zondervan Publishing House, 1991.

Ruffle, J. 'Proverbs,' *The New Bible Dictionary: Revised*. Grand Rapids: William B. Eerdmans Publishing Company, 1970.

Steinmann, Andrew E. 'Proverbs As a Solomonic Composition,' *Journal of the Evangelical Theological Society* 43.4 (December 2000): 659-674.

VanGemeren, Willem A., gen. ed. *New International Dictionary of Old Testament Theology and Exegesis*. 5 volumes. Grand Rapids: Zondervan Publishing House, 1997.

Van Leeuwen, Raymond C., 'The Book of Proverbs.' *The New Interpreter's Bible*, Volume 5. Nashville: Abingdon Press, 1997.

Waltke, Bruce K. 'Old Testament Interpretation Issues for Big Idea Preaching: Problematic Sources, Poetics, and Preaching the Old Testament, And Exposition of Proverbs 26:1-12,' *The Big Idea of Preaching*. K. Willhite and S. M. Gibson, eds. Grand Rapids: Baker Book House, 1998.

_____. 'Proverbs 10:1-15: A Coherent Collection?' *Reading and Hearing the Word from Text to Sermon: Essays in Honor of John H. Stek*, A. C. Leder, ed. Grand Rapids: CRRC Publications, 1998.

_____. 'Proverbs, Theology of,' *New International Dictionary of Old Testament Theology and Exegesis*. Volume 4. Grand Rapids: Zondervan Publishing House, 1997.

_____. 'The Book of Proverbs and Ancient Wisdom Literature,' *Bibliotheca Sacra* 136 (1979): 221-238.

_____. 'The Book of Proverbs and Old Testament Theology,' *Bibliotheca Sacra* 136 (1979): 302-318.

_____. 'The Dance Between God and Humanity,' *Doing Theology for the People of God: Studies in Honor of J. I. Packer*. D. Lewis and A. McGrath, eds. Downers Grove: InterVarsity, 1996.

_____. 'The Role of the "Valiant Wife" in the Marketplace,' *Crux* (September 1999): 23-34.

Whybray, R. N. *Proverbs*. New Century Bible Commentary. Grand Rapids: William B. Eerdmans Publishing Company, 1994.

Subject Index

Quarreling *see* contention/strife

Ransom...................................285, 476
rebellion...378–9
　see also calamity: of rebels
rebuke 281, 378, 547, 553–4,
　...605–6, 643–4
　see also reproof
Rehoboam...100, 247, 564, 620–1, 653, 659
rejoicing: in others' downfall.........548–9
　of a parent 525–6, 531–2
　　see also joy: a father's joy over a
　　wise son
　of the righteous................244–5, 634,
　...647, 652, 654
　of wisdom..................................193–5
　　see also delight; joy
relationships: avoidance of contention
　and strife...................................92
　　see also contention/strife
　to be founded on wisdom and dis-
　　cretion 87–8
　destroyed by evil men 366–8
　destroyed through tale-bearing.377–8
　with God and others......................43
　he who separates himself from
　...391–2
　love and hatred in 335
　peacemaking.....325, 336, 353–4, 359
　in times of adversity 382, 408,
　...415–16
　　see also poverty: rejection of the
　　poor; family life
repentance 49, 635–7, 701–2
reproach..................392–3, 566–7, 610–11
reproof 49, 50, 148, 205–6, 661–2
　for adding to words of God....682–3
　learning from 292–3, 327–8,
　...344–5, 431, 471
　offered and received from God's
　　fatherly love 81–2
　spurning of........52–3, 81, 227–8, 651
　value of a wise reprover.........568–9
　　see also rebuke
respect...368–9
　see also honor
restitution 152
revelation: as increasing illumination....
　...109–10
　man's knowledge of God dependent
　on..562

　the sage as a primary source of........
　...15, 19
　teaching of Proverbs based on 32
　of vision and guidance 664–5
　　see also word of God
revenge *see* vengeance
riches *see* wealth
riddles...40–1
righteousness 39, 62, 109–10, 655
　as benefit of wisdom............187, 206
　better than sacrifice 464–5
　blessings of.............217, 218–19, 232,
　...242, 273, 294–5
　boldness of the righteous........625–6
　as deliverer from death 215, 241
　descendants of the righteous......251
　desire of the righteous.............252–3
　earthly thrones established on...357–8
　the fall of a righteous man 578–9
　fruit of 257–8
　as a guard 284
　life as wages of..........226–7, 250, 278
　national exaltation through....322, 564
　plans, thoughts and intentions of the
　　righteous.........263–4, 655, 657–8
　pursuit of..........................330, 478–9
　recovery of the righteous 547
　rejoicing of and for the righteous
　...............244–5, 634, 647, 652, 654
　reward of sowing righteousness
　...250, 576
　the righteous man 243, 251, 256,
　.....................................268–9, 276–7, 578–9
　root of the righteous 262, 267–8
　self-righteousness.........443–4, 686–7
　steadfastness in.............................250
　of words of wisdom...............179–80
　　see also godliness; integrity
Ross, Allen P. 693
ruin...........224–5, 226, 234–5, 242, 471–2
　following pride.....................361, 399
　from rash speech 283, 395–6
　　see also calamity
rulers *see* kings and rulers
Ruth.......................................263, 711, 723

Sacrifice.....32, 165, 329–30, 373, 464–5
　vows of 455–6
　of the wicked...........................483–4
sages...15–16, 19
　see also wise man

Scripture Index